MOTOCOURSE™

THE WORLD'S LEADING GRAND PRIX & SUPERBIKE ANNUAL

icon
PUBLISHING LIMITED

CONTENTS

MOTOCOURSE 2015–2016

is published by:
Icon Publishing Limited
Regent Lodge
4 Hanley Road
Malvern
Worcestershire
WR14 4PQ
United Kingdom

Tel: +44 (0)1684 564511

Email: info@motocourse.com
Website: www.motocourse.com

Printed in Italy by
L.E.G.O. S.p.A.
Viale dell'Industria, 2,
I-36100 Vicenza
Email: info@legogroup.com

ISBN: 978-1910584-09-5

DISTRIBUTORS
Gardners Books
1 Whittle Drive, Eastbourne,
East Sussex BN23 6QH
Tel: +44 (0)1323 521555
email: sales@gardners.com

Bertram Books
1 Broadland Business Park, Norwich,
Norfolk, NR7 0WF
Tel: +44 (0)871 803 6709
email: books@bertrams.com

Chaters Wholesale Ltd
25/26 Murrell Green Business Park,
Hook, Hampshire RG27 9GR
Telephone: +44 (0)1256 765443
Fax: +44 (0)1256 769900
email: books@chaters.co.uk

NORTH AMERICA
Quayside Distribution Services
400 First Avenue North, Suite 300,
Minneapolis, MN 55401, USA
Telephone: (612) 344 8100
Fax: (612) 344 8691

Dust jacket: Yamaha's Jorge Lorenzo took his third world championship after a nail-biting duel with team-mate Valentino Rossi.

Title page: Jonathan Rea dominated proceedings in the World Superbike Championship after switching from Honda to the Kawasaki Ninja.

Photos: Gold & Goose

FOREWORD by 2015 MotoGP World Champion Jorge Lorenzo	4
EDITOR'S INTRODUCTION	6
THE TOP TEN RIDERS OF 2015 Ranked by the Editor	8
THE STATE OF RACING by Michael Scott	14
DANNY KENT Neil Morrison profiles the 2015 Moto3 World Champion	18
THE LOVELESS TRIANGLE Mat Oxley on the poisonous relationships of Rossi, Lorenzo and Marquez	26
FLYING ON THE GROUND Mechanical rotation and aerodynamic intervention by Neil Spalding	34
2015 MotoGP • Bike by Bike The machines of 2015 analysed by Neil Spalding	38
WHY STYLE MATTERS Technical essay by Kevin Cameron	46
MOTOGP RIDERS AND TEAMS Guide to the grid by Matthew Birt	52
MOTO2 RIDERS AND TEAMS by Peter McLaren	78
MOTO3 RIDERS AND TEAMS by Peter McLaren	82
2015 GRANDS PRIX by Michael Scott	86
WORLD CHAMPIONSHIP RIDERS' POINTS TABLES Compiled by Peter McLaren	232
RED BULL ROOKIES CUP REVIEW by Peter Clifford	234
SUPERBIKE WORLD CHAMPIONSHIP REVIEW by Gordon Ritchie	237
SUPERBIKE WORLD CHAMPIONSHIP RESULTS AND POINTS TABLES Compiled by Peter McLaren	270
SUPERSPORT WORLD CHAMPIONSHIP REVIEW by Gordon Ritchie	278
ISLE OF MAN TT REVIEW by Michael Guy	282
BRITISH SUPERBIKE REVIEW by Ollie Barstow	288
SIDECAR WORLD CHAMPIONSHIP REVIEW by John McKenzie	300
US RACING REVIEW by Larry Lawrence	302
MAJOR RESULTS WORLDWIDE compiled by Peter McLaren	308

Acknowledgements

The Editor and staff of MOTOCOURSE wish to thank the following for their assistance in compiling the 2015–2016 edition: Nereo Balanzin, Majo Botella, Alex Briggs, Alberto Cani, Mufaddal Choonia, Peter Clifford, Rhys Edwards, William Favero, Alberto Gomez, Milena Koerner, Isabelle Lariviere, Jose Maroto, Neil Morrison, Elisa Pavan, David Pato, Ricardo Pedros, Ignacio Sagnier, Julian Thomas, Mike Trimby, Michel Turco, Frine Vellila, Mike Webb, Ian Wheeler and Günther Wiesinger, among others too numerous to mention. A special thanks to Marlboro, Repsol and Honda hospitality staff; and to colleagues and friends for their comments and advice, which is never taken lightly, and often never taken at all.

Photographs published in MOTOCOURSE 2015–2016 have been contributed by:
Chief photographers: Gold & Goose.
Other photographs contributed by: Whit Bazemore, Gavan Caldwell, Clive Challinor, Dave Collister, Ducati Corse, Ecstar Suzuki, Bernd Fischer, HRC, Dominic James, MotoAmerica – Brian J. Nelson, Movistar Yamaha, Neil Spalding, Mark Walters.

publisher
STEVE SMALL
steve.small@iconpublishinglimited.com

commercial director
BRYN WILLIAMS
bryn.williams@iconpublishinglimited.com

editor
MICHAEL SCOTT

text editor
IAN PENBERTHY

results and statistics
PETER McLAREN

chief photographers
GOLD & GOOSE
David Goldman
Gareth Harford
Brian J. Nelson
David 'Chippy' Wood
www.goldandgoose.com
tel +44 (0)20 8444 2448

MotoGP bikes and circuit illustrations
ADRIAN DEAN
f1artwork@blueyonder.co.uk

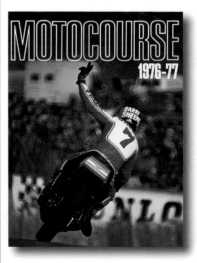

www.motocourse.com

FOREWORD by JORGE LORENZO

I THINK we can be very proud about this championship. It was a real fight all the way to the end. In spite of everything, we kept our focus and concentration. And this third MotoGP championship is a great reward.

There were times when it seemed impossible – especially when the weather turned several times from practice to race day. As in Japan, where I was fastest in dry conditions and in the wet, and led most of the race – only to drop back to third because my tactics didn't suit the changing conditions.

When conditions were stable, however, I could take seven race wins leading from the first lap to the last.

I had to do my work to the best of my ability, but this success would not have been possible without the work that Yamaha did.

As I said all year, our bike was fantastic. It is not the fastest or most powerful, but the balance of the whole package made it a winner in all sorts of different conditions. My riding style meant I could take full profit from that balance.

As a result, my picture is on the cover of the 40th edition of MOTOCOURSE, which has been the definitive record for motorcycle racing ever since 1976.

In years to come, I shall look back on this season with pleasure. This book will help me and all MotoGP fans to remember all the details.

FAREWELL TO INNOCENCE

THE thing to remember about 2015 is not the sour taste left in the mouth by the Rossi-Marquez-Lorenzo feud over the closing two races, but the much sweeter taste that had preceded it. It really was a remarkable season, and it just kept getting better.

Right up to round 16 of 18 in Australia, where everybody thought the sustained four-way front fight had been one of the greatest MotoGP races they had ever seen.

Everyone except Rossi. "Unfair," he cried. And continued to do so.

It was Rossi who had driven the escalating euphoria up to this point. His already massive worldwide popularity continued to grow and grow as, at the age of 36, he pulled off one trick after another. Nobody got ahead on points all year. Until the final race.

The nine-times champion may be numerically past his best as a rider. The lap times showed that the younger guys were faster. But his cunning, his perseverance, his racecraft, his wet-weather skills and his consistency made up for that.

What a hero. What a sportsman. After 39 years of it, he could still be the man to beat.

And what an unedifying spectacle when it all turned very nasty.

Farewell to innocence.

It is the role of MOTOCOURSE to record and analyse all these events, not just for Christmas, but also for posterity.

We have a special feature giving the full background to the storm that was released when Rossi attacked Marquez in Malaysia.

Our role is also to celebrate the good times, the good races, the good guys. And there were many in a season when Honda clocked up a record 700th grand prix win; when Superbikes turned at last to Northern Ireland; when US Racing turned the corner; when the TT reaffirmed the greatness of McGuinness and Hutchinson...

MOTOCOURSE has filled this role since before Rossi or any of his companions on any grand prix grid were born. This is the 40th edition, and there is a special symmetry to Danny Kent's nail-biting Moto3 World Championship, which broke a 31-year duck for Britain.

MOTOCOURSE was first published in the same year that Barry Sheene won his first championship – indeed, largely because of that.

We've been doing it ever since.

It's been an honour.

MICHAEL SCOTT
Gillitts, November, 2015

Above: This was the crash that changed everything for Rossi.
Photo: Gold & Goose

Left: John McGuinness: two more TT wins for a colossus of the course.
Photo: Gavan Caldwell

Far left: Fast company. Legends line up at the Goodwood Festival of Speed, with 41 titles between them. From left, Freddie Spencer (3), Phil Read (7), John Surtees (7) Valentino Rossi (9) and Giacomo Agostini (15).
Photo: Dominic James

FIM WORLD CHAMPIONSHIP 2015
TOP TEN RIDERS
THE EDITOR'S CHOICE

Rider Portraits by Gold & Goose

1 JORGE LORENZO

IMAGINE, if you can, an atomic metronome. All it can do is keep time, but it does so with microscopic accuracy.

This is no bad way to describe how Lorenzo rides a motorcycle. He is one of those riders (the opposite of Marquez) who looks as though he is just cruising, even while he is breaking the lap record.

He won seven races, and in each of them he led from the first corner. He set a new record at Catalunya for the number of consecutive laps led: 103. On his day, he was immaculate.

When anything upset that regular ticking, however, the 28-year-old suffered, most clearly exemplified by his race crash in the chaotic flag-to-flag Misano race. This inconsistency wasn't all his fault: vision problems caused by helmet failures twice intervened, among other things.

At the same time, at Motegi (another mixed-conditions miss-hit, though less costly), he was able to point out that he was fastest in both wet and dry, and that while his tactics proved wrong, nobody could have predicted that.

Lorenzo did himself no credit by shoving his oar into the Rossi-Marquez dispute; nor has he the sort of personality that generates a warm response. But he was easily the best rider in 2015 by so many measures.

2 MARC MARQUEZ

PRIMITIVE anti-lock brake systems operated by allowing the tyre to lose adhesion before releasing pressure. In this way, the tyre passed through the point of maximum adhesion repeatedly, optimising stopping power. More sophisticated measuring devices refine the process, striving to stop just short of lock-up.

Lorenzo fits into the second category, caressing the bike to its maximum.

Marquez is the opposite, finding the limit by going past it, then using his extraordinary athleticism and ability to recover.

This is devastatingly effective for lap times: Marquez claimed eight pole positions in 2015, Lorenzo five. But it is a risky strategy, and the youngster crashed many more times in the season than his older compatriot – 13 to Lorenzo's three; for Rossi, it was two.

In 2013 and 2014 (15 and 11 crashes respectively), he got away with it. In 2015, a razor-edged aggressive new Honda didn't give him the latitude he needed. And the engine-development freeze tied his hands.

Characteristically, he maintained clear sight of his simple goal: win, win, win. It meant that while almost all of his previous crashes had been in practice, while seeking the limit, seven of 2015's were in the race.

This does seem to imply a lack of maturity. The youngest ever premier-class champion was showing his age. Since that was just 22, it's forgivable.

3 VALENTINO ROSSI

ROSSI was top in many categories, some of them unique: best all-rounder, best in the wet, best over-30, best rostrum regular, best from back of the grid. He fell short in one area only, compared to team-mate Lorenzo. He couldn't go quite as fast.

All the same, his increasingly astonishing, even surreal challenge to add a tenth title at the age of 36 was inspiring and deeply impressive.

His riding style had moved on a lot since his dominant heydays, led as always by technical developments. Where his versatility had been crucial in the past, improved tyre grip and electronic interventions now demanded that riders be both more accurate and more athletic.

Having rejoined Yamaha for 2013, Rossi applied himself to adapting his approach. By his own diligence, and by a reinvented new crew chief, he taught an old dog new tricks.

His remaining weak point was in new-style go-for-it qualifying: he was on the front row only five times; on the third seven times. That cost him many chances of being able to trade blows with fast-away Lorenzo. It probably cost him the championship.

After the year-ending controversy, there was another title Rossi lost: Most Sporting Rider. But then again, behind that ready smile, he has never been anything less than completely ruthless.

4 DANI PEDROSA

A NEW Dani emerged in 2015. A change of personal manager in 2014 – leaving long-time ally Alberto Puig – was followed by a major change of pit crew.

Along with these, Pedrosa showed a more relaxed (sometimes even jovial) manner off the track. And, by season's end, he was a double winner who had added tactics and a seldom-seen aggression to the speed he has demonstrated since his first MotoGP season in 2006.

As always for the perennially luckless Spaniard, who turned 30 in 2015, circumstances prevailed to prevent a title challenge. This time, it was the return of arm-pump problems. These had never really gone away, but now they became so acute that radical invasive surgery was required.

With his racing future in doubt, a gloomy Pedrosa flew home from the first race, missed the next three and then returned while still gradually regaining strength.

He was second in Germany, but the real marker was second at Aragon, won from Rossi in a sustained and fierce fight to the flag. Two wins followed; he had preserved his record of at least one every season.

Pedrosa also emerged as the sporting gentleman in the Rossi-Marquez-Lorenzo scuffle at year's end. Only fourth, but it had turned out to be a very good year.

5 ANDREA IANNONE

THE nickname 'Maniac Joe' is self-inflicted, and there are several explanations floating around – his tag when blasting around his home town of Vasto as a teenage scooterist; named after an Italian cartoon character; or (a semi-official version) not because of manic riding, but an avidity for neatness and order everywhere from his bedside table to his pit box.

Iannone (26) clung to the nickname, but in a highly impressive first works-team season, he cast aside his former rostrum-or-hospital reputation. Far from it, he emerged as the stronger and more consistent of the two factory Ducati riders. Strong fights with both Rossi and Marquez showed he was afraid of nobody.

In spite of a twice-troublesome shoulder dislocation, he scored well in the first 15 races, including a Mugello pole start and two podiums, when a mechanical failure dropped him off the board in Japan. Same thing in Malaysia, and he only actually crashed out once, in the last race, trying too hard to regain fourth overall from Pedrosa.

Iannone significantly out-performed highly regarded team-mate Dovizioso, and had a particularly strong ride in Australia, beating Rossi to third. All this reinforced his candidacy for a serious title challenge in 2016 and beyond.

6 JOHANN ZARCO

SMALL differences between machines in Moto2 can lead to surprising variations in individual riders' performances. Look at Jonas Folger, who won two races, but spent more time fighting for lesser points. Or one-race-winner Thomas Luthi, likewise up and down. Or Mika Kallio, from race winner and title contender in 2014 to nowhere-man in 2015.

This makes the consistent superiority of Johann Zarco (25) all the more impressive.

He really should have won the first race at Qatar, robbed by a gear-linkage failure. For the next 12 races, he was on the podium every time, and six times on the uppermost step.

His TV-grabbing post-win back-flips would be seen twice more; and Zarco had amassed enough points to be crowned champion with four races to spare.

Loquacious and articulate, he explained his return to a form not seen since 2011 quite simply: he was back with the same Ajo team that had taken him to runner-up in 125s in that year. The consequent confidence meant everything.

Zarco declined offers to switch to MotoGP, following Rabat to become the second Moto2 champion to stay on to defend. Like Rabat, he might find the going tougher in 2016.

7 MAVERICK VINALES

MAVERICK VINALES showed strong gifts in his first year in Moto2. Moving on promptly to the top class, he did even more so in 2015. He finished 12th overall, on a brand-new bike in a very competitive year. As significantly, the 20-year-old was only eight points adrift of his more experienced and well-regarded Suzuki team-mate, Aleix Espargaro.

He failed to score only twice, crashing out at Brno and Motegi.

It may be that the pretty new Suzuki GSX-RR flattered his style. It lacked the brutish power of, for example, even the Open Hondas. As a corollary, it put less stress on chassis and tyres.

An experienced pit crew proved very capable of finding the sweetest settings, and both Suzuki riders were able to exploit this to the maximum, high corner speed in place of high top speed.

Aleix's pole at Catalunya was a signal moment for rider and machine; yet it was even more impressive to see Vinales qualify alongside him, only 0.083 of a second slower. He was a rookie.

It might be closer under 2016's rules, but for all its unexpected success, the new Suzuki was not ready to be considered a serious title contender. This rider, another young Spanish natural, most definitely is.

8 BRADLEY SMITH

SOME might think Smith merits a higher place on this list. They might be right. The strength of the English rider's season showed a step change in maturity, in every way.

Smith (24) became more analytical and more lucid. Working with veteran crew chief Guy Coulon, he earned a small reputation as a set-up guru.

He also became faster and more consistent, continuing to work on refining an ever shortening list of areas to improve. A string of solid results – ten times in the top six – was reinforced by second place at Misano. A missed tyre change was transformed into a tactical master-stroke by ever changing conditions, but his determination was the greater factor in that signal success.

He had some feisty battles through the year, but most important was his consistency. Smith was the only rider, other than Rossi, to score points in every race. And good points. In this way, he triumphed in a private battle with compatriot Cal Crutchlow to be top satellite-team rider.

Smith was seldom spectacular in 2016, but he was spectacularly solid. It's hard to know how much of a drawback it was to be on a lower-spec Factory Yamaha, but it would be interesting to see him on the full package.

9 ALEX RINS

THERE are very few past champions who did not get there without displaying precocious talent and an ability to learn fast.

Rins (19) may have been beaten in Moto3 in 2014 by team-mate Alex Marquez, but when the upwardly-mobile pair transferred together to the middle class in 2015, it was Rins, older by fewer than six months, who shone by far the brighter.

He was third, then second in rounds two and three, and leading the world championship when he crashed while challenging for second at round four at Jerez.

The first of two wins came in feisty fighting style at Indianapolis, and by the time of the second at Phillip Island, he had taken over second overall from the now-absent Rabat.

Rins showed a promising combination of aggression and natural ability. He made mistakes – a couple of crashes, one of which led to disqualification at Misano (he remounted, then engaged in battle with the leaders when they came to lap him). Their cause was over-enthusiasm rather than – in Stoner's memorable phrase to Rossi – "running out of talent".

Rins is earmarked by Yamaha for future promotion – possibly to supplant previous pet candidate Pol Espargaro. He looks good enough to do it.

10 DANNY KENT

IF this were a Portuguese publication, this spot would go to Miguel Oliveira, and be well deserved. But MOTOCOURSE is British, and Danny Kent did his home nation proud.

The honours were very evenly split between the pair: six wins apiece, neatly arranged at opposite ends of the season. Kent set record-breaking runaways to amass five of his victories in the first nine races. Oliveira took the same number in the last nine races.

Significantly, there were no runaways for him, how-ever. And in the final analysis, Kent won more points, and that is what really counts.

Kent (21) is a rider with a measured maturity, which showed clearly in his prophetic earlier pronouncements that it was far too soon to feel confident. By the time circumstances – and errors like his headlong Aragon crash – had proved his misgivings well founded, this was stretched close to breaking point.

He is the first British world champion since the far-off days of Barry Sheene, and fags on rostrum. This is a great honour, but also quite a heavy burden. Perhaps wisely, Kent turned down a chance to go straight to MotoGP.

His next task instead is to make it through the Moto2 morass, which has bogged down many a good rider in recent years.

IN GREAT SHAPE

With intense rivalry on and off the track, passion overflowing and new rules making closer racing, MotoGP looked healthy in 2015. There was more light than shade ... but Rossi cast a long shadow. MICHAEL SCOTT explains

Above: MotoGP has never been as competitive, and never had such strength in depth

Top right: Dorna's Carmelo Ezpeleta – plans falling into place.

Centre right: FIM president Vito Ippolito waxed lyrical about "fair play, sportsmanship and courtesy" in the wake of the furore.
Photos: Gold & Goose

Right: But what will happen when 'The Doctor' disappears over the horizon for the last time?
Photo: Movistar Yamaha

I F intense personal rivalry is the lifeblood of racing, then MotoGP in 2015 was in great shape. And looking back in history, the majority of the most memorable battles involved great personal animosity, often loudly expressed. Think only of Agostini-Read, Sheene-Roberts, Rainey-Schwantz, Stoner-Rossi, Doohan-Everybody.

Thus 2015 was especially blessed, because it went three ways: Rossi-Marquez-Lorenzo. And long before the sun set at Valencia on the last of 18 increasingly tense races, feelings had boiled over, insults had been exchanged, an internet frenzy had been provoked, and headlines had been generated around the world. All the hallmarks of a classic.

Later that night, as Rossi's last cries of "Not fair!" reached their final echo, there was a strange taste in the mouth: slightly sour, certainly, but also with a tinny tang of anxiety.

On the grounds that any publicity is good publicity, the whole farrago had given MotoGP a major shot in the arm. The widest possible audience had been reached. But was it the controversy that had made the tabloids all over the world, or was it just Rossi?

More than ever, after the old rascal had assembled one of the best and most inspiring seasons of his 20 brilliant grand prix years, and had personally initiated the whole media storm, one was left wondering again: what on earth will happen when he has gone?

But there were encouraging signs during 2015, mainly expressed in the growing success of Dorna's machinations to add strength in depth by means of ground-levelling technical restrictions. In the second and final year of the Open class, the season was blessed with regular fierce midfield battles all the way down the points and beyond.

Over and above the sustained displays of skill at the front, the racing was robust and entertaining pretty much all the way, and strong seasons by the likes of Iannone, Vinales, Smith and Miller showed there is talent aplenty still to come. Just no one like Rossi.

It's easy to be wise in hindsight, but it is obvious that much of the year-end furore – the farrago of insults, the embarrassing abandonment of any pretence of sportsmanship, the storm of hostility from opposing fans, the pious pronouncements from on high – could all have been avoided had Race Direction made an on-the-spot decision in Malaysia.

Trouble had been brewing from the start of the race, and when Rossi precipitated the final moments, slowing, glancing backwards and running radically wide, the race was still young. There was plenty of time for the authorities to respond.

There was no question. Rossi's action had caused Marquez to crash. How deliberately could be debated later; the fact was plain to see.

When Marco Simoncelli knocked Dani Pedrosa flying at Le Mans in 2011 he was immediately called in for a ride-through penalty. Had it been a deliberate act rather than a

trade-mark over-ambitious lunge then more punishment could have been applied later. But the matter was over. As were Pedrosa's title hopes.

If only this had happened in Malaysia.

There would have been a storm, certainly, and arguments. But no back-of-the-grid start, which effectively denied Rossi a chance of the title. No appeals to the Court of Arbitration for Sport, no death-threat frenzy among rival supporters, no need for Yamaha to draw a veil of silence over their previously much-vaunted 60th anniversary celebration.

Most importantly, no need for anything but on-track action to cloud the issue of the championship.

Race Director Mike Webb explained the reasoning: they wanted time to view all the footage more carefully, and to hear from both riders, because the matter was of such importance to the championship. (You could say that again.)

In a way, this is understandable. As well as this decision, the four-man group also had a race to direct. There really isn't much time to spare.

Then there are the different interests involved. As well as director Mike Webb, Race Direction comprises FIM Safety Delegate Franco Uncini, poacher-turned-gamekeeper Loris Capirossi (Riders' Representative), and most crucially Javier Alonso of Dorna, representing the commercial side. Which, when Rossi is concerned, is a very important side indeed.

It's impossible to second-guess the sway of their debate. But since the decision had been left until so long after the event, after the podium parade and all the pomp, one option was no longer open. It was much too late for that ride-through. They were left with little option but to do exactly what they did.

Triggering a tsunami.

Formula One operates a different system: Race Direction refers incidents to a panel of FIA stewards, then gets on with directing the race. The stewards decide the penalty, then and there.

Time for something similar in MotoGP. And we would like to think that if ever the FIM do manage to claw back sufficient power to make up that panel of stewards, they would have given Rossi a ride-through.

LEVELLER THAN EVER

Dorna added a new twist of classes within classes in 2015, blurring the edges between the categories with a typically ad hoc mix-and-match approach that has served well step by step during the years of transition, via CRT, towards the planned nirvana of technical equality for 2017.

One solid step came with the introduction of Magneti Marelli ECU hardware for all. Factories could write their own software, but Open teams had that handed to them by Dorna as well.

There were two categories, as in 2014: Factory Option and Open.

Factory teams were restricted to five engines, with no technical development allowed after the start of the season; 20 litres of fuel; and the harder range of available tyre options. They were only allowed to continue developing their own electronic software until a mid-year cut-off, at Assen. Thereafter, that too was frozen. Testing with factory riders outside the official tests was limited to five days.

Open teams had 12 engines, with free development, and 24 litres of fuel; and they could test as much as they liked. They were confined to the two softer of three tyre options. Their common limitation was the control software, still undergoing development throughout the season.

But Dorna had to add a sub-category, with its own subdivisions, to accommodate reality.

Ducati, Suzuki and Aprilia were classed as Factory Option teams, but with concessions, on a sliding scale. They had the same engine numbers and testing freedom, the same access to soft tyres and 24 litres of fuel, as Open teams. However, one win, two seconds or three podiums in the dry would produce a fuel cut to 22 litres – which happened to

Ducati right after the first race.

For Ducati, fastest MotoGP bike of them all (Iannone's new 350.8km/h record at Mugello eclipsed Marquez's 350.5 for Honda at Qatar), not having access to the harder tyres was actually a disadvantage on a few occasions. The disparity certainly shook up the qualifying order, however, with soft-tyre poles for Iannone and Dovizioso's Ducatis, and one for Espargaro's Suzuki.

But the restructuring of the class was still a work in progress, and although 2016 is supposed to be the start of a long spell of stability in technical regulations, after years of constant flux, there is still a need for a second tier, to accommodate low-level factories Aprilia and Suzuki. This is also adjustable on a complex system of points: applied for dry-weather podiums, culminating in compulsory promotion to the more restricted world of true Factory teams as the bikes move closer to the front.

In 2016, Factory teams get two more engines than in 2015, up to seven, but with development again frozen. Suzuki and Aprilia are allowed 12 engines, with free development and no testing restrictions.

The greatest leveller is electronic. In 2015, all teams used the same Magneti Marelli control hardware platform; in 2016, they will all have to use supplied software as well. Limited development is allowed, but it must be shared between all teams.

This will affect some manufacturers more than others: Yamaha and Ducati already use Magneti Marelli-based software and thus are familiar with the systems; Honda has to more or less start again, after using several generations of their own in-house software; while Suzuki began the adaptation during the 2015 season.

In post-Valencia tests, however, first time out, the software was not too badly received, although it is primitive compared with the current factory systems. On first acquaintance, Rossi described it as "like the software we had in 2008 or 2009"; but crews rapidly took the first step towards greater familiarity. Marquez broke the race lap record, and Lorenzo was only two-tenths slower.

CLOSED SHOP, SECURE FUTURE?

Having tweaked and tickled the technical regulations into shape, Dorna's next great step was a major rejig of racing finances, with a similar aim – no better described than with the time-worn cliche: levelling the playing field.

This came into public knowledge and then into the statute book in record time, with Dorna's Carmelo Ezpeleta announcing details of the plan at the Argentine GP, and then confirming their ratification barely ten weeks later at Assen, after a Permanent Bureau meeting. The acquiescence of the factories via the MSMA represented a major victory for Ezpeleta.

The main thrust is towards a stable financial platform and a better spread of the proceeds for the five-year period from 2017 to 2021; and the mechanism is via a sort of closed shop, protecting current teams plus 2017 arrivals KTM.

The details include compulsory cost-capped lease bikes from factory teams; also a freeze on technical developments, unless agreed by all participants or for safety reasons.

The MotoGP class will comprise six manufacturers, with participants Honda, Yamaha, Ducati, Aprilia and Suzuki, plus KTM. Each has the right to participate with a two-rider factory team, but furthermore is obliged to make between two and four machines available to private teams, for a lease price set at 2.2-million euros, to cover all except crash damage.

In return, Dorna is upping its financial contribution to the teams by (according to Ezpeleta) "more than 30 per cent from 2016 to 2017", with a special focus on private teams.

This situation applies only to existing teams. Any new manufacturers hoping to join in – BMW remains a sought-after candidate – will have to do so with one of these teams.

On the other hand, Dorna also has the right (although not

the obligation) to buy the slots of the last two teams in the championship, a way of removing dead wood and opening the way to fresh growth.

The minimum number of riders will be 22, the maximum 24, one less than in 2015.

TYRED AND EMOTIONAL

Bridgestone were able to celebrate a 242nd and final grand prix victory at Valencia. For the previous seven years, 124 consecutive wins went without saying, after they had reluctantly been the only company willing to take up Dorna's new diktat of control tyres for the 2009 season.

There were some hiccups during those years, notably the spate of early-lap crashes with hard-to-warm rubber in 2012, and the calamitous failure to anticipate the hyperabrasive new Phillip Island tarmac in 2013, when the race had to be shortened and a compulsory pit stop introduced, to change to a bike with fresh tyres.

By and large, however, Bridgestone had been not far short of exemplary, continuing development, though at perhaps a steadier pace than when they had faced competition. Asymmetric tyres were much improved, tyre endurance radically so – it was not unusual in the past two or three years for the fastest laps to come at the end of the race. As with Marquez in Australia in 2015.

To the end, innovations continued, with a much-improved pioneering asymmetric front becoming race tyre of choice in Australia.

The Japanese company finally decided in 2014 that it had had enough of always winning an unequal contest, and declined to renew their three-year contract. They stayed to give MotoGP a year of grace to find an alternative.

Step forward Michelin, with a policy about-face after turning up its nose at the very notion of a control-tyre world championship seven years ago. And most welcome, too.

In the past, Michelin likewise had achieved serial success as the tyre of choice for both 500cc two-strokes and MotoGP four-strokes – but a couple of their own blunders against a steady improvement by Bridgestone put the Frenchmen on the back foot before their withdrawal.

Tests during 2015 were not often favoured with good weather; and at Mugello, a spate of front-end crashes persuaded Rossi, Lorenzo and Marquez to decline pre-planned race-distance simulations. The moment of truth came two days after the Valencia race with the official opening of the 2016 season. There were more and similar front-end crashes, but, as with the electronics, the lap record was broken.

This can only be a good omen, for those who believe the business of racing is to keep going faster. A view increasingly going out of fashion, by the way, for safety reasons – Michelin's future task may be to make slower tyres.

The task of riders and engineers is to adapt their techniques and their technicalities to the new tyre performance envelope. The consensus from Valencia was that while the lap times were similar, the character of the Michelins compared to the Bridgestones was different, and conformed very much to type.

The Japanese front tyres always excelled (with the exception of the first-generation asymmetric fronts of 2014) and changed very little over the years. This made the front wheel a stable platform, allowing hard late braking and sharp turn-in. Riding styles evolved to take advantage of this.

Michelins need to be ridden differently. The front, using a different construction technique, is the weaker link, needing a bit of nursing, but the performance of the rear offers different possibilities. (In the abstruse world of racing-tyre performance, over-simplifications are sometimes apposite.)

Marquez's best time at Valencia tests was 1m 31.060s; three days earlier, Lorenzo's race record had been 1m 31.367s. This was impressive. Lorenzo's pole time, however, had been better than a second out of reach, at 1m 30.011s.

This start was good enough, since rapid improvement can

Above: Valencia 2015. Bridgestone's last stand. Lorenzo takes the win ahead of his 'bodyguards'.

Left: Despite superb facilities and a grand Indiana welcome, the Indianapolis Motor Speedway failed to attract enough support, and followed Laguna Seca off the MotoGP schedule.

Right: "I'm back." Michelin's Nicolas Goubert was a familiar face when the French company returned for the Valencia test.

Photos: Gold & Goose

Above: **John McPhee leads a train: Moto3 was so close, and often the best race of the day.**
Photo: Gold & Goose

be expected as more miles are piled on. Michelin will continue the same choice of two compounds for each race as Bridgestone; although with no Open bikes, the softest option will become extinct. They also promised an extra rear slick, making it 12 per race, with ten fronts. Interestingly, they also pledged the return of an intermediate tyre – something akin to a soft cut slick, or a wet with less tread pattern. This would have been an interesting prospect for races run in changing conditions in 2015, like Motegi and Misano.

DON'T FOLLOW MY LEADER

Looking for a tow from a faster rider in qualifying is nothing new in racing. Over recent years, however, there has been a substantial increase in the practice, most especially in Moto3. By 2015, it had reached such absurd proportions that some sessions looked more like a slow bicycle race, with almost all riders wheeling along at little more than walking pace, all waiting for the first one to pull the pin.

Race Direction used the cumulative penalty points system to try to eradicate the practice: in Australia in 2014, a record 11 had been applied, seven of them for loitering.

It had no effect, for in this class a judiciously timed slipstream can make the difference of almost a second a lap, especially at tracks with longer straights. And for Moto3, most straights are relatively long.

Matters reached a head at the Catalunyan round, where Race Direction called 30 riders in for yet another dressing down. The points system was summarily abandoned for this offence, and harsher measures promised forthwith. All riders would meet again at the next round, it was promised, by which time a more effective solution would have been found.

That was at Assen, where Race Director Mike Webb said,

"In the past, we have issued warnings, penalty points, various other penalties ... but the message clearly isn't getting through." Henceforth, there would be an immediate penalty: "specifically grid positions for the race. If someone going slowly disturbs other riders, they can expect to start from further back." The penalties would be cumulative; and a system examining section times would be applied. Any rider going slower than 107 per cent (later 110 per cent) of their best time would be investigated, and doing so without good reason for three sections or more would be promptly penalised.

This did prevent the absurd spectacle of Catalunya recurring, but only up to a point, and sufficient numbers of riders were still prepared (or forced by circumstances) to take the risk that the punishment became a regular feature. The minimum punishment was the loss of three grid places, and for some riders being forced to miss half of race-morning warm-up as well. Further sanctions awaited serial offenders, but were seldom deployed.

One such victim was eventual champion Danny Kent, in Australia again, where he and seven other riders fell foul of the system: he had exceeded the limit over eight sectors and was docked six grid places, which dropped him from pole to the third row.

But to a large extent, Kent was a victim also of circumstances, and he gave a lucid explanation of the difficulties he faced in qualifying, when every other rider wanted to tag on behind him. The new system was not proving effective.

Back at Assen, Webb had said, "If this doesn't work, we are prepared to change the format of qualifying, though I'd prefer not to do that during the racing season." A system edging towards Superpole, allowing riders much more limited track time, was under consideration. It is likely to be introduced for 2016.

It's time for
a challenge.

TISSOT PRS 516 AUTOMATIC.
A VERY SPECIAL PIECE WITH A VINTAGE
TOUCH THAT PAYS HOMAGE TO
RACING CARS. THE HOLES IN THE
STRAP INVENTED BY TISSOT
ILLUSTRATE THOSE OF
A STEERING WHEEL.
AUTOMATIC MOVEMENT
WITH UP TO 60 HOURS
OF POWER RESERVE.

TISSOT BOUTIQUE, OXFORD ST 373 – LONDON WIC 2JR

TISSOTSHOP.COM

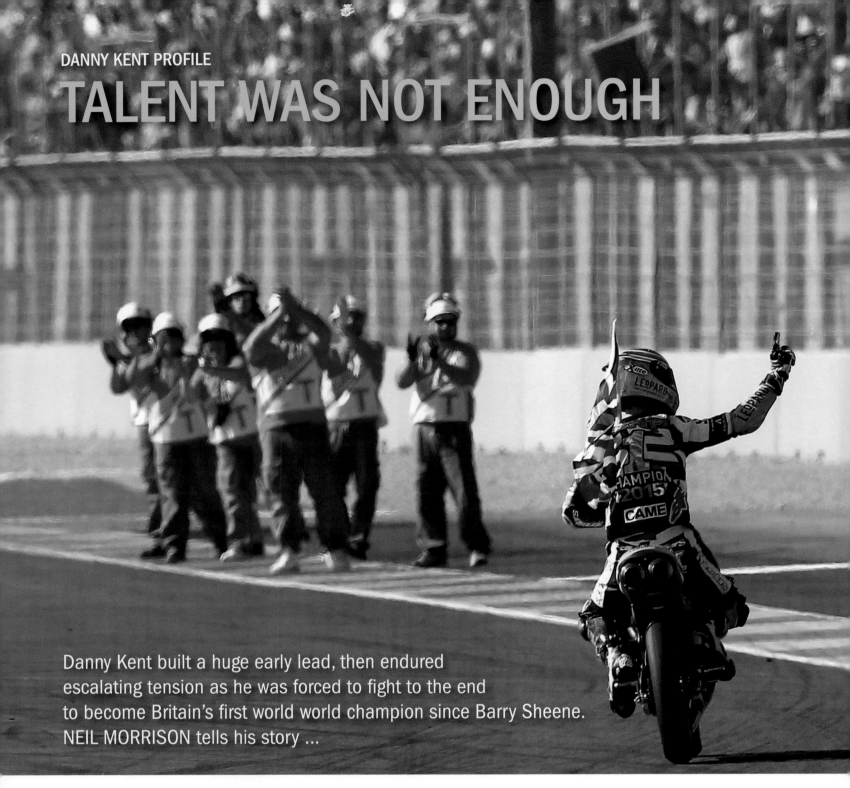

TALENT WAS NOT ENOUGH

Danny Kent built a huge early lead, then endured
escalating tension as he was forced to fight to the end
to become Britain's first world world champion since Barry Sheene.
NEIL MORRISON tells his story ...

Above: Kent's championship made him heir to Barry Sheene – after 38 years.

Centre, from top: In his first grand prix years, Kent had the benefit of vastly experienced crew chief Massimo Branchini; on the Husqvarna in 2014; perfectionist Danny pays attention to detail.

Right: The clenched fist signals a second win over uneasy team-mate Sandro Cortese at Valencia in 2012.

Far right: Kent's foray into Moto2 in 2013 was an unhappy experience. He returns with renewed hopes in 2016.

Photos: Gold & Goose

I F one rider has proved the adage that talent is no longer enough to succeed in racing, it would be 2015 Moto3 World Champion Danny Kent. The man with the enviable claim of ending Great Britain's long wait for a grand prix title had danced on the precipice of anonymity in a disappointing year in Moto2, before adding focus and belief to his armoury to finally realise his ability in 2015.

In a season of two halves, Kent was sublime in the first act, a new-found air of conviction and belief brought about by an instant gelling with the Kiefer Racing team and Honda's title winning NSF250R. His on-track antics reflected as much: five wins – three with a winning margin of more than seven seconds – and three further podiums in the first nine races ultimately were enough to secure the crown.

There were jitters and nerves in act two. A resurgent KTM-backed Miguel Oliveira, buoyed by a new chassis from Misano onwards, kept things interesting. A combination of relentless winning on his part and caution and bad fortune on Kent's resulted in Oliveira's 110-point deficit leaving Silverstone shrinking to 24 before Valencia.

A nervous showing in the race ensured that the title wasn't guaranteed until the final lap. But by then, Kent knew what was required mathematically to take the title, even if ninth place could have been achieved "with just one eye open", to

borrow his words, in the first half of the year.

The result completed not just a remarkable turn-around for Kent's own fortunes, but capped the resurgence of the British Isles as a force in grand prix racing. Those who had worked closely with him in the past regularly described a young man who possessed an abundance of natural talent, but with an equal measure of self-doubt.

Just ten months before his first victory of 2015, Kent had reached a career nadir, placing a dismal 17th in Barcelona in what was fast becoming an underwhelming return to the Moto3 class. The danger of fading away was real, and he began to realise that ability was no longer enough. From there, a focus on training, and getting the best out of the equipment available to him, resulted in his career following a largely positive trajectory.

Meanwhile for the UK, Kent's championship win curtailed a remarkable barren spell in grand prix racing. Not since the second edition of this annual could one of the four home countries boast a champion. The UK had produced six of the first ten premier-class winners. Anyone who had suggested in 1977 that the UK's next grand prix champion would come 38 years after Barry Sheene's second title triumph in Imatra would have been ridiculous.

The road for British riders into grands prix had long become

blurred by the time Kent was earmarked by Dorna scouts as a future star. Having narrowly missed out on winning the national Aprilia Superteens series – which had nurtured the talents of Casey Stoner and Cal Crutchlow - in 2007, Kent travelled to Barcelona with Dorna's MotoGP academy a year later.

The Red Bull-backed scheme was the MotoGP rights owners' solution to raising the profile of the series beyond the reaches of the Mediterranean. Due in part to a recession-hit industry and a cheaper, readily available alternative, the majority of British riders could no longer afford two-stroke racing from the mid-eighties. Grand prix results suffered, illustrated by a 15-year dearth of success, bookended by Ian McConnachie and Jeremy McWilliams' sole wins in 1986 and 2001.

In Spain, Kent received guidance from former GP winner Alberto Puig and was handed a ride in the CEV, the world's fiercest national grand prix class. While the UK now specialised in sports bike racing, those chasing the GP dream were forced to fly south to race against future world championship talent on world championship-level circuits. Fellow Brits Chaz Davies, Bradley Smith and Scott Redding had already trodden the path. Now it was the turn of 14-year-old Kent.

A promising ninth in his first season abroad led to a seat in the Red Bull Rookies programme the following year. He chalked up three podiums in his first campaign, before coming within a point of taking the title in his second. The disappointment of losing out to Jake Gagne was tempered by a full-time call-up to the Ajo Motorsports squad aboard their KTM 125 in 2011.

It was there that Kent was partnered with Italian crew chief Massimo Branchini, the man Casey Stoner had charged with teaching him the art of effectively relaying bike behaviour to the crew around him. For Branchini, Kent's pure talent was clear from the start of their working relationship. "For sure, Danny is one of the big talents. When you see the data, his talent is corner speed," he explained. "Compared to another rider, it is very, very high. Maybe in the braking, he was not so strong, but it was not a big problem because he had a very smooth style."

Fast in patches in his full debut year, Kent took seven races to score his debut podium aboard the new four-stroke KTM 250 in Moto3's inaugural campaign in 2012. By the season finale, he had notched up his first and second wins, keeping a cool head in two high-intensity brawls in Motegi and Valencia.

A graduation to Moto2 aboard Tech 3's Mistral chassis ended in disappointment, however, the rare flashes of speed rarely translating into a noteworthy performance. Just 16 points and 22nd overall was a miserly return for one of the purported big

Above: Out on his own: Kent's win at Silverstone in the wet was by almost ten seconds. Runaways were something of a habit.

Above right: Mired in the pack. Kent stays inside for safety amid typical Moto3 cut and thrust at Mugello. Oliveira (44, obscured) won, Kent was second by inches.

Top right: Kent's success was based heavily on his working relationship with crew chief Peter Bom.

Right: Victory at Jerez was number three of six in 2015.

Photos: Gold & Goose

talents in the class.

For team boss Herve Poncharal, the sight of unrealised ability was tough to watch. "I could see I had a diamond, but it was just unpolished," he said earlier in 2015. "Danny at that time was not a fighter. Every time I was talking to him, he was looking at his shoes. I think he was more focused on his hairstyle rather than training [and] after a certain stage there was no communication."

Kent felt that the jump to the intermediate category had been premature. A return to Moto3 followed, but any aims of a shot at the world title coincided with a field packed with talent. Working again alongside Branchini under the Ajo umbrella, Kent was in the Husqvarna – a rebranded KTM – side of the garage, while title favourite Jack Miller wore the Red Bull colours. "It took me a while to get used to Moto3 again after Moto2," Kent said. More tellingly, he added, "Perhaps in previous years, I felt that I wasn't the number-one rider."

The after-effects of a year scrapping for lowly points lingered until the already mentioned disappointment in Montmelo. Then it was rare to see Kent lapping in practice alone. Complaints of bike set-up were common. Then, arriving in Assen less than two weeks later, his team noticed a change.

Branchini: "Before, he said, 'In every practice, the bike is sliding, the bike is this and that.' In his mind, he found a problem. After this, he said, 'Okay, the bike is this,' [and] he was

calmer. After, he was fighting for the podium every week and we didn't touch the bike."

The Danny Kent who strode along the pit lane after the three-week summer break also caught Poncharal off guard: "It's not imagination. Danny was walking different. Before, he never looked at you right in the eyes, and he looked me in the eye. Something changed. He was more self-confident. And from that moment, also on the track he changed."

Several podiums followed as the autumn arrived. For it was then that Kent switched to Honda machinery and got to know the Kiefer team. Crucially, he had the chance to work alongside new crew chief Peter Bom, Stefan Bradl's right-hand man during his title year in Moto2.

In a single afternoon of testing at Valencia, Kent was immediately faster than his best time from the race weekend. His crew marvelled at his ability to push the Honda to its limits on cold tyres, and carry their instructions out to the fullest. What's more, Bom slowly began to gain Kent's trust, the Dutchman's machine adjustments regularly resulting in lap-time gains. The seeds were sown in Kent's head: At this rate, 2015 could be really interesting...

He arrived in Qatar in the best physical condition of his career, the potential shown in testing spurring him on during training in the winter months. "Motivation for my training was high, knowing I could have a great year," he said in Jerez. "The

fitter I am, the stronger my mind is. If before I went running now I run twice as far. I'm not making as many mistakes, and it's all down to my fitness. I now have a stronger mind."

A strong third in Qatar and that first commanding win in Texas suggested as much. But, according to Bom, Kent was still mechanically over-analysing, filling his thoughts with technical information when the more pressing issue of race tactics was at hand.

"I would say the way he behaved, Danny was damaged a little bit," explained Bom, midway through the year. "He didn't trust us making certain decisions. He tried to get involved with everything with me. That's one thing I needed to sort out quickly. Maybe he got f****d around a little bit in the past. I will never change something on the bike without telling him, just to check if he's paying attention. Or always changing the bike again and promising there will be a miracle. That's wrong, but it happens a lot."

The good results continued, another dominant win in Argentina coming before his first close-combat victory in Jerez. A freak shower during qualifying in France left him stranded in 31st on the grid. Not a problem, however, as he scorched through the field for a fine fourth. Two more wins in Barcelona and Germany followed before the summer break.

Incredibly, Bom still had to occasionally remind the championship leader of his talents. "I have worked with a lot of riders.

Me saying I thought, talent-wise, he is up there with them and that he should start to believe in it as much as I do, I saw him look at me like, 'Really, you think that?' That really surprised me that he didn't trust himself that much."

Clearly the team's more familiar approach was paying dividends. Team manager Stefan Kiefer explained: "We try to be a team which is like a family, to be fair and honest, and try to understand the riders. With Danny, it worked perfect from the first second."

Kent had never enjoyed a relationship like this with his crew chief. Small details like sharing a hotel room with Bom during race weekends were having a positive effect. "We're a lot closer," Kent said in Valencia. "We're in contact even when I'm at home. If we're in the hotel and we think of something that can improve set-up, we'll discuss it. He listens to me and he's very skilled."

As the two seasons before had proved, the Moto3 class isn't supposed to be this one-sided. Kent's 66-point lead at the halfway stage made him the subject of all types of speculation. Several Moto2 teams were interested in his services for 2016. As were several premier-class outfits, with Pramac Ducati offering him a three-year deal to follow friend and training partner Jack Miller in bypassing Moto2, a straight ticket to the big time.

Kent's belief that given time and the right equipment, he

Above: **The tightly-knit Kent clan stroll around Indy's "Gasoline Alley."**
Photo: Whit Bazemore Photography

Top right: **Kent's unforced error at Aragon could easily have cost him the championship.**

Above right: **Flying the flag. Kent after winning at Montmelo.**

Bottom right: **Kent in early-season command, leading main rival Oliveira and Red Bull team-mate Brad Binder at Jerez. They finished in that order.**
Photos: Gold & Goose

could be a force in the top class was a sure sign of how far his self-confidence had come. Yet a split with long-time manager Roger Burnett before the summer left the 21-year-old alone in negotiating deals. Results on track took a temporary hit.

A romp to victory at a soaking Silverstone aside, Kent was off the podium at Indianapolis, Brno and Misano. Then, on the day his graduation to the Moto2 class with Kiefer Racing in 2016 was announced, came a rash last-corner fall at Aragon – "a stupid thing" in Kiefer's words – that was completely out of sync with his measured, season-long approach.

Next came the nerves. Kent's first match point arrived in the rain in Motegi. A tepid opening preceded a strong end, leading to his team boss's frustration: "I was not happy with him. He was much too slow in the first four or five laps. There we lost points." Misfortune led to him being pushed off track in Phillip Island, first by an errant Francesco Bagnaia, then by Nico Antontelli, whose contact sent him spiralling through the air.

A fifth in Sepang would have been enough to collect the crown. But another nervy opening and an unwillingness to apply the measured aggression of the first half of the year on the leading group meant he came home seventh, all in contrast to Oliveira's relentless final push.

Kent, 24 points ahead, needed to place 14th to secure the crown. And that was only if Oliveira won. While the mathematics were clearly on his side, that didn't stop one last flap in qualifying. Eighteenth on the grid was the result of a head-scratching gearbox change mid-session. Suddenly, Oliveira began to believe.

A night away from the track at Bom's behest worked won-

ders. Kent returned on Sunday, his mind refocused. "We made a small change," said Kiefer. "The warm-up was really good, and afterward he came to me and said, 'Stefan, I will do it exactly as I did in warm-up,' and I said, 'Okay, I know he will do it.'"

Along with Oliveira, Kent had to overcome unhappy memories from his days as a teenage racer. Twice he had been in title-winning positions in the last lap of the last race – the first in the Superteens series, then Red Bull Rookies – only to lose out.

Knowing the stakes, Kent rode within his means to come home ninth, the colossal pressure that had weighed him down for weeks finally lifted. Sixty different riders from 12 countries had won grand prix titles between Sheene's last title and Kent's first. That made the triumph all the sweeter.

"It gives me goose bumps. It's a dream come true for any rider, and being British, it means even more than it might for a Spanish rider, as there's a Spanish champion every year. You don't get that in England, so it's a great feeling.

"A lot of people have been asking about the pressure, and I've had to say 'No, no pressure,' as Oliveira is reading all of these interviews! It's normal to have pressure, and I put a lot of it on myself. Because we had such a great start to the year, doing what we did, we had a big target on our backs."

For Kent, a move to Moto2 has already shown promise in winter testing. There he will join title favourite Sam Lowes as, along with MotoGP contingent Bradley Smith, Cal Crutchlow and Scott Redding, the British grand prix resurgence continues apace. Surely there won't be another 38-year gap.

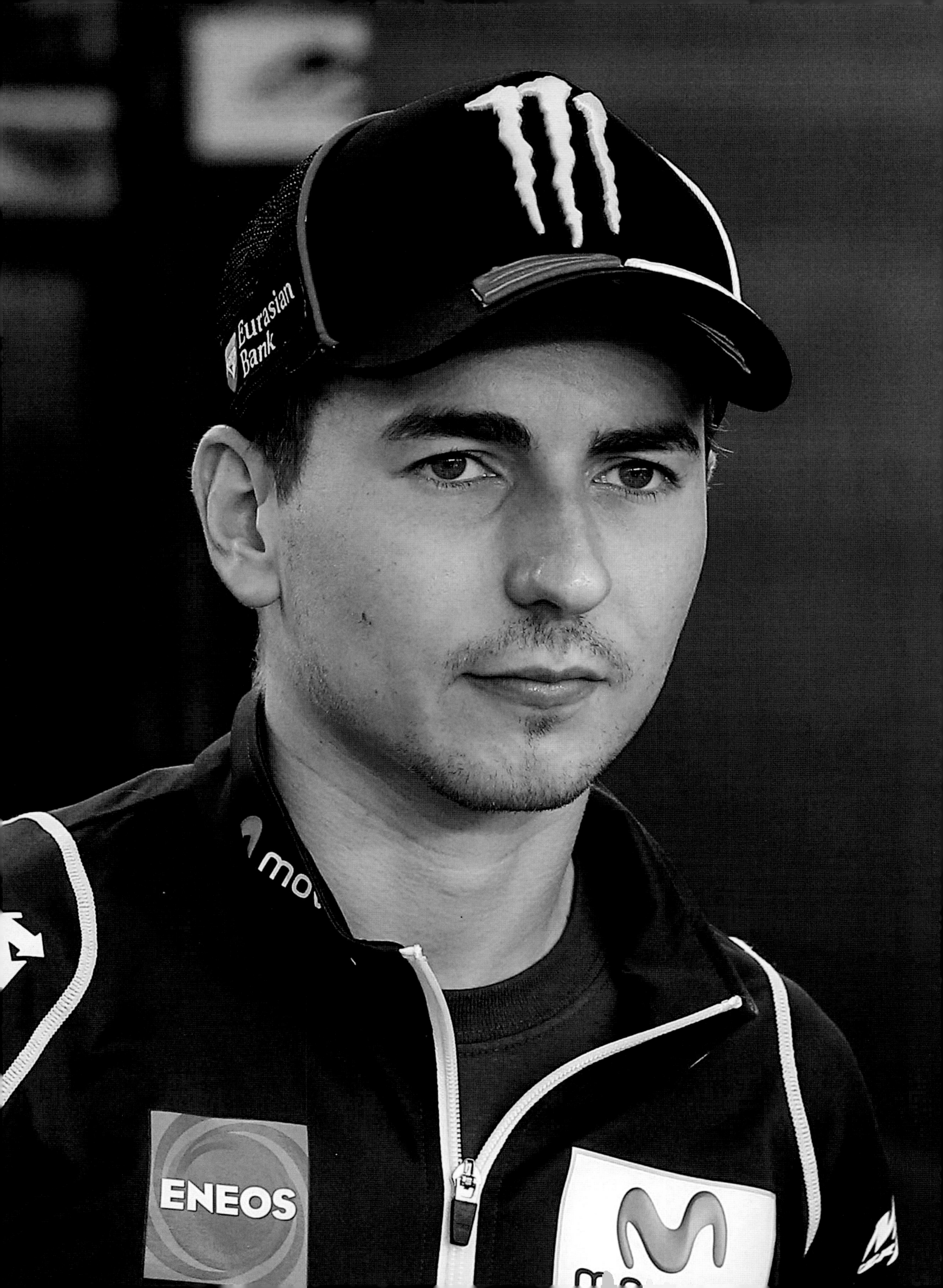
Eurasian
Bank
ENEOS

"The enemy of mine enemy is my friend." – Ancient proverb

Left: Rossi wrote the script and
played the lead in the 2015 melo-
drama. "Nobody is innocent" was
the verdict of a Spanish newspaper.
Photo: Gold & Goose

Left: Marquez couldn't win the
championship, but his influence on
the outcome was crucial.

Main: Lorenzo's fine title win was
shadowed by matters beyond his
own control.
Photos: Gold & Goose

THE LOVELESS TRIANGLE

The poisonous relationship between Rossi, Marquez and Lorenzo
dominated and coloured the climax of the 2015 MotoGP season.

How did it come to this, asks MAT OXLEY

ONCE upon a time, an Italian of great distinction and a Spaniard of burning ambition lived next door to each other. The Italian did not like the Spaniard, and the Spaniard did not like the Italian. Their mutual dislike grew and grew until one day they built a big wall so they would not have to gaze upon one another.

Some years later, a younger Spaniard with fire in his soul moved in further down the street. Soon he had a fight with his older compatriot, who became very angry. Later the younger Spaniard became best friends with the Italian of great distinction. They never invited the other Spaniard to their parties.

Then one day, the younger Spaniard and the Italian of great distinction had their own fight and became sworn enemies. Then the two Spaniards made up and became friends, making the Italian of great distinction very, very angry.

MotoGP's loveless triangle could be a fairy tale, a Greek tragedy, a Dynasty-style TV serial or just a silly little playground spat. But it may just change MotoGP for ever.

By the end of 2015, the relationship between Valentino Rossi, Marc Marquez and Jorge Lorenzo had become so poisonous that lawyers and bodyguards were called in.

Of course, bitter rivalries are nothing new in grand prix racing, though the first really public feud occurred in the late 1960s, between Yamaha team-mates Phil Read and Bill Ivy. Their battle for the 1968 250 title descended into farce at the Monza finale, where Ivy filed a protest against his victorious team-mate, claiming that Read's number plates didn't comply with regulations. If Ivy had won the race and

therefore the title, Read intended to protest that his diminutive team-mate was below the FIM's nine-stone-six minimum weight limit. Read's mechanic, Ferry Brouwer, remembers the weekend: "It would've been more fun going to a funeral."

The Valencia championship climax between Yamaha team-mates Lorenzo and Rossi was similarly hate-filled, a complete contrast to Rossi's last final-race showdown at the Spanish track. His Valencia duel with Nicky Hayden for the 2006 MotoGP championship had been every bit as intense, but it felt like a great sporting occasion, not a mean-spirited brawl.

The roots of this epic fall-out go back nearly a decade, when Lorenzo was fighting his way through the 125 and 250 ranks, his eyes already fixed on the greatest prize of them all. When Yamaha signed the fiery youngster, he was the first team-mate who posed a serious threat to Rossi, who had only recently transformed Yamaha from paddock joke to MotoGP dominator. The king of MotoGP was aggrieved, feeling that this was no reward for his hard work and dedication. But of course, Yamaha had to think of the future. Rossi was knocking on 30 years old and they couldn't wait until the king was gone before anointing a successor. The moment Lorenzo arrived, the team wasn't big enough for both of them.

The famous pit wall, erected between the Italian and the Spaniard, in fact initially had been requested by the pair's rival tyre manufacturers. In 2008, their first year as team-mates, Rossi's YZR-M1 ran Bridgestones, while Lorenzo's bike used Michelins. But when MotoGP moved to a control-

tyre format in 2009, the wall stayed in place, because the riders preferred it that way.

Animosity fizzed and crackled between the two, and yet their first heavy racing duel didn't happen until Motegi 2010, when Lorenzo had one hand on his first MotoGP crown and Rossi was recovering from a recently broken leg. The pair disputed third place – last-chance saloon for the all-important podium champagne party – colliding on several occasions during a torrid final few laps. Rossi won the duel, as he had won similar physical encounters with Sete Gibernau and Casey Stoner.

After the race, Lorenzo raged that Rossi had taken him so close to an accident with the title almost won. Yamaha admonished their four-times world champion, who left the team office like a naughty schoolboy following an encounter with an angry headmaster.

"Yamaha asked me to race with more attention," he beamed. So, what would happen if he had another duel with his team-mate? "I will try to beat him again… with more attention!"

Motegi was Rossi dealing out a little bit of revenge for what had happened a few months earlier. At Mugello, Lorenzo had led the championship and Rossi had broken a leg. The injury had come at a time when Yamaha was negotiating a new contract with its legendary rider, apparently already convinced that Lorenzo was the future. Rossi didn't fancy hanging around as number-two rider, so he cut off his nose to spite his face and signed with Ducati.

Two years of pain, suffering and embarrassment followed. When Rossi returned to Yamaha at the end of 2012, seemingly drifting towards retirement, the reunited team-mates announced that they had grown up and put their differences behind them. Lorenzo, like most people, probably no longer saw Rossi as a serious title rival, so there was surely no reason for them to rekindle their enmity.

And anyway, Lorenzo had someone new with whom to fall out. When Casey Stoner announced his retirement in May, 2012, the Majorcan no doubt could see his way to a sunny upland of further MotoGP glory. Then just weeks later, HRC signed Moto2 hero Marc 'The Merciless' Marquez.

Marquez was instantly competitive on his Repsol Honda RC213V. While champion Lorenzo won the season-opening Qatar Grand Prix, Marquez disputed second place with his childhood racing hero. The first Marquez versus Rossi encounter was a balletic clash, the pair swapping places time and again around the fast and flowing Losail circuit, the old-timer finally prevailing over the young upstart by a couple of tenths. The race proved that Rossi wasn't over the hill, and that Marquez was already very nearly at the top. Afterwards, they embraced warmly – hero and fan together for the first time – but both surely knew the romance could not last.

Two weeks later, Marquez won his first MotoGP race in Texas, and another fortnight after that he had his first encounter with Lorenzo. It wasn't a happy one. Arguing over second place, the pair headed towards Jerez's famous final hairpin. Marquez instigated a block pass on his compatriot, pretty much a replica of the manoeuvre Rossi had made on Gibernau at the same corner eight years earlier.

This was no coincidence. Marquez had spent his childhood watching Rossi, learning the tricks of a sometimes dirty trade. He had seen the 2005 Rossi/Gibernau move on television and had memorised every detail for future use.

Just as Rossi had defeated Gibernau, so Marquez took second at Jerez, Lorenzo third and wagging his finger at the youngster like an angry father. Insult had been added to injury because only days earlier, the hairpin had been christened Lorenzo Corner. It didn't seem like it anymore.

While Lorenzo seethed, Rossi and Marquez became best buddies, chatting and giggling whenever they were together. They seemed like natural friends, with similar attitudes to life and racing: happy chappies off the bike, grinning assassins on it. They were smiling cavaliers to Lorenzo's sombre Spartan.

In 2013, Marquez went on to become history's youngest premier-class champion; Lorenzo's challenge was derailed by huge crashes at Assen and the Sachsenring. The following season, the youngster dominated, winning a record 13 races. The Lorenzo era was surely over.

Then the dynamic changed again. Rossi won the very first race of 2015, while Marquez was immediately in trouble, his RC213V less of a friend than it had been during the previous two seasons. And yet the Spaniard won the second race in Texas and led the third in Argentina, until a fading rear tyre and a resurgent Rossi brought the two together, literally. On the penultimate lap, Marquez clipped the rear of Rossi's M1 and went down hard.

Ten weeks later, the pair argued over Assen's most famous piece of tarmac, colliding as they attacked the chicane for the final time. Once again, Rossi came out on top to win the race and extend his championship lead, while Marquez finished second, at least closing the points gap on Lorenzo, who finished a distant third, after having dominated the previous four races.

Marquez's bike troubles had left him struggling to keep up with Rossi and Lorenzo on the rejuvenated M1. His fourth and fifth crashes of the year – at Silverstone and Aragon – ended his slim hopes of a historic title hat trick.

For the final third of the season, it was a straightforward all-Yamaha duel. Of course, Rossi wasn't merely trying to win a tenth world title in his 20th grand prix season, he was also trying to exact further revenge on Lorenzo for having driven him out of Yamaha in 2010. Because if Rossi hadn't allowed his ego to be flattered by Ducati, he might already have become the most successful rider in history, overtaking Giacomo Agostini's record of 122 GP wins.

Meanwhile, Marquez still had a part to play. "Valentino is really smart and he taught us something," he said after his Assen defeat. "We must learn from it…"

At the 16th round of the championship at Phillip Island,

Marquez won a breathtaking four-way skirmish with Lorenzo, Rossi and Ducati's Andrea Iannone. Such a titanic scrap was nothing new at Phillip Island, where fast and wide corners have produced some of the best racing in the world championship spanning two decades.

Marquez snatched the lead from Lorenzo with just three corners to go, which made Rossi's claim that Marquez had been hindering him and aiding Lorenzo ring hollow. The words certainly rankled Marquez, but not half as much as Rossi's astonishing attack during the pre-event media conference for the following weekend's Malaysian round. There, Rossi repeated his claims of the previous Sunday, adding for good measure that he wondered if Marquez had ever been his fan.

Such was the shock of this onslaught that some journalists guffawed, thinking it a jolly good joke. What was Rossi up to? Everyone knew Marquez had been his starry-eyed fan; there was photographic evidence to prove it. So, either these were the mind-games of a Machiavellian genius or the paranoid outburst of a man buckling under the pressure. Lorenzo had been inching closer and closer to Rossi's championship lead, and certainly had the sheer speed to catch and pass him.

The Sepang race will for ever be the defining moment of the 2015 season. While Dani Pedrosa took off out front, Marquez looked as out of control as he had been for most of the year. He ran wide, Lorenzo came past and set off after the leader. Then Rossi too came by and seemed set to chase his team-mate. Marquez had other ideas. He came back at Rossi, again and again. This was nothing like the ballet of Qatar 2013, this was a heavyweight rumble in the jungle. Rossi had insulted Marquez in public; this was Marquez avenging that affront, as well as Argentina and Assen.

There is an unwritten rule in racing that you don't race a title hopeful if you've no chance of winning the title yourself. Marquez chose to ignore that rule, just as Rossi had ignored

Above: "He's behind you!" Rossi used all his gifts and experience to take the fight to Lorenzo.

Top left: Marquez makes his mark: his Rossi-inspired Jerez pass in 2013 left Lorenzo seriously miffed.

Above left: And again. According to Rossi, Marquez "helped Lorenzo" with his amazing last-lap charge to the lead in Australia.

Left: All smiles at the now infamous Malaysian press conference. At first, everyone thought Rossi's attack had been meant as a joke.

Below left: The Assen clash. Marquez's chicane attack was rough and ruthless, Rossi's response more so.

Photos: Gold & Goose

Below: Sweet summer. Lorenzo and Rossi celebrate another double podium at Aragon. By early autumn, the fizz had gone from their uneasy partnership.
Photo: Gold & Goose

Right: Baby-face no more? Marquez still looks cool, just after getting back on track with Honda's 700th win at Indianapolis.
Photo: Whit Bazemore Photography

Below right: Lorenzo controlled Marquez from the front at Valencia. Or did he?

Bottom right: What have I done? A subdued Rossi post-race in Sepang's *parc fermé.*

Below far right: After a season of high expectation and towering achievement, Lorenzo's title triumph was turned slightly sour.
Photos: Gold & Goose

it at Motegi five years earlier. The pair's vicious slugging match allowed Lorenzo to escape, and that was too much for Rossi. First he waved angrily at Marquez, as if swatting away an annoying insect. Finally, the provocation got too much; Rossi slowed, ran wide and looked at Marquez, no doubt speaking a few choice words inside his helmet. Then the bikes tangled and Marquez crashed out. As penance, Rossi would have to start the final race of the year from last.

Rumours of a Marquez/Lorenzo accord swept the paddock, the press and the internet. More likely this was nothing more than that ancient proverb, "The enemy of mine enemy is my friend" made modern.

The Sepang clash sent MotoGP into a panic: Rossi appealed to the Court of Arbitration for Sport; Lorenzo's lawyers tried to get involved; Dorna cancelled the Valencia pre-event media conference, apparently unable to contemplate its three greatest riders sitting side by side; and Yamaha cancelled the company's 60th anniversary party.

The final race of the year did nothing to reduce the bitterness and bile or placate the conspiracy theorists. Lorenzo led from start to finish, shadowed all the way by Marquez, Pedrosa briefly in with a chance. Rossi stormed through from the back row to fourth, but by the time he had reached that position, the top three were long gone. The only way he could win the championship was if Lorenzo was beaten by both Repsol Hondas.

The result was surely proof of the conspiracy: Marquez never attacked Lorenzo, he had ridden shotgun to his compatriot. Or had he? Valencia is a tight, narrow go-kart track of a grand prix circuit, where more often than not the man who leads into the first corner is never overtaken. Marquez

denied the 'shotgun' accusation, pointing out that all seven of Lorenzo's 2015 victories had been Valencia replicas. In other words, when he's on it, Lorenzo is impossible to pass.

Marquez's most persuasive argument was born of the turn his life had taken since Sepang. Rossi fans – possibly half the world's motorcyclists – had turned on him in fury. He knew very well that if he didn't beat Lorenzo at Valencia, he would pay the price for years to come. Diehard Rossi fans certainly wouldn't be cheering any of his future successes. No wonder he wore a face like thunder in the post-race *parc fermé* – minutes later, he was loudly booed while standing on the podium.

And anyway, even if he had won the race, Lorenzo would still have taken the title. If Marquez had been so determined to deny Rossi the championship, surely he would have juggled with all the Valencia permutations during the lead up to the grand finale: if he won the race, Lorenzo would be champion; if he finished second, Lorenzo would be champion, so he couldn't deny Lorenzo the title on his own.

The fallout of Sepang and its aftermath will affect MotoGP. At Valencia, FIM president Vito Ippolito announced that "changes will be made to prevent this from happening again". It is possible MotoGP will introduce a stewards system, similar to that used in Formula One, to judge racing incidents not purely from a regulatory perspective, but also from a sporting perspective.

Most MotoGP fans enjoy the elbow-to-elbow battles that make it so different to Formula One, but from now on each and every incident will be examined and dissected, with heavier punishments applied to the guilty. How long before that changes the racing?

FLYING ON THE GROUND

The forces generated by mechanical rotation or aerodynamic intervention are relatively small – but MotoGP consists of small differences. NEIL SPALDING explains...

Above: **Above: The only way is forward. Bautista's Aprilia remained wingless, but still earthbound.**

Bottom right: **Small margins make big differences: Rossi's Yamaha leads the bewinged Ducatis early in the season.**

Photos: Whit Bazemore Photography

MOTORCYCLES are not like cars; they bank and weave. They aren't like aircraft either; they can wheelie or pitch, but not climb or dive. But many of the things that affect a car or aircraft can also affect a bike, sometimes in slightly different ways. The trick is to recognise what aspects of a given design might enhance a bike's performance, and then to maximise the positive and minimise the negative aspects of the new addition.

In 2015, two particular technical aspects came to the fore. Both were design decisions that had been around for years, but suddenly they attracted new adherents and appeared to be making a difference.

Old ideas, but back in the spotlight.

Deciding which way to rotate the crankshaft became important. Three new bikes joined the grid in 2015, and the two that had 'proper' MotoGP engines had been designed with crankshafts that rotated backwards.

Wings, a technology that seems to have been tried once a decade for over 40 years, were suddenly back in vogue. Ducati made a major effort to use them; Yamaha tried them out and raced with them on occasion.

CRANKSHAFT ROTATION

So which way should the crankshaft rotate on a MotoGP bike? For years, Yamaha have employed a reverse-rotating crankshaft, Aprilia had one, too, on their three-cylinder 'Cube', Kawasaki, used one in 2009, their final year in MotoGP. The original design reason for Yamaha and Aprilia was packaging. Yamaha wanted their crankshaft to have a central power take-off and needed a jackshaft to take the power from the centre of the bike to the primary gear mounted on the clutch basket.

The effect of the primary gear is to reverse the rotation of the primary input; since the ubiquitous two-shaft gearbox rotates the final drive (output) sprocket in the opposite direction to the primary shaft, it follows that interposing a jackshaft means that the crank must turn backwards to get the drive sprocket turning forwards. There is a cost to power output: an extra set of gears sapping perhaps two per cent. Yamaha considered that cost acceptable, as did Aprilia.

During the 990cc years, it became obvious that the Yamaha operated on track differently from the other in-line fours. All the others found it extremely difficult to change direction at high speed, yet the Yamaha managed to do it easily. By comparison, the Honda 990 had a 'conventional' forward crankshaft rotation, and its relatively narrow V5 engine seemed to roll in quickly and to hold tighter lines. In any event, its greater power output seemed to encourage a more hard-stopping and hard-accelerating style. It seems that the wider engine of a conventional in-line four resists the initial turn in, as do the gyroscopic forces that prefer to continue in a straight line. The narrower V5's more centralised weight distribution took less effort to roll into the corners.

The Kawasaki conversion from forward-rotating crank to reverse occurred in the winter of 2008/9. Realising that

their bike, similar in many ways to the Yamaha, still wouldn't change direction as well, they decided to reverse the rotation of the crankshaft on their last ZX-RR.

In the brief time the bike was competitive, before Kawasaki withdrew from racing, it was apparent that it turned far better, well enough for Marco Melandri to grab a podium at Le Mans for the Hayate team. Now, Suzuki and Ducati have debuted engines with crankshafts that rotate backwards.

Initially the idea came from Honda in the mid-1960s. Running in-line four and then in-line six 250s, they wanted the power take-off in the centre of the crank, hence a jackshaft to transfer the power to the clutch. When Yamaha subsequently built their in-line-four two-stroke 700 and 750s in the 1970s, they used the same central power take-off.

On track, it was discovered that these wide bikes initially would roll over into the corners unexpectedly easily, but then had a reputation for understeering on the corner exit.

There are several effects at play here, all very small individually, but together adding up to a significant change in the bike's dynamic behaviour.

Gyroscopically, a reverse-rotating crank reduces the overall desire of the bike to continue in a straight line. You have a lot of wheels and shafts spinning in different directions on the bike, but the main ones in terms of being efficient gyroscopes are the wheels, with their brakes and tyres, and the crankshaft. The wheels and tyres, especially Bridgestones, are heavy, but they rotate relatively slowly. The crank is smaller, but still typically around 10kg (to help control throttle response), and it can easily be revving to 17,000rpm or more on a hard-braking corner entry.

Now, if you try to turn (or lean) a gyroscope, it generates a force at 90 degrees – called gyroscopic precession. Having the crankshaft turn backwards generates a force in the opposite direction to that generated by the front and rear wheels. There is a certain cancellation effect; the sum total of the precessional forces is reduced.

Of course, in the case of a motorcycle, it is not quite that simple. The overall effect depends on the relative rotational speeds of all the main parts of the equation at each point of the corner.

Once the rider tries to steer into the corner, as usual by counter-steering the 'wrong' way, gyroscopic effects again come in to play. For a turn to the right, the bike is steered initially to the left; that left turn effectively trips the bike up,

the mass falls to the right. This is aided by the gyroscopic reaction to a left turn, which is for the top of the wheel to rotate over to the right, helping the fall into the corner.

There follows another reaction. As the wheel is dropped into the corner (i.e., the bike pitches over to full lean), a second gyroscopic reaction can be noted, as the bike wants to oversteer. Both of these gyroscopic reactions are very small, but they still have an effect, and on a bike with a reverse-rotating crankshaft, less effort will be required initially, but then it will fall into the corner slightly more slowly. All things being equal, the slight oversteer tendency will be less, compared to a bike with a forward-rotating crankshaft.

There is more: when turning into a corner, the speed of the bike and the violence of the manoeuvre influence the way the bike reacts. In normal street riding, the counter-steer (to the left) generates a force in the tyre carcass, and a barely measurable movement of the tyre to the left, causing the bike to start to fall over to the right. At full MotoGP speeds, however, the front wheel changes track much more.

That means the bike has rotated about a point in space, a 'roll centre'; the question then has to be what decides where that point is? We think that the roll centre is some complex interaction between the vertical centre of gravity location and the roll inertia properties of the machine; this belief has led Honda on a decades-long pursuit of mass centralisation in roll. The late Warren Willing, however, was firmly of the view that there is a centre point for all the gyroscopic forces, too, and while the effects are likely to be smaller than those defined by the centre of gravity, they will also have an effect on the position of the roll centre.

To add to all of this gyroscopic action, we also have the relatively simple crankshaft torque reaction, a forward-rotating crank will work to enhance a desire to wheelie on acceleration while upright, and it might help hold a line leaned over. By contrast, the reverse-rotating crank will help hold the front of the bike down as it accelerates while vertical, but would tend to make it run wide while leaned over. These torque reactions are also very small, creating perhaps just a couple of kilograms of force, but that can be enough to turn an understeering bike into an oversteering one.

A torque reaction only occurs when you are accelerating or decelerating, so while corner entry sees a reaction, the effects are mostly felt from corner apex onwards while accelerating. On a bike with a conventional forward-rotating crank-

Above: Crankshaft direction reversed and name changed from Kawasaki, the Hayate took Marco Melandri to the podium at Le Mans in 2009.
Photo: Gold & Goose

Top right: Early days for Ducati's experiments in downforce: this is Iannone at COTA
Photo: Whit Bazemore Photography

Centre: The technology develops: pictures show how Ducati's wings changed, at (clockwise from top left) Qatar, Silverstone, Motegi and Phillip Island.

Bottom right: Yamaha's fairing-nose wings first appeared at Misano. Rossi gives them a try.
Photos: Gold & Goose

shaft, the torque reaction is to roll back the engine. While leaned over, that could help tighten the line, but once upright it would allow a wheelie to occur at a lower speed. However, a motorcycle fitted with a reverse-rotating crank – assuming the chassis set-up hasn't been changed to compensate – will tend to understeer as the throttle is applied, then be able to accelerate quicker, as the torque reaction tends to hold the nose of the bike down as it starts to wheelie.

These effects interweave all the way though a corner. In the entry phase, there is gyroscopic influence only when the spinning items, be they wheels crankshafts, cams or gears, are moved off their straight-ahead axis. Once on their new course, the gyroscopic forces are inactive again. The torque reactions only occur when something is being accelerated or decelerated. In a normal race situation, the bike is set up to balance the load on the tyres for the maximum grip. All the slight loading changes caused by the various reactions are balanced out in the set-up decisions, from spring rates to weight distribution; anything not resolved that way is dealt with by the way the rider chooses to ride the machine.

Taken as a whole, the gyroscopic reactions and torque reactions exert very small forces, but if everything else is equal they have an effect on the performance of the machine, and in MotoGP even a small force changes things. It is only when you have bikes equipped with forward-rotating cranks racing bikes fitted with reverse-rotating cranks that you start to notice the differences in the behaviour of each type.

Looking at the current crop of MotoGP bikes and noting their behaviour on track, their 'in corner' performance does seem to be in line with the effects of the small forces described here. The Honda, with its forward-rotating crank, can turn very tightly, while the others prefer to carve wider, smoother lines.

WINGS

Bike designers have tried using wings to create downforce for years, without much success. Now we have real work being put into wing design by Ducati, and they were joined later in the season by Yamaha.

New Zealander Rodger Freeth was one of the first to put wings on his TZ750. Two wings, one mounted high over the rear wheel and one sprouting from the front mudguard, each more than 600mm wide, made this a serious effort to generate downforce. After just three outings, however, and with competitors complaining, the New Zealand rule makers finally decided that the winged bike was too dangerous to

allow on to the racetrack.

In the four-stroke MotoGP era, Aprilia used wings on the special Mugello fairings for their three-cylinder 'Cube', while Ducati brought wings, with additional winglets, to Sachsenring in 2008. The latter were intended to help high-speed stability and extract more air through the fairing flanks, using the vortex created by the winglet hanging down from the end of the small wing. None lasted for long. The normal resolution has been a small redesign, or new settings, to replicate any improved stability endowed by the wings, while dispensing with the extra drag.

In 2015, however, Ducati at least seemed wedded to the concept of wings on the sides of their bikes. Something had changed; the question is what? And the main answer is power.

Current MotoGP bikes make much more power than can be used. Most only ever allow full power to be deployed in the last 100m of the longest straights, and in fifth and sixth gears. The rest of the time, the electronics are used to provide maximum *usable* power, finding the most effective balance of wheelie and rate of acceleration.

So a wing that holds the front down under acceleration allows the computer to hold the power on for longer and lets the bike accelerate harder before the wheelie becomes too big. Ducati were using power they wouldn't otherwise have been able to use to generate downforce (the wings have some drag), and as a result could deploy even more of the power they couldn't previously use to accelerate faster.

It's a virtuous circle. The bigger the wing, the greater the downforce. It was very little by Formula One standards, but the sizeable wings we began to see on the Ducatis were putting tens of kilograms of additional pressure on to the tyres at high speed. Thence more acceleration, and with the current high power levels overcoming the increased drag, allowing ever higher top speeds. (Ducati's extra fuel allocation was a bonus.)

After Ducati's new fairing was debuted at Brno, with its pinched centre section and wider wings, the bike's top speed advantage increased dramatically. For the first half of the season, the works Ducatis and Hondas had similar top speeds through the speed traps. From near equality at Brno, Iannone was 5.8km/h faster than Pedrosa at Silverstone, four at Misano and three at Aragon.

But a motorcycle isn't static. It is always changing its attitude. Wings might help while the bike is upright, but maybe not so much when leaned over. Historically, the top teams have controlled excess lift by changing the angle of the front face of the front cowling, offering several different cowls in search of the best combination of downforce and drag. In 2015, however, Ducati didn't want a big fairing cowl.

The first priority in the redesign of their bike was to make sure it turned into the corners properly, something no Desmosedici had ever done before. One thing that can affect turn-in performance is too much side area on the top part of the fairing: the bigger it is, the greater the wind resistance to a sharp flick into the corner. To prevent this, Ducati made the front cowl as short and small as possible.

The initial Ducati wings were an experiment, introduced at the pre-season Qatar test to try to calm the bike a little on the brakes; it was an experiment that certainly worked.

The Ducati wing was different in several important ways from the wings we had seen before. Ducati's wings were wide, in fact so wide that they had to extend the fairing in front of the rider's hands to make sure the fairing was wider than the wings, as the rules required.

Downforce that helps while the bike is upright can hurt at full lean. You do want the front wheel held down while it is upright, but when leaned over, the downforce still passes straight down through the centre line of the bike. You don't want to push the tyres so hard that they slide, or even let go.

By mounting its wings midway down the flanks of the fairing, however, and therefore close to the ground when leaned over, Ducati exerted pressure on both tyres, trying to spread the load in the hope of increasing grip.

Placing the wings low on the fairing also reduces the effect of the drag on the bike. The location cuts the tendency to elevate the centre of pressure, and therefore does not add to the bike's tendency to wheelie, which is exacerbated at high speed if the centre of pressure is higher than the centre of gravity.

Ducati are now working to improve the efficiency of their basic wing design. From the start, the wings had winglets (flat end plates) on each side. These keep the air that otherwise could have flowed off the end of the wing securely attached to the part that generates the downforce, making the aerofoil work far more efficiently.

For Catalunya's high kerbs, rubber-tipped wings were tried initially to gauge ground clearance. Several races later, at the Sachsenring, a biplane version was used, to see if increasing the downforce would have more benefit. For Brno, new fairings were debuted that were narrower at the front with pinched-in sides around the fork legs. That allowed a bigger wing to be fitted without the bike becoming wider. To push things further, new biplane versions of the bigger wing were used at Misano. It was hardly a coincidence that since that narrower fairing arrived, the Ducati top speeds began going up. For Motegi, Ducati really went for it; new additional wings, mounted just under the nose cone, were added in FP4, in addition to the biplanes on the flanks – for a total of six wings on each bike.

Yamaha also employed wings in the latter half of the year: small units mounted up on the front of the nose cone. Lorenzo set a very fast lap using them in free practice at Misano, and Rossi used them in the dry during FP4 and the race at Misano. The riders said the wings generated a 3mm drop in the suspension position, theoretically increasing tyre grip and acceleration before the ECU had to throttle back to keep the front down. Unlike the Ducati main wings, however, they were not close to the ground, so were also raising the centre of pressure and working the front far more than the back.

Yamaha were simply trying to hold the front down, to stop wheelies, but then Yamaha didn't have the massive excess of power that Ducati enjoyed, so they had to be far more careful when considering the drag cost of any additional wings.

It will be interesting to see if Yamaha continue with this development, and if they do whether it is possible for them to slim down their fairing and use bigger wings lower down like Ducati. It won't be easy because of the relatively wide across-the-frame four-cylinder engine. Perhaps low-set wings require a V4 engine layout to be really effective?

Then there are the tyres: increased mechanical grip brought about by aerodynamic aids pushing the tyre into the track surface is only an option if the tyre has enough spare grip capacity. At the time of writing, we had yet to discover whether the Bridgestones had that capacity. We shall have to wait to see what happens on Michelins.

2015 MOTOGP · BIKE BY BIKE

Above: Rossi's Yamaha had a softer swing-arm (no braced cut-out) and a slash-cut exhaust: better aerodynamics, and more noise.

Top: The 2015 Yamaha looked very similar to the 2014 bike; but was much improved.

Photos: Gold & Goose

Right: Yamaha steering head construction in detail: 2015 chassis mods improved braking stability.

Photo: Neil Spalding

YAMAHA YZR-MI

YAMAHA maintained their philosophy of usable power married to a good-handling chassis; they were not distracted by worrying about what others were doing and followed their own development path towards fast lap times.

The 2015 Yamaha was a development of the previous year's bike: the major changes were a new seamless-shift gearbox, which allowed seamless down-shifts as well as up, and a careful redesign of the chassis to improve braking stability and provide the two top riders with chassis characteristics that suited their differing riding styles more closely.

When seamless-shift gearboxes were first introduced, most thought they would be effective in improving acceleration and fuel mileage. That wasn't the case, however. Acceleration is mostly limited by a bike's wheelie limit, and fuel wasn't the major issue expected. Seamless up-shifts helped a lot mid-corner, but seamless down-shifts made a bigger difference, by avoiding triggering excessive chassis pitching and maintaining the right amount of engine braking into corners.

Chassis flexibility is one area where Jorge Lorenzo and Valentino Rossi's riding styles have differing needs. Lorenzo's super-smooth cornering works better with a stiffer chassis; Rossi's more adventurous style needed a design that allowed him to change line mid-corner. Yamaha dealt with this by employing two different swing-arm designs. The stiffer one, as used by Lorenzo, had a hole in one side with a carbon patch over it. The less rigid one had a normal shape, and since it didn't have a hole cut in it, with the appropriate welding, it wasn't as stiff. The stiff version gave better acceleration off corners, but wasn't so forgiving of mistakes. The axle clamps were also different, Rossi's swing-arm having heavy-duty clamps, while Lorenzo's had less robust items.

A new chassis was debuted mid-season at Assen, with more steering-head flex for a better turn in with almost as much braking stability. Both factory riders went on to it immediately and never looked back.

HONDA RC213V

THE 2014 RCV was a finely balanced tool for a brilliant Marquez. Somehow, that balance went missing in 2015. The main culprit seemed to be the engine character. The previous year's bike hadn't been easy to ride fast unless you were fully committed, but if you were, it was clear that it was a delight. The 2015 bike seemed to have an aggression in the power delivery that prevented it from being flung around as accurately. The most likely cause would be a low-inertia crankshaft, which can help acceleration and manoeuvrability, but which requires very accurate throttle mapping.

This was an entirely self-inflicted wound, most likely caused by a determination to stop a newly resurgent Ducati powering past on the straights. The trouble was that Honda was now one of the only two full Factory Option bikes in the series. That meant only five engines for the whole year and no changes to the engine specification after the first race. The solutions, therefore, had to be found without mechanical changes.

Problems were obvious from the start of testing. Marquez had four different bikes to test, but rather than a show of strength, it appeared that Honda didn't understand what he needed. The first chassis option hardly lasted the first day, while new narrower seat and tank units that went with the new chassis were also ditched in favour of remounted 2014 items.

The chassis chosen by Marquez and his crew was good for a fast lap, but it wasn't the best for a race. It was easily distinguishable, with an obvious indentation halfway up the main beam. Pedrosa chose another based closely on his 2014 (and therefore 2013 and 2012) chassis. Riders for the customer teams, Crutchlow and Redding, had to race the first few rounds of the series using the chassis rejected by the Repsol riders on the first day, before replacement chassis were available for them.

It wasn't until Catalunya, and after Marquez had crashed several times, that new parts became available. The first was a stiffer swing-arm, an attempt to stop the aggressive power winding up the chassis. Then Marquez got his old 2014 exhaust pipes back: much smaller in diameter, and likely to have helped mid-range and the 'throttle connection'. We couldn't see what was in the airbox, but that big a change of exhaust would likely have meant some changes on the inlet side, too, most probably some form of flow restrictor.

His reaction was positive. After the race, things went further and Marquez tried his 2014 chassis in the test. It was more forgiving and allowed him to recover from some of the mistakes caused by the power delivery; and from the next race at Assen, he used only his 2014 chassis. To smooth the transition to control software, a ban on software upgrades came in at the end of the Assen race. It certainly looked like some improvement was found in the throttle mapping before that came into force. Pedrosa made do with a new heavier clutch, most likely to increase drive train inertia. His first chassis choice was clearly better.

Above: Early Marquez chassis: note deliberate distortion to main beam.
Photo: Neil Spalding

Top: Pedrosa chose a different chassis, seen here at February Sepang tests.
Photo: Gold & Goose

Right: The Suzuki started the year looking very like the 2014 test bike.

Left: Ohlins fork-bottom detail – these on Redding's Honda.
Photos: Gold & Goose

Below: Scott Redding needed a reminder that the throttle was very abrupt.
Photo: Neil Spalding

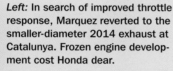

Left: In search of improved throttle response, Marquez reverted to the smaller-diameter 2014 exhaust at Catalunya. Frozen engine development cost Honda dear.

Below left: Honda only needed the smaller 320mm discs at Mugello, and kept them shrouded.

Right: New Akrapovic exhausts for Suzuki at Brno

Bottom right: Suzuki used a torque sensor in testing at Jerez.
Photos: Neil Spalding

Bottom: Crutchlow's Honda at preseason tests: note new frame and seat mounts, all replaced by Texas.
Photo: Gold & Goose

SUZUKI GSX-RR

SUZUKI returned to racing in 2015, having taken a holiday that lasted three years while they redeveloped their bike. When they were last in MotoGP, they had used a 75-degree V4. Now they had developed a 1000cc in-line four with a reverse-rotating cross-plane crankshaft and pneumatic valve springs.

Testing in public had gone on for two years. It took that long for the electronics to be transferred from the old Mitsubishi system to the new Marelli control ECU. Power had been increased, too, and despite the embarrassment of losing three engines during its first official test in November, 2014, at Valencia, reliability was also good.

The handling was clearly more than okay, but power levels were obviously well down on the main opposition. Looking at the typical top speed deficit, however, the bike needed another 20bhp to reach the typical top speeds of the Yamaha, let alone the Honda and Ducati. There was a power upgrade at Catalunya, which resulted in a pole position on the softer tyre allowed to new entrants to the series.

As a design, the Suzuki looked notably small and delicate. Several swingarms were tried during the year, with a longer version debuted at the same time as the power upgrade at Catalunya.

The next technology upgrade will be a seamless-shift gearbox. Suzuki have been developing a design themselves for a long time now. It was due to be ready before the flyaway races at the end of the year. That didn't happen, and it may be some time before we do see that technology.

The combination of power upgrade and additional stability was very successful. Usually additional power can really disrupt a good handling package. Suzuki managed that upgrade exceptionally well; the problem is that they have got to do that again to get their bike into the company it deserves.

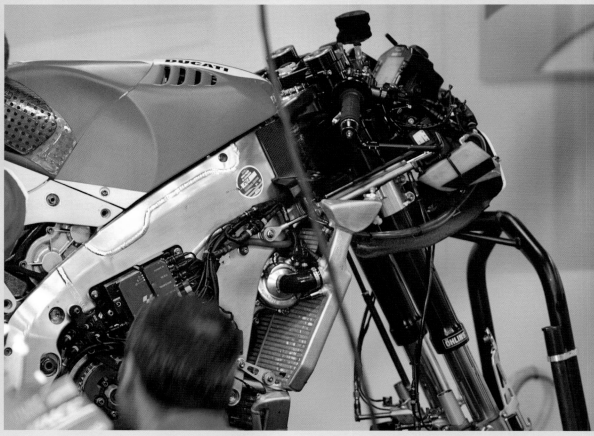

Top: All-new Ducati shows its chassis. Note long front engine mounts.

Above: Dovizioso went out with rubber depth-gauge wings at Catalunya, to see if they touched down on the kerbs.

Right: No longer an 'L4' – Desmosedici 2015 shows rearward tilting of 90-degree engine.

Far right: Aprilia experimented with longer front engine mounts at Brno.
Photos: Neil Spalding

DUCATI DESMOSEDICI GP15

DUCATI missed the first Sepang test because their new bike was not quite ready, but when it did arrive it made a massive impression. All new from the ground up, it had a new engine – still a 90-degree Desmo V4 – and a new chassis that finally allowed enough weight on to the front end to get it to turn into corners.

Repackaging and mass centralisation were the keys to the changes, Ducati couldn't move their old engine any further forward in the chassis without hitting the front tyre, and even if they could the output shaft was in the wrong place to get the right effects from 'chain pull' in the corners.

The new bike turned amazingly well. It was fast, too, finishing the first test third. The major issue mentioned right from the start was a little instability under heavy braking. Equipping the bikes with wings seemed to settle things down.

Ducati enjoyed the benefit of 'Factory Concession' rules, with extra fuel, softer tyres, plus 12 engines and the right to produce modifications during the season.

The early races were good, too; two bikes on the podium in Qatar saw an immediate reduction in fuel capacity from 24 litres to 22. There was a podium at round two in Austin as well – Dovizioso third, Iannone fifth. But the combined effects of a reduction in the fuel levels, fuel tanks that didn't pick up the last of the available fuel and a restart where the fuel wasn't chilled led to both bikes failing to finish the cool-down lap. New fuel tanks were built and rushed to the next round in Argentina on the following weekend by the boss himself, Gigi Dall'Igna.

After the initial surge, results seemed to slip away somewhat. Iannone started to get better results than Dovizioso. The problems were mostly on circuits with long corners: the Desmosedici had great power, but it wasn't easy to modulate the throttle.

Development continued. There were ever larger wings, new fairings and chassis, and slowly the results got better: the bike did well anywhere strong acceleration and top speed were required. Dovizioso also complained that his bike no longer held the corner entry line as easily. He has a history of liking a very 'rearwards' weight distribution, and Ducati had to take a far more pro-active approach to moving him backwards on the bike to get the 'feel' he liked.

On its initial performance, the Ducati looked like it could win races in 2015. It was a massively improved motorcycle, but there were still a few areas where it lagged; fine throttle control and electronic sophistication seemed to be the outstanding issues.

APRILIA RSV-GP

IT was always going to be a tough year for Aprilia. The decision to race in MotoGP had been taken, but all they had to race with were old Superbikes and the knowledge gained from the ART project. They benefited from running under the Factory Concession regulations, like Ducati and Suzuki. Very quickly, new engines were prepared, still based on the RSV4 Superbike, using the old gear-driven cams with pneumatic valve springs.

The first outing was at Sepang, where several engines broke, but after development they were able to increase their rev ceiling to 16,000rpm. The chassis changed quite quickly as the factory began to understand the needs of the Bridgestone tyres.

Weight was a major issue, with the engines coming in nearly 8kg heavier than the equivalent MotoGP engine. Overall, the bike was 9kg over the minimum weight limit, and that alone really affected its performance, especially into and through corners.

By mid-year, a new seamless-shift gearbox (licensed from British company Zeroshift) was in use, new dry clutches had been tested and the chassis was in its fourth iteration. The final chassis had much longer front engine mounts, and in several rounds the bike did surprisingly well.

Each circuit added to Aprilia's database, and it is believed that development of the new engine for 2016, which will be lighter, smaller and stronger, started in September. That bike will be one to watch.

OPEN MOTOGP

Above: In 2015, there were fewer similarities between Factory and Open Yamahas.

Top: Bradl's Yamaha used an elderly 'web-design' Yamaha works chassis. One drawback was more weight on the front wheel.

Photos: Gold & Goose

OPEN bikes, theoretically, are the same as the Factory bikes. In practice, they are all older models, and all suffered from having to employ the clunky Dorna control software. This uses many different 'screens' to allow any adjustment: quite often, it is the programmer who has to remember all the small adjustments that are needed to make any major change work. It is a long, laborious process. The 2016 version of the software will be radically improved with help from all the factories.

Ducati

DUCATI had a range of bikes on track, from GP14 to GP14.2. They all had the 'old' engine, considered too long for future use, and different versions of 2014's chassis. They were very good in the wet and suffered least from the software problems.

Honda

IN 2015, Honda took the previous season's steel-valve-spring RCV1000S, owned by each team, and leased a new main frame section and a supply of pneumatic-valve-spring engines from the 2014 works bikes. That translated into a serious power boost for the Open RC213V-RS. From insufficient power, the bikes suddenly had too much. This made them very different to set up and ride.

Yamaha

THE 2015 Open Yamahas were just like the previous year's – two-year-old parts with a smattering of aftermarket additions to make it all work. The chassis were of an early 'web-like' design, with the front engine mounts joined to the main beam by a thin web of aluminium. After flirting with Kayaba suspension, the Forward team was persuaded by their riders to revert to Ohlins, but it took until mid-season for some important rear linkage upgrades to arrive.

Left: The de Angelis Aprilia ART was the last remaining bike from the CRT days.

Below left: Abraham's Honda became the Showa and Nissin rolling test-bed.

Below: There were several Desmosedici generations in the pit lane. Di Meglio's was one of the oldest.

Bottom: Hayden's Open Honda – 2015 bike was a major upgrade from 2014, but harder to ride and no more competitive.
Photos: Gold & Goose

TECHNICAL ESSAY

WHY STYLE MATTERS

From tucked in via knee out to elbow down: KEVIN CAMERON analyses the
technical reasons that continue to drive ever evolving riding styles…

Above: Kenny Roberts pioneered and popularised the need for knee sliders.

Top right: Geoff Duke: tucked in, at one with the bike. That too was a breakthrough.

Photos: Motocourse Archive

Above centre right: Mick Doohan in 1998 keeps head and shoulders in line, body weight inboard, as he prepares to pick up the bike and accelerate out.

Photo: Gold & Goose

Bottom right: Rossi redux spent 2014 learning the latest style, and 2015 applying it.

Photo: Movistar Yamaha

Opening spread: Jorge Lorenzo. Speed with style.

Photo: Whit Bazemore Photography

I DISLIKE the term 'style' when applied to riding technique, because it implies something arbitrarily chosen, like the hemline of a woman's dress. Rider style is far from arbitrary. It is what the rider must do to produce competitive lap times.

Fashion does enter into style, because street riders and clubmen copy the look of top racers without understanding its function. When the 'knee out' style appeared in the 1960s – transferring some weight to the inside of the machine in corners – traditionalists deplored it, proposing Geoff Duke's 'with the bike' knees-in style as the classic model all should adopt.

When I asked 1969 250cc World Champion and long-time Yamaha GP crew chief Kel Carruthers about this, he replied, "What you must realise is that Duke's style was progressive in his time. Before him, many riders leaned the opposite way."

In his book, Mike Hailwood wrote, "Before the war there was a raging controversy about the relative merits of the Stanley Woods 'lean with it' and the Freddie Frith 'lean away from it' styles."

Some have argued that pre-war bikes had long wheelbases that required Frith's upright style, but in fact Stan Woods's preferred wheelbase was just 52.5 inches.

In his book *On Racing*, John Surtees wrote that his original cornering style on the Vincent Grey Flash was little different from pre-war riders. He continued, "But when I changed to a Featherbed Norton with its lower build, and heeled it over as far as the Vincent, I found that the footrests and exhaust pipe grounded; if the suspension worked at the same time the pipe tended to lift the machine and cause it to run wide. To counter this I started to let my body stay down as the machine came up.

"The MV does not ground so badly as the Norton, but the idea is to keep the machine as upright as possible for maximum traction. That way I can use more power and speed in a bend than if I stay in line with the machine or lean outward; for I would then have to put the machine itself down a little farther and that would mean easing the throttle to keep the back wheel from breaking away."

In our own time, we have seen many greats 'lift and accelerate'. Mick Doohan did it on the NSR500 Hondas in the 1990s, pushing the bike upward, but remaining on the inside to increase the rear tyre's footprint so he could accelerate early and hard. We have also seen this from Marc Marquez and Dani Pedrosa – abruptly pushing the machine upward while beginning acceleration.

Hailwood noted, "I can think of no pre-war rider who wore out his boots and megaphone on the ground, but this is so commonplace nowadays that the faster men go through several pairs of riding boots a season.

"For the same reason, I always reduce the length of my footrests to the absolute minimum required to position and hold my feet."

Rising tyre grip forced change. Duke began his racing career on the cotton-carcass Dunlops of what engineer Tony Mills called "the hard rubber era", but in the later 1950s rubber compounding adopted higher-grip, high-hysteresis materials, allowing increased lean angle.

Tyre grip is phenomenal in our era, permitting Marc Marquez's radical inward displacement of his whole body, holding himself so low on the inside of the machine that there is no room for the classic 'knee out'. Instead, the knee is drawn up to the body and it is Marc's elbow that carries a slider to protect it from track abrasion. Bikes have become taller to permit the lean angles enabled by modern tyres.

For many years, classic European racing line was geometric – the inscribed arc of a circle of maximum radius. This was a natural outgrowth of grand prix racing's multi-displacement structure. Today, the classes have become rungs of a ladder, but in 1950 the many makers of 125s and 250s gave top riders full careers in lightweight classes. Also, save for the high-powered Italian fours from Gilera and MV, acceleration was moderate. Even in 1971, I would see New Zealander Ginger Molloy ride his Kawasaki 500 H1R like a 125 – fully tucked in through corners.

For years, riders were seated almost directly above the

rear axle, forcing the rear tyre to carry more than its share of the load. Street riders diligently copied this. But change was coming. Engineer/riders Rex and Cromie McCandless, in their 'featherbed' twin-loop chassis for the 1950 works Nortons, moved the rider forward by over three inches, and the engine forward by 2.75 – changes they had found effective in testing on Irish roads. On the TT course, the new Norton was able to accelerate *around the outside* of the previous bike in corners.

MV and their new rider Giacomo Agostini took this further, moving the rider forward enough to require forward-offset clip-ons. As acceleration increased, front wheels became too light to steer off corners, so thinking riders moved forward to restore control. The Ago/MV combination defeated Hailwood and Honda in the 1966 and '67 500 championships. The 500 RC-181 Honda, classically designed long and low, was less able to transfer most of its weight to the rear wheel. As a result, Ago accelerated while the Honda spun. In 1971, the stability of long wheelbase won adherents, but the faster acceleration of shorter chassis won races.

For many years, the classic road race style was as though the rider's upper body was pivoted on an axis down between the rider's shoulders and into the fuel tank; the upper body remained centered on the bike, while the inside knee dropped and the butt slid to the inside in varying degree. Even Valentino Rossi rode most of his career in this style. Along the way, there were special cases that showed that riders would do whatever they had to do. Jarno Saarinen, on the 1973 in-line Yamaha 500 two-stroke, took to offsetting his whole body to the inside (as Marquez does today) as a means of controlling sudden wheelspin that would result if the oval-section tyre were on its narrow shoulder when the engine 'hit'.

Necessity forced the change that Kenny Roberts brought to GP racing in 1978. He had been riding the elemental Yamaha TZ750 in US races – a machine whose 120hp was far ahead of its flexing pipe chassis ("That bike had too much of every-

Above: "Playing the violin while climbing a mountain." Casey Stoner shows how elbow dragging helps the Honda, at Brno in 2011.

Photo: Gold & Goose

Bottom right: Marc Marquez likewise, at COTA in 2015.

Photo: Whit Bazemore Photography

thing," he said). That engine 'hit' very hard at 9,300rpm and peaked at 10,300. No existing tyre could take that hit while leaned over, so there was no possibility of riding that bike in classic big-line style, feeding power gradually to lift and accelerate. So Kenny braked and turned early so that he could lift the bike on to the fat part of the tyre, which had the footprint to take the hit. His apex speed was low, but by using most of the corner as an increasing-radius drag strip, his exit speed was high. Because hard acceleration made the front end too light to steer, Kenny steered the *rear* tyre with throttle-induced wheelspin.

With few exceptions, this 'point-and-shoot' style remained dominant in 500 GP racing until tyre design changed again. When the GP classes were cut to just 125, 250 and 500, the lightweight classes ceased to stand on their own and became stepping-stones to 500. Because 125s and 250s lacked the acceleration of 500s, they had to be ridden to conserve corner speed. As 250 riders advanced to 500, they brought their tyre preferences with them. Instead of the abuse tolerance necessary for the tyre-spinning point-and-shoot style, development moved toward shoulder and edge grip. By 1999, five-times 500 title winner Mick Doohan was willing to say that corner speed was faster, but only until the drop in tyre properties after a few laps. Then, marginal side grip made a modified point-and-shoot style safer, because it shortened the rider's time at high lean angle.

When American Nicky Hayden arrived in MotoGP, tyres had evolved to the point where conventional spin-steering quickly fatigued the tyre into grip loss. Hayden rode hard for midfield positions, redoubling his efforts each time he was passed, thereby fatiguing his tyre all the faster.

At the end of 2005, the growing difference between rider styles on Yamaha and Honda was revealed by Honda's re-quest for more traction from Michelin. Yet, according to Rossi's engineer Jeremy Burgess, Yamaha had all the traction they needed. Traction, in rider talk, means the longitudinal grip to accelerate, as opposed to the side grip needed to go around corners.

In 2006, conversations with Valentino Rossi and Colin Edwards revealed the underlying riding style difference, and the tyre construction needed by each man. Colin rode a dirt-track-based style, in which corner exit speed required a supple tyre construction, able to lay down a large footprint for hard acceleration. Rossi needed a much stiffer tyre that could sustain the prolonged shoulder and edge grip necessary for continuous high corner speed. When I asked Valentino what happened if he tried Colin's style of tyre, he said, "The bike jumps sideways." This suggests buckling of the softer carcass under high, steady turning load.

When Casey Stoner stopped biting his nails and losing the front of his LCR Honda, he learned to steer the very powerful 800cc Ducati, won ten races and was champion in 2007. Although it appeared that he was riding a high-lean-angle corner-speed style, Ducati race engineer Filippo Preziosi warned that "something else is going on." In 2008, Yamaha's track-side monitoring devices reported that Stoner's traction control was cycling at corner apexes. Like Miguel DuHamel before him, Stoner had learned to apply throttle to the more flexible tyre edge to 'walk' the back of the machine sideways without destructive wheelspin. As veteran Ohlins technician Jon Cornwell said, "Edge grip is a wasting asset." Therefore, it was necessary to limit its use to a short 'zone of more rapid turning', rather than apply it all the way through a corner, as in the corner-speed style. In this way, it was analogous to point-and-shoot, where the zone of faster turning was more compact.

Now came a stylistic fork in the road. For those who were

winning races on the tyre edge, tyres had to be designed for the higher temperatures that style generated. That made it more difficult for riders of the previous style to get their tyres to working temperature. When I asked Giorgio Barbier, Pirelli's race tyre manager, what was putting older riders out of MotoGP, he replied, "Their whole experience forbids them to turn the throttle on the edge of the tyre."

Such riders tried the usual methods to raise tyre temperature – low pressure to generate flex heating, high pressure for spin-driven frictional heating. They couldn't work, because the tyres had been designed to *require* combined throttle and running on the tyre edge. Those unable to adapt left the series.

Jorge Lorenzo brought a pure corner-speed riding style to its highest level. A corner-speed style works by keeping the tyres in constant contact with the track surface. Mechanical grip comes from the use of the softest springing and damping consistent with not bottoming. Older race-goers may remember that Freddie Spencer's Honda 500s *felt* stiff, but that was just the heavy preload needed to prevent in-corner bottoming with soft springs.

In 2011, Stoner applied his imagination at Honda, again winning ten races and the title. Part of his success was in tyre management and part in what he called "riding every corner as it needs to be ridden." As with Rossi, this is the role of intelligence in racing – to observe and remember everything, and to apply that knowledge flexibly and in detail.

Lorenzo worked diligently to approach perfection, but his style required earlier, less-severe braking and more gradual transitions from braking to turning, from turning to acceleration. Despite all his care, corner speed works tyres hard, causing them to 'drop' or take a step down from maximum performance after a few laps. Riders make long runs in later practice (race simulations), to give them an idea of how their style, the emerging competitive pace and the chosen tyres will perform in the closing laps.

Moto2, by requiring all to use identically tuned engines, forces riders to improvise other areas of superiority. Marc Marquez found ways to go fast at reduced cost in tyre fatigue. When he arrived in MotoGP on a factory Honda in 2013, he rode, as he later said, "Every lap as in qualifying." A year later, all could see that his new and highly athletic style of moving his whole body to a place on the inside of the bike was allowing him to use more of the Bridgestone tyres' remarkable grip. This increased the angle of lean of the machine/rider combination. The on-bike camera shows him early in a corner at a high lean angle, but then he leans over further, his outside elbow riding up over the fuel tank to allow his body to take up an extreme low on the inside position. In this process, his inside elbow drops down to the track surface. The time spent at this extreme angle is Marquez's zone of most rapid turning, the apex of what Cal Crutchlow has called "Honda's V-shaped line."

This is not just a new body position. It is also the moves required to assume it, executed without disturbance to steering or bike. It is playing the violin while climbing a mountain.

In the lap time analysis, anyone could see the lap number of each rider's tyre drop. In the case that first caught my eye, Rossi's drop occurred first, then Lorenzo's and latest of all, that of Marquez, who won. Rossi knew he would have to learn the new method of tyre conservation, spending most of 2014 in doing so. In 2015, he was newly competitive – no longer just trailing Marquez, Lorenzo and Pedrosa.

It is fascinating to see Marquez's style change from practice to race. In direction changes in late practice and qualifying, he leaps from one side of the bike to the other very quickly, like a gymnast, *before* rolling the bike. In the race, where energy conservation is essential, his body and bike move together.

Lorenzo has pushed his corner-speed style close to perfection in an amazing display of grace and accuracy. Yet when Marquez is close behind from the start, he often waits until he judges that his meticulously conserved tyres have more fast laps left in them than Lorenzo's, and is often able to pass and win. In 2015, Honda's harsher engine handicapped Marquez, while Yamaha's improved braking and acceleration helped their riders.

In 2016, Michelin replaces Bridgestone as spec tyre supplier, and riders will again race to be first to successfully exploit their tyres' possibilities.

TEAM-BY-TEAM

2015 MOTOGP REVIEW

Teams and Riders   Bike Specifications   Bike Illustrations

MATTHEW BIRT   NEIL SPALDING   ADRIAN DEAN

MOVISTAR YAMAHA MOTOGP

TEAM STAFF

Masahiko NAKAHIMA: President, Yamaha Motor Racing
Kouichi TSUJI: MotoGP Group Leader
Lin JARVIS: Managing Director, Yamaha Motor Racing
Massimo MEREGALLI: Team Director
Kouji TSUYA: Yamaha M1 Project Leader
Wilco ZEELENBERG: Rider Performance Analyst
William FAVERO: Communications Manager
Matteo VITELLO: Sponsorship Strategies
Alen BOLLINI/Alberto GOMEZ: Press Officers
Mark CANELLA:Team Co-ordinator
Takehiro SUZUKI: Parts Co-ordinator
Raffaella PASQUINO: Marketing Co-ordinator

JORGE LORENZO PIT CREW

Ramon FORCADA: Crew Chief
Mechanics: Javier ULLATE, Jurij PELLEGRINI,
Ian GILPIN, Juan Llansa HERNANDEZ
Yoichi NAKAYAMA: Yamaha Engineer
Davide MARELLI: Data Engineer

VALENTINO ROSSI PIT CREW

Silvano GALBUSERA: Crew Chief
Mechanics: Alex BRIGGS, Bernard ANSIAU,
Brent STEPHENS, Gary COLEMAN
Hiroya ATSUMI: Yamaha Engineer
Matteo FLAMIGNI: Data Technician

JORGE LORENZO
Born: 4 May, 1987 – Palma de Mallorca, Spain
GP Starts: 232 (138 MotoGP, 48 250cc, 46 125cc)
GP Wins: 61 (40 MotoGP, 17 250cc, 4 125cc)
World Championships: 5 (3 MotoGP, 2 250cc)

VALENTINO ROSSI
Born: 16 February, 1979 – Urbino, Italy
GP Starts: 330 (270 MotoGP/500cc, 30 250cc, 30 125cc)
GP Wins: 112 (86 MotoGP/500cc, 14 250cc, 12 125cc)
World Championships: 9 (6 MotoGP, 1 500cc, 1 250cc, 1 125cc)

YAMAHA could not have timed its return to dominance in MotoGP more perfectly, with Valentino Rossi and Jorge Lorenzo's tense and engrossing title fight coming in a year in which the Japanese manufacturer celebrated its 60th anniversary.

Individual glory went to Lorenzo after a nail-biting shootout at the final round in Valencia, as Yamaha finally put the brakes on Honda and Marc Marquez's supremacy.

The team championship was wrapped up in Aragon, with four races still remaining, to end a four-year reign of Repsol Honda. And the coveted triple crown was clinched in Australia, when Yamaha secured its first constructors' title since 2010.

Yamaha's resurgence was instant when Rossi produced a magnificently cavalier ride from eighth on the grid to win the opening round in Qatar. That success put him on top of the world championship standings for the first time in five years, and he never surrendered the outright lead on points until the dramatic last race in Valencia, when, having started from the back of the grid, he was helpless as his team-mate took a brilliant victory to snatch the title by just five points.

Yamaha's start was inspired – four wins in the open-

YAMAHA YZR-M1

Sponsors and Technical Suppliers: Movistar • Eneos • Monster • Yamalube • Eurasian Bank • Abarth • TW Steel • Akrapovic • Alpinestars • Bridgestone • Magneti Marelli
Beta • BMC Air Filters • NGK Spark Plugs • DID • 2D • Exedy • Capit • Blue Core • Descente • Gilles Tooling • RCB • Cromax

Engine: 1000cc transverse in-line 4; reverse-rotating cross-plane crankshaft, DOHC, 4 valves per cylinder, pneumatic valve return system
   Power: Around 260bhp, revs up to 17,000rpm

Ancillaries: Magneti Marelli electronics, NGK sparking plugs, full electronic ride-by-wire • *Lubrication:* Yamalube

Transmission: Gear primary drive, multi-plate dry slipper clutch, six-speed seamless-shift cassette-style gearbox, DID chain

Suspension: Front, Ohlins TRSP25 48mm 'through-rod' forks; Rear, Ohlins TRSP44 shock with linkage • *Wheels:* 16.5in MFR • *Tyres:* Bridgestone

Brakes: Brembo 340mm carbon carbon front; Yamaha steel rear

KATSUYUKI NAKASUGA

Born: 9 August, 1981 – Shizuoka, Japan

GP Starts: 9 (6 MotoGP/500cc, 3 250cc)

ing five races equalled the number of victories it had achieved in the whole of 2014.

Evergreen Rossi continued to deliver startling age-defying performances as his relationship with crew chief Silvano Galbusera flourished with the benefit of a year's experience. Galbusera had coped fantastically well under intense scrutiny in 2014, when Rossi had picked the Italian to replace Jerry Burgess. He worked in tandem with Yamaha engineer Hiroya Atsumi and data engineer Matteo Flamigni in helping Rossi mount his strongest title challenge since 2009.

Alex Briggs, Bernard Ansiau, Brent Stephens and Gary Coleman were the long-serving spine of the team that remained, and they were present to witness more record-breaking exploits from the 36-year-old.

Remarkably, Rossi was in his 20th world championship campaign, but he was a more potent threat than for many years, and at Jerez he became the first rider in history to reach 200 podiums.

His four wins amounted to his most successful campaign in terms of victories since 2009, and when he won a classic Dutch TT scrap after a last-corner challenge of Marquez, Yamaha was able to celebrate winning six straight races for the first time in its grand prix history.

The ultra-consistent Rossi only missed the podium three times, including a chaotic Misano battle when he stayed out too long on rain tyres on a drying track.

What made his accomplishments even more impressive was the fact that he juggled his own title challenge while remaining the very public figurehead of the SKY VR46 KTM Moto3 squad, as well as nurturing a stable of fast and gifted young Italian talent through his VR46 Academy. These included Romano Fenati, Niccolo Antonelli and Franco Morbidelli.

What made Yamaha's YZR-M1 such formidable opposition was the fact that it had two riders racing in the form of their lives.

Lorenzo started slowly. He missed the Qatar podium thanks to a piece of foam that became detached inside his HJC helmet, hampering his vision. A nasty bout of bronchitis in Austin and a wrong choice of front tyre in Argentina kept him off the podium in both races.

Then he embarked on the best streak of his career, four wins on the spin at Jerez, Le Mans, Mugello and Catalunya. The start of his dominant run coincided with confirmation that he would stay with Yamaha in 2016, announced on the first day of practice in Jerez.

Although he had signed a two-year deal, there were options in place that could have resulted in him leaving. He was already being linked with Ducati, but Yamaha moved quickly to tie up the loose ends to avoid any distractions.

Lorenzo won a further three races, all with devastating early speed and consistency. Crucially, he led from start to finish in the title showdown at Valencia.

His first race crash since the opening round of 2014

Above: **Team director Massimo Meregalli.**

Above centre: **Managing director Lin Jarvis.**

Photos: Gold & Goose

Top: **The team celebrates their double podium at Jerez – the third win in four races.**

Above right: **Rossi was the stronger rider in wet conditions.**

Photo: Movistar Yamaha

Right: **Lorenzo countered with his sheer speed.**

Photo: Gold & Goose

came in the carnage and confusion at Misano, but a commanding win in Aragon moved him ahead of Casey Stoner into fourth place in the all-time class winners list. Only Rossi, Giacomo Agostini and Mick Doohan have won more blue-riband-class races than Lorenzo.

His crew was largely unchanged from 2014, with Ramon Forcada continuing as crew chief, despite mid-season speculation in 2014 that he could be replaced. Davide Marelli was data engineer, while Yoichi Nakayama took over from Takashi Moriyama as YMC engineer.

The upper echelons at Yamaha certainly had a familiar look, with Masahiko Nakajima operating again in

the lead role as president of Yamaha Motor Racing Srl.

Lin Jarvis remained as managing director of the Milan-based outfit, while Kouichi Tsuji had the tongue-twister title of General Manager Motorsports Division YMC MotoGP Group Leader Yamaha Motor Co, Ltd.

Kouji Tsuya was YZR-M1 project leader again, and Massimo Meregalli continued as team director.

Dutchman Wilco Zeelenberg had a new job title for 2015, being officially listed as riders' performance analyst, instead of his previous role of team manager. Despite the all-encompassing title, Zeelenberg was still very much associated with Camp Lorenzo.

REPSOL HONDA TEAM

TEAM STAFF

Shuhei NAKAMOTO: HRC Executive Vice President
Livio SUPPO: Team Principal
Takeo YOKOYAMA: Technical Director
Toshiyuki YAMAJI: Assistant Technical Director
Teruaki MATSUBARA: HRC Engineer (Marquez)
Yukihide AKITSU: HRC Engineer (Pedrosa)
Masunori TAKAHASHI: HRC Engineer (Electronics)
Gianni BERTI: HRC Engineer (Satellite Teams)
Roger VAN DER BORGHT: Co-ordinator
Ruben CASTELLA: Assistant Co-ordinator
Katsura SHIBASAKI: Spare Parts Control
Rhys EDWARDS: Communication & Marketing Manager
Norihiko KATO: PR & Marketing

MARC MARQUEZ PIT CREW

Santi HERNANDEZ: Race Engineer
Christophe LINAN: Chief Mechanic
Mechanics: Roberto CLERICI, Andrea BRUNETTI,
Jordi CASTELLA, Javier ORTIZ
Carlo LUZZI: Fuel Injection Engineer
Gerold BUCHER: Data Engineer
Andy DAWSON: Ohlins engineer

DANI PEDROSA PIT CREW

Ramon AURIN: Race Engineer
Masashi OGO: Chief Mechanic
Mechanics: Emanuel BUCHNER, Pedro CALVET,
John EYRE, Denis PAZZAGLINI
Jose Manuel ALLENDE: Fuel Injection Engineer
Daniel PETZOLD: Data Engineer
Paul TREVATHAN: Ohlins Engineer

DANI PEDROSA

Born: 29 September, 1985 – Sabadell, Spain

GP Starts: 244 (166 MotoGP, 32 250cc, 46 125cc)
GP Wins: 52 (28 MotoGP, 15 250cc, 8 125cc)
World Championships: 3 (2 250cc, 1 125cc)

MARC MARQUEZ

Born: 17 February, 1993 – Cervera, Spain

GP Starts: 132 (54 MotoGP, 32 Moto2, 46 125cc)
GP Wins: 50 (24 MotoGP, 16 Moto2, 10 125cc)
World Championships: 4 (2 MotoGP, 1 Moto2, 1 125cc)

EVER since Marc Marquez first burst into MotoGP in 2013, Honda's official factory team quickly became accustomed to winning and dominating the premier class. But the mercurial Marquez and Japanese superpower HRC were brought crashing back to earth with a bump in 2015, after winning 13 of 18 races together the previous season.

The triple crown of rider, team and constructors' titles they had won in such emphatic fashion in 2014 was surrendered in the face of a renewed onslaught from rival Yamaha.

Marquez was still blindingly fast, winning five races, and his raw speed, composure and skill in the face of adversity were never better demonstrated than in his memorable pole lap in Austin, which came just seconds after he'd been forced to sprint down the pit lane, having blown the motor on his number-one RC213V.

But his aspirations of sweeping to a hat trick of titles were undermined by an unforgiving and aggressive factory RC213V, and more than one major unforced error of his own.

Not surprisingly, Marquez and HRC didn't tinker with a winning formula, and his crew remained the same as it had been in a thoroughly one-sided title battle in 2014. Santi Hernandez was race engineer

HONDA RC213V – Repsol

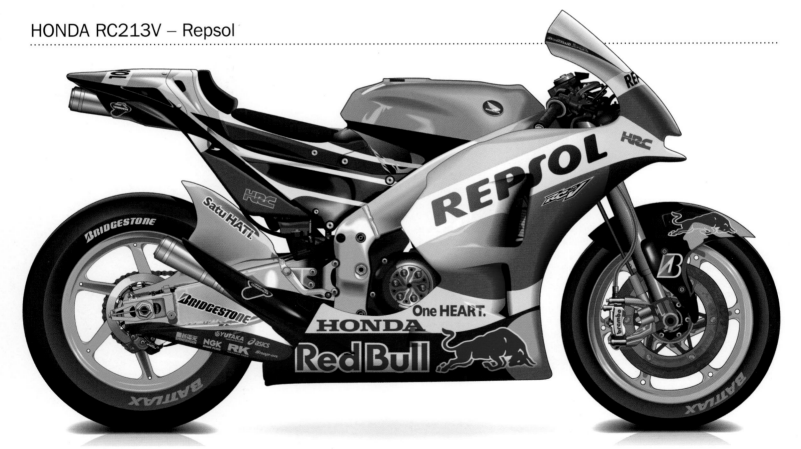

Sponsors and Technical Suppliers: Repsol • One Heart • Estrella Galicia 0.0 • Gas • Red Bull • Bridgestone • NGK Spark Plugs • RK Chains • Alpinestars • Asics Join Me • Shindengen • Snap-on • Termignoni • Yuasa • Yutaka

Engine: 1000cc 90-degree V4, 360-degree crank, DOHC, 4 valves per cylinder, pneumatic valve return system • Power: More than 260bhp, revs up to 17,500rpm

Ancillaries: HRC electronics and ride-by-wire throttle and fuel-injection system with torducter, NGK sparking plugs • Lubrication: Repsol

Transmission: Gear primary drive, multi-plate dry slipper clutch, six-speed seamless-shift cassette-type gearbox, RK chain

Suspension: Front, Ohlins TRSP25 48mm 'through-rod' forks; Rear, TRSP44 gas shock with linkage

Wheels: 16.5in Marchesini • Tyres: Bridgestone

Brakes: Brembo 320 or 340mm carbon carbon front; Yutaka 218mm steel rear

HIROSHI AOYAMA

Born: 25 October, 1981 – Chiba, Japan

GP Starts: 172 (68 MotoGP, 104 250cc)

GP Wins: 9 250cc

World Championships: 1 250cc

TAKUMI TAKAHASHI

Born: 26 November, 1989 – Saitama, Japan

GP Starts: 5 (1 MotoGP, 3 250cc, 1 125cc)

former Repsol Honda rider Tadayuki Okada's Idemitsu Honda Team Asia Moto2 squad, where he had worked with Takaaki Nakagami.

Pedrosa's low-key sixth place in the Qatar night race masked a darker secret that kept him out for the next three races. The 30-year-old was susceptible to chronic arm-pump issues, and past corrective surgery had failed to remedy the situation. He was so downbeat at Qatar that had an invasive and rare procedure not worked, it seemed possible that his career would come to a premature conclusion. He was absent from Texas, Argentina and Jerez.

Pedrosa's factory seat was taken by HRC test rider Hiroshi Aoyama, parachuted in after the intriguing prospect of a shock return by double MotoGP World Champion Casey Stoner had been rejected by HRC. Stoner had given little hint of returning to combat since his much-publicised retirement at the end of 2012, so it was something of a bombshell when he appeared to make himself available for the Circuit of The Americas encounter. After a handful of testing appearances for Honda since quitting, he was also in excellent physical condition, having trained hard for a return to racing as an HRC factory rider in the Suzuka 8 Hours endurance race. Shuhei Nakamoto, who continued as HRC executive vice president and executive chief engineer, Honda R&D Co., and team principal Livio Suppo carefully considered Stoner as a replacement, but eventually rejected the idea. Both are staunch supporters of the Australian, and both were influential in signing him from Ducati for 2011, but a lack of preparation time was cited as one reason why fantasy never became reality.

Dani was back in action at Le Mans, but he took time to regain full form and fitness. One standout performance was a seldom-seen aggressive and tenacious Pedrosa snatching a last-gasp second off Rossi at Aragon.

It was a sign of even more to come. He sustained his record of at least one win every season since his MotoGP debut in 2006 with a fine tactical ride in Japan, then a convincing runaway in Malaysia. Six podiums moved him ahead of Mick Doohan, into second in the list of all-time premier-class podium finishers.

Dani Pedrosa and his crew celebrate their win in Sepang.

again, while data engineer Carlo Luzzi, and mechanics Roberto Clerici and Andrea Brunetti remained from Casey Stoner's two-year spell with Repsol Honda in 2011 and '12.

Former 125cc World Champion Emilio Alzamora was again a constant companion for Marquez in his role as mentor and manager.

Marquez was on the back foot from the opening race in Qatar, however, when he ran off track at the first corner and recovered to fifth. He suffered the first of two fractures to his left hand in a dirt-track training accident during the build-up to the Jerez race, and was under the knife again after falling from his mountain bike while training in advance of the fly-away triple-header in Japan, Australia and Malaysia.

But injuries were the least of his worries.

Takeo Yokoyama continued as HRC's technical director, but the RC213V he rolled out for 2015 featured a brutally aggressive engine that frequently overpowered the new chassis. Back-to-back crashes out of podium contention at Mugello and Catalunya tested the Spaniard's patience to breaking point, and from Assen he reverted to the 2014-spec frame. With Honda unable to tweak its motor because of the cost-saving, in-season development freeze, the older chassis at least gave Marquez more confidence and margin for error, and he didn't finish out of the top two in the next four races.

That included a landmark 700th grand prix win for Honda at Indianapolis, before the aggressive engine

bit him viciously at Silverstone in the rain, when he suffered an off-throttle high-side while battling Rossi for the win.

Slim hopes that he could pull off a miracle revival and get back into title contention were completely extinguished when he fell early out of second in Aragon, his fifth race crash of the season to that date. His sixth fall, after his coming together with Rossi in Malaysia, would prove to be more damaging in the championship battle for the Yamaha man, who was penalised and sent to the back of the grid in Valencia.

If Marquez had resisted making changes to continue his golden run of success in MotoGP, teammate Dani Pedrosa employed completely opposite tactics. He instigated sweeping changes to his crew, leading to Christophe Leonce and Mark Barnett being axed and replaced by Pedro Calvet, hired from Cal Crutchlow's Ducati team, and Denis Pazzaglini, who had worked with the Spaniard in the early part of his grand prix career. Pazzaglini's most recent engagement had been with Nicky Hayden at Aspar Honda.

The musical chairs upset Pedrosa's crew chief, Mike Leitner, who had been his technical mastermind since 2004. He turned down a new deal and moved on to become a senior figure behind KTM's new MotoGP project, due to break cover in 2017.

Pedrosa's data engineer, Ramon Aurin, who had crew-chief pedigree with Andrea Dovizioso at Repsol Honda between 2009 and '11, was promoted. His telemetry role went to Daniel Petzold, poached from

Dani Pedrosa

Marc Marquez

DUCATI TEAM

TEAM STAFF

Luigi DALL'IGNA: Ducati Corse General Manager
Paolo CIABATTI: Ducati Corse Sports Director
Davide TARDOZZI: Team Manager
Riccardo SAVIN: Vehicle Dynamics Engineer
Fabiano STERLACCHINI: Track Technical Co-ordinator
Gabriele CONTI: Software & Strategies Manager
Massimo BARTOLINI: Track Engineer
Federico POLI: Data Analyst
Francesco RAPISARDA: Communications Director
Julian THOMAS: Press Manager
Paola BRAIATO: Administration, Logistics & Hospitality
Mauro GRASSILLI: Sponsorship Manager
Silvio SANGALLI: Crew Co-ordinator

ANDREA DOVIZIOSO PIT CREW

Christian PUPULIN: Track Engineer
Michele PERUGINI: Chief Mechanic
Mechanics: Enrico SAMPERI, Fabio ROVELLI,
Mark ELDER, Massimo TOGNACCI
Dario MASSARIN: Electronics Engineer
Peter BERGVALL: Ohlins Suspension Engineer

ANDREA IANNONE PIT CREW

Marco RIGAMONTI: Track Engineer
Marco VENTURA: Chief Mechanic
Mechanics: Ivan BRANDI, Michele BUBBOLINI,
Lorenzo CANESTRARI, Giuliano POLETTI
Tommaso PAGANO: Electronics Engineer
Giacomo MASSAROTTO: Ohlins Suspension Engineer

Photo: Gold & Goose

ANDREA DOVIZIOSO

Born: 23 March, 1986 – Forlimpopoli, Forli, Italy

GP Starts: 240 (142 MotoGP, 49 250cc, 49 125cc)
GP Wins: 10 (1 MotoGP, 4 250cc, 5 125cc)
World Championships: 1 125cc

Photo: Ducati

ANDREA IANNONE

Born: 9 August, 1989 – Vasto, Italy

GP Starts: 179 (51 MotoGP, 51 Moto2, 77 125cc)
GP Wins: 12 (8 Moto2, 4 125cc)

DUCATI finally dragged itself out of the doldrums with its most successful MotoGP campaign since 2010. Its return to prominence was largely thanks to a blistering start to the season, with a radical new GP15 making a remarkable early impact. It was the first Desmosedici that Gigi Dall'Igna had had total control over since he defected from Italian rival Aprilia at the end of 2013.

Ducati was in dreamland under the Losail floodlights in Qatar when Andrea Dovizioso and Andrea Iannone finished together on the first all-Italian premier-class podium since 2006.

The Doha double podium was the first for Ducati since former talisman Casey Stoner and 2006 World Champion Nicky Hayden had stood together on the rostrum in Aragon some five years earlier.

There were plenty of other positives for Ducati to draw on after the bleak and barren years that had gone before, including a disastrous two-year spell with Valentino Rossi.

But the Bologna factory still missed one of Dall'Igna's main pre-season goals of winning a race for the first time since 2010.

Dovizioso came closest to ending that drought in

DUCATI Desmosedici GP15

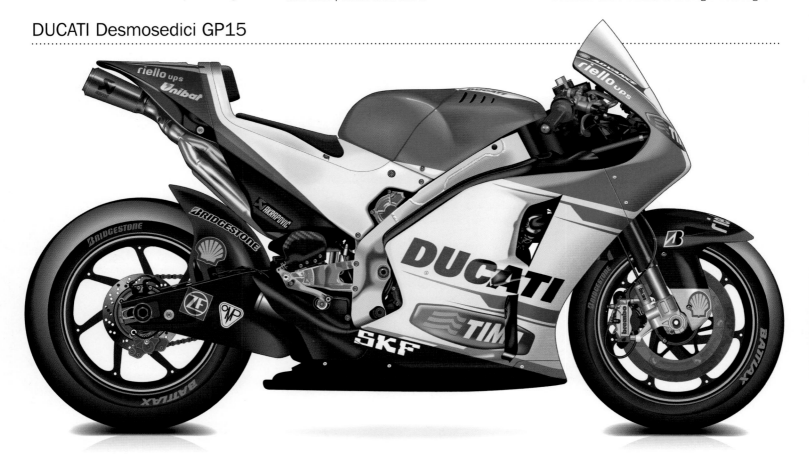

Sponsors and Technical Suppliers: Philip Morris (Marlboro) • TIM (Telecom Italia) • Shell Advance • Riello UPS • Diadora • Akrapovic • Bridgestone • Bosch • Guabello • ZF Mahle • EMC • Trenkwalder • Tudor • DID • Magneti Marelli • NGK • SKF • USAG • VAR • Unibat • Baxi •Aobo •Reflex Alert • Siemens

Engine: 1000cc 90-degree V4, irregular-fire crank, DOHC, 4-valves per cylinder, desmodromic valve gear, variable-length inlet tracts
   Power: Around 270bhp, revs up to 18,000rpm

Ancillaries: Magneti Marelli electronics, NGK sparking plugs, full electronic ride-by-wire • *Lubrication:* Shell Advance

Transmission: Gear primary drive, Xtrac seamless-shift cassette gearbox

Suspension: Front, Ohlins TRSP25 48mm 'through-rod' forks; Rear, Ohlins TRSP44 shock with linkage

Wheels: 16.5in Marchesini • *Tyres:* Bridgestone • *Brakes:* Brembo, 340mm carbon carbon front; 200mm steel rear

Photo: Gold & Goose

MICHELE PIRRO

Born: 5 July, 1986 – San Giovanni Rotondo, Italy

GP Starts: 84 (37 MotoGP, 18 Moto2, 29 125cc)

GP Wins: 1 Moto2

Right: Top Ducati triumvirate Tardozzi, Ciabatti and Dall'Igna.

Below: Andrea Dovizioso started the season with a second place in Qatar, and repeated the result at COTA and Argentina, but his form tailed off thereafter.

Below right: Despite a niggling shoulder injury, Andrea Iannone was a revelation in his first season on the works bike.

Photos: Gold & Goose

the season's opening round, when he was narrowly defeated by Rossi just 35 days after the new GP15 had first been ridden in anger in public at the second Sepang winter test session in late February.

The GP15 was finally rid of the chronic understeer that had hung around Ducati like a dark cloud since the Stoner era, and Dovizioso enjoyed a scintillating start to the season, which included pole position in the season opener.

Working again with crew chief Christian Pupulin, Dovizioso became the first Ducati rider in history to finish on the podium in the opening three races when he followed up his second in Qatar with runner-up places in Austin and Argentina. He was back on the podium at Le Mans, before a best of ninth in the next five races represented his worst spell in world championship racing.

Dovizioso returned to the podium five times, but after his early-season burst of form, he was frequently overshadowed by impressive team-mate Iannone. The younger rider completed Ducati's first all-Italian factory line-up since it had joined MotoGP in 2003. He was allowed to bring crew chief Marco Rigamonti from the Pramac Ducati squad, and he showed why he had been such a highly rated hard charger in 125cc and Moto2.

Iannone added consistency to his reputation as a wild and aggressive rider, and it wasn't until round 13 at a soaked Silverstone that he missed the top six for the first time. His maiden podium was at round one, but undoubtedly his standout weekend was the Italian Grand Prix at Mugello, where he took a career-first pole. He was the first Italian rider on an Italian bike

to do so since Giacomo Agostini's MV Agusta was on pole for the 500cc race at Imola in 1972.

Then he raced to a career-best second place, and subsequently was often the main threat behind the elite quartet of Rossi, Lorenzo, Marquez and Pedrosa, another podium in Australia and racking up five fourth-place finishes.

Typically, Iannone's first full factory season was not without incident. He badly dislocated his left shoulder in a high-speed testing crash in Mugello in mid-May, and at the next race, Le Mans, he engaged in one of the most enthralling personal duels of the season with Marquez.

The shoulder popped out again when he tripped on a training run shortly before the Aragon round, and the start of his winter lay-off would be spent recuperating from surgery to repair the ligament damage.

Once again, Ducati utilised test rider Michele Pirro in its home rounds at Mugello and Misano. Both times the former Moto2 winner qualified inside the top six, with an eye-catching fifth on the grid in Misano – the best wild-card qualifying since Ben Spies was fifth at Indianapolis on a Suzuki in 2008.

Ducati's on-track success coincided with some stability behind the scenes, after the turmoil of major management shake-ups that resulted in Filippo Preziosi and Bernhard Gobmeier being ousted.

Dall'Igna was in his second season as Ducati Corse's technical manager, while stalwarts Paolo Ciabatti and Davide Tardozzi continued in their roles of sporting director and team manager respectively. Dall'Igna only reported to Ducati CEO Claudio Domenicali, who, as a previous chief at Ducati Corse,

maintained an active interest in the factory's fortunes in both MotoGP and World Superbikes.

Fabiano Sterlacchini and Riccardo Savin were both effectively on-site track technical co-ordinators, though Savin's job title was tweaked to vehicle dynamics engineer.

Gabriele Conti was another long-serving and highly respected Ducati Corse team member, whose responsibility shifted from being Dovizioso's electronics engineer to software and strategies manager for the entire operation.

And Massimo Bartolini, who had been chief mechanic with Cal Crutchlow for the British rider's short one-year stint at Ducati in 2014, was installed as track engineer.

Dall'Igna had been able to exploit Ducati's lack of recent success, which allowed them to benefit from Open-class concessions, including extra fuel, more engines, additional testing, no in-season engine development freeze and access to softer tyres.

An original rule stated that unless Ducati won a dry race, they would still be eligible for the concessions in 2016. For that season, a points system was formulated (three points for first, two for second, one for third) for Ducati, Suzuki and Aprilia. Any team that reached six points in wet or dry conditions would forfeit the concessions the following season. But Ducati's overnight competitiveness with the GP15, with six podiums by Mugello, prompted rival factories to pressure Dorna to implement the six-point system a year early. The outcome was confirmation at Assen that Ducati would lose all concessions for 2016 and would race under the same regulations as Honda and Yamaha.

MONSTER YAMAHA TECH 3

TEAM STAFF

Herve PONCHARAL: Team Manager

Gerard VALLEE: Team Co-ordinator

Mathilde PONCHARAL: Team Assistant

Laurence COTTIN: Team Assistant

Fabien ROPERS: Parts Manager

Thomas RUBANTEL: Fuel/Tyres

Milena KOERNER, William MOODY: Press &
Communications

Joeri RIEASSUW: Ohlins Suspension

POL ESPARGARO PIT CREW

Nicolas GOYON: Crew Chief

Mechanics: Eric LABORIE, David LIEBERT,
Xavier QUIEXALOS

Maxime REYSZ: Telemetry

BRADLEY SMITH PIT CREW

Guy COULON: Crew Chief

Mechanics: Steve BLACKBURN, Jerome PONCHARAL,
Josian RUSTIQUE

Maxime DUPONCHEL: Telemetry

POL ESPARGARO

Born: 10 June, 1991 – Granollers, Spain

GP Starts: 158 (36 MotoGP, 51 Moto2, 71 125cc)

GP Wins: 10 Moto2; 5 125cc

World Championships: 1 Moto2

BRADLEY SMITH

Born: 28 November, 1990 – Oxford, England

GP Starts: 167 (54 MotoGP, 33 Moto2, 80 125cc)

GP Wins: 3 125cc

Photos: Gold & Goose

THE extent to which the major factories have commandeered the MotoGP podium in recent years was never more perfectly illustrated than by the 2015 campaign for the French-based Monster Yamaha Tech 3 team.

Herve Poncharal's respected squad, based in Bormes les Mimosas in the south of France, remained the highest-profile and most successful independent team on the grid, with title sponsorship from Monster Energy for the seventh season in succession.

Despite past success that could be measured in multiple podium finishes, in 2015 it was restricted once again to a solitary top-three result that was delivered in the craziest of circumstances at a manic Misano. Bradley Smith's sole rostrum was the highlight of another successful season for Tech 3, and in particular the British rider.

Tech 3 was in its 15th season with Yamaha, and yet again Poncharal filled a dual role in the paddock. The team owner remained as president of the International Race Teams Association, a position he had held since 2006.

Smith was in his fifth season with Tech 3, and his performances were firmly under the microscope, with

YAMAHA YZR-M1 – Tech 3

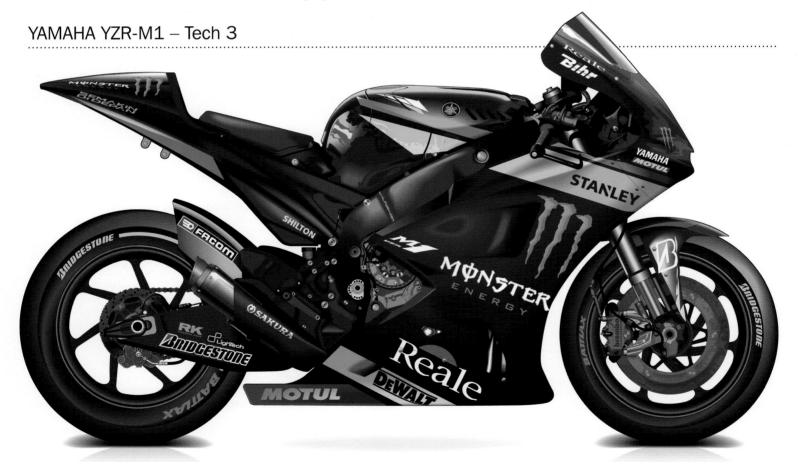

Sponsors and Technical Suppliers: Monster • DeWalt • Stanley • Facom • Bihr • Motul • LightTecht • Reale Seguros • Semakin Di Depan • Bridgestone

Engine: 1000cc transverse in-line 4, reverse-rotating cross-plane crankshaft, DOHC, 4 valves per cylinder, pneumatic valve return system
    Power: Around 260bhp, revs up to approximately 17,000rpm

Ancillaries: Magneti Marelli electronics, NGK sparking plugs, full electronic ride-by-wire • *Lubrication:* Motul

Transmission: Gear primary drive, multi-plate dry slipper clutch, six-speed constant-mesh floating-dog-ring cassette-style gearbox, RK chain

Suspension: Front, Ohlins TTxTR25 48mm forks; Rear, Ohlins TRSP44 shock with linkage

Wheels: 16.5in MFR • *Tyres:* Bridgestone

Brakes: Brembo 320 or 340mm carbon carbon front; Yamaha steel rear

many considering him somewhat fortuitous to retain his prize YZR-M1 seat after a troubled opening half to 2014. He continued to work with instantly recognisable crew chief Guy Coulon, but he adjusted quickly to a reshuffle of his backroom crew. Long-serving Tech 3 mechanic Laurent Ducloyer left to head up a new Tech 3 Classic venture, which specialises in restoring and maintaining classic motorcycles.

Telemetry engineer Andrew Griffith opted to join the new Estrella Galicia 0,0 Marc VDS Honda with Scott Redding. Maxime Duponchel filled his place, promoted from Tech 3's Moto2 team, which continued to run the self-designed, self-built and self-funded Mistral 610 machine in the intermediate category.

Smith's ambition to finish as top non-factory rider was accomplished with relative ease, emphatically silencing his critics, thanks to a season that blended raw speed and aggression with a much calmer approach. He had already scored seven top-six finishes in the opening ten races before starring on a historic podium at Misano, where there were two British riders in the top three in a premier-class race for the first

time in 36 years. During the race, he had missed the chance to pit for rain tyres, and it proved a tactical stroke of genius, as the track dried rapidly and he surged through to second.

Smith's future at Tech 3 was never under any serious threat, though he was made to sweat over the signing of an extended deal. Having frequently outpaced team-mate Pol Espargaro, he was aggrieved when the Spaniard's future was finalised before his. He had to wait until the eve of his home race before one more year was confirmed, with the assurance he had been seeking of parity in technical support from the factory.

Espargaro's new one-year extension had been announced at Indianapolis, and once again it was a direct contract with Yamaha Motor Racing – he will remain on loan to Tech 3, with no factory seat available.

With all major contracts up for renewal for 2017, Smith and Espargaro are in line for possible promotion, but Yamaha is rumoured also to be keeping close tabs on rising star Alex Rins.

Espargaro's second season in MotoGP didn't yield

the progress many had anticipated from one of the few riders to have prevailed in close combat with Marc Marquez in Moto2. He made the top six on only four occasions, and a first premier-class podium eluded him again, though luck was not always on his side. He appeared set for a season-best fourth at Aragon when he first suffered a gearbox malfunction, before the rubber grip on his gearshifter sheared off. He dropped to seventh, and suffered five non-finishes.

Espargaro worked with crew chief Nicolas Goyon again and, like Smith, had a crew shake-up, with Julien Lajunie and Sebastien Letort having departed at the end of 2014.

The Monster Yamaha Tech 3 squad played a pivotal role in a key success for Yamaha in the Japanese factory's 60th anniversary celebrations.

Smith and Espargaro have been career-long enemies, but in a show of unity, they teamed up with five-times All-Japan Superbike champion and YZR-M1 test rider Katsuyuki Nakasuga to win the prestigious Suzuka 8 Hours endurance race for Yamaha for the first time in 19 years.

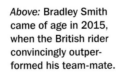

Above: Bradley Smith came of age in 2015, when the British rider convincingly outperformed his team-mate.

Left: Pol Espargaro had a troubled season, although he did clock up four top-six finishes.

Right: Smith's second place in Misano is celebrated with the Monster Tech3 crew.

Photos: Gold & Goose

TEAM SUZUKI ECSTAR

TEAM STAFF

Satoru TERADA: Team Director

Davide BRIVIO: Team Manager

Ken KAWAUCHI: Technical Manager

Sadayuki TSUJIMURA: Engine Management Engineer

Yuta SHIMBUKURO: Engine Management Engineer

Atsushi KAWASAKI: Chassis Engineer

Russell JORDAN: Parts Manager

Roberto BRIVIO, Mitia DOTTA: Co-ordinators

Lara RODINI: Marketing Consultant

Federico TONDELLI: Press Office & Social

ALEIX ESPARGARO PIT CREW

Tom O'KANE: Crew Chief:

Mechanics: Raymond HUGHES, Tsutomu MATSUGANO,

Jacques ROCA, Fernando Mendez PICON (Helper)

Claudio RAINATO: Data Engineer

MAVERICK VINALES PIT CREW

Jose Manuel CAZEAUX: Crew Chief

Mechanics: Davide MANFREDI, Massimo MIRANO,

Marco Rosa GASTALDO, Paco NOQUEIRA (Helper)

Elvio DEGANELLO: Data Engineer

ALEIX ESPARGARO

Born: 30 July, 1989 – Granollers, Spain

GP Starts: 178 (94 MotoGP, 61 Moto2/250cc, 23 125cc)

MAVERICK VINALES

Born: 12 January, 1995 – Figueres, Spain

GP Starts: 85 (18 MotoGP, 18 Moto2, 49 Moto3/125cc)

GP Wins: 16 (4 Moto2, 12 Moto3/125cc)

World Championships: 1 Moto3

SUZUKI ended its three-year, self-imposed exile from MotoGP by returning in 2015, 12 months later than had been expected. Struggling to cope with the impact of the global economic crisis, the Hamamatsu factory had withdrawn at the end of 2011 for what originally had been intended as a short break until 2014. But Suzuki changed its strategy, delaying its eagerly awaited comeback to focus on returning with a more competitive version of its new GSX-RR 1000cc prototype.

Suzuki had a very different look and feel to it compared to 2011, when it had been run under the Crescent banner out of Paul Denning's UK base.

The Suzuki of 2015 had been restored to a two-rider effort, after it had scaled back to a one-man outfit with Alvaro Bautista in 2011. The team had been completely restructured and was headed by Satoru Terada as team director, with no return for Shinichi Sahara, who had been at the helm when Suzuki had departed. It was no longer run out of the UK, with a new European HQ in Italy, which owed much to the appointment of Davide Brivio as team manager.

Brivio had not been seen in the paddock in an official capacity since he had quit Yamaha at the end of 2010, when Valentino Rossi had made an ill-fated

SUZUKI GSX-RR

Sponsors and Technical Suppliers: Ecstar • Motul • Akapovic • Bridgestone • NGK • RK • 2D • Tras Carbon • Beta • Dondup • Sakart • Virgin Radio

Engine: 1000cc transverse in-line 4, reverse-rotating cross-plane crankshaft, DOHC, 4 valves per cylinder, pneumatic valve return system
    Power: Around 260bhp, revs up to 16,500rpm

Ancillaries: Magneti Marelli electronics, NGK sparking plugs, full electronic ride-by-wire • *Lubrication:* Motul

Transmission: Gear primary drive, multi-plate dry slipper clutch, six-speed cassette-style gearbox, RK chain

Suspension: Front, Ohlins TRSP25 48mm 'through-rod' forks; Rear, Ohlins TRSP44 shock with linkage • *Wheels:* 16.5in Magtan • *Tyres:* Bridgestone

Brakes: Brembo 320 or 340mm carbon carbon front; Brembo steel rear

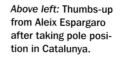

Above: Mayday in Jerez, and a welcome return to MotoGP for the Suzuki team in 2015.

Far left: Massively experienced team manager Davide Brivio imparts his wisdom to MotoGP rookie Maverick Vinales.
Photos: Team Suzuki Ecstar

Above left: Thumbs-up from Aleix Espargaro after taking pole position in Catalunya.

Left: Maverick Vinales adapted to the MotgoGP class and matched his teammate's pace.
Photos: Gold & Goose

Right: Aleix Espargaro's best finish was a sixth place in Aragon.
Photo: Team Suzuki Ecstar

switch to Ducati. The Italian had joined Suzuki in the middle of 2013, when testing of the GSX-RR began in earnest with Randy de Puniet. He brought a wealth of experience as well as some credibility to the project.

Brivio had been an influential figure in Rossi's switch from Honda to Yamaha at the end 2003, and the Italian had managed Yamaha's factory team through the most successful period in its history, when Rossi and Lorenzo had won five titles in seven years.

His wide network of contacts was evident immediately, as he orchestrated the recruitment of one of the paddock's most underrated riders in Aleix Espargaro and one of the sport's rising stars in Maverick Vinales.

Espargaro had earned his first big factory opportunity after excelling on non-factory machinery in the defunct CRT category in 2012 and '13, and the new Open class in 2014. His crew certainly had a familiar look to it, with respected and long-serving crew chief Tom O'Kane re-hired by Suzuki.

Mechanics Raymond Hughes and Tsutomu Matsugano were also survivors of Suzuki's previous MotoGP effort, as was technical manager Ken Kawauchi.

Brivio's Italian influence was apparent in the appointments made to oversee Vinales in his rookie season. Jose Manuel Cazeaux, Davide Manfredi and Massimo Mirano were all signed after a raid on Cal Crutchlow's 2014 factory Ducati technical line-up. Cazeaux had been Crutchlow's data engineer in 2014, but was promoted to the role of crew chief for Vinales, himself recruited on the back of four wins in a stellar debut Moto2 campaign.

In Suzuki's return to the top tier of global racing, they were backed by Ecstar, the Japanese factory's own brand of engine oil.

The GSX-RR was drop-dead gorgeous, with a chassis that made the bike one of the most stable under braking and fastest through the corners. An all too familiar complaint was a lack of engine performance, but Suzuki had been on the back foot chasing horsepower when it suffered very public and very embarrassing engine failures when de Puniet raced as a wild-card in the last round of 2014 at Valencia.

A winter when the main focus should have been on seeking performance was spent in a pursuit of reliability. And a seamless-shift gearbox, now acknowledged as must-have equipment for a factory MotoGP squad, was missing all season, despite initial hopes that it would be ready as early as round six in Barcelona.

Suzuki ended the season still looking for its first podium since Loris Capirossi's third place in Brno way back in 2008.

There was plenty of early promise, with Espargaro qualifying in second place at round three in Argentina. The highlight was a sensational one-two in qualifying at Catalunya. Espargaro's pole was Suzuki's first since Chris Vermuelen had headed qualifying at Assen some eight years before. And with Vinales second on the grid, it was the first Suzuki one-two since Texan legend Kevin Schwantz and Alex Barros had been first and second at Jerez in 1993! Saturday's elation turned to deflation on Sunday, however, when Espargaro crashed while set for a season-best fourth place.

Espargaro was also on the front row in Assen, but had to wait until round 14 in Aragon to register his first top six, which turned out to be his season best.

Vinales capitalised on his Catalunya front-row start by registering his first top-six finish. Subsequently he repeated the feat in Australia. The rookie gained precious experience with points-scoring finishes in the first ten races, before his first lapse with a crash in Brno. That and another non-finish in Japan were the impressive young Spaniard's only races out of the points.

OCTO PRAMAC RACING

TEAM STAFF

Paolo CAMPINOTI: Team Principal

Francesco GUIDOTTI: Team Manager

Felix RODRIGUEZ: Team Co-ordinator

Federico CAPELLI: Press Officer

Francesco NAPOLI: Marketing & Sponsorship

Alex GHINI: Hospitality & PR

Luciano BONCI: Warehouse & Spare Parts

DANILO PETRUCCI PIT CREW

Daniele ROMAGNOLI: Crew Chief

Alberto GIRIBUOLA: Technical Co-ordinator

Federico PECCI: Chief Mechanic

Mechanics: Edoardo CIFERRI, Fabrizio MALAGUTI,

Morris GRAZZI (Tyres & Fuel)

Cristian BATTAGLIA: Data Engineer

YONNY HERNANDEZ PIT CREW

Giacomo GUIDOTTI: Crew Chief

Nicola MANNA: Chief Mechanic

Mechanics: David GALACHO, Pedro RIVERA,

Francesco GALINDO, Marco POLASTRI (Tyres & Fuel)

Mario FRIGIERO: Data Engineer

DANILO PETRUCCI

Born: 24 October, 1990 – Terni, Italy

GP Starts: 68 MotoGP

YONNY HERNANDEZ

Born: 25 July, 1988 – Medellin, Colombia

GP Starts: 100 (69 MotoGP, 31 Moto2)

Photos: Gold & Goose

THE Italian-based Pramac Racing squad started its second decade as Ducati's leading satellite team in 2015 and marked the milestone with a return to a MotoGP podium for the first time in seven years.

Senior management remained unchanged, with Paolo Campinoti operating as team principal, while former Aprilia and KTM boss Francesco Guidotti remained responsible for the day-to-day running of affairs as team manager.

Danilo Petrucci was given the sizeable challenge of replacing number-one rider Andrea Iannone, unveiled as a late replacement after the likes of Scott Redding, Johann Zarco, Loris Baz and Eugene Laverty had all been linked with the ride.

Petrucci had slogged and struggled so much on uncompetitive machinery, since making his MotoGP debut for Ioda Racing in 2012, that he had seriously contemplated quitting to switch to World Superbikes for 2015. He might not have topped Pramac's wish list, but he handsomely repaid the faith shown in him.

Highly motivated not to let his big chance pass him by after securing a two-year deal with Pramac, Petrucci arrived for the first pre-season showdown in Sepang looking a shadow of his former self. He had shed close to 10kg in weight to extract the maximum from the Ducati GP14.1 he had been allocated – the factory-spec machine raced by Dovizioso and Iannone up to the Aragon round the previous season.

Petrucci was paired with crew chief Daniele Romagnoli, who was still under contract to Ducati after mov-

DUCATI Desmosedici GP14 – Pramac

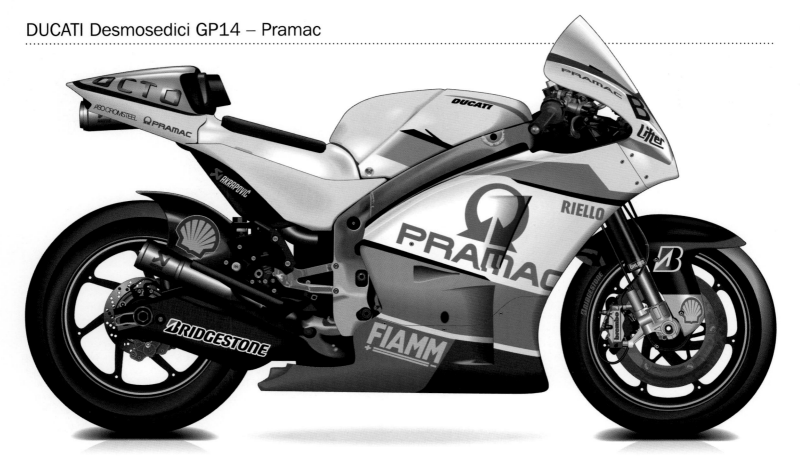

Sponsors and Technical Suppliers: Octo • Pramac • Shell Advance • Rifle • Beta • Regina • Bridgestone • Akrapovic • Termorace • Speedfiber • Quantya
Birra Baladin • La Marchesina • Cecchi • Blackzi • Flex • Riello • FIAMM • partybag • Ma Fra • Gatorade • LSR Helmets
Adidas • B3 • CNC Racing • Nero Modena • La Pizta • Ariete • print • Hawkers • Pole Position Travel • GameStop

Engine: 1000cc 90-degree V4, 360-degree crank, DOHC, 4 valves per cylinder, desmodromic valve gear, variable-length inlet system
    Power: Around 270bhp, revs up to 18,000rpm

Ancillaries: Magneti Marelli electronics, NGK sparking plugs, full electronic ride-by-wire • *Lubrication:* Shell

Transmission: Gear primary drive, Xtrac seamless-shift cassette gearbox

Suspension: Front, Ohlins TRSP25 48mm forks; Rear, Ohlins TRSP44 shock with linkage

Wheels: 16.5in Marchesini • *Tyres:* Bridgestone • *Brakes:* Brembo 320 or 340mm carbon carbon front; 200mm steel rear

ing to the Bologna factory in 2014 with Crutchlow, and thus not able to transfer with the Briton again to LCR Honda.

Edoardo Ciferri was the only mechanic carried over from the Iannone spell, with a key change being Alberto Giribuola's move from the factory team as technical co-ordinator.

Petrucci's best before a career breakthrough at Silverstone was an impressive fifth on the grid in Indianapolis. In the rain in Britain, he claimed a stunning first podium, splashing through from 18th on the grid to second, behind Rossi.

Highlighting Ducati's fall from grace in recent years, Petrucci's second was the first time a satellite bike from the Italian brand had finished on the podium since Toni Elias had been third for Pramac at Misano in 2008.

He followed his maiden podium with an immediate return to the top six in the flag-to-flag at Misano, his first ride on the GP14.2 Desmosedici, but his 100 per cent points record ended with his first race fall in nearly a year at Aragon.

Yonny Hernandez remained South America's lone participant in the second year of his deal with Pramac, and his crew was untouched from a promising 2014 season. Giacomo Guidotti stayed on as crew chief, with Nicola Manna taking on the role of chief mechanic again.

Hernandez made a strong start to the season, fully capitalising on the chance to run Bridgestone's soft option rear tyres to outqualify Rossi and Lorenzo in fifth place at Qatar.

Four top-ten finishes in the opening six rounds continued his impressive start and coincided with a name change for the team. Octo, one of the world's biggest suppliers of insurance telematics technology, signed a naming rights sponsorship deal on the eve of the team's home race in Mugello.

Aside from another strong fifth on the grid at Germany's Sachsenring, Hernandez found it tough to replicate his early-season form. Ultimately his inconsistency cost him his ride, with Pramac expressing interest in Moto2 World Champion Johann Zarco, before launching an audacious attempt to lure Danny Kent straight out of Moto3. Kent was offered a three-

year deal to take the same leap of faith made by his close pal Jack Miller a year earlier, but eventually he opted for the more conventional career route through Moto2 with Leopard Racing.

Kent was still deliberating when Pramac was alerted to the availability of fellow Briton Redding, who was seeking a quick exit from a nightmare season in the newly formed Estrella Galicia 0,0 Marc VDS Honda squad. Ducati was keen, having kept the Pramac seat open for him for a lengthy period in the summer of 2014 while he considered his options. He'd also tested a Desmosedici in Mugello in the middle of 2012, and Ducati remained a big admirer.

Redding was confirmed as Petrucci's 2016 teammate shortly after registering his first top six in MotoGP in a rain-hit home round, He will ride a GP15-spec machine, which is the factory bike campaigned in 2015 by Dovizioso and Iannone.

LCR HONDA

TEAM STAFF

Lucio CECCHINELLO: CEO

Martine FELLONI: Administration & Legal

Oscar HARO: Public Relations

Elisa PAVAN: Press Officer

Elena CECCHINELLO: Hospitality

CAL CRUTCHLOW PIT CREW

Christophe BOURGIGNON: Chief Engineer

Mechanics: Joan CASAS, Xavier CASANOVAS,

Chris RICHARDSON, Ugo GELMI (Tyres)

Brian HARDEN: Telemetry

Katsuhiko IMAI, Yuji KIKUCHI: HRC Engineers

Klaus NOEHLES: Bridgestone Technician

Andy DAWSON: Ohlins Technician

JACK MILLER PIT CREW

Cristian GAVARRINI: Chief Engineer

Mechanics: Filippo BRUNETTI, Christophe LEONCE,

Michele ANDREINI (Tyres)

Ricardo SANCASSINI: Telemetry

CAL CRUTCHLOW
Born: 29 October, 1985 – Coventry, England

GP Starts: 87 MotoGP

World Championships: 1 World Supersport

Photos: Gold & Goose

JACK MILLER
Born: 18 January, 1995 – Townsville, Queensland, Australia

GP Starts: 73 (18 MotoGP, 55 Moto3/125cc)

GP Wins: 6 Moto3

FOR the first time since entering the MotoGP World Championship, back in 2006, Lucio Cecchinello's much-respected LCR Honda squad expanded to a two-rider effort.

Briton Cal Crutchlow had ended his Ducati disappointment by invoking an early-release clause halfway through a two-year deal, to take over the factory RC213V left open by Stefan Bradl's departure.

Meanwhile, Honda's faith in the talent and promise shown by Jack Miller resulted in the Australian being fast-tracked straight out of the combative Moto3 class into MotoGP on a lucrative and unprecedented three-year HRC contract. Miller would learn his craft and gain experience on the improved Honda RC213V-RS Open-class machine. That package was effectively the 2014 factory RC213V, but equipped with the Open-class Magneti Marelli control electronics, and minus the expensive and high-maintenance seamless-shift transmission.

It seemed a dream scenario for Cecchinello.

Not only was he free of the burden of financing Miller's deal, but also he secured a title sponsorship agreement with London-based foreign exchange trading company CWM FX to bankroll Crutchlow's contract and secure the lease of the factory bike.

The honeymoon period didn't last long, however, and LCR found itself dragged reluctantly through murky waters by the affairs of CWM's playboy boss,

HONDA RC213V – LCR

Sponsors and Technical Suppliers: Castrol • Givi • Unibat • Rizoma • Carpimoto • Viar • Progrip • PBR Sprockets • Arrow • Comaco • Draco • SIFI • OZ Racing
Ohlins • Bridgestone • AGOS • Special Impianti

Engine: 1000cc 90-degree V4, 360-degree crank, pneumatic valve springs *Power:* More than 260ps up to 17,000rpm

Ancillaries: HRC electronics, ride-by-wire throttle and fuel injection system, Denso sparking plugs *Lubrication:* Castrol

Transmission: Gear primary drive, multi-plate dry slipper clutch, six-speed seamless-shift cassette-style gearbox, DID chain

Suspension: Front, Ohlins TRSP25 48mm 'through-rod' forks • Rear, TRSP44 gas shock with linkage

Wheels: 16.5in OZ Racing *Tyres:* Bridgestone

Brakes: Brembo 320 or 340mm carbon carbon front; HRC 218mm steel rear

Anthony Constantinou. A wheel hadn't even turned in anger at the opening round in Qatar before it emerged that London City police had raided CWM's headquarters and made 13 arrests relating to allegations of fraud.

The situation became worse during the summer, when Constantinou was charged on multiple counts of sexual assault. By the time Crutchlow's home race came around at Silverstone, in late August, CWM branding had vanished for good.

The fallout from the CWM controversy had significant consequences for Cecchinello. Motorcycle accessories brand Givi, a loyal and long-term partner of the Italian, had been the main sponsor on Jack Miller's Open-class bike since round one in Qatar, and the company stepped up to sponsor Crutchlow's RC213V for the remaining seven races. However, the collapse of the CWM deal meant that Cecchinello had no choice but to revert to a one-rider squad for 2016.

After a very brief flirtation with Pramac for a shock return to the Ducati, Crutchlow had agreed a new two-year deal with LCR, which was confirmed on the eve of his home round at Silverstone. His switch to a third different manufacturer in three years didn't yield the transformation in fortunes many had anticipated. He inherited all of Bradl's crew, which meant for the first time in his MotoGP career, he would not work with Daniele Romagnoli as his crew chief.

Christophe Bourguignon filled that role once again, while Brian Harden was in control of data recording.

Crutchlow enjoyed limited success on the unruly RC213V, though he joined an elite group of riders to finish on the podium for three different manufacturers when he took a last-gasp third from Andrea Iannone in Argentina. That performance also made him the first rider to finish on the podium in three successive years on bikes from three different manufacturers since Eddie Lawson in 1989, '90 and '91 on a Honda, Yamaha and Cagiva. He scored only four more top-six finishes – at Jerez, Assen, Twin Ring Motegi and Sepang.

Rookie Miller, not surprisingly, found the transition from the light and nimble 60bhp KTM Moto3 bike to the fire-breathing 1000cc MotoGP prototype a complex adjustment. Nonetheless, he finished top Open-class rider in two races, joining Crutchlow in *parc fermé* at Termas de Rio Hondo with 12th, then taking honours again at home in Australia; but the closest he got to the top ten was 11th at Catalunya.

Honda hired some big-hitting technical talent to help Miller make the big leap of faith from Moto3 to MotoGP. His crew chief was Italian Cristian Gabarrini, the technical mastermind behind Casey Stoner's Ducati and Honda titles in 2007 and 2011. Gabarrini's journey to prominence had begun when LCR gave him his break in world championship racing with Stoner, as a 125cc data technician in 2003.

Miller's crew included Filippo Brunetti, who had also worked with Stoner in MotoGP, and the vastly experienced Christophe Leonce, whom Dani Pedrosa had ruthlessly deemed surplus to requirements at Repsol Honda at the end of 2014. They would all move with Miller to the Estrella Galicia 0,0 Marc VDS squad in 2016.

Honda RCV213V-RS – Miller

Engine: 1000cc 90-degree V4, 360-degree crank, pneumatic valve recovery system

Power: More than 265ps

Ancillaries: Magneti Marelli control electronics and inertial platform, Dorna control software, NGK sparking plugs, full electronic ride-by-wire

Lubrication: Castrol

Transmission: Gear primary drive, multi-plate dry slipper clutch, six-speed constant-mesh cassette-style gearbox, DID chain

Suspension: Front, Ohlins TRSP25 48mm forks; Rear, Ohlins TRSP44 shock with linkage

Wheels: 16.5in OZ Racing

Tyres: Bridgestone

Brakes: Brembo 320 or 340mm carbon carbon front; HRC 218mm steel 218mm rear

Top: Cal Crutchlow was happier on the Honda after his downbeat Ducati season.

Top right: Team principal Lucio Cecchinello.

Above right: Aussie Jack Miller bypassed Moto2 and made a strong impression.

Right: Celebrations in Argentina, where Crutchlow took his only podium finish, and Miller the first of two Open class wins.

Photos: Gold & Goose

ESTRELLA GALICIA 0,0 MARC VDS

TEAM STAFF

Marc VAN DER STRATEN: Team President

Michael BARTHOLEMY: Team Principal

Marina ROSSI: Team Co-ordinator

Patrick KRAMER: Logistics Co-ordinator

Stefan PREIN: Rider Coach

Mike WATT: Ohlins Technician

Ian WHEELER: Marketing & Communications Manager

SCOTT REDDING PIT CREW

Chris PIKE: Chief Mechanic

Mechanics: Mark BARNETT, Craig BURTON, Koichi UJINO

Francesco FAVA: Fuel Injection Engineer

Andrew: GRIFFITH: Data Engineer

Mark LLOYD: Gearbox

Christian AUSSEMS: Tyres & Fuel

Photo: Gold & Goose

SCOTT REDDING
Born: 4 January, 1993 – Quedgeley, England
GP Starts: 135 (36 MotoGP, 66 Moto2, 33 125cc)
GP Wins: 4 (3 Moto2, 1 125cc)

EVER since wealthy entrepreneur Marc van der Straten first bankrolled his high-profile Moto2 squad in 2010, the Belgian tycoon had made no secret of his desire to break into team ownership in the MotoGP World Championship. That ambition was finally realised in 2015, following its breakthrough first world championship success with Tito Rabat in Moto2 the previous season.

Marc VDS took over the lease of Fausto Gresini's vacant factory Honda RC213V, after the Italian's sponsorship woes, and they welcomed back into the fold British rider Scott Redding. The 22-year-old had been a driving force behind the Marc VDS Moto2 project from its inception, and van der Straten, who was officially known as team president, had treated

the rider like his own son when Redding narrowly missed out on capturing the intermediate-category title in 2013.

Team principal duty went to former factory Kawasaki MotoGP boss Michael Bartholemy, who had been a pivotal figure in convincing van der Straten to enter two-wheeled competition during 2009. Bartholemy was not only the high-profile and outspoken public voice of Marc VDS, but he also operated as Redding's personal manager.

Former Ten Kate Honda World Superbike crew chief Chris Pike was given the opportunity to cut his teeth in the MotoGP paddock, after Redding missed out on Casey Stoner's ex-chief engineer Cristian Gabarrini, who had been his number-one pick.

Pike was new to MotoGP, but surrounded by familiar faces to help him adjust to the career change. HRC gearbox technician Mark Lloyd and mechanic Craig Burton, both of whom had Repsol Honda experience, had worked with Pike during heady days at the Castrol Honda World Superbike squad, when it had been run out of Louth in the UK.

Mark Barnett also joined after being axed by Dani Pedrosa at Repsol Honda.

Andrew Griffith moved from Bradley Smith's Monster Yamaha Tech 3 squad as data engineer, while long-serving Gresini fuel injection engineer Francesco Fava completed the new line-up.

Much had been expected of Redding after his encouraging first MotoGP season on the uncompetitive Open-class Honda RCV1000R. But it was a season of overwhelming underachievement as he struggled with the aggressive and unforgiving engine and handling characteristics of the factory RC213V. He didn't score a top-six until the treacherously wet British Grand Prix

HONDA RC213V – Mark VDS

Sponsors and Technical Suppliers: Estrella Galicia 0,0 • Total • PCL • Monster • Dribble Dots • Rizoma • Beta • AFAM • Regina • Akrapovic • Pascucci • Pro-Bolt • 2D Domino Group • Bischoff Scheck • Abakus • Roncato • Mode Performance • GB Racing • MRA • Zuurbier • Jeeper • Valter Moto North Week • MacManniack • Pavonet • Taleo Encoracing • Rudy Project • Earwear • Top-Racers.com • Eupen • Race Seats • Herock

Engine: 1000cc 90-degree V4, 360-degree crank, DOHC, 4 valves per cylinder, pneumatic valve return system • *Power:* More than 265bhp, revs up to 17,500rpm

Ancillaries: HRC electronics and ride-by-wire throttle and fuel injection system, NGK sparking plugs • *Lubrication:* Castrol

Transmission: Gear primary drive, multi-plate dry slipper clutch, six-speed seamless-shift constant-mesh cassette-style gearbox, RK chain

Suspension: Front, Ohlins TRSP25 48mm forks; Rear, Ohlins TRSP44 shock with linkage

Wheels: 16.5in OZ Racing • *Tyres:* Bridgestone

Brakes: Brembo 320 or 340mm carbon carbon; HRC 218mm steel rear

at Silverstone in late August, but he followed that up with a first premier-class podium in the flag-to-flag mayhem at Misano, where he crashed early, completed two pit stops and still finished third!

That result made Redding the first rider to crash in a race and still finish on the podium since Casey Stoner, during his unforgettable 2008 duel with Valentino Rossi at Laguna Seca.

He only scored one more top-ten in the remaining five races, and his fairy-tale return to Marc VDS was abruptly ended halfway through a two-year deal when he opted to move to Pramac Ducati.

Rabat, the first Moto2 rider to defend the title, will take over the factory RC213V for the 2016 season, working with Pike.

Ambition knows no bounds at Marc VDS, and the team confirmed in mid-October that it would be expanding to two riders in 2016.

Highly rated Jack Miller is contracted to HRC and therefore was assured of a grid slot somewhere, despite the disappearance of his LCR saddle. With Aspar switching allegiance to Ducati, Honda cut a deal with Marc VDS for Miller, which smacked of irony, given the acrimonious fallout between the two parties during 2014. Bartholemy had been convinced he had a binding agreement with Miller for a Moto2 project, only for the Australian to sign a three-year MotoGP deal with HRC.

The meteoric rise to prominence of Marc VDS in just five years has been one of the big success stories in recent MotoGP history, and it reaches beyond the paddock. A three-year sponsorship deal with Spanish brewery giant Estrella Galicia aligns Marc VDS with the Monlau Repsol Technical School, which was managed by former 125cc World Champion Emilio Alzamora, who discovered and then nurtured the prodigious talent of Marc Marquez.

As well as the EG Moto3 squad, Alzamora also ran a two-rider effort in the newly named FIM CEV Repsol Moto3 Junior World Championship, now the breeding ground for future grand prix stars. The link between Alzamora and Bartholemy offers a talented rider a career path through the domestic Spanish series right into MotoGP.

Photo: Gold & Goose

Photo: Team Estrella Galicia 0,0

Photo: Gold & Goose

Above: Team principal Michael Bartholemy.

Left: Redding took a fine sixth in the wet in his home round at Silverstone.

Centre: Searching for front-end feel was the main problem for Redding on the Honda.

Top: After a topsy-turvey race, the team celebrate a podium place in Misano.

APRILIA RACING
TEAM GRESINI

TEAM STAFF

Romano ALBESIANO: Aprilia Racing Manager

Fausto GRESINI: Team Manager

Marco BERTOLATTI: Project Leader

Massimo MENEGHINI: Spare Parts

Oscar BOLZONELLA: Suspension

STEFAN BRADL PIT CREW

Diego GUBELLINI: Head Technician

Paolo BIASIO: Track Engineer

Mechanics: Andrea BONASOLLI, Carlo TOCCAFONDI,
Federico VICINO, Jerome GALLANO, Eddy BOSSI

Guido FONTANA: Data Engineer

ALVARO BAUTISTA PIT CREW

Giulio NAVA: Head Technician

Nicolo BILIATO: Track Engineer

Mechanics: Ivano MANCURTI, Maurizio VISANI,
Alberto PRESUTTI, Renzo PINI, Gianpetro CANETTI

Loris CONTE: Data Engineer

ALVARO BAUTISTA

Born: 21 November, 1984 – Talavera de la Reina, Spain

GP Starts: 220 (104 MotoGP, 49 250cc, 67 125cc)

GP Wins: 16 (8 250cc, 8 125cc)
World Championships: 1 125cc

Photos: Gold & Goose

MARCO MELANDRI

Born: 7 August, 1982 – Ravenna, Italy

GP Starts: 215 (139 MotoGP/500cc, 47 250cc, 29 125cc)

GP Wins: 22 (5 MotoGP/500cc, 10 250cc, 7 125cc)
World Championships: 1 250cc

DORNA'S drive to encourage major manufacturers back into MotoGP by offering appealing technical regulations and attractive financial subsidies enticed Aprilia to return with a full factory project for the first time since 2004.

The Noale factory has had a presence in MotoGP since 2012, when it made available the ART bike (Aprilia Racing Technology) for the CRT class. This was closely derived from its RSV4 superbike as an affordable alternative to expensive factory machinery.

Aprilia's return to full factory status came a year ahead of schedule, the original intention having been to come back in 2016 with a brand-new RS-GP 1000cc prototype contender.

New Aprilia boss Romano Albesiano was given the tough task of replacing Gigi Dall'Igna, who had been head-hunted by Ducati at the end of 2013, and he quickly decided the best way for the RS-GP to progress was to be tested in cut-throat competition.

Albesiano kept faith with highly regarded engineer Marco Bertolatti, who was installed as project leader of the RS-GP.

The mission for 2015 was always crystal clear. The RS-GP was intended purely as a 'lab' bike that Aprilia

APRILIA RS-GP

Sponsors and Technical Suppliers: Barracuda • SAP • Motul • Berner • Fast Design • Gaga Milano • Inox Centre • PBR • Pascucci • Sagtubi • Akrapovic
Bike-Lift • Cobo Group • Dellorto • Do Design • Zeroshift Performance • GraphiStudio • Kopron • Neiko • NGK Spark Plugs
Regina Chain • Roland • Sprint Filter • Tenax • Vertex

Engine: 1000cc 65-degree V4, DOHC, 4 valves per cylinder, pneumatic valve return system, gear-driven cams, variable-length inlet system
Power: Around 240bhp, revs up to 16,500rpm

Ancillaries: Magneti Marelli control electronics and inertial platform, Dorna control software, full electronic ride-by-wire

Transmission: Zeroshift seamless-shift cassette gearbox • *Lubrication:* Motul

Suspension: Front, Ohlins TTxTR25 48mm forks; Rear, Ohlins TRSP44 shock with linkage • *Wheels:* 16.5in Marchesini

Tyres: Bridgestone • *Brakes:* Brembo, 320 or 340mm carbon carbon front; 200mm steel rear

STEFAN BRADL
Born: 29 November, 1989 – Augsberg, Germany

GP Starts: 156 (69 MotoGP, 33 Moto2, 54 125cc)

GP Wins: 7 (5 Moto2, 2 125cc)
World Championships: 1 Moto2

MICHAEL LAVERTY
Born: 7 June 1981 – Toomebridge, Northern Ireland

GP Starts: 37 MotoGP

would continually bombard with new parts ahead of a full-blown prototype being rolled out for 2016. A constant stream of upgrades seemed to filter through from Noale, the most notable being the addition of a seamless-shift gearbox, which appeared at Mugello.

Aprilia's return to MotoGP gave rise to a four-year collaboration with Italian team boss Fausto Gresini. He ended an 18-year association with Honda, which stretched back to his move into team ownership in 1997, to align with Aprilia. Funding issues with Gresini's 2014 backer, GO&FUN, meant that he had been unable to meet the leasing fees set by HRC to run a factory-backed RC213V. And collaborating with an existing team meant that Aprilia was guaranteed financial support from Dorna, and would avoid having to pay for expensive running costs like air freight and tyres.

Thus the arrangement was mutually beneficial to both Aprilia and Gresini.

Eager to develop the RS-GP as quickly as possible, Aprilia opted for one of the most experienced line-ups on the grid.

Alvaro Bautista had been with Gresini for three years on a Honda and was signed to a two-year deal, as was Marco Melandri. The Italian was back in MotoGP for the first time since 2010, and for a third stint with Gresini. He was more than a reluctant employee though, as his clear preference was to remain in World Superbikes.

Diego Giubellini was Melandri's crew chief, while Paolo Biasio was Aprilia's track engineer.

Melandri's return to MotoGP was nothing short of an embarrassing disaster. It was painful to watch a rider who had won races in 125cc, 250cc, MotoGP and World Superbikes struggling so woefully off the pace. He failed to score a single point, and in all but one race qualified in last place, before he was put out of his misery just before the summer break.

Rumours of a divorce first surfaced in Mugello, but an amicable settlement was finally reached after Assen, and Melandri was out.

Former PBM rider Michael Laverty was hired by Aprilia as a test rider for 2015. The Irishman, who was also riding for Tyco BMW in the British Superbike series, focused primarily on tuning the RS-GP to Michelin tyres, ahead of the switch from Bridgestone for 2016. He replaced Melandri at the Sachsenring in Germany and finished 20th, but his tenure was short-lived.

With Athina Forward Racing plunged into crisis during the summer hiatus, Stefan Bradl swiftly invoked a release clause in his contract and signed a deal to partner Bautista for the remaining nine races.

Bradl was only able to score points in two races, but he acquitted himself well enough to clinch a one-year deal for 2016, announced in late September.

Bautista went quietly about his business, despite being cast in the role of test mule for a project that didn't advance at the rate he desired. He scored points

in 13 races and twice broke into the top ten, at Barcelona and Silverstone.

With Bautista's longstanding Gresini crew chief, Antonio Jiminez, having moved to the Italtrans Moto2 squad, the Spaniard's head technician was Guilio Nava. He had previously been a data engineer at Repsol Honda with Casey Stoner and most recently had filled the same role with Nicky Hayden at Aspar Honda.

A milestone race for Aprilia came in Brno, where both Bautista and Bradl finished inside the points. That was the first time in 11 years that Aprilia had had both bikes in the top 15.

Bautista and Bradl will be fighting it out for just one vacant RS-GP seat in 2017. Weaved into the Bradl announcement came confirmation that former World Supersport champion Sam Lowes will ride for Gresini's Moto2 squad in 2016, before he is guaranteed a two-year tilt on the RS-GP in MotoGP for the 2017 and 2018 seasons.

Above and top right: **Stefan Bradl (6) moved over from Forward Racing in mid-season to replace the hapless Marco Melandri (33).**

Right: **Team Principal Fausto Gresini.**

Far right: **Aprilia's Romano Albesiano.**

Below: The loyal Alvaro Bautista was the team's mainstay in 2015.

Photos: Gold & Goose

FORWARD RACING

TEAM STAFF

Giovanni CUZARI: Team Owner

Marco CURIONI: Managing Director

Giulia DOGLIANI: Sponsorship & Logistics

Laura BERETTA: PR & Press

STEFAN BRADL/TONI ELIAS PIT CREW

Sergio VERBENA: Crew Chief

Mechanics: Guglielmo ANDREINI, Jonny DONELLI,

Florian FERRACI, Mirko FIUZZI

Manfred GEISSLER: Data Technician

LORIS BAZ PIT CREW

Andrew OLEART: Crew Chief

Mechanics: Antonio PEREZ-HABA, Danilo PIAZZA,

Paolo PIAZZA, Martin ZABALA

Bernard MARTIGNAC: Data Technician

FORWARD YAMAHA M-1

Engine: 1000cc transverse in-line 4, reverse-rotating cross-plane crankshaft, DOHC, 4 valves per cylinder, pneumatic valve return system

Power: Around 255bhp, revs up to approximately 16,200rpm

Ancillaries: Magneti Marelli control electronics and inertial platform, Dorna control software, NGK sparking plugs, full electronic ride-by-wire

Lubrication: Yamalube

Transmission: Gear primary drive, multi-plate dry slipper clutch, six-speed constant-mesh floating-dog-ring cassette-style gearbox, Tsubaki chain, AFAM sprockets

Suspension: Front, Ohlins TTxTR25 48mm forks; Rear, Ohlins TRSP44 shock with linkage

Wheels: 16.5in Marchesini

Tyres: Bridgestone

Brakes: Brembo 320 and 340mm carbon carbon front; Yamaha steel rear

STEFAN BRADL
Born: 29 November, 1989 – Augsberg, Germany
GP Starts: 156 (69 MotoGP 33 Moto2, 54 125cc)
GP Wins: 7 (5 Moto2, 2 125cc)
World Championships: 1 Moto2

LORIS BAZ
Born: 1 February, 1993 – Sallanches, France
GP Starts: 17 MotoGP

Cuzari with Stefan Bradl and his crew at Jerez.

Photo: Forward Racing

Stefan Bradl

Photo: Gold & Goose

THE rapid decline of Forward Racing in 2015 was a stark reminder of how fickle the business of elite motorcycle racing can be. In 2014, Forward had blazed a trail for the underdog when it showed what a successful concept the new Open class could be, if you had the right machinery and a highly-motivated and talented rider.

The contract with Yamaha meant it received a dated, but still competitive YZR-M1 engine and chassis package, which Aleix Espargaro had put on pole position in Assen and on the podium at Motorland Aragon. This success was one of the feel-good stories of the year, and it showed that Dorna's Open class vision to allow moderately-funded independent teams to lease competitive machinery was a viable way to go racing at an affordable price.

Success on track also resulted in success off track, with Athina Eyewear stepping in to replace NGM as title sponsor.

Espargaro had thoroughly merited a big-money move to Suzuki's factory squad on the back of his Forward form; while the competitiveness of the Forward package was enough to entice ex-LCR Honda rider Stefan Bradl to join rookie Loris Baz.

By the end of 2015, however, the team had been generating headlines for all the wrong reasons, and

for 2016, it would no longer be on the MotoGP grid.

The season had started full of optimism, but the team never threatened to reach the dizzy heights of 2014. Bradl found the transition to the standard Open-class electronics a shock to the system, after having access to Honda's sophisticated and advanced rider aids at LCR, despite the input of experienced former factory Suzuki data technician Manfred 'Tex' Geissler.

Bradl had scored just one point before a season-best eighth-place finish in Catalunya, which was immediately followed by a crash in Assen that left him with a broken right scaphoid. Nobody realised at the time, but the Dutch TT would be Bradl's swansong in Forward livery.

The wrist injury kept him out of action in his home race at Sachsenring. Immediately after the German round, the entire operation was thrown into major turmoil when news broke that charismatic and forthright team owner Giovanni Cuzari had been arrested by Swiss authorities for alleged corruption, money laundering and bribery.

Cuzari's arrest prompted swift action by Athina, who immediately severed all ties with Forward Racing to avoid a blitz of negative publicity. Other sponsors quickly distanced themselves from the saga, too, and

CLAUDIO CORTI

Born: 25 June, 1987 – Como, Italy

GP Starts: 69 (23 MotoGP, 46 Moto 2)

TONI ELIAS

Born: 26 March, 1983 – Manresa, Catalonia, Spain

GP Starts: 228 (105 MotoGP, 88 Moto2/250cc, 35 125cc)

GP Wins: 17 (1 MotoGP, 14 Moto2/250cc, 2 125cc)
World Championships: 1 Moto2

Giovanni Cuzari

Photos: Gold & Goose

Claudio Corti

Toni Elias

the MotoGP team and two-rider Moto2 squad (featuring Simone Corse and Lorenzo Baldassarri) were pitched into a fight for survival, all the team's funding effectively having been cut off.

Forward Racing skipped the Indianapolis round, but a rescue package was put together to compete at Brno, Silverstone, Misano and Motorland Aragon.

Bradl invoked a get-out clause in his contract to take Marco Melandri's factory Aprilia RS-GP berth for the final nine races.

Former Forward Racing MotoGP rider Claudio Corti, who had already replaced the injured Bradl in Germany, stood in at Brno, Silverstone and Misano, before unemployed former Moto2 World Champion Toni Elias took over for the final five rounds.

The big positive for Forward Racing was the performance of lanky Frenchman Baz. He'd had problems of his own at the end of 2014, when the Aspar squad had backed out of a deal because of fears that he was too tall.

The former factory Kawasaki World Superbike rider worked with crew chief Andrea Oleari, who had been Scott Redding's Moto2 data technician at Marc VDS and an engineer with Mahindra's Moto3 project.

Baz had the distinction of claiming the best Open class result of the season with a magnificent fourth

in a manic Misano flag-to-flag encounter – the best result by a French rider since Randy de Puniet had finished fourth at Catalunya in 2010. He also came close to an unlikely success in the Open class battle and lost out to Hector Barbera by just five points.

The allegations against Cuzari inevitably put the team's MotoGP future in jeopardy. Yamaha wasn't willing to supply machinery again, and talks with Ducati and Aprilia never came to fruition. One day after the Australian Grand Prix, it became clear that Forward Racing had no immediate future in MotoGP.

The team would remain in Moto2, however, having committed to promising teenager Baldassarri. But in a major strategic change, Forward Racing would collaborate with legendary Italian marque MV Agusta for a double-pronged attack in World Superbikes and World Supersport in 2016.

Cuzari will become team principal of both Forward MV Agusta teams, and he even hinted at lofty ambitions of bringing the iconic Varese company back to MotoGP in the future. Forward Racing also confirmed that former 250cc World Champion Marco Melandri would be test rider for the 2016 F4 RC machine. He had raced for Forward in 2009 when it was briefly named Hayate Racing Team, having taken over the remnants of the collapsed factory Kawasaki squad.

Above: Baz celebrates his tremendous fourth place – and Open class win – in San Marino.
Photo: Gold & Goose

Above centre: Loris Baz made an impressive switch from World Superbikes.
Photo: Forward Racing

AVINTIA RACING

TEAM STAFF

Antonio MARTIN: General Manager
Augustin ESCOBAR: Team Manager
Akikito ISHIDA: Technical Director
Marc VIDAL: Team Co-ordinator (Logistics)
David DE GEA: Team Co-ordinator

HECTOR BARBERA PIT CREW

Jarno POLASTRI: Chief Mechanic
Mechanics: Simone FALCONI, Jesus MORENO,
Jordi PRADES, Manuel SANTOS
Mario MARTINI: Data Engineer

MIKE DI MEGLIO PIT CREW

Alessandro TOGNELLI: Chief Mechanic
Mechanics: Rafael LOPEZ, Jose MA ROJAS,
Luis MARTINEZ, Toni MIR
Miguel Angel ARIAS: Data Engineer

Barbera at Austin

Mike di Meglio

Ducati Desmosedici GP12 Avintia

Engine: 1000cc 90-degree V4, 360-degree crank, DOHC, 4 valves per cylinder, desmodromic valve gear, variable-length inlet system

Power: Around 270bhp, revs up to 18,000rpm

Ancillaries: Magneti Marelli electronics, NGK sparking plugs, full electronic ride-by-wire

Lubrication: Shell

Transmission: Xtrac seamless-shift cassette gearbox, Regina chain

Suspension: Front, Ohlins TRSP25 48mm forks; Rear, Ohlins TRSP44 shock with linkage

Wheels: 16.5in Marchesini

Tyres: Bridgestone

Brakes: Brembo 320 or 340mm carbon carbon front; 200mm steel rear

HECTOR BARBERA

Born: 2 November, 1986 – Dos Aguas, Spain

GP Starts: 207 (85 MotoGP, 75 250cc, 47 125cc)
GP Wins: 10 (4 250cc, 6 125cc)

MIKE DI MEGLIO

Born: 17 January, 1988 – Toulouse, France

GP Starts: 184 (18 MotoGP, 59 Moto2, 16 250cc, 91 125cc)
GP Wins: 5 125cc
World Championships: 1 125cc

ARMED with its most competitive machinery since it first entered the MotoGP World Championship in 2012, the Avintia Racing squad was a prominent force in the second year of the Open category.

The Spanish-based team finally shelved its three-year Kawasaki ZX-10R-powered project to form a new alliance with Ducati, which had effectively started at the back end of 2014, when Hector Barbera had raced a Desmosedici in the last five rounds.

For 2015, both Barbera and former 125cc World Champion Mike di Meglio had access to GP14 machinery at the start of the season. Ducati boss Gigi Dall'Igna used the Avintia deal as a test mule in many respects, to understand the parameters and performance of the Open-class electronics, which would help form the basis of the unified software to be implemented across the board in 2016.

Antonio Martin continued as general manager, with co-owner Raul Romero remaining the public face of the project, while Agustin Escobar continued in the role of team manager.

A significant change in personnel led to di Meglio's 2014 crew chief, Jarno Polastri, switching to lead Barbera's side of the garage, his replacement being Alessandro Tognelli.

Jordi Prades, a former Repsol Honda mechanic, who had spent four years with HRC from 2006, working with Dani Pedrosa, also made the transfer from di Meglio's camp to Barbera.

Barbera made a brilliant start to the season, scoring in the first six races, which included a 13th at Le Mans, where he made his debut on an upgraded GP14.1 chassis. His command at the top of the Open class rankings started to unravel in Catalunya, however, where a front brake problem dropped him out of the points for the first time. Then he was fortunate to escape serious injury when his right leg became trapped momentarily in Jack Miller's rear wheel, after a rash rookie mistake by the Aussie.

Barbera found it hard to repeat his early-season points-scoring form, given MotoGP's phenomenal strength in depth, and in the unforgettable Misano flag-to-flag battle he surrendered control of the Open class title chase to Loris Baz. Then a strong ninth in the Japanese round put him back in control, and he emerged Open champion at the end of the season.

Baz was five points adrift, and there was a touch of irony to his challenge, for at the time he took over he was negotiating a deal to partner Barbera in 2016. Earlier, it had looked as though Yonny Hernandez would move in as di Meglio's replacement.

Di Meglio had to wait until round seven to score his first points, with 14th in Catalunya. He would score points on three more occasions in the remaining 11 races, but it was no surprise when Avintia management began moving to replace him. France being one of the key European markets for Spanish-based promotional rights holders Dorna, Avintia would retain a French flavour by contracting Baz.

The former factory Kawasaki World Superbike rider signed his deal during the Moto3 race in Aragon, and he will ride Ducati's GP14.2 with Barbera. It was poignant for Baz to secure his future at the race, as it had been at the Aragon round in 2014 where it first emerged that Aspar Honda had pulled out of a deal to sign him on the absurd notion that he was too tall.

Hector Barbera

EUGENE LAVERTY
Born: 3 June, 1986 – Ballymena, Northern Ireland

GP Starts: 48 (18 MotoGP, 29 250cc, 1 125cc)

NICKY HAYDEN
Born: 30 July, 1981 – Owensboro, Kentucky, USA

GP Starts: 216
GP Wins: 3 MotoGP
World Championships: 1 MotoGP

ASPAR HONDA

TEAM STAFF

Jorge MARTINEZ: Team Manager
Silvia PELUFO: Assistant Team Manager
Facundo GARCIA: Administration Manager
Gino BORSOI: Sporting Manager
Maria Jose BOTELLA: Media & Logistics
Ricardo PEDROS: Media Officer
Carmen PRYTZ, Leonor FONS: Administration
Agustin PEREZ: Maintenance

NICKY HAYDEN PIT CREW

Bruno LEONI: Chief Mechanic
Mechanics: Salvador FRANCO, Jordi CUNILL, Oscar GRAU
Francesco CARCHEDI/Andrea MATTIOLI: Data Engineers
Matthew CASEY: Track Engineer
Jeremy ROBINSON: Suspension

EUGENE LAVERTY PIT CREW

Miguel Angel GALLEGO: Chief Mechanic
Mechanics: Phil MARRON, Nacho CABEZA,
Salvador MORALEDA (Assistant)
Andrea ORLANDI: Track Engineer
Davide TAGLIATESTA: Data Engineer
Roger MARCACCINI: Supplies

THE Valencia-based Aspar squad rode out a big early financial storm in 2015, before ending its short relationship with Honda and bidding farewell to one of racing's genuine good guys.

The season hadn't even begun in Qatar when Jorge Martinez's squad was plunged into crisis by Malaysian energy drink Drive M7 withdrawing its naming rights sponsorship, halfway through a two-year deal.

Not only did the break have a big impact on the funding of the team, which was in its sixth season of campaigning in MotoGP, but also the late removal of support meant that Martinez had no opportunity to procure a replacement. The predicament was only marginally eased when Aspar's former title sponsor, Power Electronics, came back on board from the second race at the Circuit of The Americas in Texas.

Eugene Laverty

Power Electronics had backed Aspar's successful Aprilia ART project when it had dominated the defunct CRT class with Aleix Espargaro in 2012 and 2013.

Senior management at Aspar remained unchanged, with Martinez filling the role of team manager, and trusted sidekick Gino Borsoi once again operating as sporting manager.

American Nicky Hayden was back for his second season with Aspar, hoping that Honda's decision to radically upgrade its struggling RCV1000R Open-class contender to the new RC213V-RS would make him more competitive.

The RC213V-RS was a 2014 factory-spec machine, but equipped with standard Magneti Marelli Open-class electronics. It was also stripped of exotic technology like a seamless-shift gearbox.

Hayden didn't score a top-ten place all season and finished with a best of 11th place at Le Mans, though in Austin he did become the first American to reach 200 appearances. Only Valentino Rossi, Alex Barros and Loris Capirossi have started more races than Hayden.

A roller-coaster grand prix career that Hayden had started as a wide-eyed rookie at Repsol Honda in 2003 finally ended. At the Japanese round at Twin Ring Motegi, he confirmed his departure to embark on the challenge of becoming the first to win both the premier-class MotoGP and World Superbike crowns. He will join the Ten Kate Honda squad with emerging Dutch star Michael van der Mark.

The writing was on the wall for Hayden shortly before the Far East trip to Japan, after Aspar announced that it had signed Colombian Yonny Hernandez, who initially had seemed destined for a transfer to Avintia Ducati. The South American's close relationship with Ducati provided the biggest clue that Aspar was moving back to the Bologna factory for 2016.

Aspar had formed a close association with Ducati Corse boss Gigi Dall'Igna when he'd run successful 125cc, 250cc and MotoGP ventures for the Italian in his previous spell as technical guru at Aprilia.

So it came as no surprise when the split from Honda and return to Ducati for the first time since 2011

Nicky Hayden

was finally confirmed during the Australian Grand Prix at Phillip Island. The team will run GP14.2 machinery, the factory-spec bikes raced by Andrea Dovizioso and Andrea Iannone at the end of 2014.

In the same communication came confirmation that Aspar would honour the second year of Eugene Laverty's two-year deal, which at times had appeared to be a fragile promise in the weeks leading up to the Australian GP.

Laverty's first season in MotoGP was a brutally steep learning curve, though he was paired with experienced crew chief Andrea Orlandi to help shorten it. He was allowed to bring in one of his own staff, and not surprisingly opted for Phil Marron, who was not only a trusted crew chief from his World Superbike career, but also his brother-in-law.

Marron was first mechanic for the Monaco-based Ulsterman, who finished with a season-best 12th at Catalunya. His strongest overall weekend though was undoubtedly in Aragon, where he qualified and finished top Open rider.

Honda RCV213V-RS Aspar

Engine: 1000cc 90-degree V4, 360-degree crank, pneumatic valve return system

Power: More than 265ps

Ancillaries: Magneti Marelli control electronics and inertial platform, Dorna control software, NGK sparking plugs, full electronic ride-by-wire

Lubrication: Castrol

Transmission: Gear primary drive, multi-plate dry slipper clutch, six-speed constant-mesh cassette-style gearbox, RK chain

Suspension: Front, Ohlins TRSP25 48mm forks; Rear, Ohlins TRSP44 shock with linkage

Wheels: 16.5in Marchesini

Tyres: Bridgestone

Brakes: Brembo 320 or 340 mm carbon carbon; Rear, HRC 218mm steel

Photos: Gold & Goose

E-MOTION IODARACING TEAM

TEAM STAFF

Giampiero SACHI: Team Owner

Monica RIVERO: Logistics

Luca BOLOGNA: Press

ALEX DE ANGELIS PIT CREW

Gianni CALTANELA: Chief Mechanic

Mechanics: Angelo ANGELI, Michele TAVALOZZI,

Tiziano VERNIANI, Vanni CORBARA

Sander DOCKERS: Aprilia Data Engineer

Filippo AGOSTINI: Aprilia Suspension Engineer

ALEX DE ANGELIS
Born: 26 February, 1984 – Rimini, Italy

GP Starts: 262 (61 MotoGP, 136 Moto2/250cc, 65 125cc)

GP Wins: 4 (3 Moto2, 1 250cc)

DAMIAN CUDLIN
Born: 19 October, 1982 – Sydney, Australia

GP Starts: 11 (8 MotoGP, 3 Moto2)

Broc Parkes

BROC PARKES
Born: 24 December, 1981 – Newcastle, Australia

GP Starts: 19 (18 MotoGP, 1 250cc)

A SHOESTRING budget, lingering doubts about its participation in 2016, and an ageing and uncompetitive Aprilia ART machine all paled into insignificance when the small E-motion IodaRacing Project experienced the dark side of racing during the Japanese Grand Prix.

The Italian-based squad was in its fourth season in MotoGP, and San Marino rider Alex de Angelis had gamely soldiered on against all the odds on a three-year-old ART machine that Aleix Espargaro had used to win the now obsolete CRT class in 2012.

Lining up on arguably the most competitive grid in MotoGP history, de Angelis had the thankless task of trying to pull off giant-killing acts to help keep the team afloat.

He scored points in two races with 15th-place finishes in Catalunya and a rain-soaked British Grand Prix at Silverstone, but he had relied heavily on several crashes and adverse weather conditions to trouble the top 15.

His tough battle on track was completely overshadowed by an even greater fight he faced off track, after crashing heavily in FP4 during the Twin Ring Motegi round in Japan in early October. Multiple injuries included a bleed on the brain that left de Angelis in a life-threatening condition for four days after the accident. Mercifully, he was stabilised in intensive care at the Dokkyo Hospital in Mibu and allowed to fly home to continue his rehabilitation in Europe some 15 days after the crash.

The seriousness of the injuries suffered by de Angelis cast a cloud over a team that had already faced a bleak 2015.

It had started the season backed by Octo again, but one of the world's biggest suppliers of insurance telematics technology jumped ship and switched allegiance to the Pramac Ducati squad from the Mugello round onwards.

Octo was immediately replaced by e-motion, a prominent company in logistics and solutions for e-commerce, and they backed the squad for the remainder of the season.

New investment did little to banish almost constant rumours that the team was struggling to survive. On the provisional entry list released at Valencia, there was no official confirmation that Ioda would be back in 2016.

That was definitely its intention, however, with de Angelis signed on a two-year deal and team owner Giampiero Sacchi locked in negotiations to find additional funding.

When MOTOCOURSE went to press, talks were continuing with a major Venezuelan backer, and if they came to fruition, Dorna would give Ioda an entry for 2016. If that funding didn't materialise, Dorna would instead offer IodaRacing the option of expanding to a two-rider effort in Moto2, having raced a Suter chassis with former Red Bull Rookies Cup champion Florian Alt in 2015.

Sachi was again the very public figurehead of Io-

daRacing and was still revered by many for his king-maker exploits of yesteryear. He had been a key father figure in the early development of the likes of Valentino Rossi, Jorge Lorenzo, Max Biaggi and the late Marco Simoncelli.

Chief mechanic was Gianni Caltanela, who took over from the vastly experienced Giovanni Sandi; while mechanics Tiziano Verniani and Angelo Angeli remained after working with Danilo Petrucci in 2014.

Despite the old ART machinery at its disposal, Aprilia still maintained an active interest in IodaRacing, with factory electronics engineer Sander Donkers and suspension technician Filippo Agostini both assigned to the team.

With de Angelis ruled out for the rest of the season by his horrific fall, IodaRacing called on Australian Damian Cudlin to deputise at Phillip Island and Sepang. The Sydney rider had previous MotoGP experience after replacement rides for Pramac Ducati in 2011 and PBM in 2013. Another Australian rider, Broc Parkes, took the place of de Angelis in the season's finale at Valencia, but failed to finish the race.

Alex de Angelis

APRILIA ART

Engine: 1000cc 65-degree V4, DOHC, 4 valves per cylinder, gear-driven cams, variable-length inlet system

Power: Around 220bhp, revs up to 15,500rpm

Ancillaries: Magneti Marelli control electronics and inertial platform, Dorna control software, full electronic ride-by-wire

Lubrication: Fuchs Silkolene

Transmission: Constant-mesh cassette gearbox

Suspension: Front, Ohlins forks; Rear, Ohlins shock with linkage

Wheels: 16.5in Marchesini

Tyres: Bridgestone

Brakes: Brembo, 320mm carbon carbon front; 200mm steel rear

AB MOTORACING

TEAM STAFF

Karel ABRAHAM Snr: Team Manager

Jiri SMETANA: Communications

Olivier BOUTRON: Logistics

KAREL ABRAHAM PIT CREW

Marc GRANA: Chief Mechanic

Mechanics: Yannis MAIGRET, Martin HAVILECK,
Martin NESVADBA, Pietro BERTI (Tyres & Transport)

Armando Garcia CANTO: Telemetry

HONDA RC213V-RS

Engine: 1000cc 90-degree V4, 360-degree crank,
pneumatic valve return system

Power: More than 265ps

Ancillaries: Magneti Marelli control electronics and
inertial platform, Dorna control software, NGK sparking
plugs, full electronic ride-by-wire

Lubrication: Castrol

Transmission: Gear primary drive, multi-plate dry slipper clutch, six-speed constant-mesh cassette-style
gearbox, RK chain

Suspension: Front, Showa twin-tube 48mm forks;
Rear, Showa twin-tube gas shock with linkage

Wheels: 16.5in Marchesini

Tyres: Bridgestone

Brakes: Front, Nissin 320 or 340mm carbon carbon;
Rear, HRC 218mm steel

KAREL ABRAHAM

Born: 2 January, 1990 – Brno, Czech Republic

GP Starts: 159 (67 MotoGP, 61 Moto2/250cc, 31 125cc)

GP Wins: 1 Moto2

HIROSHI AOYAMA

Born: 25 October, 1981 – Chiba, Japan

GP Starts: 172 (68 MotoGP, 104 250cc)

GP Wins: 9 250cc

World Championships: 1 250cc

TONI ELIAS

Born: 26 March, 1983 – Manresa, Catalonia, Spain

GP Starts: 228 (105 MotoGP, 88 Moto2/250cc, 35 125cc)

GP Wins: 17 (1 MotoGP, 14 Moto2/250cc, 2 125cc)

World Championships: 1 Moto2

KOUSUKE AKIYOSHI

Born: 12 January, 1975 – Kurume, Japan

GP Starts: 9 MotoGP

ANTHONY WEST

Born: 17 July, 1981 – Maryborough, Australia

GP Starts: 237 (46 MotoGP, 190 Moto2/250cc, 1 125cc)

Karel Abraham

UNFORTUNATELY, AB Motoracing's fifth season in the MotoGP World Championship was a familiar tale of hard luck, with poor results and cruel injury that ultimately would lead to the Czech Republic-based squad shutting down its premier-class operation.

Backed again by leading Czech medical supplies company Cardion AB, the team's garage almost needed a revolving door, as no fewer than five riders appeared for them during a turbulent 2015.

As had been the case when the team first entered the world championship in the 125cc category in 2006, Karel Abraham was a full-time contracted rider. That was no surprise, considering that his father, Karel Abraham Senior, remained owner and chief investor in the squad.

And as owner of the Brno circuit, Abraham Senior wasn't exclusively committed to running the team, and he was actually caught in the eye of a political storm in the summer that at one stage threatened the running of the Czech Grand Prix.

On the track, 2015 was an unforgettable disaster for AB Motoracing.

The upgraded Honda RC213V-RS Open-class machine did not offer the huge leap in performance over its predecessor, the RCV1000R, that everybody had anticipated. And Abraham was out on a limb in the same manner as Scott Redding had been in 2014: as the only Open-class Honda rider to be using a technical package that included Showa suspension and Nissin brakes.

Abraham had not scored a single point when he suffered a season defining injury during FP4 at the Catalunya track near Barcelona. A vicious high-side left him with seemingly minimal damage to his left foot, and he had even intended to race the following day with a dislocated big toe. But the internal damage to ligaments and tendons was so severe that he was forced to miss the next three races in Assen, Sachsenring and Indianapolis.

Bravely, he returned in intense pain for the next four races, starting with his home round at Brno, but he retired early in Aragon in agony and was never seen on track again.

Highly rated Dutch World Superbike rider Michael van der Mark had come close to a replacement deal for Assen, only for it to collapse at the last minute. HRC test rider Hiroshi Aoyama stood in for Abraham in Germany, and 2010 Moto2 World Champion Toni Elias was rescued from the wilderness to make his 100th MotoGP start in Indianapolis.

With Abraham absent from the last four rounds, HRC development rider Kousuke Akiyoshi replaced him at the Twin Ring Motegi in Japan, before Australian Anthony West clinched a deal to ride the bike in the last three races. West had become a free agent following his release by the QMMF Moto2 squad.

Throughout all the injury turmoil, Abraham's loyal crew remain unchanged. Former Ferrari school graduate Marc Grana was crew chief for a ninth successive season, while former Aspar Moto2 employee Amando Garcia Canto came in as telemetry specialist. Yannis Maigret, Martin Havlicek, Martin Nesvadba and Pietro Berti all continued as mechanics.

The team's tenth world championship campaign would be its last for now, while Abraham confirmed that he had been in tentative talks with KTM about a collaboration with the Austrian factory when it enters MotoGP in 2017.

Abraham's immediate future, though, appeared to lie in World Superbikes. Towards the end of October, he announced that talks had taken place with Shaun Muir Racing, looking to move up from BSB after the Milwaukee Yamaha squad had taken the title with Josh Brookes.

Milwaukee Yamaha had missed out on the factory Yamaha contract in World Superbikes to Crescent Racing and was looking at a possible switch to Aprilia or Suzuki machinery, while also being linked with a privateer Yamaha entry in 2016.

FIM MOTO2 WORLD CHAMPIONSHIP

2015 TEAMS AND RIDERS

By PETER McLAREN

JOHANN ZARCO went from flighty Frenchman to back-flipping Napoleon, securing his first world title with an all-conquering Moto2 campaign. Along the way he had to defeat Tito Rabat, who broke ranks with the previous Moto2 champions by trying to defend his championship crown rather than move straight to MotoGP.

Meanwhile, murmurs of a 'Kalex Cup' grew louder, with 22 of 30 riders using the German chassis.

Written in the aftermath of the financial crisis, and as an antidote to the factory favouritism of 250GP, the strict Moto2 formula – which included control 600cc (Honda) engines, electronics and (Dunlop) tyres – may itself have played a role.

Such tight regulations have kept costs down and competition close. The unintended consequence, however, is that many teams – often in the face of pressure from riders and sponsors – view the largest remaining technical variable, the chassis, as a source of doubt to be eradicated.

At first, this weeded out uncompetitive frame designs. But by 2015, it had reached the stage where those who had a Kalex kept hold of it, and most of the rest tried to get one. Thus Kalex filled almost 75 per cent of the grid, with nearest rival Suter paying the biggest price.

Suter had begun the 2014 season with ten machines and won three races, including the final round. Yet the Swiss manufacturer, world champions with Marc Marquez in 2012, could only muster two minor entries for 2015.

Three other chassis brands didn't even make the return journey to Qatar. The Forward KLX project dropped away during 2014, with Caterham Suter and TSR disappearing at the end of the season. That left 2015's six other entries to be split equally between Tech 3 and Speed Up.

Reigning champion Rabat may have made headlines by remaining in Moto2, but he was far from alone. Of the top 19 in the previous season's standings, only Maverick Vinales (third) and Jordi Torres (16 th) sought a change of championship.

Vinales moved to MotoGP with Suzuki, while Torres – like former Aspar team-mate and fellow Moto2 race winner Nico Terol – attempted to rebuild his career in World Superbike.

Alex Marquez continued the perfect trend of reigning Moto3 champions joining Moto2, graduating alongside team-mate Alex Rins. Also on the rookie list was Florian Alt, returning to the paddock, plus grand prix newcomers Jesko Raffin and Zaqhwan Zaidi.

Of the 30 full-time riders, four fewer than 2014, Spain again topped the list of nationalities. But a reduced seven competitors were just two more than Switzerland, which continues to punch well above its motorsport-free weight. Germany (four), Italy (three), Malaysia (three) and France (two) also boasted multiple riders, while the hopes of Great Britain, Japan, Finland, Belgium, Australia and Thailand each rested on a single competitor.

Six riders were teenagers at the time of the opening round, with three riders over the age of 30.

For 2016 private testing will be limited to a maximum of ten days, in response to complaints that some of the better funded competitors can test almost constantly.

KALEX

Having won back-to-back riders' titles and swept the top three championship positions, Kalex was hounded for chassis in 2015. To satisfy the year-on-year rise from 14 to 22 riders, continuing teams began with the 2015 chassis, while new arrivals got the 2014 model.

Consistency had been the last word associated with **Johann Zarco** (24, France) – in terms of results or team partnerships – prior to 2015.

He came into the season having made his fourth team change in as many Moto2 seasons, following Caterham's exit. But the result was a return to Aki Ajo, with whom Zarco had finished runner-up in the 2011 125cc championship, the Finn having put together a new Moto2 project alongside his factory KTM commitments in Moto3.

Quick from the start of testing, Zarco was only denied victory in round one by a technical problem, with a record-breaking podium run beginning in Texas. His only previous grand prix win had been in 2011, but he got plenty of chances to show off his back-flipping celebrations en route to becoming France's first intermediate-class champion since Olivier Jacque in 2000.

Zarco will become the second successive Moto2 champion to remain in the class, having been unimpressed by the MotoGP offers available for 2016.

Sito Pons retained **Luis Salom** (23, Spain) for his Paginas Amarillas HP 40 squad (world champions with Pol Espargaro in 2013) while adding another former Moto3 title contender, **Alex Rins** (19, Spain), to replace top 2014 rookie Maverick Vinales.

Rins would follow in the footsteps of Vinales as a race-winning Moto2 newcomer, eclipsing both Salom and rookie rival Alex Marquez in the process. But his season wouldn't be without complications. The eight-times Moto3 winner twice required arm-pump surgery, while a calamitous Misano race ended in a black flag. A fall at Sepang also cost Rins easy points in the battle for second overall with the absent Rabat.

Sito's youngest son, Edgar, made wild-card appearances at Jerez, Catalunya and Brno, then finished the season with Italtrans. He will race alongside Rins in his father's team in 2016.

Valentino Rossi's half-brother, Luca Marini, rode a Kalex run by the Pons Junior Team at Misano.

Tito Rabat (25, Spain) returned in 2015 as the first Moto2 champion to attempt a title defence. He also had a new name, 'Esteve' being switched for his nickname 'Tito' in the official classifications.

The winner of a convincing seven races on the way to his and the Marc VDS team's first world title, Rabat began the year as clear favourite, but a slow start to his tenth GP season soon put him on the back foot relative to Zarco.

His pursuit would suffer a major blow when he broke his collarbone during a training accident at Almeria, one week before the Sachsenring. He bravely chose to race in Germany, only to be taken out by Morbidelli at the final turn. Marc VDS certainly didn't bear a grudge, signing the Italian for 2016.

He sustained a second training injury in October, by which time he had been confirmed as moving up to the Belgian team's MotoGP project for 2016.

Rabat was partnered by **Alex Marquez** (18, Spain), younger brother of MotoGP champion Marc and winner of Honda's first Moto3 title after a Valencia showdown with Jack Miller. Riding in place of Mika Kallio, Marquez found the class change to be an unexpected struggle, and he took until the Brno round to feature near the front.

Technomag merged with Interwetten for 2015 to form an all-Swiss dream team of **Thomas Luthi** (28), **Dominique Aegerter** (24) and **Robin Mulhauser** (23). But nationality wasn't everything, both sides of the new squad dropping the 'local' Suter chassis for a new partnership with Kalex, a move that was tipped to see Luthi and Aegerter challenge for the title.

The reality proved somewhat less glamorous, but Luthi, 125cc world champion in 2005, would stand on the top step in 2015 and thus be a winner in four of the six Moto2 seasons. He also claimed his first pole since 2012.

Aegerter, like Luthi, has raced in Moto2 since

Photos: Gold & Goose

ALEX RINS

XAVIER SIMEON

ESTEVE RABAT

DOMINIQUE AEGERTER

ROBIN MULHAUSER

EDGAR PONS

FRANCO MORBIDELLI

MIKA KALLIO

JONAS FOLGER

2010. However, Aegerter was the only rider to have started every race as the grid formed for Moto2's 100th grand prix at Aragon, but it would be memorable for the wrong reasons.

Taken out by Rins at the previous round, Aegerter was swiped by Xavier Simeon at Aragon, halting the race while he received medical attention for fractures to his vertebrae, wrist, hand and ribs. Josh Hook stepped in while the injuries healed.

Away from Moto2, Aegerter began the year testing a Kawasaki-based MotoGP prototype for French tuning company Akira, and later claimed his second Suzuka 8 Hours rostrum (in as many starts) as part of the TSR Honda team.

AGR fielded an unchanged rider and machine line-up for 2015, with **Jonas Folger** (21, Germany) continuing alongside **Axel Pons** (23, Spain).

Folger, who claimed a pair of podiums during his rookie Moto2 season, began the new championship in perfect fashion in Qatar. By round four, the former

125cc and Moto3 race winner had added another victory, but wouldn't be seen on the rostrum again until the flyaways.

Pons, son of Sito, claimed a more modest career highlight at Indianapolis and was generally far more stable than in previous seasons. However, he did miss Texas and Argentina due to a wrist injury, being replaced at the latter by Steven Odendaal, and was forced to start from the back of the grid at Motegi.

Fausto Gresini's team cut back to a single entry in 2015, retaining **Xavier Simeon** (25, Belgium) while switching from Suter to Kalex.

Simeon, who had joined Moto2 during the inaugural season, finally became a grand prix winner – the first victory for a Belgian since Didier de Radigues in 1983 – although it wouldn't be enough to keep the Gresini seat. Instead, Gresini will run Sam Lowes in 2016, the Englishman having signed a multi-year deal that starts with a season in Moto2 before moving up to the Aprilia Gresini MotoGP squad.

In addition to Simeon, multiple 125 and 250cc race winner Mattia Pasini raced as a wild-card for Gresini at the home Mugello and Misano rounds.

Over at Italtrans, 2014 title runner-up **Mika Kallio** (32, Finland) was signed to take over Julian Simon's seat, with impressive rookie **Franco Morbidelli** (20, Italy) retained for a second season.

Morbidelli's reputation grew further as he consistently outpaced the proven Kallio, culminating in a debut grand prix rostrum at Indianapolis – the event after his final-turn faux pas with Rabat.

A broken right leg in a motocross accident halted Morbidelli's momentum, but he had done enough to secure the coveted Marc VDS seat for 2016. Countryman Federico Caricasulo was hired during Morbidelli's absence.

Despite continuing with Kalex, the vastly experienced Kallio proved a shadow of the rider who had taken ten podiums (including three wins) for Marc VDS in 2014. Kallio jumped ship to QMMF (Speed

SANDRO CORTESE

AZLAN SHAH

LORENZO BALDAASSARRI

THITIPONG WAROKORN

LOUIS ROSSI

RANDY KRUMMENACHER

JESKO RAFFIN

MARCEL SCHROTTER

AXEL PONS

ZAKHWAN ZAIDI

XAVI VIERGE

Photos: Gold & Goose

Up) after Misano and will become a KTM MotoGP test rider in 2016. Edgar Pons took the Finn's Italtrans place for the remainder of the year.

Dynavolt Intact GP kept the combination of former Moto3 champion **Sandro Cortese** (25, Germany) and Kalex for a third year, but their results took a backward step until a late-season podium.

Tady Okada's Honda Team Asia was also unchanged, **Takaaki Nakagami** (23, Japan) and **Azlan Shah** (30, Malaysia) producing some notable highlights: look out for Nakagami ending a two-year podium drought and Shah getting within two laps of a shock rostrum place at Motegi.

Having swapped a short-lived Forward KLX for the official Kalex package during 2014, Forward Racing retained the equipment for 2015.

Lorenzo Baldassarri (18, Italy) moved from Gresini to replace countryman Mattia Pasini while **Simone Corsi** (27, Italy) made his comeback after missing the second half of the previous season due to injury.

Forward was rocked by Giovanni Cuzari's mid-summer arrest, the financial fallout from which caused both his teams to skip the Indianapolis round.

Despite the uncertainty, Baldassarri made respectable progress during his second Moto2 season and would spray rostrum champagne for the first time.

Corsi – on the podium in all but one of the previous Moto2 seasons – would be one place short.

Baldassarri will stay with Forward for 2016, when he will be joined by Luca Marini.

The Petronas Raceline Malaysia project continued for a second season, the stability helping 2012 home podium wild-card **Hafizh Syahrin** (20, Malaysia) to move up the championship rankings with regular points finishes.

Having persevered with a TSR chassis for much of Moto2's history, JiR shelved the project for the perceived certainty of a Kalex in 2015. Wholesale changes also resulted in rookie Tetsuta Nagashima being replaced by **Randy Krummenacher** (25, Switzerland), who moved from an Ioda-run Suter for his ninth grand prix season.

SAG's pair of Kalex seats went to the retained **Thitipong Warokorn** (26, Thailand), while alongside him rookie **Jesko Raffin** (17, Switzerland) took over from Louis Rossi.

SPEED UP

Italian manufacturer Speed Up continued with its single-rider official team for **Sam Lowes** (24, Great Britain) while also supporting the two-strong QMMF squad.

The biggest technical change was to replace the carbon-fibre swing-arm with a conventional aluminium version, which Lowes quickly credited with helping to improve his feeling and confidence on the bike.

The former World Supersport champion began his second grand prix season on pole in Qatar, then took a debut victory in Texas. Much to his credit – and despite some dodgy tyre choices and technical mishaps – the Englishman continued to provide the only serious opposition to Kalex.

It would become an increasingly difficult contest, but Lowes received his reward in the form of a factory Aprilia MotoGP contract for 2017 and 2018, preceded by a move to Gresini and Kalex for one final year in Moto2.

QMMF began the season with the most experienced rider pairing on the grid. **Julian Simon** (27, Spain) arrived from Italtrans to replace countryman Roman Ramos, while **Anthony West** (33, Australia) remained at the Qatari outfit for a fourth season. It would be his last.

West had been present for all but one Moto2 race since the category was formed, only missing Valencia in 2012 after testing positive for a prohibited stimulant, unwittingly consumed via an energy drink.

QMMF had stood by West during the doping con-

HAFIZH SYAHRIN

RATHAPARK WILAIROT

ANTHONY WEST

SIMONE CORSI

FLORIAN ALT

YUKI TAKAHASHI

RICARD CARDUS

SAM LOWES

TAKAAKI NAKAGAMI

JULIAN SIMON

troversy and they had celebrated a victory together in 2014, but West was unceremoniously dropped after Misano and replaced by Mika Kallio. Simon achieved slightly better results than West (who took on replacement rides in British Supersport and MotoGP), although neither could get close to Lowes.

Simon and Xavier Simeon will form the QMMF line-up in 2016.

SUTER

A winner of 32 Moto2 races, including the final round of 2014, the depleted Suter entry took until round 12 to even score a world championship point.

The winter migration left Suter represented by two class rookies, **Florian Alt** (18, Germany) and **Zaqhwan Zaidi** (19, Malaysia).

Alt took over from Krummenacher at Iodaracing, while Zaidi rode for the new JPMoto Malaysia entry. Or at least he did until Catalunya, when he was replaced by Ratthapark Wilairot. The Thai rider had raced in the intermediate grand prix class from 2007 to 2012, with a best finish of fourth. His GP return followed a surprising split from the Core" World Supersport team, just a few rounds after a memorable home victory.

But when Wilairot – like Zaidi and indeed Alt – failed to score a point, the newly available Cardus was handed the ride at Brno, the Spaniard using his wet-weather skills to break Suter's top-15 drought.

Suter is planning to regain some of its lost ground with a redesigned MMX2 machine in 2016.

TECH 3

Tech 3's race victory during the 2010 Moto2 season looked further away than ever as the retained line-up of **Marcel Schrotter** (22, Germany) and **Ricard Cardus** (27, Spain) took a step back from their encouraging 2014 campaign.

Schrotter couldn't get close to his tenth place and 80 points of the previous season, while Cardus was without a single point by the time he was dropped during the summer break and replaced by Spanish teenager Xavi Vierge.

Vierge, a race winner on the Mistral 610 in the CEV Moto2 category, will get a full season in 2016 alongside new signing Isaac Vinales.

Herve Poncharal, whose team briefly switched from Ohlins to KYB suspension, insisted that riders were wrong to assume that they could only be successful with Kalex:

"I will never say one bad word about Kalex, because if they have this super ultra-dominant position it is because they are best, and riders want them because they believe they will have better results, which if you look at this season is not necessarily true.

"This is the sixth year of Moto2. Do you think in those six years we, the Moto2 manufacturers, have not had a chassis from all of our rivals in our workshops to measure the dimensions, the rigidity of the chassis and the swing-arm? Everybody is very, very close…"

Tasca Racing switched from Suter to run a third Tech 3 machine for **Louis Rossi** (25, France). Rossi, a Moto3 winner in 2012 and official Tech 3 rider in 2013, returned to the French chassis after a season on a SAG-run Kalex.

MORIWAKI/NTS

They may not have raced the full season, but wet conditions at Motegi would help both Moriwaki (which won the 2010 riders' title with Toni Elias) and NTS (trialled by JiR at the end of 2014) score world championship points as wild-card entries in the hands of former grand prix regulars Yuki Takahashi and Tomoyoshi Koyama respectively.

2015 TEAMS AND RIDERS

By PETER McLAREN

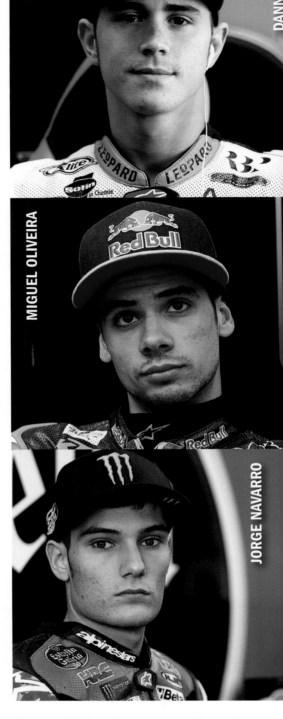

DANNY KENT

MIGUEL OLIVEIRA

JORGE NAVARRO

"**B**ARRY SHEENE, 1977!" – the answer to many a pub quiz will need to be rewritten after Danny Kent ended the UK's near four-decade wait for a new motorcycle grand prix champion. But it went down to the wire, Kent having seen three chances to wrap up the title slip away before the Valencia finale.

The Englishman's efforts also helped Honda topple KTM in the constructors' championship, ruled by the Austrian brand since the debut of 250cc four-strokes in 2012.

But when factories do battle, money is the main ammunition, and many competitors continued to claim that Moto3 was more expensive than Moto2. Both classes have control tyres and electronics, but Moto3 allows engine as well as chassis competition. That's vital in attracting manufacturers such as Honda and KTM, but cost and fairness in machinery remain a concern.

A random engine distribution rule, preventing factories from favouring individual riders, came into force in 2014, and further attempts were made to keep a lid on team bills in 2015. The engine package price was lowered to 60,000 euros per rider, with a new limit of 85,000 euros put in place for the rolling chassis.

Engine specification changes were not allowed during the season, with only one update (available to all customers at the same time) possible for homologated 'performance parts' – including the chassis, swing-arm and suspension.

Maximum engine revs were cut from 14,000 to 13,500, while minimum weight (motorcycle and rider) increased to 149kg. It will rise to 152kg in 2016.

The rev drop may seem like a minor adjustment, but less fortunate riders, using 2014's bikes, found that trimming the top end was a noticeable handicap against those with engines redesigned around the new limit.

Race Director Mike Webb's biggest headache in respect of Moto3 was human rather than technical: riders seeking a tow during qualifying. Their aim was to tuck in behind a quicker competitor to improve their lap time. But the tactic reached farcical – and clearly dangerous – proportions at Catalunya, where most of the grid was caught riding slowly and therefore obstructing anyone who dared push for a fast time.

Thirty riders faced potential penalties, prompting Webb to call a meeting with the entire class at the following Assen round. He announced that future punishments would be more immediate, rather than an accumulation of penalty points, with anyone consistently lapping below 107 per cent of their normal lap time liable to investigation.

The clamp down was greeted with applause by the riders, but some would have short memories: 11 were docked three grid positions and banned from the first half of morning warm-up next time out, in Germany. Many similar penalties would follow.

For the first time in Moto3's short history, the previous season's top three – Alex Marquez (Moto2), Jack Miller (MotoGP) and Alex Rins (Moto2) – all moved on. Efren Vazquez had been best of the rest and one of just four GP winners alongside team-mate Kent, Romano Fenati and Alexis Masbou to return in 2015.

At the opposite end of the experience scale, nine riders were enrolled in the 'rookie of the year' contest, including Fabio Quartararo. The young Frenchman was the first beneficiary of a controversial rule that allows winners of the FIM CEV (Spanish) Moto3 Championship to compete in grand prix racing, even though they have not reached the minimum age of 16.

At 15 years and 11 months, Quartararo was the youngest of 23 teenagers signed up for the opening round. Vazquez was the oldest rider at 28, the maximum age for Moto3. The line-up also included female competitors Ana Carrasco and Maria Herrera, brothers Brad and Darryn Binder, plus Remy Gardner – son of 1987 500cc World Champion Wayne Gardner.

The 34-strong entry list, one more than in 2014, was again led by Italy (nine) and Spain (seven). France (three), Great Britain (two), South Africa (two) and Japan (two) followed, with one competitor each from Germany, Australia, Malaysia, Portugal, Finland, the Czech Republic, Argentina and Belgium.

The loss of Kalex KTM meant that official constructors dropped to four. Mahindra and Husqvarna continued alongside Honda and KTM, although the Husqvarna remains a re-badged KTM.

As in Moto2, Moto3 will also introduce a new private testing limit of ten days during 2016.

HONDA

Having won the riders' title during the first season of its factory Moto3 assault, Honda entries doubled to 12 for 2015, making the NSF250RW the most popular bike on the grid.

Stability may be favoured in grand prix racing, but **Danny Kent** (21, Great Britain) had competed for six different brands, spanning two classes, during six seasons – Lambretta, Aprilia, KTM, Tech 3, Husqvarna and now Honda.

Kent had claimed Moto3 podiums either side of an ill-fated Moto2 attempt at Tech 3, but there was little warning of the spectacular success in store at Kiefer, which featured new riders (Kent, Efren Vazquez and Hiroki Ono), bikes (Honda in place of Kalex KTM) and title sponsor (Leopard) in 2015.

However, Kent's season would be very much a tale of two halves.

Head and shoulders clear of the field during the opening eight races – Kent's Austin victory, his first win since 2012, was of record proportions – the Englishman showed a level of tactical prowess rarely seen in the junior class.

"I've never seen, in Moto3 or 125, someone dominate so much," commented Repsol Honda MotoGP team principal Livio Suppo.

Yet later Kent would lose 86 points to Miguel Oliveira in the space of five rounds, producing the tense finale at Valencia.

Kiefer, which won the 2011 Moto2 championship with Stefan Bradl, will return to the intermediate class in 2016 with Kent and Oliveira as team-mates.

Finally a race winner in 2014, **Efren Vazquez** (28, Spain) continued with Honda during the switch from RTG to Leopard. Podiums followed, but he wasn't able to replicate Kent's performances, while a front-row start would be the highlight for **Hiroki Ono** (22, Japan) during his rookie season. When Ono was injured at his home round, Joan Mir stepped in for Australia.

Gresini's MotoGP team may have broken its long Honda links, but the Moto3 project returned to HRC after a season with KTM. Not surprisingly, rookie star **Enea Bastianini** (17, Italy) was retained with countryman **Andrea Locatelli** (18, Italy) in place of Niccolo Antonelli.

Bastianini would be Kent's closest rival for much of the season, and he confirmed his status as Italy's next star with a debut grand prix win in front of his home fans at Misano, which he celebrated by having his hair sprayed in the colours of the national flag.

Locatelli was watching his team-mate from the pits, having been ruled out by an injured coccyx that would also prevent him from riding at Aragon and Sepang. But after a pointless season on a Team Italia Mahindra in 2014, Locatelli was otherwise a regular scorer in 2015. Ongetta remained with Honda, but hired two new riders in the form of **Niccolo Antonelli** (19, Italy) and **Jules Danilo** (19, France).

Antonelli shrugged off the crasher label that had dogged him throughout his Gresini years to deliver a breakthrough season, including a first victory and podium (from pole position) at Brno, the same circuit where VR46 mentor Valentino Rossi had taken his first win in 1996. More success was to follow.

Arriving from Ambrogio (Mahindra), Danilo also enjoyed his best season to date, albeit at a much more modest level.

Emilio Alzamora's Estrella Galicia 0,0 team hired two impressive rookies to replace Alex Marquez and Alex Rins, first and third in the 2014 championship. **Jorge Navarro** (19, Spain) got the nod after spending the second half of that season on a Marc VDS Kalex KTM, but the main attention was focused on **Fabio Quartararo** (15, France).

Quartararo was already a double Spanish CEV (Spanish) Moto3 champion for Alzamora, but he would have

EFREN VAZQUEZ • KAREL HANIKA • ALEXIS MASBOU

HIROKI ONO • JULES DANILO • JOHN McPHEE • NICCOLÒ ANTONELLI • LIVIO LOI

ANDREA LOCATELLI • SENA YAMADA • BRAD BINDER • ENEA BASTIANINI

been too young to race the full grand prix season – until the rule change declaring that exceptions would be made for any reigning FIM CEV Moto3 champion.

The Frenchman was duly fastest in two of the three pre-season tests, then he led his first grand prix. A debut podium and pole followed in quick succession, but the final step to victory never materialised, and after a spate of falls shock rumours began to emerge of a team change for 2016.

The split – Quartararo will move to Leopard (and KTM) – was confirmed at Aragon, an event the youngster missed due to injuries at Misano.

While Quartararo's season went downhill, Navarro (runner-up to Quartararo in the CEV) would steadily improve, despite also being sidelined by a nasty accident on Friday at the San Marino round. The Spaniard celebrated a first grand prix podium on his comeback ride and will lead the team in 2016, when he will be partnered by CEV star Aron Canet.

John McPhee (20, Great Britain) was joined by teammate **Alexis Masbou** (27, France) at Saxoprint RTG.

The Frenchman previously had waited ten seasons to win a race, but the move from Ongetta paid off instantly with victory in Qatar. McPhee's highlights – a first grand

prix podium and poles – would come later in the season. But much of the year was a hard slog for both RTG riders, prompting McPhee to experiment with the previous season's frame.

Racing Team Germany will run Peugeot-branded Mahindras in 2016.

Dropped mid-season by Marc VDS, **Livio Loi** (17, Belgium) was given a second grand prix chance by RW Racing, replacing Dutch rider Scott Deroue as the team made the transition from Kalex KTM to Honda.

Indianapolis was the first event Loi had missed after his 2014 sacking, and he made a triumphant return – courtesy of an inspired tyre choice – from 26th on the grid! He was the first Belgian to win a Moto3/125cc race in the 67-year history of motorcycle grands prix.

KTM

Having suffered its first ever Moto3 title defeat in the 2014 showdown, KTM returned with 11 riders (one more than in 2014), again led by the factory Red Bull Ajo team.

Jack Miller having moved to MotoGP, **Karel Hanika** (18, Czech Republic) gained two new team-mates in the

form of **Miguel Oliveira** (20, Portugal) and **Brad Binder** (19, South Africa). Oliveira was easily the most experienced of the trio, competing in his fifth grand prix season, but – like Binder and Hanika – yet to win a race.

Former factory Mahindra rider Oliveira corrected that situation in his sixth KTM start, the dental student adding a further victory before breaking his hand in practice for the Sachsenring. It looked like KTM's title chances had departed with Oliveira to hospital, but the Portuguese would mount a stunning late-season comeback to take the championship down to the final round.

KTM made its technical roll of the dice by introducing the one allowed chassis and swing-arm update at Misano. Binder, who had repeated his two podiums for Ambrogio Mahindra, described the developments as "just what I needed" and was in contention for a debut victory at Aragon until disaster struck on the last lap.

Just 18th in his rookie season, Hanika needed to step up in 2015. The pressure perhaps had begun to tell by the opening European round at Jerez, where he received an unprecedented five penalty points from Race Direction – meaning a pit-lane start for the following French round – for a deliberate post-race collision with Aspar's Juanfran Guevara.

Photos: Gold & Goose

Days later, Hanika underwent surgery for a right scaphoid problem and, while he briefly led a GP for the first time in Germany, the Czech wouldn't make the breakthrough needed to match his team-mates.

After a race-winning debut season, Valentino Rossi's VR46 team returned with **Romano Fenati** (19, Italy) once again as its lead rider, but having swapped Francesco Bagnaia for **Andrea Migno** (19, Italy).

Fenati wouldn't match his four wins of 2014, but he still ranked higher in the championship. The Italian also created the slapstick moment of the year when – furious at Niklas Ajo after morning warm-up at Argentina – he switched off the Finn's engine as he waited to do a practice start. Race Direction didn't see the funny side, however, and penalty points meant a back-of-the-grid start.

Migno spent the end of 2014 with the factory Mahindra team, and thus effectively swapped places with Bagnaia, but he would struggle to break into the top ten.

A new Moto3 team, backed by the Sepang International Circuit and Drive M7, rose from the ashes of the former Caterham Moto2 project. Local star **Zulfahmi Khairuddin** (23, Malaysia) was signed from **Ongetta**, with **Jakub Kornfeil** (21, Czech Republic) arriving from Calvo. Kornfeil would give the team podium finishes during its 'rookie' season.

Aleix Espargaro joined Valentino Rossi in backing a Moto3 team as RBA Racing stepped up from the Spanish championship. A wild-card in 2014, **Gabriel Rodrigo** (18, Spain) was retained for the full-time effort, being joined by former RW rider **Ana Carrasco** (18, Spain) and ex-Husqvarna competitor **Niklas Ajo** (20, Finland).

After the altercation with Fenati in Argentina, Ajo – son of KTM and Moto2 team boss Aki – was again in the headlines when he pulled off a dramatic save at Assen; the Finn riding across the finish line still hanging off the side of his bike.

Ajo was the only RBA rider to score points by Brno – when he was given the axe.

Isaac Vinales was hired as Ajo's replacement, having begun the season on a Husqvarna, before joining RBA as a substitute for Carrasco at Indianapolis and Brno. Carrasco was recovering from a complicated left-arm fracture caused by a tangle with fellow female racer Maria Herrera at Sachsenring.

It marked the second troublesome injury for Carrasco during her third grand prix season: she had been forced to sit out Qatar due to a broken collarbone suffered in testing. Belgian Loris Cresson was called up as her replacement on that occasion.

Rodrigo was also feared injured after a race-stopping pile-up at Brno. He was taken away in an ambulance, but returned for Silverstone.

Philipp Oettl (19, Germany) moved from an Interwetten Kalex KTM to Schedl GP KTM for his third season of grand prix racing, which proved by far his most successful, thanks mainly to a ride from 34th to 3rd in the tricky Indianapolis conditions.

MAHINDRA

A major change at Mahindra resulted in the in-house factory team being scrapped in favour of a tie-up with Aspar, allowing the Indian manufacturer to focus on closing the mechanical gap to Honda and KTM.

Mahindra Racing also moved its design and development base from Switzerland to Italy, while Suter, main technical partner since 2013, had its role revised to that of "an important vendor for some outsourced design work and production of some components."

Aspar received its factory Mahindra status after running Kalex KTMs during the previous Moto3 seasons. The 2014 season had been particularly tough for the four-times 125cc title winners, with lone rider **Juanfran Guevara** (19, Spain) finishing as the highest ranked Kalex KTM in a forgettable 17th.

DARREN BINDER

NIKLAS AJO

ZULFAHMI KHAIRUDDIN

LORENZ DALLA PORTA

ANA CARRASCO

PHILIPP OETTL

JORGE MARTIN

ANDREA MIGNO

FRANCESCO BAGNAIA

Guevara remained with Aspar for the transition to Mahindra, but would struggle to contain his two new teammates, partly due to injuries. His third year in grand prix racing would be complicated by the post-race clash with Hanika at Jerez, which left him with a broken collarbone, and missing the German race as a result of hand and coccyx pain.

Francesco Bagnaia (18, Italy) arrived after being overshadowed by Romano Fenati at VR46, but he soon had the satisfaction of outperforming his replacement in that team, Andrea Migno. Highlights included a first grand prix podium for both Bagnaia and the Aspar-Mahindra partnership. The Italian was re-signed at the Silverstone round, by which stage he was comfortably top Mahindra rider, a position he would maintain, despite having suffered a hairline fracture to his collarbone at Phillip Island.

Jorge Martin (17, Spain) was the youngest and least experienced of the teenage trio, making the move to grands prix as the reigning Red Bull Rookies champion. The Spaniard put together a very solid first season, improving as the year progressed.

As well as Aspar, Mahindra continued to supply three customer teams.

World Wide Race, which had competed under the Ambrogio Racing banner in 2014, remained with Mahindra as the retitled Outox Reset Drink Team. It was a case of 'one out, one in' for the Binder family, with Brad moving on to Red Bull KTM and being replaced by younger brother **Darryn** (17, South Africa), who was making his grand prix debut.

On the other side of the garage was **Alessandro Tonucci** (21, Italy), already familiar with the Mahindra after riding for the CIP team in 2014.

CIP also had an all-new rider line-up in rookies **Remy Gardner** (17, Australia) and **Tatsuki Suzuki** (17, Japan). Both cracked the points, but Remy's father, 1987 world champion Wayne Gardner, made his frustration over a lack of engine performance increasingly clear. Remy, who suffered a wrist injury at Le Mans, tested a Moto2 machine in early September and is set to join the class in 2016.

San Carlo Team Italia retained the services of **Matteo Ferrari** (18, Italy) for a second season, with rookie **Stefano Manzi** (16, Italy) taking the place of Gresini-bound Andrea Locatelli.

Since Manzi turned 16 after the Qatar season opener, he was replaced at Losail by Marco Bezzecchi. Manzi would go on to become the top scoring non-Aspar Mahindra rider. Ferrari's championship ended at Misano,

and he was replaced for the remainder of the season by reigning CIV Moto3 champ Manuel Pagliani.

HUSKVARNA

For the second year running, KTM badged two of its bikes under the sister Husqvarna brand, this time moving them out from under the wing of Aki Ajo to be run by the Laglisse team, Moto3 title winners with Maverick Vinales in 2013.

After wild-card appearances for the Estrella Honda team, **Maria Herrera** (18, Spain) was given a full-time grand prix ride alongside Laglisse's 2014 signing, **Isaac Vinales** (21, Spain), cousin of Maverick.

Herrera's year was punctuated by incidents, notably being taken out by Antonelli after breaking into the top eight at Assen, then dislocating her shoulder at the German GP when she was involved in the spectacular tangle with Carrasco. But she did score her first points.

Vinales had taken a front-row start in Qatar, put Husqvarna on the podium in Argentina and collected 48 other points by the time he was dumped during the summer break, to be replaced by Italian CEV racer Lorenzo Dalla Porta. Laglisse claimed Vinales had not "achieved the expected results".

Photos: Gold & Goose

MOTOGP · MOTO2 · MOTO3

GRANDS PRIX 2015

Reports by MICHAEL SCOTT

Statistics compiled by PETER McLAREN

Inset, left: Riders and officials stand for the minute's silence, the first of several for the season.

Inset, right: Alexis Masbou's tactics translated pole position to the narrowest of wins.

Inset, below right: Stuck in third gear, and no amount of staring will fix it for Johann Zarco.

Inset, far right: Italian spoken here: The Doctor and Desmo Dovi celebrate a joint renaissance.

Main: Dovizioso looked set to win; Rossi had another idea.
Photos: Gold & Goose

FIM WORLD CHAMPIONSHIP · ROUND 1

QATAR GRAND PRIX

LOSAIL CIRCUIT

Above: Dovi's Duke could draft past Rossi's Yamaha every time, except when it really mattered.

Top right: Red bike gives you wings.

Above right: First Tissot ticker for Lowes, after his maiden pole.

Right: The Outsider: Marquez goes wide as Dovi leads Lorenzo and Pedrosa through turn one.

Below right and below far right: Sponsor trouble – Lucio Cecchinello wasn't sure whether to call his bikes LCR or CWM; team boss Martinez had his other shirt on, but Nicky Hayden continued to wear the colour-coded leathers

Below centre right: Style-master Lorenzo's race was spoiled by a loose helmet lining.

Photos: Gold & Goose

WAS Rossi bluffing? Over the last few laps there were several demonstrations that the newly re-nicknamed Desmo Dovi had the horses to gallop past down the straight, to lead over the finish line. Thereafter, he and Rossi would stay closely and most entertainingly engaged for the remainder of the lap.

Until the last. Funnily enough, it was Dovizioso's fastest lap of the race. But this time, Valentino had the legs. The old master and unsuccessful ex-Ducati alumni scored a magnificent first-race triumph; the new red bike had made a stunning debut. Double renaissance.

In this way, the scene was set in the desert night for an intriguing season. Masterclass versus the Ducati revival. Never mind that it had all been conducted in the absence of the factory Hondas: Pedrosa stricken with career-threatening arm-pump; Marquez the victim of his own first-corner error, condemned to a stirring ride from last to fifth. Never mind that long-time leader Lorenzo had faded after "human mistake" helmet problems spoiled his vision (the lining had become detached and drooped over his eyes).

This was a showdown to remember, underlined by Iannone's career-best third making an all-Italian rostrum, on a night when not a single Spaniard made the podium in all three classes.

GP people are getting used to the weirdness of Qatar: the night-shift feeling, with slow late-afternoon starts, then working into the small hours – as do the endless stream of construction lorries at the many adjacent building projects. The riders enjoy racing under lights; the track is barren, but not uninteresting, with some fast rhythmic sections. And in 2015, it was faster earlier on: washed by dust-dampening rains that continued into the four-day race weekend, though without disruption.

Rain had ruined the third of three planned days of pre-testing at the track, and with so many new bikes, or new bike-rider combinations, a lack of set-up time was a common complaint. Crutchlow, on the Factory Honda, was just one trying to come to terms with something completely new.

The Ducatis, of course, were a revelation. First out for the second Sepang test, Dall'Igna's new GP15 was fast from the start. The understeer was gone. Dovi and Iannone had a bike

that could fight. But could it do that over full race distance? Oh yes. How much of this was down to the little fairing-flank winglets was debatable, but both riders liked them, and both would have raced with them, had Iannone not wiped out his sole such fairing in free practice.

Honda's factory bikes were much as before, with evolutionary improvement addressing corner entry; Yamaha's official team bikes likewise, although now at last with a both-directions seamless shift, down as well as up. It was not, observed both Rossi and Lorenzo, the equal of Honda's super-smooth original, but it was a help.

Honda's private Open bikes were a different matter: now with pneumatic valve springs (although not the gearbox), they were virtually the same as the 2014 factory bikes. It was a major upgrade, said Nicky Hayden; and while the chassis could cope with the extra acceleration, the electronics lagged seriously. Both he and new team-mate Eugene Laverty had different electronic problems in the race. This difficulty afflicted all Open teams with the new control software.

The RS Hondas were faster, but the positions little changed. Most others had become faster as well; while the Suzukis had come out of an unimpressive year of testing fully renewed and surprisingly competitive. (The same could not be said of the Aprilia, very much a work in progress, with returned former 250 champion Melandri gaining a stranglehold on the bottom rung of the timing ladder.

By the way, Melandri had been one of the trio who had claimed the last all-Italian premier-class rostrum, at Motegi in 2006, his Honda having come in third behind Capirossi and Rossi, who said, "It is great for an all-Italian podium, specially because I was on the last one also."

There were notable sponsorship vicissitudes at the opening round. Jorge 'Aspar' Martinez announced that his MotoGP title sponsors had pulled out unexpectedly in the week before the race. There were hints that the withdrawal of Malaysian energy drink Drive M7 may not have been entirely unexpected, after the failure to secure European distribution; and while seeking help from Dorna, the exemplary team owner (with successful teams in all classes) promised a replacement by the next race.

The situation at LCR was less clear-cut. New sponsors

CWM-FX, a high-flying London-based online foreign exchange company, had launched the team with Crutchlow and Miller with lavish extravagance at a fashionable nightclub; but news now broke of arrests at the parent company, on suspicion of money laundering and fraud. All had been released pending further investigation, and boss Anthony Constantinou was in Qatar for the race. Team boss Lucio Cecchinello (another exemplary MotoGP entrepreneur) was in a lather of apprehension, uncertain of the meaning of it all. "Better just call our bikes LCR, not CWM, this weekend," he told a TV commentator.

There was already keen attention on the pit, where Crutchlow was getting to grips with a factory bike, and new boy Jack Miller was making his top-class debut. In 2014, he had won the Moto3 race here. He made a convincing start, typically aggressive, but rather spoiled it by first running wide early on, then taking out seasoned Open Honda rider Karel Abraham with an over-enthusiastic last-lap lunge.

There'd been a wholesale switch to Kalex in Moto2: with 22 of them, to three each of Speed Up and Tech 3, and only two Suters. Speed Up was the revelation. Having switched from carbon-fibre to an aluminium swing-arm that gave more feel, Sam Lowes claimed a convincing maiden pole – only to crash out early, after missing a gear and running on to the dirty part of the track. There was heartbreak also for Johann Zarco, and a lucky escape. He had a huge lead, with only three laps to go, when his gear linkage failed exiting the last corner. He stared down at it, the bike veering across the track towards the pit wall. He noticed just in time and avoided a potentially catastrophic crash by inches. Thereafter, stuck in third, he soldiered home to eighth.

Moto3 opened with new restrictions (revs down by 500rpm to 13,500), but no loss of speed. If anything, torquier engines were an improvement. Mahindra's latest was all new; but Honda and KTM were evolutionary. And the Hondas firmly took early control.

The season started with the first of what would become a series of one-minute silences, this for the victims of the German Airbus that had crashed in the Alps on the previous Tuesday, killing 150 people.

MOTOGP RACE – 22 laps

For once, Pedrosa outqualified Marquez, but qualifying was a dark-hours daydream for Ducati: three in the top six. Dovi snatched a stunning last-gasp pole ahead of the Hondas; Iannone and Hernandez were ahead of Lorenzo's top Yamaha on row two. Rossi was eighth. Dovi remained cautious: it showed how much they had improved, "but the race is what is important". After it was over, he agreed he'd have been happy then if he'd known he would be second. "But the race is long, and you can change your opinion."

Victory had seemed within his grasp. But it was not to be.

Marquez was the favourite, but he was boxed at the first corner by fast-away Bradley Smith and pushed wide on to the off-line dust. "I lost a little the front," he said. "Maybe I could have saved it, but I thought it was better not to crash." He ran across the Astroturf on to the paved run-off, and rejoined last.

His fight back through was typically impressive: he scythed past Bautista so close that the impact severed a brake line before the Aprilia had completed one lap. He was sixth by

lap eight of 22; then ahead of team-mate Pedrosa just after half-distance. But long before this, the leaders had escaped, some five seconds clear. Fifth, he affirmed later, was his worst ever finish, apart from when he had fallen off and remounted.

Dovi led away, but Lorenzo had bullied his way past Hernandez and Iannone into second by the end of lap one, and next time around he was in front. The leading three embarked on a compelling battle, Iannone a close third as Dovi chased Lorenzo, every so often nosing ahead and clearly faster down the straight.

Rossi, meantime, had finished the first lap in tenth, behind both Monster Yamahas and fast-starting Aleix Espargaro's Suzuki, as well as Petrucci and Pedrosa.

Hernandez had lost touch with the front three after three laps, but Rossi and Pedrosa were still battling to find a way through the satellite riders. By lap five, they had done it.

Now Rossi was already closing a gap that had been almost 2.5 seconds. Every lap a couple of tenths. By lap ten, he was on them, and next time around past Iannone for third.

As the race wore on, Dovi started pushing harder, and Lorenzo finally succumbed with four laps remaining, his loose helmet lining too much of a distraction. Only Rossi followed the Ducati.

He was obviously slower on the long straight, and with the finishing line a long way down it, the result seemed inevitable. Though they swapped several times, Desmo Dovi and his Duke could power past at will.

Rossi led the start of the last lap, however, and he stayed just far enough clear to cross the line 0.174 second ahead. His choice of a hard front tyre might have helped, but, he said, "The motivation is the important thing." His motivation derives from enjoyment. "I put this battle at the top of my career," he said, "because Dovi rides in a very clever way. Now MotoGP is changing. We are often fighting to the end. I prefer it like this."

A couple of seconds adrift, Ducati power did prevail, with Iannone gaining his first MotoGP podium half a second clear of Lorenzo.

With Marquez fifth, Pedrosa had lost another four seconds in sixth, and after the race he revealed that the same arm-pump that had blighted his results in 2014 had come back strongly. In a bleak post-race statement, he hinted that he might withdraw from the upcoming races to seek a more permanent solution, and the next day he flew home for further surgery.

Only two seconds down, Crutchlow emerged to lead a close battle for seventh from team-mates Smith and Espargaro. Hernandez dropped off the back for tenth, and likewise 11th-placed Aleix Espargaro, in an unexpectedly impressive Suzuki debut.

Petrucci's Ducati was a lone 12th; Redding's factory Honda debut left him a disappointed 13th.

Class rookie Vinales emerged victorious over top Open finishers Barbera and Bradl. All three had passed Hayden, battling with electronic problems.

The American was comfortably clear of new team-mate Laverty, whose electronically confused bike "didn't know where it was on the track." Abraham and Miller had both been ahead of Laverty, until they crashed together.

Melandri was saved from last place in his Aprilia return when new boy Baz pitted for a tyre change, finishing three laps down.

MOTO2 RACE – 20 laps

More tales of the unexpected, in a Moto2 race that typically lacked close battles up front, but was larded with heavy drama, the front-runners suffering a variety of cruel fates.

Sam Lowes on the revitalised Speed Up was rampant in practice and claimed his first pole by three-tenths from pre-season test star Zarco and defender Rabat. All Speed Up riders had the same new aluminium swing-arm, but the next pair – Julian Simon and Anthony West – were 21st and 22nd on the grid. The Tech 3s of Rossi, Cardus and Schrotter, meanwhile, slotted in among the Kalex phalanx in a respectable 13th, 14th and 17th respectively.

With bad luck on the prowl, Lowes was the first victim. He led away confidently, but had given way to Zarco by the end of lap two. He never finished the third, crashing after "a stupid mistake that spoiled a wonderful weekend". He'd missed a gear, got on to the marbles and paid the price.

Rabat was also doomed to failure. A poor start led to him finishing lap one in eighth, and he had picked up only one position when he also crashed out at the start of lap four while aiming for the same piece of tarmac as Simone Corsi at turn one. Partisan fans blamed Corsi for the race-ending collision, but Race Direction sided with the majority in judging it a racing incident. Either way, it was a poor start for Tito.

Milady Bad-Luck was also awaiting Zarco. But she would take her time.

The Frenchman sailed serenely, majestically onwards, with a lead of almost five seconds and no threats in sight. Folger was second, Simeon third, all politely spaced out.

Then, with three laps left, Zarco suddenly slowed as he ran on to the main straight, staring down at his failed quick-shift mechanism with such intensity that he veered unknowingly towards the pit wall, where team signallers were awaiting his pursuers.

Zarco was in third gear and unable to change out of it. He could only limp the remaining ten miles while those he had outdistanced rapidly caught up.

Folger and Simeon flashed past.

Behind, Morbidelli and team-mate Kallio had been engaged with Luthi and Cortese. They would soon be joined by class rookie Rins, who had qualified ninth, finished laps one and two placed 20th, and had been forging ahead ever since, making a strong early impression that he would sustain in the races to come. Compared with team-mate Alex Marquez, he was shining bright.

By the penultimate lap, Luthi had got clear to inherit the last podium place. Rins was inches behind. Then came Morbidelli, Kallio and Cortese, with the disconsolate Zarco another seven seconds down in eighth.

Rossi narrowly headed a gang of four for ninth, with Marquez 11th, behind Baldassarri.

West (QMMF Speed Up) crashed out of a points-scoring spot at half-distance, after suffering gearbox problems. Pons and Cardus also crashed, the former taking Salom with him.

MOTO3 RACE – 18 laps

With the top 20 qualifiers within a shade over one second of Masbou's pole time, a typical close Moto3 race was predictable: with the closest ever top nine. It was also something of a Honda whitewash, NSF250RWs from first to fifth plus seventh and eighth.

Masbou led away, but there would be many different leaders over the line alone. Antonelli led lap one. Then Brad Binder, then Danny Kent. Then Masbou again; Vazquez for a spell; Kent once more; and under-age rookie Quartararo. Plus, with four laps left, Bagnaia on the Mahindra.

At half-distance, the leading pack was 18-strong, within just over two seconds, shuffling at every corner and at all points between.

The last lap was desperate. Vazquez led at the start of it. Then Quartararo and Bagnaia, but the pair clashed, sending the Mahindra rider on to the Astroturf.

Luck or timing? Masbou did it perfectly to sneak ahead over the line, by just 0.027 of a second from Bastianini and Kent for a second career win.

A canny McPhee had been waiting it out, to come through for fifth, four-tenths behind Vazquez.

Vinales, first non-Honda, was sixth, from Quartararo and Antonelli, the position decided by a video finish, and by one-thousandth. Bagnaia recovered for ninth, still less than a second behind. Next came Binder, Locatelli, Navarro and Hanika (KTM); and only then a gap of greater than half a second to Oettl and GP first-timer Martin, taking the last point, and just 5.1 seconds off the winner.

Fancied new KTM rider Oliveira crashed out on the first corner, but came back for 16th, just out of the points. Ajo also tumbled; Fenati retired with one lap to go.

LOSAIL INTERNATIONAL CIRCUIT
22 laps
Length: 5.380 km / 3,343 miles
Width: 12m

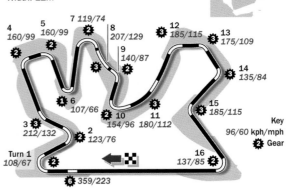

COMMERCIAL BANK
GRAND PRIX OF QATAR

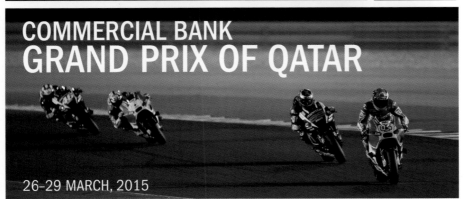

26–29 MARCH, 2015

MotoGP	RACE DISTANCE: 22 laps, 73.545 miles/118.360km · RACE WEATHER: Dry (air 22°C, humidity 83%, track 28°C)

Pos.	Rider	Nat.	No.	Entrant	Machine	Tyres	Race tyre choice	Laps	Time & speed
1	**Valentino Rossi**	ITA	46	Movistar Yamaha MotoGP	Yamaha YZR-M1	B	F: Hard/R: Medium	22	42m 35.717s 103.6mph/ 166.7km/h
2	**Andrea Dovizioso**	ITA	4	Ducati Team	Ducati Desmosedici	B	F: Medium/R: Medium	22	42m 35.891s
3	**Andrea Iannone**	ITA	29	Ducati Team	Ducati Desmosedici	B	F: Medium/R: Medium	22	42m 37.967s
4	**Jorge Lorenzo**	SPA	99	Movistar Yamaha MotoGP	Yamaha YZR-M1	B	F: Medium/R: Medium	22	42m 38.424s
5	**Marc Marquez**	SPA	93	Repsol Honda Team	Honda RC213V	B	F: Medium/R: Medium	22	42m 42.753s
6	**Dani Pedrosa**	SPA	26	Repsol Honda Team	Honda RC213V	B	F: Medium/R: Medium	22	42m 46.472s
7	**Cal Crutchlow**	GBR	35	CWM LCR Honda	Honda RC213V	B	F: Hard/R: Medium	22	42m 48.101s
8	**Bradley Smith**	GBR	38	Monster Yamaha Tech 3	Yamaha YZR-M1	B	F: Hard/R: Medium	22	42m 48.631s
9	**Pol Espargaro**	SPA	44	Monster Yamaha Tech 3	Yamaha YZR-M1	B	F: Hard/R: Medium	22	42m 48.748s
10	**Yonny Hernandez**	COL	68	Pramac Racing	Ducati Desmosedici	B	F: Hard/R: Medium	22	42m 53.152s
11	**Aleix Espargaro**	SPA	41	Team SUZUKI ECSTAR	Suzuki GSX-RR	B	F: Hard/R: Medium	22	42m 55.618s
12	**Danilo Petrucci**	ITA	9	Pramac Racing	Ducati Desmosedici	B	F: Hard/R: Medium	22	43m 00.149s
13	**Scott Redding**	GBR	45	EG 0,0 Marc VDS	Honda RC213V	B	F: Hard/R: Medium	22	43m 07.749s
14	**Maverick Vinales**	SPA	25	Team SUZUKI ECSTAR	Suzuki GSX-RR	B	F: Medium/R: Medium	22	43m 09.180s
15	**Hector Barbera**	SPA	8	Avintia Racing	Ducati Desmosedici Open	B	F: Hard/R: Medium	22	43m 09.342s
16	Stefan Bradl	GER	6	Athina Forward Racing	Yamaha Forward	B	F: Hard/R: Medium	22	43m 09.661s
17	Nicky Hayden	USA	69	Aspar MotoGP Team	Honda RC213V-RS	B	F: Hard/R: Soft	22	43m 14.687s
18	Eugene Laverty	IRL	50	Aspar MotoGP Team	Honda RC213V-RS	B	F: Hard/R: Medium	22	43m 22.287s
19	Mike di Meglio	FRA	63	Avintia Racing	Ducati Desmosedici Open	B	F: Hard/R: Soft	22	43m 34.928s
20	Alex de Angelis	RSM	15	Octo IodaRacing Team	Aprilia ART	B	F: Hard/R: Medium	22	43m 50.698s
21	Marco Melandri	ITA	33	Aprilia Racing Team Gresini	Aprilia RS-GP	B	F: Medium/R: Soft	22	44m 23.860s
22	Loris Baz	FRA	76	Athina Forward Racing	Yamaha Forward	B	F: Hard/R: Medium	19	43m 25.153s
	Karel Abraham	CZE	17	AB Motoracing	Honda RC213V-RS	B	F: Hard/R: Soft	21	DNF-crash
	Jack Miller	AUS	43	CWM LCR Honda	Honda RC213V-RS	B	F: Hard/R: Medium	21	DNF-crash
	Alvaro Bautista	SPA	19	Aprilia Racing Team Gresini	Aprilia RS-GP	B	F: Medium/R: Soft	0	DNF-mechanical

Fastest lap: Valentino Rossi, on lap 5, 1m 55.267s, 104.4mph/168.0km/h.

Lap record: Casey Stoner, AUS (Ducati), 1m 55.153s, 104.5mph/168.1km/h (2008).

Event best maximum speed: Marc Marquez, 217.8mph/350.5km/h (race).

Qualifying
Weather: Dry
Air Temp: 22° **Track Temp:** 27°
Humidity: 64%

1	Dovizioso	1m 54.113s
2	Pedrosa	1m 54.330s
3	Marquez	1m 54.437s
4	Iannone	1m 54.521s
5	Hernandez	1m 54.675s
6	Lorenzo	1m 54.711s
7	Smith	1m 54.732s
8	Rossi	1m 54.851s
9	Petrucci	1m 54.876s
10	P. Espargaro	1m 55.004s
11	A. Espargaro	1m 55.035s
12	Crutchlow	1m 55.123s
13	Vinales	1m 55.246s
14	Redding	1m 55.428s
15	Barbera	1m 55.604s
16	Di Meglio	1m 55.729s
17	Hayden	1m 55.756s
18	Bradl	1m 55.791s
19	Laverty	1m 55.848s
20	Abraham	1m 55.892s
21	Bautista	1m 56.187s
22	Miller	1m 56.287s
23	Baz	1m 56.454s
24	De Angelis	1m 56.793s
25	Melandri	1m 57.934s

Fastest race laps

1	Rossi	1m 55.267s
2	Lorenzo	1m 55.428s
3	Dovizioso	1m 55.495s
4	Iannone	1m 55.514s
5	Marquez	1m 55.661s
6	Pedrosa	1m 55.798s
7	Redding	1m 55.855s
8	Crutchlow	1m 55.926s
9	Hernandez	1m 56.037s
10	P. Espargaro	1m 56.067s
11	Smith	1m 56.091s
12	A. Espargaro	1m 56.375s
13	Petrucci	1m 56.493s
14	Vinales	1m 56.616s
15	Barbera	1m 56.738s
16	Hayden	1m 56.778s
17	Abraham	1m 56.891s
18	Bradl	1m 57.127s
19	Miller	1m 57.175s
20	Di Meglio	1m 57.237s
21	Laverty	1m 57.442s
22	Baz	1m 57.509s
23	De Angelis	1m 57.693s
24	Melandri	1m 59.323s

Grid order		1	2	3	4	5	6	7	8	9	10	11	12	13	14	15	16	17	18	19	20	21	22	
4	DOVIZIOSO	4	99	99	99	99	99	99	99	4	99	99	99	99	99	99	99	4	99	4	4	46	46	1
26	PEDROSA	99	4	4	4	4	4	4	4	99	4	4	4	4	4	4	4	99	4	46	46	4	4	2
93	MARQUEZ	29	29	29	29	29	29	29	29	29	29	46	46	46	46	46	46	46	29	29	29	29	29	3
29	IANNONE	68	68	68	46	46	46	46	46	46	46	29	29	29	29	29	29	29	99	99	99	99	99	4
68	HERNANDEZ	38	38	38	68	26	26	26	26	26	26	26	93	93	93	93	93	93	93	93	93	93	93	5
99	LORENZO	44	44	26	26	68	68	68	93	93	93	93	26	26	26	26	26	26	26	26	26	26	26	6
38	SMITH	41	26	46	38	38	93	93	68	68	68	68	68	68	68	35	35	35	35	35	35	35	35	7
46	ROSSI	9	46	44	44	93	38	38	38	38	38	38	38	38	38	68	38	38	38	38	38	38	38	8
9	PETRUCCI	26	9	35	35	35	35	35	35	35	35	35	35	35	35	38	68	44	44	44	44	44	44	9
44	P. ESPARGARO	46	35	9	93	44	44	44	44	44	44	44	44	44	44	44	44	68	44	68	68	68	68	10
41	A. ESPARGARO	35	41	93	41	41	41	41	41	41	41	41	41	41	41	41	41	41	41	41	41	41	41	11
35	CRUTCHLOW	43	93	41	9	45	45	45	45	45	45	9	9	9	9	9	9	9	9	9	9	9	9	12
25	VINALES	69	69	45	45	9	9	9	9	9	9	45	45	45	45	45	45	45	45	45	45	45	45	13
45	REDDING	45	45	69	69	69	69	69	69	69	69	69	69	69	69	8	8	8	8	8	8	8	25	14
8	BARBERA	6	6	6	6	6	6	6	6	6	6	6	6	8	8	69	6	6	6	6	6	8		15
63	DI MEGLIO	25	43	17	17	17	17	17	17	17	8	8	8	6	6	6	69	25	25	25	25	6		
69	HAYDEN	93	17	8	8	8	8	8	8	8	17	17	17	25	25	25	25	69	69	69	69	69		
6	BRADL	17	8	63	63	63	63	25	25	25	25	25	25	17	17	17	17	17	17	17	50			
50	LAVERTY	63	63	50	50	25	25	63	63	63	50	50	50	50	50	50	50	50	50	43	63			
17	ABRAHAM	76	76	76	25	50	50	50	50	50	63	63	63	43	43	43	43	43	43	50	15			
19	BAUTISTA	8	15	15	76	43	43	43	43	43	43	43	63	63	63	63	63	63	63	33				
43	MILLER	15	50	25	15	76	76	76	15	15	15	15	15	15	15	15	15	15	15					
76	BAZ	33	25	43	43	15	15	15	33	33	33	33	33	33	33	33	33	33	33					
15	DE ANGELIS	50	33	33	33	33	33	33	76	76	76	76	76	76	76	76	76	76	76					
33	MELANDRI																							

76 Pit stop   76 Lapped rider

Championship Points
1	Rossi	25
2	Dovizioso	20
3	Iannone	16
4	Lorenzo	13
5	Marquez	11
6	Pedrosa	10
7	Crutchlow	9
8	Smith	8
9	P. Espargaro	7
10	Hernandez	6
11	A. Espargaro	5
12	Petrucci	4
13	Redding	3
14	Vinales	2
15	Barbera	1

Constructor Points
1	Yamaha	25
2	Ducati	20
3	Honda	11
4	Suzuki	5

Moto2

RACE DISTANCE: 20 laps, 66.860 miles/107.600km · RACE WEATHER: Dry (air 22°C, humidity 83%, track 29°C)

Pos.	Rider	Nat.	No.	Entrant	Machine	Laps	Time & Speed
1	Jonas Folger	GER	94	AGR Team	Kalex	20	40m 18.532s 99.5mph/ 160.1km/h
2	Xavier Simeon	BEL	19	Federal Oil Gresini Moto2	Kalex	20	40m 23.583s
3	Thomas Luthi	SWI	12	Derendinger Racing Interwetten	Kalex	20	40m 30.655s
4	Alex Rins	SPA	40	Paginas Amarillas HP 40	Kalex	20	40m 30.734s
5	Franco Morbidelli	ITA	21	Italtrans Racing Team	Kalex	20	40m 32.917s
6	Mika Kallio	FIN	36	Italtrans Racing Team	Kalex	20	40m 32.945s
7	Sandro Cortese	GER	11	Dynavolt Intact GP	Kalex	20	40m 33.003s
8	Johann Zarco	FRA	5	Ajo Motorsport	Kalex	20	40m 37.073s
9	Louis Rossi	FRA	96	Tasca Racing Scuderia Moto2	Tech 3	20	40m 39.446s
10	Lorenzo Baldassarri	ITA	7	Athina Forward Racing	Kalex	20	40m 39.868s
11	Alex Marquez	SPA	73	EG 0,0 Marc VDS	Kalex	20	40m 40.379s
12	Hafizh Syahrin	MAL	55	Petronas Raceline Malaysia	Kalex	20	40m 41.758s
13	Julian Simon	SPA	60	QMMF Racing Team	Speed Up	20	40m 44.105s
14	Takaaki Nakagami	JPN	30	IDEMITSU Honda Team Asia	Kalex	20	40m 48.316s
15	Dominique Aegerter	SWI	77	Technomag Racing Interwetten	Kalex	20	40m 48.799s
16	Marcel Schrotter	GER	23	Tech 3	Tech 3	20	40m 53.093s
17	Randy Krummenacher	SWI	4	JIR Racing Team	Kalex	20	40m 55.382s
18	Azlan Shah	MAL	25	IDEMITSU Honda Team Asia	Kalex	20	41m 06.878s
19	Thitipong Warokorn	THA	10	APH PTT The Pizza SAG	Kalex	20	41m 07.304s
20	Robin Mulhauser	SWI	70	Technomag Racing Interwetten	Kalex	20	41m 08.202s
21	Florian Alt	GER	66	Octo Iodaracing Team	Suter	20	41m 34.128s
22	Jesko Raffin	SWI	2	sports-millions-EMWE-SAG	Kalex	20	41m 34.173s
23	Zaqhwan Zaidi	MAL	51	JPMoto Malaysia	Suter	20	41m 40.225s
	Ricard Cardus	SPA	88	Tech 3	Tech 3	19	DNF
	Anthony West	AUS	95	QMMF Racing Team	Speed Up	9	DNF
	Simone Corsi	ITA	3	Athina Forward Racing	Kalex	3	DNF
	Tito Rabat	SPA	1	EG 0,0 Marc VDS	Kalex	3	DNF
	Luis Salom	SPA	39	Paginas Amarillas HP 40	Kalex	3	DNF
	Axel Pons	SPA	49	AGR Team	Kalex	3	DNF
	Sam Lowes	GBR	22	Speed Up Racing	Speed Up	2	DNF

Fastest lap: Johann Zarco, on lap 2, 1m 59.918s, 100.4mph/161.5km/h (record).
Previous lap record: Maverick Vinales, SPA (Kalex), 2m 0.168s, 100.1mph/161.1km/h (2014).
Event best maximum speed: Alex Rins, 178.1mph/286.7km/h (race).

Qualifying

Weather: Dry
Air Temp: 24° **Track Temp:** 31°
Humidity: 53%

1	Lowes	1m 59.423s
2	Zarco	1m 59.755s
3	Rabat	1m 59.813s
4	Cortese	1m 59.845s
5	Folger	1m 59.938s
6	Simeon	2m 00.232s
7	Luthi	2m 00.284s
8	Morbidelli	2m 00.396s
9	Rins	2m 00.479s
10	Corsi	2m 00.584s
11	Pons	2m 00.593s
12	Marquez	2m 00.604s
13	Rossi	2m 00.605s
14	Cardus	2m 00.713s
15	Salom	2m 00.791s
16	Kallio	2m 00.844s
17	Schrotter	2m 00.948s
18	Nakagami	2m 00.985s
19	Syahrin	2m 01.000s
20	Baldassarri	2m 01.030s
21	Simon	2m 01.112s
22	West	2m 01.267s
23	Shah	2m 01.397s
24	Krummenacher	2m 01.465s
25	Aegerter	2m 02.055s
26	Warokorn	2m 02.589s
27	Zaidi	2m 02.817s
28	Mulhauser	2m 03.052s
29	Raffin	2m 03.483s
30	Alt	2m 03.486s

Fastest race laps

1	Zarco	1m 59.918s
2	Folger	2m 00.144s
3	Lowes	2m 00.182s
4	Simeon	2m 00.276s
5	Luthi	2m 00.326s
6	Rins	2m 00.448s
7	Cortese	2m 00.596s
8	Morbidelli	2m 00.742s
9	Kallio	2m 00.760s
10	Baldassarri	2m 00.789s
11	Rabat	2m 00.987s
12	Simon	2m 01.007s
13	Cardus	2m 01.041s
14	Marquez	2m 01.057s
15	Syahrin	2m 01.100s
16	West	2m 01.158s
17	Salom	2m 01.253s
18	Rossi	2m 01.291s
19	Schrotter	2m 01.425s
20	Aegerter	2m 01.428s
21	Corsi	2m 01.433s
22	Pons	2m 01.614s
23	Nakagami	2m 01.655s
24	Krummenacher	2m 01.891s
25	Shah	2m 02.011s
26	Mulhauser	2m 02.300s
27	Warokorn	2m 02.312s
28	Alt	2m 03.608s
29	Zaidi	2m 03.664s
30	Raffin	2m 03.761s

Championship Points

1	Folger	25
2	Simeon	20
3	Luthi	16
4	Rins	13
5	Morbidelli	11
6	Kallio	10
7	Cortese	9
8	Zarco	8
9	Rossi	7
10	Baldassarri	6
11	Marquez	5
12	Syahrin	4
13	Simon	3
14	Nakagami	2
15	Aegerter	1

Constructor Points

1	Kalex	25
2	Tech 3	7
3	Speed Up	3

Moto3

RACE DISTANCE: 18 laps, 60.174 miles/96.840km · RACE WEATHER: Dry (air 23°C, humidity 71%, track 34°C)

Pos.	Rider	Nat.	No.	Entrant	Machine	Laps	Time & Speed
1	Alexis Masbou	FRA	10	SAXOPRINT RTG	Honda	18	38m 25.424s 94.0mph/ 151.2km/h
2	Enea Bastianini	ITA	33	Gresini Racing Team Moto3	Honda	18	38m 25.451s
3	Danny Kent	GBR	52	Leopard Racing	Honda	18	38m 25.566s
4	Efren Vazquez	SPA	7	Leopard Racing	Honda	18	38m 25.712s
5	John McPhee	GBR	17	SAXOPRINT RTG	Honda	18	38m 26.117s
6	Isaac Vinales	SPA	32	Husqvarna Factory Laglisse	Husqvarna	18	38m 26.189s
7	Fabio Quartararo	FRA	20	Estrella Galicia 0,0	Honda	18	38m 26.196s
8	Niccolo Antonelli	ITA	23	Ongetta-Rivacold	Honda	18	38m 26.197s
9	Francesco Bagnaia	ITA	21	MAPFRE Team MAHINDRA	Mahindra	18	38m 26.333s
10	Brad Binder	RSA	41	Red Bull KTM Ajo	KTM	18	38m 26.741s
11	Andrea Locatelli	ITA	55	Gresini Racing Team Moto3	Honda	18	38m 26.970s
12	Jorge Navarro	SPA	9	Estrella Galicia 0,0	Honda	18	38m 27.032s
13	Karel Hanika	CZE	98	Red Bull KTM Ajo	KTM	18	38m 27.293s
14	Philipp Oettl	GER	65	Schedl GP Racing	KTM	18	38m 27.928s
15	Jorge Martin	SPA	88	MAPFRE Team MAHINDRA	Mahindra	18	38m 30.543s
16	Miguel Oliveira	POR	44	Red Bull KTM Ajo	KTM	18	38m 32.238s
17	Jakub Kornfeil	CZE	84	Drive M7 SIC	KTM	18	38m 34.184s
18	Juanfran Guevara	SPA	58	MAPFRE Team MAHINDRA	Mahindra	18	38m 34.683s
19	Darryn Binder	RSA	40	Outox Reset Drink Team	Mahindra	18	38m 36.809s
20	Jules Danilo	FRA	95	Ongetta-Rivacold	Honda	18	38m 53.040s
21	Matteo Ferrari	ITA	12	San Carlo Team Italia	Mahindra	18	38m 54.495s
22	Maria Herrera	SPA	6	Husqvarna Factory Laglisse	Husqvarna	18	38m 54.690s
23	Tatsuki Suzuki	JPN	24	CIP	Mahindra	18	38m 54.860s
24	Andrea Migno	ITA	16	SKY Racing Team VR46	KTM	18	38m 54.909s
25	Alessandro Tonucci	ITA	19	Outox Reset Drink Team	Mahindra	18	38m 55.194s
26	Marco Bezzecchi	ITA	53	San Carlo Team Italia	Mahindra	18	39m 11.719s
27	Gabriel Rodrigo	ARG	91	RBA Racing Team	KTM	18	39m 11.830s
28	Zulfahmi Khairuddin	MAL	63	Drive M7 SIC	KTM	18	39m 29.833s
29	Loris Cresson	BEL	61	RBA Racing Team	KTM	18	40m 06.030s
	Romano Fenati	ITA	5	SKY Racing Team VR46	KTM	17	DNF
	Livio Loi	BEL	11	RW Racing GP	Honda	10	DNF
	Hiroki Ono	JPN	76	Leopard Racing	Honda	8	DNF
	Remy Gardner	AUS	2	CIP	Mahindra	8	DNF
	Niklas Ajo	FIN	31	RBA Racing Team	KTM	1	DNF

Fastest lap: Enea Bastianini, on lap 3, 2m 35.312s, 94.0mph/151.2km/h.
Lap record: Alexis Masbou, FRA (Honda), 2m 5.862s, 95.6mph/153.8km/h (2014).
Event best maximum speed: Livio Loi, 149.3mph/240.2km/h (race).

Qualifying

Weather: Dry
Air Temp: 25° **Track Temp:** 34°
Humidity: 45%

1	Masbou	2m 06.170s
2	Vinales	2m 06.237s
3	Antonelli	2m 06.245s
4	Bagnaia	2m 06.253s
5	McPhee	2m 06.254s
6	Quartararo	2m 06.293s
7	Locatelli	2m 06.323s
8	Oliveira	2m 06.378s
9	Kent	2m 06.426s
10	Vazquez	2m 06.465s
11	Loi	2m 06.551s
12	Navarro	2m 06.574s
13	Binder	2m 06.729s
14	Hanika	2m 06.815s
15	Ono	2m 06.829s
16	Ajo	2m 06.891s
17	Fenati	2m 07.099s
18	Danilo	2m 07.195s
19	Gardner	2m 07.235s
20	Binder	2m 07.250s
21	Bastianini	2m 07.308s
22	Oettl	2m 07.320s
23	Tonucci	2m 07.325s
24	Guevara	2m 07.387s
25	Martin	2m 07.459s
26	Kornfeil	2m 07.602s
27	Rodrigo	2m 08.035s
28	Khairuddin	2m 08.040s
29	Migno	2m 08.350s
30	Ferrari	2m 08.497s
31	Suzuki	2m 08.753s
32	Herrera	2m 09.431s
33	Bezzecchi	2m 09.757s
34	Cresson	2m 13.015s

Fastest race laps

1	Bastianini	2m 06.561s
2	Masbou	2m 06.631s
3	Oliveira	2m 06.641s
4	Kent	2m 06.776s
5	Antonelli	2m 06.821s
6	Quartararo	2m 06.828s
7	McPhee	2m 06.883s
8	Vazquez	2m 06.906s
9	Vinales	2m 06.906s
10	Navarro	2m 06.918s
11	Bagnaia	2m 06.938s
12	Oettl	2m 06.962s
13	Locatelli	2m 06.969s
14	Binder	2m 06.973s
15	Martin	2m 07.011s
16	Guevara	2m 07.015s
17	Hanika	2m 07.045s
18	Kornfeil	2m 07.117s
19	Loi	2m 07.184s
20	Ono	2m 07.266s
21	Binder	2m 07.459s
22	Fenati	2m 07.705s
23	Gardner	2m 07.740s
24	Danilo	2m 07.865s
25	Khairuddin	2m 08.081s
26	Suzuki	2m 08.113s
27	Tonucci	2m 08.229s
28	Rodrigo	2m 08.253s
29	Herrera	2m 08.303s
30	Ferrari	2m 08.626s
31	Migno	2m 08.693s
32	Bezzecchi	2m 08.807s
33	Cresson	2m 11.985s

Championship Points

1	Masbou	25
2	Bastianini	20
3	Kent	16
4	Vazquez	13
5	McPhee	11
6	Vinales	10
7	Quartararo	9
8	Antonelli	8
9	Bagnaia	7
10	Binder	6
11	Locatelli	5
12	Navarro	4
13	Hanika	3
14	Oettl	2
15	Martin	1

Constructor Points

1	Honda	25
2	Husqvarna	10
3	Mahindra	7
4	KTM	6

FIM WORLD CHAMPIONSHIP · ROUND 2

GRAND PRIX OF THE AMERICAS

CIRCUIT OF THE AMERICAS

High plains drifters: Dovizioso and
Marquez lead the pack into the first
corner at CotA.
Photo: Gold & Goose

THE defining moment of Marquez's domination at Austin came not with his runaway third Texan win in a row, but at the end of qualifying, when he added another footnote as he continued to make history..

Fastest in free practice, he was lying seventh when he went out for the second of two runs. The bike proved hard to start. Then, as he completed the out-lap, a warning lamp: "Honda always say, if you see one, stop immediately. We only have five engines."

He parked near the end of the pit wall, made an athletic vault over the concrete and cantered fast the length of the pits. The true value of his fitness, he explained, was not the run, but the recovery. "After half a lap, my body was stable."

The team already had the spare bike ready. The set-up was different, and it had the wrong front tyre – soft rather than the preferred hard. "But for one lap … it's not so bad. The rear is more important."

He had barely enough time to complete an out-lap before the chequered flag. Just one chance.

It happened that Dovizioso was behind him. He tried to tag on. "I wanted to see him, his lines – especially in qualifying, because I know he pushes really 100 per cent. I wanted to see all the details, all the secrets."

What he saw was mesmerising. "With a lot of mistakes, he made a special lap time."

It was far from fault free as Marquez wrestled with the bucking RCV, out of the saddle at turn ten. But it was blazingly fast, and enough to take pole off the Ducati rider by better than three-tenths.

From the jaws of disaster... But what had happened to the engine? It was hurried back to Japan; two races later, Marquez confirmed that he would not be using it again. We would have to wait a lot longer to find out even whether the malfunction had been in the engine or the seamless transmission – the audio of the on-board footage suggested the latter – and whether this loss might play him foul later in the year.

The third visit to CotA was marked by the first ever rain, to which were added other quite random problems that combined to make a slightly surreal atmosphere. Proceedings got under way 45 minutes late anyway, after tardy marshals took their places. When MotoGP finally did get going, it was red-flagged with 33 minutes to go because of the on-track arrival of a stray dog, Labrador cross by the look of it. With rain falling steadily, it led waterproof-clad marshals a merry chase before it was finally corralled after 15 minutes. Given the venue, it was probably lucky not to have been shot.

The oddest interruption came on race day, from an incontinent footbridge. It wasn't exactly clear why, but after a damp start and with more rain threatening, before the main race a strip of water beneath it had to be dried off laboriously, imposing yet more delay.

The track's combination of sinuous rhythm with hard braking and slow corners is demanding on bike set-up and riding skills. As a consequence, riders enjoy it. A couple of race-day incidents highlighted another aspect of the highly technical series of to-and-fro flip-flops: they are intrinsically dangerous. This is because a bike crashing in one corner can very easily come across the track a little further around. Exactly this happened in Moto3, as Oliveira's KTM, sliding on its side, forced front-runner Locatelli off the track, lucky not to crash. Then, in Moto2, Simeon's riderless Kalex, still at speed and wheels down, came within an ace of spearing into Alex Rins.

Rossi was prompted to speak: "We already know this danger with chicanes. It is worse with double chicanes, or [like here] triple chicanes. But to fix the problem, we have to change the layout of the track. There are other places with this problem, but here it is dangerous."

The paddock was puzzled by a strange saga involving Casey Stoner and the spare Repsol Honda. Pedrosa was absent, and the double champion had approached Honda offering to take his place. Amazingly, HRC's response had been "Thanks, but no thanks". HRC's vice-president Shuhei Nakamoto had been surprised initially and delighted. But a series of meetings at HQ led to the refusal, on the excuse that they were unable to furnish the infrastructure to guarantee a possible podium, and that since Casey was "a VIP", anything less was beneath his dignity. Stoner's response came on Twitter: "Bummer I'm not racing, no prep was needed as I wasn't planning on winning, just replacing a good friend and having some fun in Texas!"

Retired former 250 champion and now HRC tester Hiro Aoyama was given the job instead, and would prove very undistinguished.

Lorenzo was out of sorts, suffering from bronchitis that would spoil his weekend, although publicly forgiving the helmet technician whose "human mistake, like I made here last year", had spoiled the previous weekend as well. He had jumped the start and suffered a ride-through penalty.

Ducati was feeling the first traces of punishment for their successful new bike. Two rostrum finishes at Qatar had brought the dry-weather total to three, and their fuel allocation had been cut from 24 litres to 22, although this was still two more than the full Factory Option bikes. It would be no problem, they insisted, but intriguingly both Dovi and Iannone stopped on the cool-down lap. Not out of fuel, apparently, but with so little that the reduced airflow at lower speed (through a vent for exactly this purpose) meant it boiled, vapour-locking the pump.

Crutchlow's adaptation to the Honda was complicated by the arrival of a new chassis, with a lower seat unit, that was more flexible and (according to Nakamoto) closer to the factory team bikes. Lapping fast in free practice, he found it better in corner entry, "but I'm losing in other areas, where I would've gained with the old chassis." The taller Scott Redding was in line for yet another chassis with revised seating, but it was not ready yet.

Frequent crasher Axel Pons had another in Moto2 practice and broke his scaphoid, flying straight home for surgery; Moto3 rider John McPhee survived only battered and bruised from a different sort of freak accident: hit in the pits by a scooter ridden by Rabat's riding coach, former 125GP winner Stephan Prein.

And, true to his word, team boss Aspar Martinez had his bikes running in a new livery: Power Electronics was back in place of the departed Drive M7.

MOTOGP RACE – 21 laps

Dovi had been set for a second successive pole when Marquez pulled the pin in the closing stages. Lorenzo was third, rallying somewhat with a "change of antibiotics" on Saturday. Rossi headed row two from Crutchlow and Redding; Iannone down in seventh. Both Suzukis had made it into Q2, with Espargaro eighth and Vinales 12th.

Rain and morning mist had interfered with practice, leaving all once again short of set-up time. All the same, in Saturday's Q2, the top six had all run inside Marquez's previous circuit best. Sunday was very different, after heavy rain overnight robbed the surface of grip. Marquez "was not able to push 100 per cent"; while Iannone's fastest lap of the race was seven-tenths short of the record.

Furthermore, the weeping bridge performed its stunt at just the wrong time, delaying the main race start by 40 minutes and putting it in more danger of a return of the rain, as clouds continued to loom.

Dovi shot off the line, pursued by Marquez, Rossi and Smith, the Englishman again fast away, from the fourth row of the grid. Lorenzo was consigned to fifth and would not quite be one of the party until much later in the race.

On lap one, an over-ambitious lunge by Redding took him and a fist-shaking Pol Espargaro down and out. A few laps later, Bradl was also out, blaming a ramming attack by rookie Miller. "He shouldn't treat this like Moto3," he complained.

Above: Marquez at the maximum. His attack was irresistible.

Left: An incontinent bridge delayed the MotoGP race.

Below left: The First Family of Racing: the Haydens celebrate father Earl's book of that title, and Nicky's 200th grand prix.

Far left: Cal Crutchlow was delayed on lap one, but won this battle with Aleix Espargaro's Suzuki.

Photos: Gold & Goose

Up front, Marquez outbraked Dovi on to the straight, only for the Ducati to power ahead. Marquez attacked again at the hard braking area at the other end, and from here on he took the lead to the finish. It was his third win in three attempts at the Texan track, each time from pole.

His escape over the following laps was helped by Rossi, now also setting about the vexingly fast Ducati, and finally ahead on lap eight with an aggressive outbraking move at the end of the straight. At the same time, slow-starting Iannone had got past not only Espargaro's Suzuki, but also Lorenzo and Smith to close on his fellow Italians.

None could catch Marquez, but second remained in doubt until the closing laps. On the 16th, after noticing "that Valentino was having some trouble on the right-handers", Dovi reclaimed second and set about staying just far enough ahead to prevent another last-lap attack. For Rossi, it was front tyre trouble, like the previous year, "though not as bad". Bridgestone had supplied an extra-hard, but "I need an extra-extra-hard," he quipped.

Iannone had challenged strongly, but lost pace in the closing stages. At the same time, a hitherto lacklustre Lorenzo had been speeding up, and he took fourth with three laps to spare.

Smith was a fine sixth, still only a couple of seconds adrift and better than five ahead of Crutchlow, who had been delayed by the Redding-Espargaro crash on lap one: "I lost nearly five seconds." He finally caught Espargaro's Suzuki by half-distance for seventh.

The second Suzuki was ninth for a double top ten, after an impressive Vinales caught, fought and beat Petrucci's Ducati. On the long straight, the Suzukis had been more than 20km/h slower than the top Hondas and Dukes, but they were clearly the sweetest handling of all, and had two riders willing and able to make the most of it.

Aoyama was tenth, having held off a persistent Barbera.

Almost ten seconds away, the battle raged among the Open gang. Veteran Hayden (in his 200th MotoGP) and Miller (in his second) were joined by Abraham, Bautista at his heels.

Abraham retired with a broken gear lever, while Hayden had a handful of rookie, Miller in front several times. He was less than three-tenths behind as they crossed the line 13th and 14th. Miller had his first points. "I learn a lot, fighting with guys like Nicky," he said, far from overawed.

Bautista was still less than a second away for the returned Aprilia's first point.

They had outpaced Laverty, with Baz and de Angelis trailing behind. Melandri retired; di Meglio and Hernandez crashed out, the former twice.

Two races in, and business as usual for Marquez at a track where he could assume a proprietorial air. But Rossi still led the championship…

MOTO2 RACE – 19 laps

The top 14 qualifiers were within a second of pole, where sat Simeon, for the second time in his career. He had displaced Lowes to second. The Englishman had a bruising first day. He crashed twice, the second time heavily, and from there on, battered and stiff, the weekend was an ordeal.

Rabat was alongside, less than two-tenths off and ready for another shot at opening his title defence. Zarco led row two, from Morbidelli and a briefly revived Nakagami. Rins was eighth, between Simon and Aegerter on row three.

Race day would yield continuing refreshment to the class, with a second first-time winner, after a strong race for the lead. And at the end, a class rookie title leader, meaning there could be no early foregone conclusions.

Nor in the race. Zarco led from the first lap, but this time there was no escape. Injuries notwithstanding, Lowes stuck like glue, pushing and testing. Finally, on lap 14, he pounced, pulling clear for a first win by a good two seconds.

He'd suffered some pain in the early laps, he admitted with customary good cheer, "but after that, I didn't feel a thing."

Simeon had lost a couple of seconds in the early laps while disputing third with Morbidelli; and now Rins arrived, after finishing the first lap 11th and forging through to fourth by lap four. The three closed up on the leaders again.

Lowes was barely half a second clear when Simeon went on the attack on lap 16, his eyes on the leader. His first target was Zarco, and he thought he had him. But the Frenchman fought back and was marginally ahead when they collided going through the complex of Esses. Zarco stayed on, Simeon didn't, and he complained furiously. After investigation, however, Race Direction decided to take no further interest.

Rins had to take avoiding action as Simeon's riderless bike made a good attempt at taking him out; thereafter, any further challenge was over.

The incident helped the escape of Lowes, while Rins secured a podium finish at his second attempt.

Morbidelli had dropped back into a group scrapping over an eventual fourth. Rabat led into the first corner, but soon fell among this gang, and on lap five he was eighth; with an on-form Syahrin and Aegerter also ahead.

Aegerter would crash out of the points, and Rabat come through again, but it wasn't until the closing stages that he finally managed to shake off Morbidelli, now more than four seconds adrift of Rins and the rostrum.

Syahrin was sixth; then came a furious battle, won by West from Kallio, Simon, Nakagami and Corsi: seventh to 11th covered by seven-tenths.

Luthi had a nightmare of electronic problems in qualifying and finished lap one 25th: by the end, he had fought through to 12th, bringing Schrotter with him past Cortese. The last point went to Moto3 champion Marquez.

Qatar winner Folger qualified a lowly 19th and finished 16th, a full second away from the points, while Rins took the overall lead.

MOTO3 RACE – 18 laps

Danny Kent's runaway was remarkable. He found a massive advantage for pole, then cleared off alone to win by an eventual 8.5 seconds, an unthinkable margin in a dry (-ish) Moto3 race.

The usual battle of inches was for second, and almost an all-Honda affair. Notably after the departure of early leader Oliveira, who had suffered a second race crash while recovering from dropping to the back of a highly volatile gang.

Antonelli was the early leader, Kent cautiously biding his time on a still partially damp track as Oliveira took over. At the end of the back straight, for the fourth time he swept past both of them. Within two laps, he led by more than a second, and he kept on building, his progress serene by contrast with the fireworks in his wake.

Oliveira fell foul of a tangle and dropped to ninth on lap six, then set fastest lap as he cut back through to fourth, only to crash.

Vazquez had been steadily picking up positions after dropping to 15th after the start. Just after half-distance, he took over fourth from Oliveira, now behind long-time group leader Masbou and persistent compatriot Quartararo.

The under-age rookie had seized a landmark second by the last corner of the final lap, Masbou having fallen within sight of the flag. He held off Vazquez, Bastianini and Brad Binder, fifth, and first non-Honda.

Then came two more Hondas, McPhee having lost touch with the pack, but well clear of Locatelli, who'd been pushed off as he narrowly avoided the fallen Oliveira's bike. He had finally regained seventh from Fenati on the last lap; Vinales was close behind, fending off a late challenge from Hanika and Kornfeil.

With lurking damp patches, there were several crashers, including Bagnaia, out of third place at half-distance.

Above: Gentleman Johann: defeated Zarco lofts Sam Lowes's arm to celebrate his first GP win.

Above left: Drive M7 Moto3 riders Kornfeil and Khairuddin clearly in good spirits.

Above far left: Marquez was unbeatable once more in Texas – but it was a false dawn for the Repsol team.

Top centre: Lowes leads Zarco and Simeon in Moto2.

Top: Leopard Racing boss Stefan Keifer celebrates his double Moto3 podium with Vazquez and Kent.

Left: Still 15, under-age rookie Fabio Quartararo took a dazzling second.

Photos: Gold & Goose

RED BULL
GRAND PRIX OF
THE AMERICAS

10-12 APRIL, 2015

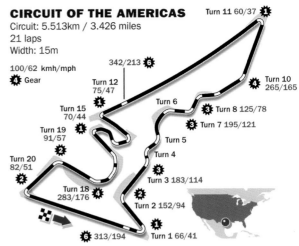

CIRCUIT OF THE AMERICAS
Circuit: 5.513km / 3.426 miles
21 laps
Width: 15m

100/62 kmh/mph
⚙ Gear

Turn 11 60/37
342/213
Turn 12 75/47
Turn 15 70/44
Turn 19 91/57
Turn 20 82/51
Turn 18 283/176
Turn 10 265/165
Turn 6
Turn 8 125/78
Turn 7 195/121
Turn 5
Turn 4
Turn 3 183/114
Turn 2 152/94
Turn 1 66/41
313/194

MotoGP

RACE DISTANCE: 21 laps, 71.938 miles/115.773km · RACE WEATHER: Dry (air 27°C, humidity 62%, track 36°C)

Pos.	Rider	Nat.	No.	Entrant	Machine	Tyres	Race tyre choice	Laps	Time & speed
1	**Marc Marquez**	SPA	93	Repsol Honda Team	Honda RC213V	B	F: Hard/R: Medium	21	43m 47.150s 98.5mph/ 158.6km/h
2	**Andrea Dovizioso**	ITA	4	Ducati Team	Ducati Desmosedici	B	F: Medium/R: Medium	21	43m 49.504s
3	**Valentino Rossi**	ITA	46	Movistar Yamaha MotoGP	Yamaha YZR-M1	B	F: Hard/R: Medium	21	43m 50.270s
4	**Jorge Lorenzo**	SPA	99	Movistar Yamaha MotoGP	Yamaha YZR-M1	B	F: Medium/R: Medium	21	43m 53.832s
5	**Andrea Iannone**	ITA	29	Ducati Team	Ducati Desmosedici	B	F: Medium/R: Medium	21	43m 54.734s
6	**Bradley Smith**	GBR	38	Monster Yamaha Tech 3	Yamaha YZR-M1	B	F: Medium/R: Medium	21	43m 57.707s
7	**Cal Crutchlow**	GBR	35	CWM LCR Honda	Honda RC213V	B	F: Hard/R: Medium	21	44m 04.117s
8	**Aleix Espargaro**	SPA	41	Team SUZUKI ECSTAR	Suzuki GSX-RR	B	F: Medium/R: Medium	21	44m 06.175s
9	**Maverick Vinales**	SPA	25	Team SUZUKI ECSTAR	Suzuki GSX-RR	B	F: Hard/R: Medium	21	44m 25.720s
10	**Danilo Petrucci**	ITA	9	Pramac Racing	Ducati Desmosedici	B	F: Medium/R: Medium	21	44m 28.946s
11	**Hiroshi Aoyama**	JPN	7	Repsol Honda Team	Honda RC213V	B	F: Medium/R: Medium	21	44m 34.349s
12	**Hector Barbera**	SPA	8	Avintia Racing	Ducati Desmosedici Open	B	F: Medium/R: Medium	21	44m 34.489s
13	**Nicky Hayden**	USA	69	Aspar MotoGP Team	Honda RC213V-RS	B	F: Medium/R: Medium	21	44m 43.634s
14	**Jack Miller**	AUS	43	CWM LCR Honda	Honda RC213V-RS	B	F: Medium/R: Medium	21	44m 43.881s
15	**Alvaro Bautista**	SPA	19	Aprilia Racing Team Gresini	Aprilia RS-GP	B	F: Medium/R: Soft	21	44m 44.522s
16	Eugene Laverty	IRL	50	Aspar MotoGP Team	Honda RC213V-RS	B	F: Medium/R: Medium	21	44m 46.048s
17	Loris Baz	FRA	76	Athina Forward Racing	Yamaha Forward	B	F: Medium/R: Medium	21	44m 55.937s
18	Alex de Angelis	RSM	15	Octo IodaRacing Team	Aprilia ART	B	F: Medium/R: Medium	21	45m 09.386s
	Karel Abraham	CZE	17	AB Motoracing	Honda RC213V-RS	B	F: Medium/R: Medium	16	DNF-mechanical
	Marco Melandri	ITA	33	Aprilia Racing Team Gresini	Aprilia RS-GP	B	F: Medium/R: Medium	10	DNF-mechanical
	Yonny Hernandez	COL	68	Pramac Racing	Ducati Desmosedici	B	F: Hard/R: Medium	6	DNF-crash
	Mike di Meglio	FRA	63	Avintia Racing	Ducati Desmosedici Open	B	F: Medium/R: Medium	6	DNF-crash
	Scott Redding	GBR	45	EG 0,0 Marc VDS	Honda RC213V	B	F: Hard/R: Medium	5	DNF-crash
	Stefan Bradl	GER	6	Athina Forward Racing	Yamaha Forward	B	F: Medium/R: Medium	3	DNF-crash
	Pol Espargaro	SPA	44	Monster Yamaha Tech 3	Yamaha YZR-M1	B	F: Medium/R: Medium	0	DNF-crash

Fastest lap: Andrea Iannone, on lap 4, 2m 4.251s, 99.2mph/159.7km/h.

Lap record: Marc Marquez, SPA (Honda), 2m 3.575s, 99.8mph/160.6km/h (2014).

Event best maximum speed: Hiroshi Aoyama, 213.9mph/344.2km/h (free practice).

Qualifying

Weather: Dry
Air Temp: 21° Track Temp: 25°
Humidity: 82%

1	Marquez	2m 02.135s
2	Dovizioso	2m 02.474s
3	Lorenzo	2m 02.540s
4	Rossi	2m 02.573s
5	Crutchlow	2m 02.613s
6	Redding	2m 02.674s
7	Iannone	2m 02.792s
8	A. Espargaro	2m 02.869s
9	P. Espargaro	2m 03.161s
10	Smith	2m 03.440s
11	Petrucci	2m 03.741s
12	Vinales	2m 03.754s
13	Barbera	2m 03.926s
14	Bradl	2m 04.275s
15	Hernandez	2m 04.313s
16	Di Meglio	2m 04.392s
17	Laverty	2m 04.875s
18	Aoyama	2m 05.086s
19	Miller	2m 05.156s
20	Baz	2m 05.214s
21	Abraham	2m 05.261s
22	Hayden	2m 05.569s
23	Bautista	2m 05.595s
24	De Angelis	2m 06.145s
25	Melandri	2m 07.267s

Fastest race laps

1	Iannone	2m 04.251s
2	Dovizioso	2m 04.323s
3	A. Espargaro	2m 04.535s
4	Rossi	2m 04.543s
5	Marquez	2m 04.563s
6	Smith	2m 04.583s
7	Lorenzo	2m 04.753s
8	Crutchlow	2m 05.133s
9	Petrucci	2m 05.512s
10	Bradl	2m 06.070s
11	Miller	2m 06.076s
12	Hernandez	2m 06.076s
13	Vinales	2m 06.146s
14	Bautista	2m 06.618s
15	Barbera	2m 06.633s
16	Aoyama	2m 06.753s
17	Di Meglio	2m 06.786s
18	Hayden	2m 06.791s
19	Redding	2m 06.855s
20	Abraham	2m 06.903s
21	Laverty	2m 07.000s
22	De Angelis	2m 07.316s
23	Baz	2m 07.352s
24	Melandri	2m 09.256s

Championship Points

1	Rossi	41
2	Dovizioso	40
3	Marquez	36
4	Iannone	27
5	Lorenzo	26
6	Smith	18
7	Crutchlow	18
8	A. Espargaro	13
9	Pedrosa	10
10	Petrucci	10
11	Vinales	9
12	P. Espargaro	7
13	Hernandez	6
14	Aoyama	5
15	Barbera	5
16	Hayden	3
17	Redding	3
18	Miller	2
19	Bautista	1

Constructor Points

1	Yamaha	41
2	Ducati	40
3	Honda	36
4	Suzuki	13
5	Aprilia	1

Grid order		1	2	3	4	5	6	7	8	9	10	11	12	13	14	15	16	17	18	19	20	21	
93	MARQUEZ	4	4	4	4	93	93	93	93	93	93	93	93	93	93	93	93	93	93	93	93	93	1
4	DOVIZIOSO	93	93	93	93	4	4	4	46	46	46	46	46	46	46	4	4	4	4	4	4	4	2
99	LORENZO	46	46	46	46	46	46	46	4	4	4	4	4	4	4	46	46	46	46	46	46	46	3
46	ROSSI	38	38	38	38	38	38	38	29	29	29	29	29	29	29	29	29	29	99	99	99	99	4
35	CRUTCHLOW	99	99	99	99	99	99	29	38	38	38	99	99	99	99	99	99	99	29	29	29	29	5
45	REDDING	41	41	41	29	29	29	99	99	99	99	38	38	38	38	38	38	38	38	38	38	38	6
29	IANNONE	29	29	29	41	41	41	41	41	41	41	35	35	35	35	35	35	35	35	35	35	35	7
41	A. ESPARGARO	35	35	35	35	35	35	35	35	35	35	41	41	41	41	41	41	41	41	41	41	41	8
44	P. ESPARGARO	68	9	9	9	9	9	9	9	9	9	9	9	9	9	9	9	9	25	25	25	25	9
38	SMITH	9	68	68	68	68	68	25	25	25	25	25	25	25	25	25	25	25	9	9	9	9	10
9	PETRUCCI	63	43	6	25	25	25	8	7	7	7	7	7	7	7	7	7	7	7	7	7	7	11
25	VINALES	50	6	43	50	50	50	50	8	8	8	8	8	8	8	8	8	8	8	8	8	8	12
8	BARBERA	43	25	25	7	7	8	7	43	69	69	69	69	43	43	69	43	69	69	69	69		13
6	BRADL	25	50	50	43	8	7	43	50	69	69	43	43	43	69	69	43	69	43	43	43	43	14
68	HERNANDEZ	6	7	7	8	43	43	69	69	50	50	17	17	17	17	17	19	19	19	19	19	19	15
63	DI MEGLIO	76	76	8	69	69	69	17	17	17	17	50	19	19	19	19	50	50	50	50	50	50	
50	LAVERTY	7	17	69	17	17	17	76	19	19	19	19	50	50	50	50	76	76	76	76	76	76	
7	AOYAMA	17	69	17	76	76	76	19	76	76	76	76	76	76	76	76	17	15	15	15	15	15	
43	MILLER	69	8	19	19	19	19	15	15	15	15	15	15	15	15	15							
76	BAZ	8	19	76	15	15	15	33	33	33	33												
17	ABRAHAM	19	15	15	33	63	63																
69	HAYDEN	15	33	33	63	33	33																
19	BAUTISTA	33	63	63	45	45																	
15	DE ANGELIS	45	45	45																			
33	MELANDRI																						

17 Pit stop

Moto2

RACE DISTANCE: 19 laps, 65.087 miles/104.747km · RACE WEATHER: Dry (air 23°C, humidity 85%, track 26°C)

Pos.	Rider	Nat.	No.	Entrant	Machine	Laps	Time & Speed
1	Sam Lowes	GBR	22	Speed Up Racing	Speed Up	19	41m 45.565s 93.5mph/150.5km/h
2	Johann Zarco	FRA	5	Ajo Motorsport	Kalex	19	41m 47.564s
3	Alex Rins	SPA	40	Paginas Amarillas HP 40	Kalex	19	41m 50.187s
4	Tito Rabat	SPA	1	EG 0,0 Marc VDS	Kalex	19	41m 54.540s
5	Franco Morbidelli	ITA	21	Italtrans Racing Team	Kalex	19	41m 58.541s
6	Hafizh Syahrin	MAL	55	Petronas Raceline Malaysia	Kalex	19	41m 59.733s
7	Anthony West	AUS	95	QMMF Racing Team	Speed Up	19	42m 02.836s
8	Mika Kallio	FIN	36	Italtrans Racing Team	Kalex	19	42m 03.078s
9	Julian Simon	SPA	60	QMMF Racing Team	Speed Up	19	42m 03.254s
10	Takaaki Nakagami	JPN	30	IDEMITSU Honda Team Asia	Kalex	19	42m 03.329s
11	Simone Corsi	ITA	3	Athina Forward Racing	Kalex	19	42m 03.547s
12	Thomas Luthi	SWI	12	Derendinger Racing Interwetten	Kalex	19	42m 10.389s
13	Marcel Schrotter	GER	23	Tech 3	Tech 3	19	42m 11.581s
14	Sandro Cortese	GER	11	Dynavolt Intact GP	Kalex	19	42m 13.021s
15	Alex Marquez	SPA	73	EG 0,0 Marc VDS	Kalex	19	42m 14.133s
16	Jonas Folger	GER	94	AGR Team	Kalex	19	42m 15.454s
17	Ricard Cardus	SPA	88	Tech 3	Tech 3	19	42m 21.970s
18	Dominique Aegerter	SWI	77	Technomag Racing Interwetten	Kalex	19	42m 24.258s
19	Azlan Shah	MAL	25	IDEMITSU Honda Team Asia	Kalex	19	42m 26.146s
20	Robin Mulhauser	SWI	70	Technomag Racing Interwetten	Kalex	19	42m 27.069s
21	Randy Krummenacher	SWI	4	JIR Racing Team	Kalex	19	42m 36.036s
22	Louis Rossi	FRA	96	Tasca Racing Scuderia Moto2	Tech 3	19	42m 54.390s
23	Thitipong Warokorn	THA	10	APH PTT The Pizza SAG	Kalex	19	42m 56.555s
24	Jesko Raffin	SWI	2	sports-millions-EMWE-SAG	Kalex	19	42m 56.703s
25	Florian Alt	GER	66	Octo Iodaracing Team	Suter	19	43m 05.007s
26	Lorenzo Baldassarri	ITA	7	Athina Forward Racing	Kalex	19	43m 10.970s
27	Luis Salom	SPA	39	Paginas Amarillas HP 40	Kalex	19	43m 18.441s
	Xavier Simeon	BEL	19	Federal Oil Gresini Moto2	Kalex	15	DNF
	Zaqhwan Zaidi	MAL	51	JPMoto Malaysia	Suter	12	DNF

Fastest lap: Sam Lowes, on lap 18, 2m 10.578s, 94.4mph/151.9km/h.
Lap record: Maverick Vinales, SPA (Kalex), 2m 10.103s, 94.8mph/152.5km/h (2014).
Event best maximum speed: Luis Salom, 175.7mph/282.7km/h (free practice).

Qualifying
Weather: Dry
Air Temp: 22° Track Temp: 27°
Humidity: 78%

1	Simeon	2m 09.888s
2	Lowes	2m 09.942s
3	Rabat	2m 10.077s
4	Zarco	2m 10.102s
5	Morbidelli	2m 10.135s
6	Nakagami	2m 10.190s
7	Simon	2m 10.261s
8	Rins	2m 10.488s
9	Aegerter	2m 10.513s
10	Schrotter	2m 10.548s
11	Kallio	2m 10.576s
12	Corsi	2m 10.590s
13	West	2m 10.594s
14	Salom	2m 10.854s
15	Syahrin	2m 10.894s
16	Cortese	2m 10.930s
17	Luthi	2m 10.985s
18	Krummenacher	2m 11.031s
19	Folger	2m 11.092s
20	Cardus	2m 11.104s
21	Baldassarri	2m 11.286s
22	Rossi	2m 11.486s
23	Marquez	2m 11.661s
24	Shah	2m 11.954s
25	Mulhauser	2m 12.509s
26	Warokorn	2m 12.735s
27	Alt	2m 13.392s
28	Zaidi	2m 13.545s
29	Raffin	2m 14.118s

Fastest race laps

1	Lowes	2m 10.578s
2	Simeon	2m 11.006s
3	Zarco	2m 11.028s
4	Rins	2m 11.296s
5	Rabat	2m 11.302s
6	Morbidelli	2m 11.441s
7	Aegerter	2m 11.524s
8	Schrotter	2m 11.558s
9	Luthi	2m 11.574s
10	Syahrin	2m 11.663s
11	Simon	2m 11.668s
12	West	2m 11.684s
13	Nakagami	2m 11.727s
14	Folger	2m 11.755s
15	Corsi	2m 11.807s
16	Kallio	2m 11.818s
17	Cardus	2m 11.909s
18	Cortese	2m 12.001s
19	Krummenacher	2m 12.060s
20	Mulhauser	2m 12.253s
21	Marquez	2m 12.354s
22	Rossi	2m 12.386s
23	Baldassarri	2m 12.490s
24	Shah	2m 12.507s
25	Salom	2m 12.779s
26	Raffin	2m 14.130s
27	Warokorn	2m 14.218s
28	Alt	2m 14.334s
29	Zaidi	2m 15.852s

Championship Points

1	Rins	29
2	Zarco	28
3	Folger	25
4	Lowes	25
5	Morbidelli	22
6	Simeon	20
7	Luthi	20
8	Kallio	18
9	Syahrin	14
10	Rabat	13
11	Cortese	11
12	Simon	10
13	West	9
14	Nakagami	8
15	Rossi	7
16	Baldassarri	6
17	Marquez	6
18	Corsi	5
19	Schrotter	3
20	Aegerter	1

Constructor Points

1	Kalex	45
2	Speed Up	28
3	Tech 3	10

Moto3

RACE DISTANCE: 18 laps, 61.661 miles/99.234km · RACE WEATHER: Dry (air 22°C, humidity 90%, track 22°C)

Pos.	Rider	Nat.	No.	Entrant	Machine	Laps	Time & Speed
1	Danny Kent	GBR	52	Leopard Racing	Honda	18	41m 32.287s 89.0mph/143.3km/h
2	Fabio Quartararo	FRA	20	Estrella Galicia 0,0	Honda	18	41m 40.819s
3	Efren Vazquez	SPA	7	Leopard Racing	Honda	18	41m 40.939s
4	Enea Bastianini	ITA	33	Gresini Racing Team Moto3	Honda	18	41m 41.098s
5	Brad Binder	RSA	41	Red Bull KTM Ajo	KTM	18	41m 41.843s
6	John McPhee	GBR	17	SAXOPRINT RTG	Honda	18	41m 46.156s
7	Andrea Locatelli	ITA	55	Gresini Racing Team Moto3	Honda	18	41m 52.729s
8	Romano Fenati	ITA	5	SKY Racing Team VR46	KTM	18	41m 52.898s
9	Isaac Vinales	SPA	32	Husqvarna Factory Laglisse	Husqvarna	18	41m 53.150s
10	Karel Hanika	CZE	98	Red Bull KTM Ajo	KTM	18	41m 53.200s
11	Jakub Kornfeil	CZE	84	Drive M7 SIC	KTM	18	41m 53.536s
12	Andrea Migno	ITA	16	SKY Racing Team VR46	KTM	18	41m 56.012s
13	Philipp Oettl	GER	65	Schedl GP Racing	KTM	18	42m 04.505s
14	Niklas Ajo	FIN	31	RBA Racing Team	KTM	18	42m 08.989s
15	Matteo Ferrari	ITA	12	San Carlo Team Italia	Mahindra	18	42m 09.570s
16	Alexis Masbou	FRA	10	SAXOPRINT RTG	Honda	18	42m 19.314s
17	Maria Herrera	SPA	6	Husqvarna Factory Laglisse	Husqvarna	18	42m 31.544s
18	Remy Gardner	AUS	2	CIP	Mahindra	18	42m 36.035s
19	Gabriel Rodrigo	ARG	91	RBA Racing Team	KTM	18	42m 36.898s
20	Zulfahmi Khairuddin	MAL	63	Drive M7 SIC	KTM	18	42m 49.255s
21	Alessandro Tonucci	ITA	19	Outox Reset Drink Team	Mahindra	18	42m 59.684s
22	Ana Carrasco	SPA	22	RBA Racing Team	KTM	18	43m 12.696s
23	Niccolo Antonelli	ITA	23	Ongetta-Rivacold	Honda	18	43m 16.128s
24	Stefano Manzi	ITA	29	San Carlo Team Italia	Mahindra	18	43m 18.392s
25	Livio Loi	BEL	11	RW Racing GP	Honda	17	42m 44.158s
	Tatsuki Suzuki	JPN	24	CIP	Mahindra	17	DNF
	Miguel Oliveira	POR	44	Red Bull KTM Ajo	KTM	10	DNF
	Francesco Bagnaia	ITA	21	MAPFRE Team MAHINDRA	Mahindra	9	DNF
	Jorge Navarro	SPA	9	Estrella Galicia 0,0	Honda	9	DNF
	Jorge Martin	SPA	88	MAPFRE Team MAHINDRA	Mahindra	8	DNF
	Hiroki Ono	JPN	76	Leopard Racing	Honda	6	DNF
	Jules Danilo	FRA	95	Ongetta-Rivacold	Honda	5	DNF
	Darryn Binder	RSA	40	Outox Reset Drink Team	Mahindra	1	DNF
	Juanfran Guevara	SPA	58	MAPFRE Team MAHINDRA	Mahindra	0	DNF

Fastest lap: Miguel Oliveira, on lap 8, 2m 17.559s, 89.6mph/144.2km/h.
Lap record: Luis Salom, SPA (KTM), 2m 16.345s, 90.4mph/145.5km/h (2013).
Event best maximum speed: Romano Fenati, 148.5mph/239.0km/h (qualifying).

Qualifying:
Weather: Dry
Air Temp: 20° Track Temp: 22°
Humidity: 89%

1	Kent	2m 15.344s
2	Oliveira	2m 15.829s
3	Locatelli	2m 16.090s
4	Antonelli	2m 16.101s
5	Navarro	2m 16.144s
6	Quartararo	2m 16.150s
7	Vinales	2m 16.335s
8	Bastianini	2m 16.400s
9	Bagnaia	2m 16.417s
10	Masbou	2m 16.576s
11	Binder	2m 16.735s
12	Martin	2m 16.849s
13	Guevara	2m 16.945s
14	Loi	2m 16.954s
15	McPhee	2m 16.992s
16	Vazquez	2m 17.012s
17	Ono	2m 17.173s
18	Danilo	2m 17.434s
19	Fenati	2m 17.469s
20	Hanika	2m 17.485s
21	Ajo	2m 17.487s
22	Migno	2m 17.518s
23	Kornfeil	2m 17.621s
24	Ferrari	2m 17.653s
25	Manzi	2m 17.659s
26	Tonucci	2m 17.894s
27	Gardner	2m 17.894s
28	Khairuddin	2m 17.941s
29	Suzuki	2m 18.024s
30	Rodrigo	2m 18.303s
31	Herrera	2m 18.631s
32	Oettl	2m 19.073s
33	Carrasco	2m 19.181s
34	Binder	2m 19.253s

Fastest race laps

1	Oliveira	2m 17.559s
2	Kent	2m 17.579s
3	Bastianini	2m 17.753s
4	Vazquez	2m 17.882s
5	Binder	2m 17.930s
6	Quartararo	2m 18.001s
7	Masbou	2m 18.015s
8	Navarro	2m 18.031s
9	Kornfeil	2m 18.076s
10	Ajo	2m 18.112s
11	McPhee	2m 18.119s
12	Bagnaia	2m 18.234s
13	Ono	2m 18.257s
14	Locatelli	2m 18.424s
15	Hanika	2m 18.479s
16	Vinales	2m 18.495s
17	Fenati	2m 18.636s
18	Oettl	2m 18.703s
19	Antonelli	2m 18.829s
20	Migno	2m 18.877s
21	Ferrari	2m 19.071s
22	Manzi	2m 19.437s
23	Martin	2m 19.508s
24	Danilo	2m 19.808s
25	Suzuki	2m 20.142s
26	Herrera	2m 20.222s
27	Khairuddin	2m 20.311s
28	Gardner	2m 20.363s
29	Loi	2m 20.474s
30	Rodrigo	2m 20.821s
31	Tonucci	2m 20.959s
32	Carrasco	2m 21.680s

Championship Points

1	Kent	41
2	Bastianini	33
3	Quartararo	29
4	Vazquez	29
5	Masbou	25
6	McPhee	21
7	Binder	17
8	Vinales	17
9	Locatelli	14
10	Hanika	9
11	Antonelli	8
12	Fenati	8
13	Bagnaia	7
14	Kornfeil	5
15	Oettl	5
16	Migno	4
17	Navarro	4
18	Ajo	2
19	Ferrari	1
20	Martin	1

Constructor Points

1	Honda	50
2	KTM	17
3	Husqvarna	17
4	Mahindra	8

ARGENTINE GRAND PRIX

TERMAS DE RIO HONDO CIRCUIT

Victor Rossi struts his stuff in *parc fermé*, while Dovi muses on finishing second for a third race in a row. In the background, team-mates Miller (*left, top Open finisher) and Crutchlow share the moment.
Photo: Gold & Goose

Above: Aleix Espargaro (41) pushes inside Marquez into the first turn. Dovizioso, Lorenzo, Crutchlow and Rossi jockey for position.

Right: Back of the class for a naughty boy. Moto3 miscreant Fenati was consigned to the back of the grid.

Below right: Soft tyres and sweet handling helped Espargaro qualify the Suzuki second, but he had to settle for seventh in the race.

Far right: Dorna's Ezpeleta: continuing to shape the future of MotoGP.

Photos: Gold & Goose

THE third and most inaccessible of the trio of flyaways offered yet more variety, in a quite different kind of race – a battle of tyre strategies that really could have gone either way.

To the benefit of the series in general, Marquez stumbled most spectacularly, while Rossi took a second win out of it. He departed leading the world championship; the first time after three races since 2009, his last title year.

In only its second year, the Termas de Rio Hondo weekend was something of a trial, now that the novelty had worn off. The venue is interesting, the fan support evocative, but getting there is vexatious, and the whole expedition so expensive that all but a handful of top teams run on skeleton staff.

The circuit also elicits mixed feelings. The layout is great, an instant classic – a fast lap with fast corners and several complex technical challenges makes for good motorcycle racing. The only slightly faster Phillip Island is the perfect example. The surface, however, is little short of disastrous. It suffers from serious under use, and is also open to the dry dusty winds of the arid Gran Chaco plains and the pampas to the south. It takes a lot cleaning by racing tyres, and then it's only on the racing line. (Only a handful of old-timers recalled the value of the long-discarded sidecars in this respect.)

While slippery, the track is also abrasive; in addition, there is the punishment of the long and fast left-hand turns six and eleven. Bridgestone brought an extra-hard asymmetrical tyre to address this problem, introducing a new element to race-tyre choice.

Differing strategies led to the crucial confrontation. Marquez gambled on the softer hard tyre – the Hondas had trouble making the extra-hards work well anyway. It was necessary to build a big advantage straight away. Which he did.

Rossi favoured the end-of-race potential of the extra-hard. That worked too. It was touch and go, but the rate at which he caught the leader on the second-last lap suggested that he had the speed to go away and win.

Now came the difference: the sheer aggression of Marquez. It is such a trademark that some think he introduced it to MotoGP. Rossi proved otherwise. He withstood the first collision as Marquez barged back underneath after Rossi had swept past at the end of the straight. And he survived the second as he seized control of the line for the next corner.

Marquez did not. His front wheel hit Rossi's swing-arm, swivelled and flicked him off. For once, no crucial cables were cut; and it was Marquez who had to pay the price.

The circuit's tyre consumption also changed the landscape somewhat for Ducati, condemned on this occasion by the differential rules to the softer tyre allocation, without access to the extra-hard. Considering the bike's speed and power, riders thought this might be a serious disadvantage.

As it transpired, race day was sufficiently cooler than qualifying to upset the equation again. Rossi won on an extra-hard, but the Ducatis were second and fourth, and Crutchlow between them was on the same hard option. In the event, only the factory and satellite Yamaha quartet employed the extra-hard; all the rest – Open bikes included – used the same hard in the race.

Also disappointed at not having that tyre was the elder Espargaro, who was unable to capitalise on his second place in qualifying. The Suzuki's evident sweet handling, a great asset at a track like this, was being compromised by baffling chatter. His strong qualifying came, much to pole-setter Marquez's amusement, after both riders had adopted the two-stop three-run strategy in the 15 minutes of Q2. Marquez

had pioneered this at Jerez in 2014, but revealed now that the idea had first come to him in qualifying here.

His Repsol companion, once more, was Aoyama, who again spent most of his race (until he was knocked off at the finish) with the Open and lower Factory bikes; the news of Pedrosa's return was muted. Originally, the team had hoped that he would reappear for the next round at Jerez, but now they were casting doubt on this.

Dorna chief Ezpeleta chose the far-flung race to announce a major investment rethink for the future. Massively increased payments to teams in exchange for fixed-price lease agreements from the factories were aimed at replacing the current multi-level, multi-rule situation with a period of stability from 2017 to 2021. This was still just an idea. The proposal suggested no technical changes in the five-year period "unless everyone agrees". Factories would "also have the obligation to lease ... two [or more, to a maximum of six] bikes to a satellite team, for a maximum agreed price." Dorna would pay "practically all" of this lease fee for the satellite teams, said Ezpeleta: "everything except crashes". This represented a 30-per cent boost to Dorna's existing contribution.

The same carefully timed statement suggested an expanded calendar in that period, with a maximum of 20 races. Austria was already to return in 2016; Thailand high on the list of potential new races. Not mentioned was that this Argentine race was already in doubt for 2016.

Seemingly, tempers were fraying after too long on the road, with several penalty points for unseemly behaviour, including one each for Oliveira, Morbidelli and Petrucci, whose headlong attack knocked Aoyama off on the last lap. Romano Fenati, however, set a new record: three at once after a prolonged attack on Niklas Ajo at the end of race-day warm-up. It began with a kick on the slow-down lap; then he parked alongside in the practice-start group. Fists flew; then he leaned across and flicked the KTM's kill switch, leaving Ajo stalled in the middle of the pack.

Fenati already had one point, and the new total meant a back-of-the-grid start, from which he recovered strongly to place eighth.

At the closest he gets to a home GP, Colombian Yonny Hernandez had an Argentine flag painted on his helmet. There was no glory, though: his Ducati suffered an early oil leak and belly-pan fire that exploded his back tyre in short order. Rossi's tribute was more appreciated: a Maradona shirt on the top podium step.

There was a local star: a burrowing owl perched sentinel on a lamp standard, unmoving for most of the weekend – not even when the TV cameras also picked up a sizeable and tasty looking tarantula crossing the track.

MOTOGP RACE – 25 laps

Qualifying, as the track gradually rubbered up, ended in a battle for pole between Marquez's Honda and the remarkable Suzuki of Espargaro. The Honda won it by better than half a second, even though, as Espargaro said, "I rode like a beast."

Iannone was alongside; Crutchlow led Lorenzo and Dovizioso on row two; Petrucci was ahead of Rossi in eighth and second Suzuki rider Vinales.

With track temperature cooler than Saturday, Marquez took an on-the-grid gamble, switching to the faster, but less durable hard rear. That obliged him, he well understood, to build as strong a lead as possible during the opening laps. All four Yamaha riders plus Redding opted to stay with the extra-hard.

Espargaro led away, brawling with Lorenzo while Marquez took control and started on his task. Rossi was bumped wide in the first corner by Iannone and finished lap one eighth. Ahead were both Ducatis, Crutchlow and Petrucci.

Crutchlow was riding aggressively: his brief was to help Marquez get away, and he took second on lap two.

Both Ducatis were soon past Lorenzo, while Rossi was picking up places one by one. On lap five, he caught his comparatively downbeat team-mate (on the softer front tyre option) and was directly past.

He made short work of the trio ahead and was up to second on lap 11, with both Dovi and Iannone now in front of

Crutchlow. The gap to the leader was 4.151 seconds, the race almost halfway done. Surely Marquez had enough of a cushion to win a second race in a row?

Even Rossi thought so: "But I had to try. I concentrated only on my own speed. I had to catch him, or scare him."

There followed a double masterclass in racing. Marquez nursed his tyres and his lead. Rossi just rode. And rode and rode. And steadily the gap shrank.

On lap 18, it was still 2.3 seconds. Next time around, 2.0. And on lap 20, Rossi broke Marc's old record to get within 1.2 seconds.

Practice had shown that Valentino's race pace was strong on that tyre, but it was still not apparent that he would catch him, as Marquez put in a fast lap of his own to stay a second clear. And he would still need to get past. The race was set for a thrilling battle to the flag.

It never reached that far. Rossi was on his tail as they started the second-last lap, and he attacked directly at the second corner. Marquez passed him straight back.

At the end of the long straight, Rossi slipped past under brakes. Again, Marquez fought straight back, attempting to force a way through inside at the apex of the tight right. The bikes touched.

"I thought, 'F***, you are aggressive.' Then I accelerated out, and sincerely I don't know what happened next," said the Yamaha rider.

Marquez tried again to get inside for the following left-hander, but Rossi had the line, and as he moved across, the Honda's front wheel clipped the Yamaha's rear. And Marquez was down – his third race-ending crash in MotoGP.

The Ducatis proved that the softer tyre was not such a disadvantage, with a third second place in a row for Dovi, who had followed Rossi, but in the end couldn't stay with him.

Behind, Crutchlow had regained fourth and was fending off Iannone and the revived Lorenzo. The Italian got ahead as they started the last lap, but Crutchlow dived inside through the last corners to claim third by five-hundredths. Lorenzo was a dispirited fifth, blaming a bad tyre.

The fast and flowing track made sure of a good race all the way down the points and beyond. Smith was a solid sixth; Aleix Espargaro managed to hang on to seventh, clear of a desultory threat from younger brother Pol. Redding was ninth after a difficult race: he'd been sprayed with oil when Hernandez's Duke suddenly expired in sheets of flame on lap seven.

Vinales had closed right up after escaping the next big battle, 12th to 19th covered by just over 2.2 seconds. Petrucci was ahead in 11th, after knocking Aoyama off in the last corner. Miller impressed again by heading the gang over the line, top Open finisher, from Barbera, fellow-rookie Baz and team-mate Bradl, who took the last points; team-mates Hayden and Laverty missed out by inches; then came di Meglio and Bautista.

Now MotoGP could head home to Europe, after a compelling start to the season.

MOTO2 RACE – 23 laps

Zarco set the pace in qualifying, almost three-tenths clear of Rabat and Luthi, but it was third-row starter Simeon away off the line, with Rabat taking over at the second corner.

That didn't last, in another bad weekend for the Spaniard. On the next corner, jostled by Zarco, he ran off, dropping back to last.

At the same time, Qatar winner Folger did exactly the same thing, and the pair charged back through together, Folger breaking the lap record.

Simeon led the first lap, chased by Lowes, Zarco, Kallio, Cortese and Luthi. Rookie title leader Rins was seventh.

Zarco was feeling comfortable and confident; he took over up front on lap three for a lead he would never lose. But the pressure was sustained until half-distance; Lowes took up the pursuit on lap five, while Simeon close behind was coming under pressure from Kallio; Rins still tagged on behind.

Zarco's lead was up to two seconds by lap eight. But he did not feel secure, for Lowes was determined, taking back almost half a second through the middle of the race.

Simeon had dropped to the back of the group, but was up to fourth again, ahead of Kallio, when he slipped off on lap 17, rejoining near the back.

Ahead of this pair, Rins was dogging the wheel tracks of Lowes, whose challenge was spent, the gap growing again by lap 20. The push to stay in touch with the flying leader, he explained, had taken "a lot of energy from me and the bike. By the last five laps, I was losing grip."

Now an unexpected passage: he slowed deliberately and let Rins past, planning to study his rival for a late attack. He didn't get the chance, as Rins pulled firmly clear, better than 1.5 seconds at the end. In three Moto2 races, he had finished fourth, third and second.

Kallio was just a second behind the fading Lowes at the finish: another three seconds away, team-mate Morbidelli had got the better of the next big group for fifth.

Luthi headed the gang behind, from Cortese, Baldassarri, Folger – who had quite outpaced earlier companion Rabat – the increasingly impressive Syahrin, Salom, Rabat and Aegerter, fifth to 13th in less than five seconds.

West narrowly led Alex Marquez for the last points, the younger brother keeping his record consistent, if overshadowed by team-mate Rins.

Corsi and Rossi were the only two to crash out; Zarco took over the points lead from Rins.

MOTO3 RACE – 21 laps

A week before, Kent had torn up the book of Moto3 conventions to claim a record dry-weather win by 8.5 seconds. In Argentina, the iconoclast remained rampant. Although pipped for pole by Oliveira, the English rider simply ran away for a second straight lone win by an even bigger margin, 10.3 seconds.

An extraordinary feat, since the rest remained engaged in the usual massive skirmish. Even after two front-runners had crashed out, there were still 14 riders battling over second, and they crossed the line within less than 2.5 seconds.

Vinales led the first couple of laps, Oliveira and Antonelli in close attendance, Kent biding his time close behind.

Kent went from fourth to first on lap three, and three laps later he was already well over two seconds clear, in a class of his own. Moto3.5, perhaps. It was a rather dull race, he admitted: "I'd prefer to be fighting for it."

The rest laid on a feast of close, high-class racing – although in the absence of Antonelli and Navarro, after the Italian knocked the Spaniard down.

Positions changed from corner to corner. Oliveira dropped to 13th on lap five after running wide; six laps later, he was up to second.

The leading players were clear enough. Vazquez was always strong; rank rookie Quartararo likewise, up to second at one point from 16th on the grid. Brad Binder closed up to join in; Bagnaia and Hanika were in the mix. Tactics would be everything.

Remarkably, Fenati was also among them, after starting on the back row of the grid.

In the end, the experienced Vazquez narrowly prevailed over Vinales, with team-mates Oliveira and Binder just off the rostrum. Quartararo, Hanika and Fenati were inches behind, so also Bastianini, Ajo, Loi, an on-form Ono, Kornfeil and McPhee, who took the final point.

Above, from top: **Showman Rossi curried local favour with a Maradona shirt on the podium; Cecchinello captures Crutchlow's third-place finish; Vinales (32) and Oliveira (44) head a titanic Moto3 battle for second.**

Top left: **Marquez versus Rossi. Soon afterwards, it was touch and go for the youngster.**

Above left: **Starting his fourth year in the class, Zarco claimed his first Moto2 victory. More were to follow.**

Left: **Yonny Hernandez's flaming Ducati shed chunks after an explosive oil fire. Pol Espargaro and Redding dodge the debris.**

Right: **Danny Kent broke the pattern again and won the Moto3 race by a massive margin.**
Photos: Gold & Goose

OFFICIAL TIMEKEEPER TISSOT

G.P. RED BULL
DE LA REPUBLICA
ARGENTINA

17–19 APRIL, 2015

AUTÓDROMO TERMAS DE RÍO HONDO

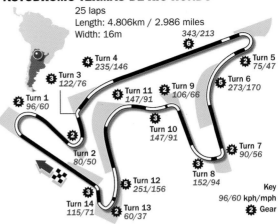

25 laps
Length: 4.806km / 2.986 miles
Width: 16m

Turn 1 96/60
Turn 2 80/50
Turn 3 122/76
Turn 4 235/146
Turn 5 75/47
Turn 6 273/170
Turn 7 90/56
Turn 8 152/94
Turn 9 106/66
Turn 10 147/91
Turn 11 147/91
Turn 12 251/156
Turn 13 60/37
Turn 14 115/71
343/213

Key
96/60 kph/mph
Gear

MotoGP

RACE DISTANCE: 25 laps, 74.658 miles/120.150km · RACE WEATHER: Dry (air 29°C, humidity 71%, track 36°C)

Pos.	Rider	Nat.	No.	Entrant	Machine	Tyres	Race tyre choice	Laps	Time & speed
1	**Valentino Rossi**	ITA	46	Movistar Yamaha MotoGP	Yamaha YZR-M1	B	F: Hard/R: Extra-Hard	25	41m 35.644s 107.7mph/ 173.3km/h
2	**Andrea Dovizioso**	ITA	4	Ducati Team	Ducati Desmosedici	B	F: Hard/R: Hard	25	41m 41.329s
3	**Cal Crutchlow**	GBR	35	CWM LCR Honda	Honda RC213V	B	F: Hard/R: Hard	25	41m 43.942s
4	**Andrea Iannone**	ITA	29	Ducati Team	Ducati Desmosedici	B	F: Hard/R: Hard	25	41m 43.996s
5	**Jorge Lorenzo**	SPA	99	Movistar Yamaha MotoGP	Yamaha YZR-M1	B	F: Medium/R: Extra-Hard	25	41m 45.836s
6	**Bradley Smith**	GBR	38	Monster Yamaha Tech 3	Yamaha YZR-M1	B	F: Hard/R: Extra-Hard	25	41m 55.520s
7	**Aleix Espargaro**	SPA	41	Team SUZUKI ECSTAR	Suzuki GSX-RR	B	F: Medium/R: Hard	25	41m 59.977s
8	**Pol Espargaro**	SPA	44	Monster Yamaha Tech 3	Yamaha YZR-M1	B	F: Medium/R: Extra-Hard	25	42m 03.314s
9	**Scott Redding**	GBR	45	EG 0,0 Marc VDS	Honda RC213V	B	F: Medium/R: Extra-Hard	25	42m 10.041s
10	**Maverick Vinales**	SPA	25	Team SUZUKI ECSTAR	Suzuki GSX-RR	B	F: Medium/R: Hard	25	42m 10.452s
11	**Danilo Petrucci**	ITA	9	Pramac Racing	Ducati Desmosedici	B	F: Hard/R: Hard	25	42m 15.850s
12	**Jack Miller**	AUS	43	CWM LCR Honda	Honda RC213V-RS	B	F: Hard/R: Hard Slick	25	42m 18.298s
13	**Hector Barbera**	SPA	8	Avintia Racing	Ducati Desmosedici Open	B	F: Medium Slick/R: Hard	25	42m 18.373s
14	**Loris Baz**	FRA	76	Athina Forward Racing	Yamaha Forward	B	F: Hard/R: Hard	25	42m 18.497s
15	**Stefan Bradl**	GER	6	Athina Forward Racing	Yamaha Forward	B	F: Hard/R: Hard	25	42m 18.681s
16	Nicky Hayden	USA	69	Aspar MotoGP Team	Honda RC213V-RS	B	F: Hard/R: Hard	25	42m 18.896s
17	Eugene Laverty	IRL	50	Aspar MotoGP Team	Honda RC213V-RS	B	F: Hard/R: Hard	25	42m 19.044s
18	Mike di Meglio	FRA	63	Avintia Racing	Ducati Desmosedici Open	B	F: Medium/R: Hard	25	42m 19.452s
19	Alvaro Bautista	SPA	19	Aprilia Racing Team Gresini	Aprilia RS-GP	B	F: Medium/R: Hard	25	42m 20.522s
20	Marco Melandri	ITA	33	Aprilia Racing Team Gresini	Aprilia RS-GP	B	F: Medium/R: Hard	25	42m 31.880s
21	Karel Abraham	CZE	17	AB Motoracing	Honda RC213V-RS	B	F: Medium/R: Hard	25	42m 39.015s
22	Alex de Angelis	RSM	15	Octo IodaRacing Team	Aprilia ART	B	F: Medium/R: Hard	25	42m 44.088s
	Hiroshi Aoyama	JPN	7	Repsol Honda Team	Honda RC213V	B	F: Medium/R: Hard	24	DNF-crash
	Marc Marquez	SPA	93	Repsol Honda Team	Honda RC213V	B	F: Hard/R: Hard	23	DNF-crash
	Yonny Hernandez	COL	68	Pramac Racing	Ducati Desmosedici	B	F: Hard/R: Hard	6	DNF-mechanical

Fastest lap: Valentino Rossi, on lap 20, 1m 39.019s, 108.6mph/174.7km/h (record).

Previous lap record: Dani Pedrosa, SPA (Honda), 1m 39.233s, 108.3mph/174.3km/h (2014).

Event best maximum speed: Marc Marquez, 206.2mph/331.9km/h (free practice).

Qualifying

Weather: Dry
Air Temp: 27° **Track Temp:** 43°
Humidity: 70%

1	Marquez	1m 37.802s
2	A. Espargaro	1m 38.316s
3	Iannone	1m 38.467s
4	Crutchlow	1m 38.485s
5	Lorenzo	1m 38.485s
6	Dovizioso	1m 38.520s
7	Petrucci	1m 38.786s
8	Rossi	1m 38.890s
9	Vinales	1m 39.187s
10	Smith	1m 39.197s
11	Redding	1m 39.380s
12	Barbera	1m 40.526s
13	Hernandez	1m 39.405s
14	Laverty	1m 39.434s
15	Aoyama	1m 39.715s
16	Bradl	1m 39.734s
17	Abraham	1m 39.758s
18	P. Espargaro	1m 39.808s
19	Bautista	1m 39.828s
20	Hayden	1m 39.876s
21	Miller	1m 39.888s
22	Baz	1m 39.972s
23	Di Meglio	1m 40.133s
24	Melandri	1m 40.403s
25	De Angelis	1m 40.485s

Fastest race laps

1	Rossi	1m 39.019s
2	Marquez	1m 39.071s
3	Crutchlow	1m 39.474s
4	Dovizioso	1m 39.495s
5	Iannone	1m 39.507s
6	Lorenzo	1m 39.595s
7	Smith	1m 40.058s
8	A. Espargaro	1m 40.261s
9	P. Espargaro	1m 40.287s
10	Hernandez	1m 40.395s
11	Vinales	1m 40.432s
12	Aoyama	1m 40.500s
13	Redding	1m 40.524s
14	Petrucci	1m 40.566s
15	Barbera	1m 40.567s
16	Bradl	1m 40.593s
17	Miller	1m 40.854s
18	Di Meglio	1m 40.865s
19	Laverty	1m 40.900s
20	Hayden	1m 40.921s
21	Baz	1m 40.927s
22	Bautista	1m 41.067s
23	Melandri	1m 41.471s
24	Abraham	1m 41.507s
25	De Angelis	1m 41.613s

Championship Points

1	Rossi	66
2	Dovizioso	60
3	Iannone	40
4	Lorenzo	37
5	Marquez	36
6	Crutchlow	34
7	Smith	28
8	A. Espargaro	22
9	P. Espargaro	15
10	Vinales	15
11	Petrucci	15
12	Pedrosa	10
13	Redding	10
14	Barbera	8
15	Hernandez	6
16	Miller	6
17	Aoyama	5
18	Hayden	3
19	Baz	2
20	Bradl	1
21	Bautista	1

Constructor Points

1	Yamaha	66
2	Ducati	60
3	Honda	52
4	Suzuki	22
5	Yamaha Forward	2
6	Aprilia	1

Grid order / Lap chart

Grid order	1	2	3	4	5	6	7	8	9	10	11	12	13	14	15	16	17	18	19	20	21	22	23	24	25
93 MARQUEZ	93	93	93	93	93	93	93	93	93	93	93	93	93	93	93	93	93	93	93	93	93	93	93	46	46
41 A. ESPARGARO	99	35	35	35	35	35	35	4	4	4	46	46	46	46	46	46	46	46	46	46	46	46	46	4	4
29 IANNONE	41	99	4	4	4	4	4	35	35	46	4	4	4	4	4	4	4	4	4	4	4	4	4	29	35
35 CRUTCHLOW	35	4	29	29	29	29	29	29	46	35	29	29	29	29	29	35	35	35	35	35	35	35	35	35	29
99 LORENZO	4	29	99	99	99	46	46	46	29	29	35	35	35	35	29	29	29	29	29	29	29	29	99	99
4 DOVIZIOSO	29	41	46	46	46	99	99	99	99	99	99	99	99	99	99	99	99	99	99	99	99	99	38	38
9 PETRUCCI	9	46	41	41	41	41	41	41	41	38	38	38	38	38	38	38	38	38	38	38	38	41	41	41
46 ROSSI	46	9	9	9	9	38	38	38	38	41	41	41	41	41	41	41	41	41	41	41	41	44	44
25 VINALES	25	68	68	68	38	9	9	9	44	44	44	44	44	44	44	44	44	44	44	44	44	45	45
38 SMITH	38	25	38	38	68	68	44	44	9	45	45	45	45	45	45	45	45	45	45	45	45	25	25
45 REDDING	68	38	45	45	45	44	45	45	9	9	9	25	9	25	25	9	25	25	25	25	25	9	9
8 BARBERA	45	45	25	25	44	45	6	6	6	6	6	25	9	25	9	9	9	9	9	9	9	7	43
68 HERNANDEZ	44	44	44	44	25	6	25	25	25	25	25	6	6	8	8	8	8	8	8	8	7	43	8
50 LAVERTY	6	6	6	6	6	25	43	43	43	43	8	8	8	6	6	6	43	43	43	43	43	8	76
7 AOYAMA	43	43	8	8	8	43	8	8	43	43	43	43	43	43	43	6	6	7	7	43	69	6
6 BRADL	76	8	43	43	43	8	69	69	69	69	69	69	69	7	7	69	7	69	7	6	6	6	76	69
17 ABRAHAM	8	76	50	69	69	69	76	76	76	76	76	7	7	69	7	69	7	69	69	69	69	6	50
44 P. ESPARGARO	50	50	76	76	76	76	50	50	50	50	50	7	76	76	76	76	76	76	76	76	76	50	63
19 BAUTISTA	17	69	69	50	50	7	63	63	7	7	7	50	50	50	50	50	50	50	63	63	63	19	19
69 HAYDEN	69	17	7	7	7	50	7	7	63	63	63	63	63	63	63	63	63	50	50	50	19	33
43 MILLER	33	7	17	63	17	63	19	19	19	19	19	19	19	19	19	19	19	19	19	19	33	17
76 BAZ	7	63	63	17	63	19	17	17	33	33	33	17	17	17	17	17	17	17	33	33	17	19
63 DI MEGLIO	63	33	19	19	17	33	33	33	17	17	17	33	33	33	33	33	33	33	17	17	15
33 MELANDRI	19	19	33	33	33	15	15	15	15	15	15	15	15	15	15	15	15	15
15 DE ANGELIS	15	15	15	15	15												

Moto2

RACE DISTANCE: 23 laps, 68.685 miles/110.538km · RACE WEATHER: Dry (air 25°C, humidity 74%, track 34°C)

Pos.	Rider	Nat.	No.	Entrant	Machine	Laps	Time & Speed
1	**Johann Zarco**	FRA	5	Ajo Motorsport	Kalex	23	39m 44.497s
							103.6mph/
							166.8km/h
2	**Alex Rins**	SPA	40	Paginas Amarillas HP 40	Kalex	23	39m 47.212s
3	**Sam Lowes**	GBR	22	Speed Up Racing	Speed Up	23	39m 48.658s
4	**Mika Kallio**	FIN	36	Italtrans Racing Team	Kalex	23	39m 49.807s
5	**Franco Morbidelli**	ITA	21	Italtrans Racing Team	Kalex	23	39m 52.455s
6	**Thomas Luthi**	SWI	12	Derendinger Racing Interwetten	Kalex	23	39m 53.905s
7	**Sandro Cortese**	GER	11	Dynavolt Intact GP	Kalex	23	39m 54.423s
8	**Lorenzo Baldassarri**	ITA	7	Athina Forward Racing	Kalex	23	39m 54.525s
9	**Jonas Folger**	GER	94	AGR Team	Kalex	23	39m 54.649s
10	**Hafizh Syahrin**	MAL	55	Petronas Raceline Malaysia	Kalex	23	39m 55.813s
11	**Luis Salom**	SPA	39	Paginas Amarillas HP 40	Kalex	23	39m 56.261s
12	**Tito Rabat**	SPA	1	EG 0,0 Marc VDS	Kalex	23	39m 56.369s
13	**Dominique Aegerter**	SWI	77	Technomag Racing Interwetten	Kalex	23	39m 58.502s
14	**Anthony West**	AUS	95	QMMF Racing Team	Speed Up	23	40m 05.285s
15	**Alex Marquez**	SPA	73	EG 0,0 Marc VDS	Kalex	23	40m 05.818s
16	Marcel Schrotter	GER	23	Tech 3	Tech 3	23	40m 10.190s
17	Azlan Shah	MAL	25	IDEMITSU Honda Team Asia	Kalex	23	40m 11.034s
18	Ricard Cardus	SPA	88	Tech 3	Tech 3	23	40m 11.183s
19	Steven Odendaal	RSA	44	AGR Team	Kalex	23	40m 11.894s
20	Takaaki Nakagami	JPN	30	IDEMITSU Honda Team Asia	Kalex	23	40m 12.276s
21	Randy Krummenacher	SWI	4	JIR Racing Team	Kalex	23	40m 13.056s
22	Xavier Simeon	BEL	19	Federal Oil Gresini Moto2	Kalex	23	40m 20.485s
23	Robin Mulhauser	SWI	70	Technomag Racing Interwetten	Kalex	23	40m 20.954s
24	Thitipong Warokorn	THA	10	APH PTT The Pizza SAG	Kalex	23	40m 31.207s
25	Florian Alt	GER	66	Octo Iodaracing Team	Suter	23	40m 32.019s
26	Julian Simon	SPA	60	QMMF Racing Team	Speed Up	23	40m 47.407s
27	Zaqhwan Zaidi	MAL	51	JPMoto Malaysia	Suter	23	40m 51.238s
28	Jesko Raffin	SWI	2	sports-millions-EMWE-SAG	Kalex	23	40m 51.336s
	Louis Rossi	FRA	96	Tasca Racing Scuderia Moto2	Tech 3	18	DNF
	Simone Corsi	ITA	3	Athina Forward Racing	Kalex	1	DNF

Fastest lap: Jonas Folger, on lap 23, 1m 43.001s, 104.3mph/167.9km/h (record).
Previous lap record: Luis Salom, SPA (Kalex), 1m 44.011s, 103.3mph/166.3km/h (2014).
Event best maximum speed: Thomas Luthi, 171.1mph/275.4km/h (race).

Qualifying

Weather: Dry
Air Temp: 27° **Track Temp:** 43°
Humidity: 70%

1	Zarco	1m 42.809s
2	Rabat	1m 43.102s
3	Luthi	1m 43.165s
4	Lowes	1m 43.253s
5	Rins	1m 43.364s
6	Folger	1m 43.384s
7	Corsi	1m 43.449s
8	Cortese	1m 43.460s
9	Simeon	1m 43.640s
10	Kallio	1m 43.699s
11	Krummenacher	1m 43.755s
12	Schrotter	1m 43.778s
13	Baldassarri	1m 43.797s
14	Simon	1m 43.847s
15	Nakagami	1m 43.857s
16	Syahrin	1m 43.874s
17	Aegerter	1m 43.984s
18	Salom	1m 44.051s
19	West	1m 44.070s
20	Marquez	1m 44.178s
21	Cardus	1m 44.212s
22	Morbidelli	1m 44.292s
23	Rossi	1m 44.349s
24	Mulhauser	1m 44.823s
25	Shah	1m 44.857s
26	Odendaal	1m 44.904s
27	Warokorn	1m 45.158s
28	Alt	1m 45.498s
29	Raffin	1m 45.882s
30	Zaidi	1m 45.930s

Fastest race laps

1	Folger	1m 43.001s
2	Zarco	1m 43.079s
3	Rabat	1m 43.176s
4	Rins	1m 43.183s
5	Luthi	1m 43.195s
6	Lowes	1m 43.248s
7	Syahrin	1m 43.349s
8	Kallio	1m 43.362s
9	Simeon	1m 43.381s
10	Cortese	1m 43.457s
11	Morbidelli	1m 43.481s
12	Salom	1m 43.502s
13	Baldassarri	1m 43.628s
14	Aegerter	1m 43.696s
15	Marquez	1m 43.823s
16	West	1m 43.955s
17	Rossi	1m 43.966s
18	Schrotter	1m 43.983s
19	Shah	1m 44.001s
20	Cardus	1m 44.005s
21	Nakagami	1m 44.087s
22	Odendaal	1m 44.094s
23	Krummenacher	1m 44.180s
24	Mulhauser	1m 44.230s
25	Simon	1m 44.449s
26	Warokorn	1m 44.898s
27	Alt	1m 45.098s
28	Raffin	1m 45.435s
29	Zaidi	1m 45.799s

Championship Points

1	Zarco	53
2	Rins	49
3	Lowes	41
4	Morbidelli	33
5	Folger	32
6	Kallio	31
7	Luthi	30
8	Simeon	20
9	Syahrin	20
10	Cortese	20
11	Rabat	17
12	Baldassarri	14
13	West	11
14	Simon	10
15	Nakagami	8
16	Rossi	7
17	Marquez	7
18	Salom	5
19	Corsi	5
20	Aegerter	4
21	Schrotter	3

Constructor Points

1	Kalex	70
2	Speed Up	44
3	Tech 3	10

Moto3

RACE DISTANCE: 21 laps, 62.713 miles/100.926km · RACE WEATHER: Dry (air 24°C, humidity 85%, track 30°C)

Pos.	Rider	Nat.	No.	Entrant	Machine	Laps	Time & Speed
1	**Danny Kent**	GBR	52	Leopard Racing	Honda	21	38m 25.621s
							97.9mph/
							157.5km/h
2	**Efren Vazquez**	SPA	7	Leopard Racing	Honda	21	38m 35.955s
3	**Isaac Vinales**	SPA	32	Husqvarna Factory Laglisse	Husqvarna	21	38m 36.017s
4	**Miguel Oliveira**	POR	44	Red Bull KTM Ajo	KTM	21	38m 36.388s
5	**Brad Binder**	RSA	41	Red Bull KTM Ajo	KTM	21	38m 36.738s
6	**Fabio Quartararo**	FRA	20	Estrella Galicia 0,0	Honda	21	38m 36.816s
7	**Karel Hanika**	CZE	98	Red Bull KTM Ajo	KTM	21	38m 37.009s
8	**Romano Fenati**	ITA	5	SKY Racing Team VR46	KTM	21	38m 37.224s
9	**Enea Bastianini**	ITA	33	Gresini Racing Team Moto3	Honda	21	38m 37.333s
10	**Niklas Ajo**	FIN	31	RBA Racing Team	KTM	21	38m 37.427s
11	**Francesco Bagnaia**	ITA	21	MAPFRE Team MAHINDRA	Mahindra	21	38m 37.579s
12	**Livio Loi**	BEL	11	RW Racing GP	Honda	21	38m 37.976s
13	**Hiroki Ono**	JPN	76	Leopard Racing	Honda	21	38m 38.122s
14	**Jakub Kornfeil**	CZE	84	Drive M7 SIC	KTM	21	38m 38.265s
15	**John McPhee**	GBR	17	SAXOPRINT RTG	Honda	21	38m 38.393s
16	Philipp Oettl	GER	65	Schedl GP Racing	KTM	21	38m 48.098s
17	Andrea Migno	ITA	16	SKY Racing Team VR46	KTM	21	38m 48.973s
18	Stefano Manzi	ITA	29	San Carlo Team Italia	Mahindra	21	38m 54.367s
19	Remy Gardner	AUS	2	CIP	Mahindra	21	38m 56.030s
20	Zulfahmi Khairuddin	MAL	63	Drive M7 SIC	KTM	21	38m 56.265s
21	Matteo Ferrari	ITA	12	San Carlo Team Italia	Mahindra	21	38m 56.407s
22	Jorge Martin	SPA	88	MAPFRE Team MAHINDRA	Mahindra	21	39m 09.716s
23	Andrea Locatelli	ITA	55	Gresini Racing Team Moto3	Honda	21	39m 10.774s
24	Darryn Binder	RSA	40	Outox Reset Drink Team	Mahindra	21	39m 14.770s
25	Alessandro Tonucci	ITA	19	Outox Reset Drink Team	Mahindra	21	39m 16.694s
26	Ana Carrasco	SPA	22	RBA Racing Team	KTM	21	39m 21.806s
27	Tatsuki Suzuki	JPN	24	CIP	Mahindra	21	39m 27.082s
28	Gabriel Rodrigo	ARG	91	RBA Racing Team	KTM	20	38m 32.761s
	Jorge Navarro	SPA	9	Estrella Galicia 0,0	Honda	15	DNF
	Juanfran Guevara	SPA	58	MAPFRE Team MAHINDRA	Mahindra	12	DNF
	Alexis Masbou	FRA	10	SAXOPRINT RTG	Honda	7	DNF
	Niccolo Antonelli	ITA	23	Ongetta-Rivacold	Honda	4	DNF
	Jules Danilo	FRA	95	Ongetta-Rivacold	Honda	3	DNF
	Maria Herrera	SPA	6	Husqvarna Factory Laglisse	Husqvarna	0	DNF

Fastest lap: Miguel Oliveira, on lap 7, 1m 48.977s, 98.6mph/158.7km/h (record).
Previous lap record: Alex Marquez, SPA (Honda), 1m 49.109s, 98.5mph/158.5km/h (2014).
Event best maximum speed: Jorge Navarro, 143.5mph/231.0km/h (race).

Qualifying:

Weather: Dry
Air Temp: 21° **Track Temp:** 37°
Humidity: 70%

1	Oliveira	1m 48.461s
2	Kent	1m 48.511s
3	Antonelli	1m 48.665s
4	Vazquez	1m 48.729s
5	Vinales	1m 48.883s
6	Hanika	1m 49.026s
7	Navarro	1m 49.202s
8	Fenati	1m 49.291s
9	Ono	1m 49.302s
10	Bastianini	1m 49.409s
11	Loi	1m 49.413s
12	Guevara	1m 49.419s
13	Masbou	1m 49.436s
14	Migno	1m 49.523s
15	Binder	1m 49.529s
16	Quartararo	1m 49.567s
17	Ajo	1m 49.597s
18	Bagnaia	1m 49.617s
19	McPhee	1m 49.650s
20	Kornfeil	1m 49.675s
21	Oettl	1m 49.708s
22	Danilo	1m 49.806s
23	Martin	1m 49.817s
24	Herrera	1m 49.866s
25	Ferrari	1m 50.027s
26	Manzi	1m 50.078s
27	Gardner	1m 50.088s
28	Khairuddin	1m 50.122s
29	Locatelli	1m 50.352s
30	Binder	1m 50.401s
31	Tonucci	1m 51.153s
32	Suzuki	1m 51.169s
33	Carrasco	1m 51.654s
34	Rodrigo	1m 51.714s

Fastest race laps

1	Oliveira	1m 48.977s
2	Kent	1m 49.037s
3	Bagnaia	1m 49.264s
4	Manzi	1m 49.332s
5	Fenati	1m 49.338s
6	Vazquez	1m 49.368s
7	Oettl	1m 49.395s
8	Bastianini	1m 49.400s
9	Ono	1m 49.407s
10	Loi	1m 49.437s
11	Quartararo	1m 49.442s
12	Kornfeil	1m 49.465s
13	Ajo	1m 49.467s
14	Binder	1m 49.479s
15	McPhee	1m 49.480s
16	Navarro	1m 49.490s
17	Hanika	1m 49.533s
18	Vinales	1m 49.538s
19	Antonelli	1m 49.683s
20	Masbou	1m 49.883s
21	Gardner	1m 49.888s
22	Migno	1m 49.929s
23	Guevara	1m 49.933s
24	Martin	1m 50.147s
25	Khairuddin	1m 50.327s
26	Ferrari	1m 50.393s
27	Locatelli	1m 50.525s
28	Danilo	1m 50.662s
29	Tonucci	1m 51.076s
30	Binder	1m 51.260s
31	Carrasco	1m 51.523s
32	Suzuki	1m 51.982s
33	Rodrigo	1m 52.917s

Championship Points

1	Kent	66
2	Vazquez	49
3	Bastianini	40
4	Quartararo	39
5	Vinales	33
6	Binder	28
7	Masbou	25
8	McPhee	22
9	Hanika	18
10	Fenati	16
11	Locatelli	14
12	Oliveira	13
13	Bagnaia	12
14	Antonelli	8
15	Ajo	8
16	Kornfeil	7
17	Oettl	5
18	Migno	4
19	Loi	4
20	Navarro	4
21	Ono	3
22	Ferrari	1
23	Martin	1

Constructor Points

1	Honda	75
2	Husqvarna	33
3	KTM	30
4	Mahindra	13

SPANISH GRAND PRIX

JEREZ CIRCUIT

Above: M1 metronomic, Honda showing its weaknesses – try as he might, Marquez had no answer for Lorenzo at Jerez.

Top right: Star-class rookie Vinales heads Laverty, Bradl and Baz en route to 11th.

Above right: Only a little finger, but "worse than a broken leg," said Marquez.

Above far right: Bad boy Hanika earned five penalty points and a damaged shoulder for his aggressive lapse.

Right: Aleix Espargaro shone once again on the Suzuki, but had to give best to the pursuing Iannone.

Photos: Gold & Goose

"IT shows that in racing you can't say things like 'This guy is down, he's finished', because the next day he is going to be at the front." Pause. Sincere look. "The opposite is true, too."

Philosopher of the weekend was Jorge Lorenzo, and speaking from a position of strength. Pole position and a dominant win. His confidence was brimming, and this would be the beginning of a run of victories that would quite eclipse his below-average start to the year, and change the course of the championship.

The opposite truth was represented by Marquez, who had arrived in Jerez in 2014 for the fourth of ten wins in a row. His Honda's weaknesses were being cruelly exposed by the improvement from Yamaha and Ducati; and now there was a painful, if short-term setback: a motocross accident the previous Saturday had broken the little finger of his left hand. In fact, it had been a lucky escape: victim of the 'just one more lap' syndrome, he'd slipped off, then been run over by his training partner, close behind. It could have been much worse than a broken finger.

He had started 2014 with a broken leg, but this was worse, he confirmed. "It's only a little finger, but it disturbs me more than the leg … I cannot ride the bike as I want." Apart from the obvious task of hanging on in braking and acceleration, and "when the bike is shaking", there was unfamiliar stress on the rest of his body as he took the strain on the right to compensate. This was the greatest problem over race distance, leaving him exhausted and weakened by the flag. Doubtless it also contributed to a crash in free practice, which persuaded the crestfallen rider to abandon his planned two-stop strategy in qualifying.

Second was a significant achievement.

Repsol team-mate Pedrosa had kept everyone guessing until days before practice began as to whether he would be returning as originally planned, after an outing on a Supercross bike had showed his recovery was still a work in progress. Aoyama stood in again; and HRC called a conference where vice-president Nakamoto stoutly defended his compatriot's performance, and was obliged to repeat his justifications of the decision not to give Stoner the vacant seat.

News broke during the weekend of the death of Geoff Duke, pioneering superstar, five-times world champion and timeless racing hero. Duke won six TTs, and he lived on the Isle of Man until his death aged 92. Very properly, he was remembered with a minute of silence on the grid – which he had to share as a late-comer, however, with the earthquake victims in Nepal, for whom this increasingly frequent slot had been pre-assigned.

More fitting, if inadvertent, was the nature of the MotoGP race: a respectful procession won in imperious style at lap-record speed by a rider revered for his smooth accuracy, and a style that makes him look slow even when he's winning. Lorenzo summed up a change in his approach for this race: "I am riding more by feel and instinct." He and Duke have much in common.

Doubtless, however, a high-speed cortege wasn't what the usual huge Jerez crowd – 122,551 on race day – had come to see. Happily, the smaller classes compensated.

Most teams were looking forward to Monday, the first official test of the season. Although there wasn't much in the way of new parts (although Honda had a chassis and swing-arm), it was a chance to catch up without the pressure of limited time and the need to qualify. This was especially important for riders on unfamiliar bikes.

Crutchlow, over from Ducati, was clearly getting to grips with his completely different factory Honda without too much difficulty. Compatriot Redding was struggling, especially with front-end feel; he thought it was because of having switched from the Open Honda he had ridden in 2014. The bikes were outwardly very similar, yet "completely different. Different suspension, brakes, tyres…" Extra power aside, he had become used to the extra grip of the Open bike's softer tyre. "I'm always asking for more grip, and there is no more grip. I did learn a few things last year, but I would have learned more coming straight on to a factory bike."

Ducati skipped the tests, however, in favour of two potentially more valuable private days at Mugello, their official test track, where they would be racing in four weeks.

Down in Moto3, where Honda claimed a fourth straight win, came news that KTM was developing a new chassis to spice up their challenge. With only one upgrade allowed per season, which must be available to all riders, "we must get it right. We get no second chance," said race chief Pit Beirer; and testing was already under way at national level. As it transpired, the early promise came to naught and the project was shelved before the due delivery date of the Italian GP. So much for a low-cost grand prix class.

Three of Honda's wins had come at the hands of Danny Kent, this time a fight rather than a runaway, and he became the first British rider to win three in a row for more than 35 years – after Barry Sheene in 1977.

Another Moto3 rider, Karel Hanika, set a different and un-enviable record, smashing that set by class-mate Fenati in Argentina, when he garnered a maximum of penalty points: five at once, and a pit-lane start next time out. His offence was egregious enough: he deliberately rammed Juanfran Guevara on the slow-down lap, causing him to crash. The consequence was more severe still: a broken collarbone, which the Aspar team rider had surgically repaired to be back in two weeks.

More from Moto3, to many the best class of all: rookie Quartararo had now turned 16, and was also on a familiar circuit. Even so, his first pole was an impressive achieve-ment, and news broke that he'd been offered a move directly into Moto2 in 2016, to partner Alex Marquez in the Marc VDS team. This would be at the expense of Rabat, but was conditional on one thing: the Frenchman had to win the title at his first attempt. He made a good stab at winning the race, but suffered from a (fully forgivable) rookie error. Rabat looked a bit safer.

MOTOGP RACE – 27 laps

Lorenzo claimed his first pole since Misano in 2014 by almost four-tenths from Marquez and Iannone, the Italian's second front row of the season. Rossi was fifth, on row two between the Espargaro brothers, in reverse age order. Crutchlow led the third from an unusually downbeat Dovizioso, struggling with set-up, and Hernandez on a 2014 Desmosedici.

Jorge's race was more than an emphatic return to form. Simply a masterclass. A perfect start, the lead into the first corner and a clear track ahead. Start the metronome. Neat and precise, he reeled off lap after lap on the limit, a new record third time around. If he'd had mirrors, he'd have seen Marquez riding his socks off, heaving himself around the now clumsy-looking Honda. And gradually getting smaller.

After six laps, his lead was better than a second; better than two after just three more. It didn't stop growing until the flag, by which time it was 5.5.

Marquez's second was to be admired: the greatest prob-lem his right arm, with double the usual workload. He chased hard at first, then pushed hard to resist a distant, but for a while increasingly threatening Rossi. Twenty points and a revived championship defence the reward.

Rossi had taken third off fast-starting Pol Espargaro on lap three, but wasn't up to the pace of the two leaders. The gap to Marquez grew to almost three seconds and hovered around 2.5 past half-distance. Then, as the Honda rider's pace slackened marginally, Rossi started to close. On lap 20, he was just over a second behind, but too many narrow escapes on a track grown increasingly slippery in race day's heat persuaded him to choose caution, and he slackened off for a secure third.

Also on lap three, Crutchlow got ahead of Aleix Espar-garo's Suzuki. The Englishman, suffering from some sort of virus, took six more to get ahead of the younger Espargaro brother. In this way, the first five positions were settled early, and they stayed that way.

Understandably, Lorenzo was "very proud of myself and the team that we finally delivered some extraordinary work." He feigned a repeat of his life-threatening jump into the small

Above: Crutchlow took seven laps to hunt down and pass Espargaro's Yamaha for fourth.

Top and above right: Rins's classic last-corner attack on Rabat didn't work. He fell; Rabat survived, but lost second to Zarco, waiting just behind.

Top far right: Jonas Folger took the top step in Moto2 for a second time in 2015.

Centre right: Rookie versus run-away: Kent (52) won again (by less than a hundredth), but the aggressive Quartararo (20) blew his chances.

Centre far right: Brad Binder celebrates his Moto3 podium.

Below right: The top four, with inches in it – Oliveira heads winner Kent, from Quartararo and Binder.

Photos: Gold & Goose

lake inside the last fast corners, turning away at the last moment. Five years before, he'd had to be rescued there.

There might have been more to-and-fro up front if both Ducati riders hadn't run into trouble.

Iannone was sixth, pushing Pol Espargaro at the end, after pulling through from 11th on lap one. He'd started from the front row, but spoiled his chances with an electronic pratfall. At the start, he'd mistakenly switched to the mapping for wet conditions instead of launch control, "and I had to do the whole race with that set-up, because the procedure to return to dry settings is very complicated."

His last victims had been Aleix Espargaro, seventh, and Smith, who had a lonely ride to eighth.

Dovizioso suffered a different Ducati electronic problem, and an even busier ride through to ninth after dropping from seventh to last on lap two. It was a problem with engine braking, which sent him wide at the far hairpin, then right off across the gravel at the last corner. The problem did not recur. "We had the speed for fourth or fifth," he said, first time off the podium.

There was a lively battle for the last points, tenth to 14th covered by just over two seconds over the line.

Team-mates Petrucci and Hernandez had been scrapping most of the race with Redding, joined just after half-distance by Vinales and Barbera, who had tagged on behind Dovizioso as he came through.

It was more Moto3 than MotoGP, finally resolved in favour of Hernandez, from Vinales, Petrucci, Redding and Barbera, first Open bike.

Two seconds away, Bautista finally escaped from Bradl to take the final point, the second for Aprilia.

The electronic difficulties affecting Open riders were exacerbated by the low traction. Hayden managed to speed up at the end to catch and pass team-mate Laverty for 17th, the rookie struggling with arm-pump.

Miller was even worse off, saving more than one near crash as he dropped behind 19th-placed Melandri. De An-

gelis and di Meglio trailed in, the latter remounting after slipping off.

Aoyama crashed out of his last race as replacement for Pedrosa as he was picking up speed to get ahead of the Open riders. Baz and unhappily Showa-suspended Abraham also crashed out.

Rossi increased his points lead, but the main rivals were closing the gap.

MOTO2 RACE – 26 laps

In contrast to the MotoGP procession, the often dour Moto2 laid on a good race with a sting in the tail, at Jerez's rightly famous final corner.

Defender Rabat was on pole for the first time in the year, by a good three-tenths from Rins and Folger. Rins was riding high, still second overall, and the object of much attention at home. Plenty of pressure for the class rookie.

Luthi, Nakagami and Lowes were behind; Cortese headed row three from Pons and Zarco.

Rabat took off in the lead in fine style – but he was not alone. Folger was on his heels and awaiting developments; Luthi and Rins were close behind. All the while, points leader Zarco was making his way through from 11th on lap one.

Rabat was somewhat troubled. "I had bad front wheel chatter, and it kept closing," he said. "It hadn't happened all weekend."

Soon enough, on lap ten, he left sufficient room for Folger to get through. The German was on the limit, but marginally faster as he reeled off "four or five really risky laps to stretch the gap."

By the 21st, he was better than a second away, and almost two over the line.

The drama was behind him. Rins, who set fastest lap on the third tour, had got ahead of Luthi for third on lap seven and would soon start pressing Rabat. But in the later stages, Zarco was the fastest out there, and he also passed Luthi

with eight laps to go. Luthi dropped away, Zarco closed up steadily, and there were three together as they started the last lap: Rabat, Rins, Zarco...

The drama reached its conclusion at that decisive final hairpin. Rabat was still in front as they started to brake. Rins had a better idea, and was following a great and often successful tradition. He dived inside to seize the apex. But he was too fast. He slipped, struck Rabat's back wheel and went down. After remounting, he finished 18th, the first no-score of his debut season.

Zarco was poised to take advantage of the confusion and nipped inside Rabat to secure a valuable second place. "On the last lap, I thought something might be possible," he said. He was three-tenths ahead over the line.

Luthi was another four seconds back; a similar distance behind came Simeon, a lone fifth. Morbidelli finally prevailed by half a second after a long battle with Salom; both had outdistanced eighth-placed Corsi. Alex Marquez dropped off the back of the group for ninth, his best so far.

There was another fight for tenth. Simon had come through after a back-of-the-grid start (a penalty for a technical infringement: under minimum weight), and had caught and passed Schrotter on lap 22 – only for the German rider to get him back when it mattered.

Syahrin led the next group, from Baldassari and Krummenacher; West had dropped off the back, but was promoted to gain the final point by Rins's crash.

Lowes had a disastrous weekend, dropping back to 20th.

MOTO3 RACE – 23 laps

Reliably race of the day, Moto3 didn't disappoint. The winner's name was repetitive, the style not so. Far from the yawning gulf in Texas and Argentina, Kent's margin here was just 0.097 of a second, after another fraught final hairpin.

Precocious pole-starter Quartararo played a prominent role among a quartet that battled all race long. Kent was a constant; the other two were Red Bull KTM team-mates Oliveira and Binder.

All except Binder led at least once, with Oliveira particularly feisty after heading Quartararo off the line.

It became a quintet for a while, after Vazquez came through from 17th on the grid to tag on the back – but the effort had taken too much out of the rider and his tyres, and he lost touch again.

The drama was similar to Moto2. Kent was in front as they arrived, all four inches apart. Now came what both Kent and Quartararo later described as a "rookie move". The new boy dived inside, ran out of room, touched Kent and only narrowly saved the crash.

So it was Oliveira second by less than a tenth, with Binder two-tenths behind him. Quartararo was still less than a second adrift.

With Vazquez a lone fifth, the rest scrapped it out.

Fenati was long-term front man and managed to hang on to sixth; Bagnaia had finally got ahead on the last lap, only to run wide at the hairpin. Navarro was less than a second further back.

Bastianini managed to save ninth from McPhee, Vinales and Danilo.

Kent now had a one-race buffer, with a lead of 31 points.

OFFICIAL TIMEKEEPER — TISSOT

GRAN PREMIO
bwin
DE ESPAÑA

1–3 MAY, 2015

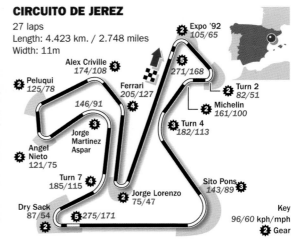

CIRCUITO DE JEREZ
27 laps
Length: 4.423 km. / 2.748 miles
Width: 11m

- Expo '92 105/65
- Alex Criville 174/108
- 271/168
- Peluqui 125/78
- Ferrari 205/127
- Turn 2 82/51
- 146/91
- Michelin 161/100
- Turn 4 182/113
- Jorge Martinez Aspar
- Angel Nieto 121/75
- Turn 7 185/115
- Jorge Lorenzo 75/47
- Sito Pons 143/89
- Dry Sack 87/54
- 275/171
- Key 96/60 kph/mph
- Gear

MotoGP

RACE DISTANCE: 27 laps, 74.205 miles/119.421km · RACE WEATHER: Dry (air 26°C, humidity 41%, track 30°C)

Pos.	Rider	Nat.	No.	Entrant	Machine Tyres		Race tyre choice	Laps	Time & speed
1	**Jorge Lorenzo**	SPA	99	Movistar Yamaha MotoGP	Yamaha YZR-M1	B	F: Hard/R: Medium	27	44m 57.246s 99.0mph/ 159.3km/h
2	**Marc Marquez**	SPA	93	Repsol Honda Team	Honda RC213V	B	F: Hard/R: Medium	27	45m 02.822s
3	**Valentino Rossi**	ITA	46	Movistar Yamaha MotoGP	Yamaha YZR-M1	B	F: Hard/R: Medium	27	45m 08.882s
4	**Cal Crutchlow**	GBR	35	CWM LCR Honda	Honda RC213V	B	F: Hard/R: Medium	27	45m 19.973s
5	**Pol Espargaro**	SPA	44	Monster Yamaha Tech 3	Yamaha YZR-M1	B	F: Hard/R: Medium	27	45m 23.866s
6	**Andrea Iannone**	ITA	29	Ducati Team	Ducati Desmosedici	B	F: Hard/R: Medium	27	45m 24.267s
7	**Aleix Espargaro**	SPA	41	Team SUZUKI ECSTAR	Suzuki GSX-RR	B	F: Medium/R: Soft	27	45m 32.691s
8	**Bradley Smith**	GBR	38	Monster Yamaha Tech 3	Yamaha YZR-M1	B	F: Hard/R: Medium	27	45m 33.542s
9	**Andrea Dovizioso**	ITA	4	Ducati Team	Ducati Desmosedici	B	F: Hard/R: Medium	27	45m 39.179s
10	**Yonny Hernandez**	COL	68	Pramac Racing	Ducati Desmosedici	B	F: Hard/R: Medium	27	45m 48.318s
11	**Maverick Vinales**	SPA	25	Team SUZUKI ECSTAR	Suzuki GSX-RR	B	F: Medium/R: Soft	27	45m 48.920s
12	**Danilo Petrucci**	ITA	9	Pramac Racing	Ducati Desmosedici	B	F: Hard/R: Medium	27	45m 49.667s
13	**Scott Redding**	GBR	45	EG 0,0 Marc VDS	Honda RC213V	B	F: Hard/R: Medium	27	45m 50.298s
14	**Hector Barbera**	SPA	8	Avintia Racing	Ducati Desmosedici Open	B	F: Hard/R: Soft	27	45m 50.446s
15	Alvaro Bautista	SPA	19	Aprilia Racing Team Gresini	Aprilia RS-GP	B	F: Hard/R: Soft	27	45m 54.590s
16	Stefan Bradl	GER	6	Athina Forward Racing	Yamaha Forward	B	F: Hard/R: Medium	27	45m 56.264s
17	Nicky Hayden	USA	69	Aspar MotoGP Team	Honda RC213V-RS	B	F: Hard/R: Soft	27	45m 58.752s
18	Eugene Laverty	IRL	50	Aspar MotoGP Team	Honda RC213V-RS	B	F: Hard/R: Soft	27	46m 00.409s
19	Marco Melandri	ITA	33	Aprilia Racing Team Gresini	Aprilia RS-GP	B	F: Hard/R: Soft	27	46m 04.141s
20	Jack Miller	AUS	43	CWM LCR Honda	Honda RC213V-RS	B	F: Hard/R: Soft	27	46m 11.428s
21	Alex de Angelis	RSM	15	Octo IodaRacing Team	Aprilia ART	B	F: Hard/R: Soft	27	46m 24.078s
22	Mike di Meglio	FRA	63	Avintia Racing	Ducati Desmosedici Open	B	F: Hard/R: Soft	26	45m 28.537s
	Hiroshi Aoyama	JPN	7	Repsol Honda Team	Honda RC213V	B	F: Hard/R: Hard	14	DNF-crash
	Loris Baz	FRA	76	Athina Forward Racing	Yamaha Forward	B	F: Hard/R: Medium	8	DNF-crash
	Karel Abraham	CZE	17	AB Motoracing	Honda RC213V-RS	B	F: Hard/R: Soft	3	DNF-crash

Fastest lap: Jorge Lorenzo, on lap 2, 1m 38.735s, 100.2mph/161.2km/h (record).
Previous lap record: Jorge Lorenzo, SPA (Yamaha), 1m 39.565s, 99.4mph/159.9km/h (2013).
Event best maximum speed: Andrea Iannone, 183.9mph/295.9km/h (race).

Qualifying

Weather: Dry
Air Temp: 31° **Humidity:** 32%
Track Temp: 48°

1	Lorenzo	1m 37.910s
2	Marquez	1m 38.300s
3	Iannone	1m 38.468s
4	P. Espargaro	1m 38.539s
5	Rossi	1m 38.632s
6	A. Espargaro	1m 38.638s
7	Crutchlow	1m 38.714s
8	Dovizioso	1m 38.823s
9	Hernandez	1m 39.464s
10	Smith	1m 39.491s
11	Petrucci	1m 39.789s
12	Redding	1m 39.825s
13	Barbera	1m 39.569s
14	Vinales	1m 39.603s
15	Bautista	1m 39.612s
16	Aoyama	1m 39.866s
17	Laverty	1m 39.974s
18	Hayden	1m 40.025s
19	Bradl	1m 40.166s
20	Abraham	1m 40.177s
21	Baz	1m 40.280s
22	Miller	1m 40.365s
23	Di Meglio	1m 40.817s
24	De Angelis	1m 41.108s
25	Melandri	1m 41.273s

Fastest race laps

1	Lorenzo	1m 38.735s
2	Marquez	1m 38.823s
3	P. Espargaro	1m 39.169s
4	Rossi	1m 39.186s
5	Crutchlow	1m 39.444s
6	A. Espargaro	1m 39.444s
7	Iannone	1m 39.829s
8	Hernandez	1m 39.882s
9	Dovizioso	1m 40.000s
10	Smith	1m 40.139s
11	Petrucci	1m 40.199s
12	Redding	1m 40.317s
13	Bautista	1m 40.548s
14	Vinales	1m 40.638s
15	Bradl	1m 40.714s
16	Miller	1m 40.715s
17	Barbera	1m 40.722s
18	Laverty	1m 40.766s
19	Baz	1m 40.887s
20	Aoyama	1m 40.949s
21	Hayden	1m 41.292s
22	Melandri	1m 41.321s
23	Abraham	1m 41.562s
24	Di Meglio	1m 41.576s
25	De Angelis	1m 41.755s

Championship Points

1	Rossi	82
2	Dovizioso	67
3	Lorenzo	62
4	Marquez	56
5	Iannone	50
6	Crutchlow	47
7	Smith	36
8	A. Espargaro	31
9	P. Espargaro	26
10	Vinales	20
11	Petrucci	19
12	Redding	13
13	Hernandez	12
14	Pedrosa	10
15	Barbera	10
16	Miller	6
17	Aoyama	5
18	Hayden	3
19	Baz	2
20	Bautista	2
21	Bradl	1

Constructor Points

1	Yamaha	91
2	Honda	72
3	Ducati	70
4	Suzuki	31
5	Yamaha Forward	2
6	Aprilia	2

Grid order / Lap chart

Grid order	1	2	3	4	5	6	7	8	9	10	11	12	13	14	15	16	17	18	19	20	21	22	23	24	25	26	27	
99 LORENZO	99	99	99	99	99	99	99	99	99	99	99	99	99	99	99	99	99	99	99	99	99	99	99	99	99	99	99	1
93 MARQUEZ	93	93	93	93	93	93	93	93	93	93	93	93	93	93	93	93	93	93	93	93	93	93	93	93	93	93	93	2
29 IANNONE	44	44	46	46	46	46	46	46	46	46	46	46	46	46	46	46	46	46	46	46	46	46	46	46	46	46	46	3
44 P. ESPARGARO	46	46	44	44	44	44	35	35	35	35	35	35	35	35	35	35	35	35	35	35	35	35	35	35	35	35	35	4
46 ROSSI	41	41	35	35	35	44	44	44	44	44	44	44	44	44	44	44	44	44	44	44	44	44	44	44	44	44	44	5
41 A. ESPARGARO	35	35	41	41	41	41	41	41	41	41	41	41	41	41	29	29	29	29	29	29	29	29	29	29	29	29	29	6
35 CRUTCHLOW	4	38	38	38	38	38	38	29	29	29	29	29	29	29	41	41	41	41	41	41	41	41	41	41	41	41	41	7
4 DOVIZIOSO	38	9	9	29	29	29	38	38	38	38	38	38	38	38	38	38	38	38	38	38	38	38	38	38	38	38	38	8
68 HERNANDEZ	9	68	68	29	9	9	9	9	9	9	9	9	9	9	4	4	4	4	4	4	4	4	4	4	4	4	4	9
38 SMITH	68	29	29	68	68	68	68	68	68	68	68	68	68	68	4	68	68	68	68	9	68	68	68	68	68	68	68	10
9 PETRUCCI	29	44	45	45	45	45	45	45	45	45	45	45	45	68	9	9	9	9	68	9	9	9	25	25				11
45 REDDING	45	8	8	8	8	8	8	25	25	25	25	25	4	25	45	45	25	25	25	25	25	25	9	9				12
8 BARBERA	8	6	6	50	25	25	25	25	25	8	4	4	25	4	25	25	45	45	45	45	45	45	45	45				13
25 VINALES	6	50	50	25	50	50	50	50	4	4	8	8	8	8	8	8	8	8	8	8	8	8	8	8				14
19 BAUTISTA	50	43	25	6	6	6	7	4	50	50	7	7	7	50	50	19	19	19	19	19	19	19	19	19				15
7 AOYAMA	7	25	43	43	7	7	7	7	7	50	50	50	19	19	50	6	6	6	6	6	6	6	6	6				
50 LAVERTY	43	7	19	19	19	19	19	6	19	19	19	19	6	6	6	50	50	50	50	50	50	69	69	69				
69 HAYDEN	25	19	7	7	76	76	4	19	19	6	6	6	69	69	69	69	69	69	69	69	69	50	50	50				
6 BRADL	69	76	76	76	43	4	76	76	43	69	69	69	43	33	33	33	33	33	33	33	33	33	33	33				
17 ABRAHAM	19	69	69	69	4	43	43	43	69	43	43	43	33	43	43	43	43	43	43	43	43	43	43	43				
76 BAZ	76	33	33	33	69	69	69	69	33	33	33	33	15	15	15	15	15	15	15	15	15	15	15	15				
43 MILLER	33	17	17	4	33	33	33	33	15	15	15	15	63	63	63	63	63	63	63	63	63	63						
63 DI MEGLIO	63	63	15	15	15	15	15	63	63	63	63	63																
15 DE ANGELIS	17	15	15	63	63	63	63																					
33 MELANDRI	15	4	4																									

63 Lapped rider

Moto2

RACE DISTANCE: 26 laps, 71.456 miles/114.998km · RACE WEATHER: Dry (air 27°C, humidity 40%, track 32°C)

Pos.	Rider	Nat.	No.	Entrant	Machine	Laps	Time & Speed
1	Jonas Folger	GER	94	AGR Team	Kalex	26	45m 01.873s 95.2mph/ 153.2km/h
2	Johann Zarco	FRA	5	Ajo Motorsport	Kalex	26	45m 03.804s
3	Tito Rabat	SPA	1	EG 0,0 Marc VDS	Kalex	26	45m 04.095s
4	Thomas Luthi	SWI	12	Derendinger Racing Interwetten	Kalex	26	45m 08.706s
5	Xavier Simeon	BEL	19	Federal Oil Gresini Moto2	Kalex	26	45m 12.959s
6	Franco Morbidelli	ITA	21	Italtrans Racing Team	Kalex	26	45m 14.352s
7	Luis Salom	SPA	39	Paginas Amarillas HP 40	Kalex	26	45m 14.838s
8	Simone Corsi	ITA	3	Athina Forward Racing	Kalex	26	45m 16.307s
9	Alex Marquez	SPA	73	EG 0,0 Marc VDS	Kalex	26	45m 19.946s
10	Marcel Schrotter	GER	23	Tech 3	Tech 3	26	45m 23.831s
11	Julian Simon	SPA	60	QMMF Racing Team	Speed Up	26	45m 23.999s
12	Hafizh Syahrin	MAL	55	Petronas Raceline Malaysia	Kalex	26	45m 27.212s
13	Lorenzo Baldassarri	ITA	7	Athina Forward Racing	Kalex	26	45m 28.652s
14	Randy Krummenacher	SWI	4	JIR Racing Team	Kalex	26	45m 29.819s
15	Anthony West	AUS	95	QMMF Racing Team	Speed Up	26	45m 32.746s
16	Dominique Aegerter	SWI	77	Technomag Racing Interwetten	Kalex	26	45m 35.899s
17	Takaaki Nakagami	JPN	30	IDEMITSU Honda Team Asia	Kalex	26	45m 35.978s
18	Alex Rins	SPA	40	Paginas Amarillas HP 40	Kalex	26	45m 37.441s
19	Edgar Pons	SPA	57	Paginas Amarillas HP 40	Kalex	26	45m 39.463s
20	Sam Lowes	GBR	22	Speed Up Racing	Speed Up	26	45m 42.884s
21	Azlan Shah	MAL	25	IDEMITSU Honda Team Asia	Kalex	26	45m 48.492s
22	Thitipong Warokorn	THA	10	APH PTT The Pizza SAG	Kalex	26	45m 49.616s
23	Robin Mulhauser	SWI	70	Technomag Racing Interwetten	Kalex	26	46m 01.724s
24	Florian Alt	GER	66	Octo Iodaracing Team	Suter	26	46m 13.334s
25	Jesko Raffin	SWI	2	sports-millions-EMWE-SAG	Kalex	26	46m 13.386s
26	Zaqhwan Zaidi	MAL	51	JPMoto Malaysia	Suter	26	46m 27.576s
	Mika Kallio	FIN	36	Italtrans Racing Team	Kalex	22	DNF
	Sandro Cortese	GER	11	Dynavolt Intact GP	Kalex	14	DNF
	Ricard Cardus	SPA	88	Tech 3	Tech 3	12	DNF
	Axel Pons	SPA	49	AGR Team	Kalex	5	DNF

Fastest lap: Alex Rins, on lap 3, 1m 43.012s, 96.0mph/154.5km/h.
Lap record: Jonas Folger, GER (Kalex), 1m 42.876s, 96.1mph/154.7km/h (2014).
Event best maximum speed: Luis Salom, 157.1mph/252.8km/h (race).

Qualifying

Weather: Dry
Air: 32° Track: 49°
Humidity: 29%

1	Rabat	1m 42.874s
2	Rins	1m 43.179s
3	Folger	1m 43.201s
4	Luthi	1m 43.259s
5	Nakagami	1m 43.278s
6	Lowes	1m 43.354s
7	Cortese	1m 43.391s
8	Pons	1m 43.401s
9	Zarco	1m 43.436s
10	Simon	1m 43.483s
11	Simeon	1m 43.514s
12	Corsi	1m 43.683s
13	Baldassarri	1m 43.689s
14	Schrotter	1m 43.713s
15	Morbidelli	1m 43.721s
16	Aegerter	1m 43.730s
17	Marquez	1m 43.737s
18	Kallio	1m 43.843s
19	Krummenacher	1m 43.899s
20	Salom	1m 43.916s
21	Syahrin	1m 44.060s
22	Cardus	1m 44.441s
23	Pons	1m 44.459s
24	West	1m 44.466s
25	Shah	1m 44.624s
26	Rossi	1m 44.695s
27	Warokorn	1m 45.299s
28	Mulhauser	1m 45.436s
29	Alt	1m 45.663s
30	Raffin	1m 45.879s
31	Zaidi	1m 46.282s

Fastest race laps

1	Rins	1m 43.012s
2	Rabat	1m 43.115s
3	Zarco	1m 43.117s
4	Luthi	1m 43.151s
5	Folger	1m 43.164s
6	Simeon	1m 43.495s
7	Corsi	1m 43.526s
8	Salom	1m 43.526s
9	Cortese	1m 43.613s
10	Morbidelli	1m 43.617s
11	Marquez	1m 43.656s
12	Schrotter	1m 43.793s
13	Simon	1m 43.928s
14	Syahrin	1m 43.934s
15	Aegerter	1m 43.962s
16	Pons	1m 44.014s
17	Krummenacher	1m 44.082s
18	Baldassarri	1m 44.092s
19	West	1m 44.101s
20	Lowes	1m 44.102s
21	Kallio	1m 44.120s
22	Nakagami	1m 44.496s
23	Cardus	1m 44.503s
24	Pons	1m 44.551s
25	Shah	1m 44.569s
26	Warokorn	1m 44.883s
27	Mulhauser	1m 44.921s
28	Alt	1m 45.585s
29	Raffin	1m 45.817s
30	Zaidi	1m 46.117s

Championship Points

1	Zarco	73
2	Folger	57
3	Rins	49
4	Luthi	43
5	Morbidelli	43
6	Lowes	41
7	Rabat	33
8	Simeon	31
9	Kallio	31
10	Syahrin	24
11	Cortese	20
12	Baldassarri	17
13	Simon	15
14	Salom	14
15	Marquez	14
16	Corsi	13
17	West	12
18	Schrotter	9
19	Nakagami	8
20	Rossi	7
21	Aegerter	4
22	Krummenacher	2

Constructor Points

		Pts
1	Kalex	95
2	Speed Up	49
3	Tech 3	16

Moto3

RACE DISTANCE: 23 laps, 63.211 miles/101.729km · RACE WEATHER: Dry (air 23°C, humidity 53%, track 25°C)

Pos.	Rider	Nat.	No.	Entrant	Machine	Laps	Time & Speed
1	Danny Kent	GBR	52	Leopard Racing	Honda	23	41m 19.552s 91.7mph/ 147.6km/h
2	Miguel Oliveira	POR	44	Red Bull KTM Ajo	KTM	23	41m 19.649s
3	Brad Binder	RSA	41	Red Bull KTM Ajo	KTM	23	41m 19.848s
4	Fabio Quartararo	FRA	20	Estrella Galicia 0,0	Honda	23	41m 20.434s
5	Efren Vazquez	SPA	7	Leopard Racing	Honda	23	41m 22.458s
6	Romano Fenati	ITA	5	SKY Racing Team VR46	KTM	23	41m 30.587s
7	Francesco Bagnaia	ITA	21	MAPFRE Team MAHINDRA	Mahindra	23	41m 30.678s
8	Jorge Navarro	SPA	9	Estrella Galicia 0,0	Honda	23	41m 31.313s
9	Enea Bastianini	ITA	33	Gresini Racing Team Moto3	Honda	23	41m 35.413s
10	John McPhee	GBR	17	SAXOPRINT RTG	Honda	23	41m 35.516s
11	Isaac Vinales	SPA	32	Husqvarna Factory Laglisse	Husqvarna	23	41m 35.567s
12	Jules Danilo	FRA	95	Ongetta-Rivacold	Honda	23	41m 35.599s
13	Livio Loi	BEL	11	RW Racing GP	Honda	23	41m 38.352s
14	Jorge Martin	SPA	88	MAPFRE Team MAHINDRA	Mahindra	23	41m 44.144s
15	Alexis Masbou	FRA	10	SAXOPRINT RTG	Honda	23	41m 44.255s
16	Andrea Locatelli	ITA	55	Gresini Racing Team Moto3	Honda	23	41m 45.537s
17	Niklas Ajo	FIN	31	RBA Racing Team	KTM	23	41m 55.347s
18	Matteo Ferrari	ITA	11	San Carlo Team Italia	Mahindra	23	41m 55.500s
19	Stefano Manzi	ITA	29	San Carlo Team Italia	Mahindra	23	41m 55.915s
20	Juanfran Guevara	SPA	58	MAPFRE Team MAHINDRA	Mahindra	23	41m 56.050s
21	Andrea Migno	ITA	16	SKY Racing Team VR46	KTM	23	41m 56.084s
22	Karel Hanika	CZE	98	Red Bull KTM Ajo	KTM	23	41m 56.573s
23	Tatsuki Suzuki	JPN	24	CIP	Mahindra	23	41m 56.727s
24	Darryn Binder	RSA	40	Outox Reset Drink Team	Mahindra	23	41m 56.870s
25	Remy Gardner	AUS	2	CIP	Mahindra	23	42m 00.494s
26	Zulfahmi Khairuddin	MAL	63	Drive M7 SIC	KTM	23	42m 13.144s
27	Ana Carrasco	SPA	22	RBA Racing Team	KTM	23	42m 29.099s
	Philipp Oettl	GER	65	Schedl GP Racing	KTM	20	DNF
	Jakub Kornfeil	CZE	84	Drive M7 SIC	KTM	15	DNF
	Hiroki Ono	JPN	76	Leopard Racing	Honda	12	DNF
	Alessandro Tonucci	ITA	19	Outox Reset Drink Team	Mahindra	7	DNF
	Niccolo Antonelli	ITA	23	Ongetta-Rivacold	Honda	4	DNF
	Gabriel Rodrigo	ARG	91	RBA Racing Team	KTM	3	DNF
	Maria Herrera	SPA	6	Husqvarna Factory Laglisse	Husqvarna	0	DNF

Fastest lap: Brad Binder, on lap 10, 1m 46.723s, 92.6mph/149.1km/h (record).
Previous lap record: Luis Salom, SPA (KTM), 1m 46.948s, 92.5mph/148.8km/h. (2013).
Event best maximum speed: Hiroki Ono, 135.5mph/218.1km/h (race).

Qualifying:

Weather: Dry
Air: 30° Track: 44°
Humidity: 36%

1	Quartararo	1m 46.791s
2	Kent	1m 46.911s
3	Oliveira	1m 46.984s
4	Binder	1m 47.180s
5	Oettl	1m 47.194s
6	Hanika	1m 47.198s
7	Bastianini	1m 47.251s
8	Fenati	1m 47.355s
9	Antonelli	1m 47.394s
10	Navarro	1m 47.400s
11	Masbou	1m 47.477s
12	Kornfeil	1m 47.528s
13	Vinales	1m 47.574s
14	Ono	1m 47.657s
15	Martin	1m 47.689s
16	Bagnaia	1m 47.704s
17	Vazquez	1m 47.709s
18	Guevara	1m 47.773s
19	Ajo	1m 47.794s
20	Ferrari	1m 47.857s
21	Danilo	1m 47.889s
22	Loi	1m 47.941s
23	Locatelli	1m 47.962s
24	Herrera	1m 48.046s
25	McPhee	1m 48.142s
26	Gardner	1m 48.142s
27	Migno	1m 48.155s
28	Binder	1m 48.224s
29	Suzuki	1m 48.357s
30	Khairuddin	1m 48.725s
31	Tonucci	1m 48.925s
32	Rodrigo	1m 49.079s
33	Manzi	1m 49.266s
34	Carrasco	1m 50.045s

Fastest race laps

1	Binder	1m 46.723s
2	Quartararo	1m 46.962s
3	Hanika	1m 46.964s
4	Vazquez	1m 46.972s
5	Bagnaia	1m 47.099s
6	Oliveira	1m 47.102s
7	Kent	1m 47.118s
8	Fenati	1m 47.215s
9	Vinales	1m 47.307s
10	McPhee	1m 47.403s
11	Kornfeil	1m 47.422s
12	Ono	1m 47.434s
13	Navarro	1m 47.458s
14	Masbou	1m 47.503s
15	Danilo	1m 47.543s
16	Bastianini	1m 47.612s
17	Locatelli	1m 47.625s
18	Oettl	1m 47.627s
19	Ajo	1m 47.659s
20	Loi	1m 47.682s
21	Antonelli	1m 47.733s
22	Martin	1m 47.748s
23	Binder	1m 47.972s
24	Migno	1m 48.094s
25	Ferrari	1m 48.095s
26	Guevara	1m 48.166s
27	Manzi	1m 48.207s
28	Suzuki	1m 48.330s
29	Herrera	1m 48.495s
30	Gardner	1m 48.631s
31	Khairuddin	1m 48.775s
32	Carrasco	1m 48.958s
33	Tonucci	1m 49.130s
34	Rodrigo	1m 49.404s

Championship Points

1	Kent	91
2	Vazquez	60
3	Quartararo	52
4	Bastianini	47
5	Binder	44
6	Vinales	38
7	Oliveira	33
8	McPhee	28
9	Masbou	26
10	Fenati	26
11	Bagnaia	21
12	Hanika	18
13	Locatelli	14
14	Navarro	12
15	Antonelli	8
16	Ajo	8
17	Kornfeil	7
18	Loi	7
19	Oettl	5
20	Migno	4
21	Danilo	4
22	Ono	3
23	Martin	3
24	Ferrari	1

Constructor Points

		Pts
1	Honda	100
2	KTM	50
3	Husqvarna	38
4	Mahindra	22

FRENCH GRAND PRIX

LE MANS CIRCUIT

Main: Lorenzo scorches away from the pursuing Ducatis at the start.

Inset, left: The Bugatti circuit was Lorenzo's Land again.
Photos: Gold & Goose

Inset, far left: Lorenzo aloft, Rossi grounded – his title lead shrinking.
Photo: Movistar Yamaha

AFTER the azure skies of Andalucia, and based on bitter experience, everyone came to Le Mans prepared for cold and wet. There was enough of both to throw a spanner in the works for Moto3, but race day especially was mild and balmy. And dry.

The stage was set for a repeat of the omens of the previous fortnight: Lorenzo imperious; Marquez unfortunate. The pressure continued to mount on the defender, as the quirky Bugatti circuit turned on the Honda. For three of the previous four years, Le Mans had favoured the point-and-squirt abilities of the RCV. Now, in another indication of the improvement of Honda's rivals, the track was revealing its weaknesses.

Marquez summed it up, both before and after a race in which he had to ride at least as hard as for any of his 21 class wins so far just to rescue fourth place. "Today I fought more against my bike than my rivals."

While the bike could still do a fast lap, "the problem is to keep the pace, because always we have the same problem. You can see on TV, I am entering corners like a truck, really sliding. With the other bike, I created that slide. Now the problem is the bike creates that slide, and I am trying to avoid it."

Marquez was sticking with a new swing-arm combination tested at Jerez (Crutchlow also), blaming the errant behaviour on the engine – too aggressive both in braking and acceleration. "We are not allowed to touch the engine, so we will have to fix it with electronics," he said.

The other three factory Hondas all succumbed to front-end crashes in the race, though Crutchlow insisted his was for a different reason. It rather spoiled Dani Pedrosa's return. He'd qualified a dogged eighth, but his slither off came early in the race. Happily he was able to remount to complete full race distance – an important and promising early test of his recovery from the last-ditch surgery. He finished six seconds out of the points after rejoining in last place.

Lorenzo's platform was altogether more stable, and both

Yamaha riders looked a little smug as they spoke about their post-Jerez tests. There were only a few details to test, said Rossi, but all were beneficial: more important had been the time to work on improving the base set-up. For Lorenzo, another considered remark: "My bike is … complete." He proved that alright.

Ducati had tested privately at Mugello, with mixed results. Some progress with their still-young machine, but still more to come, said Dovizioso, who thought that heavier tyre wear might still be a consideration.

His team-mate, Iannone, was in a parlous state: he'd crashed twice at the tests, the second time heavily at the fast Arrabbiata Two, dislocating his left shoulder, with less than a week to go before the first practice. He wasn't even sure if he'd be able to make the race. He underestimated his courage. Not only did he run up front, but it was he who made fourth so difficult for Marquez, fighting without remission all the way to the flag.

When he got home, sent back to the doctor by the pain, he discovered that he also had a hairline fracture to the top of his humerus – making his efforts all the more heroic.

A couple of Suzuki gremlins robbed Aleix Espargaro of a chance to do anything similar. He had "the biggest crash of my career" when he high-sided on the fast first run down the hill, lucky to escape with a badly wrenched thumb. This was serious enough to require seven-stitch surgery to the ligaments directly after the race; nothing daunted, he lined up to run anyway, only for his preferred bike to refuse to start. He hurriedly switched to the spare, but pitted after only one full lap, with clutch problems.

He was accompanied to hospital by younger brother Pol, who was the latest to require surgery for arm-pump problems. He'd been struggling, he said, since lap five with a condition that was becoming suddenly more prominent again, with more victims to follow.

Some blamed the grip generated by Bridgestone's tyres, still continuing to improve in the Japanese company's final

year; thus proving the adage that tyres take the blame for everything. If it's not too little grip, it's too much. All the more so at the French track, which has become notorious for left-side cold-tyre slip-offs in morning practice sessions, the track being not just cool, but even a little dew-damp. Bridgestone followed their introduction of an extra-hard in Argentina with an extra-soft at Le Mans: the front was available to all, although the rear was offered only to Open riders.

There had been idle speculation in the past about inverting the qualifying order: putting the fastest at the back of the grid, and Moto3 yielded an interesting experiment in more or less this system. The cause was the weather, when a not altogether unpredictable rain shower swept the circuit just minutes after the qualifying session had begun. Some contributed with unexpectedly poor tactics, in this most strategic of all classes, failing to react fast enough for the narrowing window of opportunity.

The best laps of the session were almost all set on the second full lap; certainly all but two of those of the 28 official qualifiers. Not among them was runaway series leader Danny Kent, nor his Leopard Racing team-mates, Vazquez and Ono; three of six riders outside the 107-per cent qualifying cut-off. They were allowed to start anyway; and with such luminaries at the back, and French *enfant terrible* Quartararo on pole, the field much mixed in between, the scene was set for a race of consuming interest, although ultimately no great surprises.

MOTOGP RACE – 28 laps

Lorenzo's bid for pole had been spoiled, he explained, by a faulty sensor. He had to be content with third, just a tenth off Dovi's Ducati, but six-tenths off a seemingly resurgent Marquez.

Crutchlow headed row two from Iannone and Smith; big guns Rossi and Pedrosa were on the third, joined for the first time by Petrucci.

Marquez was concerned about race pace, but when race day was fine and sunny he could nurture some hopes that his corner entry problems would be less severe in the warmer conditions: track temperature at 32 degrees, against the previous day's 15 in Q2. "We knew conditions would change, but we expected it to be for the better. This time it was for the worse," he said later, as he described a most unfamiliar race-long struggle.

Lorenzo's second masterclass win was sealed in the second corner. Marquez had been punted wide by Iannone in the first, but came back under the Yamaha into the sharp left. "When I saw Marc brake later than me, I thought, he's not going to make the corner." Nor did he. The Honda ran wide on the exit, letting not only Lorenzo, but also both Ducatis through.

Lorenzo was never headed, but could never relax. Dovi's pressure was relentless for the first half of the race; Iannone in turn was pushing on his team-mate.

All the while, Rossi was closing from seventh on the grid, after disposing of Marquez firmly on lap three. It took him another eight to get past Iannone for third. With strong braking and powerful acceleration, the Ducatis were hard to pass at the stop-and-go squirts of the Bugatti circuit.

But the Ducati was only five races old and still under development. Dovizioso: "I think we use a bit too much grip from the tyres, and after ten laps it's hard to keep the pace," he explained. He remained close, but had no answer when Rossi arrived to take over second on lap 13.

Now, before half-distance, the gap to Lorenzo was just under two seconds. The Yamaha pair duelled at this distance for the next six or seven laps, closely matched, if not close together. Then a slip by Rossi gave Jorge another half a second, and by the end Rossi, already beaten by his own poor qualifying, was obliged to accept second.

Dovizioso was a lone third; then came that fantastic battle for fourth.

Above: Marquez, Iannone, Smith. They finished that close, in that order, after a great battle.

Top right: Thomas Luthi celebrates his Moto2 win.

Top far right: Chasing the leaders, Simon leads Nakagami and Simeon.

Above right: Rookie star Quartararo put his Honda on Moto3 pole at home, but fell in the race.

Above far right: Luthi was out on his own ahead of the usual Moto2 favourites.

Right: Moto3 melee: the front three – Fenati, Bastianini and Bagnaia – made the podium. Quartararo, Oliveira, Kent and Antonelli (23) missed out.

Below right: Kent-free zone. For the first time Bastianini, Fenati and Bagnaia edged the title leader off the rostrum.

Photos: Gold & Goose

Marquez was clearly struggling, as he fell under attack from Smith, who had started well, behind Rossi. By lap five, the English rider was ahead and set for a long spell there as Marquez chased along, gradually dropping behind, by almost two seconds at half-distance, a most unfamiliar scenario.

By now, Iannone was tiring and losing touch with the front three. By lap 19, Smith had closed a gap that had been better than five seconds and was on his tail. Marquez was also closing again. The scene was set for a three-way battle to the end, Smith a close-up spectator over the last five laps as Iannone just kept on fighting back. It was everything Marquez could do to lead the trio over the line.

Some way back were a lone Pol Espargaro and an equally solitary Hernandez, eighth his best finish. Then came Vinales, eventually the winner of a late battle with Petrucci. Hayden had dropped away in the closing stages with a minor electronic glitch, but 11th was his best of the season so far and top Open bike.

Baz outpaced Barbera for 12th; Laverty passed Bautista for 14th and his first points. A long casualty list helped the results of these lower runners.

Pedrosa was an early victim of the wayward Honda front, on the exit from the first chicane on lap two, while lying seventh. Bradl fell on the same lap; then Redding had a similar Honda crash, from 15th. Di Meglio was next; then it was Crutchlow's turn, tucking the front on lap nine, also while seventh. It was not, he explained, the same as his fellow Honda riders, though it looked like it. "My foot slipped off the rear brake, so I grabbed the front harder and came down," he said.

Miller suffered the same fate after enjoying a strong battle with Hayden, then dropping back cautiously after "one moment after another", only to lose the front once and for all on lap 15.

Aleix Espargaro, after a last-minute switch, retired his spare bike on the second lap with clutch trouble; Abraham also retired.

MOTO2 RACE – 26 laps

Rins and Lowes set identical pole times, the position going to the rookie because his next-best lap was quicker. Zarco,

basking in home-race euphoria, was alongside; Rabat led row two from a briefly on-form Nakagami and Luthi.

The front positions were soon settled; Rins was not among them, having blown his start. He was swamped into the first corners, to finish the first lap ninth.

By then, Zarco was already building a lead from Lowes and Luthi, with Nakagami dropping to the back as Rabat also joined in. There remained a little sorting out to be done.

Luthi moved straight into second and set about the leader. It took until lap five before he could get ahead for good, and a new lap record on lap six and for Zarco to make a slip on lap seven for the gap to grow to better than a second. From there on, he paced himself steadily, eventually winning by 1.7 seconds.

He credited the win to two days of fruitful testing at Aragon: "It was good to have this feeling from the beginning. In the race, I could push very aggressively from the start. This win was very important for the championship."

By then, there had been a change for second place.

Lowes had gambled on a soft rear tyre, and it hadn't paid off. He ceded third to Rabat on lap four. The champion didn't seem able to quite match the leaders' pace, but that was deceptive. As the race wore on, he started closing up again on Zarco, finally pouncing on lap 18. The Frenchman admitted that he had lost his rhythm: "Perhaps I was a little tense on the bike, thinking of a podium in my home race."

He nearly lost third over the line to Lowes, who had caught up rapidly in the closing stages.

The excitement was all some ten seconds behind, where a gang of six was fully engaged disputing fifth.

Rins seemed to have the best of it, his team-mate Salom displacing Simon from the pursuit on lap 12. Nakagami was with them, and also Simeon, while Kallio dropped to the back, eventually crashing out. Soon after, Folger also left the gaggle in a cloud of dust. Meanwhile, Morbidelli had joined up and was picking his way through, piling on the pressure.

On lap 20, he was past Salom, next time around Rins as well, and battle was truly joined as the Italian staved off the Spanish team-mates. Rins tried again through turn one as they started lap 24; Morbidelli pushed back inside; then Rins lost the front into the next left – his second successive race crash.

Salom would not last much longer. On the next lap, he took the inside line at the Museum left-hander, but Morbidelli slammed the door, Salom hit his back end and was out, in a state of high dudgeon.

Now Simon briefly got ahead of Morbidelli, but the feisty Italian was in front again over the line by a couple of tenths; then came Nakagami and Simeon, still right up close.

Syahrin held off Aegerter for ninth; West made his way steadily to finally prevail over a four-strong battle for 11th.

Marquez and Louis Rossi also crashed out. Rins remounted for 17th; Luthi took over second overall, but Zarco's title lead was bigger again.

MOTO3 RACE – 24 laps

The grid muddle guaranteed high drama. It was Quartararo's second straight pole, but first time up front for Navarro and Bagnaia; Bastianini was down in 18th, Brad Binder 25th; the top two in the championship, Kent and Vazquez, racing under special sanction, started 31st and 29th.

Vazquez and Binder would not survive the first three corners: the latter was taken out (along with Gardner) by Rodrigo's sliding KTM; Vazquez was tagged a few yards later.

Up front, the usual tooth-and-nail. Antonelli led away, Bagnaia and Fenati pushing hard, Quartararo and Kornfeil in close attendance. Oliveira soon tagged on, and Bastianini charged through to fourth after only five laps.

Fenati led over the line for the first time on lap four and stayed there under furious pressure, Bastianini second for a spell up to half-distance; then Quartararo took his turn.

With six laps left, Quartararo crashed out, giving the four leaders a chance to escape. By now, the amazing Kent had joined them. His progress from 31st had been steady and relentless, but he admitted he had used up his tyres. If he could have started up front, "I think I would have had the pace to escape again," he said.

Bagnaia timed his attack to lead on to the last lap, but it was really anybody's race; and Fenati led over the line, by inches, from Bastianini, Bagnaia and Kent. It was the first all-Italian podium since 2004.

Antonelli got back to lead the next group from Kornfeil and late arrival Vinales, while Oliveira had lost touch by the finish.

LE MANS – BUGATTI
28 laps
Length: 4.185 km / 2.600 miles
Width: 13m

Garage Vert 80/50
288/179
Chemin aux Boeufs 108/67
La Chappelle 118/73
Le Musée 96/60
"S" du Garage Bleu 160/99
Chicane Dunlop 137/85
Courbe Dunlop 266/166
145/90
Raccordement 90/56

Key
96/60 kph/mph
Gear

MONSTER ENERGY
GRAND PRIX DE FRANCE
15–17 MAY, 2015

MotoGP

RACE DISTANCE: 28 laps, 72.812 miles/117.180km · RACE WEATHER: Dry (air 18°C, humidity 45%, track 32°C)

Pos.	Rider	Nat.	No.	Entrant	Machine	Tyres	Race tyre choice	Laps	Time & speed
1	**Jorge Lorenzo**	SPA	99	Movistar Yamaha MotoGP	Yamaha YZR-M1	B	F: Soft/R: Soft	28	43m 44.143s 99.9mph/ 160.7km/h
2	**Valentino Rossi**	ITA	46	Movistar Yamaha MotoGP	Yamaha YZR-M1	B	F: Soft/R: Soft	28	43m 47.963s
3	**Andrea Dovizioso**	ITA	4	Ducati Team	Ducati Desmosedici	B	F: Soft/R: Soft	28	43m 56.523s
4	**Marc Marquez**	SPA	93	Repsol Honda Team	Honda RC213V	B	F: Soft/R: Soft	28	44m 04.033s
5	**Andrea Iannone**	ITA	29	Ducati Team	Ducati Desmosedici	B	F: Soft/R: Soft	28	44m 04.380s
6	**Bradley Smith**	GBR	38	Monster Yamaha Tech 3	Yamaha YZR-M1	B	F: Soft/R: Soft	28	44m 05.288s
7	**Pol Espargaro**	SPA	44	Monster Yamaha Tech 3	Yamaha YZR-M1	B	F: Soft/R: Soft	28	44m 19.636s
8	**Yonny Hernandez**	COL	68	Pramac Racing	Ducati Desmosedici	B	F: Soft/R: Soft	28	44m 23.744s
9	**Maverick Vinales**	SPA	25	Team SUZUKI ECSTAR	Suzuki GSX-RR	B	F: Soft/R: Soft	28	44m 25.714s
10	**Danilo Petrucci**	ITA	9	Pramac Racing	Ducati Desmosedici	B	F: Soft/R: Soft	28	44m 26.932s
11	**Nicky Hayden**	USA	69	Aspar MotoGP Team	Honda RC213V-RS	B	F: Soft/R: Extra-Soft	28	44m 37.779s
12	**Loris Baz**	FRA	76	Athina Forward Racing	Yamaha Forward	B	F: Soft/R: Extra-Soft	28	44m 44.760s
13	**Hector Barbera**	SPA	8	Avintia Racing	Ducati Desmosedici Open	B	F: Soft/R: Soft	28	44m 48.415s
14	**Eugene Laverty**	IRL	50	Aspar MotoGP Team	Honda RC213V-RS	B	F: Soft/R: Extra-Soft	28	44m 49.402s
15	**Alvaro Bautista**	SPA	19	Aprilia Racing Team Gresini	Aprilia RS-GP	B	F: Soft/R: Extra-Soft	28	44m 49.658s
16	Dani Pedrosa	SPA	26	Repsol Honda Team	Honda RC213V	B	F: Soft/R: Soft	28	45m 05.050s
17	Alex de Angelis	RSM	15	Octo IodaRacing Team	Aprilia ART	B	F: Soft/R: Extra-Soft	28	45m 05.806s
18	Marco Melandri	ITA	33	Aprilia Racing Team Gresini	Aprilia RS-GP	B	F: Soft/R: Extra-Soft	27	44m 22.904s
	Jack Miller	AUS	43	CWM LCR Honda	Honda RC213V-RS	B	F: Soft/R: Extra-Soft	14	DNF-crash
	Karel Abraham	CZE	17	AB Motoracing	Honda RC213V-RS	B	F: Soft/R: Soft	14	DNF-mechanical
	Cal Crutchlow	GBR	35	CWM LCR Honda	Honda RC213V	B	F: Soft/R: Soft	7	DNF-crash
	Scott Redding	GBR	45	EG 0,0 Marc VDS	Honda RC213V	B	F: Soft/R: Soft	3	DNF-crash
	Mike di Meglio	FRA	63	Avintia Racing	Ducati Desmosedici Open	B	F: Soft/R: Soft	3	DNF-crash
	Aleix Espargaro	SPA	41	Team SUZUKI ECSTAR	Suzuki GSX-RR	B	F: Soft/R: Soft	2	DNF-mechanical
	Stefan Bradl	GER	6	Athina Forward Racing	Yamaha Forward	B	F: Soft/R: Soft	1	DNF-crash

Fastest lap: Valentino Rossi, on lap 4, 1m 32.879s, 100.8mph/162.2km/h (record).

Previous lap record: Marc Marquez, SPA (Honda), 1m 33.548s, 100.0mph/161km/h (2014).

Event best maximum speed: Andrea Iannone, 196.7mph/316.6km/h (free practice).

Qualifying

Weather: Dry
Air Temp: 15° **Track Temp:** 17°
Humidity: 90%

1	Marquez	1m 32.246s
2	Dovizioso	1m 32.749s
3	Lorenzo	1m 32.846s
4	Crutchlow	1m 32.897s
5	Iannone	1m 33.001s
6	Smith	1m 33.299s
7	Rossi	1m 33.352s
8	Pedrosa	1m 33.419s
9	Petrucci	1m 33.556s
10	A. Espargaro	1m 33.665s
11	Hernandez	1m 33.714s
12	P. Espargaro	1m 33.724s
13	Vinales	1m 34.245s
14	Hayden	1m 34.267s
15	Redding	1m 34.551s
16	Bradl	1m 34.575s
17	Di Meglio	1m 34.833s
18	Miller	1m 34.858s
19	Barbera	1m 34.870s
20	Abraham	1m 34.940s
21	Laverty	1m 34.947s
22	Baz	1m 35.456s
23	Bautista	1m 35.458s
24	De Angelis	1m 35.680s
25	Melandri	1m 37.522s

Fastest race laps

1	Rossi	1m 32.879s
2	Lorenzo	1m 33.004s
3	Iannone	1m 33.035s
4	Dovizioso	1m 33.039s
5	Marquez	1m 33.310s
6	Smith	1m 33.559s
7	Crutchlow	1m 33.585s
8	P. Espargaro	1m 33.940s
9	Pedrosa	1m 34.083s
10	Redding	1m 34.226s
11	Hayden	1m 34.418s
12	Hernandez	1m 34.427s
13	Vinales	1m 34.477s
14	Petrucci	1m 34.495s
15	Miller	1m 34.503s
16	Barbera	1m 34.768s
17	Bautista	1m 34.863s
18	Baz	1m 34.936s
19	Laverty	1m 35.219s
20	De Angelis	1m 35.595s
21	Abraham	1m 35.756s
22	Di Meglio	1m 35.876s
23	Melandri	1m 36.986s

Championship Points

1	Rossi	102
2	Lorenzo	87
3	Dovizioso	83
4	Marquez	69
5	Iannone	61
6	Crutchlow	47
7	Smith	46
8	P. Espargaro	35
9	A. Espargaro	31
10	Vinales	27
11	Petrucci	25
12	Hernandez	20
13	Redding	13
14	Barbera	13
15	Pedrosa	10
16	Hayden	8
17	Baz	6
18	Miller	6
19	Aoyama	5
20	Bautista	3
21	Laverty	2
22	Bradl	1

Constructor Points

1	Yamaha	116
2	Ducati	86
3	Honda	85
4	Suzuki	38
5	Yamaha Forward	6
6	Aprilia	3

Grid order	1	2	3	4	5	6	7	8	9	10	11	12	13	14	15	16	17	18	19	20	21	22	23	24	25	26	27	28	
93 MARQUEZ	99	99	99	99	99	99	99	99	99	99	99	99	99	99	99	99	99	99	99	99	99	99	99	99	99	99	99	99	1
4 DOVIZIOSO	4	4	4	4	4	4	4	4	4	4	4	46	46	46	46	46	46	46	46	46	46	46	46	46	46	46	46	46	2
99 LORENZO	29	29	29	29	29	29	29	29	29	29	46	46	4	4	4	4	4	4	4	4	4	4	4	4	4	4	4	4	3
35 CRUTCHLOW	93	93	46	46	46	46	46	46	46	46	29	29	29	29	29	29	29	29	29	29	29	93	93	93	93	93	93	93	4
29 IANNONE	46	46	93	93	38	38	38	38	38	38	38	38	38	38	38	38	38	38	38	38	38	29	29	29	29	29	29	29	5
38 SMITH	38	38	38	38	93	93	93	93	93	93	93	93	93	93	93	93	93	93	93	93	93	38	38	38	38	38	38	38	6
46 ROSSI	26	35	35	35	35	35	35	44	44	44	44	44	44	44	44	44	44	44	44	44	44	44	44	44	44	44	44	44	7
26 PEDROSA	35	44	44	44	44	44	44	68	68	68	68	68	68	68	68	68	68	68	68	68	68	68	68	68	68	68	68	68	8
9 PETRUCCI	44	68	68	68	68	68	68	9	9	9	9	9	9	9	9	9	9	9	9	9	9	9	9	9	9	25	25	25	9
41 A. ESPARGARO	68	9	9	9	9	9	9	69	69	69	69	69	69	69	69	69	25	25	25	25	25	25	25	25	25	9	9	9	10
68 HERNANDEZ	9	69	69	69	69	69	69	43	43	43	43	25	25	25	25	25	69	69	69	69	69	69	69	69	69	69	69	69	11
44 P. ESPARGARO	41	43	43	43	43	43	43	25	25	25	25	43	43	43	76	76	76	76	76	76	76	76	76	76	76	76	76	76	12
25 VINALES	6	25	25	25	25	25	25	76	76	76	76	76	76	76	8	8	8	8	8	8	8	8	8	8	8	8	8	8	13
69 HAYDEN	69	76	45	76	76	76	76	19	19	19	19	8	8	8	19	19	19	50	50	50	50	50	50	50	50	50	50	50	14
45 REDDING	43	45	76	19	19	19	19	8	8	8	8	19	19	19	50	50	50	19	19	19	19	19	19	19	19	19	19	19	15
6 BRADL	25	19	19	50	8	8	8	50	50	50	50	50	50	50	15	15	15	15	15	15	15	15	15	15	15	15	26		
63 DI MEGLIO	76	63	15	8	50	50	50	15	15	15	15	15	15	15	33	33	26	26	26	26	26	26	26	26	26	26	15		
43 MILLER	45	15	50	15	15	15	15	17	17	17	17	17	17	17	26	26	33	33	33	33	33	33	33	33	33	33			
8 BARBERA	19	50	8	17	17	17	17	33	33	33	33	33	33	33															
17 ABRAHAM	15	17	17	33	33	33	33	26	26	26	26	26	26																
50 LAVERTY	63	8	33	26	26	26	26																						
76 BAZ	17	41	63																										
19 BAUTISTA	50	33	26																										
15 DE ANGELIS	33	26																											
33 MELANDRI	8																												

41 Pit stop   33 Lapped rider

Moto2

RACE DISTANCE: 26 laps, 67.611 miles/108.810km · RACE WEATHER: Dry (air 18°C, humidity 45%, track 30°C)

Pos.	Rider	Nat.	No.	Entrant	Machine	Laps	Time & Speed
1	**Thomas Luthi**	SWI	12	Derendinger Racing Interwetten	Kalex	26	42m 27.011s 95.2mph/ 153.2km/h
2	**Tito Rabat**	SPA	1	EG 0,0 Marc VDS	Kalex	26	42m 28.778s
3	**Johann Zarco**	FRA	5	Ajo Motorsport	Kalex	26	42m 30.771s
4	**Sam Lowes**	GBR	22	Speed Up Racing	Speed Up	26	42m 31.087s
5	**Franco Morbidelli**	ITA	21	Italtrans Racing Team	Kalex	26	42m 41.503s
6	**Julian Simon**	SPA	60	QMMF Racing Team	Speed Up	26	42m 41.692s
7	**Takaaki Nakagami**	JPN	30	IDEMITSU Honda Team Asia	Kalex	26	42m 41.856s
8	**Xavier Simeon**	BEL	19	Federal Oil Gresini Moto2	Kalex	26	42m 42.146s
9	**Hafizh Syahrin**	MAL	55	Petronas Raceline Malaysia	Kalex	26	42m 46.254s
10	**Dominique Aegerter**	SWI	77	Technomag Racing Interwetten	Kalex	26	42m 46.542s
11	**Anthony West**	AUS	95	QMMF Racing Team	Speed Up	26	42m 56.489s
12	**Randy Krummenacher**	SWI	4	JIR Racing Team	Kalex	26	42m 56.657s
13	**Marcel Schrotter**	GER	23	Tech 3	Tech 3	26	42m 57.231s
14	**Sandro Cortese**	GER	11	Dynavolt Intact GP	Kalex	26	42m 57.702s
15	**Axel Pons**	SPA	49	AGR Team	Kalex	26	43m 00.108s
16	Ricard Cardus	SPA	88	Tech 3	Tech 3	26	43m 00.615s
17	Alex Rins	SPA	40	Paginas Amarillas HP 40	Kalex	26	43m 05.304s
18	Simone Corsi	ITA	3	Athina Forward Racing	Kalex	26	43m 06.012s
19	Azlan Shah	MAL	25	IDEMITSU Honda Team Asia	Kalex	26	43m 10.470s
20	Robin Mulhauser	SWI	70	Technomag Racing Interwetten	Kalex	26	43m 24.753s
21	Lorenzo Baldassarri	ITA	7	Athina Forward Racing	Kalex	26	43m 36.410s
22	Thitipong Warokorn	THA	10	APH PTT The Pizza SAG	Kalex	26	43m 44.258s
23	Florian Alt	GER	66	Octo Iodaracing Team	Suter	26	43m 44.657s
24	Jesko Raffin	SWI	2	sports-millions-EMWE-SAG	Kalex	26	43m 44.848s
25	Zaqhwan Zaidi	MAL	51	JPMoto Malaysia	Suter	26	44m 00.203s
26	Louis Bulle	FRA	20	Promoto Sport	Transfiormers	25	43m 12.052s
	Luis Salom	SPA	39	Paginas Amarillas HP 40	Kalex	24	DNF
	Mika Kallio	FIN	36	Italtrans Racing Team	Kalex	12	DNF
	Jonas Folger	GER	94	AGR Team	Kalex	9	DNF
	Louis Rossi	FRA	96	Tasca Racing Scuderia Moto2	Tech 3	4	DNF
	Alex Marquez	SPA	73	EG 0,0 Marc VDS	Kalex	4	DNF

Fastest lap: Thomas Luthi, on lap 6, 1m 37.281s, 96.2mph/154.8km/h (record).
Previous lap record: Maverick Vinales, SPA (Kalex), 1m 37.882s, 95.6mph/153.9km/h (2014).
Event best maximum speed: Alex Rins, 163.7mph/263.5km/h (qualifying).

Qualifying

Weather: Dry
Air Temp: 17°   Track Temp: 19°
Humidity: 79%

1	Rins	1m 37.114s
2	Lowes	1m 37.114s
3	Zarco	1m 37.222s
4	Rabat	1m 37.329s
5	Nakagami	1m 37.415s
6	Luthi	1m 37.442s
7	Salom	1m 37.641s
8	Simeon	1m 37.645s
9	Simon	1m 37.724s
10	Krummenacher	1m 37.764s
11	Kallio	1m 37.790s
12	Morbidelli	1m 37.900s
13	Syahrin	1m 37.937s
14	Schrotter	1m 37.941s
15	Folger	1m 37.968s
16	Pons	1m 37.969s
17	West	1m 38.065s
18	Cortese	1m 38.152s
19	Aegerter	1m 38.199s
20	Corsi	1m 38.290s
21	Marquez	1m 38.511s
22	Baldassarri	1m 38.512s
23	Rossi	1m 38.721s
24	Shah	1m 38.748s
25	Cardus	1m 38.787s
26	Mulhauser	1m 38.817s
27	Warokorn	1m 39.733s
28	Alt	1m 40.036s
29	Raffin	1m 40.081s
30	Zaidi	1m 40.546s
31	Bulle	1m 41.523s

Fastest race laps

1	Luthi	1m 37.281s
2	Rabat	1m 37.353s
3	Zarco	1m 37.522s
4	Lowes	1m 37.633s
5	Folger	1m 37.702s
6	Simon	1m 37.840s
7	Rins	1m 37.855s
8	Morbidelli	1m 37.867s
9	Salom	1m 37.893s
10	Simeon	1m 37.944s
11	Nakagami	1m 37.966s
12	Corsi	1m 38.020s
13	Aegerter	1m 38.065s
14	Syahrin	1m 38.117s
15	Kallio	1m 38.128s
16	Schrotter	1m 38.205s
17	Cortese	1m 38.207s
18	West	1m 38.276s
19	Krummenacher	1m 38.283s
20	Pons	1m 38.433s
21	Cardus	1m 38.440s
22	Shah	1m 38.578s
23	Baldassarri	1m 38.739s
24	Marquez	1m 38.910s
25	Rossi	1m 39.016s
26	Mulhauser	1m 39.371s
27	Warokorn	1m 39.759s
28	Raffin	1m 39.821s
29	Alt	1m 40.207s
30	Zaidi	1m 40.535s
31	Bulle	1m 42.028s

Championship Points

1	Zarco	89
2	Luthi	68
3	Folger	57
4	Lowes	54
5	Morbidelli	54
6	Rabat	53
7	Rins	49
8	Simeon	39
9	Kallio	31
10	Syahrin	31
11	Simon	25
12	Cortese	22
13	Nakagami	17
14	West	17
15	Baldassarri	17
16	Salom	14
17	Marquez	14
18	Corsi	13
19	Schrotter	12
20	Aegerter	10
21	Rossi	7
22	Krummenacher	6
23	Pons	1

Constructor Points

1	Kalex	120
2	Speed Up	62
3	Tech 3	19

Moto3

RACE DISTANCE: 24 laps, 62.411 miles/100.440km · RACE WEATHER: Dry (air 17°C, humidity 46%, track 24°C)

Pos.	Rider	Nat.	No.	Entrant	Machine	Laps	Time & Speed
1	**Romano Fenati**	ITA	5	SKY Racing Team VR46	KTM	24	41m 22.829s 90.5mph/ 145.6km/h
2	**Enea Bastianini**	ITA	33	Gresini Racing Team Moto3	Honda	24	41m 22.951s
3	**Francesco Bagnaia**	ITA	21	MAPFRE Team MAHINDRA	Mahindra	24	41m 23.286s
4	**Danny Kent**	GBR	52	Leopard Racing	Honda	24	41m 23.522s
5	**Niccolo Antonelli**	ITA	23	Ongetta-Rivacold	Honda	24	41m 25.073s
6	**Jakub Kornfeil**	CZE	84	Drive M7 SIC	KTM	24	41m 25.250s
7	**Isaac Vinales**	SPA	32	Husqvarna Factory Laglisse	Husqvarna	24	41m 25.416s
8	**Miguel Oliveira**	POR	44	Red Bull KTM Ajo	KTM	24	41m 26.894s
9	**Andrea Migno**	ITA	16	SKY Racing Team VR46	KTM	24	41m 37.705s
10	**Philipp Oettl**	GER	65	Schedl GP Racing	KTM	24	41m 45.417s
11	**Hiroki Ono**	JPN	76	Leopard Racing	Honda	24	41m 46.076s
12	**Juanfran Guevara**	SPA	58	MAPFRE Team MAHINDRA	Mahindra	24	41m 49.060s
13	**Livio Loi**	BEL	11	RW Racing GP	Honda	24	41m 49.299s
14	**Zulfahmi Khairuddin**	MAL	63	Drive M7 SIC	KTM	24	41m 49.506s
15	**Stefano Manzi**	ITA	29	San Carlo Team Italia	Mahindra	24	41m 49.670s
16	Andrea Locatelli	ITA	55	Gresini Racing Team Moto3	Honda	24	41m 51.313s
17	John McPhee	GBR	17	SAXOPRINT RTG	Honda	24	41m 56.022s
18	Ana Carrasco	SPA	22	RBA Racing Team	KTM	24	42m 01.808s
19	Maria Herrera	SPA	6	Husqvarna Factory Laglisse	Husqvarna	24	42m 02.279s
20	Karel Hanika	CZE	98	Red Bull KTM Ajo	KTM	24	42m 21.011s
	Jorge Martin	SPA	88	MAPFRE Team MAHINDRA	Mahindra	23	DNF
	Alexis Masbou	FRA	10	SAXOPRINT RTG	Honda	21	DNF
	Niklas Ajo	FIN	31	RBA Racing Team	KTM	21	DNF
	Tatsuki Suzuki	JPN	24	CIP	Mahindra	19	DNF
	Fabio Quartararo	FRA	20	Estrella Galicia 0,0	Honda	17	DNF
	Matteo Ferrari	ITA	12	San Carlo Team Italia	Mahindra	11	DNF
	Jules Danilo	FRA	95	Ongetta-Rivacold	Honda	10	DNF
	Darryn Binder	RSA	40	Outox Reset Drink Team	Mahindra	9	DNF
	Jorge Navarro	SPA	9	Estrella Galicia 0,0	Honda	5	DNF
	Alessandro Tonucci	ITA	19	Outox Reset Drink Team	Mahindra	2	DNF
	Remy Gardner	AUS	2	CIP	Mahindra	0	DNF
	Gabriel Rodrigo	ARG	91	RBA Racing Team	KTM	0	DNF
	Brad Binder	RSA	41	Red Bull KTM Ajo	KTM	0	DNF
	Efren Vazquez	SPA	7	Leopard Racing	Honda	0	DNF

Fastest lap: Enea Bastianini, on lap 3, 1m 42.525s, 91.3mph/146.9km/h (record).
Previous lap record: Francesco Bagnaia, ITA (KTM), 1m 42.636s, 91.2mph/146.7km/h (2014).
Event best maximum speed: Hiroki Ono, 138.4mph/222.7km/h (free practice).

Qualifying

Weather: Wet
Air Temp: 14°   Track Temp: 16°
Humidity: 92%

1	Quartararo	1m 44.763s
2	Navarro	1m 44.885s
3	Bagnaia	1m 45.457s
4	Kornfeil	1m 45.575s
5	Fenati	1m 45.665s
6	Danilo	1m 45.671s
7	Antonelli	1m 45.689s
8	Oliveira	1m 46.011s
9	Vinales	1m 46.234s
10	Suzuki	1m 46.846s
11	Herrera	1m 46.885s
12	Ferrari	1m 46.974s
13	Locatelli	1m 47.019s
14	Manzi	1m 47.027s
15	Guevara	1m 47.037s
16	Migno	1m 47.130s
17	Gardner	1m 47.171s
18	Bastianini	1m 47.220s
19	McPhee	1m 47.225s
20	Ajo	1m 47.556s
21	Tonucci	1m 47.623s
22	Loi	1m 48.004s
23	Rodrigo	1m 48.134s
24	Hanika	1m 48.380s
25	Binder	1m 48.402s
26	Masbou	1m 48.474s
27	Binder	1m 49.631s
28	Carrasco	1m 51.344s
29	Vazquez	1m 52.610s
30	Khairuddin	1m 52.778s
31	Kent	1m 52.819s
32	Ono	1m 53.276s
33	Oettl	1m 54.836s
34	Martin	2m 06.206s

Fastest race laps

1	Bastianini	1m 42.525s
2	Kent	1m 42.554s
3	Quartararo	1m 42.630s
4	Oliveira	1m 42.762s
5	Bagnaia	1m 42.777s
6	Martin	1m 42.792s
7	Oettl	1m 42.822s
8	Kornfeil	1m 42.836s
9	Vinales	1m 42.840s
10	Fenati	1m 42.870s
11	Antonelli	1m 42.872s
12	Migno	1m 42.893s
13	Masbou	1m 42.972s
14	Navarro	1m 42.977s
15	Ajo	1m 42.983s
16	Hanika	1m 43.204s
17	Guevara	1m 43.413s
18	Danilo	1m 43.426s
19	Khairuddin	1m 43.427s
20	Ono	1m 43.438s
21	Loi	1m 43.473s
22	Manzi	1m 43.516s
23	Locatelli	1m 43.524s
24	Ferrari	1m 43.586s
25	McPhee	1m 43.595s
26	Binder	1m 43.721s
27	Carrasco	1m 43.855s
28	Herrera	1m 43.885s
29	Suzuki	1m 44.651s
30	Tonucci	1m 45.438s

Championship Points

1	Kent	104
2	Bastianini	67
3	Vazquez	60
4	Quartararo	52
5	Fenati	51
6	Vinales	47
7	Binder	44
8	Oliveira	41
9	Bagnaia	37
10	McPhee	28
11	Masbou	26
12	Antonelli	19
13	Hanika	18
14	Kornfeil	17
15	Locatelli	14
16	Navarro	12
17	Migno	11
18	Oettl	11
19	Loi	10
20	Ajo	8
21	Ono	8
22	Guevara	4
23	Danilo	4
24	Martin	3
25	Khairuddin	2
26	Manzi	1
27	Ferrari	1

Constructor Points

1	Honda	120
2	KTM	75
3	Husqvarna	47
4	Mahindra	38

ITALIAN GRAND PRIX

MUGELLO CIRCUIT

Main: Another Lorenzo masterclass – but his pupils couldn't keep up.

Inset, above: Lorenzo and his Yamaha crew celebrate.

Inset, above right: Faithful fans and Rossi's continuing podium full house gave him reasons to be cheerful.

Photos: Gold & Goose

Inset, above: Iannone looks shocked after beating Rossi.

Inset, above left: The Red Sea – Ducati grandstand rivalled Rossi's yellow host on the opposite hillside.

Photos: Gold & Goose

W ITH the first third of the season coming to an end in front of 90,500 avid Italian fans, the theme remained unchanged, as Marquez took two more steps into the darkness, and Lorenzo another stride forward, after a third dominant race in succession.

As always, problems make better reading than smooth perfection, giving Marquez the lion's share of the ink. He almost drowned in it.

He had opined that long and fast Mugello would be kinder to his RCV than Le Mans where, with the short gearbox dictated by the low average speed, "the bike would wheelie all the time. Here the gearing is longer." But the following days would prove that he and Honda were still far from a solution. Although with the leaders on Friday, when the pace hotted up on Saturday, he missed the top ten for the first time, obliging him to run through Q1 with the lesser lights. It became worse. He had set second time (behind Aleix Espargaro) and was waiting powerless in his pit as Yonny Hernandez put in a late flier on the Pramac Ducati, consigning him to 13th on the grid.

The scene was set for a blazing first lap, and Marquez duly obliged, gaining six places by the entry to the first corner, and another by the exit. But he could do nothing to stop Lorenzo clearing off, and he was having trouble in the battle for second when he lost the front and slipped off, his second race crash of the year. Would the monkey never get off his back?

Mugello is a special track for a number of reasons, ranging from the strong Rossi flavour and the Ducati factions to the old-school fast layout; and the long (nearly) straight regained its place as the fastest on the calendar, with Iannone's Ducati GP15 enjoying a mild tailwind in free practice to clock 350.8km/h – all but 218mph. This just shaded the new record set at Qatar earlier in the year by Marquez's Honda, at 350.5.

Ducati took the top three speed-trap figures at Mugello, with Barbera's GP14 and wild-card Michele Pirro's GP15 both faster than 350km/h. Pedrosa's Honda was next, at 349.6. By comparison, Aleix Espargaro's Suzuki was second to last, with only de Angelis's ART slower. The factory Suzuki recorded a best of 337.0km/h. Espargaro still managed to qualify fifth, which spoke volumes about the bike's handling, and his own riding.

The straight is followed (over a daunting blind rise) by the tight San Donato corner, with speeds dropping from around 350km/h to just 124, according to Brembo's data, defining a stopping distance of 321m over 6.1 seconds, during which the rider must apply 5.7kg pressure to the lever, and withstand 1.6G. But who was the last of the late brakers? Brembo culled team telemetry data from each qualifying session to find out and came up with the following roll of honour: *1, Dovizioso; 2, Rossi; 3, Iannone; 4, Lorenzo; 5, Marquez.*

Mugello is special also as the fancy-dress GP, a trend possibly not started by Rossi, but certainly carried forward by him: once again, his outfit was the winner – a chrome-plated mirror-finish helmet "to reflect the fans at Mugello", along with an energy-saving theme, with painted-on solar panels and a colour-coded set of 'energy bars'. Many other riders (including Iannone, Dovizioso and several in the smaller classes) adopted home-race themes, but Rossi's VR46-Sky Moto3 team stole a march on them, too. Romano Fenati and his bike were mobile Tricolore flags: green on the right, white over the centre, red on the left.

The usual sea of Rossi yellow dominated the top of the first hillside; a swathe of red later on the lap on the Ducati grandstand, at the Correntaio right-hander. And an even redder face for Desmo Dovi, who waved at the fans there on his out-lap in morning warm-up, only to crash on the exit, blaming cold tyres.

There was more colour trackside – paved sections replacing Astroturf on the outside of several corners, a safety modification, were painted no-go red, warning riders off except in dire emergency, since they could be used to offer a faster

exit. Many were tempted anyway, leading to an unprecedented number of cancelled laps in practice.

Aprilia resisted the temptation to dress up at their first home GP as a Factory team, having more pressing image problems to solve. Like performance. The RS-GP had started out as little more than a glorified CRT bike, still firmly based on a production model; though race chief Romano Albesiano preferred to call it "a lab bike", aimed at developing a credible 2016 challenger after he had brought them into MotoGP a year earlier than originally planned. Already equipped with pneumatic valve springs, it now acquired (*inter alia*) a seamless-shift gearbox. The upgrades helped Bautista to a fourth scoring finish, 14th his best so far. Melandri remained in the doldrums, however; his greater problem was with handling and feel. An expected chassis redesign could not come soon enough for him, while rumours of his imminent dismissal abounded in the Italian press. In three races, these would come true.

Iannone was a hero again, a career-best pole and second place coming in spite of having discovered a hairline fracture in his left humerus, an undiagnosed addition to his still painful shoulder injury.

Other injury news: both Espargaro brothers were fresh out of hospital, Aleix for his injured thumb (seven stitches) and Pol after surgery to tackle arm-pump problems; Pedrosa was still in recovery from the same process. The newest victims of the syndrome were Open points leader Barbera, who suffered in the race, and Moto2 rookie star Rins, both under the knife directly. Also hurt, twice, Cal Crutchlow, whose minor scuffs from a fall in practice paled into insignificance when he dislocated his ankle in the race.

Moto3 brought a second straight win for KTM – the first for Oliveira, and for a Portuguese rider in any class. It was a comfort for those being regularly trounced by the Hondas, compensating for the non-arrival of the promised new chassis. Early tests had been promising, but then it had run out of steam.

Danny Kent was right in the mix of the photo-finish end of the smallest class. He added another statistic after claiming pole for the second time: with Sam Lowes also on pole in Moto2, it was the first time two Britons had done so since 1977. That was at Anderstorp in Sweden, where Mick Grant had taken pole on his Kawasaki in the 250 class, and Barry Sheene (Suzuki) in the 500s. Both went on to win their races, a feat not repeated in 2015.

MOTOGP RACE – 23 laps

At their own test track, the Ducatis looked menacing: Iannone took his first pole by a tenth from Lorenzo; Dovizioso was third fastest. The top Honda was Crutchlow's, heading row two from Aleix Espargaro and wild-card Pirro, on a third Duke. Pedrosa led row three from Rossi and Vinales; Marquez headed the fifth.

Iannone made a blazing start, but Dovi led by the time they came out of the first corner. Then an aggressive Lorenzo took over into Arrabbiata One, never to be headed again.

There was even more aggression from Marquez, who jetted off the line and dived inside the pack into turn one. By the end of lap three, he was past the Ducatis and in second place, setting a new record in the process and pushing Lorenzo hard for one more lap. But by the fifth, Lorenzo was almost a second clear, and next time almost two seconds. The gap kept on stretching,

Marquez had no answer to his metronomic speed, and – with Dovizioso regaining second – he was soon having serious problems with his companions. One of those was his team-mate. Pedrosa had recovered well from eighth on lap one, and by the fourth had just passed the fast-away Smith for fifth, immediately starting to close on the group ahead.

Rossi was another, though it seemed unlikely at first, after finishing lap one ninth, one lap lower than his grid position, and later complaining of handling problems with a full tank and new tyres. Balancing effort against risk, he passed Pol

Above: **Smith couldn't stay with Pedrosa, but best-so-far fifth continued a run of strong results.**

Top left: Speed **star Keanu Reeves advises Crutchlow not to slow down.**

Above left: **Making progress. Loris Baz was top Open finisher.**

Centre far left: **Don't crash the flag. Fenati rode in Italian Tricolore livery.**

Centre left: **Rossi's chromed helmet was to "reflect the fans at Mugello".**

Left: **Marquez visited the gravel trap once again, for his second non-finish in four races.**

Photos: Gold & Goose

Above: Pramac Ducati team-mates Petrucci and Hernandez ran in convoy, chasing ninth behind factory wild-card Pirro.

Top right: A rare 2015 podium for Aegerter, though he would succumb to the chasing Zarco.

Above right: Reigning Moto2 champion Rabat broke his losing streak.

Right: Oliveira heads Kornfeil, Vazquez and an ever shuffling Moto3 pack. He was the first ever Portuguese GP winner.

Photos: Gold & Goose

Espargaro, Smith and then Crutchlow for sixth on lap nine. The next four, with Pedrosa closing and Lorenzo gone, were almost 2.5 seconds away: "I was very behind."

Dovizioso had problems to come. He had regained second on lap six, but four laps later Iannone and Marquez were ahead again, and he would continue losing places, bound for the pits and retirement after 14 laps with a most unusual problem: his chain was jumping on a rear sprocket that was shedding teeth.

Rossi had been working away at the gap, willed on by the crowd, and as Dovi pitted he had tagged on the back of the quartet disputing second, now led by Iannone, doing a sterling job of fending off Marquez, Pedrosa a close spectator.

There is only so long that even Marquez can survive, riding at the very giddy limit. In this case, it was 17 laps. Halfway around the next, the front tucked on the right-hander exit from the first esses. For a while, it looked like he might effect one of his miraculous saves. Then for a second time in four races, the defender was down and out, with zero points.

"It was a shame about the crash, because I had already done the hardest part," he said. Dark days, with the season one-third done and a 49-point deficit.

Rossi finally found his way past Pedrosa after five laps of effort, and he was lucky not to have become involved in Marquez's crash a little further around the lap. Pedrosa harried for the next three laps, then had to give best.

In all this, Iannone had been steadfastly heading the group since lap ten. Now Rossi was closing – less than a second behind as they started the final tour. But not close enough to unseat his determined younger compatriot.

Some way back, this had left Smith engaged with Crutchlow, riding with a painful and swollen right thumb after a heavy fall in morning warm-up; Pol Espargaro was hanging on behind. Brother Aleix had crashed out on lap three at the first corner, after a bump with Petrucci, later declared blameless by Race Direction.

Crutchlow had finally escaped and was comfortably fifth when, with less than three laps left, his troublesome harder front tyre choice "finally failed me" on the entrance to the high-speed Arrabbiata One corner. His foot was caught in the bike, dislocating his ankle. Marquez, Smith and Hernandez also used the harder front.

Smith had only to fend off a late challenge from team-mate Espargaro to claim a year's best fifth, continuing a run of strong results.

There was a career-best seventh for second Suzuki rider Vinales, after a strong ride in which he caught, hounded and then passed Ducati wild-card Michele Pirro.

Petrucci was ninth, eventually having escaped team-mate Hernandez by a couple of seconds; the pair had outdistanced a still struggling Redding. Baz, Barbera, Bautista and Laverty straggled in for the rest of the points; then came di Meglio, having narrowly held off Abraham, after the latter had served a ride-through penalty for a jump start.

Miller crashed out on lap three; Hayden and Bradl together one lap later. De Angelis was an early retirement.

MOTO2 RACE – 21 laps

Lowes was on pole for a second time in the year; Rabat was on the far end of row one. The surprise, between them, was Dominique Aegerter, who hitherto had struggled with his switch from Suter to Kalex. His Technomag team had found a new setting in practice and "something happened. I felt comfortable, and I was surprised to be second," the Swiss rider said. "I was surprised also to be leading the race."

Lead away he did, though, from Lowes and fellow Suter refugee Luthi.

As they started lap two, Lowes collided with Corsi, who had just taken second, putting the Italian out and dropping out of contention to ninth. By the end of the lap, Luthi was ahead and looking set to repeat his commanding win at Le Mans.

It was a short-lived impression, for at the downhill sweeping right near the end of the lap, he slipped off and slid away.

That put Aegerter back in front; fast-starting Simeon was a close second, with Rabat up to third, followed by Folger and title leader Zarco.

Simeon would drop back; Folger crashed out for a second race in a row. And Rabat would take the lead on lap seven; with Zarco also ahead of Aegerter three laps later.

That settled the top-three order, but not without drama. Zarco was seldom more than a second adrift, and by the start of the final lap he had closed to within less than half a second. It was not quite enough, however, to prevent Rabat from taking his first win of the year by three-tenths, and putting his title defence on a sounder footing after a shaky start.

Aegerter, meanwhile, was under strong, but ultimately vain pressure from a recovered Lowes, less than three-tenths down over the line.

Only a couple of seconds behind, Salom finally, if narrowly, prevailed after a long battle with Simeon; Simon had dropped away by the finish in seventh.

Sandro Cortese headed Pons after a long struggle for eighth, erstwhile companion Baldassari a second away in tenth.

Meanwhile, a downbeat top rookie Rins came out on top for 11th from fellow ex-Moto3 rival (and champion) Marquez.

Morbidelli and Kallio crashed out together; Syahrin went down by himself.

Zarco's consolation for defeat was an increased title lead over new second-placer Rabat, as no-score Luthi fell to third.

MOTO3 RACE – 20 laps

Counterpoint to Moto2, the smallest class was a feast of ultra-close multi-marque racing on genuine grand prix bikes, tooth-and-nail tactics and ruthless precision. Seven laps in, the first 16 were still all within 1.5 seconds; at the flag, the top six within less than four-tenths; the next four, still close behind, within six.

It hardly mattered who led over the line each time, since it would all be different by the time they reached the first corner. Kent: "Mugello is very special: you can exit the last corner in first, but at the end of the straight you find yourself back in tenth. So you need to ride very clever."

There were two ways of doing so.

Oliveira chose head down and self-belief, leading more often over the line than anybody – 11 laps in all, including the last six. He started the last with enough margin to stay just clear of any final slipstream attack. The articulate and multi-lingual Portuguese dentistry student won his first grand prix by 0.071 of a second.

Kent went for wait-and-see. He dropped as low as 13th on lap nine, but was back up to tenth three laps later. "I wasn't worried. We were still close, nobody was getting away, and I knew I had the speed to get back," he said.

Quite so, and he was inches short of victory.

Bagnaia had also come on strong in the closing stages and was third out of the last corner, pushed a little wide as Kent came through inside. That was enough for earlier leader Fenati to get his draft and pinch third by three-thousandths, confirmed by a photo-finish.

Bastianini was hardly further behind in fifth, Antonelli almost alongside him.

The next quartet, a second down, were only a little more spaced out: Navarro from Vinales, Masbou and lap-record-setter Brad Binder.

Quartararo crashed out for a second race in succession, as did one-time short-lived leader Hanika, who took Vazquez out of the lead pack on the last lap.

Superlative, while Kent extended his lead yet again, from Bastianini and Fenati.

GRAN PREMIO D'ITALIA TIM

29–31 MAY, 2015

AUTODROMO INTERNAZIONALE DEL MUGELLO

23 laps
Length: 5.245 km / 3,259 miles
Width: 14m

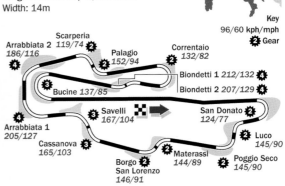

Key
96/60 kph/mph
⚙ Gear

Scarperia
Arrabbiata 2 119/74
186/116
Palagio 152/94
Correntaio 132/82
Biondetti 1 212/132
Biondetti 2 207/129
Bucine 137/85
Savelli 167/104
San Donato 124/77
Arrabbiata 1 205/127
Luco 145/90
Cassanova 165/103
Materassi 144/89
Poggio Seco 145/90
Borgo San Lorenzo 146/91

MotoGP

RACE DISTANCE: 23 laps, 74.959 miles/120.635km · RACE WEATHER: Dry (air 25°C, humidity 48%, track 48°C)

Pos.	Rider	Nat.	No.	Entrant	Machine	Tyres	Race tyre choice	Laps	Time & speed
1	**Jorge Lorenzo**	SPA	99	Movistar Yamaha MotoGP	Yamaha YZR-M1	B	F: Medium/R: Medium	23	41m 39.173s 107.9mph/ 173.7km/h
2	**Andrea Iannone**	ITA	29	Ducati Team	Ducati Desmosedici	B	F: Medium/R: Medium	23	41m 44.736s
3	**Valentino Rossi**	ITA	46	Movistar Yamaha MotoGP	Yamaha YZR-M1	B	F: Medium/R: Medium	23	41m 45.834s
4	**Dani Pedrosa**	SPA	26	Repsol Honda Team	Honda RC213V	B	F: Medium/R: Medium	23	41m 49.151s
5	**Bradley Smith**	GBR	38	Monster Yamaha Tech 3	Yamaha YZR-M1	B	F: Hard/R: Medium	23	41m 54.457s
6	**Pol Espargaro**	SPA	44	Monster Yamaha Tech 3	Yamaha YZR-M1	B	F: Medium/R: Medium	23	41m 54.838s
7	**Maverick Vinales**	SPA	25	Team SUZUKI ECSTAR	Suzuki GSX-RR	B	F: Medium/R: Medium	23	42m 02.978s
8	**Michele Pirro**	ITA	51	Ducati Team	Ducati Desmosedici	B	F: Medium/R: Soft	23	42m 08.325s
9	**Danilo Petrucci**	ITA	9	Octo Pramac Racing	Ducati Desmosedici	B	F: Medium/R: Soft	23	42m 11.181s
10	**Yonny Hernandez**	COL	68	Octo Pramac Racing	Ducati Desmosedici	B	F: Hard/R: Medium	23	42m 13.744s
11	**Scott Redding**	GBR	45	EG 0,0 Marc VDS	Honda RC213V	B	F: Medium/R: Medium	23	42m 17.726s
12	**Loris Baz**	FRA	76	Athina Forward Racing	Yamaha Forward	B	F: Medium/R: Soft	23	42m 21.331s
13	**Hector Barbera**	SPA	8	Avintia Racing	Ducati Desmosedici Open	B	F: Medium/R: Soft	23	42m 23.974s
14	**Alvaro Bautista**	SPA	19	Aprilia Racing Team Gresini	Aprilia RS-GP	B	F: Medium/R: Medium	23	42m 29.608s
15	**Eugene Laverty**	IRL	50	Aspar MotoGP Team	Honda RC213V-RS	B	F: Medium/R: Soft	23	42m 32.233s
16	Mike di Meglio	FRA	63	Avintia Racing	Ducati Desmosedici Open	B	F: Medium/R: Soft	23	42m 54.438s
17	Karel Abraham	CZE	17	AB Motoracing	Honda RC213V-RS	B	F: Medium/R: Soft	23	42m 54.554s
18	Marco Melandri	ITA	33	Aprilia Racing Team Gresini	Aprilia RS-GP	B	F: Medium/R: Soft	23	43m 21.013s
	Cal Crutchlow	GBR	35	CWM LCR Honda	Honda RC213V	B	F: Hard/R: Medium	20	DNF-crash
	Marc Marquez	SPA	93	Repsol Honda Team	Honda RC213V	B	F: Hard/R: Medium	17	DNF-crash
	Andrea Dovizioso	ITA	4	Ducati Team	Ducati Desmosedici	B	F: Medium/R: Medium	13	DNF-mechanical
	Stefan Bradl	GER	6	Athina Forward Racing	Yamaha Forward	B	F: Medium/R: Soft	3	DNF-crash
	Nicky Hayden	USA	69	Aspar MotoGP Team	Honda RC213V-RS	B	F: Medium/R: Soft	3	DNF-crash
	Aleix Espargaro	SPA	41	Team SUZUKI ECSTAR	Suzuki GSX-RR	B	F: Medium/R: Medium	2	DNF-crash
	Jack Miller	AUS	43	CWM LCR Honda	Honda RC213V-RS	B	F: Medium/R: Soft Slick	2	DNF-crash
	Alex de Angelis	RSM	15	E-Motion IodaRacing Team	Aprilia ART	B	F: Medium Slick/R: Soft	2	DNF-mechanical

Fastest lap: Marc Marquez, on lap 3, 1m 47.654s, 108.9mph/175.3km/h.
Lap record: Marc Marquez, SPA (Honda), 1m 47.639s, 109.0mph/175.4km/h (2013).
Event best maximum speed: Andrea Iannone, 218.0h/350.8km/h (free practice – new MotoGP record).

Qualifying

Weather: Dry
Air Temp: 22° **Track Temp:** 41°
Humidity: 51%

1	Iannone	1m 46.489s
2	Lorenzo	1m 46.584s
3	Dovizioso	1m 46.610s
4	Crutchlow	1m 46.657s
5	A. Espargaro	1m 46.854s
6	Pirro	1m 46.870s
7	Pedrosa	1m 46.875s
8	Rossi	1m 46.923s
9	Vinales	1m 46.934s
10	P. Espargaro	1m 47.050s
11	Smith	1m 47.090s
12	Hernandez	1m 47.423s
13	Marquez	1m 47.240s
14	Petrucci	1m 47.497s
15	Barbera	1m 47.978s
16	Bradl	1m 48.047s
17	Redding	1m 48.120s
18	Baz	1m 48.133s
19	Hayden	1m 48.298s
20	Abraham	1m 48.366s
21	Bautista	1m 48.477s
22	Di Meglio	1m 48.503s
23	Miller	1m 48.572s
24	Laverty	1m 48.638s
25	De Angelis	1m 49.198s
26	Melandri	1m 51.391s

Fastest race laps

1	Marquez	1m 47.654s
2	Lorenzo	1m 47.700s
3	Iannone	1m 47.837s
4	Dovizioso	1m 47.905s
5	Pedrosa	1m 48.043s
6	Rossi	1m 48.173s
7	Smith	1m 48.415s
8	Crutchlow	1m 48.620s
9	P. Espargaro	1m 48.698s
10	Pedrosa	1m 48.774s
11	Pirro	1m 49.005s
12	Petrucci	1m 49.077s
13	Hayden	1m 49.117s
14	Redding	1m 49.217s
15	Hernandez	1m 49.256s
16	A. Espargaro	1m 49.330s
17	Bradl	1m 49.379s
18	Baz	1m 49.569s
19	Abraham	1m 49.602s
20	Barbera	1m 49.662s
21	Miller	1m 49.839s
22	Bautista	1m 49.868s
23	Laverty	1m 50.053s
24	Di Meglio	1m 50.525s
25	Melandri	1m 52.063s
26	De Angelis	1m 52.469s

Championship Points

1	Rossi	118
2	Lorenzo	112
3	Dovizioso	83
4	Iannone	81
5	Marquez	69
6	Smith	57
7	Crutchlow	47
8	P. Espargaro	45
9	Vinales	36
10	Petrucci	32
11	A. Espargaro	31
12	Hernandez	26
13	Pedrosa	23
14	Redding	18
15	Barbera	16
16	Baz	10
17	Pirro	8
18	Hayden	8
19	Miller	6
20	Aoyama	5
21	Bautista	5
22	Laverty	3
23	Bradl	1

Constructor Points

1	Yamaha	141
2	Ducati	106
3	Honda	98
4	Suzuki	47
5	Yamaha Forward	10
6	Aprilia	5

Grid order / Lap chart

Grid order		1	2	3	4	5	6	7	8	9	10	11	12	13	14	15	16	17	18	19	20	21	22	23	
29	IANNONE	99	99	99	99	99	99	99	99	99	99	99	99	99	99	99	99	99	99	99	99	99	99	99	1
99	LORENZO	4	4	93	93	93	4	4	4	4	29	29	29	29	29	29	29	29	29	29	29	29	29	29	2
4	DOVIZIOSO	29	93	4	4	4	93	93	93	93	93	93	93	93	93	93	93	93	46	46	46	46	46	46	3
35	CRUTCHLOW	93	29	29	29	29	29	29	29	29	4	4	26	26	26	26	26	26	26	26	26	26	26	26	4
41	A. ESPARGARO	38	38	38	26	26	26	26	26	26	26	26	4	46	46	46	46	46	35	35	35	38	38	38	5
51	PIRRO	44	26	26	38	38	35	35	35	46	46	46	46	4	35	35	35	35	38	38	38	44	44	44	6
26	PEDROSA	35	44	35	35	35	38	46	46	35	35	35	35	35	38	38	38	38	44	44	44	25	25	25	7
46	ROSSI	26	35	44	44	44	46	38	38	38	38	38	38	38	44	44	44	44	25	25	25	51	51	51	8
25	VINALES	46	46	46	46	46	44	44	44	44	44	44	44	44	25	25	25	25	51	51	51	9	9	9	9
44	P. ESPARGARO	41	41	51	51	51	51	51	51	51	51	51	51	25	51	51	51	51	9	9	9	68	68	68	10
38	SMITH	51	51	68	68	25	25	25	25	25	25	25	25	51	68	68	68	68	68	68	68	45	45	45	11
68	HERNANDEZ	25	9	9	25	68	68	68	68	9	9	9	9	68	68	68	68	68	45	45	45	76	76	76	12
93	MARQUEZ	9	68	25	9	9	9	9	9	68	68	68	9	9	45	45	45	45	76	76	76	8	8	8	13
9	PETRUCCI	45	25	6	76	45	45	45	45	45	45	45	45	76	76	76	76	76	8	8	8	19	19	19	14
8	BARBERA	68	6	69	45	76	76	76	76	76	76	76	76	8	8	8	19	19	19	19	19	50	50	50	15
6	BRADL	6	69	76	8	8	8	8	8	8	8	8	8	50	50	50	50	50	50	50	50	63	63	63	
45	REDDING	69	76	45	19	19	19	19	50	50	50	50	50	19	19	19	19	19	63	63	63	17	17	17	
76	BAZ	43	43	8	50	50	50	50	19	19	19	19	19	63	63	63	63	17	17	17	17	33	33	33	
69	HAYDEN	76	45	19	17	17	63	63	63	63	63	63	63	17	17	17	17	33	33	33					
17	ABRAHAM	8	8	50	63	63	33	33	33	33	33	33	17	33	33	33									
19	BAUTISTA	19	19	17	33	33	17	17	17	17	17	17	33												
63	DI MEGLIO	50	50	63																					
43	MILLER	63	63	33																					
50	LAVERTY	17	17																						
15	DE ANGELIS	15	15																						
33	MELANDRI	33	33																						

4 Pit stop   **17** Ride-through penalty

Moto2

RACE DISTANCE: 21 laps, 68.441 miles/110.145km · RACE WEATHER: Dry (air 25°C, humidity 49%, track 46°C)

Pos.	Rider	Nat.	No.	Entrant	Machine	Laps	Time & Speed
1	**Tito Rabat**	SPA	1	EG 0,0 Marc VDS	Kalex	21	39m 40.545s 103.5mph/ 166.5km/h
2	**Johann Zarco**	FRA	5	Ajo Motorsport	Kalex	21	39m 40.853s
3	**Dominique Aegerter**	SWI	77	Technomag Racing Interwetten	Kalex	21	39m 45.825s
4	**Sam Lowes**	GBR	22	Speed Up Racing	Speed Up	21	39m 46.099s
5	**Luis Salom**	SPA	39	Paginas Amarillas HP 40	Kalex	21	39m 48.038s
6	**Xavier Simeon**	BEL	19	Federal Oil Gresini Moto2	Kalex	21	39m 48.441s
7	**Julian Simon**	SPA	60	QMMF Racing Team	Speed Up	21	39m 51.040s
8	**Sandro Cortese**	GER	11	Dynavolt Intact GP	Kalex	21	39m 57.925s
9	**Axel Pons**	SPA	49	AGR Team	Kalex	21	39m 58.320s
10	**Lorenzo Baldassarri**	ITA	7	Athina Forward Racing	Kalex	21	39m 59.381s
11	**Alex Rins**	SPA	40	Paginas Amarillas HP 40	Kalex	21	40m 01.243s
12	**Alex Marquez**	SPA	73	EG 0,0 Marc VDS	Kalex	21	40m 01.468s
13	**Takaaki Nakagami**	JPN	30	IDEMITSU Honda Team Asia	Kalex	21	40m 02.978s
14	**Randy Krummenacher**	SWI	4	JIR Racing Team	Kalex	21	40m 03.307s
15	**Azlan Shah**	MAL	25	IDEMITSU Honda Team Asia	Kalex	21	40m 08.260s
16	Marcel Schrotter	GER	23	Tech 3	Tech 3	21	40m 12.006s
17	Ricard Cardus	SPA	88	Tech 3	Tech 3	21	40m 12.125s
18	Mattia Pasini	ITA	54	Gresini Racing	Kalex	21	40m 13.323s
19	Anthony West	AUS	95	QMMF Racing Team	Speed Up	21	40m 26.572s
20	Louis Rossi	FRA	96	Tasca Racing Scuderia Moto2	Tech 3	21	40m 27.102s
21	Thitipong Warokorn	THA	10	APH PTT The Pizza SAG	Kalex	21	40m 27.474s
22	Robin Mulhauser	SWI	70	Technomag Racing Interwetten	Kalex	21	40m 27.507s
23	Jesko Raffin	SWI	2	sports-millions-EMWE-SAG	Kalex	21	40m 55.546s
24	Florian Alt	GER	66	E-Motion IodaRacing Team	Suter	20	40m 18.022s
	Hafizh Syahrin	MAL	55	Petronas Raceline Malaysia	Kalex	19	DNF
	Jonas Folger	GER	94	AGR Team	Kalex	6	DNF
	Simone Corsi	ITA	3	Athina Forward Racing	Kalex	6	DNF
	Franco Morbidelli	ITA	21	Italtrans Racing Team	Kalex	4	DNF
	Mika Kallio	FIN	36	Italtrans Racing Team	Kalex	4	DNF
	Thomas Luthi	SWI	12	Derendinger Racing Interwetten	Kalex	2	DNF
	Zaqhwan Zaidi	MAL	51	JPMoto Malaysia	Suter	0	DNF

Fastest lap: Tito Rabat, on lap 7, 1m 52.530s, 104.2mph/167.7km/h (record).
Previous lap record: Esteve Rabat, SPA (Kalex), 1m 52.587s, 104.2mph/167.7km/h (2014).
Event best maximum speed: Alex Rins, 180.2mph/290.0km/h (qualifying).

Qualifying

Weather: Dry
Air Temp: 23° **Track Temp:** 42°
Humidity: 50%

1	Lowes	1m 51.514s
2	Aegerter	1m 51.856s
3	Rabat	1m 51.874s
4	Luthi	1m 51.879s
5	Salom	1m 52.120s
6	Zarco	1m 52.140s
7	Corsi	1m 52.144s
8	Simeon	1m 52.155s
9	Rins	1m 52.240s
10	Pons	1m 52.327s
11	Cortese	1m 52.331s
12	Simon	1m 52.472s
13	Folger	1m 52.480s
14	Syahrin	1m 52.510s
15	Marquez	1m 52.536s
16	Baldassarri	1m 52.709s
17	Nakagami	1m 52.807s
18	Pasini	1m 52.845s
19	Schrotter	1m 52.880s
20	Krummenacher	1m 52.927s
21	Morbidelli	1m 53.024s
22	Cardus	1m 53.279s
23	Kallio	1m 53.333s
24	Shah	1m 53.552s
25	Mulhauser	1m 53.867s
26	Rossi	1m 53.975s
27	Alt	1m 54.662s
28	Zaidi	1m 54.807s
29	Raffin	1m 54.844s
30	West	1m 54.989s
31	Warokorn	1m 55.069s

Fastest race laps

1	Rabat	1m 52.530s
2	Salom	1m 52.619s
3	Folger	1m 52.671s
4	Zarco	1m 52.685s
5	Aegerter	1m 52.848s
6	Lowes	1m 52.860s
7	Simeon	1m 52.934s
8	Baldassarri	1m 52.994s
9	Simon	1m 53.063s
10	Luthi	1m 53.065s
11	Cortese	1m 53.218s
12	Morbidelli	1m 53.264s
13	Shah	1m 53.284s
14	Pons	1m 53.318s
15	Marquez	1m 53.349s
16	Kallio	1m 53.432s
17	Rins	1m 53.492s
18	Krummenacher	1m 53.516s
19	Syahrin	1m 53.599s
20	Nakagami	1m 53.683s
21	Schrotter	1m 53.828s
22	Cardus	1m 53.900s
23	Pasini	1m 53.902s
24	Corsi	1m 53.976s
25	West	1m 54.245s
26	Rossi	1m 54.572s
27	Warokorn	1m 54.579s
28	Mulhauser	1m 54.615s
29	Raffin	1m 55.652s
30	Alt	1m 56.121s

Championship Points

1	Zarco	109
2	Rabat	78
3	Luthi	68
4	Lowes	67
5	Folger	57
6	Rins	54
7	Morbidelli	54
8	Simeon	49
9	Simon	34
10	Kallio	31
11	Syahrin	31
12	Cortese	30
13	Aegerter	26
14	Salom	25
15	Baldassarri	23
16	Nakagami	20
17	Marquez	18
18	West	17
19	Corsi	13
20	Schrotter	12
21	Pons	8
22	Krummenacher	8
23	Rossi	7
24	Shah	1

Constructor Points

1	Kalex	150
2	Suter	92
3	Speed Up	47
4	Forward KLX	33
5	Tech 3	28
6	Caterham Suter	17

Moto3

RACE DISTANCE: 20 laps, 65.182 miles/104.900km · RACE WEATHER: Dry (air 22°C, humidity 51%, track 35°C)

Pos.	Rider	Nat.	No.	Entrant	Machine	Laps	Time & Speed
1	**Miguel Oliveira**	POR	44	Red Bull KTM Ajo	KTM	20	39m 39.510s 98.6mph/ 158.7km/h
2	**Danny Kent**	GBR	52	Leopard Racing	Honda	20	39m 39.581s
3	**Romano Fenati**	ITA	5	SKY Racing Team VR46	KTM	20	39m 39.637s
4	**Francesco Bagnaia**	ITA	21	MAPFRE Team MAHINDRA	Mahindra	20	39m 39.640s
5	**Enea Bastianini**	ITA	33	Gresini Racing Team Moto3	Honda	20	39m 39.710s
6	**Niccolo Antonelli**	ITA	23	Ongetta-Rivacold	Honda	20	39m 39.891s
7	**Jorge Navarro**	SPA	9	Estrella Galicia 0,0	Honda	20	39m 41.008s
8	**Isaac Vinales**	SPA	32	Husqvarna Factory Laglisse	Husqvarna	20	39m 41.086s
9	**Alexis Masbou**	FRA	10	SAXOPRINT RTG	Honda	20	39m 41.495s
10	**Brad Binder**	RSA	41	Red Bull KTM Ajo	KTM	20	39m 41.649s
11	**Hiroki Ono**	JPN	76	Leopard Racing	Honda	20	39m 44.476s
12	**Niklas Ajo**	FIN	31	RBA Racing Team	KTM	20	39m 44.652s
13	**Andrea Locatelli**	ITA	55	Gresini Racing Team Moto3	Honda	20	39m 44.670s
14	**Livio Loi**	BEL	11	RW Racing GP	Honda	20	39m 44.671s
15	**Andrea Migno**	ITA	16	SKY Racing Team VR46	KTM	20	39m 45.160s
16	Jakub Kornfeil	CZE	84	Drive M7 SIC	KTM	20	39m 46.760s
17	Jorge Martin	SPA	88	MAPFRE Team MAHINDRA	Mahindra	20	39m 48.078s
18	Darryn Binder	RSA	40	Outox Reset Drink Team	Mahindra	20	39m 56.740s
19	Alessandro Tonucci	ITA	19	Outox Reset Drink Team	Mahindra	20	39m 56.801s
20	John McPhee	GBR	17	SAXOPRINT RTG	Honda	20	39m 56.815s
21	Maria Herrera	SPA	6	Husqvarna Factory Laglisse	Husqvarna	20	39m 56.847s
22	Philipp Oettl	GER	65	Schedl GP Racing	KTM	20	40m 05.958s
23	Remy Gardner	AUS	2	CIP	Mahindra	20	40m 07.613s
24	Matteo Ferrari	ITA	12	San Carlo Team Italia	Mahindra	20	40m 07.646s
25	Ana Carrasco	SPA	22	RBA Racing Team	KTM	20	40m 07.686s
26	Zulfahmi Khairuddin	MAL	63	Drive M7 SIC	KTM	20	40m 07.732s
27	Anthony Groppi	ITA	73	Pos Corse	FTR Honda	20	40m 08.329s
28	Karel Hanika	CZE	98	Red Bull KTM Ajo	KTM	20	40m 14.135s
	Efren Vazquez	SPA	7	Leopard Racing	Honda	19	DNF
	Jules Danilo	FRA	95	Ongetta-Rivacold	Honda	19	DNF
	Juanfran Guevara	SPA	58	MAPFRE Team MAHINDRA	Mahindra	16	DNF
	Tatsuki Suzuki	JPN	24	CIP	Mahindra	14	DNF
	Gabriel Rodrigo	ARG	91	RBA Racing Team	KTM	10	DNF
	Fabio Quartararo	FRA	20	Estrella Galicia 0,0	Honda	9	DNF
	Stefano Manzi	ITA	29	San Carlo Team Italia	Mahindra	7	DNF
	Marco Bezzecchi	ITA	72	Minimoto Portmaggiore	Mahindra	3	DNF

Fastest lap: Brad Binder, on lap 3, 1m 57.318s, 100.0mph/160.9km/h (record).
Previous lap record: Efren Vazquez, SPA (Honda), 1m 57.633s, 99.7mph/160.5km/h (2014).
Event best maximum speed: Fabio Quartararo, 151.2mph/243.4km/h (race).

Qualifying

Weather: Dry
Air Temp: 21° **Track Temp:** 40°
Humidity: 58%

1	Kent	1m 56.615s
2	Ono	1m 56.904s
3	Fenati	1m 57.319s
4	Hanika	1m 57.329s
5	Antonelli	1m 57.333s
6	Kornfeil	1m 57.366s
7	Bastianini	1m 57.393s
8	Bagnaia	1m 57.529s
9	Locatelli	1m 57.551s
10	Vinales	1m 57.647s
11	Oliveira	1m 57.657s
12	Binder	1m 57.696s
13	Quartararo	1m 57.741s
14	Guevara	1m 57.799s
15	Vazquez	1m 57.833s
16	Loi	1m 57.875s
17	Danilo	1m 57.887s
18	Navarro	1m 57.905s
19	McPhee	1m 58.095s
20	Martin	1m 58.098s
21	Oettl	1m 58.123s
22	Ajo	1m 58.181s
23	Masbou	1m 58.322s
24	Migno	1m 58.331s
25	Khairuddin	1m 58.455s
26	Gardner	1m 58.594s
27	Herrera	1m 58.605s
28	Binder	1m 58.616s
29	Manzi	1m 58.629s
30	Ferrari	1m 58.654s
31	Carrasco	1m 58.718s
32	Tonucci	1m 58.787s
33	Rodrigo	1m 59.168s
34	Groppi	1m 59.206s
35	Bezzecchi	1m 59.591s
36	Suzuki	1m 59.975s

Fastest race laps

1	Binder	1m 57.318s
2	Vazquez	1m 57.391s
3	Kornfeil	1m 57.459s
4	Kent	1m 57.575s
5	Fenati	1m 57.594s
6	Oliveira	1m 57.671s
7	Binder	1m 57.676s
8	Antonelli	1m 57.684s
9	Bastianini	1m 57.694s
10	Oettl	1m 57.737s
11	Martin	1m 57.742s
12	Migno	1m 57.794s
13	Masbou	1m 57.839s
14	Hanika	1m 57.904s
15	Loi	1m 57.905s
16	Ajo	1m 57.919s
17	Quartararo	1m 57.926s
18	Vinales	1m 58.017s
19	Bagnaia	1m 58.042s
20	Navarro	1m 58.062s
21	Ono	1m 58.079s
22	Danilo	1m 58.095s
23	Guevara	1m 58.110s
24	Locatelli	1m 58.148s
25	Tonucci	1m 58.206s
26	Manzi	1m 58.258s
27	Herrera	1m 58.337s
28	McPhee	1m 58.395s
29	Groppi	1m 58.519s
30	Gardner	1m 58.560s
31	Carrasco	1m 58.610s
32	Suzuki	1m 58.736s
33	Ferrari	1m 58.783s
34	Bezzecchi	1m 58.880s
35	Khairuddin	1m 59.034s
36	Rodrigo	1m 59.120s

Championship Points

1	Kent	124
2	Bastianini	78
3	Fenati	67
4	Oliveira	66
5	Vazquez	60
6	Vinales	55
7	Quartararo	52
8	Bagnaia	50
9	Binder	50
10	Masbou	33
11	Antonelli	29
12	McPhee	28
13	Navarro	21
14	Hanika	18
15	Kornfeil	17
16	Locatelli	17
17	Ono	13
18	Migno	12
19	Ajo	12
20	Loi	12
21	Oettl	11
22	Guevara	4
23	Danilo	4
24	Martin	3
25	Khairuddin	2
26	Manzi	1
27	Ferrari	1

Constructor Points

1	Honda	140
2	KTM	100
3	Husqvarna	55
4	Mahindra	51

Main: Marquez, Rossi, Crutchlow (obscured) and Smith chase the departed Lorenzo in the sprint to the first corner. Note Vinales (25) already dropping back.

Insets: Lorenzo hammered home his fourth victory in a row – but this was the hardest for the Mallorcan rider.

Photos: Gold & Goose

FIM WORLD CHAMPIONSHIP · ROUND 7

CATALUNYA GRAND PRIX

CATALUNYA CIRCUIT

Above: Ecstatic Ecstar Suzuki team celebrate the marque's first qualifying one-two since 1993.

Top right: A new longer exhaust on the Repsol Honda.

Above right: Casey Stoner returned to demonstrate Honda's new road-going RCV.

Right: Marquez tried to out-muscle Lorenzo – and paid the price with a second race crash in a row.

Photos: Gold & Goose

AT what point did the 2015 season stop being about whether Marc Marquez could return to domination; when exactly did taking three titles in a row change from being difficult, but possible, to requiring a miracle? At the time, it seemed to happen quite suddenly on the third lap at Montmelo. Well, we would see about that…

For now, it was more of the same: for Lorenzo imperiously taking four in a row to come within one point of the championship lead; and for Marquez, with a second successive race crash. By the end of the weekend, the former had clocked up a record number of race laps in the lead; the latter had now crashed three times in the previous six races.

How long could this continue? And how long could Rossi stay on top of the points? The season was taking on quite a different hue from what had been expected.

All three riders were bearing scuff marks after post-Mugello tests on 2016's Michelin tyres. The Bridgestone contract banned them from making any comment, but it is easy to imagine what they might have said: "The fronts lose grip very suddenly." Lap times were reported to be at least respectable – Lorenzo credited with 1m 47.7s, less than a tenth off the race lap record, but 1.2 off Iannone's pole, with Marquez a tenth slower. But the queasy front feeling put the kybosh on plans to run full race distance, with the riders unwilling to take further risks.

Marquez did say that the tests had been useful in the quest to coax some better manners out of the beleaguered RC213V. An over-aggressive engine, both in acceleration and braking, had taken most of the blame for his poor results, and part of the progress had been electronic. Comfortingly, though, there was some visible hardware – a longer bottom tailpipe indicated a revised exhaust system.

With Barbera and Rins joining Pedrosa, and Pol Espargaro recuperating from arm-pump surgery, there was much talk about what seemed to be something of an epidemic. Especially among those lucky enough to escape it – like Rossi, in the longest career of anyone still racing. "For me, there is a technical reason. In the last years, pressure on the arms

during the braking has increased. Bridgestone's front is fantastic, the brakes get bigger and bigger. Also there is more engine braking. This is a lot of force coming to your arms."

Marquez was another non-sufferer, so far – though his enforced lopsided race at Jerez (broken little finger) had showed him just how an unnatural and awkward style was physically very deleterious. Riding style made the difference, though he too added, "The level is very high now, and you have to push so hard, for the whole race." At this track, according to Brembo's data, maximum braking for turn one lasted 5.9 seconds with a maximum of 1.6G deceleration, almost as much as at Mugello.

Suzuki's GSX-RR was already well respected as the best handling MotoGP bike. Now came a small step forward, with new engine parts that made only a 2–3km/h difference to top speed, but contributed a great deal more towards making the overall package more competitive. Along with more top end, according to Espargaro and somewhat counter-intuitively, came better throttle response and improved bottom end. The improvement was underlined not only by the marque's first pole position since 2007 (Vermeulen, Assen), but also by class rookie Vinales all but pipping his team-mate to take second. The last time Suzuki had had the front two grid positions had been way back in 1993, when Kevin Schwantz had qualified ahead of team-mate Alex Barros at Jerez. Schwantz won, Barros crashed. This time, however, with below-average acceleration exacerbated by the lack of a seamless-shift gearbox, they were both swamped on the run to the first corner, and there would be no repeat victory.

Catalunya's broad cambered kerbs make it an easy track for riders to touch down knees, elbows, and almost shoulders. But there were fears that the incline might prove an angle too far for the factory Ducatis, with their anhedral winglets mounted low on the fairing flanks. Touching these down could have been disastrous; and while Iannone completed the first session without them, Dovi ran a test with a strip of foam on the outside edge, as a tell-tale. If this touched

down, it would give way without causing a crash. It didn't; the winglets stayed put.

In spite of the season's upgrades, the Open Hondas were still struggling more than any rivals with the new standard electronics. Karel Abraham had a hurdle all of his own, having taken over sole use of Nissin brakes and Showa suspension from the Gresini team, since their switch to Aprilia. Yet to score a point, things got worse, with a heavy crash in qualifying that injured his foot so badly that it put him out of this race and until after the summer break.

Moto3 qualifying turned once again into a slow bicycle race, the worst ever seen, with almost the entire field meandering around at close to walking speed, all waiting for a tow. Hitherto this had incurred penalty points, but clearly that had not been effective, as Race Direction explained to the 30 riders summoned to the ivory control tower. They were given a severe wigging, with the promise that a less futile deterrent would be sought, with another mass meeting scheduled for the Dutch TT a fortnight later.

Casey Stoner and family were at the track, the premature retiree fresh from a visit to Lamborghini (like Ducati, owned by Audi). But suggestions that his former Italian employers were cosying up to him after Honda had rejected his offer to step in for the absent Pedrosa were silenced when he donned Honda leathers to run a sedate demonstration lap on the new road-going version of their GP bike, the 188,000-euro RC213V-S. Honda expected to make some 200 of the machine, with a similar chassis and engine to the MotoGP bike, but without such fripperies as pneumatic valve springs and a seamless-shift gearbox.

Finally, it was announced that – football World Cup problems notwithstanding – Dorna had signed up to another ten years of racing in Qatar, with the desert venue on the calendar until 2026.

MOTOGP RACE – 25 laps

With the soft-tyre-clad Suzuki pair first and second, Lorenzo completed the front row; Marquez headed the second from Dovizioso and Pedrosa. Rossi was again on row three, and again it cost him the chance of victory.

The race was in hotter, less grippy conditions than practice, and it began as had the previous three: Lorenzo took a strong start and led into the first corner. Marquez was right up close and pushing, then Dovizioso and Pol Espargaro, with Rossi past Smith by the end of the lap. Aleix Espargaro's start had been strong, but his run to the first corner was well below par, and he finished the first lap seventh; team-mate Vinales's had been far worse, and he was 14th.

Lorenzo would never be headed, and by the end of the race he had led a record total of 103 consecutive laps. It had been, he said, one of his hardest ever victories. But race-long pressure would not come from Marquez, whose full-on attacks came to an abrupt end on the third lap, at the end of the back straight. He was looking to dive inside, but was too late. It was a mistake, or as he preferred to describe it, "a small problem" – braking is one particular area of weakness for the Honda revealed by the improved competition.

Marquez just clipped the back of the Yamaha, picked up to run wide, and then the Repsol Honda was barrelling into the gravel. He'd hoped he might save it, but in vain. Though he was able to get going again, it was only to return to the pits.

Rossi had passed Pol by the end of lap two and was up to second, ahead of Dovi, at the end of the fourth. His team-mate was just 1.4 seconds away. That would see-saw for the rest of the race, at some points to just over two seconds, but the two Yamahas were very closely matched, and Rossi's pressure relentless. He crossed the line less than a second away. If he had qualified better, he said, "It would have been

interesting." Also if the race had been a lap or two longer, Lorenzo, less comfortable when it gets slippery, admitted he was hanging on for dear life by the finish.

The usually ultra-reliable Dovi did not last long, crashing out on lap six to leave the leaders alone, one of a higher than usual number of tumbles. Crutchlow had been the first to go down, after a first-lap tangle with Espargaro's Suzuki.

The chase saw plenty of variety. Espargaro Senior had recovered strongly in the early laps, having passed Smith and then brother Pol by lap three. Smith followed him past, and a lap later Pol slipped off trying to get back at his reliably and irritatingly faster team-mate.

At the same time, Pedrosa, who had finished lap one down in tenth, was moving forward cautiously: "With so many crashes, I could see the track was delicate." He took third off the Suzuki on lap seven, riding past on a wave of horsepower, and continued to a solitary, but delighted first podium of the year. He'd been pursued by Aleix's Suzuki until the Spaniard crashed out with four laps to go.

This promoted Smith, who hadn't been able to stay with him; meanwhile, Iannone had jumped from 12th on the grid to ninth on lap one. He too was gaining places, with Redding tagging on until losing touch on lap nine.

By now, Iannone had caught Smith, but found him very hard to pass. It took almost ten laps; thereafter he was able to escape for fourth.

Smith was unmolested in fifth, top satellite rider again. Redding had trouble coming from behind in the shape of Vinales, however. He caught up with ten laps remaining and had outstripped the Englishman by the finish for a career-best sixth.

Bradl had finally got the better of Petrucci by half-distance and was first Open bike in eighth, by far his best so far.

There was a long and fierce battle for tenth, finally won by the more experienced Bautista from class rookie Miller, who eventually settled for a best-yet 11th, after crashing out of the previous two races.

Laverty was a couple of seconds down, having narrowly held ex-Superbike rival Baz at bay. Di Meglio was next; de Angelis the last rider on the same lap for the final point. Barbera had pitted and rejoined in a distant 16th.

Hernandez had crashed out early; Hayden late in the race, after a troubled start with launch control issues, then a run on to the gravel on lap one, where excessive wheelspin triggered the electronics to cut the engine. He restarted near the back, but the ECU seemed deranged and eventually he succumbed: "The front folded on me at turn five."

Melandri retired with problems in the Aprilia's new seamless-shift gearbox.

MOTO2 RACE – 23 laps

Zarco started from pole, and finished first. What happened in between was enjoyably intriguing for the one-make class, the podium three decided only on the final two laps, with high drama.

The last lap was also the first time that the Frenchman had led the race, which had been dominated by defending champion Rabat, under serious pressure from class rookie Rins.

Zarco had played a waiting game, moving into fourth before half-distance, then perfectly timing his final attack. His Spanish rivals helped a bit, both faltering under the pressure. Rins (who

had set a new record on lap two) ran wide on the penultimate lap, letting him into second; then Rabat did the same on the last lap, not only allowing Zarco through for his second win of the year, but also ceding second to race-long rival Rins.

Rabat had qualified third, with Folger between him and Zarco, but the perennially luckless German was punted wide into the first corner by Zarco, who in turn had been pushed out by a determined Sam Lowes, through from the middle of the second row.

Lowes would take the lead from Rabat on lap two, with fourth fastest qualifier Aegerter in close attendance. Rins was fourth, but would vault up to second as Rabat regained the lead from the English rider on lap five.

From there, the two Spaniards were engaged, Rins taking over for two laps at half-distance. By then, Lowes was starting to lose touch; Aegerter had fallen back into the next group, where Salom had been heading Zarco.

The last-named now escaped and gradually closed a gap of around a second to Lowes, outbraking him for third at the start of lap 14.

Soon he was in touch with the leading pair, and the stage was set for a shootout.

Rins slipped first, wide into the fourth corner on the penultimate lap; Zarco was second. Then he pushed past Rabat into the turn five hairpin. Rabat tried to counter-attack at the end of the back straight, but ran wide, and Rins took over second. The rostrum was reshuffled.

Lowes was safe in fourth; Salom was battling for fifth with Luthi. They swapped several times, Salom taking the place by less than half a second.

By now, Folger had battled his way back through from 14th to seventh. He had finally outpaced a lively gang, where Morbidelli narrowly got the better of Aegerter, Baldassarri and an at last more impressive Alex Marquez, who had come sweeping up to join them at the last minute. He'd been involved in a lap-one tangle, and rode to 11th from 28th.

Kallio, Corsi, Syahrin and Simon took the last points.

Pons, Simeon and Cortese were all put out in the first-lap incident, while Morbidelli was given a penalty point for his part in knocking Pons down.

Maximum championship points extended Zarco's title lead still further, 38 clear of increasingly troubled defender Rabat.

MOTO3 RACE – 22 laps

A lap-scorer's nightmare; a tactician's playground. And an astonishingly mature fourth win of the year for Danny Kent, who was able to parlay his remarkable speed into a win that was as decisive as it was narrow: 0.035 of a second over pole man Bastianini.

It was a strategic triumph. Kent had started the first lap at the back of the sextet, drafting past into second at the first corner, taking the lead three corners later and holding it all the way around the rest of a lap that must have seemed thousands of miles long.

It was almost a Honda lock-out for the first six, all across the line within less than a second; Vazquez was third, Antonelli fourth and Navarro sixth. Only erstwhile leader Oliveira's KTM spoiled it, in fifth.

All but Navarro had led at least once over the line, but positions were notional until the flag.

Brad Binder and Oettl had dropped out of the group to fall into a fierce four-strong battle for seventh. It went to Vinales, from Fenati, Binder and Oettl, out of touch at the end.

Another huge group, at one stage a dozen strong, but depleted by a number of crashes, fought over the last points.

A career-best 11th went to rookie Martin, while Mahindra team-mate Bagnaia tumbled out of 12th in the last corners. That place went to Locatelli, from Ajo, Quartararo and an on-form Maria Herrera.

A long crash list included Ono, McPhee, Gardner, Guevara, Migno, Darryn Binder and Hanika. Vazquez set fastest lap, a new record.

GP MONSTER ENERGY DE CATALUNYA
12-14 JUNE, 2015

CIRCUIT DE CATALUNYA

25 laps
Length: 4.727km / 2.892 miles
Width: 12m

Turn 3 175/109
Seat 109/68
Repsol 130/81
Campsa 132/82
Europcar 177/110
Abolafio 185/115
Turn 7 110/68
Banc Sabadell 127/79
Elf 123/76
Würth 109/68
300/186
La Caixa 105/65
Key
96/60 kph/mph
Gear
Tourisme de Catalunya 158/98

MotoGP

RACE DISTANCE: 25 laps, 73.431 miles/118.175km · **RACE WEATHER:** Dry (air 28°C, humidity 46%, track 49°C)

Pos.	Rider	Nat.	No.	Entrant	Machine	Tyres	Race tyre choice	Laps	Time & speed
1	Jorge Lorenzo	SPA	99	Movistar Yamaha MotoGP	Yamaha YZR-M1	B	F: Medium/R: Medium	25	42m 53.208s / 102.7mph/ 165.3km/h
2	Valentino Rossi	ITA	46	Movistar Yamaha MotoGP	Yamaha YZR-M1	B	F: Medium/R: Medium	25	42m 54.093s
3	Dani Pedrosa	SPA	26	Repsol Honda Team	Honda RC213V	B	F: Medium/R: Medium	25	43m 12.663s
4	Andrea Iannone	ITA	29	Ducati Team	Ducati Desmosedici	B	F: Hard/R: Medium	25	43m 18.133s
5	Bradley Smith	GBR	38	Monster Yamaha Tech 3	Yamaha YZR-M1	B	F: Medium/R: Medium	25	43m 20.990s
6	Maverick Vinales	SPA	25	Team SUZUKI ECSTAR	Suzuki GSX-RR	B	F: Medium/R: Medium	25	43m 22.767s
7	Scott Redding	GBR	45	EG 0,0 Marc VDS	Honda RC213V	B	F: Medium/R: Medium	25	43m 29.632s
8	Stefan Bradl	GER	6	Athina Forward Racing	Yamaha Forward	B	F: Medium/R: Soft	25	43m 35.311s
9	Danilo Petrucci	ITA	9	Octo Pramac Racing	Ducati Desmosedici	B	F: Hard/R: Medium	25	43m 42.558s
10	Alvaro Bautista	SPA	19	Aprilia Racing Team Gresini	Aprilia RS-GP	B	F: Medium/R: Soft	25	43m 45.777s
11	Jack Miller	AUS	43	CWM LCR Honda	Honda RC213V-RS	B	F: Medium/R: Soft	25	43m 46.874s
12	Eugene Laverty	IRL	50	Aspar MotoGP Team	Honda RC213V-RS	B	F: Medium/R: Soft	25	43m 48.973s
13	Loris Baz	FRA	76	Athina Forward Racing	Yamaha Forward	B	F: Medium/R: Soft	25	43m 49.040s
14	Mike di Meglio	FRA	63	Avintia Racing	Ducati Desmosedici Open	B	F: Medium/R: Soft	25	44m 02.245s
15	Alex de Angelis	RSM	15	E-Motion IodaRacing Team	Aprilia ART	B	F: Medium/R: Soft	25	44m 18.471s
16	Hector Barbera	SPA	8	Avintia Racing	Ducati Desmosedici Open	B	F: Medium/R: Soft	24	43m 35.670s
	Aleix Espargaro	SPA	41	Team SUZUKI ECSTAR	Suzuki GSX-RR	B	F: Medium/R: Medium	20	DNF-crash
	Nicky Hayden	USA	69	Aspar MotoGP Team	Honda RC213V-RS	B	F: Medium/R: Soft	13	DNF-crash
	Marco Melandri	ITA	33	Aprilia Racing Team Gresini	Aprilia RS-GP	B	F: Medium/R: Soft	6	DNF-mechanical
	Andrea Dovizioso	ITA	4	Ducati Team	Ducati Desmosedici	B	F: Hard/R: Medium	6	DNF-crash
	Pol Espargaro	SPA	44	Monster Yamaha Tech 3	Yamaha YZR-M1	B	F: Medium/R: Medium	4	DNF-crash
	Marc Marquez	SPA	93	Repsol Honda Team	Honda RC213V	B	F: Medium/R: Medium	3	DNF-crash
	Cal Crutchlow	GBR	35	CWM LCR Honda	Honda RC213V	B	F: Medium/R: Medium	3	DNF-crash
	Yonny Hernandez	COL	68	Octo Pramac Racing	Ducati Desmosedici	B	F: Hard/R: Medium	2	DNF-crash
	Karel Abraham	CZE	17	AB Motoracing	Honda RC213V-RS	B	–	0	DNS-injured

Fastest lap: Marc Marquez, on lap 2, 1m 42.219s, 103.4mph/166.4km/h.

Lap record: Marc Marquez, SPA (Honda), 1m 42.182s, 103.5mph/166.5km/h (2014).

Event best maximum speed: Marc Marquez, 215.7mph/347.1km/h (free practice).

Qualifying

Weather: Dry
Air Temp: 25° **Track Temp:** 42°
Humidity: 55%

1	A. Espargaro	1m 40.546s
2	Vinales	1m 40.629s
3	Lorenzo	1m 40.646s
4	Marquez	1m 40.754s
5	Dovizioso	1m 40.907s
6	Pedrosa	1m 40.928s
7	Rossi	1m 41.058s
8	Smith	1m 41.068s
9	Crutchlow	1m 41.195s
10	Hernandez	1m 41.333s
11	P. Espargaro	1m 41.385s
12	Iannone	1m 41.524s
13	Barbera	1m 42.003s
14	Redding	1m 42.029s
15	Bradl	1m 42.053s
16	Petrucci	1m 42.155s
17	Di Meglio	1m 42.273s
18	Hayden	1m 42.485s
19	Baz	1m 42.592s
20	Bautista	1m 42.600s
21	Miller	1m 42.928s
22	Laverty	1m 42.971s
23	De Angelis	1m 43.601s
24	Melandri	1m 44.345s
	Abraham	No Time

Fastest race laps

1	Marquez	1m 42.219s
2	Lorenzo	1m 42.225s
3	Rossi	1m 42.356s
4	Dovizioso	1m 42.527s
5	Redding	1m 42.672s
6	A. Espargaro	1m 42.692s
7	Smith	1m 42.818s
8	Pedrosa	1m 42.855s
9	Hernandez	1m 42.977s
10	Iannone	1m 42.979s
11	P. Espargaro	1m 43.166s
12	Vinales	1m 43.268s
13	Petrucci	1m 43.512s
14	Bradl	1m 43.535s
15	Hayden	1m 43.905s
16	Miller	1m 43.929s
17	Bautista	1m 44.028s
18	Laverty	1m 44.178s
19	Barbera	1m 44.277s
20	Baz	1m 44.486s
21	Di Meglio	1m 44.517s
22	De Angelis	1m 44.850s
23	Melandri	1m 45.936s
24	Crutchlow	1m 53.571s

Championship Points

1	Rossi	138
2	Lorenzo	137
3	Iannone	94
4	Dovizioso	83
5	Marquez	69
6	Smith	68
7	Crutchlow	47
8	Vinales	46
9	P. Espargaro	45
10	Pedrosa	39
11	Petrucci	39
12	A. Espargaro	31
13	Redding	27
14	Hernandez	26
15	Barbera	16
16	Baz	13
17	Bautista	11
18	Miller	11
19	Bradl	9
20	Pirro	8
21	Hayden	8
22	Laverty	7
23	Aoyama	5
24	Di Meglio	2
25	De Angelis	1

Constructor Points

1	Yamaha	166
2	Ducati	119
3	Honda	114
4	Suzuki	57
5	Yamaha Forward	18
6	Aprilia	11
7	ART	1

Grid order	1	2	3	4	5	6	7	8	9	10	11	12	13	14	15	16	17	18	19	20	21	22	23	24	25	
41 A. ESPARGARO	99	99	99	99	99	99	99	99	99	99	99	99	99	99	99	99	99	99	99	99	99	99	99	99	99	1
25 VINALES	93	93	4	46	46	46	46	46	46	46	46	46	46	46	46	46	46	46	46	46	46	46	46	46	46	2
99 LORENZO	4	4	46	4	4	41	26	26	26	26	26	26	26	26	26	26	26	26	26	26	26	26	26	26	26	3
93 MARQUEZ	44	46	41	41	41	26	41	41	41	41	41	41	41	41	41	41	41	41	41	29	29	29	29	29	29	4
4 DOVIZIOSO	46	44	44	38	26	38	38	38	38	38	38	38	38	38	38	38	29	29	29	38	38	38	38	38	38	5
26 PEDROSA	38	41	38	44	38	29	29	29	29	29	29	29	29	29	29	29	38	38	38	25	25	25	25	25	25	6
46 ROSSI	41	68	26	26	29	45	45	45	45	45	45	45	45	45	25	25	25	25	25	45	45	45	45	45	45	7
38 SMITH	68	38	29	29	25	25	25	25	25	25	25	25	25	25	45	45	45	45	45	6	6	6	6	6	6	8
35 CRUTCHLOW	29	29	45	45	9	9	9	9	9	9	6	6	6	6	6	6	6	6	6	9	9	9	9	9	9	9
68 HERNANDEZ	26	26	9	9	25	6	6	6	6	6	9	9	9	9	9	9	9	9	9	43	43	43	19	19		10
44 P. ESPARGARO	9	45	25	25	6	19	43	43	43	43	43	43	43	43	43	43	43	19	19	19	19	43	43			11
29 IANNONE	19	9	6	6	19	43	19	19	19	19	19	19	19	19	19	19	19	43	50	50	50	50	50			12
8 BARBERA	45	25	19	19	43	50	50	50	50	50	50	50	50	50	50	50	50	50	76	76	76	76	76			13
45 REDDING	25	6	43	43	63	63	63	63	63	63	63	76	76	76	76	76	76	63	63	63	63	63	63			14
6 BRADL	43	19	63	63	50	76	76	76	76	76	76	63	63	63	63	63	63	15	15	15	15	15	15			15
9 PETRUCCI	6	43	76	50	76	8	8	8	8	8	15	15	15	15	15	15	15	8	8	8	8					
63 DI MEGLIO	63	63	50	76	8	15	15	15	15	15	69	69	8	8	8	8	8									
69 HAYDEN	76	76	8	8	15	33	69	69	69	69	8	8														
76 BAZ	50	50	15	15	33	69																				
19 BAUTISTA	69	15	33	33	69	4																				
43 MILLER	15	8	93	69																						
50 LAVERTY	8	33	69																							
15 DE ANGELIS	33	69	35																							
33 MELANDRI	35	35																								

93 Pit stop   8 Lapped rider

Moto2

RACE DISTANCE: 23 laps, 67.556 miles/108.721km · RACE WEATHER: Dry (air 27°C, humidity 48%, track 45°C)

Pos.	Rider	Nat.	No.	Entrant	Machine	Laps	Time & Speed
1	**Johann Zarco**	FRA	5	Ajo Motorsport	Kalex	23	41m 15.487s / 98.2mph/ 158.1km/h
2	**Alex Rins**	SPA	40	Paginas Amarillas HP 40	Kalex	23	41m 15.913s
3	**Tito Rabat**	SPA	1	EG 0,0 Marc VDS	Kalex	23	41m 16.602s
4	**Sam Lowes**	GBR	22	Speed Up Racing	Speed Up	23	41m 19.401s
5	**Luis Salom**	SPA	39	Paginas Amarillas HP 40	Kalex	23	41m 22.567s
6	**Thomas Luthi**	SWI	12	Derendinger Racing Interwetten	Kalex	23	41m 22.870s
7	**Jonas Folger**	GER	94	AGR Team	Kalex	23	41m 24.326s
8	**Franco Morbidelli**	ITA	21	Italtrans Racing Team	Kalex	23	41m 25.839s
9	**Dominique Aegerter**	SWI	77	Technomag Racing Interwetten	Kalex	23	41m 26.125s
10	**Lorenzo Baldassarri**	ITA	7	Athina Forward Racing	Kalex	23	41m 26.217s
11	**Alex Marquez**	SPA	73	EG 0,0 Marc VDS	Kalex	23	41m 26.539s
12	**Mika Kallio**	FIN	36	Italtrans Racing Team	Kalex	23	41m 31.825s
13	**Simone Corsi**	ITA	3	Athina Forward Racing	Kalex	23	41m 32.136s
14	**Hafizh Syahrin**	MAL	55	Petronas Raceline Malaysia	Kalex	23	41m 35.071s
15	**Julian Simon**	SPA	60	QMMF Racing Team	Speed Up	23	41m 35.144s
16	Marcel Schrotter	GER	23	Tech 3	Tech 3	23	41m 35.453s
17	Edgar Pons	SPA	57	Paginas Amarillas HP 40	Kalex	23	41m 42.720s
18	Randy Krummenacher	SWI	4	JIR Racing Team	Kalex	23	41m 45.768s
19	Azlan Shah	MAL	25	IDEMITSU Honda Team Asia	Kalex	23	41m 45.831s
20	Takaaki Nakagami	JPN	30	IDEMITSU Honda Team Asia	Kalex	23	41m 55.393s
21	Florian Alt	GER	66	E-Motion IodaRacing Team	Suter	23	41m 58.950s
22	Anthony West	AUS	95	QMMF Racing Team	Speed Up	23	41m 59.128s
23	Louis Rossi	FRA	96	Tasca Racing Scuderia Moto2	Tech 3	23	42m 00.336s
24	Jesko Raffin	SWI	2	sports-millions-EMWE-SAG	Kalex	20	42m 03.689s
25	Thitipong Warokorn	THA	10	APH PTT The Pizza SAG	Kalex	19	42m 16.944s
26	Ramdan Rosli	MAL	93	Petronas AHM Malaysia	Kalex	6	42m 23.363s
	Ricard Cardus	SPA	88	Tech 3	Tech 3	17	DNF
	Ratthapark Wilairot	THA	15	JPMoto Malaysia	Suter	9	DNF
	Robin Mulhauser	SWI	70	Technomag Racing Interwetten	Kalex	7	DNF
	Sandro Cortese	GER	11	Dynavolt Intact GP	Kalex	0	DNF
	Axel Pons	SPA	49	AGR Team	Kalex	0	DNF
	Xavier Simeon	BEL	19	Federal Oil Gresini Moto2	Kalex	0	DNF

Fastest lap: Alex Rins, on lap 2, 1m 46.474s, 99.3mph/159.8km/h (record).
Previous lap record: Thomas Luthi, SWI (Suter), 1m 46.631s, 99.2mph/159.6km/h (2012).
Event best maximum speed: Robin Mulhauser, 180.1mph/289.9km/h (race).

Qualifying
Weather: Dry
Air Temp: 25° **Track Temp:** 41°
Humidity: 59%

1	Zarco	1m 45.895s
2	Folger	1m 46.060s
3	Rabat	1m 46.123s
4	Aegerter	1m 46.191s
5	Lowes	1m 46.333s
6	Salom	1m 46.478s
7	Rins	1m 46.490s
8	Corsi	1m 46.526s
9	Cortese	1m 46.537s
10	Luthi	1m 46.591s
11	Pons	1m 46.673s
12	Marquez	1m 46.686s
13	Baldassarri	1m 46.745s
14	Simeon	1m 46.784s
15	Simon	1m 46.805s
16	Schrotter	1m 46.806s
17	Shah	1m 46.905s
18	Krummenacher	1m 47.077s
19	Syahrin	1m 47.151s
20	Mulhauser	1m 47.244s
21	Pons	1m 47.244s
22	Kallio	1m 47.426s
23	Morbidelli	1m 47.427s
24	Wilairot	1m 47.508s
25	Nakagami	1m 47.600s
26	Rossi	1m 47.624s
27	West	1m 47.711s
28	Alt	1m 47.968s
29	Warokorn	1m 48.008s
30	Cardus	1m 48.044s
31	Raffin	1m 48.081s
32	Rosli	1m 48.831s

Fastest race laps

1	Rins	1m 46.474s
2	Zarco	1m 46.714s
3	Salom	1m 46.797s
4	Morbidelli	1m 46.809s
5	Luthi	1m 46.816s
6	Kallio	1m 46.827s
7	Marquez	1m 46.882s
8	Rabat	1m 46.917s
9	Aegerter	1m 46.921s
10	Baldassarri	1m 46.929s
11	Lowes	1m 46.982s
12	Corsi	1m 47.016s
13	Folger	1m 47.046s
14	Simon	1m 47.329s
15	Schrotter	1m 47.410s
16	Mulhauser	1m 47.449s
17	Syahrin	1m 47.534s
18	Pons	1m 47.607s
19	Krummenacher	1m 47.765s
20	West	1m 47.777s
21	Shah	1m 47.898s
22	Cardus	1m 47.902s
23	Wilairot	1m 47.980s
24	Rossi	1m 47.983s
25	Alt	1m 48.050s
26	Nakagami	1m 48.070s
27	Raffin	1m 48.355s
28	Warokorn	1m 48.934s
29	Rosli	1m 49.248s

Championship Points

1	Zarco	134
2	Rabat	94
3	Lowes	80
4	Luthi	78
5	Rins	74
6	Folger	66
7	Morbidelli	62
8	Simeon	49
9	Salom	36
10	Kallio	35
11	Simon	35
12	Aegerter	33
13	Syahrin	33
14	Cortese	30
15	Baldassarri	29
16	Marquez	23
17	Nakagami	20
18	West	17
19	Corsi	16
20	Schrotter	12
21	Pons	8
22	Krummenacher	8
23	Rossi	7
24	Shah	1

Constructor Points

1	Kalex	170
2	Speed Up	88
3	Tech 3	19

Moto3

RACE DISTANCE: 22 laps, 64.619 miles/103.994km · RACE WEATHER: Dry (air 26°C, humidity 46%, track 37°C)

Pos.	Rider	Nat.	No.	Entrant	Machine	Laps	Time & Speed
1	**Danny Kent**	GBR	52	Leopard Racing	Honda	22	40m 59.419s / 94.6mph/ 152.2km/h
2	**Enea Bastianini**	ITA	33	Gresini Racing Team Moto3	Honda	22	40m 59.454s
3	**Efren Vazquez**	SPA	7	Leopard Racing	Honda	22	41m 00.019s
4	**Niccolo Antonelli**	ITA	23	Ongetta-Rivacold	Honda	22	41m 00.106s
5	**Miguel Oliveira**	POR	44	Red Bull KTM Ajo	KTM	22	41m 00.246s
6	**Jorge Navarro**	SPA	9	Estrella Galicia 0,0	Honda	22	41m 00.332s
7	**Isaac Vinales**	SPA	32	Husqvarna Factory Laglisse	Husqvarna	22	41m 08.290s
8	**Romano Fenati**	ITA	5	SKY Racing Team VR46	KTM	22	41m 08.336s
9	**Brad Binder**	RSA	41	Red Bull KTM Ajo	KTM	22	41m 10.487s
10	**Philipp Oettl**	GER	65	Schedl GP Racing	KTM	22	41m 14.387s
11	**Jorge Martin**	SPA	88	MAPFRE Team MAHINDRA	Mahindra	22	41m 16.015s
12	**Andrea Locatelli**	ITA	55	Gresini Racing Team Moto3	Honda	22	41m 16.759s
13	**Niklas Ajo**	FIN	31	RBA Racing Team	KTM	22	41m 18.505s
14	**Fabio Quartararo**	FRA	20	Estrella Galicia 0,0	Honda	22	41m 18.739s
15	**Maria Herrera**	SPA	6	Husqvarna Factory Laglisse	Husqvarna	22	41m 18.785s
16	Jules Danilo	FRA	95	Ongetta-Rivacold	Honda	22	41m 21.676s
17	Alessandro Tonucci	ITA	19	Outox Reset Drink Team	Mahindra	22	41m 22.764s
18	Alexis Masbou	FRA	10	SAXOPRINT RTG	Honda	22	41m 25.833s
19	Livio Loi	BEL	11	RW Racing GP	Honda	22	41m 26.499s
20	Francesco Bagnaia	ITA	21	MAPFRE Team MAHINDRA	Mahindra	22	41m 36.375s
21	Matteo Ferrari	ITA	12	San Carlo Team Italia	Mahindra	22	41m 37.314s
22	Tatsuki Suzuki	JPN	24	CIP	Mahindra	22	41m 37.365s
23	Ana Carrasco	SPA	22	RBA Racing Team	KTM	22	41m 37.507s
24	Zulfahmi Khairuddin	MAL	63	Drive M7 SIC	KTM	22	41m 52.765s
25	Remy Gardner	AUS	2	CIP	Mahindra	22	42m 02.181s
26	Juanjun Guevara	SPA	58	MAPFRE Team MAHINDRA	Mahindra	22	42m 15.906s
27	Stefano Manzi	ITA	29	San Carlo Team Italia	Mahindra	21	41m 22.813s
28	Andrea Migno	ITA	16	SKY Racing Team VR46	KTM	21	41m 24.959s
	Karel Hanika	CZE	98	Red Bull KTM Ajo	KTM	19	DNF
	Darryn Binder	RSA	40	Outox Reset Drink Team	Mahindra	17	DNF
	John McPhee	GBR	17	SAXOPRINT RTG	Honda	9	DNF
	Hiroki Ono	JPN	76	Leopard Racing	Honda	6	DNF
	Jakub Kornfeil	CZE	84	Drive M7 SIC	KTM	0	DNF
	Gabriel Rodrigo	ARG	91	RBA Racing Team	KTM	0	DNF

Fastest lap: Efren Vazquez, on lap 12, 1m 50.606s, 95.6mph/153.8km/h (record).
Previous lap record: John McPhee, GBR (Honda), 1m 51.299s, 94.9mph/152.8km/h (2014).
Event best maximum speed: Hiroki Ono, 150.1mph/241.6km/h (qualifying).

Qualifying:
Weather: Dry
Air Temp: 27° **Track Temp:** 42°
Humidity: 50%

1	Bastianini	1m 50.137s
2	Kent	1m 50.281s
3	Navarro	1m 50.840s
4	Antonelli	1m 50.848s
5	Oliveira	1m 50.857s
6	Vazquez	1m 50.894s
7	Quartararo	1m 50.896s
8	Ajo	1m 51.113s
9	Oettl	1m 51.265s
10	Ono	1m 51.290s
11	McPhee	1m 51.517s
12	Hanika	1m 51.528s
13	Fenati	1m 51.551s
14	Herrera	1m 51.586s
15	Martin	1m 51.597s
16	Guevara	1m 51.721s
17	Bagnaia	1m 51.772s
18	Binder	1m 51.822s
19	Locatelli	1m 51.833s
20	Vinales	1m 51.914s
21	Migno	1m 52.137s
22	Danilo	1m 52.149s
23	Masbou	1m 52.172s
24	Tonucci	1m 52.191s
25	Gardner	1m 52.283s
26	Kornfeil	1m 52.813s
27	Manzi	1m 52.564s
28	Suzuki	1m 52.620s
29	Loi	1m 52.752s
30	Binder	1m 52.813s
31	Ferrari	1m 52.869s
32	Rodrigo	1m 53.023s
33	Khairuddin	1m 53.203s
34	Carrasco	1m 53.473s

Fastest race laps

1	Vazquez	1m 50.606s
2	Oliveira	1m 50.615s
3	Kent	1m 50.672s
4	Antonelli	1m 50.708s
5	Bastianini	1m 50.732s
6	Navarro	1m 50.902s
7	Ono	1m 51.149s
8	Oettl	1m 51.211s
9	Vinales	1m 51.236s
10	Bagnaia	1m 51.238s
11	Martin	1m 51.249s
12	Ajo	1m 51.256s
13	Fenati	1m 51.268s
14	Binder	1m 51.326s
15	Hanika	1m 51.342s
16	Guevara	1m 51.347s
17	Migno	1m 51.457s
18	Quartararo	1m 51.466s
19	Locatelli	1m 51.622s
20	Herrera	1m 51.642s
21	Tonucci	1m 51.699s
22	Masbou	1m 51.702s
23	Danilo	1m 51.715s
24	McPhee	1m 51.806s
25	Gardner	1m 51.974s
26	Loi	1m 51.980s
27	Carrasco	1m 52.120s
28	Suzuki	1m 52.221s
29	Binder	1m 52.279s
30	Ferrari	1m 52.423s
31	Khairuddin	1m 52.930s
32	Manzi	1m 55.116s

Championship Points

1	Kent	149
2	Bastianini	98
3	Oliveira	77
4	Vazquez	76
5	Fenati	75
6	Vinales	64
7	Binder	57
8	Quartararo	54
9	Bagnaia	50
10	Antonelli	42
11	Masbou	33
12	Navarro	31
13	McPhee	28
14	Locatelli	21
15	Hanika	18
16	Kornfeil	17
17	Oettl	17
18	Ajo	15
19	Ono	13
20	Migno	12
21	Loi	12
22	Martin	8
23	Danilo	4
24	Guevara	4
25	Khairuddin	2
26	Herrera	1
27	Manzi	1
28	Ferrari	1

Constructor Points

1	Honda	165
2	KTM	111
3	Husqvarna	64
4	Mahindra	56

Main: Rossi's win made him Assen's most successful rider. The fans loved it.

Inset: A muted smile from a massacred Marquez.

Photos: Gold & Goose

EVERY lap of the Dutch TT was memorable. The last was an all-time classic, a moment to be replayed for years to come. With an outcome of the greatest possible significance. For the 24 previous laps, it had been a duel between old master and young pretender. In the past, almost all of these had had the same outcome: the old guy lost. This weekend was a sea change. Marquez tried everything, including one of his hitherto reliably successful last-corner physical attacks. Rossi proved not only equal to it, but also able to turn it to his advantage. The old guy won.

After four Lorenzo races, the element of change was more widespread. The fact that Marquez was a serious factor, instead of a headlong faller, was the consequence of a chassis change: not new, but from 2014, fitted with 2015's rear suspension. He admitted later that he'd begun to doubt himself after the previous two races, but although post-Catalunya tests had been washed out after only a couple of laps, those were enough for him to feel encouraged for the first time all year. "The new bike was very precise, good for one fast lap. On this one, I can make mistakes and recover from them." The first day of practice was "the first that I wasn't making changes: I felt comfortable." Not that comfortable, though, after a lucky escape on his first out-lap: at the fast and notorious Ramshoek left-hander, he'd suffered a high-speed high-sider, luckily landed back on the seat and managed to stay on board across the run-off before being tipped off at walking speed.

Rossi also had a transformation that allowed him to claim pole position for the first time after a costly spell of second- and third-row starts: a new chassis, visibly different around the steering head, with revised stiffness ratios made it "more easy to ride ... lighter, and it looks like the tyres have more grip. But it is maybe a little more unstable under braking." Yamaha had found dry weather at Aragon for tests, and after back-to-back trials at Assen, Rossi switched to the new one.

The stage was set, but this time Lorenzo wasn't on it. He too liked the new chassis, but low grip from tyres with a different sort of heat treatment did not suit his style.

With the track in good condition and weather conditions mainly favourable, records tumbled, including one in MotoGP's Q2. All 12 of them were within just over six-tenths of Rossi's pole, and given that he'd mustered a yawning gap of 0.235 second, that meant that 0.378 made the difference between qualifying second or 12th, at a circuit where the tight first corner emphasises the need for a good start.

It was a factor that made it all the more tempting for Moto3 qualifiers to look for somebody to slipstream, but all managed to resist, having freshly emerged from a mass meeting with Race Direction, during which a new system of penalties was outlined in an attempt to stamp it out. From now, instead of penalty points, punishment would be immediate as well as cumulative, starting with the loss of three grid positions for a first offence. If this system proved ineffective, said race director Mike Webb, they would consider a major rethink: "not exactly Superpole" (where each rider, alone on track, gets just one fast lap), "but much more limited track time."

At strategic level, the GP Commission announced "a New Era", with adoption of the proposal revealed at the Argentine GP, represented as an *entente cordiale* between Dorna, manufacturers, teams and the federation; in reality, it was a major victory for the first named. This was the fourth, or perhaps fifth, New Era since the advent of MotoGP four-strokes, analysed more fully earlier in this book.

If we hadn't yet quite finished with the previous New Era, certainly some of the lights were going out: after this race, factory electronic development remained frozen for the rest of the season.

Another great change was announced, causing furrowed brows among the more traditional, but enthusiasm elsewhere: this would be the last Dutch TT to run on Saturday, a unique feature dating back to the strict observance of the no-sport Sundays in the still-conservative northern province

of Drenthe when racing began at Assen in the 1920s. This not only brings it into line with all other races, but also rationalises TV schedules and is expected to draw more crowds for qualifying, when this is shifted from a working Friday to the more usual Saturday. The TT, agreed elderly Assen management stalwart Egbert Braakman (race secretary from 1970 to 2006), had become a little more international, but "a little less Drenthe".

It was a disastrous weekend for Stefan Bradl, at last beginning to get to grips with his Open Forward Yamaha after his first top ten at the previous round. He was lying 15th when he crashed early in the race and suffered a broken scaphoid in his right wrist. That ruled him out of his forthcoming home German GP.

Karel Abraham was not race fit, and a plot to give Superbike bright hope Michael van der Mark a home grand prix debut on the Czech rider's vacant Open Honda foundered over sponsor clashes and a dispute over potential accident damage costs. Brighter news from the rider's home (his house is adjacent to the circuit) was that 2015's Brno GP was at last confirmed as a definite on the calendar after some shaky financing problems with the local government in the preceding weeks.

Monster team-mates Smith and Pol Espargaro had to rush off after the race to fly to Japan, where they would test the factory Yamaha they would use to win the Suzuka 8 Hours race; Rossi was another hasty departure, bound for a starring role at the Goodwood Festival of Speed on Sunday. But if you were thinking he could do no wrong, Race Direction did not agree. He and Aleix Espargaro had led the field out of the pits for Q2, but the pair were judged to have jumped the red light and were fined 2,000 euros apiece. Taking the top two grid positions was some sort of consolation.

MOTOGP RACE – 26 laps

Marquez joined Rossi and Aleix on the front row; Pedrosa was consigned to the second by a tenth, ahead of Pol Espargaro and Iannone. Lorenzo was in the middle of row three, between Crutchlow and Vinales; Dovizioso led row four. Pedrosa's hopes of capitalising on a strong practice were

scotched by a heavy crash in morning warm-up, which left his preferred bike *hors de combat* and the rider somewhat knocked about.

Rossi's start was flawless, he seized the first corner from Aleix Espargaro and Marquez; Lorenzo started even better to slot into fifth. First time into the tight left and Marquez was second; Lorenzo slotted into third at Mandeveen – first and tighter of the old-school rights (Duikersloot the second) – on the old section of the track.

Thus the first three were settled, but after two laps it was clear that Lorenzo couldn't match the pace of the first two. They embarked on a duel that long will be replayed, enjoyed and remembered.

Each broke the record early on; thereafter Rossi rode and Marquez stalked for the first 19 laps. Nobody could remember seeing the Repsol Honda man riding with such restraint, compact, athletic and smooth; it had been a long time, too, since he had been so obviously master of his bike. Rossi likewise was master of his craft, in both senses of the word. It was fascinating, the pair separated by the narrowest of margins, very seldom more than two-tenths.

At the start of lap 20, Marquez finally pounced at the end of the front straight: Rossi's entry had been slowed by a run across the Astroturf. But escape was as impossible for him as it had been for the old-timer. And four laps later, Rossi returned the compliment, with a masterful move inside on the brakes for Mandeveen.

He started the last lap seemingly in control, with a four-tenths advantage. But Marquez reeled that in and was poised as they approached the last chicane for a final lunge up the inside.

The camera angle suggested that he may even have been briefly ahead. But he was now much slower; Rossi ignored the block-pass and turned in anyway. He was clearly ahead as they made contact. Marquez wobbled and completed the remaining two corners.

Rossi was sent off at a tangent. He opened the throttle to pick up the front wheel ("I didn't know how deep the gravel was."), cut the middle corner, and when he regained the hard surface he had a lead of 1.2 seconds. His seventh Assen win (his career 111th) lifted him one clear of compatriot

Above: Wide-eyed warrior – an amazing win, even for its perpetrator.

Left, from top: The last-corner clash and how it unfolded. One made the corner, the other made the flag.

Photos: Gold & Goose

Agostini as the most successful Dutch TT rider.

Race Direction has more camera angles, and after analysing them decreed that it had been "a racing incident". Not surprisingly, the riders had differing views. Asked who would have won had they not collided, they responded thus:

Rossi: "I think me, because I was ahead."

Marquez: "I think me, because I was inside."

Lorenzo was almost 15 seconds adrift; Iannone was a fine fourth, a huge battle behind him having aided his escape.

And what a battle, at one stage eight riders strong.

Dovizioso had come through from a poor start; Crutchlow, Smith and both Espargaro brothers were in the mix; Petrucci and Vinales were close at hand. And in the middle of it, Pedrosa, riding his second bike, and not all was well with it.

They were to and fro Moto3-style. By lap 11, Dovi had got to the front, after jousting with former team-mate Crutchlow, who was back in front when Dovi hit trouble on lap 18 – another strange failure, this time structural, to the rear sub-frame carrying an exhaust. Flapping around, it transferred vibration to the front, and he dropped away.

Now Pol Espargaro was attacking Crutchlow again, while Pedrosa had moved through behind him, all resolved with their own last-chicane reshuffle: Pol in front, then Crutchlow, Smith and Pedrosa, who was mugged.

A little way back, Aleix Espargaro was half a second clear of team-mate Vinales, who had finally outdistanced Petrucci, who took 11th off Dovizioso on the final lap.

Redding was a distant 13th, having eventually dropped Hernandez; last point and Open class honours went to Baz. Hayden, in 16th, had been pushed off on lap one by a head-long Miller, who then crashed into the back of Barbera when they got to the chicane, taking both out. Bautista, di Meglio and Melandri trailed in behind the American.

Rossi's fine third win gave him a ten-point advantage over team-mate Lorenzo; Marquez was 74 points, almost three races, adrift.

MOTO2 RACE – 16 laps

Qualifying times were widely spaced compared with MotoGP: the first three occupied almost as much time as the big class's top dozen. Zarco was on pole for a second race in a row, from Rabat and Lowes, the usual suspects. Corsi led row two from Folger and Simeon; Rins the third from Luthi and Baldassarri.

The scheduled 22-lapper didn't even make one. A tangle with Ant West near the back of the first-corner melee sent Salom's yellow Kalex looping to a fiery landing, and left oil on the track. Red flag, frantic scrubbing, then a restart for a relative sprint race. Salom was unable to make the restart.

Above: Zarco and Rabat rub fairings in their Moto2 battle.

Above left: Four-way battle for fifth, between Pol Espargaro, Crutchlow, Smith and Pedrosa.

Far and bottom left: Miller clobbered Barbera on the opening lap, sending both flying. Barbera's leg was caught in Miller's bike, and he was lucky to escape serious injury.

Left: Carry On Bike Racing! Niklas Ajo's amazing Moto3 finish.

Below: Winner Oliveira leads Kent, Bastianini, Quartararo, Fenati, Navarro and Binder.

Photos: Gold & Goose

Folger led away first, and he had a good go at making another runaway, as at Jerez, as Rabat, Zarco and Simeon dropped to more than a second behind after five laps.

By then, Zarco's first attack on Rabat had gone wrong and he was behind Simeon, with Lowes tagged on his back wheel. A lap later, Zarco and Lowes were both past Simeon, and Rabat, with a clear track, had closed up on the leader.

Rabat took to the front at the end of lap seven; Folger would continue to drop as Zarco and Lowes both got past. Then Zarco closed the gap on Rabat, and on lap 14 he made a clear and authoritative pass, soon stretching enough of a gap to secure his second win in a row, third of the year, by less than a second.

Lowes was another second-and-a-bit behind, happy to be the best non-Kalex on a day when "nobody else could stay with those guys ahead".

The battle for fourth had slimmed down to four riders by the end, with Rins taking over on lap ten, and Luthi also getting ahead of Simeon, Folger just off the back by the finish.

Kallio and the improving younger Marquez had a race-long battle for eighth, narrowly won by the veteran. Corsi was a little adrift to complete the top ten; Simon and Aegerter were spaced out behind. West and Baldassari crashed out of this group together.

Zarco's third win further extended his points advantage, now 45 clear of Rabat.

MOTO3 RACE – 22 laps

Bastianini took his second straight pole by three-tenths from a close batch, Navarro and Hanika alongside, the last named for the first time; Kent headed Vinales and Oliveira on the second; then Quartararo, Fenati and Vazquez. It was a good mix of Hondas and KTMs, Bagnaia's Mahindra being the first interloper in tenth.

Kent described a thrilling race as "more like a war". A seven-strong lead group had formed after only four laps, and from there to the end they remained inches apart, swapping to and fro. Typical Moto3, and typically breathtaking.

When the septet crossed the line for the last time, they were still covered by 0.540 of a second.

They exchanged blows from the first corner to the last. Oliveira led away, and headed more laps than any other – nine in total. The one that mattered was the last: it was the Portuguese rider's second win of the year, by just 0.066 of a second.

Second, for a second time in the season, went to rookie Quartararo, Kent just five-hundredths behind him.

It can't have been luck, so it must have been tactics; but it was very fraught.

Laps 17 to 20 were led by another rookie, Navarro, who ended up fourth, having managed to fend off Fenati, who also had led for a total of six laps.

Bastianini had a few goes up front, too, but was shuffled down to sixth at the last; Brad Binder was seventh pretty much throughout, able to stay close, but no more.

There was an even bigger group battling behind, with similar up-and-down fortunes. Eighth went to erstwhile front-runner Hanika, who had climbed back after dropping to 18th following a run-off.

Six-hundredths behind, Antonelli managed to hold off McPhee, Bagnaia, Migno, Loi, Ono and Oettl, who took the last point. Danilo was just out of luck, eighth to 16th all within 1.2 seconds.

Vazquez was an early casualty, crashing out of the front group on lap three. Vinales and on-form Husqvarna teammate Maria Herrera also crashed out. Niklas Ajo crossed the line 17th, to great applause, sliding alongside his bike on his knees. He'd high-sided at the chicane, but didn't let go, managing to finish the race while wrestling to regain control – the video soon went viral.

On the rostrum at every race but one (fourth in France), Kent again extended his points lead over Bastianini.

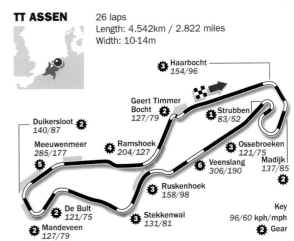

TT ASSEN

26 laps
Length: 4.542km / 2.822 miles
Width: 10-14m

Track key points:
- Haarbocht 154/96
- Geert Timmer Bocht 127/79
- Strubben 83/52
- Duikersloot 140/87
- Ramshoek 204/127
- Ossebroeken 121/75
- Meeuwenmeer 285/177
- Veenslang 306/190
- Madijk 137/85
- Ruskenhoek 158/98
- De Bult 121/75
- Stekkenwal 131/81
- Mandeveen 127/79

Key: 96/60 kph/mph ⚙ Gear

MOTUL
TT ASSEN
25–27 JUNE, 2015

MotoGP

RACE DISTANCE: 26 laps, 73.379 miles/118.092km · RACE WEATHER: Dry (air 20°C, humidity 66%, track 30°C)

Pos.	Rider	Nat.	No.	Entrant	Machine	Tyres	Race tyre choice	Laps	Time & speed
1	**Valentino Rossi**	ITA	46	Movistar Yamaha MotoGP	Yamaha YZR-M1	B	F: Soft/R: Medium	26	40m 54.037s 107.6mph/ 173.2km/h
2	**Marc Marquez**	SPA	93	Repsol Honda Team	Honda RC213V	B	F: Medium/R: Medium	26	40m 55.279s
3	**Jorge Lorenzo**	SPA	99	Movistar Yamaha MotoGP	Yamaha YZR-M1	B	F: Soft/R: Medium	26	41m 08.613s
4	**Andrea Iannone**	ITA	29	Ducati Team	Ducati Desmosedici	B	F: Soft/R: Medium	26	41m 13.146s
5	**Pol Espargaro**	SPA	44	Monster Yamaha Tech 3	Yamaha YZR-M1	B	F: Soft/R: Medium	26	41m 18.305s
6	**Cal Crutchlow**	GBR	35	CWM LCR Honda	Honda RC213V	B	F: Soft/R: Medium	26	41m 18.410s
7	**Bradley Smith**	GBR	38	Monster Yamaha Tech 3	Yamaha YZR-M1	B	F: Soft/R: Medium	26	41m 18.479s
8	**Dani Pedrosa**	SPA	26	Repsol Honda Team	Honda RC213V	B	F: Soft/R: Medium	26	41m 18.693s
9	**Aleix Espargaro**	SPA	41	Team SUZUKI ECSTAR	Suzuki GSX-RR	B	F: Soft/R: Soft	26	41m 20.762s
10	**Maverick Vinales**	SPA	25	Team SUZUKI ECSTAR	Suzuki GSX-RR	B	F: Soft/R: Soft	26	41m 21.275s
11	**Danilo Petrucci**	ITA	9	Octo Pramac Racing	Ducati Desmosedici	B	F: Soft/R: Medium	26	41m 23.075s
12	**Andrea Dovizioso**	ITA	4	Ducati Team	Ducati Desmosedici	B	F: Soft/R: Medium	26	41m 23.455s
13	**Scott Redding**	GBR	45	EG 0,0 Marc VDS	Honda RC213V	B	F: Soft/R: Medium	26	41m 40.700s
14	**Yonny Hernandez**	COL	68	Octo Pramac Racing	Ducati Desmosedici	B	F: Soft/R: Medium	26	41m 43.342s
15	**Loris Baz**	FRA	76	Athina Forward Racing	Yamaha Forward	B	F: Soft/R: Soft	26	41m 46.433s
16	Nicky Hayden	USA	69	Aspar MotoGP Team	Honda RC213V-RS	B	F: Soft/R: Soft	26	41m 50.042s
17	Alvaro Bautista	SPA	19	Aprilia Racing Team Gresini	Aprilia RS-GP	B	F: Soft/R: Soft	26	41m 53.894s
18	Mike di Meglio	FRA	63	Avintia Racing	Ducati Desmosedici Open	B	F: Soft/R: Soft	26	42m 08.550s
19	Marco Melandri	ITA	33	Aprilia Racing Team Gresini	Aprilia RS-GP	B	F: Soft/R: Soft	25	41m 04.386s
	Alex de Angelis	RSM	15	E-Motion IodaRacing Team	Aprilia ART	B	F: Soft/R: Soft	23	DNF-crash
	Eugene Laverty	IRL	50	Aspar MotoGP Team	Honda RC213V-RS	B	F: Soft/R: Soft	15	DNF-crash
	Stefan Bradl	GER	6	Athina Forward Racing	Yamaha Forward	B	F: Soft/R: Soft	5	DNF-crash
	Hector Barbera	SPA	8	Avintia Racing	Ducati Desmosedici Open	B	F: Soft/R: Soft	0	DNF-crash
	Jack Miller	AUS	43	CWM LCR Honda	Honda RC213V-RS	B	F: Soft/R: Soft	0	DNF-crash

Fastest lap: Marc Marquez, on lap 4, 1m 33.617s, 108.5mph/174.6km/h (record).
Previous lap record: Dani Pedrosa, SPA (Honda), 1m 34.548s, 107.460mph/172.940km/h (2012).
Event best maximum speed: Andrea Iannone, 198.7mph/319.8km/h (free practice).

Qualifying
Weather: Dry
Air Temp: 23° **Track Temp:** 37°
Humidity: 63%

1	Rossi	1m 32.627s
2	A. Espargaro	1m 32.858s
3	Marquez	1m 32.886s
4	Pedrosa	1m 32.987s
5	P. Espargaro	1m 33.013s
6	Iannone	1m 33.016s
7	Crutchlow	1m 33.028s
8	Lorenzo	1m 33.042s
9	Vinales	1m 33.076s
10	Dovizioso	1m 33.112s
11	Petrucci	1m 33.126s
12	Smith	1m 33.236s
13	Bradl	1m 33.789s
14	Hernandez	1m 33.875s
15	Baz	1m 33.999s
16	Redding	1m 34.071s
17	Barbera	1m 34.223s
18	Di Meglio	1m 34.289s
19	Laverty	1m 34.428s
20	Miller	1m 34.645s
21	Bautista	1m 34.736s
22	Hayden	1m 34.972s
23	De Angelis	1m 35.189s
24	Melandri	1m 36.376s

Fastest race laps

1	Marquez	1m 33.617s
2	Rossi	1m 33.673s
3	Lorenzo	1m 33.813s
4	Dovizioso	1m 34.140s
5	Iannone	1m 34.394s
6	P. Espargaro	1m 34.470s
7	A. Espargaro	1m 34.477s
8	Crutchlow	1m 34.536s
9	Smith	1m 34.616s
10	Pedrosa	1m 34.651s
11	Vinales	1m 34.652s
12	Petrucci	1m 34.683s
13	Redding	1m 34.839s
14	Hernandez	1m 35.010s
15	Bradl	1m 35.213s
16	Baz	1m 35.349s
17	Hayden	1m 35.587s
18	Bautista	1m 35.639s
19	Laverty	1m 35.812s
20	De Angelis	1m 35.893s
21	Di Meglio	1m 35.975s
22	Melandri	1m 37.285s

Championship Points

1	Rossi	163
2	Lorenzo	153
3	Iannone	107
4	Marquez	89
5	Dovizioso	87
6	Smith	77
7	Crutchlow	57
8	P. Espargaro	56
9	Vinales	52
10	Pedrosa	47
11	Petrucci	44
12	A. Espargaro	38
13	Redding	30
14	Hernandez	28
15	Barbera	16
16	Baz	14
17	Bautista	11
18	Miller	11
19	Bradl	9
20	Pirro	8
21	Hayden	8
22	Laverty	7
23	Aoyama	5
24	Di Meglio	2
25	De Angelis	1

Constructor Points

1	Yamaha	191
2	Honda	134
3	Ducati	132
4	Suzuki	64
5	Yamaha Forward	19
6	Aprilia	11
7	ART	1

Grid order	1	2	3	4	5	6	7	8	9	10	11	12	13	14	15	16	17	18	19	20	21	22	23	24	25	26
46 ROSSI	46	46	46	46	46	46	46	46	46	46	46	46	46	46	46	46	46	46	93	93	93	93	46	46	46	1
41 A. ESPARGARO	93	93	93	93	93	93	93	93	93	93	93	93	93	93	93	93	93	93	46	46	46	46	93	93	93	2
93 MARQUEZ	99	99	99	99	99	99	99	99	99	99	99	99	99	99	99	99	99	99	99	99	99	99	99	99	99	3
26 PEDROSA	44	44	29	29	29	29	29	29	29	29	29	29	29	29	29	29	29	29	29	29	29	29	29	29	29	4
44 P. ESPARGARO	29	29	41	41	41	41	41	41	41	41	4	4	4	35	35	35	35	35	35	35	44	44	44	44	44	5
29 IANNONE	41	41	44	44	44	44	44	44	4	41	35	35	35	4	44	44	44	44	44	26	26	35	35			6
35 CRUTCHLOW	35	35	35	35	4	4	4	35	4	44	44	44	44	44	4	26	26	26	26	35	35	26	38			7
99 LORENZO	38	38	4	4	35	35	35	4	35	35	26	26	26	38	44	38	4	4	4	38	38	26				8
25 VINALES	25	4	38	38	38	38	38	38	38	38	41	41	41	38	26	26	38	38	38	38	41	41	41			9
4 DOVIZIOSO	4	9	9	9	9	9	9	26	26	26	38	38	38	41	41	41	41	41	41	4	25	25				10
9 PETRUCCI	9	25	25	25	26	26	26	26	9	9	9	9	9	9	9	9	9	9	25	25	25	4	9			11
38 SMITH	26	26	26	26	25	25	25	25	25	25	25	25	25	25	25	25	25	25	9	9	9	9	4			12
6 BRADL	68	68	45	45	45	45	45	45	45	45	45	45	45	45	45	45	45	45	45	45	45	45	45			13
68 HERNANDEZ	45	45	68	68	68	68	68	68	68	68	68	68	68	68	68	68	68	68	68	68	68	68	68			14
76 BAZ	6	6	6	6	6	76	76	76	76	76	76	76	76	76	76	76	76	76	76	76	76	76	76			15
45 REDDING	76	76	76	76	76	50	50	19	19	19	19	19	19	69	69	69	69	69	69	69	69	69	69			
8 BARBERA	63	50	50	50	50	19	19	50	50	50	50	69	69	19	19	19	19	19	19	19	19	19	19			
63 DI MEGLIO	50	63	63	63	19	69	69	69	69	69	50	50	50	63	63	63	15	63	63	63	63	63				
50 LAVERTY	15	19	19	19	63	63	63	63	15	15	15	15	15	15	15	15	63	33	33							
43 MILLER	19	15	15	69	15	15	15	15	63	63	63	63	33	33	33	33	33	33	33							
19 BAUTISTA	33	69	69	69	15	33	33	33	33	33	33	33														
69 HAYDEN	69	33	33	33	33																					
15 DE ANGELIS																										
33 MELANDRI																										

33 Lapped rider

Moto2 — RACE DISTANCE: 16 laps, 45.156 miles/72.672km · RACE WEATHER: Dry (air 21°C, humidity 68%, track 30°C)

Pos.	Rider	Nat.	No.	Entrant	Machine	Laps	Time & Speed
1	Johann Zarco	FRA	5	Ajo Motorsport	Kalex	16	26m 13.410s 103.3mph/ 166.2km/h
2	Tito Rabat	SPA	1	EG 0,0 Marc VDS	Kalex	16	26m 14.167s
3	Sam Lowes	GBR	22	Speed Up Racing	Speed Up	16	26m 15.490s
4	Alex Rins	SPA	40	Paginas Amarillas HP 40	Kalex	16	26m 17.148s
5	Thomas Luthi	SWI	12	Derendinger Racing Interwetten	Kalex	16	26m 17.940s
6	Xavier Simeon	BEL	19	Federal Oil Gresini Moto2	Kalex	16	26m 18.455s
7	Jonas Folger	GER	94	AGR Team	Kalex	16	26m 19.550s
8	Mika Kallio	FIN	36	Italtrans Racing Team	Kalex	16	26m 21.515s
9	Alex Marquez	SPA	73	EG 0,0 Marc VDS	Kalex	16	26m 21.786s
10	Simone Corsi	ITA	3	Athina Forward Racing	Kalex	16	26m 23.080s
11	Julian Simon	SPA	60	QMMF Racing Team	Speed Up	16	26m 25.159s
12	Dominique Aegerter	SWI	77	Technomag Racing Interwetten	Kalex	16	26m 30.947s
13	Takaaki Nakagami	JPN	30	IDEMITSU Honda Team Asia	Kalex	16	26m 31.514s
14	Randy Krummenacher	SWI	4	JIR Racing Team	Kalex	16	26m 33.878s
15	Hafizh Syahrin	MAL	55	Petronas Raceline Malaysia	Kalex	16	26m 34.304s
16	Azlan Shah	MAL	25	IDEMITSU Honda Team Asia	Kalex	16	26m 35.815s
17	Sandro Cortese	GER	11	Dynavolt Intact GP	Kalex	16	26m 36.340s
18	Marcel Schrotter	GER	23	Tech 3	Tech 3	16	26m 39.073s
19	Franco Morbidelli	ITA	21	Italtrans Racing Team	Kalex	16	26m 44.341s
20	Robin Mulhauser	SWI	70	Technomag Racing Interwetten	Kalex	16	26m 48.424s
21	Jesko Raffin	SWI	2	sports-millions-EMWE-SAG	Kalex	16	26m 48.699s
22	Axel Pons	SPA	49	AGR Team	Kalex	16	26m 58.204s
23	Thitipong Warokorn	THA	10	APH PTT The Pizza SAG	Kalex	16	27m 01.043s
24	Ratthapark Wilairot	THA	15	JPMoto Malaysia	Suter	16	27m 07.459s
25	Jasper Iwema	NED	13	Abbink GP	Speed Up	16	27m 23.489s
	Lorenzo Baldassarri	ITA	7	Athina Forward Racing	Kalex	11	DNF
	Anthony West	AUS	95	QMMF Racing Team	Speed Up	11	DNF
	Louis Rossi	FRA	96	Tasca Racing Scuderia Moto2	Tech 3	9	DNF
	Ricard Cardus	SPA	88	Tech 3	Tech 3	5	DNF
	Florian Alt	GER	66	E-Motion IodaRacing Team	Suter	2	DNF
	Luis Salom	SPA	39	Paginas Amarillas HP 40	Kalex	0	DNF

Fastest lap: Tito Rabat, on lap 6, 1m 37.449s, 104.2mph/167.7km/h (record).
Previous lap record: Marc Marquez, SPA (Suter), 1m 38.391s, 103.3mph/166.2km/h (2012)
Event best maximum speed: Jasper Iwema, 162.1mph/260.8km/h (race).

Qualifying:
Weather: Dry
Air Temp: 23° Track Temp: 35°
Humidity: 52%

1	Zarco	1m 36.346s
2	Rabat	1m 36.633s
3	Lowes	1m 36.878s
4	Corsi	1m 37.393s
5	Folger	1m 37.434s
6	Simeon	1m 37.509s
7	Rins	1m 37.543s
8	Luthi	1m 37.585s
9	Baldassarri	1m 37.591s
10	Nakagami	1m 37.598s
11	Pons	1m 37.604s
12	Simon	1m 37.632s
13	Marquez	1m 37.638s
14	Cortese	1m 37.650s
15	Kallio	1m 37.717s
16	Aegerter	1m 37.764s
17	Schrotter	1m 37.790s
18	Krummenacher	1m 38.042s
19	Syahrin	1m 38.104s
20	Morbidelli	1m 38.142s
21	Salom	1m 38.175s
22	Cardus	1m 38.222s
23	West	1m 38.262s
24	Shah	1m 38.551s
25	Rossi	1m 38.997s
26	Mulhauser	1m 39.019s
27	Wilairot	1m 39.169s
28	Alt	1m 39.273s
29	Raffin	1m 39.298s
30	Warokorn	1m 39.991s
31	Iwema	1m 40.717s

Fastest race laps:

1	Rabat	1m 37.449s
2	Zarco	1m 37.576s
3	Lowes	1m 37.676s
4	Simeon	1m 37.802s
5	Rins	1m 37.831s
6	Luthi	1m 37.870s
7	Folger	1m 37.901s
8	Kallio	1m 37.918s
9	Marquez	1m 37.934s
10	Pons	1m 38.000s
11	Corsi	1m 38.213s
12	Simon	1m 38.222s
13	Morbidelli	1m 38.288s
14	West	1m 38.392s
15	Aegerter	1m 38.414s
16	Baldassarri	1m 38.469s
17	Cardus	1m 38.487s
18	Nakagami	1m 38.494s
19	Syahrin	1m 38.556s
20	Krummenacher	1m 38.560s
21	Cortese	1m 38.670s
22	Shah	1m 38.719s
23	Schrotter	1m 38.975s
24	Rossi	1m 39.113s
25	Raffin	1m 39.449s
26	Mulhauser	1m 39.653s
27	Warokorn	1m 40.255s
28	Wilairot	1m 40.398s
29	Iwema	1m 40.928s

Championship Points:

1	Zarco	159
2	Rabat	114
3	Lowes	96
4	Luthi	89
5	Rins	87
6	Folger	75
7	Morbidelli	62
8	Simeon	59
9	Kallio	43
10	Simon	40
11	Aegerter	37
12	Salom	36
13	Syahrin	34
14	Cortese	30
15	Marquez	30
16	Baldassarri	29
17	Nakagami	23
18	Corsi	22
19	West	17
20	Schrotter	12
21	Krummenacher	10
22	Pons	8
23	Rossi	7
24	Shah	1

Constructor Points:

1	Kalex	195
2	Speed Up	104
3	Tech 3	19

Moto3 — RACE DISTANCE: 22 laps, 62.090 miles/99.924km · RACE WEATHER: Dry (air 19°C, humidity 81%, track 25°C)

Pos.	Rider	Nat.	No.	Entrant	Machine	Laps	Time & Speed
1	Miguel Oliveira	POR	44	Red Bull KTM Ajo	KTM	22	37m 54.427s 98.2mph/ 158.1km/h
2	Fabio Quartararo	FRA	20	Estrella Galicia 0,0	Honda	22	37m 54.493s
3	Danny Kent	GBR	52	Leopard Racing	Honda	22	37m 54.544s
4	Jorge Navarro	SPA	9	Estrella Galicia 0,0	Honda	22	37m 54.606s
5	Romano Fenati	ITA	5	SKY Racing Team VR46	KTM	22	37m 54.679s
6	Enea Bastianini	ITA	33	Gresini Racing Team Moto3	Honda	22	37m 54.953s
7	Brad Binder	RSA	41	Red Bull KTM Ajo	KTM	22	37m 54.967s
8	Karel Hanika	CZE	98	Red Bull KTM Ajo	KTM	22	38m 15.833s
9	Niccolo Antonelli	ITA	23	Ongetta-Rivacold	Honda	22	38m 15.899s
10	John McPhee	GBR	17	SAXOPRINT RTG	Honda	22	38m 16.090s
11	Francesco Bagnaia	ITA	21	MAPFRE Team MAHINDRA	Mahindra	22	38m 16.120s
12	Andrea Migno	ITA	16	SKY Racing Team VR46	KTM	22	38m 16.150s
13	Livio Loi	BEL	11	RW Racing GP	Honda	22	38m 16.451s
14	Hiroki Ono	JPN	76	Leopard Racing	Honda	22	38m 16.631s
15	Philipp Oettl	GER	65	Schedl GP Racing	KTM	22	38m 17.023s
16	Jules Danilo	FRA	95	Ongetta-Rivacold	Honda	22	38m 17.093s
17	Niklas Ajo	FIN	31	RBA Racing Team	KTM	22	38m 19.921s
18	Jorge Martin	SPA	88	MAPFRE Team MAHINDRA	Mahindra	22	38m 21.698s
19	Darryn Binder	RSA	40	Outox Reset Drink Team	Mahindra	22	38m 21.813s
20	Jakub Kornfeil	CZE	84	Drive M7 SIC	KTM	22	38m 28.390s
21	Alessandro Tonucci	ITA	19	Outox Reset Drink Team	Mahindra	22	38m 29.195s
22	Stefano Manzi	ITA	2	San Carlo Team Italia	Mahindra	22	38m 33.168s
23	Ana Carrasco	SPA	22	RBA Racing Team	KTM	22	38m 46.230s
24	Matteo Ferrari	ITA	12	San Carlo Team Italia	Mahindra	22	38m 46.641s
25	Gabriel Rodrigo	ARG	91	RBA Racing Team	KTM	22	38m 48.043s
26	Remy Gardner	AUS	2	CIP	Mahindra	22	39m 33.344s
27	Jorel Boerboom	NED	25	FPW Racing	Kalex KTM	21	38m 12.430s
28	Kevin Hanus	GER	86	Team Hanusch	Honda	21	38m 13.538s
	Andrea Locatelli	ITA	55	Gresini Racing Team Moto3	Honda	21	DNF
	Maria Herrera	SPA	6	Husqvarna Factory Laglisse	Husqvarna	12	DNF
	Juanfran Guevara	SPA	58	MAPFRE Team MAHINDRA	Mahindra	12	DNF
	Isaac Vinales	SPA	32	Husqvarna Factory Laglisse	Husqvarna	11	DNF
	Zulfahmi Khairuddin	MAL	63	Drive M7 SIC	KTM	5	DNF
	Alexis Masbou	FRA	10	SAXOPRINT RTG	Honda	5	DNF
	Efren Vazquez	SPA	7	Leopard Racing	Honda	2	DNF
	Tatsuki Suzuki	JPN	24	CIP	Mahindra	0	DNF

Fastest lap: Jorge Navarro, on lap 16, 1m 42.135s, 99.4mph/160.0km/h (record).
Previous lap record: Romano Fenati, ITA (KTM), 1m 42.914s, 98.7mph/158.8km/h (2014).
Event best maximum speed: Hiroki Ono, 138.1mph/222.2km/h (race).

Qualifying:
Weather: Dry
Air Temp: 22° Track Temp: 32°
Humidity: 53%

1	Bastianini	1m 41.283s
2	Navarro	1m 41.618s
3	Hanika	1m 41.683s
4	Kent	1m 41.699s
5	Vinales	1m 41.794s
6	Oliveira	1m 41.805s
7	Quartararo	1m 41.811s
8	Fenati	1m 41.846s
9	Vazquez	1m 41.980s
10	Bagnaia	1m 42.202s
11	Binder	1m 42.278s
12	Oettl	1m 42.325s
13	Herrera	1m 42.339s
14	Locatelli	1m 42.345s
15	Martin	1m 42.371s
16	Ajo	1m 42.397s
17	Migno	1m 42.413s
18	Guevara	1m 42.442s
19	Antonelli	1m 42.445s
20	Loi	1m 42.462s
21	Masbou	1m 42.528s
22	Ono	1m 42.675s
23	McPhee	1m 42.743s
24	Binder	1m 42.803s
25	Kornfeil	1m 43.016s
26	Tonucci	1m 43.128s
27	Rodrigo	1m 43.257s
28	Danilo	1m 43.262s
29	Suzuki	1m 43.397s
30	Khairuddin	1m 43.438s
31	Gardner	1m 43.665s
32	Manzi	1m 43.871s
33	Carrasco	1m 43.988s
34	Ferrari	1m 44.442s
35	Boerboom	1m 46.694s
36	Hanus	1m 46.710s

Fastest race laps:

1	Navarro	1m 42.135s
2	Binder	1m 42.435s
3	Fenati	1m 42.456s
4	Bastianini	1m 42.510s
5	Oliveira	1m 42.523s
6	Quartararo	1m 42.542s
7	Kent	1m 42.616s
8	Kornfeil	1m 43.073s
9	Oettl	1m 43.074s
10	Guevara	1m 43.079s
11	Migno	1m 43.080s
12	Hanika	1m 43.103s
13	Herrera	1m 43.164s
14	Vazquez	1m 43.193s
15	McPhee	1m 43.259s
16	Loi	1m 43.294s
17	Antonelli	1m 43.327s
18	Danilo	1m 43.330s
19	Binder	1m 43.344s
20	Ono	1m 43.379s
21	Ajo	1m 43.413s
22	Tonucci	1m 43.437s
23	Locatelli	1m 43.441s
24	Vinales	1m 43.483s
25	Bagnaia	1m 43.486s
26	Martin	1m 43.513s
27	Rodrigo	1m 43.812s
28	Manzi	1m 43.816s
29	Gardner	1m 44.516s
30	Carrasco	1m 44.582s
31	Khairuddin	1m 44.588s
32	Ferrari	1m 44.713s
33	Masbou	1m 44.759s
34	Boerboom	1m 47.363s
35	Hanus	1m 47.898s

Championship Points:

1	Kent	165
2	Bastianini	108
3	Oliveira	102
4	Fenati	86
5	Vazquez	76
6	Quartararo	74
7	Binder	66
8	Vinales	64
9	Bagnaia	55
10	Antonelli	49
11	Navarro	44
12	McPhee	34
13	Masbou	33
14	Hanika	26
15	Locatelli	21
16	Oettl	18
17	Kornfeil	17
18	Migno	16
19	Ajo	15
20	Ono	15
21	Loi	15
22	Martin	8
23	Danilo	4
24	Guevara	4
25	Khairuddin	2
26	Herrera	1
27	Manzi	1
28	Ferrari	1

Constructor Points:

1	Honda	185
2	KTM	136
3	Husqvarna	64
4	Mahindra	61

GERMAN GRAND PRIX

SACHSENRING

Inset, left: All smiles as Rossi adds yet another podium to his 2015 selfie album.
Photo: Movistar Yamaha

Main: Marquez was back in control; Lorenzo, Rossi and Pedrosa scrap for the other podium places.
Photo: Gold & Goose

Above: Suzuki's retro livery recalled Kevin Schwantz's AMA glory days of the 1980s.

Centre, from left: Michael Laverty had a one-off ride for Aprilia; Marquez talked up his title chances, Lorenzo looked unconvinced; Forward team owner Cuzari and injured rider Bradl – after the race, the Italian was arrested.

Below right: Super-sub Aoyama took the injured Abraham's Open Honda.

Bottom right: Pick me up and lay me down: the luckless Rabat after his last-corner savaging by Morbidelli.

Far right: Eugene Laverty, wearing a tribute helmet, battles Baz and de Angelis at the tail-end of the race.

Photos: Gold & Goose

PRE-RACE press conferences are generally painfully stilted affairs, full of obvious answers from the riders ("I am going to try my maximum to get the best result possible.") and self-congratulatory toadying from website jockeys. Then somebody asked Marquez which of the two title leaders – Rossi or Lorenzo – he would prefer to see win the championship.

He smirked politely and pointed out that it was not over yet: the season was not quite halfway done. He had every intention of becoming champion himself.

Three days later came a performance that suggested perhaps the tide had turned, and there could easily be a cliff-hanger finale. His second pole-to-chequer win of the year (his third in a row at the curiously interesting little German track) was emphatic, and it triggered some mathematics. He had cut his deficit on leader Rossi to 65 points and needed to take back an average of just over seven points per race. In Germany, thanks to Pedrosa, he took back nine. Keep it up, and...

The first half of the year closed in unpredictable, but ultimately balmy weather; a preceding heat wave had Bridgestone cautiously adding an extra harder-spec tyre to their usual allocation, which included for the first time since Valencia 2014 a mixed-compound front tyre. It had not been popular there, while the previous outing at Phillip Island had coincided with a number of front-running crashes (Marquez included) as the temperature fell rapidly during the late-running race. Now the construction had been revised to cushion the transition to the soft strip on the right.

All this because of the now-famous Waterfall turn 11, the first right-hander after a series of seven increasingly rapid lefts. It is a fast and difficult corner that drops away rapidly at the apex. The new front tyres were popular and the almost universal race choice; only four riders (Redding, Crutchlow, Hernandez and Miller) chose the medium front. More significantly, on a hot race day, Marquez and Pedrosa gambled on the hard front. It paid off.

The corner continued to catch out riders anyway, with Pol Espargaro, Bautista and Miller falling there in practice in MotoGP, and others in the smaller classes. Bautista was fresh from arm-pump surgery, and his crash re-opened the wound.

Ducati had something new: their winglets had become bi-planes. Strangely, nobody seemed to have copied them yet. A different kind of doubling up saw many riders fit two layers of knee-slider to their left legs – the interminable left-handers double the usual wear rate. One who didn't was Bradley Smith, who came to regret it, when in the race he was down to the leather for the last laps, much hampering his style.

Suzuki also had a novelty, although only a paint job, along with hopes that a track with more corners and a slow top speed would favour them. The retro blue-and-white livery replicated that used in the 1980s by Kevin Schwantz, in his legendary AMA Superbike battles with career-long rival Wayne Rainey. It celebrated 30 years of the GSX-R750 and was hugely popular, including with its riders.

Bradl was playing reluctant wallflower at his home GP, saying with more hope than conviction that perhaps watching the other riders might teach him something; his place was taken by Claudio Corti, and little did anyone know that his Athina Forward squad would shortly run into near-terminal problems, with team owner Giovanni Cuzari arrested on charges of tax fraud and money laundering on his return to Switzerland. Next time out, the former Moto2 champion would be on an Aprilia; the other Forward riders (Baz in MotoGP, Corsi and Baldassarri in Moto2) would miss Indy, but return at Brno.

The Aprilia vacancy was the result of the departure (by mutual consent) of Melandri. For this race, Michael Laverty – elder brother of Eugene – took over. Between BSB duties, the former PBM rider was already testing for Aprilia, but this would be a one-race outing. The brothers met in the gravel trap during practice. Eugene wore a special orange helmet for the race, as worn by Irish road-racing's revered 'Flying

Doctor' John Hinds, killed the weekend before in a crash at the Skerries 100.

Abraham was absent for another race, with Aoyama back again as substitute, to as little effect as when he had been on a full factory Honda for Pedrosa. The level of MotoGP is so high that it does not welcome casual visitors.

Rabat arrived in poor condition, after a heavy crash while training less than a week before. As well as extensive road rash on one arm, he'd smashed his collarbone into five fragments. Orthopaedic repair was immediate and he was heavily strapped, and cause for concern when he crashed in practice. He survived that and was fighting at the front in the final corner when Morbidelli "did a ridiculous", slid off inside him and sent him flying – zero points scant reward for his bravery.

Scant reward either for Assen Moto3 winner Oliveira, who crashed at the first corner during the first session, breaking a bone in his hand, which put him out until after the summer break.

There was a rash of penalties as Race Direction donned its jackboots to put into action the threats of harsh discipline of a fortnight before. Seventeen penalties were issued for the familiar offence of loitering on the racing line, and 11 of them in the smallest class, where the new punishment applies. The guilty parties were Carrasco, Navarro, Migno, McPhee, Herrera, Ajo, Vinales, Bastianini, Locatelli, Kornfeil and Ono, with Bastianini losing his front-row start, as he was bumped down three grid places. In addition, all had to miss the first half of race morning's 20-minute warm-up session. In the other classes, penalty points were applied as usual to Corsi, Cortese, Luthi and Simeon in Moto2; di Meglio and Barbera in MotoGP, the latter actually receiving two points, because he was a serial offender. Meanwhile, Ajo got a point as well after bashing into team-mate Carrasco in practice, putting them both down.

MOTOGP RACE – 30 laps

Marquez dominated from the start – heading free practice and claiming his fourth pole of the year by almost three-tenths. In the end, team-mate Pedrosa slotted alongside, with Lorenzo third. Pedrosa had always used a different chassis from Marquez: his improving form came more from his own improving physical condition.

Rossi was at the far end of row two, headed by the Ducatis of Iannone and the flying Hernandez; Aleix Espargaro led his brother and Smith on row three.

The usual Honda/Yamaha quartet made all the running, Lorenzo seizing the lead with a daring swoop around the outside at the first tight corner, with Marquez and Pedrosa close company. Rossi grabbed fourth at turn 12, at the bottom of the hill, from Iannone's Ducati, and the race was on.

On lap five, a shuffle. Rossi consigned Pedrosa to fourth at turn 12, Marquez seized the lead at turn 13, on to the start-finish straight. Rossi at once set about his team-mate, but his first attack was repulsed. It took another lap, the eighth, before he was clear, Marquez by now 1.6 seconds away and clearly unassailable, with a new record on lap ten.

It was a demonstration of the still-young rider at his best, and it looked as though all his problems were over. But he sounded a cautionary note. The Sachsenring had only two corners on the lap – fast and opening out – where the Honda had a weak point, so the circuit had favoured him. "It looks as though we have arrived, but we need another step."

Lorenzo was struggling, saying later that rear grip problems had affected both his braking and corner exit drive. "I regret not trying a shorter bike in warm-up." At the start of lap 11, Pedrosa – gaining pace as the fuel burned off – dived inside into the first corner.

Lorenzo would steadily lose ground, while Pedrosa quickly

Above: Pedrosa versus Rossi – their duel was the feature of the race.

Top right: Morbidelli and Rabat crash out of the battle for third on Moto2's final corner.

Above right: Simeon holds off Zarco as they dash for the line.

Far right: Simeon was the first Belgian to win a grand prix since Didier de Radigues in 1983.

Right: Kent took another win to add to his huge Moto3 points advantage.

Below right: Starting his escape, Kent heads Bastianini (33), Binder (41), Vazquez (7), Hanika, Quartararo, Antonelli (23) and Locatelli (55).

Photos: Gold & Goose

closed on Rossi. He shadowed him steadily, then on lap 17 pounced at the bottom of the Waterfall to take over second.

"It was a good moment for me, because I could put a hook on his seat and make a gap on Jorge," said Rossi. He even thought he might be able to get by again, "but then Dani did two really fast laps, and he was gone." But for his discomfort in the early laps, Pedrosa felt, he might have had a chance of a fight with Marquez.

With Iannone falling away throughout in a lone fifth, and Dovizioso suffering yet another out-of-character race crash just before half-distance, it was a relatively processional race behind them, but for a stirring internecine battle by the Suzuki pair. They were separated over the line by two-hundredths after some late-laps to-and-fro for tenth. Espargaro narrowly prevailed, while Vinales set a rookie record, the first to finish in the points in his first nine races.

Hernandez held sixth for a while before losing places. First past was Smith, who had his hands full for a spell with a strong attack from Crutchlow. But the Honda rider had crashed heavily, chased in by his bike, at the Omega curve on Saturday and was still battered; eventually he lost touch, six seconds away at the end.

Second Pramac Ducati rider Petrucci had come through in the early stages and was ahead of Pol Espargaro for eighth for a spell, and less than a second adrift at the end. Then came the Suzukis, five seconds ahead of 12th-placed Hernandez at the finish.

Bautista and Miller, locked in combat, were caught and eventually passed by Barbera, top Open bike. Bautista prevailed and Miller took the last point.

Hayden was a lone 16th, again pushed out at the first corner. He managed to get ahead of Barbera, only to drop back, subsequently complaining of a loss of grip, "like we lost some weight off the rear".

Eugene Laverty finally won out after a long battle with de Angelis, whose ART had the benefit of a chassis upgrade; Baz and Michael Laverty trailed in behind.

Corti retired with handling problems; Aoyama crashed out, likewise di Meglio; while a hitherto slightly more promising weekend for Redding ended abruptly when he crashed on the final corner before completing the first lap.

Thus ended the first half, in a quite unexpected position. Rossi had extended his lead again over Lorenzo, 179 to 166, and nothing much else between them. Iannone's third was by just four points from Marquez, and seriously under threat. But were the two Yamaha riders also?

MOTO2 RACE – 29 laps

It's not often that Moto2 has so many riders still so close into the final corner. This time, there were two less on the way out of it than on the way in, as early leader Morbidelli took out defending champion Tito Rabat.

That made no difference to the pair of riders up front, but potentially plenty of difference to the championship, allowing Zarco to extend his overall points lead again, even though he lost his own long-time lead of the race to first-time winner Xavier Simeon.

Zarco had qualified on pole from Simeon and Morbidelli, with the already battered Rabat at the far end of row two.

Morbidelli led away; then Simeon for two laps before Zarco took over on the fourth. By then, second-row starter Corsi had been among them, but had dropped away to fourth, where he was briefly challenged by an at-last on-form Kallio. Meanwhile, Rabat had been picking his way up to sixth from ninth on lap one, taking Rins with him.

By half-distance, Zarco, Morbidelli and Simeon were locked together up front, while a little way back Corsi was

about to fall victim to both Rabat and Rins; Kallio was losing ground behind Luthi and Lowes, who were locked in combat.

Rabat and Rins outpaced Corsi as the defending champion pulled his class-rookie countryman up to the battle for the lead.

With nine laps left, Zarco started to gap Morbidelli, and Simeon took his chance to seize second and close on the leader. Five laps later, he dived inside under brakes at the first corner and would fend off the Frenchman to the finish.

Now the fight was for third, not far behind, with Morbidelli coming under increasing threat as the end drew nigh. Rabat finally was passed on the second-last corner; the Italian immediately fought back, taking a tight line into the final left-hander. Too tight. The front slipped away and his bike slid directly into Rabat, sending both cartwheeling into the gravel and handing a close third to Rins.

Corsi was a lone fourth; Lowes finally got the better of Luthi, who managed to fend off a late attack from Nakagami. Baldassari had lost touch with the Japanese rider in the end in eighth; Simon won out narrowly after a long battle with Aegerter and Cortese for ninth, Kallio off the back of it by the flag.

Krummenacher nicked 13th off Folger, who had dropped out of a strong top-ten position with a first-corner braking error and run-off; Pons narrowly saved the last point from Hafiz Syahrin.

West crashed out, as did Shah and Schrotter.

Zarco added 20 points to his title lead, 179 to no-score Rabat's 114, with Lowes and Rins closing on 107 and 103. A good fight for second overall, anyway.

MOTO3 RACE – 27 laps

Is it possible to be imperious on a Moto3 bike? Danny Kent obviously thought so, because it's the best description of yet another runaway, his third of the season and his fifth win of the year.

It was another furiously close race, but not for Kent and Leopard Honda team-mate Vazquez.

Kent had dominated every practice session and remained on pole as penalties reshuffled the grid. Hanika was alongside and Quartararo promoted to row one; Bastianini was in the middle of the second, between Vazquez and rookie Martin's Mahindra.

The English rider was cautious in the early laps, taking the lead from fast-away Hanika on lap one, then ceding it to second Red Bull rider Brad Binder on the second.

Then he took over again, and when Vazquez claimed second from Bastianini, it wasn't long before the pair were moving away together, and soon thereafter Kent started to put a gap on Vazquez.

The usual gang was hard at it in their wake: 11-strong at half-distance, at which point Antonelli had taken over from Binder, with Bastianini also ahead of the South African. Hanika, Navarro and Masbou were also prominent, while Fenati was coming through rapidly from 14th on lap one.

Quartararo was absent, having crashed out of the group on lap six, while lying ninth. The remainder were swapping constantly, as is their wont, then Fenati took over with four laps to go. At the last gasp, Bastianini got a better exit from the last corner and claimed third from Fenati by inches, followed by Antonelli, Navarro, Binder and Masbou, Locatelli, Ajo and Phillip Oettl. Only two seconds spanned third to 11th.

Martin, who had been running sixth in the early stages, but then lost touch with the group, recovered 12th from Hanika on the final lap; almost ten seconds away, Kornfeil and Danilo headed the next gang to claim the last points.

Other crashers included both women racers, Maria Herrera and Ana Carrasco, who collided at the last corner with just over two laps to go, the latter suffering a broken upper left arm, which put her out of action for a spell.

Kent went on holiday with the biggest lead of anyone, a full 66 points clear of Bastianini.

GOPRO MOTORRAD
GRAND PRIX DEUTSCHLAND

10–12 JULY, 2015

SACHSENRING GP CIRCUIT

30 laps
Length: 3.671 km / 3,259 miles
Width: 12m

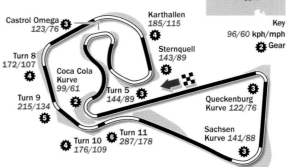

Key
96/60 kph/mph
2 Gear

Castrol Omega 123/76
Karthallen 185/115
Turn 8 172/107
Sternquell 143/89
Coca Cola Kurve 99/61
Turn 5 144/89
Turn 9 215/134
Queckenburg Kurve 122/76
Turn 11 287/178
Sachsen Kurve 141/88
Turn 10 176/109

MotoGP RACE DISTANCE: 30 laps, 68.432 miles/110.130km · RACE WEATHER: Dry (air 27°C, humidity 38%, track 42°C)

Pos.	Rider	Nat.	No.	Entrant	Machine	Tyres	Race tyre choice	Laps	Time & speed
1	**Marc Marquez**	SPA	93	Repsol Honda Team	Honda RC213V	B	F: Hard/R: Medium	30	41m 01.087s 100.0mph/ 161.0km/h
2	**Dani Pedrosa**	SPA	26	Repsol Honda Team	Honda RC213V	B	F: Hard/R: Medium	30	41m 03.313s
3	**Valentino Rossi**	ITA	46	Movistar Yamaha MotoGP	Yamaha YZR-M1	B	F: Asymmetric/R: Medium	30	41m 06.695s
4	**Jorge Lorenzo**	SPA	99	Movistar Yamaha MotoGP	Yamaha YZR-M1	B	F: Asymmetric/R: Medium	30	41m 11.015s
5	**Andrea Iannone**	ITA	29	Ducati Team	Ducati Desmosedici	B	F: Asymmetric/R: Medium	30	41m 21.872s
6	**Bradley Smith**	GBR	38	Monster Yamaha Tech 3	Yamaha YZR-M1	B	F: Asymmetric/R: Medium	30	41m 24.302s
7	**Cal Crutchlow**	GBR	35	CWM LCR Honda	Honda RC213V	B	F: Medium/R: Medium	30	41m 30.968s
8	**Pol Espargaro**	SPA	44	Monster Yamaha Tech 3	Yamaha YZR-M1	B	F: Asymmetric/R: Medium	30	41m 36.040s
9	**Danilo Petrucci**	ITA	9	Octo Pramac Racing	Ducati Desmosedici	B	F: Asymmetric/R: Medium	30	41m 36.962s
10	**Aleix Espargaro**	SPA	41	Team SUZUKI ECSTAR	Suzuki GSX-RR	B	F: Asymmetric/R: Medium	30	41m 38.340s
11	**Maverick Vinales**	SPA	25	Team SUZUKI ECSTAR	Suzuki GSX-RR	B	F: Asymmetric/R: Medium	30	41m 38.361s
12	**Yonny Hernandez**	COL	68	Octo Pramac Racing	Ducati Desmosedici	B	F: Medium/R: Medium	30	41m 43.168s
13	**Hector Barbera**	SPA	8	Avintia Racing	Ducati Desmosedici Open	B	F: Asymmetric/R: Soft	30	41m 49.698s
14	**Alvaro Bautista**	SPA	19	Aprilia Racing Team Gresini	Aprilia RS-GP	B	F: Asymmetric/R: Soft	30	41m 51.774s
15	**Jack Miller**	AUS	43	CWM LCR Honda	Honda RC213V-RS	B	F: Medium/R: Soft	30	41m 54.856s
16	Nicky Hayden	USA	69	Aspar MotoGP Team	Honda RC213V-RS	B	F: Asymmetric/R: Soft	30	42m 00.008s
17	Eugene Laverty	IRL	50	Aspar MotoGP Team	Honda RC213V-RS	B	F: Asymmetric/R: Soft	30	42m 03.825s
18	Alex de Angelis	RSM	15	E-Motion IodaRacing Team	Aprilia ART	B	F: Asymmetric/R: Soft	30	42m 04.209s
19	Loris Baz	FRA	76	Athina Forward Racing	Yamaha Forward	B	F: Asymmetric/R: Soft	30	42m 12.249s
20	Michael Laverty	GBR	70	Aprilia Racing Team Gresini	Aprilia RS-GP	B	F: Asymmetric/R: Soft	30	42m 16.997s
	Claudio Corti	ITA	71	Athina Forward Racing	Yamaha Forward	B	F: Asymmetric/R: Soft	22	DNF-mechanical
	Andrea Dovizioso	ITA	4	Ducati Team	Ducati Desmosedici	B	F: Asymmetric/R: Medium	14	DNF-crash
	Hiroshi Aoyama	JPN	7	AB Motoracing	Honda RC213V-RS	B	F: Asymmetric/R: Soft	4	DNF-crash
	Mike di Meglio	FRA	63	Avintia Racing	Ducati Desmosedici Open	B	F: Asymmetric/R: Soft	3	DNF-crash
	Scott Redding	GBR	45	EG 0,0 Marc VDS	Honda RC213V	B	F: Medium/R: Medium	0	DNF-crash

Fastest lap: Marc Marquez, on lap 10, 1m 21.530s, 100.7mph/162.0km/h (record)
Previous lap record: Dani Pedrosa, SPA (Honda), 1m 21.846s, 100.3mph/161.5km/h (2011).
Event best maximum speed: Andrea Dovizioso, 185.3mph/298.2km/h (free practice).

Qualifying
Weather: Dry
Air Temp: 24° Track Temp: 36°
Humidity: 34%

1	Marquez	1m 20.336s
2	Pedrosa	1m 20.628s
3	Lorenzo	1m 20.921s
4	Iannone	1m 21.029s
5	Hernandez	1m 21.115s
6	Rossi	1m 21.220s
7	A. Espargaro	1m 21.239s
8	P. Espargaro	1m 21.274s
9	Smith	1m 21.329s
10	Crutchlow	1m 21.409s
11	Dovizioso	1m 21.503s
12	Vinales	1m 21.796s
13	Barbera	1m 21.628s
14	Redding	1m 21.632s
15	Petrucci	1m 21.760s
16	Bautista	1m 22.049s
17	De Angelis	1m 22.195s
18	Miller	1m 22.225s
19	Hayden	1m 22.362s
20	Baz	1m 22.394s
21	Di Meglio	1m 22.441s
22	Aoyama	1m 22.543s
23	E. Laverty	1m 22.693s
24	M. Laverty	1m 22.947s
25	Corti	1m 23.374s

Fastest race laps

1	Marquez	1m 21.530s
2	Rossi	1m 21.641s
3	Pedrosa	1m 21.714s
4	Lorenzo	1m 21.811s
5	Iannone	1m 22.024s
6	Crutchlow	1m 22.319s
7	Dovizioso	1m 22.395s
8	Smith	1m 22.403s
9	Hernandez	1m 22.502s
10	Petrucci	1m 22.595s
11	P. Espargaro	1m 22.743s
12	A. Espargaro	1m 22.763s
13	Barbera	1m 22.880s
14	Vinales	1m 22.940s
15	Miller	1m 22.963s
16	Bautista	1m 23.086s
17	Hayden	1m 23.305s
18	De Angelis	1m 23.405s
19	E. Laverty	1m 23.405s
20	Baz	1m 23.449s
21	Aoyama	1m 23.556s
22	M. Laverty	1m 23.895s
23	Di Meglio	1m 24.036s
24	Corti	1m 25.036s

Championship Points

1	Rossi	179
2	Lorenzo	166
3	Iannone	118
4	Marquez	114
5	Dovizioso	87
6	Smith	87
7	Pedrosa	67
8	Crutchlow	66
9	P. Espargaro	64
10	Vinales	57
11	Petrucci	51
12	A. Espargaro	44
13	Hernandez	32
14	Redding	30
15	Barbera	19
16	Baz	14
17	Bautista	13
18	Miller	12
19	Bradl	9
20	Pirro	8
21	Hayden	8
22	E. Laverty	7
23	Aoyama	5
24	Di Meglio	2
25	De Angelis	1

Constructor Points

1	Yamaha	207
2	Honda	159
3	Ducati	143
4	Suzuki	70
5	Yamaha Forward	19
6	Aprilia	13
7	ART	1

Grid Order	1	2	3	4	5	6	7	8	9	10	11	12	13	14	15	16	17	18	19	20	21	22	23	24	25	26	27	28	29	30	
93 MARQUEZ	99	99	99	99	93	93	93	93	93	93	93	93	93	93	93	93	93	93	93	93	93	93	93	93	93	93	93	93	93	93	1
26 PEDROSA	93	93	93	93	99	99	99	46	46	46	46	46	46	46	46	46	26	26	26	26	26	26	26	26	26	26	26	26	26	26	2
99 LORENZO	26	26	26	26	46	46	46	99	99	99	26	26	26	26	26	26	46	46	46	46	46	46	46	46	46	46	46	46	46	46	3
29 IANNONE	46	46	46	46	26	26	26	26	26	26	99	99	99	99	99	99	99	99	99	99	99	99	99	99	99	99	99	99	99	99	4
68 HERNANDEZ	29	29	29	29	29	29	29	29	29	29	29	29	29	29	29	29	29	29	29	29	29	29	29	29	29	29	29	29	29	29	5
46 ROSSI	68	68	68	68	68	68	38	38	38	38	38	38	38	38	38	38	38	38	38	38	38	38	38	38	38	38	38	38	38	38	6
41 A. ESPARGARO	38	38	38	38	38	38	68	68	35	35	35	35	35	35	35	35	35	35	35	35	35	35	35	35	35	35	35	35	35	35	7
44 P. ESPARGARO	44	35	35	35	35	35	35	68	4	4	4	4	68	68	68	68	68	68	68	68	68	44	44	44	44	44	44	44	44	44	8
38 SMITH	35	44	44	41	41	41	4	4	68	68	68	68	68	4	44	44	44	44	44	44	44	68	9	9	9	9	9	9	9	9	9
35 CRUTCHLOW	41	41	41	44	4	4	41	41	41	41	41	41	41	9	44	9	9	9	9	9	9	9	25	25	41	41	41	41	41	41	10
4 DOVIZIOSO	4	4	4	44	44	44	44	44	44	9	9	9	41	41	41	41	41	41	41	41	41	25	68	41	41	25	25	25			11
25 VINALES	19	19	9	9	9	9	9	9	44	44	44	25	25	25	25	25	25	25	41	41	68	41	68	68	68	68	68				12
8 BARBERA	25	19	19	19	25	25	25	25	25	25	25	25	19	19	43	43	43	43	43	43	19	19	8	8	8	8	8				13
45 REDDING	9	25	25	25	19	19	19	19	19	19	19	19	43	43	19	19	19	19	19	19	8	8	19	19	19	19	19				14
9 PETRUCCI	43	43	43	43	43	43	43	43	43	43	43	43	9	8	8	8	8	8	8	8	43	43	43	43	43	43	43				15
19 BAUTISTA	15	15	76	76	76	76	76	76	69	69	69	8	8	69	69	69	69	69	69	69	69	69	69	69	69	69	69				
15 DE ANGELIS	76	76	15	15	15	69	69	69	76	8	8	69	69	50	50	50	50	50	50	15	50	50	50								
43 MILLER	70	70	50	50	69	15	8	8	8	76	76	76	76	76	15	15	15	15	15	50	15	15	15								
69 HAYDEN	50	50	70	69	50	8	15	15	15	15	15	50	50	76	76	76	76	76	76	76	76	76	76								
76 BAZ	8	8	69	8	8	50	50	50	50	50	50	70	70	70	70	70	70	70	70	70	70	70	70								
63 DI MEGLIO	7	69	8	7	70	70	70	70	70	70	70	71	71	71	71	71	71	71	71												
7 AOYAMA	63	7	7	70	71	71	71	71	71	71	71	71	71																		
50 E. LAVERTY	69	63	71	71																											
70 M. LAVERTY	71	71	63																												
71 CORTI																															

63 Pit stop   71 Lapped rider

Moto2 — RACE DISTANCE: 29 laps, 66.151 miles/106.459km · RACE WEATHER: Dry (air 27°C, humidity 39%, track 40°C)

Pos.	Rider	Nat.	No.	Entrant	Machine	Laps	Time & Speed
1	Xavier Simeon	BEL	19	Federal Oil Gresini Moto2	Kalex	29	41m 09.295s 96.4mph/ 155.2km/h
2	Johann Zarco	FRA	5	Ajo Motorsport	Kalex	29	41m 09.378s
3	Alex Rins	SPA	40	Paginas Amarillas HP 40	Kalex	29	41m 10.941s
4	Simone Corsi	ITA	3	Athina Forward Racing	Kalex	29	41m 15.681s
5	Sam Lowes	GBR	22	Speed Up Racing	Speed Up	29	41m 18.579s
6	Thomas Luthi	SWI	12	Derendinger Racing Interwetten	Kalex	29	41m 19.727s
7	Takaaki Nakagami	JPN	30	IDEMITSU Honda Team Asia	Kalex	29	41m 19.887s
8	Lorenzo Baldassarri	ITA	7	Athina Forward Racing	Kalex	29	41m 21.813s
9	Julian Simon	SPA	60	QMMF Racing Team	Speed Up	29	41m 24.157s
10	Dominique Aegerter	SWI	77	Technomag Racing Interwetten	Kalex	29	41m 24.248s
11	Sandro Cortese	GER	11	Dynavolt Intact GP	Kalex	29	41m 26.824s
12	Mika Kallio	FIN	36	Italtrans Racing Team	Kalex	29	41m 28.115s
13	Randy Krummenacher	SWI	4	JIR Racing Team	Kalex	29	41m 31.144s
14	Jonas Folger	GER	94	AGR Team	Kalex	29	41m 31.657s
15	Axel Pons	SPA	49	AGR Team	Kalex	29	41m 32.570s
16	Hafizh Syahrin	MAL	55	Petronas Raceline Malaysia	Kalex	29	41m 32.724s
17	Luis Salom	SPA	39	Paginas Amarillas HP 40	Kalex	29	41m 37.802s
18	Alex Marquez	SPA	73	EG 0,0 Marc VDS	Kalex	29	41m 42.035s
19	Ricard Cardus	SPA	88	Tech 3	Tech 3	29	41m 42.760s
20	Robin Mulhauser	SWI	70	Technomag Racing Interwetten	Kalex	29	41m 42.803s
21	Jesko Raffin	SWI	2	sports-millions-EMWE-SAG	Kalex	29	42m 04.486s
22	Thitipong Warokorn	THA	10	APH PTT The Pizza SAG	Kalex	29	42m 06.744s
23	Ratthapark Wilairot	THA	15	JPMoto Malaysia	Suter	29	42m 07.071s
	Franco Morbidelli	ITA	21	Italtrans Racing Team	Kalex	28	DNF
	Tito Rabat	SPA	1	EG 0,0 Marc VDS	Kalex	28	DNF
	Louis Rossi	FRA	96	Tasca Racing Scuderia Moto2	Tech 3	25	DNF
	Marcel Schrotter	GER	23	Tech 3	Tech 3	5	DNF
	Azlan Shah	MAL	25	IDEMITSU Honda Team Asia	Kalex	5	DNF
	Anthony West	AUS	95	QMMF Racing Team	Speed Up	4	DNF

Fastest lap: Franco Morbidelli, on lap 6, 1m 24.538s, 97.1mph/156.3km/h (record).
Previous lap record: Julian Simon, SPA (Kalex), 1m 24.809s, 96.8mph/155.5km/h (2013).
Event best maximum speed: Sandro Cortese, 158.3mph/254.8km/h (free practice).

Qualifying
Weather: Dry
Air Temp: 24° Track Temp: 36°
Humidity: 36%

1	Zarco	1m 24.044s
2	Simeon	1m 24.133s
3	Morbidelli	1m 24.291s
4	Luthi	1m 24.403s
5	Corsi	1m 24.449s
6	Rabat	1m 24.507s
7	Cortese	1m 24.515s
8	Folger	1m 24.618s
9	Lowes	1m 24.661s
10	Kallio	1m 24.669s
11	Nakagami	1m 24.696s
12	Rins	1m 24.710s
13	Aegerter	1m 24.710s
14	Pons	1m 24.733s
15	Simon	1m 24.782s
16	Baldassarri	1m 24.921s
17	Syahrin	1m 24.922s
18	West	1m 24.970s
19	Krummenacher	1m 25.027s
20	Cardus	1m 25.097s
21	Schrotter	1m 25.216s
22	Salom	1m 25.231s
23	Shah	1m 25.343s
24	Marquez	1m 25.506s
25	Wilairot	1m 25.536s
26	Raffin	1m 25.616s
27	Mulhauser	1m 25.827s
28	Warokorn	1m 26.208s
29	Rossi	1m 26.234s
	Alt	No Time

Fastest race laps

1	Morbidelli	1m 24.538s
2	Zarco	1m 24.659s
3	Rabat	1m 24.774s
4	Simeon	1m 24.795s
5	Kallio	1m 24.798s
6	Corsi	1m 24.815s
7	Rins	1m 24.871s
8	Baldassarri	1m 24.904s
9	Aegerter	1m 24.912s
10	Lowes	1m 25.002s
11	Luthi	1m 25.080s
12	Nakagami	1m 25.090s
13	Cortese	1m 25.091s
14	Folger	1m 25.125s
15	Simon	1m 25.128s
16	Syahrin	1m 25.308s
17	Krummenacher	1m 25.334s
18	Pons	1m 25.342s
19	Marquez	1m 25.353s
20	West	1m 25.465s
21	Cardus	1m 25.486s
22	Shah	1m 25.524s
23	Salom	1m 25.530s
24	Mulhauser	1m 25.557s
25	Schrotter	1m 25.603s
26	Wilairot	1m 25.867s
27	Raffin	1m 25.953s
28	Rossi	1m 26.090s
29	Warokorn	1m 26.371s

Championship Points

1	Zarco	179
2	Rabat	114
3	Lowes	107
4	Rins	103
5	Luthi	99
6	Simeon	84
7	Folger	77
8	Morbidelli	62
9	Kallio	47
10	Simon	47
11	Aegerter	43
12	Baldassarri	37
13	Salom	36
14	Corsi	35
15	Cortese	35
16	Syahrin	34
17	Nakagami	32
18	Marquez	30
19	West	17
20	Krummenacher	13
21	Schrotter	12
22	Pons	9
23	Rossi	7
24	Shah	1

Constructor Points

1	Kalex	220
2	Speed Up	115
3	Tech 3	19

Moto3 — RACE DISTANCE: 27 laps, 61.588 miles/99.117km · RACE WEATHER: Dry (air 25°C, humidity 45%, track 32°C)

Pos.	Rider	Nat.	No.	Entrant	Machine	Laps	Time & Speed
1	Danny Kent	GBR	52	Leopard Racing	Honda	27	39m 29.359s 93.5mph/ 150.5km/h
2	Efren Vazquez	SPA	7	Leopard Racing	Honda	27	39m 36.913s
3	Enea Bastianini	ITA	33	Gresini Racing Team Moto3	Honda	27	39m 38.962s
4	Romano Fenati	ITA	5	SKY Racing Team VR46	KTM	27	39m 38.988s
5	Niccolo Antonelli	ITA	23	Ongetta-Rivacold	Honda	27	39m 39.023s
6	Jorge Navarro	SPA	9	Estrella Galicia 0,0	Honda	27	39m 39.166s
7	Brad Binder	RSA	41	Red Bull KTM Ajo	KTM	27	39m 39.196s
8	Alexis Masbou	FRA	10	SAXOPRINT RTG	Honda	27	39m 39.625s
9	Andrea Locatelli	ITA	55	Gresini Racing Team Moto3	Honda	27	39m 39.711s
10	Niklas Ajo	FIN	31	RBA Racing Team	KTM	27	39m 40.917s
11	Philipp Oettl	GER	65	Schedl GP Racing	KTM	27	39m 41.136s
12	Jorge Martin	SPA	88	MAPFRE Team MAHINDRA	Mahindra	27	39m 47.775s
13	Karel Hanika	CZE	98	Red Bull KTM Ajo	KTM	27	39m 47.785s
14	Jakub Kornfeil	CZE	84	Drive M7 SIC	KTM	27	39m 58.141s
15	Jules Danilo	FRA	95	Ongetta-Rivacold	Honda	27	39m 58.251s
16	Livio Loi	BEL	11	RW Racing GP	Honda	27	39m 58.317s
17	John McPhee	GBR	17	SAXOPRINT RTG	Honda	27	39m 58.577s
18	Isaac Vinales	SPA	32	Husqvarna Factory Laglisse	Husqvarna	27	39m 58.837s
19	Zulfahmi Khairuddin	MAL	63	Drive M7 SIC	KTM	27	39m 59.109s
20	Darryn Binder	RSA	40	Outox Reset Drink Team	Mahindra	27	40m 15.203s
21	Andrea Migno	ITA	16	SKY Racing Team VR46	KTM	27	40m 16.017s
22	Stefano Manzi	ITA	29	San Carlo Team Italia	Mahindra	27	40m 16.139s
23	Remy Gardner	AUS	2	CIP	Mahindra	27	40m 16.199s
24	Alessandro Tonucci	ITA	19	Outox Reset Drink Team	Mahindra	27	40m 16.324s
25	Matteo Ferrari	ITA	12	San Carlo Team Italia	Mahindra	27	40m 16.698s
26	Gabriel Rodrigo	ARG	91	RBA Racing Team	KTM	27	40m 35.484s
27	Jonas Geitner	GER	45	Freudenberg Racing Team	KTM	27	40m 53.796s
	Ana Carrasco	SPA	22	RBA Racing Team	KTM	23	DNF
	Maria Herrera	SPA	6	Husqvarna Factory Laglisse	Husqvarna	23	DNF
	Tatsuki Suzuki	JPN	24	CIP	Mahindra	20	DNF
	Maximilian Kappler	GER	97	SAXOPRINT-RTG	FTR Honda	12	DNF
	Fabio Quartararo	FRA	20	Estrella Galicia 0,0	Honda	5	DNF
	Francesco Bagnaia	ITA	21	MAPFRE Team MAHINDRA	Mahindra	5	DNF
	Hiroki Ono	JPN	76	Leopard Racing	Honda	1	DNF

Fastest lap: Danny Kent, on lap 3, 1m 26.916s, 94.4mph/152.0km/h.
Lap record: Brad Binder, RSA (Mahindra), 1m 26.877s, 94.5mph/152.1km/h (2014).
Event best maximum speed: Hiroki Ono, 133.3mph/214.5km/h (free practice).

Qualifying
Weather: Dry
Air Temp: 22° Track Temp: 32°
Humidity: 37%

1	Kent	1m 26.420s
2	Bastianini	1m 26.939s
3	Hanika	1m 26.941s
4	Quartararo	1m 26.968s
5	Vazquez	1m 27.005s
6	Locatelli	1m 27.130s
7	Martin	1m 27.160s
8	Navarro	1m 27.253s
9	Antonelli	1m 27.313s
10	Ajo	1m 27.334s
11	Binder	1m 27.355s
12	Masbou	1m 27.356s
13	Fenati	1m 27.378s
14	Vinales	1m 27.496s
15	Loi	1m 27.536s
16	Oettl	1m 27.567s
17	Khairuddin	1m 27.653s
18	Kornfeil	1m 27.714s
19	Binder	1m 27.828s
20	McPhee	1m 27.857s
21	Danilo	1m 27.863s
22	Bagnaia	1m 27.887s
23	Ono	1m 27.921s
24	Carrasco	1m 28.031s
25	Tonucci	1m 28.074s
26	Guevara	1m 28.103s
27	Gardner	1m 28.160s
28	Herrera	1m 28.162s
29	Manzi	1m 28.171s
30	Suzuki	1m 28.211s
31	Ferrari	1m 28.227s
32	Migno	1m 28.232s
33	Rodrigo	1m 28.535s
34	Kappler	1m 29.750s
35	Geitner	1m 30.011s
	Oliveira	No Time

Fastest race laps

1	Kent	1m 26.916s
2	Hanika	1m 26.971s
3	Vazquez	1m 26.991s
4	Antonelli	1m 27.104s
5	Navarro	1m 27.247s
6	Fenati	1m 27.282s
7	Binder	1m 27.292s
8	Bastianini	1m 27.297s
9	Masbou	1m 27.316s
10	Oettl	1m 27.348s
11	Martin	1m 27.417s
12	Ajo	1m 27.444s
13	Locatelli	1m 27.586s
14	Quartararo	1m 27.617s
15	McPhee	1m 27.631s
16	Kornfeil	1m 27.739s
17	Khairuddin	1m 27.771s
18	Danilo	1m 27.871s
19	Vinales	1m 27.888s
20	Suzuki	1m 27.991s
21	Bagnaia	1m 28.024s
22	Loi	1m 28.038s
23	Migno	1m 28.182s
24	Binder	1m 28.213s
25	Ferrari	1m 28.323s
26	Carrasco	1m 28.361s
27	Manzi	1m 28.387s
28	Rodrigo	1m 28.449s
29	Kappler	1m 28.468s
30	Tonucci	1m 28.491s
31	Herrera	1m 28.587s
32	Gardner	1m 28.648s
33	Geitner	1m 30.002s

Championship Points

1	Kent	190
2	Bastianini	124
3	Oliveira	102
4	Fenati	99
5	Vazquez	96
6	Binder	75
7	Quartararo	74
8	Vinales	64
9	Antonelli	60
10	Bagnaia	55
11	Navarro	54
12	Masbou	41
13	McPhee	34
14	Hanika	29
15	Locatelli	28
16	Oettl	23
17	Ajo	21
18	Kornfeil	19
19	Migno	16
20	Ono	15
21	Loi	15
22	Martin	12
23	Danilo	5
24	Guevara	4
25	Khairuddin	2
26	Herrera	1
27	Manzi	1
28	Ferrari	1

Constructor Points

1	Honda	210
2	KTM	149
3	Mahindra	65
4	Husqvarna	64

INDIANAPOLIS GRAND PRIX

INDIANAPOLIS CIRCUIT

Could this be the last time? With a
return to the Brickyard uncertain,
the Hondas and MotoGP pack follow
Lorenzo into turn one.
Photo: Gold & Goose

THE season recommenced with a big 'H' stamped across the result sheets. It stood for History, and for Honda. When Marquez defeated a persistent Lorenzo to cross the line for a second straight win, it was the marque's 700th, in a list that had begun two years after the 1959 Isle of Man TT debut, putting the company 211 wins ahead of nearest rival Yamaha. Aprilia was next with 294, then MV Agusta (275) and Suzuki (155).

Not everyone had been on holiday for the full three weeks. The Repsol Honda pair had spent two days testing at Misano – one with developments for the 2016 season, the other on refinements for 2015, which had the effect of strengthening Marquez's resolve to stick with his 2014 chassis.

And in a throwback to a previous era, a few had spent the time going around and around and around Suzuka instead of relaxing on the beach, in the 8 Hours endurance race.

Two of them, team-mates Smith and the younger Espargaro, had done it better than anybody else, winning for Yamaha for the first time since 1996 and fulfilling the factory's hopes in their return with a full works effort. Dominique Aegerter had been in the FCC Honda team that finished second; while Toni Elias, riding a Moriwaki Honda shared with now-and-then GP rider Ratthapark Wilairot, finished 14th. First Moto2 champion Elias had not raced for ten months; now he was also back at Indy, as the latest substitute for Abraham, and hoping for more.

Back in the 1980s and 1990s, it had been common practice (and an unwelcome contractual obligation) for top factory riders to visit the hot, humid and intensely competitive 8 Hours, a major event for the factories and the Japanese fans. Past winners include world champions Eddie Lawson, Wayne Rainey, Wayne Gardner and Mick Doohan, while more recently Rossi's name had been added to the roll. It was a potentially risky interruption to the GP series, and an awk-

ward deviation from two-stroke riding technique, from which it was necessary to recover.

Smith said otherwise, opining that there were more similarities than differences between R1 and M1, but he was not so dutiful when asked to comment on the fact that team-mate Pol's contract had been renewed for 2016, while his was still in abeyance, even though he was reliably the faster of the pair. "I've made it very clear from the start of the season that I want to stay with the same team and factory – but I haven't felt the same enthusiasm coming the other way." That comment earned private censure from Yamaha, and he would have to wait two more races before his own continued tenure was confirmed.

If the 8 Hours does have any lessons for grand prix racing, they are for the pits rather than on the track. A pit stop to re-fuel, and change rider and tyres is accomplished in little over ten seconds. Of course the bikes are designed for the job. GP bikes are not, and in MotoGP the riders simply change bikes. Not in the smaller classes, though – and exceedingly inconvenient weather played havoc with Moto3. It rained before the start, and since nobody had any wet practice, 20 minutes were allowed for sighting laps. During this time, it more or less stopped raining. When it came to time to race, the track was drying fast.

Livio Loi changed to slicks on the grid. He would win the race, his first rostrum. McPhee, Oettl, Migno and Danilo left it too late, but decided to do the same, starting from the pit lane. Migno had trouble in the race, but the first two completed the podium, a first time for all three. The gamble had paid off.

For the rest, it meant a pit stop, and that meant chaos.

One of the quickest to be turned around was Fenati, who lost only 1m 35s, the rider laying on a histrionic performance as his mechanics twirled the spanners. Others edged closer

Above: **Flashback to Suzuka. Smith, Nakasuga and Espargaro celebrate Yamaha's first victory in the 8 Hours endurance race since 1996.**

Above left: **Wayne Rainey was overseeing his Moto America series: the bikes helped to rubber-up the track.**

Top: **Marquez stalked, pounced and won again.**

Above right, from top: **Kevin Schwantz joined the Suzuki GSX-R's 30th birthday party; Toni Elias was back for a one-off ride; Superbike talk between Josh Hayes and Eugene Laverty.**

Right: **Marquez chalked up a landmark – Honda's 700th GP win.**
Photos: Gold & Goose

to two minutes. Leopard Honda teamsters Vazquez and Ono lost 2m 17s and 2m 08s respectively. But team-mate and title leader Danny Kent drew the shortest of straws. His stop took 2m 36s. That put him out of the points for the first time, in a lowly 21st. In the ensuing few days, the team produced a ten-page document analysing the problem and seeking solutions. Should this happen again, they would be better prepared.

The Forward racing team was missing, having been granted a one-race leave of absence by Dorna and IRTA to allow manager Marco Curioni to attempt a rescue after the arrest of team owner Cuzari; while Bradl had been released from his contract to move directly across to the vacant seat at Aprilia, where he outqualified, but did not outrace, incumbent Bautista.

There were changes also in the smaller classes. The Tech 3 team had replaced the underperforming Ricky Cardus with Spanish rookie Xavier Verge; and in Moto3, Isaac Vinales had been dumped by Laglisse Husqvarna for Italian rookie Lorenzo Dalla Porta, on the dubious grounds that his results had fallen short. Since Maverick's cousin was eighth overall, with one podium and five other top-ten finishes, rumours of sponsorship woes and financial disputes between rider and team were more plausible. To the team's embarrassment, Vinales was at Indianapolis on a KTM as substitute for the injured Ana Carrasco; he finished fifth.

Talking of records, Dovizioso claimed one from Rossi with his 231st consecutive start. Rossi had clocked up 230 before breaking his leg at Mugello in 2010. Dovi's Ducati, meanwhile, had reverted to monoplane winglets.

The usual problems of a slippery surface on the little-used infield circuit were ameliorated somewhat by the weekend being shared with the new MotoAmerica series, running Superbike/Superstock and Supersport classes, which helped to rubber it up. But this may have been the last time at this spectacular and unusual venue, a wrench made easier because for once the race did not coincide with the Indy Mile flat-track, so there was a little bit less to be missed.

MOTOGP RACE – 27 laps

Marquez and Pedrosa led qualifying, Lorenzo joining them on the front row; Crutchlow headed the second from the top Ducati, the satellite bike of Petrucci, and Smith. Rossi was on row three, eighth for a fourth time in the season, and increasingly aware of the difficulties this was causing him. Dovizioso, like Petrucci, was through from Q1, but languishing on row four.

The race was between two pairs.

Lorenzo had come back from a fast crash in warm-up, his first of the year, blaming a bad rear tyre. He took a blazing start to seize the lead into the first corner. Riding with trademark precision, he managed to hold it until there were only two laps to go. The pressure from Marquez was constant, closing up again promptly when the Yamaha rider eked out an advantage of more than half a second.

The pace was furious, and the final new lap record went to Marquez as he closed up again on lap 23. Now he was in position to use his horsepower advantage to power past down the front straight, seizing the lead into the first corner. He held it to the end, although by only six-tenths, adding to his American legend. It was, counting Moto2, his fourth in succession at Indianapolis, and his ninth in succession in the USA. And his second of the year, an important boost to any hopes of recovering lost ground in the championship.

Five seconds behind at the end came the second pair: Pedrosa versus Rossi. It had taken the Yamaha rider until almost half-distance to catch up, and then the battle was on. They changed places five times, with Pedrosa leading at the start of the final lap.

Rossi had used up his tyres, but had enough left for a block pass into the tight second corner. He crossed the line in third, Pedrosa on his back wheel, maintaining his perfect all-rostrum record for the season, and preserving his title lead over Lorenzo, by a shrinking margin of nine points. "For a lot of laps, I thought I would lose more points," he said. "I could catch Dani, and I tried to go away. But always he came back."

Iannone had started well in fourth, but lost the place to Rossi by the end of lap two. He remained fifth – under severe pressure in the closing laps from Smith, just over two-tenths behind after another strong race.

The Englishman had outpaced not only fast qualifier Petrucci in the early laps, but also his team-mate and 8 Hours partner, Pol Espargaro.

Petrucci would lose more places by the end of the race, while Espargaro was soon receiving close attention from Crutchlow, whose strong starting position had been nullified when he was caught out by cold brakes after the start. He almost ran into Smith, "for an all-British second-corner crash", and dropped to 13th. Espargaro managed to get back in front for the last two laps, to save seventh.

Dovizioso had suffered even worse from the same incident, having been forced to swerve wide on to the grass and rejoining plumb last, "in the wrong place at the wrong time". He spent his afternoon carving through and finished up ninth, his last victim the fading Petrucci.

Vinales came through for a lone 11th, having outpaced Hernandez in the last laps. Redding's struggle to extract grip from his RCV continued, and he dropped to a distant 13th from ninth in the early laps. Aleix Espargaro faded to a troubled 14th, blaming a lack of confidence and a locking back wheel, which he put down to a defective rear tyre.

A lively Open-class battle for the last points was won again by Barbera, from disappointed local hero Hayden, who had got back to within a second at the flag.

Di Meglio had led the group for most of the race, but had dropped away in 17th at the end; likewise both Aprilias, with Bautista finally ahead and Laverty also in front of Bradl. De Angelis was close, as was one-race AB Motoracing Honda substitute Toni Elias – the gap from Laverty in 19th to Elias in 22nd was just 1.3 seconds.

Miller had qualified 16th, his best yet, but crashed out on the seventh lap.

Marquez's win moved him past Iannone into third overall, 56 points behind Rossi. With eight races left, he needed to recover an average of seven points a race. At Indy, as at the previous round in Germany, he had recovered nine. Even more ominously for the evergreen Italian, Lorenzo was now only nine points behind.

MOTO2 RACE – 25 laps

The middle-class race was everything that the identical engines and almost universal Kalex frames suggest it usually should be, but seldom is: a big group fighting tooth and nail for the lead all the way to the end.

Rins had qualified on pole for the second time in the year, from Rabat and 2014's Indy winner Kallio, in a rare return to form, and hopeful that a good starting position might make the difference to his result.

Barely three-tenths covered the front row, and the top 18 were within one second. Times were even closer behind Kallio; Luthi, Folger and Nakagami were on row two, and Zarco only on the third, between Lowes and Morbidelli.

Conditions were iffy, and though the rain had stopped, with the track still not completely dry it was declared a wet race. Bravery won out in the early laps as Malaysian Hafizh Syahrin pushed through from the fifth row of the grid to lead the first lap, Lowes on his tail and sometimes ahead, and briefly also Simon.

After five laps, the first two were still with the leading group and Syahrin in front again, joined by points leader Zarco, Aegerter, Rins, briefly Azlan Shah, Rabat and Morbidelli, the rest close behind. Simon had already fallen, but had remounted only to retire.

Next time around, Zarco was in front. Then, on lap ten, Aegerter took over for the first of two good spells.

By half-distance, it was Aegerter from Zarco and Rins, with Rabat close behind, from Syahrin, Morbidelli and Lowes, with Luthi closing. It was still anybody's race, although Kallio was absent, having crashed out after a touch with Lowes.

Rins led for the first time on lap 15; two laps later, it was Aegerter again, scrapping with Zarco, while Rabat was ahead of Rins. Lowes slipped to the back of the group, but fell off while trying to close up, at the same time fending off Syahrin, who also fell a couple of laps later.

By the end, the front four had escaped by a marginal amount, and for the last two laps Rins took over for the win that had been predicted for some races, taking a half-second gap from Zarco over the line. Morbidelli was a similar distance behind for his first podium.

Aegerter was almost a second away, Rabat a little further behind him, and half a second clear of Luthi.

Meanwhile, Axel Pons had broken free from the next group to close right up for seventh. Sachsenring winner Simeon had also found some clear air in eighth. Less than two seconds behind, a gang of four: Nakagami, Marquez, Shah and Folger; West off the back in 13th. Schrotter and Mulhauser trailed in for the rest of the points, in a depleted field of 19 finishers. Cortese, Rossi, Wilairot, Krummenacher and new boy Vierge swelled the crash list.

A great race, and for Zarco "like a victory", because again he extended his points lead over new second-placer Rins.

MOTO3 RACE – 23 laps

Chaos reigned in Moto3, a truly bizarre race with only half the 32 finishers on the same lap as first-time winner Loi.

It began raining some 30 minutes before the start. It had stopped by the time they were on the grid, and as it had never been very hard and the day was warm, the track started drying very quickly.

Masbou led the first three laps, chased by Vazquez as Oliveira led Ajo, Bagnaia and Guevara into the pits. Kent finished lap two 30th as he joined a mass dash to the pits for a tyre change. Other riders put this off for a lap or two, some even longer. Earlier the better, it seemed: Masbou waited until lap six, and came last.

Loi took over the lead on lap four and ran away to become the second Belgian to win a GP in two races, after Simeon in Moto2 in Germany. The previous had been de Radigues, in 1983.

McPhee came through to second a lap later, 40 seconds behind at the end, staying ahead of Oettl by 20 seconds.

There was high drama in the pit lane: Fenati layed on a particularly histrionic display, but it seemed to help, because he was fourth, only 20 seconds behind Oettl. Then came Vinales, followed by a battling gang, more like the usual Moto3 spectacle.

Bastianini got the best of them on the last lap for sixth, then Antonelli, Brad Binder and Navarro close behind. Rookie Martin completed the top ten, still narrowly ahead of a charging Quartararo, who had pushed past Hanika, Locatelli and Danilo, tenth to 14th within less than a second.

Oliveira was ahead of Tonucci, the last rider on the same lap. Amazingly, Vazquez and Bagnaia were the only crashers, the latter after a ride-through for a jumped start.

RED BULL
INDIANAPOLIS
GRAND PRIX

7–9 AUGUST, 2015

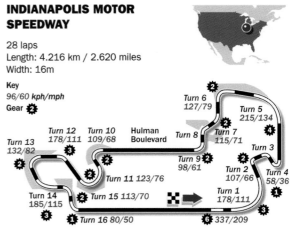

INDIANAPOLIS MOTOR SPEEDWAY

28 laps
Length: 4.216 km / 2.620 miles
Width: 16m

Key
96/60 kph/mph
Gear ⚙

Turn 6 127/79
Turn 5 215/134
Turn 12 178/111
Turn 10 109/68
Hulman Boulevard
Turn 8
Turn 7 115/71
Turn 13 132/82
Turn 3
Turn 9 98/61
Turn 2 107/66
Turn 4 58/36
Turn 11 123/76
Turn 1 178/111
Turn 14 185/115
Turn 15 113/70
Turn 16 80/50
337/209

MotoGP

RACE DISTANCE: 27 laps, 69.960 miles / 112.590km · **RACE WEATHER:** Dry (air 28°C, humidity 70%, track 35°C)

Pos.	Rider	Nat.	No.	Entrant	Machine	Tyres	Race tyre choice	Laps	Time & speed
1	**Marc Marquez**	SPA	93	Repsol Honda Team	Honda RC213V	B	F: Hard/R: Hard	27	41m 55.371s
									100.1mph/
									161.1km/h
2	**Jorge Lorenzo**	SPA	99	Movistar Yamaha MotoGP	Yamaha YZR-M1	B	F: Hard/R: Hard	27	41m 56.059s
3	**Valentino Rossi**	ITA	46	Movistar Yamaha MotoGP	Yamaha YZR-M1	B	F: Hard/R: Hard	27	42m 01.337s
4	**Dani Pedrosa**	SPA	26	Repsol Honda Team	Honda RC213V	B	F: Hard/R: Hard	27	42m 01.518s
5	**Andrea Iannone**	ITA	29	Ducati Team	Ducati Desmosedici	B	F: Hard/R: Medium	27	42m 16.899s
6	**Bradley Smith**	GBR	38	Monster Yamaha Tech 3	Yamaha YZR-M1	B	F: Hard/R: Hard	27	42m 17.122s
7	**Pol Espargaro**	SPA	44	Monster Yamaha Tech 3	Yamaha YZR-M1	B	F: Hard/R: Hard	27	42m 25.749s
8	**Cal Crutchlow**	GBR	35	CWM LCR Honda	Honda RC213V	B	F: Hard/R: Hard	27	42m 26.978s
9	**Andrea Dovizioso**	ITA	4	Ducati Team	Ducati Desmosedici	B	F: Hard/R: Medium	27	42m 28.192s
10	**Danilo Petrucci**	ITA	9	Octo Pramac Racing	Ducati Desmosedici	B	F: Hard/R: Medium	27	42m 29.888s
11	**Maverick Vinales**	SPA	25	Team SUZUKI ECSTAR	Suzuki GSX-RR	B	F: Hard/R: Medium	27	42m 34.381s
12	**Yonny Hernandez**	COL	68	Octo Pramac Racing	Ducati Desmosedici	B	F: Hard/R: Medium	27	42m 37.186s
13	**Scott Redding**	GBR	45	EG 0,0 Marc VDS	Honda RC213V	B	F: Hard/R: Hard	27	42m 45.580s
14	**Aleix Espargaro**	SPA	41	Team SUZUKI ECSTAR	Suzuki GSX-RR	B	F: Hard/R: Medium	27	42m 55.836s
15	**Hector Barbera**	SPA	8	Avintia Racing	Ducati Desmosedici Open	B	F: Hard/R: Soft	27	42m 59.518s
16	Nicky Hayden	USA	69	Aspar MotoGP Team	Honda RC213V-RS	B	F: Hard/R: Soft	27	43m 00.437s
17	Mike di Meglio	FRA	63	Avintia Racing	Ducati Desmosedici Open	B	F: Medium/R: Soft	27	43m 02.312s
18	Alvaro Bautista	SPA	19	Aprilia Racing Team Gresini	Aprilia RS-GP	B	F: Hard/R: Soft	27	43m 09.233s
19	Eugene Laverty	IRL	50	Aspar MotoGP Team	Honda RC213V-RS	B	F: Hard/R: Soft	27	43m 14.077s
20	Stefan Bradl	GER	6	Aprilia Racing Team Gresini	Aprilia RS-GP	B	F: Hard/R: Soft	27	43m 15.101s
21	Alex de Angelis	RSM	15	E-Motion IodaRacing Team	Aprilia ART	B	F: Hard/R: Soft	27	43m 15.253s
22	Toni Elias	SPA	24	AB Motoracing	Honda RC213V-RS	B	F: Medium/R: Soft	27	43m 15.305s
	Jack Miller	AUS	43	CWM LCR Honda	Honda RC213V-RS	B	F: Hard/R: Soft	7	DNF-crash

Fastest lap: Marc Marquez, on lap 23, 1m 32.625s, 100.7mph/162.0km/h (record).

Previous lap record: Marc Marquez, SPA (Honda), 1m 32.831s, 100.5mph/161.7km/h (2014).

Event best maximum speed: Andrea Iannone, 217.0mph/349.3km/h (free practice).

Qualifying

Weather: Dry
Air Temp: 29° **Humidity:** 50%
Track Temp: 40°

1	Marquez	1m 31.884s
2	Pedrosa	1m 32.055s
3	Lorenzo	1m 32.186s
4	Crutchlow	1m 32.208s
5	Petrucci	1m 32.243s
6	Smith	1m 32.269s
7	Iannone	1m 32.468s
8	Rossi	1m 32.511s
9	Vinales	1m 32.571s
10	Dovizioso	1m 32.636s
11	P. Espargaro	1m 32.670s
12	A. Espargaro	1m 32.814s
13	Redding	1m 33.170s
14	Barbera	1m 33.199s
15	Hernandez	1m 33.278s
16	Miller	1m 33.381s
17	Bradl	1m 33.822s
18	Bautista	1m 33.839s
19	Laverty	1m 33.978s
20	Hayden	1m 34.030s
21	De Angelis	1m 34.226s
22	Di Meglio	1m 34.322s
23	Elias	1m 35.167s

Fastest race laps

1	Marquez	1m 32.625s
2	Lorenzo	1m 32.652s
3	Pedrosa	1m 32.829s
4	Rossi	1m 32.847s
5	Smith	1m 33.301s
6	Crutchlow	1m 33.437s
7	Iannone	1m 33.492s
8	P. Espargaro	1m 33.539s
9	Petrucci	1m 33.671s
10	Vinales	1m 33.673s
11	Dovizioso	1m 33.684s
12	Hernandez	1m 33.782s
13	Redding	1m 34.030s
14	A. Espargaro	1m 34.237s
15	Miller	1m 34.503s
16	Bautista	1m 34.534s
17	Barbera	1m 34.573s
18	Di Meglio	1m 34.593s
19	Hayden	1m 34.607s
20	Bradl	1m 34.702s
21	Laverty	1m 34.782s
22	De Angelis	1m 34.957s
23	Elias	1m 35.239s

Championship Points

1	Rossi	195
2	Lorenzo	186
3	Marquez	139
4	Iannone	129
5	Smith	97
6	Dovizioso	94
7	Pedrosa	80
8	Crutchlow	74
9	P. Espargaro	73
10	Vinales	62
11	Petrucci	57
12	A. Espargaro	46
13	Hernandez	36
14	Redding	33
15	Barbera	20
16	Baz	14
17	Bautista	13
18	Miller	12
19	Bradl	9
20	Pirro	8
21	Hayden	8
22	E. Laverty	7
23	Aoyama	5
24	Di Meglio	2
25	De Angelis	1

Constructor Points

1	Yamaha	227
2	Honda	184
3	Ducati	154
4	Suzuki	75
5	Yamaha Forward	19
6	Aprilia	13
7	ART	1

Grid order	1	2	3	4	5	6	7	8	9	10	11	12	13	14	15	16	17	18	19	20	21	22	23	24	25	26	27	
93 MARQUEZ	99	99	99	99	99	99	99	99	99	99	99	99	99	99	99	99	99	99	99	99	99	99	99	99	93	93	93	1
26 PEDROSA	93	93	93	93	93	93	93	93	93	93	93	93	93	93	93	93	93	93	93	93	93	93	93	93	99	99	99	2
99 LORENZO	26	26	26	26	26	26	26	26	26	26	26	26	26	26	26	26	46	46	46	46	46	46	46	46	26	46		3
35 CRUTCHLOW	29	46	46	46	46	46	46	46	46	46	46	46	46	46	46	46	26	26	26	26	26	26	26	26	46	26		4
9 PETRUCCI	46	29	29	29	29	29	29	29	29	29	29	29	29	29	29	29	29	29	29	29	29	29	29	29	29	29		5
38 SMITH	44	38	38	38	38	38	38	38	38	38	38	38	38	38	38	38	38	38	38	38	38	38	38	38	38	38		6
29 IANNONE	38	44	44	44	44	44	44	44	44	35	35	35	35	44	44	44	44	44	44	35	35	35	35	35	44	44		7
46 ROSSI	9	9	9	9	9	9	9	35	35	44	44	44	44	35	35	35	35	35	35	44	44	44	44	44	35	35		8
25 VINALES	45	45	45	45	35	35	35	9	9	9	9	9	9	9	9	9	9	9	4	4	4	4	4	4	4	4		9
4 DOVIZIOSO	41	41	35	35	45	45	45	68	4	4	4	4	4	4	4	4	9	9	9	9	9	9	9	9	9	9		10
44 P. ESPARGARO	35	35	41	41	68	68	68	45	4	68	68	68	68	68	68	68	68	68	68	25	25	25	25	25	25			11
41 A. ESPARGARO	43	43	68	68	41	41	4	4	45	45	45	25	25	25	25	25	25	25	25	68	68	68	68	68	68			12
45 REDDING	6	25	43	43	4	4	41	41	41	25	25	45	45	45	41	41	41	41	41	45	45	45	45	45	45			13
8 BARBERA	25	6	25	25	25	25	25	25	25	41	41	41	41	41	45	45	45	41	41	41	41	41	41	41	41			14
68 HERNANDEZ	50	68	4	4	43	43	43	63	63	63	63	63	63	63	63	63	63	63	63	8	8	8	8	8	8			15
43 MILLER	68	50	6	6	6	63	63	50	50	50	50	50	50	8	8	8	8	8	8	63	69	69	69	69				
6 BRADL	19	4	50	50	50	6	50	6	8	8	8	8	8	50	69	69	69	69	69	69	63	63	63	63				
19 BAUTISTA	69	69	63	63	63	50	6	19	6	6	6	69	50	69	19	19	19	19	19	19	19	19	19	19				
50 LAVERTY	63	19	19	19	19	19	8	19	19	19	19	6	69	19	50	50	50	50	50	50	50	50	50	50				
69 HAYDEN	15	63	69	69	69	69	69	69	69	69	69	19	6	6	6	6	6	6	6	6	6	6	6	6				
15 DE ANGELIS	4	15	15	8	8	8	24	24	24	24	24	24	24	24	24	24	24	24	24	24	24	24	24	15				
63 DI MEGLIO	24	8	8	15	15	15	15	15	15	15	15	15	15	15	15	15	15	15	15	15	15	15	15	24				
24 ELIAS	8	24	24	24	24	24	24																					

Moto2

RACE DISTANCE: 25 laps, 64.778 miles/104.250km · RACE WEATHER: Wet (air 27°C, humidity 74%, track 32°C)

Pos.	Rider	Nat.	No.	Entrant	Machine	Laps	Time & Speed
1	Alex Rins	SPA	40	Paginas Amarillas HP 40	Kalex	25	41m 18.866s
							94.0mph/
							151.3km/h
2	Johann Zarco	FRA	5	Ajo Motorsport	Kalex	25	41m 19.348s
3	Franco Morbidelli	ITA	21	Italtrans Racing Team	Kalex	25	41m 19.754s
4	Dominique Aegerter	SWI	77	Technomag Racing Interwetten	Kalex	25	41m 20.585s
5	Tito Rabat	SPA	1	EG 0,0 Marc VDS	Kalex	25	41m 21.829s
6	Thomas Luthi	SWI	12	Derendinger Racing Interwetten	Kalex	25	41m 22.344s
7	Axel Pons	SPA	49	AGR Team	Kalex	25	41m 23.930s
8	Xavier Simeon	BEL	19	Federal Oil Gresini Moto2	Kalex	25	41m 26.428s
9	Takaaki Nakagami	JPN	30	IDEMITSU Honda Team Asia	Kalex	25	41m 28.182s
10	Alex Marquez	SPA	73	EG 0,0 Marc VDS	Kalex	25	41m 28.667s
11	Azlan Shah	MAL	25	IDEMITSU Honda Team Asia	Kalex	25	41m 28.765s
12	Jonas Folger	GER	94	AGR Team	Kalex	25	41m 28.974s
13	Anthony West	AUS	95	QMMF Racing Team	Speed Up	25	41m 35.972s
14	Marcel Schrotter	GER	23	Tech 3	Tech 3	25	41m 44.053s
15	Robin Mulhauser	SWI	70	Technomag Racing Interwetten	Kalex	25	41m 51.453s
16	Luis Salom	SPA	39	Paginas Amarillas HP 40	Kalex	25	41m 56.477s
17	Jesko Raffin	SWI	2	sports-millions-EMWE-SAG	Kalex	25	41m 57.755s
18	Thitipong Warokorn	THA	10	APH PTT The Pizza SAG	Kalex	25	42m 07.960s
19	Florian Alt	GER	66	E-Motion IodaRacing Team	Suter	25	42m 18.033s
	Hafizh Syahrin	MAL	55	Petronas Raceline Malaysia	Kalex	24	DNF
	Sam Lowes	GBR	22	Speed Up Racing	Speed Up	20	DNF
	Xavier Vierge	SPA	97	Tech 3	Tech 3	20	DNF
	Randy Krummenacher	SWI	4	JIR Racing Team	Kalex	18	DNF
	Louis Rossi	FRA	96	Tasca Racing Scuderia Moto2	Tech 3	15	DNF
	Ratthapark Wilairot	THA	15	JPMoto Malaysia	Suter	14	DNF
	Mika Kallio	FIN	36	Italtrans Racing Team	Kalex	11	DNF
	Sandro Cortese	GER	11	Dynavolt Intact GP	Kalex	10	DNF
	Julian Simon	SPA	60	QMMF Racing Team	Speed Up	6	DNF

Fastest lap: Franco Morbidelli, on lap 12, 1m 37.498s, 95.6mph/153.9km/h.
Lap record: Mika Kallio, FIN (Kalex), 1m 37.275s, 95.9mph/154.3km/h (2014).
Event best maximum speed: Thomas Luthi: 180.2mph/290.0km/h (race).

Qualifying
Weather: Dry
Air: 30° **Track:** 40°
Humidity: 51%

1	Rins	1m 36.549s
2	Rabat	1m 36.686s
3	Kallio	1m 36.865s
4	Luthi	1m 36.886s
5	Folger	1m 37.005s
6	Nakagami	1m 37.022s
7	Lowes	1m 37.038s
8	Zarco	1m 37.055s
9	Morbidelli	1m 37.081s
10	Cortese	1m 37.095s
11	Aegerter	1m 37.125s
12	Shah	1m 37.157s
13	Marquez	1m 37.329s
14	Syahrin	1m 37.365s
15	Krummenacher	1m 37.367s
16	Simeon	1m 37.419s
17	Simon	1m 37.462s
18	Pons	1m 37.528s
19	Schrotter	1m 37.622s
20	Salom	1m 37.806s
21	Mulhauser	1m 37.945s
22	Wilairot	1m 37.998s
23	West	1m 38.101s
24	Raffin	1m 38.350s
25	Vierge	1m 38.586s
26	Rossi	1m 38.843s
27	Warokorn	1m 38.943s
28	Alt	1m 39.956s

Fastest race laps

1	Morbidelli	1m 37.498s
2	Rins	1m 37.531s
3	Luthi	1m 37.580s
4	Zarco	1m 37.587s
5	Aegerter	1m 37.611s
6	Pons	1m 37.721s
7	Rabat	1m 37.760s
8	Lowes	1m 37.801s
9	Syahrin	1m 37.853s
10	Folger	1m 37.933s
11	Marquez	1m 37.988s
12	Cortese	1m 38.021s
13	Kallio	1m 38.052s
14	Shah	1m 38.073s
15	Nakagami	1m 38.073s
16	Simeon	1m 38.100s
17	Mulhauser	1m 38.118s
18	West	1m 38.352s
19	Schrotter	1m 38.446s
20	Krummenacher	1m 38.467s
21	Salom	1m 38.511s
22	Raffin	1m 38.709s
23	Warokorn	1m 39.174s
24	Vierge	1m 39.283s
25	Simon	1m 39.399s
26	Wilairot	1m 39.743s
27	Rossi	1m 39.784s
28	Alt	1m 39.810s

Championship Points

1	Zarco	199
2	Rins	128
3	Rabat	125
4	Luthi	109
5	Lowes	107
6	Simeon	92
7	Folger	81
8	Morbidelli	78
9	Aegerter	56
10	Kallio	47
11	Simon	47
12	Nakagami	39
13	Baldassarri	37
14	Salom	36
15	Marquez	36
16	Corsi	35
17	Cortese	35
18	Syahrin	34
19	West	20
20	Pons	18
21	Schrotter	14
22	Krummenacher	13
23	Rossi	7
24	Shah	6
25	Mulhauser	1

Constructor Points

1	Kalex	245
2	Speed Up	118
3	Tech 3	21

Moto3

RACE DISTANCE: 23 laps, 59.596 miles/95.910km · RACE WEATHER: Wet (air 25°C, humidity 86%, track 26°C)

Pos.	Rider	Nat.	No.	Entrant	Machine	Laps	Time & Speed
1	Livio Loi	BEL	11	RW Racing GP	Honda	23	40m 50.747s
							87.5mph/
							140.8km/h
2	John McPhee	GBR	17	SAXOPRINT RTG	Honda	23	41m 29.607s
3	Philipp Oettl	GER	65	Schedl GP Racing	KTM	23	41m 48.528s
4	Romano Fenati	ITA	5	SKY Racing Team VR46	KTM	23	42m 06.043s
5	Isaac Vinales	SPA	32	RBA Racing Team	KTM	23	42m 10.561s
6	Enea Bastianini	ITA	33	Gresini Racing Team Moto3	Honda	23	42m 14.548s
7	Niccolo Antonelli	ITA	23	Ongetta-Rivacold	Honda	23	42m 15.333s
8	Brad Binder	RSA	41	Red Bull KTM Ajo	KTM	23	42m 15.406s
9	Jorge Navarro	SPA	9	Estrella Galicia 0,0	Honda	23	42m 16.039s
10	Jorge Martin	SPA	88	MAPFRE Team MAHINDRA	Mahindra	23	42m 25.852s
11	Fabio Quartararo	FRA	20	Estrella Galicia 0,0	Honda	23	42m 26.531s
12	Karel Hanika	CZE	98	Red Bull KTM Ajo	KTM	23	42m 26.548s
13	Andrea Locatelli	ITA	55	Gresini Racing Team Moto3	Honda	23	42m 26.660s
14	Jules Danilo	FRA	95	Ongetta-Rivacold	Honda	23	42m 26.806s
15	Miguel Oliveira	POR	44	Red Bull KTM Ajo	KTM	23	42m 33.950s
16	Alessandro Tonucci	ITA	19	Outox Reset Drink Team	Mahindra	23	42m 39.753s
17	Remy Gardner	AUS	2	CIP	Mahindra	22	40m 59.461s
18	Juanfran Guevara	SPA	58	MAPFRE Team MAHINDRA	Mahindra	22	41m 01.076s
19	Stefano Manzi	ITA	29	San Carlo Team Italia	Mahindra	22	41m 01.312s
20	Andrea Migno	ITA	16	SKY Racing Team VR46	KTM	22	41m 02.487s
21	Danny Kent	GBR	52	Leopard Racing	Honda	22	41m 09.017s
22	Jakub Kornfeil	CZE	84	Drive M7 SIC	KTM	22	41m 09.047s
23	Tatsuki Suzuki	JPN	24	CIP	Mahindra	22	41m 09.101s
24	Maria Herrera	SPA	6	Husqvarna Factory Laglisse	Husqvarna	22	41m 26.919s
25	Zulfahmi Khairuddin	MAL	63	Drive M7 SIC	KTM	22	41m 37.635s
26	Hiroki Ono	JPN	76	Leopard Racing	Honda	22	41m 42.303s
27	Darryn Binder	RSA	40	Outox Reset Drink Team	Mahindra	22	41m 42.358s
28	Lorenzo Dalla Porta	ITA	48	Husqvarna Factory Laglisse	Husqvarna	22	41m 42.391s
29	Matteo Ferrari	ITA	12	San Carlo Team Italia	Mahindra	22	41m 45.128s
30	Niklas Ajo	FIN	31	RBA Racing Team	KTM	22	41m 52.405s
31	Gabriel Rodrigo	ARG	91	RBA Racing Team	KTM	22	42m 09.270s
32	Alexis Masbou	FRA	10	SAXOPRINT RTG	Honda	22	42m 18.400s
	Efren Vazquez	SPA	7	Leopard Racing	Honda	15	DNF
	Francesco Bagnaia	ITA	21	MAPFRE Team MAHINDRA	Mahindra	11	DNF

Fastest lap: Danny Kent, on lap 6, 1m 41.449s, 91.9mph/147.9km/h.
Lap record: Alex Rins, SPA (Honda), 1m 40.800s, 92.5mph/148.9km/h (2014).
Event best maximum speed: Hiroki Ono, 149.6mph/240.8km/h (warm-up).

Qualifying:
Weather: Dry
Air: 29° **Track:** 41°
Humidity: 49%

1	Kent	1m 40.703s
2	Oliveira	1m 40.791s
3	Khairuddin	1m 40.811s
4	Bastianini	1m 40.875s
5	Quartararo	1m 41.062s
6	Binder	1m 41.092s
7	Vazquez	1m 41.093s
8	Antonelli	1m 41.129s
9	Navarro	1m 41.186s
10	Martin	1m 41.242s
11	Fenati	1m 41.287s
12	Masbou	1m 41.308s
13	Hanika	1m 41.310s
14	Ono	1m 41.412s
15	Danilo	1m 41.415s
16	Kornfeil	1m 41.474s
17	Gardner	1m 41.527s
18	McPhee	1m 41.555s
19	Ajo	1m 41.585s
20	Vinales	1m 41.770s
21	Locatelli	1m 41.806s
22	Guevara	1m 41.822s
23	Herrera	1m 41.847s
24	Bagnaia	1m 41.909s
25	Tonucci	1m 41.942s
26	Loi	1m 41.958s
27	Suzuki	1m 42.026s
28	Migno	1m 42.150s
29	Rodrigo	1m 42.230s
30	Dalla Porta	1m 42.318s
31	Ferrari	1m 42.517s
32	Binder	1m 42.533s
33	Manzi	1m 42.702s
34	Oettl	1m 42.726s

Fastest race laps

1	Kent	1m 41.449s
2	Bastianini	1m 41.964s
3	Antonelli	1m 42.023s
4	Vazquez	1m 42.137s
5	Navarro	1m 42.149s
6	Oliveira	1m 42.233s
7	Fenati	1m 42.444s
8	Quartararo	1m 42.444s
9	Martin	1m 42.622s
10	Vinales	1m 42.668s
11	Kornfeil	1m 42.726s
12	Locatelli	1m 42.733s
13	Binder	1m 42.762s
14	Danilo	1m 42.765s
15	Gardner	1m 42.964s
16	Dalla Porta	1m 43.007s
17	Suzuki	1m 43.051s
18	Hanika	1m 43.087s
19	Oettl	1m 43.122s
20	Tonucci	1m 43.245s
21	Herrera	1m 43.262s
22	Guevara	1m 43.286s
23	Ajo	1m 43.405s
24	Khairuddin	1m 43.439s
25	Ono	1m 43.522s
26	Migno	1m 43.718s
27	Binder	1m 43.773s
28	Bagnaia	1m 43.776s
29	McPhee	1m 43.850s
30	Loi	1m 43.893s
31	Masbou	1m 43.938s
32	Manzi	1m 43.991s
33	Ferrari	1m 45.306s
34	Rodrigo	1m 46.158s

Championship Points

1	Kent	190
2	Bastianini	134
3	Fenati	112
4	Oliveira	103
5	Vazquez	96
6	Binder	83
7	Quartararo	79
8	Vinales	75
9	Antonelli	69
10	Navarro	61
11	Bagnaia	55
12	McPhee	54
13	Masbou	41
14	Loi	40
15	Oettl	39
16	Hanika	33
17	Locatelli	31
18	Ajo	21
19	Kornfeil	19
20	Martin	18
21	Migno	16
22	Ono	15
23	Danilo	7
24	Guevara	4
25	Khairuddin	2
26	Herrera	1
27	Manzi	1
28	Ferrari	1

Constructor Points

1	Honda	235
2	KTM	165
3	Mahindra	71
4	Husqvarna	64

FIM WORLD CHAMPIONSHIP · ROUND 11

CZECH REPUBLIC GRAND PRIX

BRNO CIRCUIT

Inset, above: Lorenzo's Gang had all the bullets…

Inset, right: …and he emerged as the boss of Brno.

Main: Lorenzo took control from the start for yet another dominant performance.

Photos: Gold & Goose

Above: Marquez celebrates being number two.

Top right: Aleix Espargaro and Danilo Petrucci battled hard for ninth.

Above right: Maverick Vinales slipped off: the first time all year not to claim points.

Right: Plucky Karel Abraham limped back into action at home – and made the finish.

Far right: Claudio Corti took over the unbranded Forward Yamaha, to no great effect.

Below right: Bradley Smith came out on top after a race-long battle with Monster Yamaha team-mate Pol Espargaro, taking seventh and top satellite bike.

Photos: Gold & Goose

ACROSS the Atlantic and over towards the far edge of Europe with barely four days for the transition, and we were racing again.

The pleasure of being back at this fine circuit, for an event only rescued from oblivion two-and-a-bit months before, was increased with the race-day news of a new accord between Dorna, the Moravian government and City of Brno guaranteeing the future of the Czech Republic Grand Prix for the next five years.

And by a compelling, if not actually very exciting, MotoGP race that added a new twist to the finely balanced championship battle. "It's unbelievable," said winner Lorenzo, "that after 11 races, we [him and Rossi] should be equal on points."

At the time, it was far from clear which of these later races would have the casting vote, but – as with Lorenzo's four straight wins earlier – this one was such a convincing display that one could have been forgiven for thinking it might be something of a formality from now on.

The weekend began badly for Rossi and Pedrosa, through no fault of their own. Both crashed on Friday morning – Rossi's first fall of the year – for the same most unusual reason: a leaking front fork seal on the usually totally reliable Ohlins.

It was Dani's Honda at fault, and he paid the greater price, landing heavily on his left ankle. Nothing was broken, but it re-awakened old injuries, became badly swollen and spoiled his weekend. The leak had spattered fork oil on to his bike, the track and ultimately his back wheel, so when he tipped it into the second corner of the final left-right combination he fell directly. By then, Rossi had already gone down. He'd smelled oil on the way up the hill, he said, but hadn't taken it seriously "because it never happens now". Unluckily, his wheel found a little patch of the spillage, and he was most surprised to slide off, unhurt.

Ducati brought an upgrade to Brno, with revised bodywork housing an equally revised engine – the same unit, but with improved power delivery, as run at Indianapolis. The fairing was slimmer, thanks to narrower water and oil radiators, while a revised seat unit exposed more exhaust. Most obviously, the winglets looked larger, although the overall width was as before, and the leading edge also had a more pronounced concave arc.

Karel Abraham made his long delayed return, still on crutches after missing four races. The free-practice left-foot injury had seemed nothing worse than a broken toe or two at first, but he looked pained as he explained how it was much more complicated. "The broken bones were not the problem. I had dislocated toes, plus muscle and ligament damage." Yet to score a point in 2015, he soldiered on, happy just to finish the race, if a lap behind, for he did have other more encouraging news. He revealed that he was in talks with KTM, the Austrian firm preparing for a MotoGP return in 2017. "We talked, but nothing is fixed or set," he said.

There was plenty of other talk about futures and contracts, with Danny Kent one axis and Pramac Ducati the other. The link was a "no pressure" offer of a three-year contract to the dominant Moto3 rider, the chance to follow Jack Miller directly from Moto3 to MotoGP.

Unlike Miller, Kent had already run a season in Moto2 – a disappointing 2013 on the uncompetitive French Mistral – and was also keenly sought for a return to the middle class. For now, he would wait and see, though his analysis was typically thoughtful: "With Michelin coming back next year, I think that it's the best year that a Moto3 rider could think of to make the jump. It's all new tyres, the electronics should bring the satellite bikes closer to the factory bikes. Hopefully next year, with the changes, it gives the satellite teams a chance to compete." At the same time, his highly successful Keifer-owned Leopard Racing squad was planning a move to Moto2, and would have loved to have Kent along for the ride.

With all factory-team seats settled, the satellite Pramac Ducati team was the only squad at a reasonably high level that a rider looking to the big class could consider, and Kent's was far from the only name in the frame. Crutchlow had already been mentioned, but now he ruled himself out: a renewal of his LCR contract would follow before the next race. Another strong candidate was Zarco, dominant in Moto2, who ruminated out loud on the possibilities. He might delay his move, he said, until he was sure of being with a good team. "I have learned again this year, when I came back to the Ajo team, how important it is to have a good team behind you," he said. When he rode for Ajo in 2011 in 125, he was second overall. "Now I am back with the same team, I am leading the championship," he said. Always a voluble interviewee, he added, "I am 25 now, but Valentino

shows that you can still be strong when you are more than 30. There is no need to hurry."

Beleaguered Forward Racing returned, ex-Moto2 rider Claudio Corti replacing Bradl alongside Baz, and both Moto2 riders on hand. The future was still unclear, their plan being to run up to Aragon and the end of the European season.

This was the 50th anniversary of motorcycle GP racing at Brno, the first races having been run on a public-roads circuit closer to the city. With race-day crowds of almost 140,000, and fans journeying to the fine sweeping track's natural grandstands from neighbouring Poland and Slovenia as well as Austria and Germany, it was fitting that the milestone was marked by a renewal of a contract that had long been in doubt.

MOTOGP RACE – 22 laps

Lorenzo saw off a threat from Marquez to lead free practice, but his pole was less than a tenth faster, with Rossi completing the first row. Iannone, Smith and Dovizioso were behind. It was only Rossi's second time up front in the season, but any hopes that this might let him get away with the leaders evaporated with a below-average start, into the first corner not only behind Lorenzo and Marquez, but also Smith and Dovizioso. It took him two laps to move into third, but by then he was more than two seconds behind the leading pair. He would never recover them.

Conditions were warmer than in practice after a heavy overnight storm, causing Lorenzo to worry about his softer tyre choice front and rear. There was no need, however. The metronome kept ticking: he reeled off the 22 laps, breaking Marc Marquez's determined pursuit by an eventual 4.4 seconds and also Repsol Honda's four-year domination at Brno.

Marquez, with a sniff of a chance to close the points gap, was out for a third straight win. "I have nothing to lose. I have to take the risk," he explained. He knew that Lorenzo was faster. "I tried to follow him, and for the first five or six laps I could." He set fastest lap, just short of a new record, fourth time around, "but when the rear tyre started to drop again, I had this problem with corner entry and acceleration." Now his job was to control the gap to Rossi.

This he did, by an eventual six seconds. It had been an austere race up front, once he'd got into third. There was plenty of variety behind.

Dovi, riding an updated Desmosedici, resisted Rossi's early attacks with vigour and a handful of extra horsepower, but after six or seven laps he was out of touch. Team-mate

Above: Rossi passes his fans on the way to a lonely third.

Top right: Zarco, with Rabat in vain pursuit, was flawless again.

Above right: Back-of-the-pack drama in Moto2 as Mulhauser falls in front of Raffin.

Centre, right and far right: Rins took a sixth podium in third; Marquez was a strong fourth and within sight of the podium.

Below right: Niccolo Antonelli (23) took a convincing first Moto3 podium – in first place. Vazquez (7), Bastianini (33), Binder (obscured), Oliveira (44) and Fenati (5) pursued.

Photos: Gold & Goose

Iannone (on the older version) had also got ahead of Smith by the end of lap one and soon began leaning on the older Andrea for top Ducati honours.

It took until lap eight before he was able to get ahead, and another eight or more before he established a comfortable gap, but basically that battle was done.

With Smith dropping away, occupied in keeping team-mate Pol Espargaro at bay as again he came out top satellite-team rider, there was an important stirring behind.

Pedrosa, still hurting, made an average start from row three, but soon began gaining speed and positions, past Vinales and one lap later Pol Espargaro. Next he closed on Smith, had nailed him by lap seven and started to work on a gap of some 2.5 seconds to the Ducatis. By lap 15, he had started a long battle with Dovi. It came to a head in the closing three laps. Several times Pedrosa would get alongside and even ahead, only to lose it again – once running wide, more often succumbing to the Ducati's speed on the last run up the hill.

On the last lap, they changed places twice; over the line, it was Dani in front, after a daring attack at the final bend. Iannone was still almost three seconds ahead.

Smith was a safe seventh, comfortably clear of Pol, who had endured a torrid time with Vinales, until the Suzuki rider slipped off with seven laps to go. The pair had been drawing clear of Crutchlow, until the Englishman sealed a disappointing weekend by crashing on lap 15.

That left a big gap to the elder Espargaro, Aleix, who had a lot of trouble getting free from Petrucci, the pair completing the top ten.

Some five seconds behind, Hernandez narrowly prevailed in a race-long battle with Redding, ahead of a lively tussle for the last points, eventually won by Bautista, who had hunted down new Aprilia team-mate Bradl to lead him over the line by just over a tenth. They had outpaced the rest, as had Baz, the Forward Yamaha rookie's first time as top Open finisher, though not his best result, taking the last point and leaving Barbera and erstwhile group leader Hayden out of luck in his wake.

Di Meglio and Miller were out of touch behind; miles away, Corti and then Abraham finished. Laverty and de Angelis also crashed out.

Lorenzo led the championship for the first time, equal on points to Rossi, but with more wins.

MOTO2 RACE – 20 laps

After the excitement of Indy, the middle class was back to normal at Brno – a processional race up front with few changes of position, and the podium exactly matching the front row of the grid.

It was not without tension, however, as championship leader Zarco lapped steadily up front, while defending champion Tito Rabat pursued remorselessly, still barely a second adrift at the finish. At the same time, Rins chased behind after working through to third shortly before half-distance.

Zarco had started from pole, and though Rabat had led through the first corners, and Luthi headed the first lap, the Frenchman took over immediately. Rabat followed him past on lap three, but a near high-side a little further around gave Zarco a lead of almost a second, and in a flawless display he held it to the finish.

"I was ready to fight if he came, but when the fuel load lightened, I could get a good rhythm," he explained.

Rins took fourth off Aegerter on lap two; the Swiss rider thereafter faded steadily to an eventual 13th. Compatriot Luthi was also unable to sustain the pace, and by lap eight Rins was past and pulling clear.

Younger Marquez brother Alex was having the best day of his first Moto2 season, moving steadily forward from eighth on lap one. By the fourth, he had cleared Morbidelli to tag on behind former Moto3 team-mate and rival Rins. He stayed close until the closing stages, just over two seconds away at the end for a career-best fourth. The 2016 Kalex was a step forward for the Moto3 champion.

One of the strongest rides came from Sam Lowes. He had qualified only 13th after a disastrous session had ended prematurely with a crash when his rear suspension link collapsed, and he finished the first lap 12th. He soon began moving forward, however, to an eventual fifth, his last victim Folger; the German remained on his back wheel to finish two-tenths behind.

Luthi was another two seconds adrift, having fended off Cortese, who had got past Salom and left him behind to his own battle with Morbidelli. He took ninth off the Italian with two laps to go.

The next group was another five seconds away: Corsi, Nakagami, Aegerter, Syahrin and Kallio, all covered by less than two seconds.

As at every race so far, the seemingly flawless Zarco extended his points lead still further; Rabat regained second by one point from Rins. But neither was close enough to pose a real threat.

MOTO3 RACE – 12 laps (shortened from 19)

Brno lends itself to ultra-close Moto3 racing. But it was a bit too close on the first lap, when four riders went down together on the first corner, and another four a couple of corners later. Argentinean Gabriel Rodrigo lay doggo in the gravel, and the red flags came out as medical staff attended to him. Later he was transferred to a local hospital with leg injuries.

Team-mate Ajo didn't make the restart; nor did Ono or Locatelli. The rest lined up again 30 minutes later, with race distance cut from 19 to 12 laps.

It was another feast of close action, with a leading pack of ten fiercely engaged throughout. Vazquez and Kent each took an early turn at leading over the line; then Antonelli, followed for several laps by team-mates Brad Binder and Oliveira. But that was only over the line; elsewhere on the track, sustained mayhem meant constant reshuffling.

Which made Antonelli's successful bid to claim a slender margin over the last two laps all the more impressive. It was the 19-year-old Italian's first win, and indeed his first time on the podium.

Bastianini bullied his way to second ahead of Binder, with Vazquez fourth, then Navarro and Fenati, with Kent caught up in the thick of it in seventh, ahead of Oliveira and Kornfeil, the first nine over the line within 1.42 seconds; tenth-placed McPhee was off the back by the end.

Fenati's ride was remarkable – along with Loi, he'd been put back three grid positions for loitering in qualifying, and he'd come from 22nd on the grid.

Mahindra team-mates Martin, Bagnaia and Guevara led the next big gang, just over two seconds adrift. They finished in that order, but with Migno slipping ahead of the last named for 13th. The final point went to first-corner crasher Oettl, with Darryn Binder, Gardner and Loi hard up behind.

There were several more crashers, including local hero Hanika, Vinales, Quartararo and 2014's winner of a similar brawl, Masbou.

For a second race in a row, Kent's title lead shrank.

bwin
GRAND PRIX
CESKE REPUBLIKY

14–16 AUGUST, 2015

AUTODROM BRNO
22 laps
Length: 5.403 km / 3.357 miles
Width: 15m

Key
96/60 kph/mph
⚙ Gear

Turn 5 131/81
Turn 9 128/80
Kevin Schwantz 124/77
Turn 8 128/80
Turn 4 115/71
Stadion 138/86
Turn 11 128/80
Turn 3 121/75
Turn 12 125/78
František Štasny 148/92
Horizont 114/71
Turn 14 121/75
315/196

MotoGP	RACE DISTANCE: 22 laps, 73.860 miles/118.866km · RACE WEATHER: Dry (air 26°C, humidity 54%, track 39°C)

Pos.	Rider	Nat.	No.	Entrant	Machine	Tyres	Race tyre choice	Laps	Time & speed
1	**Jorge Lorenzo**	SPA	99	Movistar Yamaha MotoGP	Yamaha YZR-M1	B	F: Medium/R: Medium	22	42m 53.042s 103.3mph/ 166.3km/h
2	**Marc Marquez**	SPA	93	Repsol Honda Team	Honda RC213V	B	F: Medium/R: Hard	22	42m 57.504s
3	**Valentino Rossi**	ITA	46	Movistar Yamaha MotoGP	Yamaha YZR-M1	B	F: Hard/R: Hard	22	43m 03.439s
4	**Andrea Iannone**	ITA	29	Ducati Team	Ducati Desmosedici	B	F: Medium/R: Medium	22	43m 06.113s
5	**Dani Pedrosa**	SPA	26	Repsol Honda Team	Honda RC213V	B	F: Medium/R: Medium	22	43m 08.692s
6	**Andrea Dovizioso**	ITA	4	Ducati Team	Ducati Desmosedici	B	F: Medium/R: Medium	22	43m 08.767s
7	**Bradley Smith**	GBR	38	Monster Yamaha Tech 3	Yamaha YZR-M1	B	F: Medium/R: Medium	22	43m 14.863s
8	**Pol Espargaro**	SPA	44	Monster Yamaha Tech 3	Yamaha YZR-M1	B	F: Hard/R: Medium	22	43m 16.282s
9	**Aleix Espargaro**	SPA	41	Team SUZUKI ECSTAR	Suzuki GSX-RR	B	F: Hard/R: Medium	22	43m 36.826s
10	**Danilo Petrucci**	ITA	9	Octo Pramac Racing	Ducati Desmosedici	B	F: Hard/R: Medium	22	43m 38.303s
11	**Yonny Hernandez**	COL	68	Octo Pramac Racing	Ducati Desmosedici	B	F: Medium/R: Medium	22	43m 43.015s
12	**Scott Redding**	GBR	45	EG 0,0 Marc VDS	Honda RC213V	B	F: Medium/R: Medium	22	43m 43.216s
13	**Alvaro Bautista**	SPA	19	Aprilia Racing Team Gresini	Aprilia RS-GP	B	F: Medium/R: Soft	22	43m 47.479s
14	**Stefan Bradl**	GER	6	Aprilia Racing Team Gresini	Aprilia RS-GP	B	F: Medium/R: Soft	22	43m 47.666s
15	**Loris Baz**	FRA	76	Forward Racing	Yamaha Forward	B	F: Medium/R: Soft	22	43m 53.358s
16	Hector Barbera	SPA	8	Avintia Racing	Ducati Desmosedici Open	B	F: Medium/R: Soft	22	43m 54.637s
17	Nicky Hayden	USA	69	Aspar MotoGP Team	Honda RC213V-RS	B	F: Medium/R: Soft	22	43m 55.430s
18	Mike di Meglio	FRA	63	Avintia Racing	Ducati Desmosedici Open	B	F: Medium/R: Soft	22	43m 58.986s
19	Jack Miller	AUS	43	CWM LCR Honda	Honda RC213V-RS	B	F: Medium/R: Soft	22	44m 04.449s
20	Claudio Corti	ITA	71	Forward Racing	Yamaha Forward	B	F: Medium/R: Soft	22	44m 43.075s
21	Karel Abraham	CZE	17	AB Motoracing	Honda RC213V-RS	B	F: Medium/R: Soft	22	44m 55.697s
	Maverick Vinales	SPA	25	Team SUZUKI ECSTAR	Suzuki GSX-RR	B	F: Medium/R: Medium	15	DNF-crash
	Cal Crutchlow	GBR	35	CWM LCR Honda	Honda RC213V	B	F: Medium/R: Hard	14	DNF-crash
	Eugene Laverty	IRL	50	Aspar MotoGP Team	Honda RC213V-RS	B	F: Medium/R: Soft	4	DNF-crash
	Alex de Angelis	RSM	15	E-Motion IodaRacing Team	Aprilia ART	B	F: Medium/R: Soft	3	DNF-crash

Fastest lap: Marc Marquez, on lap 4, 1m 56.048s, 104.1mph/167.6km/h.
Lap record: Dani Pedrosa, SPA (Honda), 1m 56.027s, 104.1mph/167.6km/h (2014).
Event best maximum speed: Andrea Iannone, 196.6mph/316.4km/h (free practice).

Qualifying
Weather: Dry
Air Temp: 30° Track Temp: 40°
Humidity: 37%

1	Lorenzo	1m 54.989s
2	Marquez	1m 55.063s
3	Rossi	1m 55.353s
4	Iannone	1m 55.390s
5	Smith	1m 55.460s
6	Dovizioso	1m 55.935s
7	Vinales	1m 55.954s
8	P. Espargaro	1m 55.955s
9	Pedrosa	1m 55.969s
10	Crutchlow	1m 56.192s
11	Barbera	1m 56.399s
12	Hernandez	1m 56.739s
13	Petrucci	1m 56.713s
14	Redding	1m 56.765s
15	A. Espargaro	1m 56.806s
16	Bradl	1m 57.133s
17	Di Meglio	1m 57.215s
18	Baz	1m 57.540s
19	Bautista	1m 57.552s
20	Laverty	1m 57.634s
21	Hayden	1m 57.645s
22	Miller	1m 57.855s
23	De Angelis	1m 58.599s
24	Corti	1m 59.145s
25	Abraham	1m 59.903s

Fastest race laps

1	Marquez	1m 56.048s
2	Lorenzo	1m 56.169s
3	Rossi	1m 56.747s
4	Iannone	1m 56.860s
5	Dovizioso	1m 56.943s
6	Pedrosa	1m 56.975s
7	Smith	1m 57.250s
8	Vinales	1m 57.436s
9	P. Espargaro	1m 57.454s
10	Crutchlow	1m 57.652s
11	A. Espargaro	1m 57.844s
12	Redding	1m 57.976s
13	Petrucci	1m 58.121s
14	Hayden	1m 58.338s
15	Bradl	1m 58.380s
16	Barbera	1m 58.405s
17	Hernandez	1m 58.530s
18	Baz	1m 58.679s
19	Bautista	1m 58.710s
20	Di Meglio	1m 58.943s
21	Laverty	1m 58.977s
22	Miller	1m 59.007s
23	De Angelis	1m 59.257s
24	Corti	2m 00.377s
25	Abraham	2m 01.716s

Championship Points

1	Lorenzo	211
2	Rossi	211
3	Marquez	159
4	Iannone	142
5	Smith	106
6	Dovizioso	104
7	Pedrosa	91
8	P. Espargaro	81
9	Crutchlow	74
10	Petrucci	63
11	Vinales	62
12	A. Espargaro	53
13	Hernandez	41
14	Redding	37
15	Barbera	20
16	Bautista	16
17	Baz	15
18	Miller	12
19	Bradl	11
20	Pirro	8
21	Hayden	8
22	E. Laverty	7
23	Aoyama	5
24	Di Meglio	2
25	De Angelis	1

Constructor Points

1	Yamaha	252
2	Honda	204
3	Ducati	167
4	Suzuki	82
5	Yamaha Forward	20
6	Aprilia	16
7	ART	1

Grid order	1	2	3	4	5	6	7	8	9	10	11	12	13	14	15	16	17	18	19	20	21	22	
99 LORENZO	99	99	99	99	99	99	99	99	99	99	99	99	99	99	99	99	99	99	99	99	99	99	1
93 MARQUEZ	93	93	93	93	93	93	93	93	93	93	93	93	93	93	93	93	93	93	93	93	93	93	2
46 ROSSI	4	46	46	46	46	46	46	46	46	46	46	46	46	46	46	46	46	46	46	46	46	46	3
29 IANNONE	46	4	4	4	4	4	4	29	29	29	29	29	29	29	29	29	29	29	29	29	29	29	4
38 SMITH	29	29	29	29	29	29	29	4	4	4	4	4	4	4	4	4	4	4	4	4	4	26	5
4 DOVIZIOSO	38	38	38	38	38	38	26	9	26	9	26	9	26	9	26	9	26	26	26	26	26	4	6
25 VINALES	44	44	44	44	26	26	38	38	38	38	38	38	38	38	38	38	38	38	38	38	38		7
44 P. ESPARGARO	25	25	25	26	44	44	44	44	44	44	44	44	44	44	44	44	44	44	44	44	44		8
26 PEDROSA	9	26	26	25	25	25	25	25	25	25	25	25	25	25	25	41	41	41	41	41	41	41	9
35 CRUTCHLOW	26	9	9	35	35	35	35	35	35	35	35	35	35	35	41	9	9	9	9	9	9	9	10
8 BARBERA	68	35	35	9	9	9	41	41	41	41	41	41	41	9	68	68	68	68	68	68	68		11
68 HERNANDEZ	41	68	41	41	41	41	9	9	9	9	9	9	9	68	45	45	45	45	45	45	45		12
9 PETRUCCI	35	41	68	45	45	45	45	45	45	45	45	45	68	45	6	6	6	6	19	19	19		13
45 REDDING	45	45	45	68	68	68	68	68	68	68	68	68	68	45	6	19	19	19	19	6	6		14
41 A. ESPARGARO	8	8	8	6	6	6	6	6	6	6	6	6	6	19	8	69	69	69	76	76	76		15
6 BRADL	69	69	6	8	8	8	8	8	8	8	8	8	19	8	69	8	8	8	8	8	8		
63 DI MEGLIO	6	6	69	69	69	69	69	69	69	19	19	19	8	69	76	76	76	76	69	69	69		
76 BAZ	63	63	63	76	76	76	76	76	76	19	69	69	69	69	76	43	63	63	63	63	63		
19 BAUTISTA	50	76	76	63	19	19	19	19	19	76	76	76	76	76	43	63	43	43	43	43	43		
50 LAVERTY	76	50	50	19	63	63	43	43	43	43	43	43	43	63	71	71	71	71	71	71	71		
69 HAYDEN	43	43	19	50	43	43	63	63	63	63	63	63	63	71	17	17	17	17	17	17			
43 MILLER	19	19	43	43	71	71	71	71	71	71	71	71	17										
15 DE ANGELIS	15	15	15	71	17	17	17	17	17	17	17	17											
71 CORTI	71	71	71	17																			
17 ABRAHAM	17	17	17																				

Moto2 — RACE DISTANCE: 20 laps, 67.145 miles/108.060km · RACE WEATHER: Dry (air 25°C, humidity 56%, track 37°C)

Pos.	Rider	Nat.	No.	Entrant	Machine	Laps	Time & Speed
1	**Johann Zarco**	FRA	5	Ajo Motorsport	Kalex	20	41m 02.500s 98.1mph/ 157.9km/h
2	**Tito Rabat**	SPA	1	EG 0,0 Marc VDS	Kalex	20	41m 03.921s
3	**Alex Rins**	SPA	40	Paginas Amarillas HP 40	Kalex	20	41m 04.285s
4	**Alex Marquez**	SPA	73	EG 0,0 Marc VDS	Kalex	20	41m 06.893s
5	**Sam Lowes**	GBR	22	Speed Up Racing	Speed Up	20	41m 10.344s
6	**Jonas Folger**	GER	94	AGR Team	Kalex	20	41m 10.556s
7	**Thomas Luthi**	SWI	12	Derendinger Racing Interwetten	Kalex	20	41m 12.382s
8	**Sandro Cortese**	GER	11	Dynavolt Intact GP	Kalex	20	41m 12.574s
9	**Luis Salom**	SPA	39	Paginas Amarillas HP 40	Kalex	20	41m 14.421s
10	**Franco Morbidelli**	ITA	21	Italtrans Racing Team	Kalex	20	41m 14.979s
11	**Simone Corsi**	ITA	3	Forward Racing	Kalex	20	41m 20.194s
12	**Takaaki Nakagami**	JPN	30	IDEMITSU Honda Team Asia	Kalex	20	41m 20.263s
13	**Dominique Aegerter**	SWI	77	Technomag Racing Interwetten	Kalex	20	41m 20.852s
14	**Hafizh Syahrin**	MAL	55	Petronas Raceline Malaysia	Kalex	20	41m 21.022s
15	**Mika Kallio**	FIN	36	Italtrans Racing Team	Kalex	20	41m 21.877s
16	Xavier Simeon	BEL	19	Federal Oil Gresini Moto2	Kalex	20	41m 23.311s
17	Axel Pons	SPA	49	AGR Team	Kalex	20	41m 23.772s
18	Julian Simon	SPA	60	QMMF Racing Team	Speed Up	20	41m 24.619s
19	Marcel Schrotter	GER	23	Tech 3	Tech 3	20	41m 28.446s
20	Randy Krummenacher	SWI	4	JIR Racing Team	Kalex	20	41m 29.086s
21	Anthony West	AUS	95	QMMF Racing Team	Speed Up	20	41m 41.925s
22	Edgar Pons	SPA	57	Paginas Amarillas HP 40	Kalex	20	41m 46.790s
23	Azlan Shah	MAL	25	IDEMITSU Honda Team Asia	Kalex	20	41m 47.157s
24	Ricard Cardus		88	JPMoto Malaysia	Suter	20	41m 47.247s
25	Thitipong Warokorn	THA	10	APH PTT The Pizza SAG	Kalex	20	41m 49.460s
26	Jesko Raffin	SWI	2	sports-millions-EMWE-SAG	Kalex	20	41m 56.047s
	Xavi Vierge	SPA	97	Tech 3	Tech 3	16	DNF
	Lorenzo Baldassarri	ITA	7	Forward Racing	Kalex	12	DNF
	Florian Alt	GER	66	E-Motion IodaRacing Team	Suter	12	DNF
	Louis Rossi	FRA	96	Tasca Racing Scuderia Moto2	Tech 3	11	DNF
	Robin Mulhauser	SWI	70	Technomag Racing Interwetten	Kalex	3	DNF

Fastest lap: Thomas Luthi, on lap 5, 2m 2.422s, 98.7mph/158.8km/h.
Lap record: Esteve Rabat, SPA (Kalex), 2m 2.383s, 98.7mph/158.9km/h (2014).
Event best maximum speed: Sandro Cortese, 162.5mph/261.5km/h (race).

Qualifying

Weather: Dry
Air Temp: 30° **Track Temp:** 41°
Humidity: 38%

1	Zarco	2m 01.614s
2	Rabat	2m 01.873s
3	Rins	2m 01.901s
4	Cortese	2m 01.990s
5	Luthi	2m 02.078s
6	Aegerter	2m 02.442s
7	Marquez	2m 02.535s
8	Morbidelli	2m 02.543s
9	Pons	2m 02.611s
10	Folger	2m 02.634s
11	Baldassarri	2m 02.711s
12	Corsi	2m 02.728s
13	Lowes	2m 02.855s
14	Krummenacher	2m 02.860s
15	Salom	2m 02.867s
16	Nakagami	2m 02.917s
17	Syahrin	2m 03.008s
18	Kallio	2m 03.011s
19	Simeon	2m 03.083s
20	Rossi	2m 03.423s
21	Schrotter	2m 03.440s
22	Simon	2m 03.558s
23	West	2m 03.816s
24	Mulhauser	2m 03.859s
25	Shah	2m 03.982s
26	Warokorn	2m 04.073s
27	Pons	2m 04.118s
28	Cardus	2m 04.234s
29	Alt	2m 04.309s
30	Vierge	2m 04.435s
31	Raffin	2m 04.928s

Fastest race laps

1	Luthi	2m 02.422s
2	Zarco	2m 02.427s
3	Rins	2m 02.483s
4	Rabat	2m 02.539s
5	Marquez	2m 02.541s
6	Folger	2m 02.551s
7	Lowes	2m 02.593s
8	Morbidelli	2m 02.645s
9	Cortese	2m 02.750s
10	Salom	2m 02.817s
11	Aegerter	2m 02.920s
12	Corsi	2m 02.936s
13	Baldassarri	2m 02.970s
14	Kallio	2m 03.087s
15	Nakagami	2m 03.164s
16	West	2m 03.195s
17	Syahrin	2m 03.204s
18	Pons	2m 03.216s
19	Simon	2m 03.227s
20	Simeon	2m 03.309s
21	Krummenacher	2m 03.509s
22	Schrotter	2m 03.677s
23	Pons	2m 03.958s
24	Cardus	2m 04.036s
25	Rossi	2m 04.122s
26	Shah	2m 04.131s
27	Warokorn	2m 04.211s
28	Vierge	2m 04.212s
29	Raffin	2m 04.387s
30	Mulhauser	2m 04.388s
31	Alt	2m 05.309s

Championship Points

1	Zarco	224
2	Rabat	145
3	Rins	144
4	Lowes	118
5	Luthi	118
6	Simeon	92
7	Folger	91
8	Morbidelli	84
9	Aegerter	59
10	Marquez	49
11	Kallio	48
12	Simon	47
13	Salom	43
14	Cortese	43
15	Nakagami	43
16	Corsi	40
17	Baldassarri	37
18	Syahrin	36
19	West	20
20	Pons	18
21	Schrotter	14
22	Krummenacher	13
23	Rossi	7
24	Shah	6
25	Mulhauser	1

Constructor Points

1	Kalex	270
2	Speed Up	129
3	Tech 3	21

Moto3 — RACE DISTANCE: 12 laps, 40.287 miles/64.836km · RACE WEATHER: Dry (air 22°C, humidity 68%, track 26°C)

Pos.	Rider	Nat.	No.	Entrant	Machine	Laps	Time & Speed
1	**Niccolo Antonelli**	ITA	23	Ongetta-Rivacold	Honda	12	25m 56.866s 93.1mph/ 149.9km/h
2	**Enea Bastianini**	ITA	33	Gresini Racing Team Moto3	Honda	12	25m 57.018s
3	**Brad Binder**	RSA	41	Red Bull KTM Ajo	KTM	12	25m 57.242s
4	**Efren Vazquez**	SPA	7	Leopard Racing	Honda	12	25m 57.406s
5	**Jorge Navarro**	SPA	9	Estrella Galicia 0,0	Honda	12	25m 57.426s
6	**Romano Fenati**	ITA	5	SKY Racing Team VR46	KTM	12	25m 57.687s
7	**Danny Kent**	GBR	52	Leopard Racing	Honda	12	25m 58.045s
8	**Miguel Oliveira**	POR	44	Red Bull KTM Ajo	KTM	12	25m 58.054s
9	**Jakub Kornfeil**	CZE	84	Drive M7 SIC	KTM	12	25m 58.286s
10	**John McPhee**	GBR	17	SAXOPRINT RTG	Honda	12	26m 00.251s
11	**Jorge Martin**	SPA	88	MAPFRE Team MAHINDRA	Mahindra	12	26m 02.617s
12	**Francesco Bagnaia**	ITA	21	MAPFRE Team MAHINDRA	Mahindra	12	26m 02.712s
13	**Andrea Migno**	ITA	16	SKY Racing Team VR46	KTM	12	26m 02.776s
14	**Juanfran Guevara**	SPA	58	MAPFRE Team MAHINDRA	Mahindra	12	26m 03.039s
15	**Philipp Oettl**	GER	65	Schedl GP Racing	KTM	12	26m 03.134s
16	Darryn Binder	RSA	40	Outox Reset Drink Team	Mahindra	12	26m 04.514s
17	Remy Gardner	AUS	2	CIP	Mahindra	12	26m 04.568s
18	Livio Loi	BEL	11	RW Racing GP	Honda	12	26m 05.073s
19	Lorenzo Dalla Porta	ITA	48	Husqvarna Factory Laglisse	Husqvarna	12	26m 11.168s
20	Tatsuki Suzuki	JPN	24	CIP	Mahindra	12	26m 12.879s
21	Matteo Ferrari	ITA	12	San Carlo Team Italia	Mahindra	12	26m 12.993s
22	Zulfahmi Khairuddin	MAL	63	Drive M7 SIC	KTM	12	26m 13.608s
23	Maria Herrera	SPA	6	Husqvarna Factory Laglisse	Husqvarna	12	26m 13.793s
24	Stefano Manzi	ITA	29	San Carlo Team Italia	Mahindra	12	26m 15.833s
25	Alessandro Tonucci	ITA	19	Outox Reset Drink Team	Mahindra	12	26m 28.326s
26	Karel Hanika	CZE	98	Red Bull KTM Ajo	KTM	12	26m 33.952s
27	Jules Danilo	FRA	95	Ongetta-Rivacold	Honda	12	26m 58.531s
	Kevin Hanus	GER	86	Team Hanusch	Honda	9	DNF
	Alexis Masbou	FRA	10	SAXOPRINT RTG	Honda	8	DNF
	Fabio Quartararo	FRA	20	Estrella Galicia 0,0	Honda	7	DNF
	Isaac Vinales	SPA	32	RBA Racing Team	KTM	1	DNF
	Maximilian Kappler	GER	97	SAXOPRINT-RTG	FTR Honda	0	DNS
	Hiroki Ono	JPN	76	Leopard Racing	Honda	0	DNS
	Andrea Locatelli	ITA	55	Gresini Racing Team Moto3	Honda	0	DNS
	Gabriel Rodrigo	ARG	91	RBA Racing Team	KTM	0	DNS
	Niklas Ajo	FIN	31	RBA Racing Team	KTM	0	DNS

Fastest lap: Miguel Oliveira, on lap 3, 2m 8.466s, 94.1mph/151.4km/h.
Lap record: Romano Fenati, ITA (KTM), 2m 8.064s, 94.3mph/151.8km/h (2014).
Event best maximum speed: Jorge Navarro, 140.6mph/226.2km/h (free practice).

Qualifying

Weather: Dry
Air Temp: 31° **Track Temp:** 43°
Humidity: 38%

1	Antonelli	2m 07.667s
2	Kent	2m 07.669s
3	Navarro	2m 07.700s
4	Quartararo	2m 07.815s
5	Masbou	2m 07.886s
6	Binder	2m 08.115s
7	Hanika	2m 08.116s
8	Vazquez	2m 08.283s
9	Martin	2m 08.322s
10	McPhee	2m 08.420s
11	Danilo	2m 08.483s
12	Oliveira	2m 08.495s
13	Guevara	2m 08.517s
14	Vinales	2m 08.554s
15	Bastianini	2m 08.598s
16	Binder	2m 08.616s
17	Gardner	2m 08.643s
18	Ono	2m 08.645s
19	Fenati	2m 08.720s
20	Kornfeil	2m 08.750s
21	Suzuki	2m 08.856s
22	Locatelli	2m 08.901s
23	Dalla Porta	2m 08.950s
24	Oettl	2m 08.953s
25	Rodrigo	2m 09.061s
26	Migno	2m 09.277s
27	Bagnaia	2m 09.433s
28	Ajo	2m 09.433s
29	Loi	2m 09.473s
30	Tonucci	2m 09.583s
31	Manzi	2m 09.653s
32	Herrera	2m 09.724s
33	Khairuddin	2m 10.318s
34	Kappler	2m 10.426s
35	Ferrari	2m 10.695s
36	Hanus	2m 13.210s

Fastest race laps

1	Oliveira	2m 08.466s
2	Bastianini	2m 08.540s
3	Kornfeil	2m 08.583s
4	Binder	2m 08.715s
5	Antonelli	2m 08.761s
6	Fenati	2m 08.876s
7	Masbou	2m 08.883s
8	Vazquez	2m 08.899s
9	McPhee	2m 08.911s
10	Navarro	2m 08.927s
11	Guevara	2m 08.962s
12	Kent	2m 08.976s
13	Binder	2m 08.992s
14	Oettl	2m 09.000s
15	Manzi	2m 09.105s
16	Gardner	2m 09.146s
17	Martin	2m 09.177s
18	Bagnaia	2m 09.187s
19	Migno	2m 09.209s
20	Loi	2m 09.368s
21	Dalla Porta	2m 09.570s
22	Suzuki	2m 09.734s
23	Khairuddin	2m 09.906s
24	Tonucci	2m 09.988s
25	Herrera	2m 10.005s
26	Ferrari	2m 10.030s
27	Danilo	2m 10.050s
28	Hanika	2m 10.513s
29	Quartararo	2m 10.793s
30	Hanus	2m 12.670s

Championship Points

1	Kent	199
2	Bastianini	154
3	Fenati	122
4	Oliveira	111
5	Vazquez	109
6	Binder	99
7	Antonelli	94
8	Quartararo	79
9	Vinales	75
10	Navarro	72
11	McPhee	60
12	Bagnaia	59
13	Masbou	41
14	Loi	40
15	Oettl	40
16	Hanika	33
17	Locatelli	31
18	Kornfeil	26
19	Martin	23
20	Ajo	21
21	Migno	19
22	Ono	15
23	Danilo	7
24	Guevara	6
25	Khairuddin	2
26	Herrera	1
27	Manzi	1
28	Ferrari	1

Constructor Points

1	Honda	260
2	KTM	181
3	Mahindra	76
4	Husqvarna	64

FIM WORLD CHAMPIONSHIP · ROUND 12

BRITISH GRAND PRIX

SILVERSTONE CIRCUIT

AFTER a highly notional shift, first to the unbuilt Circuit of Wales and then to the unready Donington Park, the British Grand Prix returned to Silverstone one more time, and the track lived up to its reputation for playing the weather card.

The timing was so inconvenient for the main race of the day that the race director was obliged to deploy his sweeping powers to change the rules as required.

After the riders had been flagged off for the warm-up lap with 'Dry Race' signboards displayed, it started raining halfway around. The entire field pulled into the pits to change to wet-shod bikes. By right, then there would have been a shoving and pushing match to get to the end of the pit lane first, followed by a mass start from the pit lane once the pace car had gone by.

Quite apart from the obvious dangers, this would have been absurd. The start procedure was aborted and a full-distance race rescheduled 20 minutes later.

By then, it was properly wet, and guess who took the benefit? Rossi left Lorenzo trailing in discomfort to a distant fourth and kept on up front while Marquez suffered race crash number four of the year. It was the evergreen veteran's fourth win of the season: still two less than Lorenzo, but enough to regain a handy 12-point lead.

Rossi led from the second lap to the last; Lorenzo had led the first. This was in line with a set of statistics released at Silverstone: 19 of Lorenzo's 38 premier-class wins, half of them, had been won leading every lap. For Rossi, only two of his 112 wins in all classes had been achieved that way.

The conditions created another new hero, a compatriot of Rossi, in satellite Ducati rider Danilo Petrucci. Reliably impressive on his B-grade 2014 factory machine, he had the ride of his life, outpacing Dovizioso's GP15 and even scaring himself when he realised there was a danger he might catch and pass Rossi. He shrank back from the temptation: second was by far his best ever, and plenty good enough, compared with the risk of a crash that might take both of them down. With Dovi third, it was the second all-Italian podium of the year.

A record 75,000 fans had braved the conditions for what may (or indeed may not) be the last visit to the British GP's original home, after it had moved from the Isle of Man in 1977; they were rewarded with a British race win – Danny Kent again. MotoGP hopes were denied. Redding was sixth, a career best; and Smith seventh, but that was a long way

from the real action, and both had been promoted by Marquez's crash.

Crutchlow managed only one lap. On the second, he was taken down and out by team-mate Jack Miller, who had made a blazing start from 16th on the grid to be disputing fifth with the Englishman.

The teamsters had dropped their CWM livery after fresh scandal broke around Anthony Constantinou, head of the city financial brokers. Already facing charges of financial skulduggery, he had now appeared in court on sexual harassment charges as well. With most of the sponsorship money reportedly already paid, team owner Lucio Cecchinello henceforth would revert to his former *modus operandi* – individual title sponsors race by race.

Crutchlow, along with his MotoGP compatriots, arrived at the track with his contract negotiations concluded: he would stay with LCR for another two years.

Smith, in turn, had his renewal with the Tech 3 team confirmed, leaving him a little red in the face about his complaints earlier in the season.

In fact, Redding put off his decision until race day. He was the latest target to replace Yonny Hernandez alongside Petrucci on the Pramac Ducati. Given his difficulties in meshing with the factory Honda in 2015, and an encouraging Ducati test in 2014, he finally steeled himself to turn his back on his long-time supporters at the Marc VDS team, which had moved to the top class mainly to give him a ride.

The Pramac seat, in turn, had become available because the other Englishman, Kent, had turned down their offer, reluctant to be tied up for three years as they wanted. With his Leopard-backed Kiefer team's Moto2 plans hardening, it made more sense to stay with them for the present.

The other local hero, Sam Lowes, cemented his reputation for spectacular action, although in a slightly skewed manner, in qualifying. His Speed Up team had sent him out with a light fuel load, but he blamed himself for missing the pit board instructing him to call in for a 'splash and go'. With barely 15 minutes left, he ran out of gas at the far end of the Hangar Straight. Somehow he got self and bike back to the pit, went out again, and secured pole, his third of the year.

In Moto2, just two races after his first podium finish, Morbidelli was absent. A motocross training crash had broken left tibia and fibula. He had been riding with his guru, Rossi, who transferred him to hospital for immediate surgery. Nineteen-year-old Italian rookie Federico Caricasulo took his

Above: Fast-away Miller takes out team-mate Crutchlow on lap three.

Above left: Sam Lowes cut it fine to take pole in Moto2.

Above right: A minute's silence for Juan Garriga and teenager Hahle.

Top: Rossi took command for a fine wet win.

Left: Silverstone? Wet race? Who'd have thought it?

Below left: Press room was a make-shift marquee.

Far left: Should I stay or should I go? Clash of loyalties for Redding.

Opening spread: Umbrellas, Union Jacks – and a British winner! Danny Kent takes the plaudits.

Photos: Gold & Goose

place, while Ricky Cardus was rescued after being dropped by Tech 3, for a second race replacing Wilairot in the JPMoto Malaysia team.

And in Moto3, Niklas Ajo was gone – summarily dumped from the RBA team after too many crashes and in spite of his heroic knee-surfing finish at Assen. His place went to another displaced rider, Isaac Vinales.

There was sad news and another minute of silence on the grid after the death of former 250 and 500 racer Juan Garriga, hard-man counterpart to Mr Clean Sito Pons in the late 1980s, though it was Pons who emerged triumphant. After retirement, Garriga was convicted of drug and firearm offences: recent reports from Barcelona were of a deeply troubled man in poor physical shape before he suffered ultimately fatal injuries in a street-bike crash; a sombre fate for a great racer. Also rememembered was Jonas Hahle, a 14-year-old rider killed in an ADAC Junior Cup race at Oschersleben.

MOTOGP RACE – 20 laps

Practice had been dry and Marquez was on pole, from Lorenzo and Pedrosa; Rossi was on row two.

The 'Dry Race' board was shown just before the final sighting lap. Just then it started to drizzle, and by the time they were halfway around it was turning to real rain. The full field pulled into the pits to change to wet bikes. Proceedings were abruptly halted, and with the start subsequently delayed by

20 minutes, it was properly wet rather than vexingly half-and-half.

Lorenzo grabbed control at the first corner, Rossi up to second by the end of the lap, and Marquez third. Then Pol Espargaro, Pedrosa, Crutchlow, Smith and … yes, Jack Miller, up from 16th and really mixing it with the front guys.

This came to an end on lap three, when Miller lunged inside far too fast at the tight Vale left-hander, knocking team-mate Crutchlow off and effectively out of the race (he restarted, swapped bikes, but then crashed again). Miller was also out, and docked a penalty point for his over-exuberance, which Crutchlow kindly dubbed "understandable" after the race. "I've done it before, and I'll do it again," he said. The Australian accepted the punishment, saying, "I probably should have had one before, after Assen," (where he had done something similar to Nicky Hayden).

Rossi and Marquez had passed Lorenzo by the end of lap two, and immediately started drawing away. Rossi was always in front, but Marquez looked ready to attack. The Yamaha rider thought it would come in the last lap, "and with Marquez that is always difficult".

After half-distance, 12 laps done, it looked as though Marquez might pounce earlier than that. Then, through Copse, first corner of lap 13, the front slipped and he was down and sliding away, just like any lingering title hopes. "The championship situation was already complicated. Now it is even more difficult," he said. "But it is also true that this was a

Above: Petrucci walks on water: here ahead of factory teamsters Dovizioso and Lorenzo.

Photo: Clive Challinor Motorsport Photography

Top right: Petrucci's podium joy.

Above right: More of the same for rostrum first-timer Jakub Kornfeil.

Above far right: Johann Zarco controlled a fraught Moto2 race.

Right: Slick-shod Florian Alt (66) enlivened proceedings in Moto2, and set the fastest lap.

Below right: Danny Kent, chased by Kornfeil, Martin and Fenati, soon became uncatchable.

Photos: Gold & Goose

race where we had to take a risk. I felt I had the race under control and I crashed out."

Rossi glanced at the big screen, saw his rival in the gravel and thought, with the rain getting heavier, that now he might be able to relax.

Not so. For Petrucci had been picking up places rapidly after finishing lap one ninth. He was impressed to find himself behind Lorenzo and Pedrosa by lap four, a situation so far he'd only encountered "on the PlayStation"; but he was faster. Nervously, he passed them both before half-distance.

At the same time, Dovi was storming through. A slip off the line almost put him into the pit wall, and he was last into the first corner. By lap eight, he had followed Petrucci past Lorenzo; and when Marquez fell five laps later, he had got ahead of the satellite rider. Only for two laps, however. Petrucci regained second and had stretched out a little gap by the end.

More to the point, he had closed steadily on Rossi: a gap of just under four seconds when Marquez fell was only 1.6 seconds five laps later, and Rossi was becoming worried. He'd got the message earlier and upped his pace, but he was still losing ground.

He was fast enough, however, to persuade Petrucci to settle for a brilliant second. Lorenzo's problem was caused by a badly misting visor; but he perked up towards the finish, repassing Pedrosa to close slightly on Dovizioso.

A long way back there was a big and varied battle for sixth. Smith had been deposed eventually at half-distance by team-mate Pol, only for the Spaniard to crash four laps later. Aleix Espargaro had been unable to do more than push for a while; and Iannone was now fading off the back.

Then came another charger: Redding had qualified seventh, but finished lap one 14th, feeling most uneasy with his bike. By half-distance, that had changed, and he sliced through the lot of them to take a career-best sixth.

Smith was over a second behind; while Iannone got ahead of the fading Aleix.

Another battle for the final points: won going away at the end by Bautista, whose Aprilia team-mate, Stefan Bradl, had crashed out of the gang.

Second Suzuki rider Vinales came through at the end, both having passed top Open finisher Hayden during the closing laps. Barbera and di Meglio took the last points, trailed home by Baz, Laverty, Corti (Forward Yamaha) and Abraham, one lap down.

Hernandez had been punted off on the first corner.

MOTO2 RACE – 18 laps

Unusually, because of the time difference with Europe, Moto2 was the first race of the day, and it suffered the worst conditions – a light drizzle before the start, then 18 laps on a track that was dry before the race was half done.

All started on wets. Florian Alt was the first of a handful of riders to pit for slicks, and he played an unwitting part as he came blazing past the leaders, six or seven seconds a lap faster, as he unlapped himself in the closing stages.

At least one of the group by now fighting for second didn't realise he was a lap behind; up front, Zarco – by now comfortably ahead – had the composure to be fully informed.

Lowes had qualified on pole, but was swamped away from the start as Rabat came through from row two to head the first lap. Rabat was back from a heavy crash in qualifying, but undaunted, as a leading pack of six drew away.

Rins had taken over the lead by the end of lap two, Zarco's bid for the front having lasted only until the next corner, where Rabat had barged past to consign him to fifth.

Also running strongly, Rabat's team-mate Marquez, who was second on lap three, then followed Zarco as he came past again. Behind Rabat, Luthi was right in the action; Folger was hanging on behind.

Luthi was the first to suffer a wet rear tyre beginning to disintegrate, and he was dropping back badly by half-distance. Slo-mo camera shots a couple of laps later also showed Rabat's spinning rear shedding great gobs of tread.

Before half-distance, however, Zarco had slipped cleanly past Rins and immediately started to draw away. At its best, on lap 12, the gap was almost eight seconds; by the end, he had allowed it to dwindle to better than three, secure in his fifth win of the season, and record-extending 11th consecutive podium.

Rabat and Rins duked it out behind, Marquez a close spectator; Folger also closed for a while. With two laps to go, Rins put his escape plan into action and managed to draw a couple of seconds clear, to assume second overall.

Rabat held off Marquez, the younger brother's best so far; Folger was fifth.

Pole-starter Lowes had dropped back to ninth, but by the time he finally got past Baldassari for seventh on lap six, he was already more than ten seconds adrift.

Cardus had come with him; and by half-distance, wet specialist Anthony West had closed up and was beginning to cut through.

Lowes got clear to secure what had become sixth as they all passed Luthi; West got the better of Cortese for seventh; battling Luthi regained ninth from Cardus on the last lap.

Slick-shod Alt was 24th at the end, but had the satisfaction of the fastest lap, by a handsome margin.

Wild-card Bradley Ray was an early victim of conditions, crashing out; Corsi also fell.

MOTO3 RACE – 17 laps

Moved from first race to last, Moto3 had settled weather. The downside? It was proper rain, and getting heavier. That meant a race of attrition, with 20 finishers from 36 starters. Several had fallen at least once, some twice, and a heroic Jorge Martin three times, the last proving terminal.

That made Kent's steady ride from the front row to a massive victory – his sixth of the year – all the more impressive. It was not completely calm – he was out of the seat at least once – but it was still superbly judged, and well rewarded when his closest title rival, Bastianini, never in the hunt, crashed out towards the end of a gruelling race.

First-time pole-starter Navarro and second qualifier Hanika both crashed on lap one; Vinales took over the lead for three laps, by now a second ahead of Kent, who was even further ahead of Kornfeil.

Vinales slipped off on lap four; Kent was alone. He stayed that way.

There was adventure galore behind. Martin deposed Fenati from fourth when he fell for the first time on lap two; now fast-starter Maria Herrera pressed the Italian, only to crash on lap six, after Locatelli had got by. He too would fall.

Now Antonelli took up the challenge, chased by Bagnaia and for a while Quartararo, until he faded with a misted visor.

The Italian pair were fighting for third when Fenati fell on lap nine; and with two laps to go, Antonelli was within half a second of Kornfeil. Bagnaia pushed past one more time, only to crash; and now Antonelli settled for a safe third, Kornfeil a career-best second.

Miles behind, Quartararo survived in fourth after Bastianini came past then crashed.

Loi was less than two seconds behind, while McPhee won out in a long battle with Guevara. Dalla Porta, Vazquez and Suzuki completed the top ten; then came Masbou, Fenati and Oliveira.

Wild-card Taz Taylor, son of former 500 GP star Niall, made the finish in 19th, one lap down.

FIM WORLD CHAMPIONSHIP ROUND 12

OFFICIAL TIMEKEEPER TISSOT

OCTO
BRITISH GRAND PRIX

28–30 AUGUST, 2015

SILVERSTONE GRAND PRIX CIRCUIT

20 laps
Length: 5.900km / 3.666 miles
Width: 17m

Key
96/60 kph/mph
Gear

Club 121/75
Vale 79/49
Abbey 160/99
Stowe 152/94
Farm 160/99
Hangar straight 329/204
The Loop 87/54
Chapel 165/103
Becketts 174/108
Maggotts 245/152
Copse 96/60
Wellington Straight
Brooklands 96/60
Luffield 111/69
Woodcote 265/165

MotoGP | RACE DISTANCE: 20 laps, 73.322 miles/118.000km · RACE WEATHER: Wet (air 16°C, humidity 85%, track 18°C)

Pos.	Rider	Nat.	No.	Entrant	Machine	Tyres	Race tyre choice	Laps	Time & speed
1	**Valentino Rossi**	ITA	46	Movistar Yamaha MotoGP	Yamaha YZR-M1	B	F: Soft Wet/R: Soft Wet	20	46m 15.617s 95.1mph/ 153.0km/h
2	**Danilo Petrucci**	ITA	9	Octo Pramac Racing	Ducati Desmosedici	B	F: Soft Wet/R: Soft Wet	20	46m 18.627s
3	**Andrea Dovizioso**	ITA	4	Ducati Team	Ducati Desmosedici	B	F: Soft Wet/R: Soft Wet	20	46m 19.734s
4	**Jorge Lorenzo**	SPA	99	Movistar Yamaha MotoGP	Yamaha YZR-M1	B	F: Soft Wet/R: Soft Wet	20	46m 21.343s
5	**Dani Pedrosa**	SPA	26	Repsol Honda Team	Honda RC213V	B	F: Soft Wet/R: Soft Wet	20	46m 26.749s
6	**Scott Redding**	GBR	45	EG 0,0 Marc VDS	Honda RC213V	B	F: Soft Wet/R: Soft Wet	20	46m 41.084s
7	**Bradley Smith**	GBR	38	Monster Yamaha Tech 3	Yamaha YZR-M1	B	F: Soft Wet/R: Soft Wet	20	46m 42.334s
8	**Andrea Iannone**	ITA	29	Ducati Team	Ducati Desmosedici	B	F: Soft Wet/R: Soft Wet	20	46m 45.010s
9	**Aleix Espargaro**	SPA	41	Team SUZUKI ECSTAR	Suzuki GSX-RR	B	F: Soft Wet/R: Soft Wet	20	46m 54.432s
10	**Alvaro Bautista**	SPA	19	Aprilia Racing Team Gresini	Aprilia RS-GP	B	F: Soft Wet/R: Soft Wet	20	46m 57.329s
11	**Maverick Vinales**	SPA	25	Team SUZUKI ECSTAR	Suzuki GSX-RR	B	F: Soft Wet/R: Soft Wet	20	47m 00.393s
12	**Nicky Hayden**	USA	69	Aspar MotoGP Team	Honda RC213V-RS	B	F: Soft Wet/R: Soft Wet	20	47m 08.106s
13	**Hector Barbera**	SPA	8	Avintia Racing	Ducati Desmosedici Open	B	F: Soft Wet/R: Soft Wet	20	47m 26.828s
14	**Mike di Meglio**	FRA	63	Avintia Racing	Ducati Desmosedici Open	B	F: Soft Wet/R: Soft Wet	20	47m 30.909s
15	**Alex de Angelis**	RSM	15	E-Motion IodaRacing Team	Aprilia ART	B	F: Soft Wet/R: Soft Wet	20	47m 33.480s
16	Loris Baz	FRA	76	Forward Racing	Yamaha Forward	B	F: Soft Wet/R: Soft Wet	20	47m 34.927s
17	Eugene Laverty	IRL	50	Aspar MotoGP Team	Honda RC213V-RS	B	F: Soft Wet/R: Soft Wet	20	47m 35.352s
18	Claudio Corti	ITA	71	Forward Racing	Yamaha Forward	B	F: Soft Wet/R: Soft Wet	20	48m 13.703s
19	Karel Abraham	CZE	17	AB Motoracing	Honda RC213V-RS	B	F: Soft Wet/R: Soft Wet	19	48m 20.040s
	Pol Espargaro	SPA	44	Monster Yamaha Tech 3	Yamaha YZR-M1	B	F: Soft Wet/R: Soft Wet	14	DNF-crash
	Marc Marquez	SPA	93	Repsol Honda Team	Honda RC213V	B	F: Soft Wet/R: Soft Wet	12	DNF-crash
	Stefan Bradl	GER	6	Aprilia Racing Team Gresini	Aprilia RS-GP	B	F: Soft Wet/R: Soft Wet	12	DNF-crash
	Cal Crutchlow	GBR	35	LCR Honda	Honda RC213V	B	F: Soft Wet/R: Soft Wet	4	DNF-crash
	Jack Miller	AUS	43	LCR Honda	Honda RC213V-RS	B	F: Soft Wet/R: Soft Wet	2	DNF-crash
	Yonny Hernandez	COL	68	Octo Pramac Racing	Ducati Desmosedici	B	F: Soft Wet/R: Soft Wet	0	DNF-crash

Fastest lap: Valentino Rossi, on lap 9, 2m 16.486s, 96.7mph/155.6km/h.
Lap record: Dani Pedrosa, SPA (Honda), 2m 1.941s, 108.2mph/174.1km/h (2013).
Event best maximum speed: Andrea Iannone, 206.5mph/332.4km/h (free practice).

Qualifying

Weather: Dry
Air Temp: 21° **Track Temp:** 32°
Humidity: 48%

1	Marquez	2m 00.234s
2	Lorenzo	2m 00.522s
3	Pedrosa	2m 00.716s
4	Rossi	2m 00.947s
5	P. Espargaro	2m 01.031s
6	Smith	2m 01.140s
7	Redding	2m 01.329s
8	Crutchlow	2m 01.376s
9	Iannone	2m 01.874s
10	A. Espargaro	2m 01.880s
11	Hernandez	2m 01.894s
12	Dovizioso	2m 01.979s
13	Vinales	2m 02.016s
14	Bradl	2m 02.657s
15	Baz	2m 02.677s
16	Miller	2m 02.697s
17	Barbera	2m 02.784s
18	Petrucci	2m 02.800s
19	Laverty	2m 02.894s
20	Bautista	2m 02.908s
21	Hayden	2m 02.946s
22	Di Meglio	2m 03.641s
23	Corti	2m 03.789s
24	Abraham	2m 04.133s
25	De Angelis	2m 04.304s

Fastest race laps

1	Rossi	2m 16.486s
2	Marquez	2m 16.569s
3	Lorenzo	2m 16.916s
4	Dovizioso	2m 16.971s
5	Petrucci	2m 16.995s
6	Pedrosa	2m 17.195s
7	Iannone	2m 17.809s
8	Redding	2m 17.951s
9	P. Espargaro	2m 18.058s
10	Hayden	2m 18.452s
11	Smith	2m 18.534s
12	Bradl	2m 18.536s
13	Vinales	2m 18.542s
14	A. Espargaro	2m 18.563s
15	Barbera	2m 18.811s
16	Bautista	2m 18.942s
17	Di Meglio	2m 19.044s
18	Baz	2m 20.095s
19	De Angelis	2m 20.437s
20	Laverty	2m 20.964s
21	Crutchlow	2m 21.957s
22	Miller	2m 22.096s
23	Corti	2m 22.277s
24	Abraham	2m 23.339s

Championship Points

1	Rossi	236
2	Lorenzo	224
3	Marquez	159
4	Iannone	150
5	Dovizioso	120
6	Smith	115
7	Pedrosa	102
8	Petrucci	83
9	P. Espargaro	81
10	Crutchlow	74
11	Vinales	67
12	A. Espargaro	60
13	Redding	47
14	Hernandez	41
15	Barbera	23
16	Bautista	22
17	Baz	15
18	Hayden	12
19	Miller	12
20	Bradl	11
21	Pirro	8
22	E. Laverty	7
23	Aoyama	5
24	Di Meglio	4
25	De Angelis	2

Constructor Points

1	Yamaha	277
2	Honda	215
3	Ducati	187
4	Suzuki	89
5	Aprilia	22
6	Yamaha Forward	20
7	ART	2

Grid order	1	2	3	4	5	6	7	8	9	10	11	12	13	14	15	16	17	18	19	20	
93 MARQUEZ	99	46	46	46	46	46	46	46	46	46	46	46	46	46	46	46	46	46	46	46	1
99 LORENZO	93	93	93	93	93	93	93	93	93	93	93	93	4	9	9	9	9	9	9	9	2
26 PEDROSA	46	99	99	99	99	99	99	9	9	9	9	9	9	4	4	4	4	4	4	4	3
46 ROSSI	44	44	44	26	26	26	9	4	4	4	4	9	26	99	99	99	99	99	99	99	4
44 P. ESPARGARO	26	35	26	9	9	9	4	99	26	26	26	26	99	26	26	26	26	26	26	26	5
38 SMITH	38	43	9	4	4	4	26	26	99	99	99	99	44	44	45	45	45	45	45	45	6
45 REDDING	35	26	38	38	38	38	38	38	38	44	44	44	38	38	38	38	38	38	38	38	7
35 CRUTCHLOW	43	9	4	41	41	41	41	44	44	38	38	38	45	45	29	29	29	29	29	29	8
29 IANNONE	9	38	41	29	44	44	44	41	41	41	41	41	41	29	41	41	41	41	41	41	9
41 A. ESPARGARO	29	4	29	44	29	29	29	45	45	45	45	45	29	41	19	19	19	19	19	19	10
68 HERNANDEZ	4	29	45	45	45	45	45	29	29	29	29	29	69	69	19	69	69	25	25	11	
4 DOVIZIOSO	6	41	6	19	19	19	19	19	19	19	19	69	19	19	25	25	25	25	69	69	12
25 VINALES	41	45	19	6	6	6	63	69	69	69	19	19	25	25	8	8	8	8	8	8	13
6 BRADL	45	6	63	63	63	63	69	63	63	6	6	6	8	8	63	63	63	63	63	63	14
76 BAZ	69	19	69	69	69	69	6	6	6	25	25	25	63	63	15	15	15	15	15	15	15
43 MILLER	19	63	76	76	76	76	76	25	25	63	8	8	15	15	76	76	50	50	50	76	
8 BARBERA	76	69	15	25	25	25	25	8	8	8	63	63	76	76	50	50	76	76	76	50	
9 PETRUCCI	63	76	8	8	8	8	8	76	76	76	76	76	50	50	71	71	71	71	71	71	
50 LAVERTY	15	15	25	15	15	15	15	15	15	15	15	15	71	71	17	17	17	17	17		
19 BAUTISTA	71	8	71	50	50	50	50	50	50	50	50	50	17	17							
69 HAYDEN	8	25	50	71	71	71	71	71	71	71	71	71									
63 DI MEGLIO	25	71	17	17	17	17	17	17	17	17	17	17									
71 CORTI	17	50	35	35																	
17 ABRAHAM	50	17																			
15 DE ANGELIS																					

35 Pit stop   35 Lapped rider

Moto2

RACE DISTANCE: 18 laps, 65.990 miles/106.200km · RACE WEATHER: Wet (air 17°C, humidity 82%, track 19°C)

Pos.	Rider	Nat.	No.	Entrant	Machine	Laps	Time & Speed
1	**Johann Zarco**	FRA	5	Ajo Motorsport	Kalex	18	42m 53.674s 92.3mph/ 148.5km/h
2	**Alex Rins**	SPA	40	Paginas Amarillas HP 40	Kalex	18	42m 57.034s
3	**Tito Rabat**	SPA	1	EG 0,0 Marc VDS	Kalex	18	42m 59.201s
4	**Alex Marquez**	SPA	73	EG 0,0 Marc VDS	Kalex	18	43m 00.163s
5	**Jonas Folger**	GER	94	AGR Team	Kalex	18	43m 01.902s
6	**Sam Lowes**	GBR	22	Speed Up Racing	Speed Up	18	43m 21.935s
7	**Anthony West**	AUS	95	QMMF Racing Team	Speed Up	18	43m 27.576s
8	**Sandro Cortese**	GER	11	Dynavolt Intact GP	Kalex	18	43m 27.613s
9	**Thomas Luthi**	SWI	12	Derendinger Racing Interwetten	Kalex	18	43m 28.563s
10	**Ricard Cardus**	SPA	88	JPMoto Malaysia	Suter	18	43m 28.758s
11	**Marcel Schrotter**	GER	23	Tech 3	Tech 3	18	43m 32.488s
12	**Randy Krummenacher**	SWI	4	JIR Racing Team	Kalex	18	43m 32.864s
13	**Dominique Aegerter**	SWI	77	Technomag Racing Interwetten	Kalex	18	43m 41.454s
14	**Takaaki Nakagami**	JPN	30	IDEMITSU Honda Team Asia	Kalex	18	43m 50.777s
15	**Axel Pons**	SPA	49	AGR Team	Kalex	18	43m 53.745s
16	Hafizh Syahrin	MAL	55	Petronas Raceline Malaysia	Kalex	18	43m 55.942s
17	Luis Salom	SPA	39	Paginas Amarillas HP 40	Kalex	18	43m 58.063s
18	Julian Simon	SPA	60	QMMF Racing Team	Speed Up	18	43m 58.480s
19	Azlan Shah	MAL	25	IDEMITSU Honda Team Asia	Kalex	18	44m 01.584s
20	Mika Kallio	FIN	36	Italtrans Racing Team	Kalex	18	44m 02.268s
21	Jesko Raffin	SWI	2	sports-millions-EMWE-SAG	Kalex	18	44m 04.624s
22	Xavi Vierge	SPA	97	Tech 3	Tech 3	18	44m 05.028s
23	Robin Mulhauser	SWI	70	Technomag Racing Interwetten	Kalex	18	44m 33.145s
24	Florian Alt	GER	66	E-Motion IodaRacing Team	Suter	18	44m 44.999s
25	Xavier Simeon	BEL	19	Federal Oil Gresini Moto2	Kalex	17	42m 57.059s
26	Federico Caricasulo	ITA	64	Italtrans Racing Team	Kalex	17	45m 03.308s
27	Louis Rossi	FRA	96	Tasca Racing Scuderia Moto2	Tech 3	16	44m 24.420s
	Thitipong Warokorn	THA	10	APH PTT The Pizza SAG	Kalex	16	DNF
	Lorenzo Baldassarri	ITA	7	Forward Racing	Kalex	13	DNF
	Simone Corsi	ITA	3	Forward Racing	Kalex	13	DNF
	Bradley Ray	GBR	28	FAB-Racing	FTR	2	DNF

Fastest lap: Florian Alt, on lap 18, 2m 13.742s, 98.7mph/158.8km/h.

Lap record: Tito Rabat, SPA (Kalex), 2m 7.186s, 103.7mph/166.9km/h (2013).

Event best maximum speed: Thomas Luthi, 167.9mph/270.2km/h (free practice).

Qualifying

Weather: Dry

Air Temp: 21° **Track Temp:** 31°

Humidity: 49%

1	Lowes	2m 06.345s
2	Rins	2m 06.403s
3	Zarco	2m 06.419s
4	Rabat	2m 06.588s
5	Luthi	2m 06.801s
6	Nakagami	2m 06.839s
7	Folger	2m 07.010s
8	Baldassarri	2m 07.059s
9	Marquez	2m 07.076s
10	Cortese	2m 07.258s
11	Aegerter	2m 07.264s
12	Syahrin	2m 07.297s
13	Pons	2m 07.314s
14	Krummenacher	2m 07.421s
15	Corsi	2m 07.443s
16	Simon	2m 07.540s
17	Salom	2m 07.548s
18	Schrotter	2m 07.582s
19	Kallio	2m 07.643s
20	Shah	2m 07.704s
21	Simeon	2m 08.016s
22	West	2m 08.202s
23	Cardus	2m 08.377s
24	Vierge	2m 08.397s
25	Raffin	2m 08.855s
26	Rossi	2m 09.038s
27	Warokorn	2m 09.431s
28	Mulhauser	2m 09.502s
29	Alt	2m 09.848s
30	Caricasulo	2m 11.046s
31	Ray	2m 11.519s

Fastest race laps

1	Alt	2m 13.742s
2	Simeon	2m 14.444s
3	Rossi	2m 16.722s
4	Zarco	2m 19.251s
5	Rins	2m 19.263s
6	Rabat	2m 19.425s
7	Marquez	2m 19.580s
8	Folger	2m 20.032s
9	Lowes	2m 20.480s
10	Shah	2m 20.887s
11	Cortese	2m 21.068s
12	Raffin	2m 21.108s
13	Simon	2m 21.134s
14	Schrotter	2m 21.261s
15	Caricasulo	2m 21.383s
16	Cardus	2m 21.529s
17	Vierge	2m 21.570s
18	West	2m 21.573s
19	Krummenacher	2m 21.625s
20	Aegerter	2m 22.242s
21	Luthi	2m 22.429s
22	Kallio	2m 22.854s
23	Salom	2m 22.926s
24	Baldassarri	2m 23.088s
25	Nakagami	2m 23.294s
26	Pons	2m 23.347s
27	Syahrin	2m 23.678s
28	Corsi	2m 25.135s
29	Mulhauser	2m 25.506s
30	Warokorn	2m 26.723s
31	Ray	2m 31.055s

Championship Points

1	Zarco	249
2	Rins	164
3	Rabat	161
4	Lowes	128
5	Luthi	125
6	Folger	102
7	Simeon	92
8	Morbidelli	84
9	Aegerter	62
10	Marquez	62
11	Cortese	51
12	Kallio	48
13	Simon	47
14	Nakagami	45
15	Salom	43
16	Corsi	40
17	Baldassarri	37
18	Syahrin	36
19	West	29
20	Pons	19
21	Schrotter	19
22	Krummenacher	17
23	Rossi	7
24	Cardus	6
25	Shah	6
26	Mulhauser	1

Constructor Points

1	Kalex	295
2	Speed Up	139
3	Tech 3	26
4	Suter	6

Moto3

RACE DISTANCE: 17 laps, 62.324 miles/100.300km · RACE WEATHER: Wet (air 16°C, humidity 97%, track 18°C)

Pos.	Rider	Nat.	No.	Entrant	Machine	Laps	Time & Speed
1	**Danny Kent**	GBR	52	Leopard Racing	Honda	17	44m 13.623s 84.5mph/ 136.0km/h
2	**Jakub Kornfeil**	CZE	84	Drive M7 SIC	KTM	17	44m 22.115s
3	**Niccolo Antonelli**	ITA	23	Ongetta-Rivacold	Honda	17	44m 26.812s
4	**Fabio Quartararo**	FRA	20	Estrella Galicia 0,0	Honda	17	45m 03.641s
5	**Livio Loi**	BEL	11	RW Racing GP	Honda	17	45m 05.378s
6	**John McPhee**	GBR	17	SAXOPRINT RTG	Honda	17	45m 07.349s
7	**Juanfran Guevara**	SPA	58	MAPFRE Team MAHINDRA	Mahindra	17	45m 14.709s
8	**Lorenzo Dalla Porta**	ITA	48	Husqvarna Factory Laglisse	Husqvarna	17	45m 19.781s
9	**Efren Vazquez**	SPA	7	Leopard Racing	Honda	17	45m 22.257s
10	**Tatsuki Suzuki**	JPN	24	CIP	Mahindra	17	45m 27.212s
11	**Alexis Masbou**	FRA	10	SAXOPRINT RTG	Honda	17	45m 32.584s
12	**Romano Fenati**	ITA	5	SKY Racing Team VR46	KTM	17	45m 41.085s
13	**Miguel Oliveira**	POR	44	Red Bull KTM Ajo	KTM	17	45m 44.833s
14	**Zulfahmi Khairuddin**	MAL	63	Drive M7 SIC	KTM	17	45m 51.146s
15	**Andrea Migno**	ITA	16	SKY Racing Team VR46	KTM	17	45m 51.627s
16	Philipp Oettl	GER	65	Schedl GP Racing	KTM	17	45m 53.999s
17	Remy Gardner	AUS	2	CIP	Mahindra	17	46m 04.111s
18	Luke Hedger	GBR	26	FPW Racing	Kalex KTM	17	46m 44.205s
19	Taz Taylor	GBR	66	RS Racing	KTM	16	44m 38.667s
20	Hiroki Ono	JPN	76	Leopard Racing	Honda	16	44m 54.330s
	Francesco Bagnaia	ITA	21	MAPFRE Team MAHINDRA	Mahindra	15	DNF
	Enea Bastianini	ITA	33	Gresini Racing Team Moto3	Honda	15	DNF
	Stefano Manzi	ITA	29	San Carlo Team Italia	Mahindra	15	DNF
	Andrea Locatelli	ITA	55	Gresini Racing Team Moto3	Honda	14	DNF
	Darryn Binder	RSA	40	Outox Reset Drink Team	Mahindra	14	DNF
	Alessandro Tonucci	ITA	19	Outox Reset Drink Team	Mahindra	12	DNF
	Jorge Martin	SPA	88	MAPFRE Team MAHINDRA	Mahindra	10	DNF
	Jules Danilo	FRA	95	Ongetta-Rivacold	Honda	8	DNF
	Brad Binder	RSA	41	Red Bull KTM Ajo	KTM	8	DNF
	Karel Hanika	CZE	98	Red Bull KTM Ajo	KTM	6	DNF
	Isaac Vinales	SPA	32	RBA Racing Team	KTM	6	DNF
	Maria Herrera	SPA	6	Husqvarna Factory Laglisse	Husqvarna	6	DNF
	Ana Carrasco	SPA	22	RBA Racing Team	KTM	6	DNF
	Matteo Ferrari	ITA	12	San Carlo Team Italia	Mahindra	1	DNF
	Jorge Navarro	SPA	9	Estrella Galicia 0,0	Honda	0	DNF
	Gabriel Rodrigo	ARG	91	RBA Racing Team	KTM	0	DNF

Fastest lap: Danny Kent, on lap 3, 2m 33.508s, 85.9mph/138.3km/h.

Lap record: Jakub Kornfeil, CZE (KTM), 2m 13.664s, 98.7mph/158.9km/h (2014).

Event best maximum speed: John McPhee, 141.7mph/228.1km/h (qualifying).

Qualifying

Weather: Dry

Air Temp: 20° **Track Temp:** 31°

Humidity: 52%

1	Navarro	2m 12.440s
2	Hanika	2m 12.979s
3	Kent	2m 13.044s
4	Vazquez	2m 13.124s
5	Vinales	2m 13.144s
6	Masbou	2m 13.446s
7	Bastianini	2m 13.525s
8	Fenati	2m 13.548s
9	Oliveira	2m 13.591s
10	Binder	2m 13.593s
11	Quartararo	2m 13.850s
12	McPhee	2m 13.956s
13	Kornfeil	2m 14.058s
14	Herrera	2m 14.080s
15	Bagnaia	2m 14.176s
16	Martin	2m 14.216s
17	Migno	2m 14.242s
18	Antonelli	2m 14.244s
19	Guevara	2m 14.428s
20	Locatelli	2m 14.498s
21	Rodrigo	2m 14.535s
22	Gardner	2m 14.702s
23	Danilo	2m 14.786s
24	Oettl	2m 14.929s
25	Binder	2m 14.959s
26	Manzi	2m 14.973s
27	Dalla Porta	2m 15.118s
28	Loi	2m 15.174s
29	Khairuddin	2m 15.350s
30	Tonucci	2m 15.352s
31	Ono	2m 15.394s
32	Ferrari	2m 15.462s
33	Suzuki	2m 16.290s
34	Carrasco	2m 16.765s
35	Taylor	2m 16.973s
36	Hedger	2m 19.032s

Fastest race laps

1	Kent	2m 33.508s
2	Bagnaia	2m 33.800s
3	Vinales	2m 33.897s
4	Antonelli	2m 34.079s
5	Kornfeil	2m 34.669s
6	Fenati	2m 34.783s
7	Locatelli	2m 34.870s
8	Martin	2m 35.089s
9	McPhee	2m 35.900s
10	Loi	2m 36.022s
11	Hedger	2m 36.178s
12	Guevara	2m 36.262s
13	Bastianini	2m 36.293s
14	Quartararo	2m 36.568s
15	Manzi	2m 36.632s
16	Binder	2m 36.939s
17	Herrera	2m 37.204s
18	Binder	2m 37.266s
19	Masbou	2m 37.348s
20	Dalla Porta	2m 37.359s
21	Suzuki	2m 37.477s
22	Vazquez	2m 37.521s
23	Hanika	2m 38.483s
24	Oliveira	2m 38.836s
25	Khairuddin	2m 38.859s
26	Danilo	2m 39.185s
27	Oettl	2m 39.223s
28	Tonucci	2m 39.277s
29	Gardner	2m 39.422s
30	Migno	2m 39.621s
31	Ono	2m 40.126s
32	Taylor	2m 41.819s
33	Carrasco	2m 56.896s

Championship Points

1	Kent	224
2	Bastianini	154
3	Fenati	126
4	Vazquez	116
5	Oliveira	114
6	Antonelli	110
7	Binder	99
8	Quartararo	92
9	Vinales	75
10	Navarro	72
11	McPhee	70
12	Bagnaia	59
13	Loi	51
14	Masbou	46
15	Kornfeil	46
16	Oettl	40
17	Hanika	33
18	Locatelli	31
19	Martin	23
20	Ajo	21
21	Migno	20
22	Guevara	15
23	Ono	15
24	Dalla Porta	8
25	Danilo	7
26	Suzuki	6
27	Khairuddin	4
28	Herrera	1
29	Manzi	1
30	Ferrari	1

Constructor Points

1	Honda	285
2	KTM	201
3	Mahindra	85
4	Husqvarna	72

Main: Marquez and Lorenzo exit the pit lane side by side following the first bike change, Pirro and Rossi in pursuit.

Inset, right: Marquez timed his second stop to perfection and romped to a comfortable victory.

Inset, below right: Redding recovered from an early crash for a first MotoGP podium.

Inset, bottom right: Rossi mistimed his second stop, losing the lead.

Photos: Gold & Goose

Above: Fortune favours the brave. Bradley Smith ran the entire race on slicks and reaped the reward…

Inset, top: …a career-best second place.

Inset, above: Smith and Redding bury the hatchet in congratulations after a crazy race.

Right: Redding passed Baz for the podium, but fourth was still a great result for the French rookie.

Photos: Gold & Goose

THERE were three different ways to get on to the podium at Misano. Marquez's was to second-guess the changing conditions successfully. He timed his two bike changes – dry to wet, then back to dry – just right to take his fourth win of the year.

For Bradley Smith, it was a matter of independent thinking – the only rider not to stop to change tyres even once, let alone twice. And chanting a mantra to himself inside his helmet: "Fortune favours the brave. Fortune favours the brave."

For Scott Redding, it was an early crash and return to the pits for a fortuitously timely bike change, and then his own more matter-of-fact approach: "I had nothing to lose, and when the wet tyres didn't feel right, I changed back to dry."

It was a career best for both Englishmen, and a first podium for Redding.

For the championship, it was another unexpected twist, with Lorenzo crashing out. Rossi timed it wrong, but secured valuable points for fifth, to extend his lead again.

For grand prix racing, it was yet more proof (if any were needed) that the best guarantee of edge-of-your seat racing and fresh faces on the rostrum is to throw in mixed conditions mid-race. After Silverstone, some thought it ought to be made compulsory – but sadly not even Dorna's omnipotence stretches that far.

One complication was the new asphalt, very dark in colour, which made it difficult for riders to judge just how wet or dry it was. The track had been fully resurfaced, after complaints at 2014's Safety Commission; it was popular all round, because not only the patchwork surfacing, but also the bumps had been removed.

The title rivals were fresh from factory Yamaha tests at Aragon, though Rossi said they had been focused on 2016's bikes, after earlier planned shakedown tests at Brno had been rained off. The engineers, he explained, wanted some miles put on the machines, even though these tests were necessarily on Bridgestone tyres "and the chassis will need to be modified for the Michelins." Nor would there be much advantage for the forthcoming race there, for when they switched to the 2015 bikes, it rained.

They had tested the M1 with its newly sprouted winglets – at last somebody was imitating Ducati, and Lorenzo's team chief, Wilco Zeelenberg, said that they exerted "several kilograms" of downforce at top speed. Lorenzo didn't use them for the race, however; Rossi did. Lorenzo pointed out that winglets were not new to Yamaha, since they had experimented with them in the two-stroke years, but since Ducati had been the ones to bring them back, "they started it".

The sprinklings that made mayhem of the race came out of nowhere after a balmy two days of practice; both Motos 2 and 3 were run on a warm, dry track. It was a weekend when only the gossip was hotter than the weather.

One rumour linked Dani Pedrosa with a move to KTM, an interesting and not entirely far-fetched proposition. Another, rather harder edged, had Miller joining Tito Rabat, now con-

firmed for a move to MotoGP with his Marc VDS team. The Australian HRC protégé's ride had been displaced by the shrinking of the LCR team, and his expected Aspar destination had been ruled out with that team's expected move to Ducati. And there was talk linking Loris Baz to a move to Avintia Ducati.

Another Moto2 career was bound in a different direction: veteran Anthony West, at 34 the oldest rider in the class, was unexpectedly dismissed from the QMMF team, where his results had fallen short of expectations, in spite of two seventh places. His Speed Up slot would go to Mika Kallio (32), second oldest in the class, from the next race.

Likewise Claudio Corti, whose brief and rather undistinguished time replacing Bradl on the Forward Yamaha also came to an end: from the next race, the seat would go to Toni Elias.

Rossi's half-brother, Luca Marini, was back for a second wild-card ride, a year after his first – but this time in Moto2. More suitable, his elder half-sibling explained, "because he is very big ... he is taller than me." Marini qualified 26th and raced to 21st.

The weekend got off to a bad start seven minutes into the first Moto3 free practice, when Navarro fell under the wheels of rookie Dalla Porta. The latter walked away, but the rising Spanish star lay prone by the trackside, bringing out the red flags. He suffered shoulder injuries and was out. In a further blow to the Estrella Galicia team, Fabio Quartararo's return from his ankle injury lasted only until the next session, when he fell and suffered further damage, which effectively ended his first season early. Baldassarri also crashed in Moto2 practice, dislocating his shoulder, but came back for a career-best seventh.

On the brighter side, KTM's second attempt at a significant chassis upgrade arrived, available to all riders, and was well received. Brad Binder, on the front row of the grid for the first time, praised not only the improved handling, but also the fact that it would be better at sustaining pace through the race. So it proved, in a strong challenge to the pre-eminent Hondas, which failed only by a matter of a few feet.

This further escalation in the factory Moto3 battle made nonsense yet again of any idea that Moto3 should be a low-cost class. Not only Honda and KTM were ready to swallow the cost of their rivalry, but also Mahindra, recently having moved headquarters from Switzerland to Italy, The cost strictures had proved more effective in Moto2, with control engines. But the racing was much better in Moto3.

MOTOGP RACE – 28 laps

Lorenzo had led free practice and claimed his third pole of the year – at a circuit where he had never finished lower than second and won three times. Marquez ran him close, but the omens seemed to favour another trademark breakaway win. Especially when he made a perfect start to lead front-row companions Marquez and Rossi, with Pedrosa and Iannone also past fast-starting Smith by the end of the lap.

Disaster had hit wild-card Michele Pirro, who had qualified a promising fifth as top Ducati. Electrical gremlins struck before the warm-up lap, and he was pushed off the line and obliged to start from the pit lane on his spare bike, set up for wet conditions. It might have worked, but it was too early. After two laps, he pitted for his dry bike, only to discover they still hadn't been able to start it.

Different mayhem was waiting to ambush almost everybody's plans, and to make more unexpected heroes.

Inconvenient spotting began early on; by lap six, it was pouring. Aleix Espargaro led team-mate Vinales, Bradl, Baz, Hernandez, di Meglio and Bautista into the pits. The leaders carried on: Lorenzo shadowed by Marquez and Rossi, each waiting for another to make the first move. Iannone was already five seconds adrift after taking over the pursuit when Pedrosa ran wide.

Next time around, they did all pull in, exiting in the same order, Lorenzo and Marquez almost side by side until the former motioned the Honda rider back; Rossi now was lagging a little. This handed a short-lived lead to Dovizioso until he called in. Then it was Smith for a lap, the only one not to have changed, but struggling on slicks, more than ten seconds slower than the trio of leaders, who would take over next time around as he dropped to eighth, and two laps later to 21st.

So it was back to business as usual, Marquez the first to lead, but Lorenzo taking over for another long spell, from laps ten to 15. But by then, the rain had stopped, the track was drying and their wet tyres were starting to shred badly.

Rossi had closed rapidly when it was wet, and he took over the lead shortly after Marquez had clearly let both Yamahas ahead, to note what they made of the conditions, where he was able to see for himself just how their tyres were shedding rubber. By now, slick-shod Smith was lapping better than ten seconds faster and slicing back up the order.

Marquez ducked into the pits at the end of lap 16 to change back to slicks. Others, including Baz and Redding, had already done so. Rather unaccountably, however, the

Above: Marquez was the filling in a British podium sandwich.

Top right: Aegerter was knocked down by Rins; he rejoined only for his exhaust to fall off.

Above right: Sam Lowes's smoky rear tyre was rubbing on the fender. Eventually it exploded.

Above far right: Nakagami, here leading Syahrin and Simon, made a long delayed return to the rostrum.

Right: Bastianini claimed his first win by this much from Oliveira.

Below right: The young Italian was overjoyed.

Photos: Gold & Goose

two Yamahas continued to circulate – Lorenzo for two laps more, Rossi for three.

Lorenzo's timing might have been good enough for a podium, but instead he slipped off on his second lap, blaming a cold tyre and saying goodbye to the chance of championship points.

When Rossi finally did make the swap, not only did he lose the lead to Marquez, but also he dropped behind Smith, who had caught and passed Baz; and Redding as well. And he was too far behind to do anything about it.

Marquez won by better than seven seconds; a jubilant Smith was some ten seconds clear of an equally ecstatic Redding. The second Briton on the rostrum had a race of variety: he missed the first wave into the pits and fell on the next lap. Scrambling back on board, he made the pits for his own wet switch; then his gut instinct served him well when it was time to go back to his patched-up dry bike.

Redding had firmly passed Baz with four laps to go, then pulled away. The French rookie had every reason to celebrate all the same, a best ever fourth, top Open bike, and what is more still a strong seven seconds ahead of Rossi.

Petrucci was sixth, just 1.5 seconds behind Rossi and narrowly clear of the factory Ducatis, Iannone ahead of Dovizioso. A second away, Pedrosa, another who had been late for his second change, regained ninth from Aleix Espargaro on the last lap.

Crutchlow was another couple of seconds down; then came a worthwhile 12th for Miller, who had been up to seventh at one point. Di Meglio, Vinales and Bautista took the last points; Bradl, Hayden, Barbera and Laverty followed; then Corti and Abraham, a lap down.

Pol Espargaro retired; Hernandez crashed and took de Angelis with him; Pirro had long given up the unequal struggle.

MOTO2 RACE – 26 laps

Misano gave Zarco another chance to demonstrate a perfect race, win in dominant style, then do a near-perfect back-flip off the guardrail – the sixth time in the season for his trademark celebration.

He headed a familiar front row, from Rins and Rabat; it was less usual behind, where Corsi, Aegerter and Syahrin were poised. Lowes led the third, from Nakagami and Folger.

Temperatures dropped as a light cloud cover came over;

some opted to gamble on the softer tyre choice – though not the first four qualifiers.

Zarco led away, but on lap two an inspired Aegerter took over, and there he would stay. Zarco had resisted his attack with some marginal elbow work at high speed, saying later that he knew "Domi" was making the most of his soft tyres, but "I wanted to fight with him to keep my concentration."

After four laps, however, an eager Rins had pushed into second, and on the sixth came a rather unnecessary and fatally flawed attack under brakes. As Aegerter swung in to the apex, Rins arrived half-sideways and out of control, and hit him. Both fell; both remounted, Aegerter only to pit and later retire when his exhaust fell off.

Now Zarco led, and he would continue to do so to the end; he had parlayed his constant speed into a margin of 1.5 seconds by half-distance and four odd by the end. Another step closer to a dominant championship.

The fight for second was close, varied and absorbing.

Syahrin led the pursuit for the first five laps and was still close until the experienced Corsi took over on lap eight. This marked the start of a backward slide for the Malaysian, whose heroics had impressed, but burned up his tyres.

Rabat had started badly and was struggling for feel. He finished lap one eighth and soon would drop to tenth as first Folger and then Simon got through.

Folger was forging ahead and took what now had become fourth off fast-away Nakagami on lap six, gapping him before half-distance to lean on Corsi – and through into second from laps 13 to 16, before the Italian swapped back again.

By now, Nakagami had closed up, while Rabat was steadily gaining places as the fuel load burned off. He picked off Simon and soon afterwards went to work on the three disputing second, where Nakagami had just got ahead of Folger.

The group caught Rins, who seemed to slow to let them lap him without interference. Inexplicably, however, he then involved himself in the four-way battle. As both Nakagami and Rabat got ahead of Corsi, Rins managed to follow them, aiding their escape while Corsi and Folger were delayed behind him. After a couple of laps, he was black-flagged, but by then the damage had been done.

Rabat took second with three laps to go, Nakagami's soft tyres out of grip; Simon got ahead of Folger at the end to take fifth, behind Corsi; Baldassari was a brave seventh.

Cortese kept Salom and Luthi a respectable distance be-

hind him over the line for eighth; Pons was next, with Sime-on, Shah, Krummenacher and West taking the final points without any special drama.

Marquez crashed out; Lowes retired after a spectacular tyre explosion as he crossed the line in seventh place on lap 17. His rear fender had been rubbing, it transpired.

MOTO3 RACE – 23 laps

Bastianini was on pole for a third time, with Binder alongside, his first front row, then Kent. Antonelli led the KTMs of Fenati and Oliveira behind; the first 15 were all within a second.

In blazing sunshine, in the usual way, a gang of seven broke clear, changing places over and again. Over the line, Bastianini and Oliveira did most of the leading; Binder, Fenati and once Vazquez took turns. Antonelli was up and down, and for the first seven laps Kent was pacing himself carefully at the back of it.

Now Masbou brought the next group up into contact, and both he and Bagnaia got ahead of Kent. He took a couple of laps to get clear of them, before rapidly closing on the leaders again.

Then on lap 14, disaster, when Race Direction decided he'd "exceeded track limits" at turn six once too often and applied the penalty "lose one place". This meant he had to slow to drop behind the chase group's new leader, Vinales, now some 3.5 seconds away. Any chance of fighting to win was gone.

Up front, Oliveira was forcing the pace. Bastianini and Antonelli stayed with him, Fenati and Binder struggling slightly to stay in touch. Oliveira seemed in control, getting straight back past Antonelli as they started the final lap.

But at the end of the back straight, Bastianini dived underneath and just held off the KTM over the line.

Antonelli, Fenati and Binder were right behind; Kent was a lone sixth, eight disheartening seconds down.

Masbou headed the next quartet, from Bagnaia, Vinales, Oettl and impressive rookie Dalla Porta, with Loi and Migno having closed right up at the end. Manzi was 14th; Martin saved the last point, following a run across the grass after Mahindra team-mate Guevara had crashed under his wheels in the last corner.

Bastianini's first win shrunk Kent's points lead to an intriguing 55.

GP TIM
DI SAN MARINO E
DELLA RIVIERA DI RIMINI

11-13 SEPTEMBER, 2015

MISANO WORLD CIRCUIT
28 laps
Length: 4.226 km / 2.626 miles
Width: 14m

Key
96/60 kph/mph
Gear

Tramonto 95/59
Turn 9
Rio 95/59
Turn 5
Turn 6 141/88
Rimini 287/178
Quercia 112/70
Curvone 280/174
Turn 12
Turn 2
Misano 125/78
Variante del Parco 175/109
Turn 1 152/94
Turn 15 155/96
Carro 100/62
Turn 13 182/113

MotoGP
RACE DISTANCE: 28 laps, 73.526 miles/118.328km · RACE WEATHER: Dry-wet (air 27°C, humidity 34%, track 31°C)

Pos.	Rider	Nat.	No.	Entrant	Machine	Tyres	Race tyre choice*	Laps	Time & speed
1	**Marc Marquez**	SPA	93	Repsol Honda Team	Honda RC213V	B	F: Medium/R: Medium	28	48m 23.819s 91.1mph/ 146.6km/h
2	**Bradley Smith**	GBR	38	Monster Yamaha Tech 3	Yamaha YZR-M1	B	F: Hard/R: Medium	28	48m 31.107s
3	**Scott Redding**	GBR	45	EG 0,0 Marc VDS	Honda RC213V	B	F: Hard/R: Medium	28	48m 42.612s
4	**Loris Baz**	FRA	76	Forward Racing	Yamaha Forward	B	F: Medium/R: Soft	28	48m 50.246s
5	**Valentino Rossi**	ITA	46	Movistar Yamaha MotoGP	Yamaha YZR-M1	B	F: Hard/R: Medium	28	48m 57.015s
6	**Danilo Petrucci**	ITA	9	Octo Pramac Racing	Ducati Desmosedici	B	F: Medium/R: Medium	28	48m 58.906s
7	**Andrea Iannone**	ITA	29	Ducati Team	Ducati Desmosedici	B	F: Hard/R: Medium	28	49m 00.346s
8	**Andrea Dovizioso**	ITA	4	Ducati Team	Ducati Desmosedici	B	F: Hard/R: Medium	28	49m 01.253s
9	**Dani Pedrosa**	SPA	26	Repsol Honda Team	Honda RC213V	B	F: Hard/R: Medium	28	49m 03.335s
10	**Aleix Espargaro**	SPA	41	Team SUZUKI ECSTAR	Suzuki GSX-RR	B	F: Hard/R: Medium	28	49m 03.511s
11	**Cal Crutchlow**	GBR	35	LCR Honda	Honda RC213V	B	F: Medium/R: Medium	28	49m 05.814s
12	**Jack Miller**	AUS	43	LCR Honda	Honda RC213V-RS	B	F: Medium/R: Soft	28	49m 09.894s
13	**Mike di Meglio**	FRA	63	Avintia Racing	Ducati Desmosedici Open	B	F: Hard/R: Medium	28	49m 12.200s
14	**Maverick Vinales**	SPA	25	Team SUZUKI ECSTAR	Suzuki GSX-RR	B	F: Medium/R: Medium	28	49m 16.144s
15	**Alvaro Bautista**	SPA	19	Aprilia Racing Team Gresini	Aprilia RS-GP	B	F: Hard/R: Soft	28	49m 17.167s
16	Stefan Bradl	GER	6	Aprilia Racing Team Gresini	Aprilia RS-GP	B	F: Medium/R: Soft	28	49m 22.647s
17	Nicky Hayden	USA	69	Aspar MotoGP Team	Honda RC213V-RS	B	F: Medium/R: Medium	28	49m 26.468s
18	Hector Barbera	SPA	8	Avintia Racing	Ducati Desmosedici Open	B	F: Medium/R: Medium	28	49m 28.587s
19	Eugene Laverty	IRL	50	Aspar MotoGP Team	Honda RC213V-RS	B	F: Medium/R: Medium	28	49m 29.496s
20	Claudio Corti	ITA	71	Forward Racing	Yamaha Forward	B	F: Medium/R: Soft	27	49m 17.998s
21	Karel Abraham	CZE	17	AB Motoracing	Honda RC213V-RS	B	F: Medium/R: Medium	27	49m 47.935s
	Pol Espargaro	SPA	44	Monster Yamaha Tech 3	Yamaha YZR-M1	B	F: Hard/R: Medium	26	DNF-mechanical
	Jorge Lorenzo	SPA	99	Movistar Yamaha MotoGP	Yamaha YZR-M1	B	F: Hard/R: Medium	20	DNF-crash
	Yonny Hernandez	COL	68	Octo Pramac Racing	Ducati Desmosedici	B	F: Medium/R: Medium	9	DNF-crash
	Alex de Angelis	RSM	15	E-Motion IodaRacing Team	Aprilia ART	B	F: Medium/R: Soft	9	DNF-crash
	Michele Pirro	ITA	51	Ducati Team	Ducati Desmosedici	B	F: Medium/R: Soft	9	DNF-mechanical

*Tyre choice at start of race.

Fastest lap: Jorge Lorenzo, on lap 4, 1m 33.273s, 101.3mph/163.1km/h (record).
Previous lap record: Jorge Lorenzo, SPA (Yamaha), 1m 33.906s, 100.7mph/162.0km/h (2011).
Event best maximum speed: Andrea Dovizioso, 186.1mph/299.5km/h (race).

Qualifying

Weather: Dry
Air Temp: 25° **Track Temp:** 39°
Humidity: 56%

1	Lorenzo	1m 32.146s
2	Marquez	1m 32.252s
3	Rossi	1m 32.358s
4	Pedrosa	1m 32.434s
5	Pirro	1m 32.736s
6	Smith	1m 32.801s
7	Iannone	1m 32.821s
8	Dovizioso	1m 32.934s
9	Petrucci	1m 33.169s
10	A. Espargaro	1m 33.187s
11	Crutchlow	1m 33.220s
12	P. Espargaro	1m 33.222s
13	Redding	1m 33.340s
14	Vinales	1m 33.439s
15	Hernandez	1m 33.710s
16	Baz	1m 34.093s
17	Miller	1m 34.137s
18	Barbera	1m 34.296s
19	Bradl	1m 34.333s
20	Bautista	1m 34.368s
21	Laverty	1m 34.468s
22	Di Meglio	1m 34.722s
23	Hayden	1m 34.732s
24	Corti	1m 35.385s
25	Abraham	1m 35.406s
26	De Angelis	1m 35.684s

Fastest race laps

1	Lorenzo	1m 33.273s
2	Marquez	1m 33.396s
3	Pedrosa	1m 33.636s
4	Iannone	1m 33.800s
5	Rossi	1m 33.833s
6	Dovizioso	1m 34.041s
7	Redding	1m 34.042s
8	Smith	1m 34.105s
9	Crutchlow	1m 34.399s
10	P. Espargaro	1m 34.606s
11	Petrucci	1m 34.949s
12	A. Espargaro	1m 35.027s
13	Baz	1m 35.138s
14	Vinales	1m 35.189s
15	Miller	1m 35.218s
16	Hernandez	1m 35.362s
17	Laverty	1m 35.406s
18	Bradl	1m 35.508s
19	Bautista	1m 35.524s
20	Hayden	1m 35.680s
21	Di Meglio	1m 35.684s
22	Barbera	1m 35.686s
23	De Angelis	1m 36.393s
24	Abraham	1m 37.725s
25	Corti	1m 38.268s
26	Pirro	1m 47.946s

Championship Points

1	Rossi	247
2	Lorenzo	224
3	Marquez	184
4	Iannone	159
5	Smith	135
6	Dovizioso	128
7	Pedrosa	109
8	Petrucci	93
9	P. Espargaro	81
10	Crutchlow	79
11	Vinales	69
12	A. Espargaro	66
13	Redding	63
14	Hernandez	41
15	Baz	28
16	Bautista	23
17	Barbera	23
18	Miller	16
19	Hayden	12
20	Bradl	11
21	Pirro	8
22	E. Laverty	7
23	Di Meglio	7
24	Aoyama	5
25	De Angelis	2

Constructor Points

1	Yamaha	297
2	Honda	240
3	Ducati	197
4	Suzuki	95
5	Yamaha Forward	33
6	Aprilia	23
7	ART	2

Grid order / Lap chart

Grid order	1	2	3	4	5	6	7	8	9	10	11	12	13	14	15	16	17	18	19	20	21	22	23	24	25	26	27	28	
99 LORENZO	99	99	99	99	99	99	4	38	93	99	99	99	99	99	99	46	46	46	46	46	93	93	93	93	93	93	93	93	1
93 MARQUEZ	93	93	93	93	93	93	38	93	99	93	93	93	93	46	46	99	99	99	99	93	38	38	38	38	38	38	38	38	2
46 ROSSI	46	46	46	46	46	46	35	99	46	46	46	46	46	93	93	93	93	9	26	38	76	76	76	45	45	45	45	3
26 PEDROSA	26	26	26	26	26	29	43	46	9	9	9	9	9	9	9	9	26	93	99	45	45	45	45	76	76	76	76	4
51 PIRRO	29	29	29	29	29	4	99	9	44	29	29	29	29	26	26	26	26	93	76	76	46	46	46	46	46	46	46	5
38 SMITH	38	38	38	38	38	45	93	29	29	44	44	44	26	44	44	44	44	44	45	9	9	9	9	9	9	9	9	6
29 IANNONE	4	4	4	4	4	38	46	44	26	26	26	44	29	29	4	4	38	26	43	43	43	43	29	29	29	29	7
4 DOVIZIOSO	41	41	45	45	45	26	29	26	38	4	4	4	4	4	29	35	9	9	41	35	35	35	4	4	4	8
9 PETRUCCI	44	45	41	44	44	9	9	35	4	76	35	35	35	35	29	38	43	35	29	4	4	41	41	41	9
41 A. ESPARGARO	45	44	44	41	35	44	44	4	76	35	76	76	8	41	41	41	8	45	4	41	29	4	29	41	41	35	26	41	10
35 CRUTCHLOW	68	35	35	35	41	35	26	76	35	25	8	8	41	41	41	41	60	35	35	26	41	35	26	35	35	35	11
44 P. ESPARGARO	35	68	9	9	9	43	9	41	41	41	41	41	69	69	69	76	29	43	29	4	26	63	63	26	43	43	43	12
45 REDDING	25	9	68	68	25	8	15	25	25	8	69	69	25	25	19	19	69	41	4	63	26	63	63	63	63	13
25 VINALES	9	25	25	25	43	15	50	8	8	69	63	63	19	19	25	50	8	29	63	25	25	25	25	25	25	14
68 HERNANDEZ	43	43	43	43	76	50	41	15	68	63	25	63	63	63	6	43	63	44	25	19	19	19	19	19	19	15
76 BAZ	76	76	76	76	68	41	76	68	15	50	19	19	6	6	50	38	41	8	8	19	8	8	6	6	6	16
43 MILLER	6	6	6	6	76	25	50	50	19	50	6	50	50	50	6	45	19	19	19	69	69	69	8	69	69	69	17
8 BARBERA	8	8	69	69	69	25	68	63	63	6	6	50	76	76	76	76	41	63	69	25	6	6	69	69	8	8	8	18
6 BRADL	69	69	19	19	19	6	19	19	69	38	45	45	45	38	38	38	63	6	25	69	44	44	50	44	44	50	50	19
19 BAUTISTA	19	19	8	8	68	6	8	19	45	43	43	43	45	45	45	25	50	6	6	50	50	44	44	50	50	71	20
50 LAVERTY	15	63	63	63	63	19	63	6	6	43	38	38	38	43	43	43	43	25	50	50	71	71	71	71	71	71	17	21
63 DI MEGLIO	50	15	15	50	50	63	69	43	45	71	71	17	17	17	17	71	71	71	71	17	17	17	17	17	17	22
69 HAYDEN	63	50	50	15	15	69	45	45	43	17	17	71	71	71	17	17	17	17	17	23
71 CORTI	71	71	17	71	71	71	17	17	71																				24
17 ABRAHAM	17	17	71	17	17	17	71	71	17																				25
15 DE ANGELIS	51	51	51	51	51	51	51	51	51																				

99 Pit stop   71 Lapped rider

Moto2

RACE DISTANCE: 26 laps, 68.274 miles/109.876km · RACE WEATHER: Dry (air 26°C, humidity 59%, track 32°C)

Pos.	Rider	Nat.	No.	Entrant	Machine	Laps	Time & Speed
1	Johann Zarco	FRA	5	Ajo Motorsport	Kalex	26	42m 38.099s 96.1mph/ 154.6km/h
2	Tito Rabat	SPA	1	EG 0,0 Marc VDS	Kalex	26	42m 41.949s
3	Takaaki Nakagami	JPN	30	IDEMITSU Honda Team Asia	Kalex	26	42m 43.487s
4	Simone Corsi	ITA	3	Forward Racing	Kalex	26	42m 45.157s
5	Julian Simon	SPA	60	QMMF Racing Team	Speed Up	26	42m 47.324s
6	Jonas Folger	GER	94	AGR Team	Kalex	26	42m 48.565s
7	Lorenzo Baldassarri	ITA	7	Forward Racing	Kalex	26	42m 51.883s
8	Sandro Cortese	GER	11	Dynavolt Intact GP	Kalex	26	42m 54.433s
9	Luis Salom	SPA	39	Paginas Amarillas HP 40	Kalex	26	42m 55.995s
10	Thomas Luthi	SWI	12	Derendinger Racing Interwetten	Kalex	26	42m 56.452s
11	Axel Pons	SPA	49	AGR Team	Kalex	26	43m 02.128s
12	Xavier Simeon	BEL	19	Federal Oil Gresini Moto2	Kalex	26	43m 05.708s
13	Azlan Shah	MAL	25	IDEMITSU Honda Team Asia	Kalex	26	43m 07.136s
14	Randy Krummenacher	SWI	4	JIR Racing Team	Kalex	26	43m 10.239s
15	Anthony West	AUS	95	QMMF Racing Team	Speed Up	26	43m 11.411s
16	Mattia Pasini	ITA	54	Gresini Racing Moto2	Kalex	26	43m 14.414s
17	Marcel Schrotter	GER	23	Tech 3	Tech 3	26	43m 15.344s
18	Hafizh Syahrin	MAL	55	Petronas Raceline Malaysia	Kalex	26	43m 22.046s
19	Louis Rossi	FRA	96	Tasca Racing Scuderia Moto2	Tech 3	26	43m 22.085s
20	Thitipong Warokorn	THA	10	APH PTT The Pizza SAG	Kalex	26	43m 30.453s
21	Luca Marini	ITA	9	Pons Racing Junior Team	Kalex	26	43m 39.270s
22	Florian Alt	GER	66	E-Motion IodaRacing Team	Suter	26	43m 43.267s
23	Xavi Vierge	SPA	97	Tech 3	Tech 3	25	43m 09.054s
24	Dominique Aegerter	SWI	77	Technomag Racing Interwetten	Kalex	23	44m 12.932s
	Federico Caricasulo	ITA	64	Italtrans Racing Team	Kalex	18	DNF
	Sam Lowes	GBR	22	Speed Up Racing	Speed Up	17	DNF
	Jesko Raffin	SWI	2	sports-millions-EMWE-SAG	Kalex	15	DNF
	Alex Marquez	SPA	73	EG 0,0 Marc VDS	Kalex	6	DNF
	Robin Mulhauser	SWI	70	Technomag Racing Interwetten	Kalex	5	DNF
	Mika Kallio	FIN	36	Italtrans Racing Team	Kalex	2	DNF
	Ricard Cardus	SPA	88	JPMoto Malaysia	Suter	2	DNF
	Alex Rins	SPA	40	Paginas Amarillas HP 40	Kalex	-	DSQ

Fastest lap: Jonas Folger, on lap 10, 1m 37.422s, 97.0mph/156.1km/h (record).
Previous lap record: Pol Espargaro, SPA (Kalex), 1m 38.070s, 96.4mph/155.1km/h (2013).
Event best maximum speed: Thomas Luthi, 153.7mph/247.3km/h (race).

Qualifying

Weather: Dry
Air Temp: 25° Track Temp: 39°
Humidity: 56%

1	Zarco	1m 36.754s
2	Rins	1m 36.756s
3	Rabat	1m 36.854s
4	Corsi	1m 37.121s
5	Aegerter	1m 37.172s
6	Syahrin	1m 37.220s
7	Lowes	1m 37.393s
8	Nakagami	1m 37.422s
9	Folger	1m 37.484s
10	Simon	1m 37.510s
11	Cortese	1m 37.534s
12	Salom	1m 37.578s
13	Luthi	1m 37.622s
14	Pons	1m 37.627s
15	Baldassarri	1m 37.704s
16	Krummenacher	1m 37.786s
17	Marquez	1m 37.786s
18	Cardus	1m 37.979s
19	Schrotter	1m 38.032s
20	Simeon	1m 38.137s
21	West	1m 38.286s
22	Shah	1m 38.321s
23	Kallio	1m 38.393s
24	Pasini	1m 38.414s
25	Mulhauser	1m 38.673s
26	Marini	1m 38.678s
27	Caricasulo	1m 38.857s
28	Vierge	1m 38.897s
29	Alt	1m 39.045s
30	Rossi	1m 39.058s
31	Warokorn	1m 39.343s
32	Raffin	1m 40.079s

Fastest race laps

1	Folger	1m 37.422s
2	Rabat	1m 37.574s
3	Zarco	1m 37.638s
4	Rins	1m 37.665s
5	Corsi	1m 37.771s
6	Lowes	1m 37.819s
7	Simon	1m 37.837s
8	Aegerter	1m 37.855s
9	Syahrin	1m 37.862s
10	Nakagami	1m 37.909s
11	Pons	1m 37.997s
12	Baldassarri	1m 38.049s
13	Luthi	1m 38.056s
14	Cortese	1m 38.058s
15	Salom	1m 38.108s
16	Marquez	1m 38.246s
17	Shah	1m 38.297s
18	Schrotter	1m 38.356s
19	Krummenacher	1m 38.467s
20	Simeon	1m 38.502s
21	West	1m 38.556s
22	Pasini	1m 38.781s
23	Caricasulo	1m 38.795s
24	Vierge	1m 38.890s
25	Rossi	1m 39.040s
26	Marini	1m 39.298s
27	Kallio	1m 39.336s
28	Warokorn	1m 39.354s
29	Alt	1m 39.677s
30	Raffin	1m 39.721s
31	Cardus	1m 40.335s
32	Mulhauser	1m 40.902s

Championship Points

1	Zarco	274
2	Rabat	181
3	Rins	164
4	Luthi	131
5	Lowes	128
6	Folger	112
7	Simeon	96
8	Morbidelli	84
9	Aegerter	62
10	Marquez	62
11	Nakagami	61
12	Cortese	59
13	Simon	58
14	Corsi	53
15	Salom	50
16	Kallio	48
17	Baldassarri	46
18	Syahrin	36
19	West	30
20	Pons	24
21	Schrotter	19
22	Krummenacher	19
23	Shah	9
24	Rossi	7
25	Cardus	6
26	Mulhauser	1

Constructor Points

1	Kalex	320
2	Speed Up	150
3	Tech 3	26
4	Suter	6

Moto3

RACE DISTANCE: 23 laps, 60.396 miles/97.198km · RACE WEATHER: Dry (air 26°C, humidity 49%, track 27°C)

Pos.	Rider	Nat.	No.	Entrant	Machine	Laps	Time & Speed
1	Enea Bastianini	ITA	33	Gresini Racing Team Moto3	Honda	23	39m 43.673s 91.2mph/ 146.7km/h
2	Miguel Oliveira	POR	44	Red Bull KTM Ajo	KTM	23	39m 43.710s
3	Niccolo Antonelli	ITA	23	Ongetta-Rivacold	Honda	23	39m 44.018s
4	Romano Fenati	ITA	5	SKY Racing Team VR46	KTM	23	39m 44.257s
5	Brad Binder	RSA	41	Red Bull KTM Ajo	KTM	23	39m 44.310s
6	Danny Kent	GBR	52	Leopard Racing	Honda	23	39m 51.673s
7	Alexis Masbou	FRA	10	SAXOPRINT RTG	Honda	23	39m 55.327s
8	Francesco Bagnaia	ITA	21	MAPFRE Team MAHINDRA	Mahindra	23	39m 55.449s
9	Isaac Vinales	SPA	32	RBA Racing Team	KTM	23	39m 55.512s
10	Philipp Oettl	GER	65	Schedl GP Racing	KTM	23	39m 55.646s
11	Lorenzo Dalla Porta	ITA	48	Husqvarna Factory Laglisse	Husqvarna	23	39m 55.860s
12	Livio Loi	BEL	11	RW Racing GP	Honda	23	39m 55.887s
13	Andrea Migno	ITA	16	SKY Racing Team VR46	KTM	23	39m 56.205s
14	Stefano Manzi	ITA	29	San Carlo Team Italia	Mahindra	23	40m 02.933s
15	Jorge Martin	SPA	88	MAPFRE Team MAHINDRA	Mahindra	23	40m 07.969s
16	Hiroki Ono	JPN	76	Leopard Racing	Honda	23	40m 09.397s
17	Jakub Kornfeil	CZE	84	Drive M7 SIC	KTM	23	40m 09.491s
18	Darryn Binder	RSA	40	Outox Reset Drink Team	Mahindra	23	40m 09.821s
19	John McPhee	GBR	17	SAXOPRINT RTG	Honda	23	40m 09.901s
20	Gabriel Rodrigo	ARG	91	RBA Racing Team	KTM	23	40m 10.447s
21	Karel Hanika	CZE	98	Red Bull KTM Ajo	KTM	23	40m 12.924s
22	Alessandro Tonucci	ITA	19	Outox Reset Drink Team	Mahindra	23	40m 17.859s
23	Matteo Ferrari	ITA	12	San Carlo Team Italia	Mahindra	23	40m 19.057s
24	Maria Herrera	SPA	6	Husqvarna Factory Laglisse	Husqvarna	23	40m 24.992s
25	Ana Carrasco	SPA	22	RBA Racing Team	KTM	23	40m 39.892s
26	Adrian Gyutai	HUN	90	Turvital di Vitali Ordeo	TVR	22	40m 47.741s
	Juanfran Guevara	SPA	58	MAPFRE Team MAHINDRA	Mahindra	22	DNF
	Zulfahmi Khairuddin	MAL	63	Drive M7 SIC	KTM	22	DNF
	Tatsuki Suzuki	JPN	24	CIP	Mahindra	15	DNF
	Efren Vazquez	SPA	7	Leopard Racing	Honda	14	DNF
	Remy Gardner	AUS	2	CIP	Mahindra	6	DNF
	Jules Danilo	FRA	95	Ongetta-Rivacold	Honda	3	DNF

Fastest lap: Niccolo Antonelli, on lap 3, 1m 42.841s, 91.9mph/147.9km/h (record).
Previous lap record: Juanfran Guevara, SPA (Kalex KTM), 1m 43.196s, 91.6mph/147.4km/h (2014).
Event best maximum speed: Hiroki Ono, 130.4mph/209.8km/h (free practice).

Qualifying

Weather: Dry
Air Temp: 23° Track Temp: 36°
Humidity: 60%

1	Bastianini	1m 42.486s
2	Binder	1m 42.523s
3	Kent	1m 42.782s
4	Antonelli	1m 42.812s
5	Fenati	1m 42.983s
6	Oliveira	1m 43.008s
7	Vazquez	1m 43.074s
8	Dalla Porta	1m 43.211s
9	Oettl	1m 43.227s
10	Ono	1m 43.271s
11	Vinales	1m 43.294s
12	Bagnaia	1m 43.319s
13	Masbou	1m 43.351s
14	Danilo	1m 43.417s
15	Martin	1m 43.432s
16	Guevara	1m 43.519s
17	Binder	1m 43.538s
18	Rodrigo	1m 43.572s
19	Suzuki	1m 43.634s
20	Loi	1m 43.796s
21	Migno	1m 43.846s
22	Khairuddin	1m 43.867s
23	Hanika	1m 43.898s
24	Herrera	1m 43.949s
25	McPhee	1m 43.986s
26	Manzi	1m 44.072s
27	Gardner	1m 44.190s
28	Ferrari	1m 44.192s
29	Locatelli	1m 44.270s
30	Tonucci	1m 44.548s
31	Carrasco	1m 44.920s
32	Gyutai	1m 49.065s
	Navarro	No Time
	Quartararo	No Time
	Kornfeil	DSQ

Fastest race laps

1	Antonelli	1m 42.841s
2	Vazquez	1m 42.867s
3	Fenati	1m 42.891s
4	Oliveira	1m 42.919s
5	Kent	1m 42.928s
6	Bastianini	1m 42.961s
7	Binder	1m 42.982s
8	Masbou	1m 43.014s
9	Manzi	1m 43.174s
10	Bagnaia	1m 43.212s
11	Dalla Porta	1m 43.229s
12	Migno	1m 43.283s
13	Guevara	1m 43.301s
14	Vinales	1m 43.318s
15	Oettl	1m 43.329s
16	Loi	1m 43.380s
17	Binder	1m 43.519s
18	Martin	1m 43.542s
19	Hanika	1m 43.580s
20	Khairuddin	1m 43.612s
21	Gardner	1m 43.619s
22	McPhee	1m 43.657s
23	Rodrigo	1m 43.700s
24	Kornfeil	1m 43.728s
25	Ono	1m 43.751s
26	Danilo	1m 43.773s
27	Tonucci	1m 44.127s
28	Suzuki	1m 44.161s
29	Herrera	1m 44.210s
30	Ferrari	1m 44.237s
31	Carrasco	1m 45.249s
32	Gyutai	1m 50.006s

Championship Points

1	Kent	234
2	Bastianini	179
3	Fenati	139
4	Oliveira	134
5	Antonelli	126
6	Vazquez	116
7	Binder	110
8	Quartararo	92
9	Vinales	82
10	Navarro	72
11	McPhee	70
12	Bagnaia	67
13	Loi	55
14	Masbou	55
15	Kornfeil	46
16	Oettl	46
17	Hanika	33
18	Locatelli	31
19	Martin	24
20	Migno	23
21	Ajo	21
22	Guevara	15
23	Ono	15
24	Dalla Porta	13
25	Danilo	7
26	Suzuki	6
27	Khairuddin	4
28	Manzi	3
29	Herrera	1
30	Ferrari	1

Constructor Points

1	Honda	310
2	KTM	221
3	Mahindra	93
4	Husqvarna	77

ARAGON GRAND PRIX

ARAGON CIRCUIT

Main: Out on his own. Lorenzo was imperious once again.

Inset, left: Best of enemies. Pedrosa is congratulated by Lorenzo on beating rival Rossi for second.

JUST in case anybody had doubted the riders' assertions that 2015's aggressively powerful Honda was a bit of handful, Marc Marquez underlined the point emphatically for a fifth time on only the second lap of the race in Aragon. Manfully pursuing Mr Breakaway Lorenzo, he crashed out abruptly. "It was my fault. I want to apologise to my team and the fans," he said. "When the season is not going well for you, nothing goes your way.".

And how, in his case. But fortunes reversed for his quarry, Lorenzo. After two races when changing weather had undermined his obvious superiority, here, at his serene best, three fine days allowed him to perform yet another first-to-last-corner demonstration. What happened behind him was a further boost to title hopes that had been waning after the previous two rounds.

This comprised a Honda-Yamaha battle between Pedrosa and Rossi. Not anything we hadn't seen before, usually with a predictable outcome. What we hadn't seen was a Pedrosa seemingly infused with an altogether new way of racing. Every time Rossi attacked, Dani came straight back. It happened repeatedly as the chequered flag drew nigh, with four changes of position on the last lap alone. To cut a long story short, Dani beat him, squarely, in a straight fight.

He was helped in this unexpected turn of events by the track layout – the long straight (almost a full kilometre) precedes the final corner. Honda's horsepower might have been unpleasantly aggressive, but there were times when the sheer quantity came in handy. What had destroyed Marquez's race was used by Pedrosa to make himself finally impregnable – and a folk hero on social media. He had many messages, he revealed with a smile two weeks later, "saying I should ride like that more of the time."

The last round of the European series was marked by an extension of the injury and absentee list, with the usual mid-season hazards of training. Hayden arrived hurt – a fracture in his right thumb: a painful and potentially troublesome injury for the most overworked appendage on a rider's body. It had happened while Minimoto training: he shrugged it off, "The thumb doesn't help, but I can ride."

Less able to shrug was Iannone, who had dislocated his left shoulder once again, and had an unexpected explanation for the return of the injury suffered while testing before Le Mans. He too had been training, but on foot, and hadn't even fallen over. Road running with his trainer, he had stumbled, "and when I put my arms in front really fast, the shoulder go out," he said. "I didn't touch the ground, so it was really strange." Cartilage damage and a displaced tendon were, as before, heroically ignored in yet another strong race in a season of growing maturity.

Morbidelli was still out of Moto2, while star Moto3 rookie Quartararo was also absent, his place on the Estrella Galicia Honda having been taken by Japan's Sena Yamada, his third grand prix start.

The paddock was buzzing with contract news, that from Aprilia being the most comprehensive. Firstly, they had signed Bradl for one more season, impressed by his approach. Said racing manager Romano Albesiano about their by-chance mid-season recruit: "We found a methodical and fast rider, extremely precise in his comments and therefore particularly suited for the role of 'race tester' that our rookie season requires."

Bradl and current team-mate Bautista will have to fight to stay on in 2017, for the Italian company's second announcement was a three-year deal with Sam Lowes. He would stay in Moto2 in 2016, riding a Kalex for the Gresini team (Gresini runs Aprilia's MotoGP team) while also operating as a MotoGP test rider. Then in 2017 and 2018, he would join the factory MotoGP team.

More from the Galicia Marc VDS team, where Rabat would step into the MotoGP squad in place of Redding, with all but the final details agreed for a second bike, for Jack Miller. Both would be on satellite Factory machines, the handpicked Honda-contracted Australian to bring his own crew with him.

Danny Kent was also confirmed as heading for Moto2 with the Leopard squad; later it would be announced that his team-mate would be Miguel Oliveira, soon to take over as his closest rival in Moto3.

And in Moto2, Mika Kallio was relieved to abandon a largely unsuccessful season so far on the Italtrans Kalex to take over sacked West's Speed Up in the Qatar-backed QMMF team, his place going to the younger Pons brother, Edgar, continuing the dynasty started by double 250 champion Sito, now team owner of the Paginas Amarillas squad, where Edgar was earmarked to join Rins in 2016.

Forward Racing chief Giovanni Cuzari was back in town, after his spell in custody in Switzerland, and larger than life as ever. The team remained beleaguered, its future in even greater doubt.

The increasingly usual grid-place/warm-up suspension penalties were handed out in Moto3, under the tight no-slow-riding rules, with Vinales, Herrera, Migno, Rodrigo and Dalla Porto in the frame, along with Corsi in Moto2.

Zarco was in the spotlight, as his finger-hold on the title became ever firmer. The articulate and loquacious Frenchman admitted that he was feeling the pressure. "Perhaps I don't show it, but I have a big spot here," he said, pointing to his forehead. More telling, if less disfiguring, was the first race of the year he had finished off the podium since a broken gearshift had dropped him from the lead to eighth at Qatar. All weekend, he admitted, "I never had a good feeling, never felt confident so I could push."

With four races left and his own second win in his pocket, this meant a reprieve for Rabat's title defence. The respite would not last even until the next race, however: the following Saturday, the defending champion was training as usual with endless laps at Almeria when he crashed and broke his arm. It would prove his ruin, and render Zarco's nerves redundant.

MOTOGP RACE – 23 laps

Marquez had led both free practice and qualifying, by a slender tenth from Lorenzo. Iannone completed the front row; Rossi was at the far end of the second, behind Pol Espargaro and Pedrosa.

For a sixth time in 2015, Lorenzo was on autopilot – two or three laps in 'Get Away' mode, then defaulting to 'Maintain Gap'. Riding as if on rails, one consistent lap after another, again he was unbeatable at the scenically beautiful and technically challenging Motorland Aragon circuit.

It might not have been so easy but for Marquez's fifth race crash. Held up off the line by Iannone's fast-away Desmosedici, he was past by the end of lap one. The gap to Lorenzo over the line was just over half a second, and over the next 11 corners he closed it right up. Going into Turn 12, asking too much of a still-cool front tyre, he was down and out, and furious with himself.

That promoted Iannone to second; Pedrosa and Rossi tagged on behind. Pedrosa was past on lap three, Rossi next time around, but by then Lorenzo was already 2.7 seconds clear. He sailed along imperiously, the gap sometimes under, but more often over three seconds. His second lap was his fastest, a new record.

Above: Pedrosa under attack by Rossi. This time he refused to surrender.

Top left: Over and out? The injured Karel Abraham awaits the start of his last race of the season.

Above centre left: Bautista celebrated a century of GP starts.

Above left: Thumbs-up from top Open finisher Eugene Laverty.

Left: Rossi congratulates Pedrosa on his feisty ride. Privately, he was not so pleased.
Photos: Gold & Goose

Above: Laverty heads team-mate Hayden, Baz and Bradl. The class rookie would win a lively battle.

Top right: Rabat and Rins locked in Moto2 combat.

Above right: Rabat applauds Rins for finishing behind him.

Right: Oliveira and Navarro contest the lead as Danny Kent is about to launch into orbit.

Below right and far right: A crucial moment for the champion elect: Kent was lucky to escape injury in his last-corner misadventure.

Photos: Gold & Goose

Iannone stayed close for a spell, but second was between the two old-timers, and on past experience Rossi would triumph, in familiar stalk-and-pounce fashion. This time, however, it turned out differently.

After a few tentative stabs at the first corner, he started to attack in earnest with four laps to go. He pushed past; a newly aggressive Pedrosa pushed straight back in front. Same on lap 21 and 22. This was a Pedrosa no one could remember having seen before.

On the last lap, Rossi nosed ahead twice, only for the same treatment. The last attack was desperate, on the right-left on to the long straight. "I played every card, and one that I did not expect," said Rossi, referring to that final lunge. Dani cut straight back inside and powered away – as he had on every lap, leaving the Yamaha gasping and beaten.

A long way behind the fading Iannone, Dovizioso had come forcing through from 13th on the grid, after missing the cut to go through to Q2. He had inherited fifth on lap four when Pol Espargaro ran wide, and spent the rest of the race there, fending off a variety of lively opposition.

By the end, Aleix Espargaro was still right up behind, then Crutchlow and Smith: four different makes, and fifth to eighth covered by just over a second. Pol Espargaro was still barely a second behind in ninth.

Petrucci had been part of this battle, giving Crutchlow a hard time, before he slipped off and out on lap ten.

Another big gap, then an almost race-long battle between second Pramac Ducati rider Hernandez and Redding's factory Honda. The latter had been challenging until the closing laps, but lost touch when Vinales came through to attack. Vinales was within less than half a second of taking tenth off the Colombian over the line.

There was another huge Open fight for the final points – a vindication of the forthcoming all-Open regulations due to come into force in 2017. At half-distance, 12th to 19th places were covered by less than two seconds, and it stood like this: Bradl (Aprilia), Laverty (Honda), Vinales (Suzuki), Bautista (Aprilia), Hayden (Honda), Miller (Honda), di Meglio (Ducati) and Loris Baz (Yamaha).

From there, as tyres went down and the going got tougher,

the group splintered somewhat, with Vinales moving away to catch the riders ahead; while Bautista took 13th place ahead of first-time top Open finisher Laverty by half a second. Hayden had the last point, less than a tenth behind.

By the end, Barbera had come through for a close 16th, from Baz and Bradl. Miller was now off the back in 19th, but well clear of di Meglio and last-placed Toni Elias, in his first race as permanent replacement in Forward Yamaha. De Angelis crashed out; a still-injured Abraham pitted and limped away in agony. It was his last race of the year.

In this way, Rossi still led on points, but he had lost nine to Lorenzo. But for Pedrosa, it might otherwise have been only five. After the previous two wet races, the weather had held, and that was all Lorenzo needed to revitalise his challenge, now only 14 points behind.

MOTO2 RACE – 14 laps (shortened from 20)

This was first match point for Zarco. He needed to gain only seven points compared with Rabat to stretch his advantage from 93 to 100. That would be enough. If only he could win and Rabat finish third...

Instead, the Frenchman had a rare off weekend, explaining later that he had been troubled by a lack of confidence, in himself and in the feel of his bike.

Zarco qualified on the front row, but both Rins and poleman Rabat were quicker, the latter by four-tenths, and both buoyed up by the home race effect.

Rabat set off at great speed from pole, but ran wide, letting second-row starter Lowes and Rins through. By the end of the lap, Rins led. Zarco was fourth, but about to fall prey to a flying Marquez Junior (race-developing the 2016 Kalex chassis, and qualified sixth) and the ever aggressive Corsi, through from row four.

A little way back, however, Simeon had been caught out in the heavy traffic and clipped the back end of Aegerter. Both went sprawling, but only Simeon got up. For a second successive race, the Swiss rider was innocent victim, and this time he suffered a multitude of injuries, both internal and spinal. He would be out until the end of the year.

The race was shortened to 14 laps; the second start featured similar personnel: Rabat fast away, but Rins taking the lead before the end of lap one; Lowes, Folger and Corsi in close pursuit. Corsi would run off and drop back; and after five laps, the front pair had gapped the next two by almost two seconds.

Thereafter it was a two-man race, with Rabat taking over, but never more than a tenth or two ahead. The defending champion was intent on victory to salvage a so-far erratic season; the new boy was racing close to his home village. Rins shadowed his senior rival, awaiting the inevitable last-lap resolution and setting a record on the penultimate lap.

His attack came at the braking point for Turn 12, and he got through briefly. But Rabat had been expecting it, took the place straight back and held on to the line by less than a tenth. It was only his second win of the year, but one of the sweetest of his career.

Folger kept Lowes honest defending the position until half-distance. With the pursuit a long way adrift, the German then settled for fourth.

And Zarco? He finished lap one in sixth, heading a huge pursuit pack at an ever increasing distance. Marquez was past him by lap two, then Luthi as well. He finished lap three in eighth; and although Marquez would crash out, Zarco would briefly lose another spot to the consistently impressive Syahrin.

By the finish, he had recovered to sixth, about to attack Luthi for fifth, but a shadow of his usual self.

Syahrin was still close, Nakagami and the recovered Corsi not far behind; a second adrift, Baldassarri completed the top ten.

The last points went to the rest of this big group: Kallio in his first Speed Up outing, Axel Pons, Cortese and, just off the back, Shah, with Schrotter a more distant 15th.

Salom, Edgar Pons and Simon crashed out, and Simeon for a second time.

MOTO3 RACE – 20 laps

What is the collective noun for a pack of Moto3 bikes? Probably 'swarm', because the ten in the lead group were changing back and forth so much that it was like trying to count bees. Typical Moto3 madness. Then on the final lap, it went really crazy.

Bastianini had qualified on pole from Oliveira and Kent, with Mahindra-mounted rookie Jorge Martin a surprise leader of the second row.

Bastianini headed the first lap; but as usual it was somewhat notional, with shuffling at every overtaking point, and elsewhere.

Oliveira was the next to lead, then Antonelli a few times. Most of it went to Oliveira, with points leader Kent also showing towards the end. Then Brad Binder pushed through to the front.

By the last lap, Martin had lost touch, but the first nine were still covered by less than 1.5 seconds. Tactics were everything, with Oliveira once again the best at it for a third win of the year.

Tactics. Or some rough bumping and barging, which is what did for Bastianini and Binder, when the former cannoned into the latter's back wheel and both fell. Kent now had a clear run to regain important points as he took second going into the last corner.

Then a gasp. He too crashed, sensationally, in an unforced error, handing the place to rostrum first-timer Navarro. It was a crucial error for the would-be champion.

The rest were promoted three places: Fenati third, then Vazquez and Oettl. Antonelli was sixth – forced off track by Kent's crash; Martin was a career-best seventh.

Masbou regained the lead of the big gang disputing eighth, with Ono and Migno completing the top ten.

The crashes retained the status quo in the championship, but Oliveira was ominously closer.

TISSOT OFFICIAL TIMEKEEPER

GRAN PREMIO
MOVISTAR
DE ARAGON

25-27 SEPTEMBER, 2015

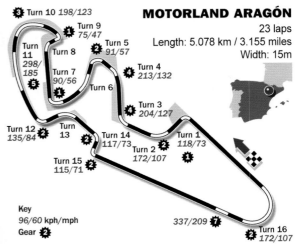

MOTORLAND ARAGÓN

23 laps
Length: 5.078 km / 3.155 miles
Width: 15m

Turn 10 198/123
Turn 9 75/47
Turn 11 298/185
Turn 8
Turn 5 91/57
Turn 7 90/56
Turn 4 213/132
Turn 6
Turn 3 204/127
Turn 12 135/84
Turn 13
Turn 14 117/73
Turn 2 172/107
Turn 1 118/73
Turn 15 115/71
337/209
Turn 16 172/107

Key
96/60 kph/mph
Gear

MotoGP · RACE DISTANCE: 23 laps, 72.572 miles/116.794km · RACE WEATHER: Dry (air 23°C, humidity 50%, track 39°C)

Pos.	Rider	Nat.	No.	Entrant	Machine	Tyres	Race tyre choice*	Laps	Time & speed
1	**Jorge Lorenzo**	SPA	99	Movistar Yamaha MotoGP	Yamaha YZR-M1	B	F: Medium/R: Medium	23	41m 44.933s
									104.3mph/
									167.8km/h
2	**Dani Pedrosa**	SPA	26	Repsol Honda Team	Honda RC213V	B	F: Medium/R: Medium	23	41m 47.616s
3	**Valentino Rossi**	ITA	46	Movistar Yamaha MotoGP	Yamaha YZR-M1	B	F: Medium/R: Medium	23	41m 47.700s
4	**Andrea Iannone**	ITA	29	Ducati Team	Ducati Desmosedici	B	F: Medium/R: Medium	23	41m 52.791s
5	**Andrea Dovizioso**	ITA	4	Ducati Team	Ducati Desmosedici	B	F: Medium/R: Medium	23	42m 09.255s
6	**Aleix Espargaro**	SPA	41	Team SUZUKI ECSTAR	Suzuki GSX-RR	B	F: Medium/R: Medium	23	42m 09.762s
7	**Cal Crutchlow**	GBR	35	LCR Honda	Honda RC213V	B	F: Medium/R: Medium	23	42m 10.300s
8	**Bradley Smith**	GBR	38	Monster Yamaha Tech 3	Yamaha YZR-M1	B	F: Medium/R: Medium	23	42m 10.436s
9	**Pol Espargaro**	SPA	44	Monster Yamaha Tech 3	Yamaha YZR-M1	B	F: Medium/R: Medium	23	42m 11.385s
10	**Yonny Hernandez**	COL	68	Octo Pramac Racing	Ducati Desmosedici	B	F: Medium/R: Medium	23	42m 28.822s
11	**Maverick Vinales**	SPA	25	Team SUZUKI ECSTAR	Suzuki GSX-RR	B	F: Medium/R: Medium	23	42m 29.188s
12	**Scott Redding**	GBR	45	EG 0,0 Marc VDS	Honda RC213V	B	F: Medium/R: Medium	23	42m 33.109s
13	**Alvaro Bautista**	SPA	19	Aprilia Racing Team Gresini	Aprilia RS-GP	B	F: Medium/R: Soft	23	42m 34.688s
14	**Eugene Laverty**	IRL	50	Aspar MotoGP Team	Honda RC213V-RS	B	F: Medium/R: Soft	23	42m 35.204s
15	**Nicky Hayden**	USA	69	Aspar MotoGP Team	Honda RC213V-RS	B	F: Medium/R: Medium	23	42m 35.297s
16	Hector Barbera	SPA	8	Avintia Racing	Ducati Desmosedici Open	B	F: Medium/R: Soft	23	42m 35.655s
17	Loris Baz	FRA	76	Forward Racing	Yamaha Forward	B	F: Medium/R: Soft	23	42m 36.930s
18	Stefan Bradl	GER	6	Aprilia Racing Team Gresini	Aprilia RS-GP	B	F: Medium/R: Soft	23	42m 38.339s
19	Jack Miller	AUS	43	LCR Honda	Honda RC213V-RS	B	F: Medium/R: Medium	23	42m 41.792s
20	Mike di Meglio	FRA	63	Avintia Racing	Ducati Desmosedici Open	B	F: Medium/R: Soft	23	42m 44.540s
21	Toni Elias	SPA	24	Forward Racing	Yamaha Forward	B	F: Soft/R: Soft	23	43m 00.170s
	Karel Abraham	CZE	17	AB Motoracing	Honda RC213V-RS	B	F: Medium/R: Soft	11	DNF-injured
	Danilo Petrucci	ITA	9	Octo Pramac Racing	Ducati Desmosedici	B	F: Medium/R: Medium	9	DNF-crash
	Alex de Angelis	RSM	15	E-Motion IodaRacing Team	Aprilia ART	B	F: Medium/R: Soft	5	DNF-crash
	Marc Marquez	SPA	93	Repsol Honda Team	Honda RC213V	B	F: Medium/R: Medium	1	DNF-crash

Fastest lap: Jorge Lorenzo, on lap 2, 1m 48.120s, 105.0mph/169.0km/h (record).
Previous lap record: Dani Pedrosa, SPA (Honda), 1m 48.565s, 104.6mph/168.3km/h (2013).
Event best maximum speed: Andrea Iannone, 214.9mph/345.8km/h (free practice).

Qualifying

Weather: Dry	
Air Temp: 23° **Track Temp:** 36°	
Humidity: 39%	

1	Marquez	1m 46.635s
2	Lorenzo	1m 46.743s
3	Iannone	1m 47.178s
4	P. Espargaro	1m 47.334s
5	Pedrosa	1m 47.357s
6	Rossi	1m 47.492s
7	A. Espargaro	1m 47.573s
8	Crutchlow	1m 47.574s
9	Petrucci	1m 47.775s
10	Smith	1m 47.830s
11	Hernandez	1m 48.556s
12	Vinales	1m 48.648s
13	Dovizioso	1m 48.294s
14	Redding	1m 48.674s
15	Laverty	1m 49.035s
16	Hayden	1m 49.102s
17	Bradl	1m 49.109s
18	Di Meglio	1m 49.253s
19	Barbera	1m 49.426s
20	Miller	1m 49.436s
21	Bautista	1m 49.437s
22	Baz	1m 49.496s
23	Abraham	1m 49.761s
24	De Angelis	1m 50.134s
25	Elias	1m 50.755s

Fastest race laps

1	Lorenzo	1m 48.120s
2	Rossi	1m 48.165s
3	Pedrosa	1m 48.451s
4	Iannone	1m 48.581s
5	Crutchlow	1m 48.980s
6	Dovizioso	1m 48.986s
7	Petrucci	1m 49.000s
8	P. Espargaro	1m 49.035s
9	A. Espargaro	1m 49.120s
10	Smith	1m 49.138s
11	Vinales	1m 49.879s
12	Bautista	1m 49.961s
13	Redding	1m 50.029s
14	Barbera	1m 50.139s
15	Hernandez	1m 50.148s
16	Baz	1m 50.313s
17	Di Meglio	1m 50.397s
18	Bradl	1m 50.406s
19	Hayden	1m 50.408s
20	Miller	1m 50.460s
21	Laverty	1m 50.506s
22	Elias	1m 50.909s
23	De Angelis	1m 51.176s
24	Abraham	1m 51.714s

Championship Points

1	Rossi	263
2	Lorenzo	249
3	Marquez	184
4	Iannone	172
5	Smith	143
6	Dovizioso	139
7	Pedrosa	129
8	Petrucci	93
9	Crutchlow	88
10	P. Espargaro	88
11	A. Espargaro	76
12	Vinales	74
13	Redding	67
14	Hernandez	47
15	Baz	28
16	Bautista	26
17	Barbera	23
18	Miller	16
19	Hayden	13
20	Bradl	11
21	E. Laverty	9
22	Pirro	7
23	Di Meglio	7
24	Aoyama	5
25	De Angelis	2

Constructor Points

1	Yamaha	322
2	Honda	260
3	Ducati	210
4	Suzuki	105
5	Yamaha Forward	33
6	Aprilia	26
7	ART	2

Grid order		1	2	3	4	5	6	7	8	9	10	11	12	13	14	15	16	17	18	19	20	21	22	23	
93	MARQUEZ	99	99	99	99	99	99	99	99	99	99	99	99	99	99	99	99	99	99	99	99	99	99	99	1
99	LORENZO	93	29	26	26	26	26	26	26	26	26	26	26	26	26	26	26	26	26	26	26	26	26	26	2
29	IANNONE	29	26	29	46	46	46	46	46	46	46	46	46	46	46	46	46	46	46	46	46	46	46	46	3
44	P. ESPARGARO	26	46	46	29	29	29	29	29	29	29	29	29	29	29	29	29	29	29	29	29	29	29	29	4
26	PEDROSA	46	44	44	4	4	4	4	4	4	4	4	4	4	4	4	4	4	4	4	4	4	4	4	5
46	ROSSI	44	4	4	41	41	41	38	38	38	38	38	38	41	41	41	41	41	41	41	41	41	41	41	6
41	A. ESPARGARO	4	41	41	38	38	38	41	41	41	41	41	41	35	35	35	35	35	35	35	35	35	35	35	7
35	CRUTCHLOW	41	38	38	35	35	35	35	35	35	35	35	35	38	38	38	38	38	38	38	38	38	38	38	8
9	PETRUCCI	38	35	35	9	9	9	9	9	9	44	44	44	44	44	44	44	44	44	44	44	44	44	44	9
38	SMITH	35	9	9	44	44	44	44	44	44	68	68	68	68	68	68	68	68	68	68	68	68	68	68	10
68	HERNANDEZ	9	68	68	68	68	68	68	68	68	45	45	45	45	45	45	45	45	45	45	25	25	25	25	11
25	VINALES	68	6	45	45	45	45	45	45	45	6	6	6	6	25	25	25	25	25	25	45	45	45	45	12
4	DOVIZIOSO	6	45	6	6	6	6	6	6	6	50	50	50	25	19	19	19	19	19	19	19	19	19	19	13
45	REDDING	69	69	69	69	19	50	50	50	50	19	25	25	50	6	6	6	6	6	6	50	50	50	50	14
50	LAVERTY	50	50	19	19	69	50	19	19	19	25	19	19	19	50	50	50	50	50	50	69	69	69	69	15
69	HAYDEN	45	19	50	50	50	19	69	25	25	69	69	69	69	69	69	69	76	76	8	8				
6	BRADL	25	25	25	25	25	25	25	69	69	43	43	43	43	43	43	76	76	76	6	8	76	76		
63	DI MEGLIO	43	43	43	43	43	43	43	43	63	63	63	76	76	76	76	43	43	8	76	6	6	6		
8	BARBERA	19	76	76	76	76	76	76	63	63	76	76	63	63	8	8	8	8	43	43	43	43	43		
43	MILLER	76	24	63	63	63	63	63	76	76	8	8	8	8	63	63	63	63	63	63	63	63	63		
19	BAUTISTA	15	63	24	24	24	8	8	8	8	24	24	24	24	24	24	24	24	24	24	24	24	24		
76	BAZ	24	15	15	15	8	24	24	24	24	17	17													
17	ABRAHAM	63	17	8	8	15	17	17	17	17															
15	DE ANGELIS	8	8	17	17	17																			
24	ELIAS	17																							

17 Pit stop

Moto2

RACE DISTANCE: 14 laps, 44.175 miles/71.092km · **RACE WEATHER:** Dry (air 21°C, humidity 57%, track 34°C)

Pos.	Rider	Nat.	No.	Entrant	Machine	Laps	Time & Speed
1	**Tito Rabat**	SPA	1	EG 0,0 Marc VDS	Kalex	14	26m 25.125s 100.3mph/ 161.4km/h
2	**Alex Rins**	SPA	40	Paginas Amarillas HP 40	Kalex	14	26m 25.221s
3	**Sam Lowes**	GBR	22	Speed Up Racing	Speed Up	14	26m 30.489s
4	**Jonas Folger**	GER	94	AGR Team	Kalex	14	26m 32.488s
5	**Thomas Luthi**	SWI	12	Derendinger Racing Interwetten	Kalex	14	26m 41.848s
6	**Johann Zarco**	FRA	5	Ajo Motorsport	Kalex	14	26m 42.114s
7	**Hafizh Syahrin**	MAL	55	Petronas Raceline Malaysia	Kalex	14	26m 42.211s
8	**Takaaki Nakagami**	JPN	30	IDEMITSU Honda Team Asia	Kalex	14	26m 43.181s
9	**Simone Corsi**	ITA	3	Forward Racing	Kalex	14	26m 43.783s
10	**Lorenzo Baldassarri**	ITA	7	Forward Racing	Kalex	14	26m 44.781s
11	**Mika Kallio**	FIN	36	QMMF Racing Team	Speed Up	14	26m 45.215s
12	**Axel Pons**	SPA	49	AGR Team	Kalex	14	26m 45.347s
13	**Sandro Cortese**	GER	11	Dynavolt Intact GP	Kalex	14	26m 46.168s
14	**Azlan Shah**	MAL	25	IDEMITSU Honda Team Asia	Kalex	14	26m 47.509s
15	**Marcel Schrotter**	GER	23	Tech 3	Tech 3	14	26m 51.142s
16	Xavi Vierge	SPA	97	Tech 3	Tech 3	14	26m 59.589s
17	Randy Krummenacher	SWI	4	JIR Racing Team	Kalex	14	26m 59.783s
18	Ricard Cardus	SPA	88	JPMoto Malaysia	Suter	14	26m 59.852s
19	Robin Mulhauser	SWI	70	Technomag Racing Interwetten	Kalex	14	27m 02.460s
20	Jesko Raffin	SWI	2	sports-millions-EMWE-SAG	Kalex	14	27m 09.143s
21	Florian Alt	GER	66	E-Motion IodaRacing Team	Suter	14	27m 09.400s
22	Thitipong Warokorn	THA	10	APH PTT The Pizza SAG	Kalex	14	27m 09.729s
23	Louis Rossi	FRA	96	Tasca Racing Scuderia Moto2	Tech 3	14	27m 19.445s
	Federico Fuligni	ITA	32	Team Ciatti	Suter	13	DNF
	Alex Marquez	SPA	73	EG 0,0 Marc VDS	Kalex	7	DNF
	Julian Simon	SPA	60	QMMF Racing Team	Speed Up	4	DNF
	Edgar Pons	SPA	57	Italtrans Racing Team	Kalex	3	DNF
	Xavier Simeon	BEL	19	Federal Oil Gresini Moto2	Kalex	2	DNF
	Luis Salom	SPA	39	Paginas Amarillas HP 40	Kalex	2	DNF
	Dominique Aegerter	SWI	77	Technomag Racing Interwetten	Kalex	0	DNS

Fastest lap: Alex Rins, on lap 13, 1m 52.767s, 100.7mph/162.1km/h (record).
Previous lap record: Marc Marquez, SPA (Suter), 1m 53.956s, 99.7mph/160.4km/h (2011).
Event best maximum speed: Luis Salom, 175.5mph/282.5km/h (race).

Qualifying

Weather: Dry
Air Temp: 24° **Track Temp:** 35°
Humidity: 40%

1	Rabat	1m 52.232s
2	Rins	1m 52.267s
3	Zarco	1m 52.659s
4	Lowes	1m 52.672s
5	Nakagami	1m 52.780s
6	Marquez	1m 52.782s
7	Folger	1m 52.804s
8	Luthi	1m 52.917s
9	Pons	1m 52.937s
10	Cortese	1m 52.943s
11	Corsi	1m 53.010s
12	Baldassarri	1m 53.114s
13	Syahrin	1m 53.117s
14	Aegerter	1m 53.197s
15	Kallio	1m 53.224s
16	Simon	1m 53.378s
17	Shah	1m 53.378s
18	Simeon	1m 53.381s
19	Krummenacher	1m 53.665s
20	Salom	1m 53.670s
21	Schrotter	1m 53.683s
22	Cardus	1m 53.845s
23	Pons	1m 53.980s
24	Fuligni	1m 54.149s
25	Rossi	1m 54.162s
26	Mulhauser	1m 54.171s
27	Vierge	1m 54.200s
28	Warokorn	1m 54.803s
29	Alt	1m 54.830s
30	Raffin	1m 55.358s

Fastest race laps

1	Rins	1m 52.767s
2	Rabat	1m 52.800s
3	Lowes	1m 53.016s
4	Folger	1m 53.201s
5	Marquez	1m 53.274s
6	Corsi	1m 53.482s
7	Syahrin	1m 53.591s
8	Zarco	1m 53.679s
9	Luthi	1m 53.710s
10	Pons	1m 53.725s
11	Nakagami	1m 53.848s
12	Kallio	1m 53.908s
13	Shah	1m 54.027s
14	Cortese	1m 54.034s
15	Baldassarri	1m 54.037s
16	Cardus	1m 54.259s
17	Schrotter	1m 54.286s
18	Pons	1m 54.467s
19	Krummenacher	1m 54.478s
20	Salom	1m 54.479s
21	Simon	1m 54.528s
22	Vierge	1m 54.587s
23	Mulhauser	1m 54.882s
24	Simeon	1m 54.898s
25	Rossi	1m 54.955s
26	Alt	1m 55.098s
27	Raffin	1m 55.182s
28	Fuligni	1m 55.232s
29	Warokorn	1m 55.335s

Championship Points

1	Zarco	284
2	Rabat	206
3	Rins	184
4	Lowes	144
5	Luthi	142
6	Folger	125
7	Simeon	96
8	Morbidelli	84
9	Nakagami	69
10	Aegerter	62
11	Marquez	62
12	Cortese	62
13	Corsi	60
14	Simon	58
15	Kallio	53
16	Baldassarri	52
17	Salom	50
18	Syahrin	45
19	West	30
20	Pons	28
21	Schrotter	20
22	Krummenacher	19
23	Shah	11
24	Rossi	7
25	Cardus	6
26	Mulhauser	1

Constructor Points

1	Kalex	345
2	Speed Up	166
3	Tech 3	27
4	Suter	6

Moto3

RACE DISTANCE: 20 laps, 63.106 miles/101.560km · **RACE WEATHER:** Dry (air 16°C, humidity 72%, track 20°C)

Pos.	Rider	Nat.	No.	Entrant	Machine	Laps	Time & Speed
1	**Miguel Oliveira**	POR	44	Red Bull KTM Ajo	KTM	20	39m 54.343s 94.8mph/ 152.6km/h
2	**Jorge Navarro**	SPA	9	Estrella Galicia 0,0	Honda	20	39m 54.536s
3	**Romano Fenati**	ITA	5	SKY Racing Team VR46	KTM	20	39m 55.848s
4	**Efren Vazquez**	SPA	7	Leopard Racing	Honda	20	39m 56.135s
5	**Philipp Oettl**	GER	65	Schedl GP Racing	KTM	20	39m 56.809s
6	**Niccolo Antonelli**	ITA	23	Ongetta-Rivacold	Honda	20	39m 59.246s
7	**Jorge Martin**	SPA	88	MAPFRE Team MAHINDRA	Mahindra	20	40m 00.855s
8	**Alexis Masbou**	FRA	10	SAXOPRINT RTG	Honda	20	40m 10.089s
9	**Andrea Migno**	ITA	16	SKY Racing Team VR46	KTM	20	40m 10.227s
10	**Hiroki Ono**	JPN	76	Leopard Racing	Honda	20	40m 10.118s
11	**Francesco Bagnaia**	ITA	21	MAPFRE Team MAHINDRA	Mahindra	20	40m 10.603s
12	**Stefano Manzi**	ITA	29	San Carlo Team Italia	Mahindra	20	40m 10.697s
13	**Maria Herrera**	SPA	6	Husqvarna Factory Laglisse	Husqvarna	20	40m 11.242s
14	**Jakub Kornfeil**	CZE	84	Drive M7 SIC	KTM	20	40m 11.192s
15	**Livio Loi**	BEL	11	RW Racing GP	Honda	20	40m 11.468s
16	Tatsuki Suzuki	JPN	24	CIP	Mahindra	20	40m 11.903s
17	John McPhee	GBR	17	SAXOPRINT RTG	Honda	20	40m 12.033s
18	Sena Yamada	JPN	81	Estrella Galicia 0,0	Honda	20	40m 25.393s
19	Remy Gardner	AUS	2	CIP	Mahindra	20	40m 25.502s
20	Gabriel Rodrigo	ARG	91	RBA Racing Team	KTM	20	40m 25.523s
21	Juanfran Guevara	SPA	58	MAPFRE Team MAHINDRA	Mahindra	20	40m 25.692s
22	Jules Danilo	FRA	95	Ongetta-Rivacold	Honda	20	40m 25.726s
23	Alessandro Tonucci	ITA	19	Outox Reset Drink Team	Mahindra	20	40m 26.102s
24	Lorenzo Dalla Porta	ITA	48	Husqvarna Factory Laglisse	Husqvarna	20	40m 38.058s
25	Khairul Idham Pawi	MAL	89	Honda Team Asia	Honda	20	40m 42.288s
26	Davide Pizzoli	ITA	37	Husqvarna Factory Laglisse	Husqvarna	20	40m 42.425s
27	Ana Carrasco	SPA	22	RBA Racing Team	KTM	20	40m 42.508s
	Brad Binder	RSA	41	Red Bull KTM Ajo	KTM	19	DNF
	Danny Kent	GBR	52	Leopard Racing	Honda	19	DNF
	Enea Bastianini	ITA	33	Gresini Racing Team Moto3	Honda	19	DNF
	Karel Hanika	CZE	98	Red Bull KTM Ajo	KTM	13	DNF
	Manuel Pagliani	ITA	96	San Carlo Team Italia	Mahindra	13	DNF
	Zulfahmi Khairuddin	MAL	63	Drive M7 SIC	KTM	13	DNF
	Isaac Vinales	SPA	32	RBA Racing Team	KTM	12	DNF
	Darryn Binder	RSA	40	Outox Reset Drink Team	Mahindra	12	DNF

Fastest lap: Niccolò Antonelli, on lap 15, 1m 58.726s, 95.6mph/153.9km/h (record).
Previous lap record: Philipp Oettl, GER (Kalex KTM), 1m 59.681s, 94.9mph/152.7km/h (2013).
Event best maximum speed: Livio Loi, 149.9mph/241.2km/h (race).

Qualifying

Weather: Dry
Air Temp: 21° **Track Temp:** 32°
Humidity: 55%

1	Bastianini	1m 57.755s
2	Oliveira	1m 57.955s
3	Kent	1m 57.956s
4	Martin	1m 58.412s
5	Navarro	1m 58.444s
6	Antonelli	1m 58.465s
7	Masbou	1m 58.473s
8	Vazquez	1m 58.477s
9	Oettl	1m 58.505s
10	Fenati	1m 58.515s
11	Binder	1m 58.579s
12	Kornfeil	1m 58.698s
13	Hanika	1m 58.733s
14	McPhee	1m 58.945s
15	Loi	1m 58.968s
16	Khairuddin	1m 58.978s
17	Migno	1m 59.020s
18	Bagnaia	1m 59.026s
19	Guevara	1m 59.054s
20	Dalla Porta	1m 59.214s
21	Ono	1m 59.236s
22	Manzi	1m 59.366s
23	Yamada	1m 59.398s
24	Vinales	1m 59.462s
25	Danilo	1m 59.475s
26	Binder	1m 59.505s
27	Herrera	1m 59.563s
28	Suzuki	1m 59.580s
29	Rodrigo	1m 59.624s
30	Tonucci	1m 59.683s
31	Gardner	1m 59.940s
32	Pagliani	1m 59.959s
33	Pizzoli	2m 00.096s
34	Pawi	2m 00.791s
35	Carrasco	2m 01.794s

Fastest race laps

1	Antonelli	1m 58.726s
2	Ono	1m 58.807s
3	Oettl	1m 58.823s
4	Vazquez	1m 58.845s
5	Fenati	1m 58.866s
6	Navarro	1m 58.919s
7	Kornfeil	1m 58.978s
8	McPhee	1m 58.980s
9	Vinales	1m 59.000s
10	Bastianini	1m 59.059s
11	Binder	1m 59.065s
12	Kent	1m 59.109s
13	Suzuki	1m 59.121s
14	Migno	1m 59.137s
15	Martin	1m 59.144s
16	Oliveira	1m 59.204s
17	Binder	1m 59.222s
18	Khairuddin	1m 59.257s
19	Manzi	1m 59.285s
20	Bagnaia	1m 59.327s
21	Herrera	1m 59.389s
22	Dalla Porta	1m 59.398s
23	Yamada	1m 59.399s
24	Loi	1m 59.477s
25	Hanika	1m 59.511s
26	Gardner	1m 59.596s
27	Masbou	1m 59.599s
28	Rodrigo	1m 59.659s
29	Danilo	1m 59.766s
30	Pagliani	1m 59.787s
31	Guevara	1m 59.925s
32	Tonucci	1m 59.930s
33	Pizzoli	2m 00.134s
34	Pawi	2m 00.838s
35	Carrasco	2m 00.978s

Championship Points

1	Kent	234
2	Bastianini	179
3	Oliveira	159
4	Fenati	155
5	Antonelli	136
6	Vazquez	129
7	Binder	110
8	Quartararo	92
9	Navarro	92
10	Vinales	82
11	Bagnaia	72
12	McPhee	70
13	Masbou	63
14	Oettl	57
15	Loi	56
16	Kornfeil	48
17	Hanika	33
18	Martin	33
19	Locatelli	31
20	Migno	30
21	Ajo	21
22	Ono	21
23	Guevara	15
24	Dalla Porta	13
25	Danilo	7
26	Manzi	7
27	Suzuki	6
28	Herrera	4
29	Khairuddin	4
30	Ferrari	1

Constructor Points

1	Honda	330
2	KTM	246
3	Mahindra	102
4	Husqvarna	80

Main: From workaday to super-hero: Pedrosa's first win of the year was both lucky and masterful.

Inset, top: Smiling fit to bust, Dani and his Honda crew in *parc fermé*.

Inset, bottom: Zarco underlined his title with a champion's win, and another trademark back-flip.

Photo: Gold & Goose

Above: Pedrosa passes Rossi for second to set his sights on Lorenzo.

Top: A detuned Marquez claimed fourth from Dovizioso, only because the Ducati had run out of grip.

Top right: Hector Barbera took his Avintia Ducati to ninth place for top Open honours.

Above right: Satellite Yamaha rider Smith chases factory Yamaha wild-card Katsuyuki Nakasuga. By the end, the Briton was comfortably clear.

Right: The Movistar Yamahas took control at the start, but that wouldn't last the distance.

Photos: Gold & Goose

HONDA'S hubris in choosing a misty mountaintop location for their motoring multiplex was revealed again on race day, when proceedings were delayed by more than two hours because the medevac helicopter was grounded. Similar difficulties had caused a full weekend of problems in 2013.

The race result was compensation for the track's owners, however, after an increasingly gripping race in changing conditions and with massively changing fortunes yielding an unlikely, but emphatic win by Pedrosa, his first of the season and 50th in his career. It was a climax to almost 47 minutes of growing tension, and it had the secondary effect of reversing the flow of the championship, as Rossi finished ahead of long-time runaway leader Lorenzo.

Practice had been dry. Sunday was not just misty, but also wet. The mist lifted eventually; before then, a solution had been found. With the co-operation of the local police, casualties could be evacuated to the nearest hospital by road in "no more than 50 minutes", according to an official statement from the medical director and chief medical officer. Combined with "significantly improved medical centre facilities and updated ambulance", this was felt sufficient. It was all rather piquant, because the day before the helicopter had been required to rush the seriously injured Alex de Angelis to intensive care. Happily, no further emergencies arose.

Lunch plans went out of the window as the schedule was rearranged to get it back on target for the 2pm MotoGP TV slot. Warm up was truncated and race distance cut by a third in the smaller classes. MotoGP started on time at two.

De Angelis had hurt himself in FP4. It was his 19th crash of the season on the obsolete and underpowered ART, and as described by witness Rossi, something of a freak, because, exiting turn nine, "instead of going to the outside of the track, he went to the inside." There the barrier is alongside, and the San Marino rider hit it hard, suffering multiple injuries, including cranial bleeding, spinal damage and lung contusions. After a worrying few days, his condition improved, and complete recovery was predicted.

Although safety standards at Motegi were generally good, opined Rossi a week later, there were several places with a similar proximity of guardrail, where accidental impact was generally considered unlikely. Not only at Motegi, chimed in fellow Safety Commission member Dovizioso. Every track had similar spots, and if such objective dangers were to be avoided entirely, "every track would need four times as much space". To add to the conundrum, air-fence in some cases was more dangerous than a barrier, he said. It had been explained to the commission that while a head-on collision with the fence used its full capacity for protection, a glancing blow could be a different matter.

The first championship of the year was settled without firing a shot. Rabat had arrived with his left arm and freshly plated radius bone in a temporary cast, and he lined up for FP1. He did only eight laps, then withdrew. It was not the pain, he said, but he lacked the strength needed, especially at a circuit known for its heavy braking.

Thus Zarco's triumph was confirmed at Friday lunchtime. Relieved of the pressure of Aragon, he went out and won like a champion. But his favourite race was not one of his seven victories so far, but his worst result, at Qatar. "I was leading, then I had a technical problem and finished eighth. I should have won. Everyone expected me to be angry and disappointed, but it was a fantastic feeling. I led from the second lap, and I was the strongest. From this race, I could say: 'Yes, I can be champion.'"

There were more experiments with wings, and some

reverse copycat by Ducati. The Desmo's latest variation mounted an upper wing at the base of the front cowling, one either side, as used by Yamaha. Deployed in conjunction with the lower fairing-flank wings, which again were in biplane format, it turned them into triplanes – shades of Baron von Richthofen. There were still no firm conclusions. As Yamaha's Massimo Meregalli told Dorna's interviewer, "The riders have a different feeling … but the lap time is the same."

There were more high-level training injuries: Marquez had suffered another left-hand fracture, this time sustained while mountain-biking and requiring "a six-hole titanium plate" on the fifth metacarpal, between wrist and first knuckle, according to the ever-active Dr Xavier Mir. His team had rigged up a specially reshaped and padded handlebar grip to ease the discomfort, again braking a particular issue, and his race was accordingly downbeat.

Lorenzo had fallen off a minibike and feared the worst on the way to hospital – that his left shoulder would require surgery. To his relief, the diagnosis was only a sprain, and he was wearing a sling upon arrival. He joked, "It's not 100 per cent, but my right side is also not 100 per cent, so perhaps it will balance me more."

After his unsuccessful return, Abraham opted out of the flyaways, his place being taken here by ex-Suzuki and Honda rider, 40-year-old Kousuke Akiyoshi, his ninth GP start. From the following race, the recently sacked Anthony West would take over.

Aegerter was absent from Moto2; Australian Suzuka 8 Hours rostrum partner Josh Hook took over. In Moto3, Quartararo was back, but he withdrew from the race on the wet Sunday, after qualifying down in 29th, and eventually from the two subsequent races as well. Locatelli had returned and raced, but this proved also temporary.

Contract news was led by Nicky Hayden's far from surprise announcement that 2015 would be his last year in grand prix racing. But not to retirement: he would be moving to World Superbikes in 2016, to join Michael van der Mark in the Ten Kate Honda team. He admitted that his hopes of earning a competitive MotoGP bike again had ended: now there was

a chance to become the first rider to win both MotoGP and WSBK crowns. Although only three times a race winner, Hayden had the unforgettable distinction of having beaten Rossi in their final-race showdown, when the Italian crashed.

Elsewhere: Hernandez, dumped by Pramac, had been picked up by Aspar, the Colombian's Ducati experience being valued for the senior private team's switch from Honda. Quartararo had signed to join Leopard Racing's 2016 Moto3 squad, along with Spaniard Joan Mir, current riders Kent and Vazquez both being bound for Moto2; and Rossi's half-brother, Luca Marini, was to join the promising Baldassarri in Forward's Moto2 team, ousting veteran Simone Corsi.

MOTOGP RACE – 24 laps

Changing conditions turned what had started as another workaday race for Pedrosa into a serendipitous tactical triumph, finally preserving his record of at least one win every year as he caught and passed both runaway Yamaha riders. Tyres, and their preservation, were the key.

Lorenzo was on pole, a tenth ahead of Rossi and four-tenths ahead of Marquez. Pedrosa was on the far end of row two, behind the Ducatis, Dovi the faster this time.

The conditions – still wet, but with a drying line, especially in the seven hard braking areas – were challenging from the start. Pedrosa had elected to use a harder rear wet, but when he saw that everyone else (bar the distant Redding and Hayden) had softs, he changed on the grid "to have the same tools". But the tyre was brand new, and it forced a cautious pace in the early laps. By mid-race, he had decided simply to maintain fourth place.

By then, the result seemed settled. Rossi led into the first corner, but Lorenzo firmly seized control into the third and quickly built a commanding lead, up to three seconds after just five laps.

From there on, Rossi could match his pace, but not get any closer – he'd been able to resist strong early pressure from Dovizioso, before he ran into early grip problems and started to drop away.

Just before half-distance, the complexion of the race began to change as the track continued to dry. Pedrosa caught and easily took third from gripless Dovizioso. The gap to Rossi was more than four seconds, but over the next laps it shrank with increasing rapidity. The Yamahas were slowing, the Honda getting into its stride.

Lorenzo was worst off, saying ruefully, "If I had known it was going to dry, I would not have made such a push in the first laps." He added, "I was the fastest in the dry and then also in the wet. I should have won this race but for the bad luck of the conditions changing."

Dorna's cameras focused on Lorenzo's front wheel, where the tyre was clearly starting to shred.

Pedrosa's focus was on Rossi, and on the 15th lap he took better than a second out of him to close up on his tail, going on to pass with great assurance before they had completed the 16th.

The gap to Lorenzo was still 2.7 seconds, but there was time aplenty, for by the end of that lap it was down to 0.8, and the outcome inevitable. Pedrosa lined him up out of the hairpin and rode cleanly past on the final downhill plunge to take a lead that would grow to 8.5 seconds at the flag. It was his second straight defeat of Rossi.

Rossi's tyres were not as bad as Lorenzo's. He took a bit of a tow from the Honda, but needed two more laps to pass his fast fading team-mate, riding on tiptoes and almost four seconds away at the flag.

Marquez started badly and never featured, circulating fifth and troubling nobody. He only gained fourth because of Dovizioso's ever slowing pace.

Crutchlow and Smith were battling, survivors of a hectic group that had been seven strong just before mid-race. Smith conceded sixth with three corners to go, when he almost fell at turn 11, saving it with his elbow.

By then, Aleix Espargaro had already run off and rejoined far behind. Petrucci played a highly active role until he fell on lap nine. Vinales had closed from behind, but also crashed. And Pol Espargaro ran off, rejoined far behind, then crashed terminally, also hitting the barrier and lucky to escape serious consequences.

Iannone had fallen back into the group, only to coast to a stop trackside with an electronic failure, his first non-finish of the year.

That left wild-card and 8 Hours winner Katsuyuki Nakasuga (Yamaha Factory) to a strong eighth, never seriously threatened by the closing Barbera, top Open finisher.

Another lap might have seen Redding take that ninth place. On the harder rear option, a slow start had resulted in him circulating in 19th, but he was slicing through in the final laps, and barely a second behind Barbera, having left Aleix Espargaro more than ten adrift. Redding passed second wild-card Takumi Takahashi (Team HRC Honda) on the last lap.

Hayden was 13th, having caught and passed Hernandez in the closing stages. Di Meglio came through at the end to take the last point, ahead of Bautista. Jack Miller also crashed, twice – the first time from an impressive fighting top ten; the second time terminally.

MOTO2 RACE – 15 laps (shortened from 23)

Already crowned champion, Zarco's plan was to focus on the race as if nothing had happened. The result was a champion's performance: pole position in the dry with a new best-ever lap; a clear victory in the wet. Status confirmed.

Luthi was alongside, then a resurgent Folger. Lowes, Rins and Syahrin filled row two.

The weather was difficult for the middle class, too. The track was wet, although the drizzle fitful as they set off, with Folger making the perfect start to lead Zarco and Luthi into the first corner.

The German stayed up front for the first four laps, by which time he and his shadow Zarco were some five seconds clear. Then, with the track starting to dry, Zarco decided that it would be safer to go away alone. This he did with great clarity, slipping past into the notorious turn 11 at the bottom of the back straight. Thereafter he pulled away at around a second a lap until he had a comfortable cushion, 4.5 seconds at the flag.

Folger had little left to do but to stay wheels down, since the pursuit was already more than six seconds adrift when the lead changed hands; and sundry dramas would cause that gap to grow to a yawning 11 seconds at the end.

Luthi led the early pursuit, only for Nakagami to please the crowd by taking over. On lap five, however, he ran off into the gravel at the end of the back straight and was down. By then, Luthi had also fallen, caught out by the treacherous surface on the right-hander before the first underpass.

Rins was now at the head of a pack. He had been fastest in wet warm-up, but had misadventures in store. He lost the position to an inspired Azlan Shah and then ran wide at the first corner on two consecutive laps to drop all the way back to tenth.

Syahrin had started well, and though he never quite caught his Malaysian compatriot, he was in a strong fourth

Above: Tyre wear determined the result: Lorenzo's Yamaha and (centre) winner Pedrosa's Honda.

Top: A sober-faced Lorenzo reflects on a disappointing third place.
Photos: Gold & Goose

Above: Azlan Shah took a career-best fourth, but ultimately had to give best to Cortese.

Left: Divided loyalties for this enthusiastic couple.

until there were three laps to go. By then, Cortese had arrived, picking up places steadily from 12th on the second lap. On the 11th, he was firmly past Syahrin, and he rapidly closed a 1.7-second gap on Shah to take third by the end of the penultimate lap, still pulling away. Fourth was a career best for Shah.

A couple of seconds away, Cardus finally got back ahead of Corsi on the last lap for sixth. Lowes did the same to Schrotter for eighth, with Krummenacher on his back wheel.

Only then, another three seconds adrift, came a thoroughly detuned Rins in 11th, having asked too much of his tyres in the early stages.

Baldassarri, wild-cards Tomoyoshi Koyama and Yuki Takahashi, and a fading Kallio took the last of the points.

Marquez had been with the pursuit group up front, but ran wide and then off, finishing 18th. Salom crashed out, as did Hook, Vierge and both Pons brothers, Axel after having been sent to the back of the grid for an illegal extra sighting lap.

MOTO3 RACE – 20 laps

Fenati was on his first ever pole, from Oliveira and Navarro – but a rotten start meant he finished the first lap tenth. Then he fell off on the third without making any progress.

Young compatriot Antonelli showed the way on the wet track, taking an immediate lead from the second row and emulating Lorenzo by rapidly making himself uncatchable, then controlling the gap for his second GP win.

Loi had been heading the pursuit from Oliveira and early crasher Ono, but he lasted only a couple more laps before he too slipped off. Oliveira was now second, more than three seconds behind.

Then Oliveira came under threat from team-mate Brad Binder, but had seen him off when the South African also fell, the third podium candidate to do so.

Vinales had come with him; but Navarro had been carving through from his rotten start, finishing lap one 13th. Fourth seemed the best he could hope for until Vinales slipped off at the hairpin, remounting to lose only one position.

Khairuddin was close, a couple of seconds clear of the main group.

This was led over the line by Kent, cautious in the early laps, but typically gaining places in the closing stages. His last victim was Bastianini. Taking sixth off him on the last lap only gained Kent one point; the psychological advantage was more important.

Hanika was still close, McPhee just dropping off the back as he fended off a late attack from Vazquez and Martin. They had finished lap one 26th and 25th respectively, and had been slashing their way through, the rookie and the veteran changing places several times as they did so.

Kornfeil, Suzuki, Locatelli and Bagnaia took the remainder of the points; the remounted Binder was 17th.

Thus Kent would have to wait one more race to be crowned. Or, as it transpired, even longer.

Above: Antonelli's second win was achieved in the style of Lorenzo.

Left: Hafizh Syahrin was another victim of a charging Cortese.

Right: Zulfahmi Khairuddin scored a fine fifth in Moto3.

Photos: Gold & Goose

TWIN RING MOTEGI
24 laps
Length: 4.801 km / 2.983 miles
Width: 15m

Key
96/60 kph/mph
Gear

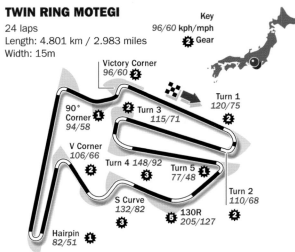

Victory Corner 96/60
90° Corner 94/58
Turn 3 115/71
Turn 1 120/75
V Corner 106/66
Turn 4 148/92
Turn 5 77/48
Turn 2 110/68
S Curve 132/82
130R 205/127
Hairpin 82/51

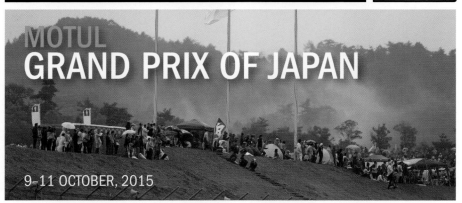

MOTUL
GRAND PRIX OF JAPAN

9–11 OCTOBER, 2015

MotoGP

RACE DISTANCE: 24 laps, 71.597 miles/115.224km · RACE WEATHER: Wet (air 19°C, humidity 93%, track 21°C)

Pos. Rider	Nat.	No.	Entrant	Machine	Tyres	Race tyre choice	Laps	Time & speed
1 Dani Pedrosa	SPA	26	Repsol Honda Team	Honda RC213V	B	F: Hard Wet/R: Soft Wet	24	46m 50.767s / 91.7mph/ 147.5km/h
2 Valentino Rossi	ITA	46	Movistar Yamaha MotoGP	Yamaha YZR-M1	B	F: Hard Wet/R: Soft Wet	24	46m 59.340s
3 Jorge Lorenzo	SPA	99	Movistar Yamaha MotoGP	Yamaha YZR-M1	B	F: Hard Wet/R: Soft Wet	24	47m 02.894s
4 Marc Marquez	SPA	93	Repsol Honda Team	Honda RC213V	B	F: Hard Wet/R: Soft Wet	24	47m 18.608s
5 Andrea Dovizioso	ITA	4	Ducati Team	Ducati Desmosedici	B	F: Hard Wet/R: Soft Wet	24	47m 25.852s
6 Cal Crutchlow	GBR	35	LCR Honda	Honda RC213V	B	F: Hard Wet/R: Soft Wet	24	47m 28.030s
7 Bradley Smith	GBR	38	Monster Yamaha Tech 3	Yamaha YZR-M1	B	F: Hard Wet/R: Soft Wet	24	47m 28.434s
8 Katsuyuki Nakasuga	JPN	21	Yamaha Factory Racing Team	Yamaha YZR-M1	B	F: Hard Wet/R: Soft Wet	24	47m 35.421s
9 Hector Barbera	SPA	8	Avintia Racing	Ducati Desmosedici Open	B	F: Hard Wet/R: Hard Wet	24	47m 39.339s
10 Scott Redding	GBR	45	EG 0,0 Marc VDS	Honda RC213V	B	F: Hard Wet/R: Hard Wet	24	47m 40.888s
11 Aleix Espargaro	SPA	41	Team SUZUKI ECSTAR	Suzuki GSX-RR	B	F: Hard Wet/R: Soft Wet	24	47m 51.302s
12 Takumi Takahashi	JPN	72	Team HRC with Nissin	Honda RC213V	B	F: Hard Wet/R: Soft Wet	24	47m 51.978s
13 Nicky Hayden	USA	69	Aspar MotoGP Team	Honda RC213V-RS	B	F: Hard Wet/R: Hard Wet	24	48m 02.028s
14 Yonny Hernandez	COL	68	Octo Pramac Racing	Ducati Desmosedici	B	F: Hard Wet/R: Soft Wet	24	48m 04.663s
15 Mike di Meglio	FRA	63	Avintia Racing	Ducati Desmosedici Open	B	F: Hard Wet/R: Soft Wet	24	48m 06.188s
16 Alvaro Bautista	SPA	19	Aprilia Racing Team Gresini	Aprilia RS-GP	B	F: Hard Wet/R: Soft Wet	24	48m 11.274s
17 Eugene Laverty	IRL	50	Aspar MotoGP Team	Honda RC213V-RS	B	F: Hard Wet/R: Soft Wet	24	48m 21.991s
18 Stefan Bradl	GER	6	Aprilia Racing Team Gresini	Aprilia RS-GP	B	F: Hard Wet/R: Soft Wet	24	48m 37.600s
19 Kousuke Akiyoshi	JPN	64	AB Motoracing	Honda RC213V-RS	B	F: Soft Wet/R: Soft Wet	24	48m 50.839s
20 Toni Elias	SPA	24	Forward Racing	Yamaha Forward	B	F: Soft Wet/R: Soft Wet	23	47m 36.873s
Pol Espargaro	SPA	44	Monster Yamaha Tech 3	Yamaha YZR-M1	B	F: Hard Wet/R: Soft Wet	22	DNF-crash
Jack Miller	AUS	43	LCR Honda	Honda RC213V-RS	B	F: Hard Wet/R: Soft Wet	16	DNF-crash
Maverick Vinales	SPA	25	Team SUZUKI ECSTAR	Suzuki GSX-RR	B	F: Hard Wet/R: Soft Wet	13	DNF-crash
Loris Baz	FRA	76	Forward Racing	Yamaha Forward	B	F: Hard Wet/R: Soft Wet	13	DNF-mechanical
Andrea Iannone	ITA	29	Ducati Team	Ducati Desmosedici	B	F: Hard Wet/R: Soft Wet	10	DNF-mechanical
Danilo Petrucci	ITA	9	Octo Pramac Racing	Ducati Desmosedici	B	F: Hard Wet/R: Soft Wet	8	DNF-crash
Alex de Angelis	RSM	15	E-Motion IodaRacing Team	Aprilia ART	B	-	-	DNS-injured

Fastest lap: Jorge Lorenzo, on lap 3, 1m 54.867s, 93.5mph/150.4km/h.
Lap record: Jorge Lorenzo, SPA (Yamaha), 101.9mph/164.0km/h (2014).
Event best maximum speed: Andrea Iannone, 195.3mph/314.3km/h (free practice).

Qualifying
Weather: Dry
Air Temp: 20° Track Temp: 24°
Humidity: 75%

1	Lorenzo	1m 43.790s
2	Rossi	1m 43.871s
3	Marquez	1m 44.216s
4	Dovizioso	1m 44.322s
5	Iannone	1m 44.436s
6	Pedrosa	1m 44.582s
7	A. Espargaro	1m 44.809s
8	Crutchlow	1m 44.932s
9	Smith	1m 45.067s
10	Vinales	1m 45.081s
11	P. Espargaro	1m 45.219s
12	Redding	1m 45.333s
13	Bradl	1m 45.432s
14	Hernandez	1m 45.438s
15	Nakasuga	1m 45.496s
16	Bautista	1m 45.608s
17	Petrucci	1m 45.691s
18	Barbera	1m 45.724s
19	Takahashi	1m 45.743s
20	Laverty	1m 45.751s
21	Hayden	1m 45.843s
22	Miller	1m 46.039s
23	Baz	1m 46.048s
24	Di Meglio	1m 46.179s
25	Elias	1m 46.256s
26	Akiyoshi	1m 47.760s
	De Angelis	No Time

Fastest race laps

1	Lorenzo	1m 54.867s
2	Dovizioso	1m 55.187s
3	Rossi	1m 55.221s
4	Pedrosa	1m 55.394s
5	Marquez	1m 56.129s
6	Crutchlow	1m 56.412s
7	Smith	1m 56.524s
8	A. Espargaro	1m 56.525s
9	Miller	1m 56.596s
10	Vinales	1m 56.748s
11	Barbera	1m 56.775s
12	Petrucci	1m 56.904s
13	Nakasuga	1m 56.914s
14	P. Espargaro	1m 56.966s
15	Iannone	1m 57.217s
16	Hernandez	1m 57.238s
17	Takahashi	1m 57.419s
18	Hayden	1m 57.479s
19	Redding	1m 57.566s
20	Bradl	1m 57.656s
21	Baz	1m 57.752s
22	Laverty	1m 57.783s
23	Di Meglio	1m 58.117s
24	Bautista	1m 58.261s
25	Akiyoshi	1m 59.572s
26	Elias	2m 01.116s

Championship Points

1	Rossi	283
2	Lorenzo	265
3	Marquez	197
4	Iannone	172
5	Pedrosa	154
6	Smith	152
7	Dovizioso	150
8	Crutchlow	98
9	Petrucci	93
10	P. Espargaro	88
11	A. Espargaro	81
12	Vinales	74
13	Redding	73
14	Hernandez	49
15	Barbera	30
16	Baz	28
17	Bautista	26
18	Miller	16
19	Hayden	16
20	Bradl	11
21	E. Laverty	9
22	Nakasuga	8
23	Pirro	8
24	Di Meglio	8
25	Aoyama	5
26	Takahashi	4
27	De Angelis	2

Constructor Points

1	Yamaha	342
2	Honda	285
3	Ducati	221
4	Suzuki	110
5	Yamaha Forward	33
6	Aprilia	26
7	ART	2

Grid order	1	2	3	4	5	6	7	8	9	10	11	12	13	14	15	16	17	18	19	20	21	22	23	24	
99 LORENZO	99	99	99	99	99	99	99	99	99	99	99	99	99	99	99	99	99	26	26	26	26	26	26	26	1
46 ROSSI	46	46	46	46	46	46	46	46	46	46	46	46	46	46	46	26	26	99	99	46	46	46	46	46	2
93 MARQUEZ	4	4	4	4	4	4	4	4	4	4	26	26	26	26	26	46	46	46	46	99	99	99	99	99	3
4 DOVIZIOSO	26	26	26	26	26	26	26	26	26	26	4	4	4	4	4	4	4	4	4	93	93	93	93	93	4
29 IANNONE	29	93	93	93	93	93	93	93	93	93	93	93	93	93	93	93	93	93	4	4	4	4	4		5
26 PEDROSA	93	29	41	41	41	35	35	35	35	35	35	35	35	35	38	38	38	38	38	38	38	38	35		6
41 A. ESPARGARO	41	41	29	29	35	29	29	29	29	29	38	38	38	38	35	35	35	35	35	35	35	35	38		7
35 CRUTCHLOW	44	44	9	35	29	9	9	44	38	38	21	21	21	21	21	21	21	21	21	21	21	21	21		8
38 SMITH	38	35	35	9	9	44	44	38	44	44	25	25	25	8	8	8	8	8	8	8	8	8	8		9
25 VINALES	9	44	44	44	44	21	9	21	21	21	8	8	8	41	41	41	41	41	45	45	45	45	45		10
44 P. ESPARGARO	35	21	21	21	21	38	38	21	25	25	41	41	41	72	72	72	44	45	45	41	41	44	41		11
45 REDDING	25	38	38	43	43	43	25	25	8	68	68	72	44	44	45	44	45	44	44	44	44	41	72	72	12
6 BRADL	21	25	43	38	38	25	8	8	68	68	72	68	68	44	68	72	72	72	72	72	69	69			13
68 HERNANDEZ	68	43	25	25	25	8	68	68	72	72	69	69	69	45	45	68	69	69	69	68	68	68			14
21 NAKASUGA	69	68	8	8	8	68	72	72	41	41	44	44	44	45	69	69	68	68	63	63					15
19 BAUTISTA	43	8	68	68	68	72	69	41	69	69	45	45	45	50	50	19	19	19	19						
9 PETRUCCI	8	69	69	69	72	69	41	69	50	50	50	50	19	19	50	19	50	50							
8 BARBERA	72	72	72	72	69	41	50	50	45	19	19	43	43	43	63	63	50	50	50	6	6				
72 TAKAHASHI	50	50	50	50	50	6	45	45	19	19	43	43	43	63	63	63	6	6	6	6	64				
50 LAVERTY	6	6	6	6	6	50	19	19	43	43	63	63	63	64	6	64	64	64	64	64	24				
69 HAYDEN	45	76	76	63	45	45	43	43	64	64	64	64	6	64	64	24	24	24	24	24	24				
43 MILLER	76	45	45	45	19	19	64	64	63	6	6	6	24	24	24										
76 BAZ	64	64	63	19	64	64	63	63	6	6	24	24	24												
63 DI MEGLIO	63	63	64	64	24	63	24	6	24	24	76	76	76												
24 ELIAS	19	19	19	24	63	24	6	24	76	76															
64 AKIYOSHI	24	24	24	76	76	76	76	76																	

76 Pit stop 24 Lapped rider

Moto2

RACE DISTANCE: 15 laps, 44.748 miles/72.015km · RACE WEATHER: Wet (air 19°C, humidity 95%, track 21°C)

Pos.	Rider	Nat.	No.	Entrant	Machine	Laps	Time & Speed
1	Johann Zarco	FRA	5	Ajo Motorsport	Kalex	15	31m 17.900s 85.7mph/ 138.0km/h
2	Jonas Folger	GER	94	AGR Team	Kalex	15	31m 22.405s
3	Sandro Cortese	GER	11	Dynavolt Intact GP	Kalex	15	31m 33.333s
4	Azlan Shah	MAL	25	IDEMITSU Honda Team Asia	Kalex	15	31m 35.248s
5	Hafizh Syahrin	MAL	55	Petronas Raceline Malaysia	Kalex	15	31m 40.758s
6	Ricard Cardus	SPA	88	JPMoto Malaysia	Suter	15	31m 42.870s
7	Simone Corsi	ITA	3	Forward Racing	Kalex	15	31m 43.659s
8	Sam Lowes	GBR	22	Speed Up Racing	Speed Up	15	31m 44.924s
9	Marcel Schrotter	GER	23	Tech 3	Tech 3	15	31m 45.385s
10	Randy Krummenacher	SWI	4	JIR Racing Team	Kalex	15	31m 45.962s
11	Alex Rins	SPA	40	Paginas Amarillas HP 40	Kalex	15	31m 48.668s
12	Lorenzo Baldassarri	ITA	7	Forward Racing	Kalex	15	31m 50.585s
13	Tomoyoshi Koyama	JPN	71	NTS T.Pro Project	NTS	15	31m 51.895s
14	Yuki Takahashi	JPN	72	Moriwaki Racing	Moriwaki	15	31m 54.482s
15	Mika Kallio	FIN	36	QMMF Racing Team	Speed Up	15	32m 01.572s
16	Julian Simon	SPA	60	QMMF Racing Team	Speed Up	15	32m 06.156s
17	Jesko Raffin	SWI	2	sports-millions-EMWE-SAG	Kalex	15	32m 07.321s
18	Alex Marquez	SPA	73	EG 0,0 Marc VDS	Kalex	15	32m 09.612s
19	Edgar Pons	SPA	57	Italtrans Racing Team	Kalex	15	32m 38.882s
20	Louis Rossi	FRA	96	Tasca Racing Scuderia Moto2	Tech 3	15	32m 49.119s
21	Florian Alt	GER	66	E-Motion IodaRacing Team	Suter	15	32m 54.016s
22	Takaaki Nakagami	JPN	30	IDEMITSU Honda Team Asia	Kalex	15	32m 59.027s
23	Robin Mulhauser	SWI	70	Technomag Racing Interwetten	Kalex	13	33m 11.291s
	Luis Salom	SPA	39	Paginas Amarillas HP 40	Kalex	9	DNF
	Thitipong Warokorn	THA	10	APH PTT The Pizza SAG	Kalex	8	DNF
	Thomas Luthi	SWI	12	Derendinger Racing Interwetten	Kalex	7	DNF
	Xavier Simeon	BEL	19	Federal Oil Gresini Moto2	Kalex	5	DNF
	Xavi Vierge	SPA	97	Tech 3	Tech 3	4	DNF
	Axel Pons	SPA	49	AGR Team	Kalex	4	DNF
	Joshua Hook	AUS	16	Technomag Racing Interwetten	Kalex	3	DNF
	Tito Rabat	SPA	1	EG 0,0 Marc VDS	Kalex	-	DNS

Fastest lap: Jonas Folger, on lap 2, 2m 4.166s, 86.4mph/139.1km/h.
Lap record: Maverick Vinales, SPA (Kalex), 1m 50.866s, 96.8mph/155.8km/h (2014).
Event best maximum speed: Azlan Shah, 159.6mph/256.9km/h (free practice).

Qualifying

Weather: Dry
Air Temp: 20° Track Temp: 24°
Humidity: 78%

1	Zarco	1m 50.339s
2	Luthi	1m 50.510s
3	Folger	1m 50.916s
4	Lowes	1m 50.953s
5	Rins	1m 50.953s
6	Syahrin	1m 51.286s
7	Nakagami	1m 51.381s
8	Pons	1m 51.384s
9	Cortese	1m 51.386s
10	Baldassarri	1m 51.486s
11	Simeon	1m 51.577s
12	Shah	1m 51.635s
13	Salom	1m 51.635s
14	Simon	1m 51.700s
15	Marquez	1m 51.755s
16	Corsi	1m 51.927s
17	Cardus	1m 52.029s
18	Krummenacher	1m 52.056s
19	Warokorn	1m 52.248s
20	Kallio	1m 52.261s
21	Schrotter	1m 52.330s
22	Mulhauser	1m 52.387s
23	Hook	1m 52.581s
24	Pons	1m 52.778s
25	Takahashi	1m 52.911s
26	Rossi	1m 53.070s
27	Vierge	1m 53.551s
28	Raffin	1m 53.613s
29	Koyama	1m 53.949s
30	Alt	1m 54.106s
	Rabat	No Time

Fastest race laps

1	Folger	2m 04.166s
2	Zarco	2m 04.252s
3	Cortese	2m 04.305s
4	Cardus	2m 05.081s
5	Rins	2m 05.127s
6	Shah	2m 05.159s
7	Marquez	2m 05.384s
8	Nakagami	2m 05.523s
9	Schrotter	2m 05.566s
10	Syahrin	2m 05.651s
11	Krummenacher	2m 05.673s
12	Lowes	2m 05.729s
13	Baldassarri	2m 05.779s
14	Koyama	2m 05.888s
15	Salom	2m 05.910s
16	Corsi	2m 05.984s
17	Takahashi	2m 06.054s
18	Kallio	2m 06.219s
19	Luthi	2m 06.276s
20	Pons	2m 06.601s
21	Pons	2m 06.679s
22	Warokorn	2m 06.774s
23	Mulhauser	2m 06.799s
24	Vierge	2m 06.835s
25	Raffin	2m 06.842s
26	Simeon	2m 06.914s
27	Simon	2m 06.978s
28	Hook	2m 07.208s
29	Alt	2m 07.772s
30	Rossi	2m 08.373s

Championship Points

1	Zarco	309
2	Rabat	206
3	Rins	189
4	Lowes	152
5	Folger	145
6	Luthi	142
7	Simeon	96
8	Morbidelli	84
9	Cortese	78
10	Nakagami	69
11	Corsi	69
12	Aegerter	62
13	Marquez	62
14	Simon	58
15	Syahrin	56
16	Baldassarri	56
17	Kallio	54
18	Salom	50
19	West	30
20	Pons	28
21	Schrotter	27
22	Krummenacher	25
23	Shah	24
24	Cardus	16
25	Rossi	7
26	Koyama	3
27	Takahashi	2
28	Mulhauser	1

Constructor Points

1	Kalex	370
2	Speed Up	174
3	Tech 3	34
4	Suter	16
5	NTS	3
6	Moriwaki	2

Moto3

RACE DISTANCE: 13 laps, 38.782 miles/62.413km · RACE WEATHER: Wet (air 19°C, humidity 95%, track 22°C)

Pos.	Rider	Nat.	No.	Entrant	Machine	Laps	Time & Speed
1	Niccolo Antonelli	ITA	23	Ongetta-Rivacold	Honda	13	28m 03.391s 82.9mph/ 133.4km/h
2	Miguel Oliveira	POR	44	Red Bull KTM Ajo	KTM	13	28m 04.444s
3	Jorge Navarro	SPA	9	Estrella Galicia 0,0	Honda	13	28m 11.920s
4	Isaac Vinales	SPA	32	RBA Racing Team	KTM	13	28m 14.465s
5	Zulfahmi Khairuddin	MAL	63	Drive M7 SIC	KTM	13	28m 16.434s
6	Danny Kent	GBR	52	Leopard Racing	Honda	13	28m 18.615s
7	Enea Bastianini	ITA	33	Gresini Racing Team Moto3	Honda	13	28m 19.264s
8	Karel Hanika	CZE	98	Red Bull KTM Ajo	KTM	13	28m 20.954s
9	John McPhee	GBR	17	SAXOPRINT RTG	Honda	13	28m 21.544s
10	Efren Vazquez	SPA	7	Leopard Racing	Honda	13	28m 21.947s
11	Jorge Martin	SPA	88	MAPFRE Team MAHINDRA	Mahindra	13	28m 23.287s
12	Jakub Kornfeil	CZE	84	Drive M7 SIC	KTM	13	28m 24.283s
13	Tatsuki Suzuki	JPN	24	CIP	Mahindra	13	28m 28.536s
14	Andrea Locatelli	ITA	55	Gresini Racing Team Moto3	Honda	13	28m 31.846s
15	Francesco Bagnaia	ITA	21	MAPFRE Team MAHINDRA	Mahindra	13	28m 32.240s
16	Gabriel Rodrigo	ARG	91	RBA Racing Team	KTM	13	28m 33.379s
17	Brad Binder	RSA	41	Red Bull KTM Ajo	KTM	13	28m 34.110s
18	Stefano Manzi	ITA	29	San Carlo Team Italia	Mahindra	13	28m 35.340s
19	Jules Danilo	FRA	95	Ongetta-Rivacold	Honda	13	28m 35.537s
20	Andrea Migno	ITA	16	SKY Racing Team VR46	KTM	13	28m 38.439s
21	Juanfran Guevara	SPA	58	MAPFRE Team MAHINDRA	Mahindra	13	28m 50.633s
22	Manuel Pagliani	ITA	96	San Carlo Team Italia	Mahindra	13	28m 52.187s
23	Philipp Oettl	GER	65	Schedl GP Racing	KTM	13	28m 52.763s
24	Lorenzo Dalla Porta	ITA	48	Husqvarna Factory Laglisse	Husqvarna	13	29m 00.251s
25	Keisuke Kurihara	JPN	27	Musashi RT Harc-Pro	Honda	13	29m 03.122s
26	Maria Herrera	SPA	6	Husqvarna Factory Laglisse	Husqvarna	13	29m 10.426s
27	Darryn Binder	RSA	40	Outox Reset Drink Team	Mahindra	13	29m 23.012s
28	Romano Fenati	ITA	5	SKY Racing Team VR46	KTM	13	29m 33.055s
29	Ana Carrasco	SPA	22	RBA Racing Team	KTM	13	29m 55.696s
	Remy Gardner	AUS	2	CIP	Mahindra	10	DNF
	Livio Loi	BEL	11	RW Racing GP	Honda	4	DNF
	Hiroki Ono	JPN	76	Leopard Racing	Honda	2	DNF
	Ryo Mizuno	JPN	34	Musashi RT Harc-Pro	Honda	1	DNF
	Alexis Masbou	FRA	10	SAXOPRINT RTG	Honda	1	DNF
	Alessandro Tonucci	ITA	19	Outox Reset Drink Team	Mahindra	1	DNF

Fastest lap: Isaac Vinales, on lap 9, 2m 7.602s, 84.1mph/135.4km/h.
Lap record: Alex Marquez, SPA (Honda), 1m 57.112s, 91.7mph/147.5km/h (2014).
Event best maximum speed: John McPhee, 136.5mph/219.6km/h (qualifying).

Qualifying

Weather: Dry
Air Temp: 21° Track Temp: 27°
Humidity: 62%

1	Fenati	1m 56.484s
2	Oliveira	1m 56.657s
3	Navarro	1m 56.720s
4	Antonelli	1m 56.887s
5	Bastianini	1m 56.927s
6	Kent	1m 56.998s
7	Vinales	1m 57.017s
8	Kornfeil	1m 57.089s
9	Loi	1m 57.092s
10	Binder	1m 57.147s
11	Bagnaia	1m 57.191s
12	Ono	1m 57.192s
13	Oettl	1m 57.288s
14	Guevara	1m 57.525s
15	Khairuddin	1m 57.585s
16	Dalla Porta	1m 57.635s
17	Migno	1m 57.659s
18	Pagliani	1m 57.687s
19	Masbou	1m 57.694s
20	Hanika	1m 57.715s
21	Suzuki	1m 57.732s
22	Manzi	1m 57.772s
23	Martin	1m 57.812s
24	McPhee	1m 57.968s
25	Rodrigo	1m 57.990s
26	Herrera	1m 57.993s
27	Vazquez	1m 58.002s
28	Danilo	1m 58.039s
29	Quartararo	1m 58.153s
30	Gardner	1m 58.388s
31	Binder	1m 58.603s
32	Tonucci	1m 58.965s
33	Mizuno	1m 59.282s
34	Carrasco	1m 59.308s
35	Locatelli	1m 59.889s
36	Kurihara	2m 00.389s

Fastest race laps

1	Vinales	2m 07.602s
2	Navarro	2m 07.797s
3	Oliveira	2m 07.826s
4	Binder	2m 08.019s
5	Antonelli	2m 08.070s
6	Kent	2m 08.382s
7	Khairuddin	2m 08.775s
8	Vazquez	2m 08.848s
9	Hanika	2m 08.925s
10	Martin	2m 09.002s
11	Bastianini	2m 09.079s
12	Suzuki	2m 09.284s
13	McPhee	2m 09.357s
14	Manzi	2m 09.514s
15	Kornfeil	2m 09.578s
16	Rodrigo	2m 09.647s
17	Locatelli	2m 09.732s
18	Loi	2m 09.765s
19	Bagnaia	2m 10.038s
20	Ono	2m 10.105s
21	Danilo	2m 10.399s
22	Guevara	2m 10.508s
23	Migno	2m 10.683s
24	Pagliani	2m 10.887s
25	Dalla Porta	2m 10.900s
26	Gardner	2m 11.012s
27	Oettl	2m 11.017s
28	Fenati	2m 11.863s
29	Kurihara	2m 12.507s
30	Herrera	2m 13.232s
31	Binder	2m 13.542s
32	Carrasco	2m 15.784s

Championship Points

1	Kent	244
2	Bastianini	188
3	Oliveira	179
4	Antonelli	161
5	Fenati	155
6	Vazquez	135
7	Binder	110
8	Navarro	108
9	Vinales	95
10	Quartararo	92
11	McPhee	77
12	Bagnaia	73
13	Masbou	63
14	Oettl	57
15	Loi	56
16	Kornfeil	52
17	Hanika	41
18	Martin	38
19	Locatelli	33
20	Migno	30
21	Ajo	21
22	Ono	21
23	Khairuddin	15
24	Guevara	15
25	Dalla Porta	13
26	Suzuki	9
27	Danilo	7
28	Manzi	7
29	Herrera	4
30	Ferrari	1

Constructor Points

1	Honda	355
2	KTM	266
3	Mahindra	107
4	Husqvarna	80

AUSTRALIAN GRAND PRIX

PHILLIP ISLAND CIRCUIT

AUSTRALIAN MOTORCYCLE GRAND PRIX

Phillip Island 2015

Inset, left: Cunning, or just gifted? Marquez celebrated his first Phillip Island MotoGP finish with an inch-perfect last-lap win.

Main: Mid-race, and Marquez leads for a spell; Iannone and Rossi in close pursuit.

Photos: Gold & Goose

Above: **Feathers flew when Iannone met a seagull while in the lead.**

Photo: Gold & Goose

I N the light of what happened a week later, so many aspects of the Australian GP that had seemed innocent at the time became tainted with the faint reek of conspiracy. Especially to those – the majority of racing fans and all of Italy, it seemed – who took Valentino Rossi's part.

Even the cheeky new-found confidence of rookie Jack Miller gained significance. He was in the pre-race conference to confirm his move to the Marc VDS team with all of his crew. A year before, Miller had been guarded while in the company of contemporary legends. This time, wondering about the treacherous recent race weather, he jerked a thumb towards Rossi and said that perhaps "this bastard" had been making special arrangements "with somebody upstairs".

A week later, he was far from the only rider or racing luminary to attach unfavourable epithets to Rossi's name; but they were not speaking in jest.

What we thought we had seen was one of the best MotoGP races for the previous ten or maybe 20 years – four riders, all with a strong chance of victory, fighting from start to finish and crossing the line within barely a second. Somebody counted 52 passes. On the last lap, the race could have gone almost any way – and at the last gasp it went the other way instead.

Actually, Lorenzo had appeared to have it sewn up, while Rossi, Marquez and Iannone traded blows a little way back. Marquez was at a loss to explain where he had found the urge for his blazing last lap, closing a gap of six-tenths to leader Lorenzo and then slicing past with apparent ease. But

he volunteered an explanation for having dropped back mid-race. His front tyre was becoming queasy. "It was time to cool down for a bit."

Just behind, Iannone did the same to Rossi, then used his Ducati's blatantly obvious extra speed to stay clear down the straight. For the second time in two races, Valentino had been beaten in a straight fight by a rival whom normally one would have expected him to defeat.

Brooding in the days that followed, Rossi assembled the evidence to support his assertion of where Marquez had found that last-lap speed. In fact, he'd had it in his pocket all race long. Instead of using it, he'd been "playing with us", to help Lorenzo escape. The reason was a personal grudge against Rossi, stemming from incidents in Argentina and Assen, where they had clashed physically and Marquez had come off worse; and fed by a desire to prevent a tenth title for the old warhorse, to make an easier target for Marquez to do even better.

The debacle to come at Sepang had its origins back then, but the catalyst had been this race within a race – whether Marquez's actions had been innocent or not.

This important turning point occurred on almost every rider's favourite circuit, and Phillip Island was showing its smiliest face. Of course there were chill winds and the odd smattering of wetness, but race day in particular was beautifully benign; and in response, the racing was of the highest order.

The weekend had started in high spirits after the bad weather of Motegi, with Rossi on fine form when asked a

Left: Former GP winners West and Elias had an enjoyable scrap, albeit at the tail of the field.

Below left: Maverick Vinales rode like a demon to overcome a top-speed deficit and finish sixth on the Suzuki GSX-RR.

Below centre left: Damian Cudlin stood in for the injured de Angelis, but retired after nine laps.

Below: Home-crowd favourite Jack Miller took Open honours for the second time.

Bottom: "He was playing with us." Marquez checks over his shoulder to see Rossi and Iannone on his back wheel.

Photos: Gold & Goose

gormless question about the state of his relationship with team-mate/title rival Lorenzo. "We are very happy about your interest," he replied, looking impish. "We have a secret diary about our relationship … we will keep it secret until the last race."

There was more feel-good with the announcement that Nicky Hayden was to be inducted as the 22nd MotoGP Legend at his last GP at Valencia. Hayden's name joins an illustrious list, where his tally of just three grand prix wins is conspicuously small. He had earned his place for other reasons: his untiring hard work, good manners and amenable nature, and his stature as an exemplar of the best aspects of the sport. Plus, of course, beating Rossi to the championship when he had been the stronger in a last-round shootout in 2006.

Two years after the resurfacing that had caused unprecedented tyre wear, the track had lost much of that early grip – no lap records, while Bridgestone had taken another step. In 2014, an asymmetric front had been popular, but had been blamed for a number of accidents under braking later in the race as the temperature dropped, robbing Marquez and Crutchlow of victory and a podium respectively. Crutchlow admitted being apprehensive about the second-generation version, which now spread the soft compound from the right shoulder across 70 per cent of the tyre. It worked well.

It was not all sweetness and light, though. Tito Rabat's brave attempt to salvage at least second place overall went awry on the first day, with a fast crash out of the final corner. This aggravated his existing left-arm fracture, and he finally gave up to fly home for further treatment.

In Moto3, Quartararo's agony continued. He ran only on the first day of practice and was languishing well out of the top 20 when he elected to withdraw from this race and the next. His ankle injury was still clearly far from race fit.

He missed an interesting race with quite unexpected consequences. Once again, Kent missed the chance to tie up the title, brought down in a controversial three-bike collision; while Oliveira's second win in four races (he had been second in the other two) was making the back of his season resemble the front half of Kent's. The upgrade to his KTM had played a major part, but Oliveira's tactical strength had been in evidence even before that arrived.

Arithmetically, Oliveira had now supplanted Bastianini (also down in the Kent crash) as a rival to steal Kent's seemingly pre-ordained crown at the last gasp. As for the crash, it caused a bitter round of recriminations. Bastianini blamed Kent for being overzealous; Kent blamed Antonelli for clipping his rear wheel after he'd been taken by surprise; but Race Direction agreed without difficulty that it had been a simple racing incident.

MOTOGP RACE – 27 laps

Marquez, yet to finish a MotoGP race at the Australian track, took over free practice and then claimed pole number eight; Iannone was alongside and then Lorenzo, peevish because the Ducati rider had achieved his lap by following the Yamaha. Rossi was on row four, behind Pedrosa, Crutchlow and an inspired Vinales, who had made up with interest through the sweeping corners the 15km/h he had been losing on the straight.

Ducati horsepower meant a lot here. Iannone seized control in the first corner, consigning Lorenzo to second. Marquez took third on lap two, leaving Pedrosa ahead of Crutchlow and Rossi.

Lorenzo was ahead of Iannone over the line, only for the red bike to surge past again before the first corner, a pattern that would be repeated for the next four laps, and spasmodically with other riders thereafter. The Ducatis were very fast: 348.0km/h the best, in free practice, ten faster than Marquez's best, and 14 more than Lorenzo; and the downhill straight with its fast entry meant he could make the most of it.

Above: **Pedrosa, Crutchlow and Vinales fought over fifth.**

Top right: **Lorenzo Baldassarri took a worthy first podium in Moto2.**

Above right: **With Rabat absent and Zarco off form, Rins and Lowes were left to battle in Moto2. Rins would soon escape.**

Right: **Oliveira leads McPhee, Fenati, Bagnaia and Navarro.**

Below right: **Brad Binder appeared a possible winner, but Oliveira (44) and Vazquez (7) narrowly got the better of him over the line.**

Photos: Gold & Goose

Rossi was on the move by lap three, past Pedrosa first and next time Crutchlow, who had got ahead of the factory Honda. Rossi was still close, and next time around he passed Marquez for the first time, though shortly afterwards Iannone was ahead of both again.

The junior factory Ducati man was riding the race of his life, including demolishing a seagull on the drop from Lukey Heights – it looked as though he had head-butted the bird, but in fact it had hit his cowling and taken a small chunk out of it, although leaving the top wing unmolested.

By the time the front four started to put a gap on Crutchlow, after one-third distance, Lorenzo's earlier runaway – at one point almost 1.5 seconds – was coming into jeopardy. Marquez was slicing a few tenths every lap, and the other two were coming with him. At least for a while. But by lap 17, when Marquez was ready to pounce, Iannone was back in front of Rossi and 1.3 seconds adrift.

Marquez led laps 18 to 20, but he couldn't get away and his front tyre was becoming too hot. Lorenzo took over again, and by then all four were together again, for that classic finale. Marquez had started the last lap third, behind Iannone, surged past him before the Southern Loop, taken whole chunks out of Lorenzo's lead braking for Honda Hairpin, then dived inside to block the exit from MG corner, to control the track's tyre-punishing trademark final bends.

Iannone's best of many overtakes was on lap 25. He was fourth; just ahead, Rossi pushed inside Marquez at MG in a textbook blocker. It slowed both of them. Iannone was perfectly poised to dive through the gap as they ran wide, to take over second.

His most important pass was on the final lap, a few yards further on. Rossi had outbraked him into the corner, but he was ready and took back third place right on the exit. From there, the Desmosedici surge meant he was invulnerable, for his third podium of the season.

And Rossi? He was the big loser, by a heartbreaking 88-hundredths of a second. From victory in 2014 to fourth place in 2015 was especially sobering, because it meant a

loss of seven of the 18-points advantage he had brought to his favourite circuit.

Behind them, it had taken Pedrosa until lap 16 to get ahead of Crutchlow, who complained afterwards of constant wheelspin. More trouble was in store. Early on, Vinales had got the better of Suzuki team-mate Espargaro and had been inches behind the Honda pair all race long, and ahead of the fading Crutchlow with three laps to go. Remarkably, he was only two seconds off Pedrosa at the finish.

Aleix had dropped away to be passed for eighth by brother Pol, the pair still close at the end; Smith was less than a second away. Redding had also closed to within a second by the finish after a dire start. He'd defeated Petrucci in the closing laps, both leaving a fading and shame-faced Dovizioso trailing in an inexplicable 13th.

Miller had a strong race to be top Open bike for the second time, although eventually he had ceded a long-held 14th to Bautista. "Okay, it's only 15th," he said. "But no one crashed: it was one of those races."

Hayden had stopped trackside with electronic gremlins; de Angelis replacement Damien Cudlin had retired to the pits. The rest trailed in with various tales of woe.

The title was in the balance, even more than before. Nobody could imagine quite how tense things would become in Malaysia.

MOTO2 RACE – 25 laps

Rabat's absence gave rookie Rins the perfect opportunity to take over second place in the championship. He seized it with both hands.

Having dominated free practice and started from pole, the Spaniard finished the first lap third, behind front-row companions Lowes and surprise second-fastest qualifier Axel Pons. By the end of the straight, though, he drafted past both and would never see another bike in front of him again.

Ever the author of his own misfortune, Pons was called in for a jump-start ride-through, while Lowes succumbed to

MOTO3 RACE – 23 laps

Circumstances broke up Phillip Island's usual huge group of leaders, and also meant that the still-close finish (five within three-tenths) wasn't the only climax to a typically thrilling race, rich in tactics, variety and breakneck daring.

The first came on lap 14, in the middle of a close pursuit pack. Runaway points leader Kent was making his way back through, having been put off track four laps before by crashing erstwhile early leader Bagnaia.

He'd had another tangle with Bastianini in the process; now he moved inside Antonelli to regain sixth. But Antonelli was committed to his line, his front touched Kent's rear and the Englishman went flying. As he slumped in the gravel, he didn't realise that Bastianini had also been brought down in the same crash, later blaming Kent directly for the cause of it.

The second climax was the finish. First-time pole-starter McPhee had crashed out early; but with three more fast Hondas also having gone, there still wasn't much room to move up front.

Binder led for several laps before running wide; Oliveira was there to take over, interrupted by Fenati, once over the line by Kornfeil and elsewhere by Navarro.

On the last lap, Oliveira took control; and in the final scramble, Vazquez squeezed second from Binder and Navarro, Kornfeil feet behind.

Fenati had lost touch in sixth. Oettl shaded Vinales and Masbou, survivors of the pursuit pack.

Remy Gardner had the ride of his short GP career at the track where his father Wayne had won the first two 500 GPs. Only just over a second off this group for tenth, his first points of the year, he had snitched the position on the last lap from Maria Herrera.

strong pressure from Luthi at the start of lap nine. By that time, Rins already had a gap of almost 1.4 seconds and had only to keep going to claim his second win of the year, by fully six seconds.

Luthi's reign in second lasted only until lap 17, when he ran on to the grass outside MG and slipped off, remounting for an eventual 15th.

Lowes would not be troubled and was glad of the 20 points. They'd changed the gearing slightly only to be caught out by a shift in the wind. "It was okay for the lap, but impossible on the straight. I realised that the first time they came flying past me at the end of the first lap."

Behind all this, Folger had come charging through from the fifth row of the grid, taking what was then fourth off Kallio's Speed Up on lap six. He quickly outpaced a pack of hard men that included new champion Zarco, Baldassarri, Cortese, Simeon and Nakagami.

While Zarco had an undistinguished race, it was Baldassarri who emerged from the brawl to catch and pass Folger on lap 17. The German stayed poised to counterattack for three laps, then suddenly slowed and cruised to the pits – with a flapping flat back tyre!

That left a career-first podium for the Italian teenager, while a long way back Nakagami finally, if narrowly, got the better of Simeon for fourth.

Salom had cut through to take sixth, well clear of Zarco by the end, with Kallio dropping away in eighth.

Krummenacher had lost touch with this group to fall into the clutches of Marquez, who prevailed at the end for ninth.

A long way back, a brave ride yielded 11th for Franco Morbidelli – the Italtrans Kalex rider back from injury after missing four races. He was able to stay over a second clear of the next battle, where Schrotter had Corsi and Cardus almost alongside, past the flag in 0.059 second.

Cortese crashed out; Luthi took the last point.

Rins now had 214 to Rabat's 206 – and Rabat would miss the next race as well. Things were going from bad to worse for the defeated defender.

PHILLIP ISLAND
27 laps
Length: 4.448 km / 2.764 miles
Width: 13m

Key
96/60 kph/mph
Gear

PRAMAC AUSTRALIAN MOTORCYCLE GRAND PRIX

16–18 OCTOBER, 2015

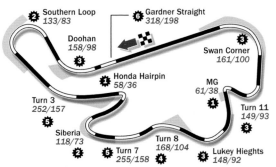

Southern Loop 133/83
Gardner Straight 318/198
Doohan 158/98
Swan Corner 161/100
Honda Hairpin 58/36
MG 61/38
Turn 3 252/157
Turn 11 149/93
Siberia 118/73
Turn 8 168/104
Turn 7 255/158
Lukey Hieghts 148/92

MotoGP

RACE DISTANCE: 27 laps, 74.624 miles/120.096km · RACE WEATHER: Dry (air 15°C, humidity 59%, track 42°C)

Pos.	Rider	Nat.	No.	Entrant	Machine Tyres	Race tyre choice	Laps	Time & speed
1	**Marc Marquez**	SPA	93	Repsol Honda Team	Honda RC213V B	F: Asymmetric/R: Medium	27	40m 33.849s
								110.4mph/
								177.6km/h
2	**Jorge Lorenzo**	SPA	99	Movistar Yamaha MotoGP	Yamaha YZR-M1 B	F: Asymmetric/R: Medium	27	40m 34.098s
3	**Andrea Iannone**	ITA	29	Ducati Team	Ducati Desmosedici B	F: Asymmetric/R: Medium	27	40m 34.779s
4	**Valentino Rossi**	ITA	46	Movistar Yamaha MotoGP	Yamaha YZR-M1 B	F: Asymmetric/R: Medium	27	40m 34.907s
5	**Dani Pedrosa**	SPA	26	Repsol Honda Team	Honda RC213V B	F: Asymmetric/R: Medium	27	40m 38.911s
6	**Maverick Vinales**	SPA	25	Team SUZUKI ECSTAR	Suzuki GSX-RR B	F: Asymmetric/R: Medium	27	40m 40.649s
7	**Cal Crutchlow**	GBR	35	LCR Honda	Honda RC213V B	F: Asymmetric/R: Medium	27	40m 43.224s
8	**Pol Espargaro**	SPA	44	Monster Yamaha Tech 3	Yamaha YZR-M1 B	F: Asymmetric/R: Medium	27	40m 52.250s
9	**Aleix Espargaro**	SPA	41	Team SUZUKI ECSTAR	Suzuki GSX-RR B	F: Asymmetric/R: Medium	27	40m 53.888s
10	**Bradley Smith**	GBR	38	Monster Yamaha Tech 3	Yamaha YZR-M1 B	F: Asymmetric/R: Medium	27	40m 54.506s
11	**Scott Redding**	GBR	45	EG 0,0 Marc VDS	Honda RC213V B	F: Asymmetric/R: Medium	27	40m 55.695s
12	**Danilo Petrucci**	ITA	9	Octo Pramac Racing	Ducati Desmosedici B	F: Asymmetric/R: Medium	27	40m 56.689s
13	**Andrea Dovizioso**	ITA	4	Ducati Team	Ducati Desmosedici B	F: Asymmetric/R: Medium	27	41m 03.017s
14	**Alvaro Bautista**	SPA	19	Aprilia Racing Team Gresini	Aprilia RS-GP B	F: Asymmetric/R: Soft	27	41m 11.093s
15	**Jack Miller**	AUS	43	LCR Honda	Honda RC213V-RS B	F: Asymmetric/R: Soft	27	41m 14.041s
16	Hector Barbera	SPA	8	Avintia Racing	Ducati Desmosedici Open B	F: Asymmetric/R: Medium	27	41m 22.112s
17	Yonny Hernandez	COL	68	Octo Pramac Racing	Ducati Desmosedici B	F: Asymmetric/R: Medium	27	41m 22.421s
18	Loris Baz	FRA	76	Forward Racing	Yamaha Forward B	F: Asymmetric/R: Soft	27	41m 22.526s
19	Eugene Laverty	IRL	50	Aspar MotoGP Team	Honda RC213V-RS B	F: Asymmetric/R: Soft	27	41m 24.050s
20	Mike di Meglio	FRA	63	Avintia Racing	Ducati Desmosedici Open B	F: Asymmetric/R: Medium	27	41m 24.111s
21	Stefan Bradl	GER	6	Aprilia Racing Team Gresini	Aprilia RS-GP B	F: Asymmetric/R: Soft	27	41m 24.126s
22	Toni Elias	SPA	24	Forward Racing	Yamaha Forward B	F: Asymmetric/R: Soft	27	41m 54.791s
23	Anthony West	AUS	13	AB Motoracing	Honda RC213V-RS B	F: Asymmetric/R: Soft	27	41m 57.303s
	Nicky Hayden	USA	69	Aspar MotoGP Team	Honda RC213V-RS B	F: Asymmetric/R: Soft	9	DNF-technical
	Damian Cudlin	AUS	55	E-Motion IodaRacing Team	ART B	F: Asymmetric/R: Soft	9	DNF-mechanical

Fastest lap: Marc Marquez, on lap 27, 1m 29.280s, 111.4mph/179.3km/h.
Lap record: Marc Marquez, SPA (Honda), 1m 28.108s, 112.9mph/181.7km/h (2013).
Event best maximum speed: Andrea Dovizioso, 216.2mph/348.0km/h (free practice).

Qualifying

Weather: Dry
Air Temp: 16° **Humidity:** 63%
Track Temp: 41°

1	Marquez	1m 28.364s
2	Iannone	1m 28.680s
3	Lorenzo	1m 28.680s
4	Pedrosa	1m 28.712s
5	Crutchlow	1m 28.912s
6	Vinales	1m 28.932s
7	Rossi	1m 29.014s
8	A. Espargaro	1m 29.015s
9	P. Espargaro	1m 29.222s
10	Dovizioso	1m 29.267s
11	Redding	1m 29.499s
12	Smith	1m 29.626s
13	Petrucci	1m 29.918s
14	Barbera	1m 30.064s
15	Miller	1m 30.104s
16	Laverty	1m 30.105s
17	Hernandez	1m 30.135s
18	Bautista	1m 30.147s
19	Baz	1m 30.173s
20	Hayden	1m 30.376s
21	Bradl	1m 30.634s
22	Di Meglio	1m 30.959s
23	West	1m 31.205s
24	Elias	1m 31.837s
25	Cudlin	1m 33.884s

Fastest race laps

1	Marquez	1m 29.280s
2	Rossi	1m 29.369s
3	Iannone	1m 29.509s
4	Vinales	1m 29.622s
5	Lorenzo	1m 29.711s
6	Pedrosa	1m 29.796s
7	Crutchlow	1m 29.875s
8	Dovizioso	1m 30.067s
9	A. Espargaro	1m 30.078s
10	Redding	1m 30.169s
11	P. Espargaro	1m 30.170s
12	Smith	1m 30.207s
13	Petrucci	1m 30.319s
14	Bautista	1m 30.319s
15	Miller	1m 30.480s
16	Hernandez	1m 30.791s
17	Baz	1m 30.816s
18	Hayden	1m 30.837s
19	Laverty	1m 30.838s
20	Barbera	1m 31.042s
21	Di Meglio	1m 31.070s
22	Bradl	1m 31.214s
23	West	1m 31.927s
24	Elias	1m 32.008s
25	Cudlin	1m 33.323s

Championship Points

1	Rossi	296
2	Lorenzo	285
3	Marquez	222
4	Iannone	188
5	Pedrosa	165
6	Smith	158
7	Dovizioso	153
8	Crutchlow	107
9	Petrucci	97
10	P. Espargaro	96
11	A. Espargaro	88
12	Vinales	84
13	Redding	78
14	Hernandez	49
15	Barbera	30
16	Baz	28
17	Bautista	28
18	Miller	17
19	Hayden	16
20	Bradl	11
21	E. Laverty	9
22	Nakasuga	8
23	Pirro	8
24	Di Meglio	8
25	Aoyama	5
26	Takahashi	4
27	De Angelis	2

Constructor Points

1	Yamaha	362
2	Honda	310
3	Ducati	237
4	Suzuki	120
5	Yamaha Forward	33
6	Aprilia	28
7	ART	2

Grid order	1	2	3	4	5	6	7	8	9	10	11	12	13	14	15	16	17	18	19	20	21	22	23	24	25	26	27	
93 MARQUEZ	99	99	99	99	99	99	99	99	99	99	99	99	99	99	99	99	99	99	99	93	93	93	99	99	99	99	93	1
29 IANNONE	29	29	29	29	93	29	93	93	93	93	93	93	93	93	93	93	93	99	99	99	93	29	93	93	29	29	99	2
99 LORENZO	26	93	93	93	46	46	29	46	46	46	46	46	46	46	46	29	29	29	29	29	93	46	46	46	93	29		3
26 PEDROSA	93	26	35	46	35	93	46	29	29	29	29	29	29	29	29	46	46	46	46	46	29	93	46	46				4
35 CRUTCHLOW	35	35	26	35	29	35	26	35	35	35	35	35	35	35	35	26	26	26	26	26	26	26	26	26	26	26	26	5
25 VINALES	46	46	46	26	26	26	35	26	26	35	35	26	26	26	26	35	35	35	35	35	35	25	25	25	25	25	25	6
46 ROSSI	41	41	41	25	25	25	25	25	25	26	25	25	25	25	25	25	25	25	25	25	25	35	35	35	35	35	35	7
41 A. ESPARGARO	25	25	25	41	41	41	41	41	41	41	41	41	41	41	44	44	44	44	44	44	44	44	44	44	44	44	44	8
44 P. ESPARGARO	9	9	44	44	44	4	4	44	44	44	44	44	44	44	41	41	41	41	41	41	41	41	41	41	41	41	41	9
4 DOVIZIOSO	4	44	4	4	4	44	44	4	4	4	4	4	38	38	38	38	38	38	38	38	38	38	38	38	38	38		10
45 REDDING	44	4	38	38	38	38	38	38	4	38	38	38	4	4	45	45	45	45	45	45	45	45	45	45	45			11
38 SMITH	38	38	38	9	9	9	9	9	9	9	45	45	45	4	4	9	9	9	9	9	9	9	9	9	9	9	9	12
9 PETRUCCI	43	43	43	43	43	45	45	45	45	45	9	9	9	9	9	4	4	4	4	4	4	4	4	4	4	4		13
8 BARBERA	19	19	19	45	45	43	43	43	43	43	43	43	43	43	43	43	43	43	43	43	43	43	19	19	19			14
43 MILLER	45	45	45	19	19	19	19	19	19	19	19	19	19	19	19	19	19	19	19	19	43	43	43					15
50 LAVERTY	68	68	68	68	68	68	68	69	68	68	68	68	76	68	68	68	76	68	68	68	68	8						
68 HERNANDEZ	6	6	50	76	69	50	76	76	76	68	8	76	68	76	76	76	68	76	76	8	68	68						
19 BAUTISTA	76	50	76	50	76	76	76	68	69	8	76	8	8	76	8	8	8	8	76	76	76							
76 BAZ	50	76	6	69	50	6	50	50	50	6	50	50	50	6	50	6	6	50	50	50	50							
69 HAYDEN	63	69	69	6	6	8	50	8	50	50	6	50	50	63	50	50	50	6	50	50	63							
6 BRADL	69	63	63	63	63	69	6	6	63	63	63	63	63	8	63	63	63	6	6	6	6							
63 DI MEGLIO	8	8	8	63	8	63	63	63	8	13	13	6	13	13	6	13	24	13	13	24	24	24						
13 WEST	24	24	13	13	13	13	13	13	13	24	24	24	24	24	13	24	13	24	24	13	13							
24 ELIAS	13	13	24	24	24	24	24	24	24																			
55 CUDLIN	55	55	55	55	55	55	55	55	55																			

55 Pit stop 55 Lapped rider

Moto2

RACE DISTANCE: 25 laps, 69.096 miles/111.200km · RACE WEATHER: Dry (air 15°C, humidity 60%, track 42°C)

Pos.	Rider	Nat.	No.	Entrant	Machine	Laps	Time & Speed
1	Alex Rins	SPA	40	Paginas Amarillas HP 40	Kalex	25	39m 00.084s 106.3mph/ 171.0km/h
2	Sam Lowes	GBR	22	Speed Up Racing	Speed Up	25	39m 06.717s
3	Lorenzo Baldassarri	ITA	7	Forward Racing	Kalex	25	39m 10.492s
4	Takaaki Nakagami	JPN	30	IDEMITSU Honda Team Asia	Kalex	25	39m 15.620s
5	Xavier Simeon	BEL	19	Federal Oil Gresini Moto2	Kalex	25	39m 16.289s
6	Luis Salom	SPA	39	Paginas Amarillas HP 40	Kalex	25	39m 17.325s
7	Johann Zarco	FRA	5	Ajo Motorsport	Kalex	25	39m 20.540s
8	Mika Kallio	FIN	36	QMMF Racing Team	Speed Up	25	39m 21.967s
9	Alex Marquez	SPA	73	EG 0,0 Marc VDS	Kalex	25	39m 24.557s
10	Randy Krummenacher	SWI	4	JIR Racing Team	Kalex	25	39m 24.643s
11	Franco Morbidelli	ITA	21	Italtrans Racing Team	Kalex	25	39m 35.187s
12	Marcel Schrotter	GER	23	Tech 3	Tech 3	25	39m 36.667s
13	Simone Corsi	ITA	3	Forward Racing	Kalex	25	39m 36.672s
14	Ricard Cardus	SPA	88	JPMoto Malaysia	Suter	25	39m 36.726s
15	Thomas Luthi	SWI	12	Derendinger Racing Interwetten	Kalex	25	39m 38.199s
16	Hafizh Syahrin	MAL	55	Petronas Raceline Malaysia	Kalex	25	39m 47.299s
17	Jesko Raffin	SWI	2	sports-millions-EMWE-SAG	Kalex	25	39m 47.338s
18	Julian Simon	SPA	60	QMMF Racing Team	Speed Up	25	39m 47.389s
19	Xavi Vierge	SPA	97	Tech 3	Tech 3	25	39m 47.466s
20	Joshua Hook	AUS	16	Technomag Racing Interwetten	Kalex	25	39m 48.047s
21	Azlan Shah	MAL	25	IDEMITSU Honda Team Asia	Kalex	25	39m 55.357s
22	Edgar Pons	SPA	57	Italtrans Racing Team	Kalex	25	39m 58.525s
23	Louis Rossi	FRA	96	Tasca Racing Scuderia Moto2	Tech 3	25	39m 59.313s
24	Axel Pons	SPA	49	AGR Team	Kalex	25	40m 00.405s
25	Thitipong Warokorn	THA	10	APH PTT The Pizza SAG	Kalex	25	40m 26.562s
	Jonas Folger	GER	94	AGR Team	Kalex	21	DNF
	Sandro Cortese	GER	11	Dynavolt Intact GP	Kalex	14	DNF
	Florian Alt	GER	66	E-Motion IodaRacing Team	Suter	10	DNF
	Robin Mulhauser	SWI	70	Technomag Racing Interwetten	Kalex	9	DNF
	Tito Rabat	SPA	1	EG 0,0 Marc VDS	Kalex	-	DNS

Fastest lap: Alex Rins, on lap 10, 1m 32.880s, 107.1mph/172.4km/h.
Lap record: Alex de Angelis, RSM (Speed Up), 1m 32.814s,107.2mph/172.5km/h (2013).
Event best maximum speed: Luis Salom, 179.1mph/288.3km/h (race).

Qualifying

Weather: Dry
Air: 16° **Track:** 41°
Humidity: 64%

1	Rins	1m 32.523s
2	Pons	1m 32.737s
3	Lowes	1m 32.787s
4	Luthi	1m 32.884s
5	Kallio	1m 32.957s
6	Nakagami	1m 32.968s
7	Zarco	1m 33.039s
8	Cortese	1m 33.086s
9	Baldassarri	1m 33.202s
10	Simon	1m 33.262s
11	Cardus	1m 33.290s
12	Corsi	1m 33.291s
13	Syahrin	1m 33.291s
14	Folger	1m 33.425s
15	Shah	1m 33.440s
16	Salom	1m 33.495s
17	Simeon	1m 33.520s
18	Marquez	1m 33.755s
19	Morbidelli	1m 33.764s
20	Schrotter	1m 33.886s
21	Krummenacher	1m 33.918s
22	Rossi	1m 34.410s
23	Raffin	1m 34.467s
24	Hook	1m 34.525s
25	Vierge	1m 34.687s
26	Pons	1m 34.808s
27	Warokorn	1m 35.014s
28	Alt	1m 35.360s
29	Mulhauser	1m 35.895s
	Rabat	No Time

Fastest race laps

1	Rins	1m 32.880s
2	Folger	1m 33.054s
3	Luthi	1m 33.070s
4	Lowes	1m 33.157s
5	Baldassarri	1m 33.173s
6	Simeon	1m 33.415s
7	Salom	1m 33.451s
8	Nakagami	1m 33.453s
9	Cortese	1m 33.486s
10	Zarco	1m 33.546s
11	Krummenacher	1m 33.552s
12	Shah	1m 33.593s
13	Kallio	1m 33.597s
14	Pons	1m 33.655s
15	Marquez	1m 33.717s
16	Morbidelli	1m 34.079s
17	Corsi	1m 34.140s
18	Cardus	1m 34.228s
19	Schrotter	1m 34.267s
20	Raffin	1m 34.478s
21	Syahrin	1m 34.509s
22	Hook	1m 34.609s
23	Vierge	1m 34.615s
24	Simon	1m 34.643s
25	Rossi	1m 35.046s
26	Pons	1m 35.053s
27	Warokorn	1m 35.196s
28	Mulhauser	1m 35.417s
29	Alt	1m 35.734s

Championship Points

1	Zarco	318
2	Rins	214
3	Rabat	206
4	Lowes	172
5	Folger	145
6	Luthi	143
7	Simeon	107
8	Morbidelli	89
9	Nakagami	82
10	Cortese	78
11	Baldassarri	72
12	Corsi	72
13	Marquez	69
14	Aegerter	62
15	Kallio	62
16	Salom	60
17	Simon	58
18	Syahrin	56
19	Schrotter	31
20	Krummenacher	31
21	West	30
22	Pons	28
23	Shah	24
24	Cardus	18
25	Rossi	7
26	Koyama	3
27	Takahashi	2
28	Mulhauser	1

Constructor Points

1	Kalex	395
2	Speed Up	194
3	Tech 3	38
4	Suter	18
5	NTS	3
6	Moriwaki	2

Moto3

RACE DISTANCE: 23 laps, 63.569 miles/102.304km · RACE WEATHER: Dry (air 15°C, humidity 59%, track 36°C)

Pos.	Rider	Nat.	No.	Entrant	Machine	Laps	Time & Speed
1	Miguel Oliveira	POR	44	Red Bull KTM Ajo	KTM	23	37m 34.742s 101.5mph/ 163.3km/h
2	Efren Vazquez	SPA	7	Leopard Racing	Honda	23	37m 34.874s
3	Brad Binder	RSA	41	Red Bull KTM Ajo	KTM	23	37m 34.903s
4	Jorge Navarro	SPA	9	Estrella Galicia 0,0	Honda	23	37m 34.912s
5	Jakub Kornfeil	CZE	84	Drive M7 SIC	KTM	23	37m 35.030s
6	Romano Fenati	ITA	5	SKY Racing Team VR46	KTM	23	37m 35.748s
7	Philipp Oettl	GER	65	Schedl GP Racing	KTM	23	37m 40.942s
8	Isaac Vinales	SPA	32	RBA Racing Team	KTM	23	37m 40.995s
9	Alexis Masbou	FRA	10	SAXOPRINT RTG	Honda	23	37m 41.064s
10	Remy Gardner	AUS	2	CIP	Mahindra	23	37m 42.309s
11	Maria Herrera	SPA	6	Husqvarna Factory Laglisse	Husqvarna	23	37m 42.315s
12	Zulfahmi Khairuddin	MAL	63	Drive M7 SIC	KTM	23	37m 44.830s
13	Manuel Pagliani	ITA	96	San Carlo Team Italia	Mahindra	23	37m 51.036s
14	Karel Hanika	CZE	98	Red Bull KTM Ajo	KTM	23	37m 52.534s
15	Jorge Martin	SPA	88	MAPFRE Team MAHINDRA	Mahindra	23	37m 52.556s
16	Alessandro Tonucci	ITA	19	Outox Reset Drink Team	Mahindra	23	37m 52.947s
17	Niccolo Antonelli	ITA	23	Ongetta-Rivacold	Honda	23	38m 12.663s
18	Ana Carrasco	SPA	22	RBA Racing Team	KTM	23	38m 17.205s
19	Olly Simpson	AUS	35	Olly Simpson Racing	KTM	23	38m 58.766s
	Lorenzo Dalla Porta	ITA	48	Husqvarna Factory Laglisse	Husqvarna	15	DNF
	Danny Kent	GBR	52	Leopard Racing	Honda	13	DNF
	Enea Bastianini	ITA	33	Gresini Racing Team Moto3	Honda	13	DNF
	Andrea Locatelli	ITA	55	Gresini Racing Team Moto3	Honda	13	DNF
	Matt Barton	AUS	14	Suus Honda	FTR	13	DNF
	Francesco Bagnaia	ITA	21	MAPFRE Team MAHINDRA	Mahindra	9	DNF
	Jules Danilo	FRA	95	Ongetta-Rivacold	Honda	8	DNF
	John McPhee	GBR	17	SAXOPRINT RTG	Honda	6	DNF
	Joan Mir	SPA	36	Leopard Racing	Honda	6	DNF
	Juanfran Guevara	SPA	58	MAPFRE Team MAHINDRA	Mahindra	6	DNF
	Andrea Migno	ITA	16	SKY Racing Team VR46	KTM	6	DNF
	Livio Loi	BEL	11	RW Racing GP	Honda	4	DNF
	Stefano Manzi	ITA	29	San Carlo Team Italia	Mahindra	0	DNF
	Gabriel Rodrigo	ARG	91	RBA Racing Team	KTM	0	DNF
	Darryn Binder	RSA	40	Outox Reset Drink Team	Mahindra	0	DNF
	Tatsuki Suzuki	JPN	24	CIP	Mahindra	0	DNF

Fastest lap: Francesco Bagnaia, on lap 3, 1m 36.532s, 103.0mph/165.8km/h.
Lap record: Jack Miller, AUS (KTM), 1m 36.302s, 103.3mph/166.2km/h (2014).
Event best maximum speed: Enea Bastianini, 152.1mph/244.8km/h (race).

Qualifying:

Weather: Dry
Air: 16° **Track:** 33°
Humidity: 65%

1	Kent	1m 36.180s
2	McPhee	1m 36.540s
3	Oliveira	1m 36.606s
4	Vazquez	1m 36.693s
5	Navarro	1m 36.705s
6	Fenati	1m 36.822s
7	Loi	1m 36.942s
8	Herrera	1m 36.960s
9	Kornfeil	1m 37.011s
10	Binder	1m 37.134s
11	Vinales	1m 37.162s
12	Hanika	1m 37.169s
13	Guevara	1m 37.176s
14	Khairuddin	1m 37.193s
15	Mir	1m 37.212s
16	Manzi	1m 37.224s
17	Antonelli	1m 37.282s
18	Masbou	1m 37.344s
19	Quartararo	1m 37.429s
20	Martin	1m 37.480s
21	Danilo	1m 37.495s
22	Dalla Porta	1m 37.513s
23	Tonucci	1m 37.538s
24	Oettl	1m 37.571s
25	Binder	1m 37.635s
26	Gardner	1m 37.644s
27	Rodrigo	1m 37.644s
28	Suzuki	1m 37.646s
29	Bastianini	1m 37.697s
30	Bagnaia	1m 37.800s
31	Migno	1m 37.806s
32	Locatelli	1m 38.242s
33	Carrasco	1m 38.378s
34	Pagliani	1m 38.503s
35	Simpson	1m 39.201s
36	Barton	1m 42.588s

Fastest race laps

1	Bagnaia	1m 36.532s
2	Hanika	1m 36.705s
3	Mir	1m 36.721s
4	Binder	1m 36.734s
5	Danilo	1m 36.827s
6	Antonelli	1m 36.887s
7	Kornfeil	1m 36.896s
8	Kent	1m 36.904s
9	Dalla Porta	1m 36.951s
10	Bastianini	1m 37.016s
11	Oettl	1m 37.023s
12	Guevara	1m 37.062s
13	Tonucci	1m 37.064s
14	Gardner	1m 37.124s
15	Oliveira	1m 37.155s
16	Loi	1m 37.159s
17	Pagliani	1m 37.183s
18	Vazquez	1m 37.186s
19	Fenati	1m 37.194s
20	McPhee	1m 37.201s
21	Navarro	1m 37.206s
22	Vinales	1m 37.210s
23	Masbou	1m 37.269s
24	Khairuddin	1m 37.318s
25	Migno	1m 37.325s
26	Martin	1m 37.352s
27	Herrera	1m 37.406s
28	Carrasco	1m 38.471s
29	Locatelli	1m 38.672s
30	Simpson	1m 39.717s
31	Barton	1m 43.167s

Championship Points

1	Kent	244
2	Oliveira	204
3	Bastianini	188
4	Fenati	165
5	Antonelli	161
6	Vazquez	155
7	Binder	126
8	Navarro	121
9	Vinales	103
10	Quartararo	92
11	McPhee	77
12	Bagnaia	73
13	Masbou	70
14	Oettl	66
15	Kornfeil	63
16	Loi	56
17	Hanika	43
18	Martin	39
19	Locatelli	33
20	Migno	30
21	Ajo	21
22	Ono	21
23	Khairuddin	19
24	Guevara	15
25	Dalla Porta	13
26	Suzuki	9
27	Herrera	9
28	Danilo	7
29	Manzi	7
30	Gardner	6
31	Pagliani	3
32	Ferrari	1

Constructor Points

1	Honda	375
2	KTM	291
3	Mahindra	113
4	Husqvarna	85

MALAYSIAN GRAND PRIX

SEPANG CIRCUIT

Inset top: A moment that will live in infamy. Rossi races away from his fallen nemesis.

Inset right: Rossi hid behind shades in parc ferme, but his camp followers' sullen faces show they know there's trouble ahead.

Main: Dense smog helped to cloud the issue, but at least the helicopters could still take off.

Photos: Gold & Goose

THIS was not the first time that Rossi had grabbed the limelight from the race winner. For example, also in Malaysia in 2010, where his celebrations for Yamaha win number 46 had quite overshadowed Lorenzo, who had just won the championship.

He did it again at Sepang, but this time not in a good way – his overshadowed victim this time Dani Pedrosa, whose start-to-finish second win in three races had been imperious, but had been virtually ignored in the aftermath.

The clip of Rossi's extraordinary attack on Marquez will be watched many hundreds of thousands of times: the great racing superstar staring him down, then effectively stopping in his path, and the subsequent collision that tipped the youngster off for his sixth race crash of the year.

The first to pore over the videos was Race Direction, from every angle; and soon afterwards the FIM stewards at the track, who promptly refused Rossi's appeal against his penalty. And after that, the Court of Arbitration for Sport (CAS), who were still considering Rossi's further appeal as MOTOCOURSE went to press.

The clash, on the seventh of 20 laps, was the brutish culmination of four days of sniping and insults from Rossi, and of surprised and aggrieved self-defence by Marquez. This had begun, in an atmosphere of bemused surprise, at the pre-race press conference. At first, it seemed as though Rossi was joking as he suggested that Marquez had deliberately interfered in the previous weekend with him and Iannone, "playing with us" when he had the pace to get away (Iannone, by the way, agreed). He had meant to help Lorenzo, said Rossi, though this view was rather undermined because Marquez had robbed Lorenzo of five points by stealing a last-gasp victory. Lorenzo, likewise, thought the suggestion facetious. "Sure he helped me. Especially on the last lap."

But Rossi was serious, as became clear in an all-Italian huddle after the conference, where he produced a now notorious annotated lap-by-lap analysis of the race, pointing out exactly when and where he had been baulked. Marquez, he said, was not just childish, but a phony, a vengeful enemy hiding behind a bland smile and the pretence of friendship. At least his rivalry with Biaggi had been honest and open.

"We were obnoxious, but I prefer."

Marquez looked genuinely bemused, and protested his innocence. The atmosphere deteriorated through practice, with some hard stares out on track, and partisan supporters divining conspiracy at every turn.

Come the race, and a change of attitude was clear. If Marquez hadn't been messing with Rossi before, he was certainly going to do so now.

Their battle began after the initial sorting out had resulted in Lorenzo lying second to eventual winner Pedrosa, with three laps done.

On the fourth lap, Rossi took third off Marquez, ready to chase the leaders. He wouldn't get the chance. He had insulted Marquez at his peril. Now he would pay the price.

On lap five, they changed places nine times. Marquez block-passed, dived inside, rode around the outside – whatever it took to get back in front. And all the while, Jorge was stretching away out of reach.

Rossi made no secret of his frustration. After another pass on lap six, he turned and gestured angrily. To no avail. Marquez pushed past again. And Rossi boiled over.

It was on the entry to the corner before the back straight, down which Marquez could blow past at will. Rossi's plan, he said later, had been to slow him right down, then get the jump on the run to the final hairpin and get some clear track.

Rossi looked back again twice, and slowed and slowed and slowed, all the while forcing the Honda to go wider and wider. Slower and slower he went: that lap took two seconds longer. No wonder Marquez was taken by surprise; no wonder they collided.

Rossi looked bad. The halo had slipped; his reputation as a hard, but fair sportsman in tatters. Especially since the trackside TV image suggested that he had actually batted Marquez off with his leg. The overhead view cast doubt, however, adding weight to Rossi's explanation, that his foot had been knocked by the crashing rider, already out of control. He hadn't meant to knock him off.

The pair went before Race Direction, who had delayed any decision until after the race, so as to examine detailed evidence and hear explanations, because the matter was of

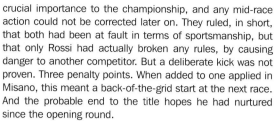

Left: Light the blue touch-paper – Rossi's public condemnation of Marquez took everyone by surprise.

Below left: Race Director Mike Webb explains why the penalty decision was deferred until after the race.

Far left: No quarter: Marquez and Rossi changed places nine times in one lap alone.

Below: Lorenzo looked happy to congratulate Pedrosa. The good mood would not last.

Photos: Gold & Goose

crucial importance to the championship, and any mid-race action could not be corrected later on. They ruled, in short, that both had been at fault in terms of sportsmanship, but that only Rossi had actually broken any rules, by causing danger to another competitor. But a deliberate kick was not proven. Three penalty points. When added to one applied in Misano, this meant a back-of-the-grid start at the next race. And the probable end to the title hopes he had nurtured since the opening round.

In the following days, Rossi appealed to the CAS, requesting either a removal or reduction of penalty, but more importantly that the penalty should be suspended until the court's judgement. He would have to wait until Thursday at Valencia to hear that his penalty would stand, and longer still for a final decision.

Rossi was in bad odour after the race, not least because many shared Lorenzo's bitter condemnation, and suggestion that disqualification or at least a ride-through would have been more appropriate (his pettish mood enhanced after being booed on the podium for snubbing Rossi). Luminaries ranging from FIM president Vito Ippolito to Spanish former multi-champion Angel Nieto wrote open letters deploring the behaviour of both riders; while an internet petition that Rossi's penalty should be reversed (unfortunately very clumsily argued) rapidly moved towards three-quarters of a million signatures from around the world, demonstrating the groundswell of support.

As the hours turned into days, Marquez's repeated insistence on a deliberate kick by Rossi made the younger rider look increasingly petulant, like a sneaky schoolboy making up stories to get a senior classmate into trouble. It was a signal moment.

In other news, forest fires in neighbouring Indonesia filled the Malaysian airspace with thick smog, though never thick enough actually to ground the medevac helicopter; de Angelis was flown back to Italy from Japan on race day; Mika Kallio revealed that he had signed up as KTM's test rider for 2016; and first moves were made to return Indonesia to the calendar at a to-be-revamped Sentul circuit.

Given the main story of the weekend, though, Rossi's cynical lapse eclipsed all that as well.

MOTOGP RACE – 20 laps

Pedrosa's return to strength was signalled in FP1, when he was fastest, and underlined in Q2, with his first pole position since Catalunya more than a year before. Marquez and Rossi were alongside; Lorenzo led Crutchlow and Iannone on row two.

Pedrosa's start was a return to his jackrabbit days. He led into the first corner, and from there to the end. A new lap record, however, went to an impressively aggressive Lorenzo, who had been dropped to sixth, behind both Hondas, Rossi, Dovizioso and Iannone off the line. He scythed past both Ducatis at once at turn four, then eased inside Rossi at the start of his record second lap. Next time around, he was up with the Hondas, and when Marquez ran wide at turn four, he was easily through.

At first, this overtake had looked as though Marquez, as he had said earlier, had been having trouble with front grip, which had spoiled his braking, causing him to miss the apex. At the same time, Lorenzo had taken the position off Marquez suspiciously easily. Had he just let him by? Another unproven case.

Nothing would change from there for the front pair, though Lorenzo pushed hard until half-distance. At the end, Pedrosa was 3.6 seconds ahead after a fine demonstration.

The leaders were already 2.7 seconds clear on the lap before the fateful collision; Rossi got third. And more controversy than he had bargained for.

Behind all this, the race. In spite of blazing heat sapping tyre adhesion as well as the riders' energy, it remained lively in parts.

Above: Pedrosa was masterful; Lorenzo chased in vain.

Top, centre: Petulant Lorenzo exits the podium early; his dismissive gesture to Rossi elicited boos from the crowd.

Above centre right: Pedrosa's second win in three races was overshadowed by what happened behind him.

Right: Long-time leader Luthi had to succumb to Zarco on the final lap – the new champion's eighth win.

Centre right: Navarro holds the lead from Binder and Oliveira, whilst Danny Kent struggles to stay with the pack.

Centre right: Navarro holds the Moto3 lead from Binder and Oliveira, at the back of the swarm, Kent lacked the speed he needed.

Bottom right: Leopard pair Vazquez and Ono crash out; Bastianini miraculously avoids the carnage.

Photos: Gold & Goose

Dovizioso had started strongly, though the Ducati had been consigned to fifth by the end of lap one. Iannone was on his tail, but soon dropped off rapidly to another trackside retirement: his radiator had been holed on the first lap. The non-finish to Pedrosa's win meant that he lost fourth overall in the championship.

Dovi was soon out of touch with the leaders, and by lap seven he was coming under pressure from Crutchlow, who attacked through the left-right turns nine and ten just after half-distance. As he slipped inside for the second one, he made contact with one of the Desmosedici's two wings, tipping Dovi off for yet another zero points. He apologised directly after the race.

Crutchlow was battling with grip, but couldn't forgive himself for succumbing to Smith closing from behind after escaping from team-mate Pol Espargaro. The Spaniard was riding in pain after suffering a hairline crack in his neck, knocked off in warm-up by Hector Barbera.

Smith was ahead two laps after Dovizioso's crash, and after a couple more laps of pressure was able to escape for a clear and impressive fourth, Crutchlow alone in fifth.

There was a good fight behind, led for much of the race by Aleix Espargaro, but Petrucci was stronger, taking over sixth with seven laps left and moving clear for a first ever dry-race top ten.

That left the brothers Espargaro to battle with an on-form Bradl and his ever improving Aprilia, until Vinales slipped past and the German started to lose ground.

By the end, Aleix Espargaro had managed to wave away the embarrassingly close attentions of team-mate Vinales; Pol, Bradl and then an again lacklustre Redding in 11th trailed in respectfully spaced apart.

Hernandez was able to stay clear of Barbera, the top Open finisher through from a back-of-the-grid start as punishment for his morning collision with Espargaro. Just over a second behind came Elias, his first strong ride to his first points since taking over the Forward Yamaha four races before. The former Moto2 champion had come through a gaggle of Open Hondas on the way, and passed Bautista's Aprilia for 14th on the last lap.

Hayden was finally best of the B-team Hondas, only getting ahead of a persistent Miller with three laps to go. Di Meglio, Laverty and second-race Abraham substitute Anthony West followed along.

Baz and de Angelis replacement Damian Cudlin both crashed, the latter on the first lap, Baz on the second. Loren-

zo was accused of having overtaken under yellow flags for this incident, but later was exonerated.

Tension for the title equalled the tension at the track. Rossi's lead was now down to seven points, with one last showdown. In 2006, the margin ahead of Nicky Hayden had been eight points, and Rossi had blinked first – a fact fresh in the memory in the aftermath of a race that had been memorable for all the wrong reasons.

MOTO2 RACE – 19 laps

Thomas Luthi had claimed his first pole in three years in calm and steadfast fashion, but new World Champion Zarco had the Derendinger Racing Kalex rider in sight, and sometimes behind, throughout qualifying.

The race followed the same pattern, though with a different outcome: Zarco waited until the last lap to pounce to claim his eighth win of the year, by just over half a second.

The leading pair battled on lap one, Zarco getting ahead at turn four, Luthi taking it back at the final hairpin. That was it for most of the race. They continued in this order as the laps counted down. At one stage, shortly after half-distance, Luthi had stretched the gap to just over a second; but from there, it began to shrink again, and as they started the last Zarco was breathing down his neck. They swapped to and fro once, but at the second attempt Zarco was clear, and with obviously better corner speed he went on to win number eight by almost half a second.

Luthi admitted he had overworked his tyres; short of corner speed, he had no answer at the end.

Rins had qualified third, but was slow off the line, and he had to fight his way past an eager Nakagami before he could start closing on fast-away second-row starter Folger for third.

By lap five, he was ahead of the German, but not only could he make no impression on a gap growing towards two seconds on the leaders, but also he couldn't shake off Folger. The German was right behind when Rins ran too hot into the left-right complex behind the pits, lost the front and tumbled out of contention.

Some way back by now, Baldassari, in another strong race on the Forward Kalex, had got past Nakagami, and the pair of them were leaving a fading Sam Lowes. After three laps, Nakagami was ahead again, and by the finish he had managed to gap the Italian teenager by better than two seconds.

The next group, led for a spell by Cortese, was now enlivened by the arrival from behind of Salom. By the finish,

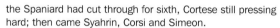

the Spaniard had cut through for sixth, Cortese still pressing hard; then came Syahrin, Corsi and Simeon.

Axel Pons, Kallio, Lowes and Ricky Cardus took the rest of the points, Lowes regaining 14th on the last lap.

Marquez, Schrotter and Warokorn filled the crash list.

The win brought Zarco's podium total for the season to 14, equalling the record shared by Marquez and Rabat. He also totted up 343 points, three short of Rabat's 2014 class record, with one race to spare. Rabat's second place likewise remained in jeopardy; no-score Rins was still ahead by eight points.

MOTO3 RACE – 18 laps

Another chance for Kent: if Oliveira won, he needed to finish only in the top five to be champion. Oliveira did win. Kent was seventh. The former foregone conclusion would now go to a tense final round.

Antonelli was on pole, from Navarro and Oliveira: two Hondas and a refreshed KTM. Kent again was punished for slow sections in practice and dropped three places, to start ninth. More damaging, he admitted later, was the circuit's long straight before the final hairpin. His weight and size told badly against him.

There was the usual furious front action, a lead group of eight taking shape before half-distance.

Oliveira did most of the leading, but Kornfeil nosed ahead briefly, both Fenati and Bagnaia more than once. With five laps to go, Antonelli put on a charge. Two laps later, Bagnaia crashed out. By then, Brad Binder was putting in a run, to lead laps 15 or 16. Then Navarro slipped to the front to start the last lap.

Outwardly, Kent had looked comfortable at the back of the group, seemingly poised for his own late charge. Appearances were deceptive; the track layout made it impossible.

The order was a lottery, but once again Oliveira was best at playing the odds, and with team-mate Binder riding shotgun, they pushed Navarro to third. Then came Antonelli, Fenati, Kornfeil and a "frustrated" Kent – first to seventh covered by less than six-tenths.

Almost five seconds down, Bastianini was eighth and alone, likewise Masbou and team-mate McPhee behind him.

Kent now led the resurgent Oliveira by 24 points. He had six wins; Oliveira had five. If Oliveira were to win and they tied on points, Kent would lose out with fewer second places. He would need at least two points to be champion.

SEPANG INTERNATIONAL CIRCUIT

20 laps
Length: 5.548 km / 3.447 miles
Width: 25m

Key
96/60 kph/mph
Gear ⚙

Langkawi curve 105/65
Genting Curve 168/104
Turn 2 75/47
Turn 3 198/123
Turn 5 178/111
Hairpin 96/60
Turn 7 144/89
KLIA Curve 153/95
Pangkor Laut Chicane 85/53
Berjaya Tioman Corner 73/45
Sunway Lagoon Corner 118/73
Turn 12 183/114
Kenyir Lake 128/80

SHELL MALAYSIAN MOTORCYCLE GRAND PRIX

23–25 OCTOBER, 2015

MotoGP

RACE DISTANCE: 20 laps, 68.885 miles/110.860km · RACE WEATHER: Dry (air 35°C, humidity 48%, track 47°C)

Pos.	Rider	Nat.	No.	Entrant	Machine	Tyres	Race tyre choice	Laps	Time & speed
1	**Dani Pedrosa**	SPA	26	Repsol Honda Team	Honda RC213V	B	F: Medium/R: Medium	20	40m 37.691s 101.7mph/ 163.7km/h
2	**Jorge Lorenzo**	SPA	99	Movistar Yamaha MotoGP	Yamaha YZR-M1	B	F: Medium/R: Medium	20	40m 41.303s
3	**Valentino Rossi**	ITA	46	Movistar Yamaha MotoGP	Yamaha YZR-M1	B	F: Medium/R: Medium	20	40m 51.415s
4	**Bradley Smith**	GBR	38	Monster Yamaha Tech 3	Yamaha YZR-M1	B	F: Medium/R: Medium	20	41m 01.686s
5	**Cal Crutchlow**	GBR	35	LCR Honda	Honda RC213V	B	F: Medium/R: Medium	20	41m 06.412s
6	**Danilo Petrucci**	ITA	9	Octo Pramac Racing	Ducati Desmosedici	B	F: Medium/R: Medium	20	41m 14.063s
7	**Aleix Espargaro**	SPA	41	Team SUZUKI ECSTAR	Suzuki GSX-RR	B	F: Medium/R: Medium	20	41m 16.981s
8	**Maverick Vinales**	SPA	25	Team SUZUKI ECSTAR	Suzuki GSX-RR	B	F: Medium/R: Medium	20	41m 17.127s
9	**Pol Espargaro**	SPA	44	Monster Yamaha Tech 3	Yamaha YZR-M1	B	F: Medium/R: Medium	20	41m 20.153s
10	**Stefan Bradl**	GER	6	Aprilia Racing Team Gresini	Aprilia RS-GP	B	F: Medium/R: Medium	20	41m 22.292s
11	**Scott Redding**	GBR	45	EG 0,0 Marc VDS	Honda RC213V	B	F: Medium/R: Medium	20	41m 25.381s
12	**Yonny Hernandez**	COL	68	Octo Pramac Racing	Ducati Desmosedici	B	F: Hard/R: Medium	20	41m 29.803s
13	**Hector Barbera**	SPA	8	Avintia Racing	Ducati Desmosedici Open	B	F: Medium/R: Soft	20	41m 30.051s
14	**Toni Elias**	SPA	24	Forward Racing	Yamaha Forward	B	F: Medium/R: Soft	20	41m 31.310s
15	**Alvaro Bautista**	SPA	19	Aprilia Racing Team Gresini	Aprilia RS-GP	B	F: Medium/R: Soft	20	41m 31.322s
16	Nicky Hayden	USA	69	Aspar MotoGP Team	Honda RC213V-RS	B	F: Medium/R: Medium	20	41m 39.122s
17	Jack Miller	AUS	43	LCR Honda	Honda RC213V-RS	B	F: Medium/R: Medium	20	41m 40.519s
18	Mike di Meglio	FRA	63	Avintia Racing	Ducati Desmosedici Open	B	F: Medium/R: Soft	20	41m 42.766s
19	Eugene Laverty	IRL	50	Aspar MotoGP Team	Honda RC213V-RS	B	F: Medium/R: Soft	20	41m 47.568s
20	Anthony West	AUS	13	AB Motoracing	Honda RC213V-RS	B	F: Medium/R: Soft	20	42m 02.440s
	Andrea Dovizioso	ITA	4	Ducati Team	Ducati Desmosedici	B	F: Medium/R: Medium	10	DNF-crash
	Marc Marquez	SPA	93	Repsol Honda Team	Honda RC213V	B	F: Medium/R: Medium	7	DNF-crash
	Loris Baz	FRA	76	Forward Racing	Yamaha Forward	B	F: Medium/R: Soft	2	DNF-crash
	Andrea Iannone	ITA	29	Ducati Team	Ducati Desmosedici	B	F: Medium/R: Medium	1	DNF-mechanical
	Damian Cudlin	AUS	55	E-Motion IodaRacing Team	ART	B	F: Medium/R: Soft	0	DNF-crash

Fastest lap: Jorge Lorenzo, on lap 2, 2m 0.606s, 102.8mph/165.4km/h (record).
Previous lap record: Marc Marquez, SPA (Honda), 2m 1.150s, 102.3mph/164.7km/h (2014).
Event best maximum speed: Andrea Iannone, 211mph/339.6km/h (free practice).

Qualifying

Weather: Dry
Air Temp: 34° **Track Temp:** 42°
Humidity: 60%

1	Pedrosa	1m 59.053s
2	Marquez	1m 59.462s
3	Rossi	1m 59.726s
4	Lorenzo	1m 59.737s
5	Crutchlow	2m 00.199s
6	Iannone	2m 00.224s
7	Dovizioso	2m 00.423s
8	Vinales	2m 00.478s
9	Smith	2m 00.652s
10	Barbera	2m 00.724s
11	A. Espargaro	2m 00.724s
12	P. Espargaro	2m 00.794s
13	Petrucci	2m 01.223s
14	Bradl	2m 01.346s
15	Redding	2m 01.367s
16	Miller	2m 01.725s
17	Bautista	2m 01.727s
18	Hernandez	2m 01.748s
19	Hayden	2m 01.829s
20	Baz	2m 01.862s
21	Elias	2m 02.415s
22	Laverty	2m 02.460s
23	Di Meglio	2m 02.964s
24	West	2m 03.855s
25	Cudlin	2m 06.051s

Fastest race laps

1	Lorenzo	2m 00.606s
2	Pedrosa	2m 00.795s
3	Marquez	2m 00.818s
4	Rossi	2m 01.127s
5	Dovizioso	2m 01.493s
6	Crutchlow	2m 01.803s
7	Smith	2m 02.051s
8	P. Espargaro	2m 02.303s
9	A. Espargaro	2m 02.350s
10	Petrucci	2m 02.601s
11	Vinales	2m 02.814s
12	Redding	2m 02.860s
13	Hernandez	2m 03.038s
14	Bradl	2m 03.079s
15	Bautista	2m 03.080s
16	Hayden	2m 03.188s
17	Barbera	2m 03.217s
18	Elias	2m 03.493s
19	Miller	2m 03.657s
20	Di Meglio	2m 03.987s
21	Laverty	2m 04.063s
22	West	2m 04.707s

Championship Points

1	Rossi	312
2	Lorenzo	305
3	Marquez	222
4	Pedrosa	190
5	Iannone	188
6	Smith	171
7	Dovizioso	153
8	Crutchlow	118
9	Petrucci	107
10	P. Espargaro	103
11	A. Espargaro	97
12	Vinales	92
13	Redding	83
14	Hernandez	53
15	Barbera	33
16	Bautista	29
17	Baz	28
18	Bradl	17
19	Miller	17
20	Hayden	16
21	E. Laverty	9
22	Nakasuga	8
23	Pirro	8
24	Di Meglio	8
25	Aoyama	5
26	Takahashi	4
27	Elias	2
28	De Angelis	2

Grid order

Grid order	1	2	3	4	5	6	7	8	9	10	11	12	13	14	15	16	17	18	19	20	
26 PEDROSA	26	26	26	26	26	26	26	26	26	26	26	26	26	26	26	26	26	26	26	26	1
93 MARQUEZ	93	93	99	99	99	99	99	99	99	99	99	99	99	99	99	99	99	99	99	99	2
46 ROSSI	46	99	93	46	93	93	46	46	46	46	46	46	46	46	46	46	46	46	46	46	3
99 LORENZO	99	46	46	93	46	46	4	4	4	4	38	38	38	38	38	38	38	38	38	38	4
35 CRUTCHLOW	4	4	4	4	4	4	35	35	35	35	35	35	35	35	35	35	35	35	35	35	5
29 IANNONE	29	35	35	35	35	35	38	38	38	38	41	41	9	9	9	9	9	9	9	9	6
4 DOVIZIOSO	44	44	38	38	38	38	44	41	41	41	9	9	41	41	41	41	41	41	41	41	7
25 VINALES	6	38	44	44	44	44	41	44	44	9	44	44	44	44	25	25	25	25	25	25	8
38 SMITH	35	6	41	41	41	41	9	9	9	44	25	25	25	25	44	44	44	44	44	44	9
41 A. ESPARGARO	38	9	9	9	9	9	6	6	6	6	6	6	6	6	6	6	6	6	6	6	10
44 P. ESPARGARO	41	41	6	6	6	6	25	25	25	25	45	45	45	45	45	45	45	45	45	45	11
9 PETRUCCI	9	45	45	45	45	45	45	45	45	45	19	19	19	19	68	68	68	68	68	68	12
6 BRADL	45	19	19	25	25	25	19	19	19	19	68	68	68	68	19	8	8	8	8	8	13
45 REDDING	19	25	25	19	19	19	68	68	68	68	8	8	8	8	8	19	19	19	19	24	14
43 MILLER	43	43	43	43	69	68	69	8	8	8	69	24	24	24	24	24	24	24	24	19	15
19 BAUTISTA	25	69	69	69	68	69	43	69	69	69	24	43	69	69	43	43	69	69	69		
68 HERNANDEZ	76	68	68	68	43	43	8	43	43	24	43	69	43	43	69	69	43	43	43		
69 HAYDEN	50	50	8	8	8	8	24	24	24	43	63	63	63	63	63	63	63	63	63		
76 BAZ	69	24	50	24	24	24	63	63	63	63	50	50	50	50	50	50	50	50	50		
24 ELIAS	24	8	24	63	63	63	50	50	50	50	13	13	13	13	13	13	13	13	13		
50 LAVERTY	68	63	63	50	50	50	13	13	13	13											
63 DI MEGLIO	63	13	13	13	13	13	93														
13 WEST	8	76																			
55 CUDLIN	13																				
8 BARBERA																					

76 Pit stop

Constructor Points

1	Yamaha	382
2	Honda	335
3	Ducati	247
4	Suzuki	129
5	Yamaha Forward	35
6	Aprilia	34
7	ART	2

Moto2

RACE DISTANCE: 19 laps, 65.441 miles/105.317km · RACE WEATHER: Dry (air 35°C, humidity 45%, track 46°C)

Pos.	Rider	Nat.	No.	Entrant	Machine	Laps	Time & Speed
1	Johann Zarco	FRA	5	Ajo Motorsport	Kalex	19	40m 37.772s 96.6mph/155.5km/h
2	Thomas Luthi	SWI	12	Derendinger Racing Interwetten	Kalex	19	40m 38.370s
3	Jonas Folger	GER	94	AGR Team	Kalex	19	40m 47.618s
4	Takaaki Nakagami	JPN	30	IDEMITSU Honda Team Asia	Kalex	19	40m 51.911s
5	Lorenzo Baldassarri	ITA	7	Forward Racing	Kalex	19	40m 54.212s
6	Luis Salom	SPA	39	Paginas Amarillas HP 40	Kalex	19	41m 00.066s
7	Sandro Cortese	GER	11	Dynavolt Intact GP	Kalex	19	41m 00.480s
8	Hafizh Syahrin	MAL	55	Petronas Raceline Malaysia	Kalex	19	41m 04.457s
9	Simone Corsi	ITA	3	Forward Racing	Kalex	19	41m 06.328s
10	Xavier Simeon	BEL	19	Federal Oil Gresini Moto2	Kalex	19	41m 07.853s
11	Axel Pons	SPA	49	AGR Team	Kalex	19	41m 08.645s
12	Mika Kallio	FIN	36	QMMF Racing Team	Speed Up	19	41m 09.559s
13	Sam Lowes	GBR	22	Speed Up Racing	Speed Up	19	41m 11.616s
14	Ricard Cardus	SPA	88	JPMoto Malaysia	Suter	19	41m 11.658s
15	Franco Morbidelli	ITA	21	Italtrans Racing Team	Kalex	19	41m 15.859s
16	Azlan Shah	MAL	25	IDEMITSU Honda Team Asia	Kalex	19	41m 19.384s
17	Randy Krummenacher	SWI	4	JIR Racing Team	Kalex	19	41m 20.011s
18	Louis Rossi	FRA	96	Tasca Racing Scuderia Moto2	Tech 3	19	41m 22.348s
19	Robin Mulhauser	SWI	70	Technomag Racing Interwetten	Kalex	19	41m 24.084s
20	Edgar Pons	SPA	57	Italtrans Racing Team	Kalex	19	41m 27.129s
21	Jesko Raffin	SWI	2	sports-millions-EMWE-SAG	Kalex	19	41m 34.248s
22	Xavi Vierge	SPA	97	Tech 3	Tech 3	19	41m 54.891s
23	Joshua Hook	AUS	16	Technomag Racing Interwetten	Kalex	19	41m 56.115s
24	Ramdan Rosli	MAL	93	Petronas AHM Malaysia	Kalex	19	41m 56.306s
25	Julian Simon	SPA	60	QMMF Racing Team	Speed Up	19	41m 58.371s
26	Florian Alt	GER	66	E-Motion IodaRacing Team	Suter	19	42m 14.800s
27	Thitipong Warokorn	THA	10	APH PTT The Pizza SAG	Kalex	14	42m 29.737s
	Alex Rins	SPA	40	Paginas Amarillas HP 40	Kalex	9	DNF
	Marcel Schrotter	GER	23	Tech 3	Tech 3	8	DNF
	Alex Marquez	SPA	73	EG 0,0 Marc VDS	Kalex	5	DNF

Fastest lap: Thomas Luthi, on lap 2, 2m 7.321s, 97.4mph/156.7km/h (record).
Previous lap record: Mika Kallio, FIN (Kalex), 2m 7.949s, 96.9mph/155.9km/h (2014).
Event best maximum speed: Ricard Cardus, 170.9mph/275.0km/h (free practice).

Qualifying
Weather: Dry
Air Temp: 32° Track Temp: 41°
Humidity: 63%

1	Luthi	2m 06.383s
2	Zarco	2m 06.510s
3	Rins	2m 06.837s
4	Folger	2m 07.070s
5	Baldassarri	2m 07.199s
6	Cortese	2m 07.224s
7	Nakagami	2m 07.422s
8	Lowes	2m 07.499s
9	Marquez	2m 07.515s
10	Simeon	2m 07.522s
11	Corsi	2m 07.533s
12	Simon	2m 07.549s
13	Salom	2m 07.635s
14	Kallio	2m 07.636s
15	Shah	2m 07.643s
16	Pons	2m 07.695s
17	Schrotter	2m 08.195s
18	Syahrin	2m 08.206s
19	Morbidelli	2m 08.326s
20	Warokorn	2m 08.377s
21	Mulhauser	2m 08.416s
22	Rossi	2m 08.512s
23	Krummenacher	2m 08.512s
24	Cardus	2m 08.700s
25	Vierge	2m 09.066s
26	Pons	2m 09.086s
27	Alt	2m 09.367s
28	Raffin	2m 09.682s
29	Hook	2m 10.203s
30	Rosli	2m 10.268s

Fastest race laps

1	Luthi	2m 07.321s
2	Rins	2m 07.449s
3	Zarco	2m 07.588s
4	Folger	2m 07.703s
5	Baldassarri	2m 07.822s
6	Lowes	2m 08.146s
7	Nakagami	2m 08.228s
8	Simeon	2m 08.400s
9	Cortese	2m 08.429s
10	Corsi	2m 08.520s
11	Marquez	2m 08.561s
12	Syahrin	2m 08.656s
13	Salom	2m 08.678s
14	Shah	2m 08.689s
15	Cardus	2m 08.731s
16	Kallio	2m 08.881s
17	Pons	2m 08.910s
18	Simon	2m 08.926s
19	Morbidelli	2m 09.159s
20	Rossi	2m 09.292s
21	Krummenacher	2m 09.525s
22	Warokorn	2m 09.655s
23	Mulhauser	2m 09.762s
24	Pons	2m 09.782s
25	Vierge	2m 10.021s
26	Schrotter	2m 10.023s
27	Raffin	2m 10.048s
28	Alt	2m 10.120s
29	Hook	2m 11.119s
30	Rosli	2m 11.195s

Championship Points

1	Zarco	343
2	Rins	214
3	Rabat	206
4	Lowes	175
5	Luthi	163
6	Folger	161
7	Simeon	113
8	Nakagami	95
9	Morbidelli	90
10	Cortese	87
11	Baldassarri	83
12	Corsi	79
13	Salom	70
14	Marquez	69
15	Kallio	66
16	Syahrin	64
17	Aegerter	62
18	Simon	58
19	Pons	33
20	Schrotter	31
21	Krummenacher	31
22	West	30
23	Shah	24
24	Cardus	20
25	Rossi	7
26	Koyama	3
27	Takahashi	2
28	Mulhauser	1

Constructor Points

1	Kalex	420
2	Speed Up	198
3	Tech 3	38
4	Suter	20
5	NTS	3
6	Moriwaki	2

Moto3

RACE DISTANCE: 18 laps, 61.997 miles/99.774km · RACE WEATHER: Dry (air 33°C, humidity 50%, track 43°C)

Pos.	Rider	Nat.	No.	Entrant	Machine	Laps	Time & Speed
1	Miguel Oliveira	POR	44	Red Bull KTM Ajo	KTM	18	40m 33.277s 91.7mph/147.6km/h
2	Brad Binder	RSA	41	Red Bull KTM Ajo	KTM	18	40m 33.366s
3	Jorge Navarro	SPA	9	Estrella Galicia 0,0	Honda	18	40m 33.550s
4	Niccolo Antonelli	ITA	23	Ongetta-Rivacold	Honda	18	40m 33.582s
5	Romano Fenati	ITA	5	SKY Racing Team VR46	KTM	18	40m 33.693s
6	Jakub Kornfeil	CZE	84	Drive M7 SIC	KTM	18	40m 33.807s
7	Danny Kent	GBR	52	Leopard Racing	Honda	18	40m 33.867s
8	Enea Bastianini	ITA	33	Gresini Racing Team Moto3	Honda	18	40m 37.281s
9	Alexis Masbou	FRA	10	SAXOPRINT RTG	Honda	18	40m 40.267s
10	John McPhee	GBR	17	SAXOPRINT RTG	Honda	18	40m 43.307s
11	Jules Danilo	FRA	95	Ongetta-Rivacold	Honda	18	40m 49.405s
12	Jorge Martin	SPA	88	MAPFRE Team MAHINDRA	Mahindra	18	40m 52.272s
13	Stefano Manzi	ITA	29	San Carlo Team Italia	Mahindra	18	40m 52.276s
14	Isaac Vinales	SPA	32	RBA Racing Team	KTM	18	40m 52.406s
15	Philipp Oettl	GER	65	Schedl GP Racing	KTM	18	40m 52.430s
16	Lorenzo Dalla Porta	ITA	48	Husqvarna Factory Laglisse	Husqvarna	18	40m 52.869s
17	Francesco Bagnaia	ITA	21	MAPFRE Team MAHINDRA	Mahindra	18	41m 05.330s
18	Maria Herrera	SPA	6	Husqvarna Factory Laglisse	Husqvarna	18	41m 06.159s
19	Livio Loi	BEL	11	RW Racing GP	Honda	18	41m 06.201s
20	Juanfran Guevara	SPA	58	MAPFRE Team MAHINDRA	Mahindra	18	41m 06.584s
21	Tatsuki Suzuki	JPN	24	CIP	Mahindra	18	41m 07.730s
22	Remy Gardner	AUS	2	CIP	Mahindra	18	41m 28.982s
23	Ana Carrasco	SPA	22	RBA Racing Team	KTM	18	41m 30.839s
24	Andrea Migno	ITA	16	SKY Racing Team VR46	KTM	18	42m 19.567s
25	Gabriel Rodrigo	ARG	91	RBA Racing Team	KTM	17	40m 48.356s
	Karel Hanika	CZE	98	Red Bull KTM Ajo	KTM	6	DNF
	Manuel Pagliani	ITA	96	San Carlo Team Italia	Mahindra	6	DNF
	Efren Vazquez	SPA	7	Leopard Racing	Honda	5	DNF
	Hiroki Ono	JPN	76	Leopard Racing	Honda	5	DNF
	Zulfahmi Khairuddin	MAL	63	Drive M7 SIC	KTM	5	DNF
	Darryn Binder	RSA	40	Outox Reset Drink Team	Mahindra	2	DNF

Fastest lap: Brad Binder, on lap 3, 2m 13.571s, 92.8mph/149.3km/h (record).
Previous lap record: Alex Rins, SPA (Honda), 2m 13.731s, 92.7mph/149.2km/h (2014).
Event best maximum speed: Hiroki Ono, 144.5mph/232.6km/h (race).

Qualifying
Weather: Dry
Air Temp: 33° Track Temp: 40°
Humidity: 58%

1	Antonelli	2m 12.653s
2	Navarro	2m 12.700s
3	Oliveira	2m 12.893s
4	Vazquez	2m 12.956s
5	Kornfeil	2m 12.987s
6	Kent	2m 12.994s
7	Fenati	2m 13.106s
8	Bagnaia	2m 13.167s
9	Bastianini	2m 13.232s
10	Khairuddin	2m 13.280s
11	Ono	2m 13.282s
12	McPhee	2m 13.538s
13	Martin	2m 13.573s
14	Hanika	2m 13.641s
15	Vinales	2m 13.668s
16	Binder	2m 13.745s
17	Manzi	2m 13.980s
18	Oettl	2m 14.040s
19	Masbou	2m 14.045s
20	Rodrigo	2m 14.053s
21	Binder	2m 14.091s
22	Guevara	2m 14.103s
23	Dalla Porta	2m 14.116s
24	Migno	2m 14.200s
25	Herrera	2m 14.217s
26	Loi	2m 14.468s
27	Suzuki	2m 14.551s
28	Pagliani	2m 14.617s
29	Danilo	2m 14.763s
30	Gardner	2m 14.912s
31	Carrasco	2m 15.629s
	Tonucci	No Time
	Locatelli	No Time

Fastest race laps

1	Binder	2m 13.571s
2	Vazquez	2m 13.574s
3	Antonelli	2m 13.711s
4	Khairuddin	2m 13.791s
5	Kent	2m 13.806s
6	Ono	2m 13.822s
7	Kornfeil	2m 13.911s
8	Navarro	2m 13.939s
9	Bastianini	2m 13.968s
10	Oliveira	2m 14.002s
11	Bagnaia	2m 14.058s
12	Hanika	2m 14.058s
13	McPhee	2m 14.062s
14	Fenati	2m 14.120s
15	Vinales	2m 14.278s
16	Martin	2m 14.320s
17	Manzi	2m 14.378s
18	Danilo	2m 14.391s
19	Masbou	2m 14.393s
20	Migno	2m 14.446s
21	Oettl	2m 14.519s
22	Dalla Porta	2m 14.527s
23	Suzuki	2m 14.594s
24	Loi	2m 14.903s
25	Pagliani	2m 14.918s
26	Guevara	2m 15.078s
27	Rodrigo	2m 15.161s
28	Herrera	2m 15.212s
29	Gardner	2m 15.522s
30	Carrasco	2m 16.668s

Championship Points

1	Kent	253
2	Oliveira	229
3	Bastianini	196
4	Fenati	176
5	Antonelli	174
6	Vazquez	155
7	Binder	146
8	Navarro	137
9	Vinales	105
10	Quartararo	92
11	McPhee	83
12	Masbou	77
13	Kornfeil	73
14	Bagnaia	73
15	Oettl	67
16	Loi	56
17	Hanika	43
18	Martin	43
19	Locatelli	33
20	Migno	30
21	Ajo	21
22	Ono	21
23	Khairuddin	19
24	Guevara	15
25	Dalla Porta	13
26	Danilo	12
27	Manzi	10
28	Suzuki	9
29	Herrera	9
30	Gardner	6
31	Pagliani	3
32	Ferrari	1

Constructor Points

1	Honda	391
2	KTM	316
3	Mahindra	117
4	Husqvarna	85

Above: Bodyguard? A brief three-way battle as Pedrosa closes in on team-mate Marquez. He got past, but ran wide.

Top right: Off to the headmaster's study: Honda's Marquez, Suppo and Pedrosa head for the Permanent Bureau talking-to, followed by Lorenzo. Riders were reminded of "the noble values" of MotoGP.

Above centre right: With the usual pre-race press conference cancelled, Rossi held forth in the Yamaha hospitality unit instead.

Centre far right: Gone, but not forgotten – but Nicky Hayden's induction as a MotoGP Legend was somewhat overshadowed.

Right: The back of the grid has seldom been so busy: Rossi lines up for an insuperable task.

Bottom, centre: The atmosphere was feverish among the sell-out crowd.

Bottom, far right: The next 'next Rossi'? Nicolo Bulega made his GP debut for the VR46 team and finished 12th.

Photos: Gold & Goose

A S at Sepang, there was only one story at Valencia, with many implications. It was not so much about who would win the championship, but how he would win it. That turned out to be Lorenzo, and the manner of his victory would stoke the fires of the conspiracy theorists and provide discussion for years to come. With some help from the rider, who was followed over the line, very closely, by the two Repsol Hondas.

Directly afterwards, interviewed for TV, Lorenzo declared that it had been "a Spanish championship". If this didn't mean he'd been confident of the help of his compatriots, Marquez and Pedrosa, and soon afterwards he said it didn't mean that, Rossi for one didn't believe him.

Marquez, Rossi said, had been Jorge's "bodyguard", and the race had been "embarrassing".

The back-row starter, whose pre-race accusations had driven a wedge between rival fans and raised unnecessary fears of potential violence at the track, had done everything he could, carving through to fourth. Had the Honda pair been ahead of Lorenzo, that would have been enough. "I was ready to lose the championship to Jorge," he said later. "But this way was not fair." To demonstrate his disgust, he cut the official FIM awards ceremony that night. Yamaha team manager Massimo Meregalli took the stage in his absence, to a deafening silence.

The atmosphere, to say the least, had been strange since Thursday, the day Rossi heard that his appeal to the CAS to suspend his penalty had been declined; the day Dorna, without precedent, had cancelled the usual pre-event conference, fearing who knows what. Spitting? Fisticuffs? Weaponry? Bad headlines?

But Dorna was not alone in believing that publicity was best avoided.

The week before, Honda had released an official "interview" with Nakamoto, in which he repeated his insistence that a kick from Rossi had fetched Marquez off at Sepang; proven by data showing a sudden stab of brake pressure. Now the press was invited to a conference to be shown the data; upon arrival, however, there had been an abrupt

about-face. Surely pressure from above, from the Honda Motor Company, desperate to back-pedal from the controversy after a storm on social media showed comments like "I shall never buy another Honda." Bullish team principal Livio Suppo even said that the post-race accusations at Sepang "may have been a mistake".

Certainly there had been top-level talks in Japan between the two companies, and Yamaha's decision to cancel their Saturday 'All Star' gala dinner was surely from the same direction. Top management had been due to fly in from Japan, along with Yamaha champions from all around the world, when the plug was pulled with only four days to go.

Also on Thursday, all MotoGP riders had been called in for a talking-to from the Permanent Bureau, in the form of FIM president Vito Ippolito and Dorna chief Ezpeleta. "First and foremost," said Ippolito, "sport must prevail. This Sunday is the last race of the year, and it is the sport that needs to win.

"Over the past days, there have been unfortunately some controversies that have surpassed the limits of a healthy passion, and on occasions, logic itself," he added, with more words about "the noble values of our sport". (The statement also included a vague threat: "We would like to emphasise that for next year some changes will be made to prevent this from happening again." Given the criticism also levelled at Race Direction for not having applied an on-the-spot ride-through penalty, which would have avoided much of the later storm, this led to speculation that heads may roll.

None of this stopped the gossip, turbocharged by the race. Had Marquez been pulling his punches? He'd been close to Lorenzo most of the way, but had not attempted even one pass. Was this the same rider who had changed places nine times on one lap with Rossi in Malaysia?

Then again, in every one of Lorenzo's seven wins of 2015, he had led from the first lap, usually from the first corner, to the flag. Why should this have been different?

And Marquez had been planning to attack, he said later, but leaving it to the end of the race, as at Indianapolis. This was foiled first by a yellow flag, and then by Pedrosa, who rapidly closed a gap that with four laps to go had been 2.949

seconds, and who pounced on Marquez on the second-last lap. That cost Marquez half a second, putting Lorenzo out of reach.

Then again, why had Pedrosa been able to catch up so easily, if Marquez hadn't been letting a fading Lorenzo set the pace?

So many questions, so many possible answers. If Marquez and Pedrosa were guilty, as one Spanish newspaper said, then it was the perfect crime. No admissible evidence beyond dubious hearsay.

This one would run and run, but the championship was done and dusted: Lorenzo's third in the class and his career fifth after seven picture-perfect wins. The dream was over for Rossi, and for the 750,000 fans who had signed a petition beseeching Race Direction to set his penalty aside.

At the other end of the paddock, the nightmare was over for Danny Kent. After round 12 in Britain, Kent had been 110 points clear of Oliveira. Now his margin had shrunk to 24. Should Oliveira win (and he was looking unstoppable) and Kent finish 15th or, worse still, fail to score, Oliveira would be champion. As at three of the previous four races, Oliveira did win. Kent, scared of getting mixed up in the usual frenzy, pootled around at the back of the points.

Later on, his Leopard team-mate Ono dropped out of the front group and came back to him. Kent moved ahead and it all looked fine. But clearly there was no love lost, and the Japanese mounted an unexpected and successful attack on the last lap.

It made no difference. Kent became the first British world champion since Barry Sheene in 1977, MOTOCOURSE's second year, by just six points.

Moto2 went through the motions, and while Rabat claimed a CV-enhancing final class win, Rins was second in the race and in the championship. But now everyone was focused on 2016, with MotoGP tests due to start on Tuesday, and new Michelin tyres and control software to get to grips with.

MOTOGP RACE – 30 laps

Iannone was a surprise leader of free practice, vowing his intent to ignore the greater championship battle and concentrate his attentions on Pedrosa, to try to recover fourth overall. Rossi was second, but didn't bother with the usual dash in qualifying, preferring to work on race set-up, and it was Lorenzo who surged to pole with a new best lap; Marquez and Pedrosa alongside, Aleix Espargaro heading row two from Englishmen Crutchlow and Smith.

Crutchlow, however, would lose a cylinder on the sighting lap and have to switch bikes, to start at the back of the grid with Rossi.

As at almost every one of his six other wins in 2015, Lorenzo seized the lead into the first corner and held it to the end. Both Hondas went with him, but while Marquez stayed there, Pedrosa was soon falling back with front grip issues and his familiar full-tank difficulties. "It was bottoming under braking," he said.

Lorenzo kept his head down for "one of the most difficult races of my life." As well as the usual wheelspin problems as the tyres started to drop off, he was also having difficulty reading his lap board. "At the end, I thought there were some laps left. Then I saw the chequer. It was very emotional. I don't usually cry, but this time I couldn't greet the fans as usual because I was crying so much."

Marquez was usually within half a second, often closer. He planned to pounce with three laps to go, but "at the place where I was stronger, turns five and six, there was a yellow flag." Di Meglio was touring back to the pits.

Shortly after that, Pedrosa arrived, having found his pace by stopping trying so hard. With two laps to go, he attacked and passed Marquez. But it didn't last – he ran wide on the next corner, and was third again. But it had given Lorenzo breathing space. Marquez came close in the last corner, but not quite close enough. Much to the suspicion of Rossi and his fans.

Rossi's race was much as expected. Starting from 25th, he was up to 16th before a quarter of a lap, then 15th by the end of it, already ahead of most of the Open-class riders.

The track is narrow and passing opportunities few, but by the end of lap three, he was up to ninth, the competition stiffer. It was three laps before he slashed past Smith; next time around his pal Petrucci moved so wide to let him by that he almost ran off, and Smith followed Rossi through.

It took four more laps before a rough pass on Pol Espargaro put him sixth, and three more before he could finally get past Aleix Espargaro's Suzuki.

With Iannone having crashed out of fourth on lap three, that left just Dovizioso. That pass came on lap 13. Rossi was fourth. But he was more than ten seconds adrift of the leading trio, an interval that would stretch, slowly at first, until it had doubled at the end.

"I knew already my chances were small," he said, in a long and impassioned (although outwardly good-humoured) post-race briefing. "It was a great season. The championship had the potential to be one of the best. But in the last three races something happened that nobody expected. Marquez decided to protect Lorenzo. The problems started at Phillip Island. I knew already my championship was finished before this race, because Marquez would finish his work."

Marquez of course denied it. You choose whom to believe. Either way, probably he would have been fourth, even if he had started from the first or second row.

Again, the rest of the race was something of a sideshow. Pol was fifth, three seconds ahead of team-mate Smith, who stole sixth from Dovizioso on the last lap. Aleix Espargaro had lost touch, five seconds away in eighth.

Crutchlow had a blazing ride through to ninth; Petrucci fell back to tenth, only narrowly ahead of Vinales, who had come through and outpaced a big midfield pack. Pirro was 12th; next Hernandez; and then the remnants of that pack –Bautista still half a second clear of Redding, who had also cut through in the closing stages for the final point.

Barbera had been his last victim, still inches behind; Hayden was a couple of seconds down by the end, having fended off Bradl on the second Aprilia.

Then came Baz and late challenger Elias; Jack Miller was less than a second down. West was last. Di Meglio, Parkes (subbing for de Angelis) and Laverty retired.

MOTO2 RACE – 18 laps (shortened from 27)

Rabat was back, still not fully recovered as he lined up for his last Moto2 race after a difficult and unsuccessful title defence. Second place had now also slipped away – unless he could recover eight points on Rins.

He qualified on pole from Zarco and Rins, with Luthi, the ever-stronger Baldassarri and Simon behind. "I arrived here not knowing if I would be able to ride at the top level – but I felt good on Friday and got better every day," he said. "I'm still not 100 per cent fit, but fit enough to ride fast."

He led away from the first start, but it lasted not one lap, with a pile-up on the second corner, a looping left, when a midfield chain reaction caused chaos, but luckily no serious injuries. Six riders crashed – Syahrin, Schrotter, Morbidelli, Simeon, Vierge and Mulhauser – and the wreckage took some clearing. Morbidelli and Syahrin did not make the restart.

For a second time, Rabat led away. This time, however, Luthi was his closest pursuer, with Rins and Baldassari chasing along behind.

There would be few changes in another austere race for the production-powered class.

The first came on lap three, when Rins took second. Now he was close to Rabat and pushed him all the way. But he never did get ahead, finishing still just three-tenths adrift, but fully aware that it was more than enough to retain second spot in the standings.

Rabat was only three points adrift after his 13th and final class win. His vanquisher Zarco had another downbeat ride to seventh, but it was enough to exceed Rabat's class record points tally for the season, with 352 to 346.

After six laps, Luthi was a second adrift, and that had grown to more than three by the end, his hands full with the ever-pressing Baldassarri.

There was some moderate shuffling behind this quartet.

Simon finished the first lap fourth, but was promptly displaced by Corsi. Salom was also in the mix and took over fifth for one lap shortly before half-distance.

Next time around, however, Sam Lowes was ahead, and he drew clear. By the finish, he was barely a second behind Baldassarri and Luthi – and the position meant Lowes took fourth overall ahead of the Swiss rider.

Salom held to sixth, with Zarco just three-tenths behind

over the line, having finally got past Corsi.

The Italian had more trouble to come as Axel Pons closed up and pounced on the final lap for eighth.

Kallio was a lone tenth; Nakagami prevailed over Marquez, Cortese and Folger in a close battle for 11th. First-race crasher Schrotter took the final point.

Edgar Pons crashed out, likewise Lucas Mahias on the unconventional Promoto Sport Transfiormers: the Frenchman had qualified the front wishbone-suspended wild-card bike an impressive 16th.

MOTO3 RACE – 24 laps

The race was about two people – Oliveira and Kent. The omens were mixed: the Portuguese rider had qualified fourth, heading the second row behind first-time pole qualifier McPhee. The Scotsman had started from pole in Australia, though qualified second.

Kent however had qualified a deeply worrying 18th.

The English title leader would play no part in the race up front, where Oliveira took an early lead, but was engaged with the usual brawling gang. The first to displace him was Kent's team-mate Vazquez, for one lap; then a bit later Fenati, for two.

Navarro – already invulnerable as top rookie – also had a couple of goes up front over the line, on laps 13 and 23. But Oliveira was dominant and took over again at the first corner of the final lap.

Navarro followed him home closely, but mayhem erupted behind them. Antonelli had caught up and made a wild lunge into the final corner. He lost it, crashed, and took Fenati and Vazquez with him.

That left a second podium to Kornfeil, close throughout. Brad Binder was inches behind, having come through from midfield; then a second's gap to Bastianini. Vinales, also through from the rear, took sixth, ahead of McPhee.

Almost ten seconds away, also promoted three places by the crash, came the other two Leopard Honda riders.

Inexplicably, Hiroki Ono had dropped back and then dutifully behind Kent, only to attack and overtake him on the final lap, taking eighth by just over half a second. Ninth was enough for Kent, however, for whom it was "the best day of my life".

Above: Bridgestone packed up their tent for the final time. Michelin took over on Tuesday.

Above left: Hector Barbera and his Avintia team celebrate their informal Open championship win.

Top centre: Defeated champion Tito Rabat signed off from Moto2 with his 13th class win.

Top right: Race winner Oliveira did his job, but came up short. The sporting Portuguese star congratulates title rival (and 2016 team-mate) Kent.

Left: Despite the attentions of pesky team-mate Ono, Danny Kent studiously avoided trouble. Ninth was good enough to clinch it.

Top left: All eyes were on Rossi as the Doctor battled through the field.
Photos: Gold & Goose

GP MOTUL DE LA
COMUNITAT VALENCIANA

6–8 NOVEMBER, 2015

CIRCUITO DE LA COMUNITAT VALENCIANA

30 laps
Length: 4.005 km / 2.489 miles
Width: 12m

Key
96/60 kph/mph
Gear

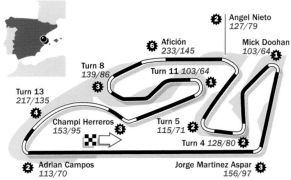

Angel Nieto 127/79
Afición 233/145
Mick Doohan 103/64
Turn 8 139/86
Turn 11 103/64
Turn 13 217/135
Champi Herreros 153/95
Turn 5 115/71
Turn 4 128/80
Adrian Campos 113/70
Jorge Martinez Aspar 156/97

| MotoGP | RACE DISTANCE: 30 laps, 74.658 miles/120.150km · RACE WEATHER: Dry (air 23°C, humidity 63%, track 29°C) |

Pos.	Rider	Nat.	No.	Entrant	Machine	Tyres	Race tyre choice	Laps	Time & speed
1	**Jorge Lorenzo**	SPA	99	Movistar Yamaha MotoGP	Yamaha YZR-M1	B	F: Soft/R: Medium	30	45m 59.364s 97.4mph/ 156.7km/h
2	**Marc Marquez**	SPA	93	Repsol Honda Team	Honda RC213V	B	F: Soft/R: Medium	30	45m 59.627s
3	**Dani Pedrosa**	SPA	26	Repsol Honda Team	Honda RC213V	B	F: Soft/R: Medium	30	46m 00.018s
4	**Valentino Rossi**	ITA	46	Movistar Yamaha MotoGP	Yamaha YZR-M1	B	F: Soft/R: Medium	30	46m 19.153s
5	**Pol Espargaro**	SPA	44	Monster Yamaha Tech 3	Yamaha YZR-M1	B	F: Asymmetric/R: Medium	30	46m 25.368s
6	**Bradley Smith**	GBR	38	Monster Yamaha Tech 3	Yamaha YZR-M1	B	F: Soft/R: Medium	30	46m 28.199s
7	**Andrea Dovizioso**	ITA	4	Ducati Team	Ducati Desmosedici	B	F: Soft/R: Medium	30	46m 28.250s
8	**Aleix Espargaro**	SPA	41	Team SUZUKI ECSTAR	Suzuki GSX-RR	B	F: Soft/R: Medium	30	46m 33.586s
9	**Cal Crutchlow**	GBR	35	LCR Honda	Honda RC213V	B	F: Soft/R: Medium	30	46m 35.288s
10	**Danilo Petrucci**	ITA	9	Octo Pramac Racing	Ducati Desmosedici	B	F: Soft/R: Medium	30	46m 38.943s
11	**Maverick Vinales**	SPA	25	Team SUZUKI ECSTAR	Suzuki GSX-RR	B	F: Soft/R: Medium	30	46m 39.110s
12	**Michele Pirro**	ITA	51	Ducati Team	Ducati Desmosedici	B	F: Soft/R: Medium	30	46m 46.417s
13	**Yonny Hernandez**	COL	68	Octo Pramac Racing	Ducati Desmosedici	B	F: Soft/R: Medium	30	46m 53.445s
14	**Alvaro Bautista**	SPA	19	Aprilia Racing Team Gresini	Aprilia RS-GP	B	F: Soft/R: Soft	30	46m 56.010s
15	**Scott Redding**	GBR	45	EG 0,0 Marc VDS	Honda RC213V	B	F: Soft/R: Medium	30	46m 56.642s
16	Hector Barbera	SPA	8	Avintia Racing	Ducati Desmosedici Open	B	F: Soft/R: Medium	30	46m 56.727s
17	Nicky Hayden	USA	69	Aspar MotoGP Team	Honda RC213V-RS	B	F: Soft/R: Soft	30	46m 58.106s
18	Stefan Bradl	GER	6	Aprilia Racing Team Gresini	Aprilia RS-GP	B	F: Soft/R: Soft	30	46m 58.450s
19	Loris Baz	FRA	76	Forward Racing	Yamaha Forward	B	F: Soft/R: Soft	30	47m 03.703s
20	Toni Elias	SPA	24	Forward Racing	Yamaha Forward	B	F: Asymmetric/R: Soft	30	47m 03.777s
21	Jack Miller	AUS	43	LCR Honda	Honda RC213V-RS	B	F: Soft/R: Soft	30	47m 04.576s
22	Anthony West	AUS	13	AB Motoracing	Honda RC213V-RS	B	F: Soft/R: Soft	30	47m 26.645s
	Mike di Meglio	FRA	63	Avintia Racing	Ducati Desmosedici Open	B	F: Soft/R: Medium	24	DNF-crash
	Eugene Laverty	IRL	50	Aspar MotoGP Team	Honda RC213V-RS	B	F: Soft/R: Soft	23	DNF-injured
	Broc Parkes	AUS	23	E-Motion IodaRacing Team	ART	B	F: Soft/R: Soft	21	DNF-technical
	Andrea Iannone	ITA	29	Ducati Team	Ducati Desmosedici	B	F: Asymmetric/R: Medium	2	DNF-crash

Fastest lap: Jorge Lorenzo, on lap 3, 1m 31.367s, 98.1mph/157.8km/h (record).
Previous lap record: Marc Marquez, SPA (Honda), 1m 31.515s, 97.9mph/157.5km/h (2014).
Event best maximum speed: Andrea Dovizioso, 208.7mph/335.9km/h (race).

Qualifying
Weather: Dry
Air Temp: 26° **Track Temp:** 31°
Humidity: 47%

1	Lorenzo	1m 30.011s
2	Marquez	1m 30.499s
3	Pedrosa	1m 30.516s
4	A. Espargaro	1m 30.917s
5	Crutchlow	1m 30.948s
6	Smith	1m 31.012s
7	Iannone	1m 31.056s
8	P. Espargaro	1m 31.080s
9	Dovizioso	1m 31.245s
10	Petrucci	1m 31.292s
11	Vinales	1m 31.340s
12	Rossi	1m 31.471s
13	Pirro	1m 31.780s
14	Bradl	1m 31.824s
15	Barbera	1m 31.851s
16	Baz	1m 31.856s
17	Hayden	1m 32.083s
18	Hernandez	1m 32.142s
19	Bautista	1m 32.282s
20	Redding	1m 32.448s
21	Miller	1m 32.564s
22	Di Meglio	1m 32.716s
23	West	1m 33.049s
24	Laverty	1m 33.066s
25	Elias	1m 33.092s
26	Parkes	1m 33.577s

Fastest race laps

1	Lorenzo	1m 31.367s
2	Marquez	1m 31.455s
3	Pedrosa	1m 31.478s
4	Iannone	1m 31.491s
5	Rossi	1m 31.820s
6	Dovizioso	1m 32.041s
7	A. Espargaro	1m 32.121s
8	P. Espargaro	1m 32.236s
9	Crutchlow	1m 32.240s
10	Smith	1m 32.338s
11	Vinales	1m 32.381s
12	Petrucci	1m 32.385s
13	Hernandez	1m 32.776s
14	Pirro	1m 32.884s
15	Redding	1m 32.942s
16	Barbera	1m 32.944s
17	Hayden	1m 33.105s
18	Bradl	1m 33.263s
19	Baz	1m 33.265s
20	Bautista	1m 33.312s
21	Miller	1m 33.427s
22	Elias	1m 33.435s
23	Laverty	1m 33.500s
24	Di Meglio	1m 33.567s
25	West	1m 33.722s
26	Parkes	1m 34.359s

Championship Points

1	Lorenzo	330
2	Rossi	325
3	Marquez	242
4	Pedrosa	206
5	Iannone	188
6	Smith	181
7	Dovizioso	162
8	Crutchlow	125
9	P. Espargaro	114
10	Petrucci	113
11	A. Espargaro	105
12	Vinales	97
13	Redding	84
14	Hernandez	56
15	Barbera	33
16	Bautista	31
17	Baz	28
18	Bradl	17
19	Miller	17
20	Hayden	16
21	Pirro	12
22	E. Laverty	9
23	Nakasuga	8
24	Di Meglio	8
25	Aoyama	5
26	Takahashi	4
27	Elias	2
28	De Angelis	2

Constructor Points

1	Yamaha	407
2	Honda	355
3	Ducati	256
4	Suzuki	137
5	Aprilia	36
6	Yamaha Forward	35
7	ART	2

Grid Order

Grid Order	1	2	3	4	5	6	7	8	9	10	11	12	13	14	15	16	17	18	19	20	21	22	23	24	25	26	27	28	29	30	
99 LORENZO	99	99	99	99	99	99	99	99	99	99	99	99	99	99	99	99	99	99	99	99	99	99	99	99	99	99	99	99	99	99	1
93 MARQUEZ	93	93	93	93	93	93	93	93	93	93	93	93	93	93	93	93	93	93	93	93	93	93	93	93	93	93	93	93	93	93	2
26 PEDROSA	26	26	26	26	26	26	26	26	26	26	26	26	26	26	26	26	26	26	26	26	26	26	26	26	26	26	26	26	26	26	3
41 A. ESPARGARO	29	29	4	4	4	4	4	4	4	4	4	46	46	46	46	46	46	46	46	46	46	46	46	46	46	46	46	46	46	46	4
35 CRUTCHLOW	4	4	41	41	41	41	41	41	41	41	41	41	46	4	4	4	4	44	44	44	44	44	44	44	44	44	44	44	44	44	5
38 SMITH	41	41	44	44	44	44	44	44	44	46	46	41	41	44	44	44	4	4	4	4	4	4	4	4	38	38	38	4	38	6
29 IANNONE	9	44	9	9	9	9	46	46	44	44	44	44	41	41	41	41	38	38	38	38	38	38	4	4	4	38	4	7
44 P. ESPARGARO	44	9	38	38	38	46	38	38	38	38	38	38	38	38	38	41	41	41	41	41	41	41	41	41	41	41	41	41	41	8
4 DOVIZIOSO	38	38	46	46	46	38	9	9	9	9	9	9	9	9	9	9	9	9	35	35	35	35	35	35	35	9
9 PETRUCCI	6	51	51	51	51	51	51	51	51	51	51	51	51	51	35	35	35	35	9	9	9	9	9	9	9	10
25 VINALES	51	6	6	6	68	68	68	68	68	68	68	68	35	35	51	51	51	51	51	25	25	25	25	25	25	25	11
51 PIRRO	19	46	19	68	68	6	6	6	6	25	35	35	35	68	68	25	25	25	25	51	51	51	51	51	51	51	12
6 BRADL	69	19	68	19	19	19	19	19	6	25	25	25	25	25	25	68	68	68	68	68	68	68	68	68	68	13
8 BARBERA	68	68	69	69	69	69	69	25	35	6	6	6	6	6	19	19	19	19	6	6	6	6	6	6	8	45	14
76 BAZ	46	69	76	76	25	25	25	35	19	19	19	19	19	19	6	6	6	6	6	6	6	6	6	8	45	15
69 HAYDEN	76	76	25	25	76	35	35	35	69	69	69	69	69	69	69	69	69	69	69	69	69	69	8	45	8
68 HERNANDEZ	25	25	43	43	35	76	76	76	76	76	76	76	76	76	76	76	76	8	8	8	8	69	6	69
19 BAUTISTA	43	43	45	45	43	43	43	43	43	43	43	43	8	8	8	8	8	76	45	45	45	45	45	69	6
45 REDDING	45	45	35	35	45	45	45	45	45	45	8	43	43	43	43	45	45	45	76	76	76	76	76	76
43 MILLER	63	50	50	50	50	50	50	8	8	8	45	45	45	45	45	43	43	43	43	43	43	24	24	24
63 DI MEGLIO	50	13	13	8	8	8	50	50	50	50	50	50	50	50	24	24	24	24	24	24	43	43	43
13 WEST	13	35	63	13	63	63	63	63	63	63	63	24	24	24	24	24	50	50	50	63	13	13	13	13
50 LAVERTY	8	63	8	63	13	13	13	24	24	24	63	63	63	63	63	63	63	50	13
24 ELIAS	35	8	24	24	24	24	24	13	13	13	13	13	13	13	13	13	13	13
23 PARKES	24	24	23	23	23	23	23	23	23	23	23	23	23	23	23	23	23	23
46 ROSSI	23	23																													

23 Pit stop

Moto2 — RACE DISTANCE: 18 laps, 44.795 miles/72.090km · RACE WEATHER: Dry (air 20°C, humidity 68%, track 29°C)

Pos.	Rider	Nat.	No.	Entrant	Machine	Laps	Time & Speed
1	Tito Rabat	SPA	1	EG 0,0 Marc VDS	Kalex	18	28m 48.831s
							93.3mph/
							150.1km/h
2	Alex Rins	SPA	40	Paginas Amarillas HP 40	Kalex	18	28m 49.140s
3	Thomas Luthi	SWI	12	Derendinger Racing Interwetten	Kalex	18	28m 52.178s
4	Lorenzo Baldassarri	ITA	7	Forward Racing	Kalex	18	28m 52.475s
5	Sam Lowes	GBR	22	Speed Up Racing	Speed Up	18	28m 53.971s
6	Luis Salom	SPA	39	Paginas Amarillas HP 40	Kalex	18	28m 58.330s
7	Johann Zarco	FRA	5	Ajo Motorsport	Kalex	18	28m 58.665s
8	Axel Pons	SPA	49	AGR Team	Kalex	18	29m 00.028s
9	Simone Corsi	ITA	3	Forward Racing	Kalex	18	29m 00.442s
10	Mika Kallio	FIN	36	QMMF Racing Team	Speed Up	18	29m 06.142s
11	Takaaki Nakagami	JPN	30	IDEMITSU Honda Team Asia	Kalex	18	29m 09.615s
12	Alex Marquez	SPA	73	EG 0,0 Marc VDS	Kalex	18	29m 10.127s
13	Sandro Cortese	GER	11	Dynavolt Intact GP	Kalex	18	29m 10.286s
14	Jonas Folger	GER	94	AGR Team	Kalex	18	29m 10.391s
15	Marcel Schrotter	GER	23	Tech 3	Tech 3	18	29m 13.500s
16	Xavier Simeon	BEL	19	Federal Oil Gresini Moto2	Kalex	18	29m 17.021s
17	Xavi Vierge	SPA	97	Tech 3	Tech 3	18	29m 17.368s
18	Julian Simon	SPA	60	QMMF Racing Team	Speed Up	18	29m 17.593s
19	Ricard Cardus	SPA	88	JPMoto Malaysia	Suter	18	29m 17.848s
20	Florian Alt	GER	66	E-Motion IodaRacing Team	Suter	18	29m 18.128s
21	Randy Krummenacher	SWI	4	JIR Racing Team	Kalex	18	29m 19.619s
22	Robin Mulhauser	SWI	70	Technomag Racing Interwetten	Kalex	18	29m 20.859s
23	Thitipong Warokorn	THA	10	APH PTT The Pizza SAG	Kalex	18	29m 25.875s
24	Jesko Raffin	SWI	2	sports-millions-EMWE-SAG	Kalex	18	29m 25.938s
25	Federico Fuligni	ITA	32	Ciatti	Suter	18	29m 36.070s
26	Joshua Hook	AUS	16	Technomag Racing Interwetten	Kalex	18	29m 36.732s
	Lucas Mahias	FRA	90	Promoto Sport	Transfiormers	13	DNF
	Edgar Pons	SPA	57	Italtrans Racing Team	Kalex	3	DNF
	Franco Morbidelli	ITA	21	Italtrans Racing Team	Kalex	0	DNS
	Hafizh Syahrin	MAL	55	Petronas Raceline Malaysia	Kalex	0	DNS

Fastest lap: Tito Rabat, on lap 15, 1m 35.416s, 93.9mph/151.1km/h.
Lap record: Thomas Luthi, SWI (Suter), 1m 35.312s, 94.0mph/151.2km/h (2014).
Event best maximum speed: Sandro Cortese, 169.4mph/272.6km/h (race).

Qualifying
Weather: Dry
Air Temp: 27° **Track Temp:** 30°
Humidity: 47%

1	Rabat	1m 35.234s
2	Zarco	1m 35.372s
3	Rins	1m 35.441s
4	Luthi	1m 35.532s
5	Baldassarri	1m 35.694s
6	Simon	1m 35.728s
7	Pons	1m 35.752s
8	Nakagami	1m 35.786s
9	Corsi	1m 35.896s
10	Lowes	1m 35.930s
11	Morbidelli	1m 35.935s
12	Salom	1m 36.036s
13	Cortese	1m 36.071s
14	Marquez	1m 36.166s
15	Kallio	1m 36.226s
16	Mahias	1m 36.284s
17	Cardus	1m 36.289s
18	Folger	1m 36.360s
19	Alt	1m 36.422s
20	Krummenacher	1m 36.427s
21	Schrotter	1m 36.470s
22	Vierge	1m 36.563s
23	Simeon	1m 36.588s
24	Syahrin	1m 36.600s
25	Pons	1m 36.741s
26	Mulhauser	1m 36.912s
27	Raffin	1m 37.573s
28	Warokorn	1m 37.658s
29	Fuligni	1m 37.835s
30	Hook	1m 38.208s
	Shah	No Time
	Rossi	No Time

Fastest race laps

1	Rabat	1m 35.416s
2	Rins	1m 35.549s
3	Lowes	1m 35.583s
4	Baldassarri	1m 35.765s
5	Luthi	1m 35.777s
6	Zarco	1m 35.887s
7	Salom	1m 35.911s
8	Corsi	1m 35.914s
9	Pons	1m 35.961s
10	Kallio	1m 35.996s
11	Cortese	1m 36.161s
12	Nakagami	1m 36.321s
13	Folger	1m 36.355s
14	Simon	1m 36.405s
15	Marquez	1m 36.444s
16	Schrotter	1m 36.656s
17	Alt	1m 36.749s
18	Vierge	1m 36.753s
19	Simeon	1m 36.774s
20	Cardus	1m 36.778s
21	Raffin	1m 36.925s
22	Krummenacher	1m 36.973s
23	Mulhauser	1m 36.986s
24	Mahias	1m 37.165s
25	Warokorn	1m 37.350s
26	Hook	1m 37.574s
27	Pons	1m 37.629s
28	Fuligni	1m 37.689s

Championship Points

1	Zarco	352
2	Rins	234
3	Rabat	231
4	Lowes	186
5	Luthi	179
6	Folger	163
7	Simeon	113
8	Nakagami	100
9	Baldassarri	96
10	Morbidelli	90
11	Cortese	90
12	Corsi	86
13	Salom	80
14	Marquez	73
15	Kallio	72
16	Syahrin	64
17	Aegerter	62
18	Simon	58
19	Pons	41
20	Schrotter	32
21	Krummenacher	31
22	West	30
23	Shah	24
24	Cardus	20
25	Rossi	7
26	Koyama	3
27	Takahashi	2
28	Mulhauser	1

Constructor Points

		Points
1	Kalex	445
2	Speed Up	209
3	Tech 3	39
4	Suter	20
5	NTS	3
6	Moriwaki	2

Moto3 — RACE DISTANCE: 24 laps, 59.726 miles/96.120km · RACE WEATHER: Dry (air 20°C, humidity 75%, track 22°C)

Pos.	Rider	Nat.	No.	Entrant	Machine	Laps	Time & Speed
1	Miguel Oliveira	POR	44	Red Bull KTM Ajo	KTM	24	40m 09.792s
							89.2mph/
							143.5km/h
2	Jorge Navarro	SPA	9	Estrella Galicia 0,0	Honda	24	40m 09.990s
3	Jakub Kornfeil	CZE	84	Drive M7 SIC	KTM	24	40m 11.882s
4	Brad Binder	RSA	41	Red Bull KTM Ajo	KTM	24	40m 11.913s
5	Enea Bastianini	ITA	33	Gresini Racing Team Moto3	Honda	24	40m 12.767s
6	Isaac Vinales	SPA	32	RBA Racing Team	KTM	24	40m 13.135s
7	John McPhee	GBR	17	SAXOPRINT RTG	Honda	24	40m 13.879s
8	Hiroki Ono	JPN	76	Leopard Racing	Honda	24	40m 19.419s
9	Danny Kent	GBR	52	Leopard Racing	Honda	24	40m 19.706s
10	Philipp Oettl	GER	65	Schedl GP Racing	KTM	24	40m 20.372s
11	Andrea Migno	ITA	16	SKY Racing Team VR46	KTM	24	40m 20.453s
12	Nicolo Bulega	ITA	8	SKY Racing Team VR46	KTM	24	40m 21.434s
13	Francesco Bagnaia	ITA	21	MAPFRE Team MAHINDRA	Mahindra	24	40m 26.533s
14	Jorge Martin	SPA	88	MAPFRE Team MAHINDRA	Mahindra	24	40m 29.988s
15	Alexis Masbou	FRA	10	SAXOPRINT RTG	Honda	24	40m 31.323s
16	Jules Danilo	FRA	95	Ongetta-Rivacold	Honda	24	40m 31.344s
17	Zulfahmi Khairuddin	MAL	63	Drive M7 SIC	KTM	24	40m 31.660s
18	Darryn Binder	RSA	40	Outox Reset Drink Team	Mahindra	24	40m 34.906s
19	Stefano Manzi	ITA	29	San Carlo Team Italia	Mahindra	24	40m 35.093s
20	Livio Loi	BEL	11	RW Racing GP	Honda	24	40m 35.123s
21	Maria Herrera	SPA	6	Husqvarna Factory Laglisse	Husqvarna	24	40m 35.447s
22	Lorenzo Dalla Porta	ITA	48	Husqvarna Factory Laglisse	Husqvarna	24	40m 42.765s
23	Fabio di Giannantonio	ITA	4	Gresini Racing Team Moto3	Honda	24	40m 42.811s
24	Ana Carrasco	SPA	22	RBA Racing Team	KTM	24	40m 43.341s
25	Manuel Pagliani	ITA	96	San Carlo Team Italia	Mahindra	24	40m 43.745s
	Efren Vazquez	SPA	7	Leopard Racing	Honda	23	DNF
	Romano Fenati	ITA	5	SKY Racing Team VR46	KTM	23	DNF
	Niccolo Antonelli	ITA	23	Ongetta-Rivacold	Honda	23	DNF
	Alessandro Tonucci	ITA	19	Outox Reset Drink Team	Mahindra	20	DNF
	Karel Hanika	CZE	98	Red Bull KTM Ajo	KTM	10	DNF
	Fabio Quartararo	FRA	20	Estrella Galicia 0,0	Honda	10	DNF
	Juanfran Guevara	SPA	58	MAPFRE Team MAHINDRA	Mahindra	7	DNF
	Tatsuki Suzuki	JPN	24	CIP	Mahindra	7	DNF
	Remy Gardner	AUS	2	CIP	Mahindra	5	DNF

Fastest lap: Romano Fenati, on lap 16, 1m 39.622s, 89.9mph/144.7km/h.
Lap record: Efren Vazquez, SPA (Honda), 1m 39.400s, 90.1mph/145.0km/h (2014).
Event best maximum speed: John McPhee, 145.0mph/233.3km/h (race).

Qualifying
Weather: Dry
Air Temp: 22° **Track Temp:** 28°
Humidity: 63%

1	McPhee	1m 39.364s
2	Fenati	1m 39.450s
3	Vazquez	1m 39.463s
4	Oliveira	1m 39.503s
5	Navarro	1m 39.525s
6	Bastianini	1m 39.581s
7	Antonelli	1m 39.591s
8	Hanika	1m 39.617s
9	Binder	1m 39.666s
10	Ono	1m 39.668s
11	Quartararo	1m 39.686s
12	Kornfeil	1m 39.763s
13	Vinales	1m 39.763s
14	Oettl	1m 39.920s
15	Migno	1m 39.952s
16	Bulega	1m 39.964s
17	Danilo	1m 40.006s
18	Kent	1m 40.013s
19	Bagnaia	1m 40.014s
20	Masbou	1m 40.063s
21	Khairuddin	1m 40.071s
22	Herrera	1m 40.324s
23	Dalla Porta	1m 40.359s
24	Martin	1m 40.380s
25	Loi	1m 40.496s
26	Manzi	1m 40.535s
27	Di Giannantonio	1m 40.552s
28	Binder	1m 40.588s
29	Pagliani	1m 40.619s
30	Guevara	1m 40.674s
31	Carrasco	1m 40.795s
32	Gardner	1m 41.041s
33	Tonucci	1m 41.063s
34	Suzuki	1m 41.162s
35	Rodrigo	1m 42.517s

Fastest race laps

1	Fenati	1m 39.622s
2	Navarro	1m 39.739s
3	Binder	1m 39.746s
4	Kornfeil	1m 39.756s
5	Antonelli	1m 39.781s
6	Oliveira	1m 39.812s
7	Vazquez	1m 39.833s
8	Ono	1m 39.861s
9	Bagnaia	1m 39.906s
10	Vinales	1m 39.911s
11	Oettl	1m 39.940s
12	McPhee	1m 39.943s
13	Bastianini	1m 39.964s
14	Kent	1m 39.990s
15	Migno	1m 39.997s
16	Bulega	1m 40.036s
17	Quartararo	1m 40.154s
18	Khairuddin	1m 40.170s
19	Hanika	1m 40.278s
20	Martin	1m 40.319s
21	Herrera	1m 40.330s
22	Manzi	1m 40.335s
23	Binder	1m 40.353s
24	Danilo	1m 40.408s
25	Gardner	1m 40.434s
26	Loi	1m 40.436s
27	Masbou	1m 40.497s
28	Suzuki	1m 40.554s
29	Di	1m 40.571s
30	Guevara	1m 40.576s
31	Dalla Porta	1m 40.624s
32	Tonucci	1m 40.920s
33	Pagliani	1m 40.920s
34	Carrasco	1m 40.926s

Championship Points

1	Kent	260
2	Oliveira	254
3	Bastianini	207
4	Fenati	176
5	Antonelli	174
6	Binder	159
7	Navarro	157
8	Vazquez	155
9	Vinales	115
10	Quartararo	92
11	McPhee	92
12	Kornfeil	89
13	Masbou	78
14	Bagnaia	76
15	Oettl	73
16	Loi	56
17	Martin	45
18	Hanika	43
19	Migno	35
20	Locatelli	33
21	Ono	29
22	Ajo	21
23	Khairuddin	19
24	Guevara	15
25	Dalla Porta	13
26	Danilo	12
27	Manzi	10
28	Suzuki	9
29	Herrera	9
30	Gardner	6
31	Bulega	4
32	Pagliani	3
33	Ferrari	1

Constructor Points

		Points
1	Honda	411
2	KTM	341
3	Mahindra	120
4	Husqvarna	85

WORLD CHAMPIONSHIP POINTS 2015

Compiled by PETER McLAREN

Photos: Gold & Goose

MotoGP – Riders

Position	Rider	Nationality	Machine	Qatar	Texas	Argentina	Spain	France	Italy	Catalunya	Netherlands	Germany	Indianapolis	Czech Republic	Great Britain	San Marino	Aragon	Japan	Australia	Malaysia	Valencia	Points total
1	Jorge Lorenzo	SPA	Yamaha	13	13	11	25	25	25	25	16	13	20	25	13	–	25	16	20	20	25	330
2	Valentino Rossi	ITA	Yamaha	25	16	25	16	20	16	20	25	16	16	16	25	11	16	20	13	16	13	325
3	Marc Marquez	SPA	Honda	11	25	–	20	13	–	–	20	25	25	20	–	25	–	13	25	–	20	242
4	Dani Pedrosa	SPA	Honda	10	–	–	–	–	13	16	8	20	13	11	11	7	20	25	11	25	16	206
5	Andrea Iannone	ITA	Ducati	16	11	13	10	11	20	13	13	11	11	13	8	9	13	–	16	–	–	188
6	Bradley Smith	GBR	Yamaha	8	10	10	8	10	11	11	9	10	10	9	9	20	8	9	6	13	10	181
7	Andrea Dovizioso	ITA	Ducati	20	20	20	7	16	–	–	4	7	10	16	8	11	11	3	–	–	9	162
8	Cal Crutchlow	GBR	Honda	9	9	16	13	–	–	–	10	9	8	–	–	5	9	10	9	11	7	125
9	Pol Espargaro	SPA	Yamaha	7	–	8	11	9	10	–	11	8	9	8	–	–	7	–	8	7	11	114
10	Danilo Petrucci	ITA	Ducati	4	6	5	4	6	7	7	5	7	6	6	20	10	–	–	4	10	6	113
11	Aleix Espargaro	SPA	Suzuki	5	8	9	9	–	–	–	7	6	2	7	7	6	10	5	7	9	8	105
12	Maverick Vinales	SPA	Suzuki	2	7	6	5	7	9	10	6	5	5	–	5	2	5	–	10	8	5	97
13	Scott Redding	GBR	Honda	3	–	7	3	–	5	9	3	–	3	4	10	16	4	6	5	5	1	84
14	Yonny Hernandez	COL	Ducati	6	–	–	6	8	6	–	2	4	4	5	–	–	6	2	–	4	3	56
15	Hector Barbera	SPA	Ducati	1	4	3	2	3	3	–	3	1	–	3	–	–	–	7	–	3	–	33
16	Alvaro Bautista	SPA	Aprilia	–	1	–	1	1	2	6	–	2	–	3	6	1	3	–	2	1	2	31
17	Loris Baz	FRA	Yamaha	–	–	2	–	4	4	3	1	–	1	–	13	–	–	–	–	–	–	28
18	Stefan Bradl	GER	Yamaha/Aprilia	–	–	1	–	–	–	8	–	–	2	–	–	–	–	–	–	6	–	17
19	Jack Miller	AUS	Honda	–	2	4	–	–	–	5	–	1	–	–	4	–	–	1	–	–	–	17
20	Nicky Hayden	USA	Honda	–	3	–	–	5	–	–	–	–	–	–	4	–	1	3	–	–	–	16
21	Michele Pirro	ITA	Ducati	–	–	–	–	–	8	–	–	–	–	–	–	–	–	–	–	–	4	12
22	Eugene Laverty	IRL	Honda	–	–	–	–	2	1	4	–	–	–	–	–	–	2	–	–	–	–	9
23	Katsuyuki Nakasuga	JPN	Yamaha	–	–	–	–	–	–	–	–	–	–	–	–	–	–	8	–	–	–	8
24	Mike di Meglio	FRA	Ducati	–	–	–	–	–	–	2	–	–	–	–	–	2	3	–	1	–	–	8
25	Hiroshi Aoyama	JPN	Honda	–	5	–	–	–	–	–	–	–	–	–	–	–	–	–	–	–	–	5
26	Takumi Takahashi	JPN	Honda	–	–	–	–	–	–	–	–	–	–	–	–	–	–	4	–	–	–	4
27	Toni Elias	SPA	Yamaha Forward	–	–	–	–	–	–	–	–	–	–	–	–	–	–	–	–	2	–	2
28	Alex de Angelis	RSM	ART	–	–	–	–	–	1	–	–	–	–	–	1	–	–	–	–	–	–	2

MotoGP – Teams

Position	Team	Qatar	Texas	Argentina	Spain	France	Italy	Catalunya	Netherlands	Germany	Indianapolis	Czech Republic	Great Britain	San Marino	Aragon	Japan	Australia	Malaysia	Valencia	Points total
1	Movistar Yamaha MotoGP	38	29	36	41	45	41	45	41	29	36	41	38	11	41	36	33	36	38	655
2	Repsol Honda Team	21	30	–	20	13	13	16	28	45	38	31	11	32	20	38	36	25	36	453
3	Ducati Team	36	31	33	17	27	20	13	17	11	18	23	24	17	24	11	19	–	9	350
4	Monster Yamaha Tech 3	15	10	18	19	19	21	11	20	18	19	17	9	20	15	9	14	20	21	295
5	Team Suzuki Ecstar	7	15	15	14	7	9	10	13	11	7	7	12	8	15	5	17	17	13	202
6	Octo Pramac Racing	10	6	5	10	14	13	7	7	11	10	11	20	10	6	2	4	14	9	169
7	LCR Honda	9	11	20	13	–	–	5	10	10	8	–	–	9	9	10	10	11	7	142
8	EG 0,0 Marc VDS	3	–	7	3	–	5	9	3	–	3	4	10	16	4	6	5	5	1	84
9	Avintia Racing	1	4	3	2	3	3	2	–	3	1	–	5	3	–	–	–	3	–	41
10	Forward Racing	–	–	3	–	4	4	11	1	–	–	1	–	13	–	–	–	2	–	39
11	Aprilia Racing Team Gresini	–	1	–	1	1	2	6	–	2	–	5	6	1	3	–	2	7	2	39
12	Aspar MotoGP Team	–	3	–	–	7	1	4	–	–	–	4	–	3	3	–	–	–	–	25
13	E-Motion Iodaracing Team	–	–	–	–	–	1	–	–	–	–	1	–	–	–	–	–	–	–	2

Moto2

Position	Rider	Nationality	Machine	Qatar	Texas	Argentina	Spain	France	Italy	Catalunya	Netherlands	Germany	Indianapolis	Czech Republic	Great Britain	San Marino	Aragon	Japan	Australia	Malaysia	Valencia	Points total
1	Johann Zarco	FRA	Kalex	8	20	25	20	16	20	25	25	20	20	25	25	25	10	25	9	25	9	352
2	Alex Rins	SPA	Kalex	13	16	20	–	–	5	20	13	16	25	16	20	–	20	5	25	–	20	234
3	Tito Rabat	SPA	Kalex	–	13	4	16	20	25	16	20	–	11	20	16	20	25	–	–	–	25	231
4	Sam Lowes	GBR	Speed Up	–	25	16	–	13	13	13	16	11	–	11	10	–	16	8	20	3	11	186
5	Thomas Luthi	SWI	Kalex	16	4	10	13	25	–	10	11	10	10	9	7	6	11	–	1	20	16	179
6	Jonas Folger	GER	Kalex	25	–	7	25	–	–	9	9	2	4	10	11	10	13	20	–	16	2	163
7	Xavier Simeon	BEL	Kalex	20	–	–	11	8	10	–	10	25	8	–	–	4	–	–	11	6	–	113
8	Takaaki Nakagami	JPN	Kalex	2	6	–	–	9	3	–	3	9	7	4	2	16	8	–	13	13	5	100
9	Lorenzo Baldassarri	ITA	Kalex	6	–	8	3	–	6	6	–	8	–	–	–	9	6	4	16	11	13	96
10	Franco Morbidelli	ITA	Kalex	11	11	11	10	11	–	8	–	16	6	–	–	–	–	5	1	–	–	90
11	Sandro Cortese	GER	Kalex	9	2	9	–	2	8	–	5	–	8	8	8	3	16	–	9	3	–	90
12	Simone Corsi	ITA	Kalex	–	5	–	8	–	–	3	6	13	–	5	–	13	7	9	3	7	7	86
13	Luis Salom	SPA	Kalex	–	–	5	9	–	11	11	–	–	–	7	–	7	–	10	10	10	–	80
14	Alex Marquez	SPA	Kalex	5	1	1	7	–	4	5	7	–	6	13	13	–	–	7	–	–	4	73
15	Mika Kallio	FIN	Kalex/Speed Up	10	8	13	–	–	4	8	4	–	1	–	–	5	1	8	4	6	–	72
16	Hafizh Syahrin	MAL	Kalex	4	10	6	4	7	–	2	1	–	–	2	–	–	9	11	–	8	–	64
17	Dominique Aegerter	SWI	Kalex	1	–	3	–	6	16	7	4	6	13	3	3	–	–	–	–	–	–	62
18	Julian Simon	SPA	Speed Up	3	7	–	5	10	9	1	5	7	–	–	–	11	–	–	–	–	–	58
19	Axel Pons	SPA	Kalex	–	–	–	–	1	7	–	–	1	9	–	1	5	4	–	–	5	8	41
20	Marcel Schrotter	GER	Tech 3	–	3	–	6	3	–	–	–	2	–	5	–	1	7	4	–	–	1	32
21	Randy Krummenacher	SWI	Kalex	–	–	–	2	4	2	–	–	–	–	–	4	2	–	5	6	6	–	31
22	Anthony West	AUS	Speed Up	–	9	2	1	5	–	–	–	3	–	9	1	–	–	–	–	–	–	30
23	Azlan Shah	MAL	Kalex	–	–	–	–	–	1	–	–	–	5	–	–	3	2	13	–	–	–	24
24	Ricard Cardus	SPA	Tech 3/Suter	–	–	–	–	–	–	–	–	–	–	–	6	–	–	10	2	2	–	20
25	Louis Rossi	FRA	Tech 3	7	–	–	–	–	–	–	–	–	–	–	–	–	–	–	–	–	–	7
26	Tomoyoshi Koyama	JPN	NTS	–	–	–	–	–	–	–	–	–	–	–	–	–	–	3	–	–	–	3
27	Yuki Takahashi	JPN	Moriwaki	–	–	–	–	–	–	–	–	–	–	–	–	–	–	2	–	–	–	2
28	Robin Mulhauser	SWI	Kalex	–	–	–	–	–	–	–	–	–	1	–	–	–	–	–	–	–	–	1

Moto3

Position	Rider	Nationality	Machine	Qatar	Texas	Argentina	Spain	France	Italy	Catalunya	Netherlands	Germany	Indianapolis	Czech Republic	Great Britain	San Marino	Aragon	Japan	Australia	Malaysia	Valencia	Points total
1	Danny Kent	GBR	Honda	16	25	25	25	13	20	25	16	25	–	9	25	10	–	10	–	9	7	260
2	Miguel Oliveira	POR	KTM	–	–	13	20	8	25	11	25	–	1	8	3	20	25	20	25	25	25	254
3	Enea Bastianini	ITA	Honda	20	13	7	7	20	11	20	10	16	10	20	–	25	–	9	–	8	11	207
4	Romano Fenati	ITA	KTM	–	8	8	10	25	16	8	11	13	13	10	4	13	16	–	10	11	–	176
5	Niccolo Antonelli	ITA	Honda	8	–	–	–	11	10	13	7	11	9	25	16	16	10	25	–	13	–	174
6	Brad Binder	RSA	KTM	6	11	11	16	–	6	7	9	9	8	16	–	11	–	–	16	20	13	159
7	Jorge Navarro	SPA	Honda	4	–	–	8	–	9	10	13	10	7	11	–	–	20	16	13	16	20	157
8	Efren Vazquez	SPA	Honda	13	16	20	11	–	–	16	–	20	–	13	7	–	13	6	20	–	–	155
9	Isaac Vinales	SPA	Husqvarna/KTM	10	7	16	5	9	8	9	–	11	–	–	7	–	13	8	2	–	10	115
10	Fabio Quartararo	FRA	Honda	9	20	10	13	–	–	2	20	–	5	–	13	–	–	–	–	–	–	92
11	John McPhee	GBR	Honda	11	10	1	6	–	–	–	6	–	20	6	10	–	–	7	–	6	9	92
12	Jakub Kornfeil	CZE	KTM	–	5	2	–	10	–	–	2	–	7	20	–	2	4	–	11	10	16	89
13	Alexis Masbou	FRA	Honda	25	–	–	1	–	7	–	8	–	–	5	9	8	–	7	7	1	–	78
14	Francesco Bagnaia	ITA	Mahindra	7	–	5	9	16	13	–	5	–	–	4	–	8	5	1	–	–	3	76
15	Philipp Oettl	GER	KTM	2	3	–	–	6	6	–	1	5	16	1	–	6	11	–	9	1	6	73
16	Livio Loi	BEL	Honda	–	–	4	3	3	2	–	3	–	25	–	11	4	1	–	–	–	–	56
17	Jorge Martin	SPA	Mahindra	1	–	–	2	–	–	5	5	–	4	6	–	1	9	5	1	4	2	45
18	Karel Hanika	CZE	KTM	3	6	9	–	–	–	–	8	3	4	–	–	–	–	8	2	–	–	43
19	Andrea Migno	ITA	KTM	–	4	–	–	7	1	–	4	–	–	3	1	3	7	–	–	–	5	35
20	Andrea Locatelli	ITA	Honda	5	9	–	–	–	3	4	–	7	–	–	–	–	–	2	–	–	3	33
21	Hiroki Ono	JPN	Honda	–	–	3	–	5	5	–	2	–	–	–	–	–	6	–	–	–	8	29
22	Niklas Ajo	FIN	KTM	–	2	6	–	–	4	3	–	6	–	–	–	–	–	–	–	–	–	21
23	Zulfahmi Khairuddin	MAL	KTM	–	–	–	–	2	–	–	–	–	–	–	2	–	–	11	4	–	–	19
24	Juanfran Guevara	SPA	Mahindra	–	–	–	–	4	–	–	–	–	–	2	9	–	–	–	–	–	–	15
25	Lorenzo Dalla Porta	ITA	Husqvarna	–	–	–	–	–	–	–	–	–	–	–	8	5	–	–	–	–	–	13
26	Jules Danilo	FRA	Honda	–	–	–	–	4	–	–	–	–	1	2	–	–	–	–	–	5	–	12
27	Stefano Manzi	ITA	Mahindra	–	–	–	–	–	1	–	–	–	–	–	–	–	–	2	4	3	–	10
28	Tatsuki Suzuki	JPN	Mahindra	–	–	–	–	–	–	–	–	–	–	6	–	–	–	–	3	–	–	9
29	Maria Herrera	SPA	Husqvarna	–	–	–	–	–	–	1	–	–	–	–	–	–	–	3	–	5	–	9
30	Remy Gardner	AUS	Mahindra	–	–	–	–	–	–	–	–	–	–	–	–	–	–	6	–	–	–	6
31	Nicolo Bulega	ITA	KTM	–	–	–	–	–	–	–	–	–	–	–	–	–	–	–	–	–	4	4
32	Manuel Pagliani	ITA	Mahindra	–	–	–	–	–	–	–	–	–	–	–	–	–	–	–	3	–	–	3
33	Matteo Ferrari	ITA	Mahindra	–	1	–	–	–	–	–	–	–	–	–	–	–	–	–	–	–	–	1

BENDSNEYDER'S YEAR

By PETER CLIFFORD

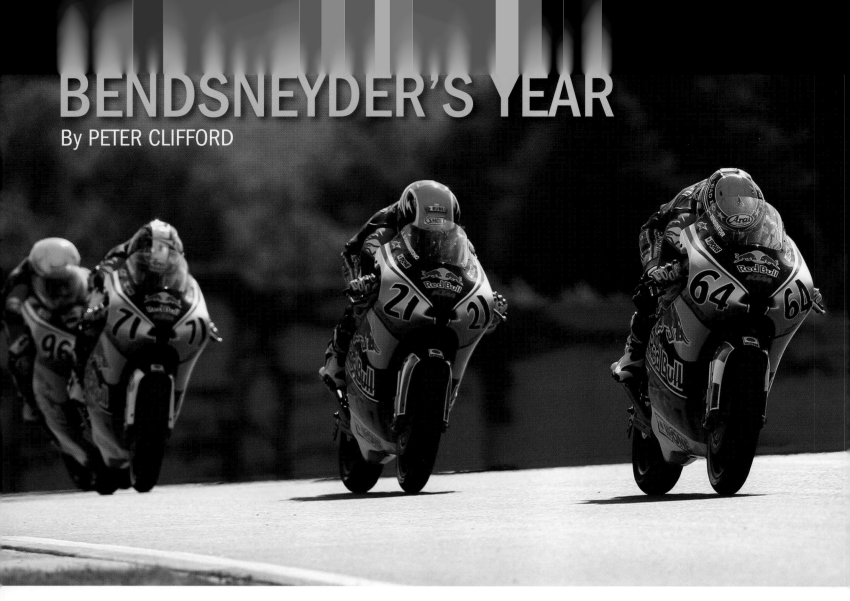

N O one has ever stamped their domination on the Red Bull MotoGP Rookies Cup in the way that Bo Bendsneyder did in 2015. He blitzed the opposition with five straight victories to kick off the ninth Cup season, the Dutchman's second in the series. It was not that the 16-year-old had an easy ride, far from it – 2015 was an extremely competitive season with lap records regularly broken, and Bendsneyder often had to fight for every corner.

With all riders on KTM RC250Rs and only a certain amount of weight ballast allowed, the lanky Netherlander appeared to have a disadvantage, but he demonstrated that being on the tall and heavy side were handicaps that could be overcome.

The opening round in Jerez was a Rookies classic. In race one, Bendsneyder was embroiled in a seven-rider battle for the win. Looking over the replay that evening, he realised that he had spent too much time looking around for the opposition. In race two on Sunday, he was very different, head down and totally focused. Three seconds behind him at the flag was Fabio di Giannantonio, the 16-year-old Italian who had to fight all the way to come out ahead of the seven-rider scrap for second.

Di Giannantonio had finished fifth in race one, and he would become the most significant challenge to Bendsneyder throughout the season. They proved themselves to be not only great racers, but also wonderful sportsmen – teenagers with an easy professional manner.

Bendsneyder and di Giannantonio set great examples to the other Rookies, and the whole Cup series benefited. They respected each other both on and off the track, with the result that while the races were intense, they were devoid of the overly aggressive riding that can be driven by a youthful lack of imagination.

If anyone was fazed by Bendsneyder's record-breaking run of victories, it wasn't di Giannantonio. Bendsneyder had taken his first Cup victory at Assen in 2014, and he returned home ready to dominate the second event of the season. He took pole, almost half a second quicker than the rest, but di Giannantonio showed that he would not be cowed, raced him hard and took second, well clear of the rest.

Just as in Jerez, Bendsneyder reviewed race one and ratcheted it up a notch for race two, with di Giannantonio still second, but nearly two seconds adrift at the flag. The Italian knew that he had to stop his arch rival's flight at the top of the points table when the Cup arrived in Germany for the third weekend of action.

Race one at the Sachsenring comprised 19 dramatic laps, where any of six riders could have taken the 25 points, yet in the end it was the Dutch national anthem that rang out again. Di Giannantonio was fourth, behind 14-year-old Ayumu Sasaki and 15-year-old Spaniard Marc Garcia. Bendsneyder had a perfect points score, 125, with di Giannantonio back on 84.

The gap looked massive going into Sunday and the sixth of 13 races. With the championship headed towards half-distance, some saw Bendsneyder already with one hand on the Cup. That hand slipped off at the last corner in race two, however, when the Dutchman fell in his determination to extend his unbroken run.

The pair had opened up an 11-second lead over their rivals and the Italian had the advantage going into the final turn; Bendsneyder slid off as he fought back. Suddenly the points difference was down to just 16 and the Cup was wide open again.

Di Giannantonio carried his momentum into qualifying at Brno and put his KTM on pole, 0.316 second ahead of Bendsneyder. He maintained it with a brilliant win in race one by 0.141 second over Bo. The pair had been so far ahead of the opposition that they started playing a quite odd game as the 14 laps wound down.

Di Giannantonio had done most of the leading and thought that it was about time Bendsneyder took some of the load. The Dutchman wasn't keen, the pace slowed, then slowed even more – "After you," "No, after you." The pack was catching up.

The Italian put the hammer down at the right time and Bendsneyder couldn't catch him before the line. They were still over two seconds ahead of a storming contest for third, resolved when 14-year-old Spaniard Raul Fernandez, a first-year Rookie, kept Marc Garcia off the podium.

Now the gap was down to just 11 points with seven races gone and six to go. Di Giannantonio had seized the initiative, and he seemed to have raised his game to the point where he could race with Bendsneyder every time and had a small victory run of his own going. That ended at the third corner of race two at Brno, where the Italian's KTM slid and flicked him off. "It was simple," the 16-year-old explained later. "I made a mistake, no one to blame but myself."

That didn't leave Bendsneyder with an easy race, though. It was an eight-man battle for the win that went down to the last corner, where victory was contested by 18-year-old Frenchman Enzo Boulom and Raul Fernandez. But the pair clashed and ran wide. That left Bendsneyder perfectly positioned to charge across the line first, with Boulom fourth and Fernandez seventh.

When the series headed across the channel to Silverstone, Bendsneyder had a 36-point lead, but knew very well how easily that could change. He made his intentions clear, taking pole by half a second. Di Giannantonio looked troubled, ninth fastest and over 1.3 seconds adrift.

Above: Leading lights. Di Giannantonio, Bendsneyder and Simpson took the top steps at Jerez.

Left: Japan's Ayumu Sasaki (14) was an impressive third overall.

Far left: Fast and Furious – again. Di Giannantonio chases winner Bendsneyder in the first race in Germany. Sasaki (71) and Spaniard Gutierrez (96) chase the chaser.

Photos: Gold & Goose

The Italian did far better in the race, but couldn't match Bendsneyder, who reeled off 14 perfect laps for his seventh win of the season. Five competitors were determined to chase him all the way, but though di Giannantonio was second, ahead of Ayumu Sasaki, they were well astern at the finish.

Sasaki was proving to be one of the great finds of the season. He had been on the pace right from the pre-season test in Jerez and a podium contender at the first GP, until collected by fellow countryman 15-year-old Kaito Toba at the last corner in race twi. After two sixth places in Assen, the second in race one at the Sachsenring was well deserved. He slid off in race two, but apart from those two falls was not outside the top six all season.

Toba seemed as fast, but didn't get the results. As reigning Asia Cup champion, he put a lot of pressure on himself, and the more success Sasaki had, the greater was the pressure on Toba. He was on the podium with third in race twi at the Sachsenring, but apart from that battled to match Sasaki and fell too often while trying. A cooler approach to 2016 would be a big advantage.

As so often at Silverstone, the weather jumped into the action for race two, and it was very slippery. Sasaki and Enzo Boulom were in a class of their own as they led Bo Bendsneyder home. The Japanese tailed the 18-year-old Frenchman all the way and then upped the pace with a lap to go, winning by three seconds, with Bendsneyder a further 23 behind. Crucially, di Giannantonio was 11th, struggling with the conditions and bike setting.

There were only 13 finishers in Silverstone, and as Bendsneyder pointed out, tapping his helmet as he crossed the line, third was very much a thinking man's result – there was no need to take chances.

Although it was only third, the 16 points were a lot better than di Giannantonio's five, and the gap was

up to 52 with three races remaining. There was not a lot of thinking to do in Misano. Bendsneyder just had to keep it all together while 'DiGi21' had to finish in front of him if the contest was going to carry over to the last two races in Aragon.

There was just a single race on Saturday in Italy, where post-MotoGP race track invasions make an outing late on Sunday problematic to say the least. The event did not start well for the local hero, who struggled through practice with bike setting and was only ninth fastest, over six-tenths off Bendsneyder's pole time.

It was those new kids, Fernandez and Sasaki completing the front row as they continued to stake their claims to be the boys to watch in 2016. Fernandez had taken a few more races to get going than Sasaki, but was well into his stride by Misano, shrugging off the embarrassment of sliding off on the wet sighting lap for race two at Silverstone, where he had been a good fourth in race one.

Unintimidated by starting from row three in Misano, di Giannantonio cut through quickly to hunt down Bendsneyder. He got in front of him, too. Finishing in front would be good, but really he needed Bendsneyder further back; he needed the pack to catch up. It all came unravelled on lap 11 of the 17, when the Italian slid off. Bendsneyder had the Cup.

Though the title had been decided, there was plenty to play for in Aragon. Bendsneyder made it clear that he was not going to be taking it easy. He already had eight wins for the season and one from 2014. He was looking at Karel Hanika's tally of three in 2012 and seven in his championship-winning year, 2013.

He already had the record for the number of eight wins in a season, but winning the last two would give him a career total of 11 and thus put him ahead of the Czech ace. Less obviously, Bendsneyder was

also chasing a place in the Red Bull KTM Ajo factory Moto3 team, a place that Hanika was still enjoying.

It was going to be a hard-fought last weekend, and it started in qualifying, with Bendsneyder denied pole by Rory Skinner. The Scott would only turn 14 on the Sunday, but he had shown great skill to take a slippery fourth in race two at Silverstone. He had begun the year further back than Sasaki and Fernandez, but had impressed the Cup rider coaches with his measured progress.

He was a quarter of a second quicker than the new Cup champion in qualifying and set off from pole to show everyone that it was no fluke. Unfortunately, a bad crash soon brought out the red flags. Fourteen-year-old Spaniard Aleix Viu had high-sided, and Bendsneyder, Boulom and Bruno Ieraci became tangled up in the mess. Viu had been quickest in the free practice sessions and was looking to improve on his fifth from Misano, but he was taken to hospital with a number of injuries, including hip and foot fractures. While his injuries were nasty, he soon expressed his firm intention to be fit and ready for 2016.

The other three fallers didn't make the restart either, and Skinner again shot off from pole. It was a great race, even though shortened to eight laps. Skinner did plenty of leading, but so did Fernandez, and there was a fierce pack behind. Skinner managed a one-second lead with two laps to go, but that had evaporated by the start of the last lap and 15-year-old Spaniard Marc Garcia cut out of his slipstream to take the lead into turn one.

Garcia held off Fernandez to take his first Cup win. It was his fourth appearance on the podium for the year, and it helped him to fourth in the title chase. Skinner was an excellent third, with di Giannantonio a disappointed sixth.

So there was no slackening of excitement for the final race of the year on the Sunday. Again Skinner shot away from pole and once more it was anyone's race for the full 15 laps. At the flag, the top six were covered by 0.742 second – typical Rookies Cup.

The win went to di Giannantonio in a photo-finish over Sasaki, another Cup classic with Skinner third, making it a sensational weekend for him and a perfect birthday present. It didn't look anything like a fluke, and he put his name alongside Sasaki and Fernandez as one to watch. Fernandez had ended up at the back of that six-rider pack, behind Garcia.

Fourth in his final Rookies outing was 17-year-old Australian Olly Simpson, seemingly the unluckiest of Rookies. He had started his third season with two excellent third places in Jerez, but an early crash in race one at Assen put him out of both races.

He had got over the worst of the shoulder injury by the following event in Germany, but had struggled to find form. Being in the hunt for the win in Aragon in the final race was where he belonged. Bendsneyder was back in ninth, almost seven seconds off the winner, thanks to a strained wrist from the race one crash.

It was a fitting end to a wonderful Cup season, and no one had any doubt that Bo Bendsneyder was the right man to carry hopes of all aspiring champions into the Moto3 class in 2016.

As the Cup looked towards its tenth season in 2016, it was interesting to see ex-Rookies Johann Zarco and Danny Kent take the 2015 Moto2 and Moto3 world titles. Indeed, of the 34 riders in the 2015 Moto3 entry list, 14 were ex-Rookies – that's 41 per cent If you discount all the Spanish and Italian riders, there were 18, and of those, nine were ex-Rookies – a full 50 per cent.

It's time for a challenge.

TISSOT PRS 516 AUTOMATIC.
A VERY SPECIAL PIECE WITH A VINTAGE TOUCH THAT PAYS HOMAGE TO RACING CARS. THE HOLES IN THE STRAP INVENTED BY TISSOT ILLUSTRATE THOSE OF A STEERING WHEEL. AUTOMATIC MOVEMENT WITH UP TO 60 HOURS OF POWER RESERVE.

T + TISSOT THIS IS YOUR TIME

REVIEW OF 2015

By GORDON RITCHIE

Photo: Gold & Goose

REWORK IN PROGRESS

SINCE Dorna took over commercial control of the FIM Superbike World Championship, the maxim had been cost reduction, particularly in relation to technical matters, achieved by reducing top performance and component exclusivity. Cost-capped electronics came into their own in 2015, after two rounds of using the previous season's kit.

These initiatives were supposed to stop the factory teams from running away with it every time, to make a 13,000-euro Superbike donor machine compete on level terms with bikes that were three times more expensive in stock trim.

However, with our open minds looking for optimism beyond the often-empty grandstands and puzzling lack of coverage in even hardcore motorcycle publications, there was little change in the perception of WSBK in 2015.

All manufacturers created their own electronics packages, supplying customers with cheap ECUs and software, but that made little difference to the electronics warfare among the top teams. It was good for the privateers, of course, but come any Sunday they were still finishing relatively miles behind the teams and manufacturers who invested most, especially in their rider talent.

That's racing for you.

The best bikes, some of which had lost an immediate 20bhp over the winter thanks to much reduced levels of allowable tuning, just became faster around the track anyway. Not everywhere, but in lots of places.

That's racing for you.

Accessibility became a keyword, making the tech packages so enticing to ambitious teams from national championships that they can come and compete right away. But with such a disjointed and expensive calendar to follow, with two huge summer breaks, WSBK still has areas to focus on.

Strong domestic wild-card entries? A memory for the most part. That's one of the key reasons WSBK has lost popularity in key markets like the UK, USA and Australia – and anywhere else with a mature national Superbike scene. Nothing like watching the local underdogs duff up the big boys to get the crowd rocking.

On balance, there remain many things for Dorna to turn around yet. Some are well in hand, however, if still in the background. All the same, WSBK presents genuine opportunities for teams and riders of the high second order, in the second biggest bike series of all.

Even with Jonathan Rea winning the championship what felt like several times over in one season, and taking 14 race wins of the 26 in total, four other riders won races somewhere or other. Some days, Rea simply was beaten in a straight fight.

Much more importantly, ten different riders proved capable of a top-three rides, with podiums spread across five manufacturers.

WSBK may have an ongoing image problem, but beneath the anti-hype the racing is often as open as ever, even in a season in which the champ won by an eventual 132 points from his nearest rival.

THE SEVEN-YEAR SWITCH

By GORDON RITCHIE

Photo: Gold & Goose

THAT it took Jonathan Rea seven years of full-time competition to become the FIM Superbike world champion is amazing in some ways, yet completely understandable.

When you ride for the world's biggest manufacturer for your entire career and demonstrate an ability to win races in every single WSBK season since your first in 2009, obviously you are a talented player of racing games. But not quite being able to challenge for the championship all the way suggests that something is not right with some aspect of the overall package.

That was the story of Rea's WSBK experience since his first ride for the Honda Europe/Ten Kate Superbike operation at the end of his first full Supersport World Championship. He almost became the 2008 WSS champion, but Ten Kate preferred to move him to Superbike in 2009, even though Aussie Andrew Pitt had won the middleweight title. Ten Kate and Honda Europe thought he was that good, and they were proved right over and over.

Rea demonstrated that he was much better than 'good' in 2015, in his first ever season away from the big H, while riding the most official and highly developed Japanese bike in the WSBK paddock, the Kawasaki Ninja ZX-10R.

A Honda rider for his entire road racing career, Ulsterman Rea is the son of former TT race winner Johnny Rea. With the road paddocks his early playgrounds, racing on mud became his first love, and he won the British 60cc junior motocross title as a teenager.

Eschewing the dangers of pure road racing when the irresistible smell of asphalt filled his lungs, Rea took part in the British 125 GP championship in 2003, then suffered a serious leg injury the next season as he moved on to the British Supersport class.

Backed by Red Bull, he was brought into the British Superbike division relatively early in his career, in 2005. He learned quickly, finishing fourth overall in 2006 and then as runner-up in 2007. By then, he was spreading his Honda wings, winning the pre-Suzuka 300km race that year.

His inclusion in the official Honda Europe/Ten Kate WSS team in 2008 set some

tongues wagging in Britain, but the clear step up to global competition, if a step down in engine capacity, was the making of him. He was runner-up in year one.

He even took the jump to Superbike before the season had been properly completed. He qualified third at the final Portimao event and finished race one fourth. Even an over-exuberant 15th in race two could not disguise his talent at the best Superbike level there is.

Ten Kate, Honda and James Toseland arguably had over-performed to win the Superbike World Championship the year before, and things did not get any easier for the best Honda team in the paddock after that. Both the Honda and Rea had been capable of wins every year since, but always against teams with greater factory input and a wider breadth of resources and personnel.

It is now clear that Rea had been holding out for a Honda MotoGP ride all along, hoping that a sufficiently consistent Superbike package would allow him to win the production world title before moving upstairs. He got neither of those things with Honda, and most observers considered that he should have left long before he did.

Rea was not short of other offers, some even in GPs, but when other British riders from inside the MotoGP paddock were given the kinds of RCV rides he felt he should have been at least offered, he bowed to the inevitability of giving up his ambition.

Rea's gigantic loyalty to Honda and Ten Kate had been reciprocated with as much love and support as the team and Honda Europe could muster through all the previous six seasons. But in his seventh WSBK season, fighting for a different samurai, he went from nearly man to hyper champion in one bound – with five races to spare.

Was Rea the most convincing WSBK title winner since total rookie Ben Spies? If we look at what he faced in 2015, absolutely yes: new manufacturer, new machine and tech rules, new crew and crew chief, new suspension supplier, new brake supplier.

Although some might have expected him to win in 2015, he did so in a way that made him an instant WSBK legend. One that had been seven years in the making.

2015 WORLD SUPERBIKE CHAMPION

JONATHAN REA

1

SBK WORLD CHAMPION
2015

JONATHAN REA

CHAZ DAVIES

TOM SYKES

NICCOLO CANEPA

ROMAN RAMOS

NICOLAS TEROL

RANDY DE PUNIET

MICHAEL van der MARK

LEANDRO MERCADO

MATTEO BAIOCCO

SUPERBIKE WORLD CHAMPIONSHIP
2015 TEAMS & RIDERS

By GORDON RITCHIE

APRILIA

Aprilia Racing Team – Red Devils

It is difficult to give an appraisal of the status of the official 2015 entry, but it was less directly official than it had been in 2014, but much more so than some other teams who claimed to be officially supported. It was an amalgam of the Aprilia Racing skeleton staff, a large handful left behind from the great MotoGP exodus and Red Devils Roma's own people. They fielded Englishman Leon Haslam (32) and Spanish ex-Moto2 star Jordi Torres (28) all year, and won races with both.

Aprilia Racing Team

The official Aprilia Racing test team really, which Max Biaggi (44) brought along to races twice, thanks to the financial input of some sponsors at the Misano and Malaysia rounds. A planned ride at Losail fell through after Biaggi had reportedly injured himself in a mountain-bike accident, after completing extensive test sessions in the desert.

BMW

BMW Motorrad Italia SBK

Sylvain Barrier (25) started the year, but by the return to Europe he was out and Ayrton Badovini (29) was in. A strong one-rider team, run by M&T Racing and Piero Guidi, they were no longer the nearest thing to the official BMW team at the end of the year, as BMW had cut their close connection.

BMW Team Toth

Imre Toth (30) and fellow Hungarian Gabor Rizmayer (30) came back for more, but were reliably among the back-markers every weekend. Poland's Ireneusz Sekora (44) was a one-off Toth team rider in Buriram of all places.

Van Zon Remeha BMW

Leading German IDM light Markus Reiterberger (21) was out in WSBK action at Misano and Magny-Cours, before a planned leap to WSBK racing in 2016. His best rides were to 13th place, securing one at each of the rounds in which he competed.

RAC Oil Racing Team BMW

Thai rider Chanon Chumjai (30) was another wild-card at his home round, but he was soon out of race one on the opening lap, and then in 20th place in race two.

DUCATI

Aruba.it Racing –
Ducati World Superbike Team

The second year of comeback as the fully combined Feel Racing and Ducati Corse squad. Chaz Davies (28) made the jump to championship runner-up, while Davide Giugliano (25) would have been more potent had he not suffered two back injuries from which he was lucky to escape relatively unscathed. Ernesto Marinelli from Ducati Corse pulled the strings as things got back to – pretty much – the old days.

Troy Bayliss (45) was a Giugliano stand-in at PI and Buriram; Xavi Fores (30) at Motorland, Assen and Losail. Luca Scassa (32) was supposed to ride at Misano, but could not. He was given another chance at Magny-Cours, scoring points and a ninth in race two. Michele Pirro (29) replaced the injured Scassa mid-weekend at Misano and rode well, then came back instead of Giugliano in Jerez, piling in with a sixth and seventh place.

Althea Racing Ducati

The team started the season with Nicolas Terol (27) and Matteo Baiocco (31), a good-looking mix of a former 125cc GP world champion and a rider returning from largely testing duties for Ducati to race again. Terol could not master the big V-twin fast enough for boss Genesio Bevilacqua, and he was replaced by Michel Fabrizio (31) at Imola and then suddenly free agent (more than once) Niccolo Canepa (27) for most of the year.

Barni Racing Ducati

Leandro Mercado (23) won Superstock 1000 the year before with Barni, so he was a full-season rookie to WSBK, with a full-season rookie WSBK team. They

fared better than some, but did not quite burst into the top five, with a best of sixth at the very last race of the year. Eighth overall was a brilliant result for such an inexperienced WSBK squad, making them top privateers all round.

EBR

Team Hero EBR

Larry Pegram (42) and Niccolo Canepa started, but did not finish, the first quarter of the season, after the home factory in America went bust on the eve of the Assen weekend. Not making their next homologation targets as a result, they were officially non-participants in some regards.

HONDA

Pata Honda World Superbike Team

Honda Europe's loss of Jonathan Rea was tempered by the arrival of 2014 champion Sylvain Guintoli (33). He took one podium in all, in the wet in France, but had he not suffered a nasty neck injury in winter testing, who knows what would have been possible? Michael van der Mark (22) was a red-hot rookie, scoring no less than three podiums in a year, which made him top Honda and a more-than worthy promotee into WSBK from WSS champion status in 2014..

YSS TS Racing

Anucha Nakcharoensri (27) took his CBR into the fray in his home round of Thailand, as a wild-card, and finished race two in 17th.

KAWASAKI

Kawasaki Racing Team

Tom Sykes (30) and Jonathan Rea (28) were easily the most potent mix of proven champion and reputedly the most talented rider in the entire championship. As close to a full factory team as WSBK gets, the Barcelona-based Provec squad were the logistical and team co-ordinators, while KHI did the technical development directly, in conjunction with the team and Ichiro Yoda.

Team Pedercini Kawasaki

The team fielded David Salom (30) as a reward for his EVO championship win in 2014, but it was a tough year for the old family firm, fronted by former WSBK racer Lucio Pedercini. Greg Gildenhuys (26), Francisco Alviz (25) and eventually Christophe Ponsson (26) made appearances for the team through the year. Matthew Walters (23) was a one-off at PI again.

Grillini SBK Team Kawasaki

Christophe Ponsson (26) and Santiago Barragan (28) started the season as the regular rider line-up, but Ponsson moved on to Pedercini. After Laguna Seca, Barragan was also away. Niccolo Canepa (27) took over from Ponsson for a short time, with Gianluca Vizziello (35) and eventually Alex Phillis (21) finally joining the squad.

Team GO Eleven Kawasaki

Roman Ramos (24) was a worthy addition to the class and yet another new Spanish rider in 2015. His GO Eleven team was having its first WSBK year and did well, if not spectacularly, to take Ramos to 15th overall.

Race Center – Demolition Plus Kawasaki

One-time Superstock 600 rider Jed Metcher (25) had a one-off ride at his home round, securing a couple of points before heading to BSB for the season.

MV AGUSTA

MV Agusta Reparto Corse

Leon Camier (29) was a full-season signing for MV. Brian Gillen, who oversaw the team for most of the year, was brought back to home base for the final round. Fifth place was a strong ride in the wet for Camier at Magny-Cours. A welcome addition to the grid, it was a form of racing while developing, rather than straight racing, as the F4 RR found its feet after a year in the EVO class in 2014.

SUZUKI

Voltcom Crescent Suzuki

Randy de Puniet (34) and second-year Suzuki rider Alex Lowes (25) ran in Voltcom colours in Paul Denning's Crescent team. Without a change in electronics required by Suzuki, and then by the regulations from round three onwards, who knows how many more podiums might have been within reach than Lowes's single in Thailand? A long relationship with Suzuki was ended, and as a last hurrah it was more of a long and dusty goodbye than a rolling street party. They will be back in WSBK with Yamahas in 2016, with official support.

YAMAHA

Szkopek POLand Position

Pawel Szkopek (40) was a one-off wild-card at the penultimate round in France, but he retired in each race.

KAWASAKI NINJA ZX-10R

DUCATI 1199R

Aprilia RSV4

HONDA CBR1000RR SP

MV AGUSTA F4 RR

SUZUKI GSX-R1000K14

BMW S1000RR

THE SUPERBIKES OF 2015 · by Gordon Ritchie

APRILIA RSV4 FACTORY

The new technical rules in 2015 were designed to draw the longest fangs of the biggest power monsters. In the case of the only V4 in the championship, the regulations caused Aprilia the most pain, in respect of 2014's abilities at least.

Losing maybe 20bhp at the top end, having to use one set of gearbox internals per rider, reducing the number of electronics sensors for their own APX ECU and having to re-create a whole new suite of electronics to meet the same kind of cost caps that affected brakes and suspension, WSBK's very own 'Special One' became much more 'of the bottle' in 2015.

To add to the agony, it happened to the most seriously revamped RSV-4 model since the original 65-degree DOHC V4 machine first showed up in WSBK racing, which would have given it a boost in previous, more liberal eras. Its 78 x 52.3mm bore-and-stroke engine now seemed not quite as radical as beforehand, but the overall package was still highly effective when everything worked in harmony.

Trouble was, all the adjustments that had allowed the RSV-4 to fly before had been limited or reduced by the regulations in 2015. The mono-gearbox spec was the worst blow, as gear options could no longer be changed to get one to suit every corner, with one set of internal ratios chosen for each rider before the first round and used all year. What you started with, you finished with.

Results also suffered badly in cold weather, in terms of chassis set-up. Since the engine was in a fixed position, not adjustable in the chassis as in all previous seasons, it was not easy to make the bike change direction in chicanes and still retain stability on acceleration and braking.

The previous Aprilias could be tailored almost infinitely to any rider's needs, but now it appeared that there were just too many compromises to allow the more race-orientated parts of the machine to shine at the very front. Infinite adjustability and near-full-factory support are only benefits if they can be used to the full.

DUCATI 1199R

Italy's most avant-garde box of tricks, the Ducati started to behave like a real race bike – more consistently every weekend – after a huge amount of work and experimentation to settle on some form of base set-up.

Many claimed the very nature of the bike was the limitation, with a monocoque chassis up front (forming the headstock tube holder, airbox and top engine mount), monoshock rear suspension and single-sided swing-arm mounted to the engine. More brackets were attached to the engine and the top of the rear subframe. Effectively, the engine was not just a stressed member; it was the chassis itself.

The top-spec cost-capped 42mm RSP Ohlins forks graced the front, while the 40mm RSP rear shock, operated by the swing-arm, was to the same high level of available tech. Compressed at one end by a triangulated link, and located by the chassis subframe, the rear shock lay horizontally on the left-hand side of the V-engine, in the breeze, but also away from the heat behind the engine. T-type Brembo brakes with Evo calipers bit at the front end, sometimes in thick options, sometimes thin.

The 112 x 60.8mm engine was made easier to ride in 2015 because of a drop in top-end power, which had increased by around 8bhp before the end of the year, had not affected the healthy mid-range. The hated air restrictors, on standby to ensure the balancing rules were fair for all, did not have to make an appearance.

An EVR clutch transmitted the power from engine to gearbox. A very convoluted and longer titanium Akrapovic exhaust was used from mid-season onwards, the two silencers being mounted under the engine, rather than at the very end of the system. This boosted the mid-range and peak power, improving acceleration, which was the biggest handicap at the start of the year.

The ECU was Marelli's latest cost-capped MLE unit, with software developed by Ducati and passed on to satellite teams almost immediately.

BMW S1000RR

There were a few BMW S1000RRs in WSBK in 2015, but the most directly linked to the factory was from the BMW Motorrad Italia squad, a one-man effort that was capable of top-six finishes. A new-model street bike for 2015, it made more power to start with than their Evo machine, but less than a full WSBK engine from 2014.

The direct factory link was not in any real way a 'backdoor' factory effort, as the same technical package was offered to all customer teams in the usual BMW manner. Teams could buy tuned engines and electronics/instrumentation packages, including software and programming modules, but they had to supply their own chassis mods and parts.

Hence the less expensive Ohlins FGR300 front forks and smaller-diameter Ohlins RSP 36mm-piston rear shocks were the most obvious differences from the equipment used by other top teams representing manufacturers offering more direct factory support.

Brembo supplied 328mm brakes. The rear swing-arm looked stock, but had been adjusted and modified by the team itself, with links and some structural alterations to improve stiffness.

Motorrad Italia also created many small engineering marvels on their own, like engine protectors with small-radius ends, so that a crashing machine would skip over trackside kerbs and lips, and not catch on them, subsequently barrelling to destruction.

The BMW had a very Japanese-style across-the-frame four-cylinder engine layout and corresponding twin-spar chassis, but the 999cc engine had an over-square bore and stroke of 80mm x 49.7mm.

HONDA CBR1000RR SP

With two new riders, and despite a host of power-limiting regulations designed to make all manufacturers have the same ultimate horsepower goal, Honda's Ten Kate team had a serious lack of competitive push from the early engines, much to their surprise.

The 76 x 55.1mm engine had made a claimed 228bhp in 2014, but in 2015 it was closer to about 215bhp in the mid-range. There was a much more linear engine output, and by season's end the power and electronics had helped stop the CBR from losing too much time on the straights.

Once again, Ten Kate and Honda Europe used Cosworth and Pectel expertise to develop the electronics, with their cost-capped systems in reality only supplied to their own team. The split ride-by-wire throttle was a neat solution to the problem of controlling a four, as per 2014.

As previously, sponsors and tech partners Nissin supplied the calipers and their own brake rotors. The former were matched with Yutaka discs on occasion.

The great levelling of performance expected and promoted by Honda did not materialise in WSBK, much to their early chagrin, but the bike was still podium capable for each of their riders and improved in most respects throughout the year.

KAWASAKI NINJA ZX-10R

The 76 x 55mm Kawasaki engine architecture remained in 2015, but the extensive tuning for the official KRT squad had to be done under the new rules, which cut the previous 15 per cent reduction in crankshaft weight to five per cent, robbing established Kawasaki champion Sykes of his easy-corner-entry, high-revving corner-exit engine.

The other rider, new boy Rea, got on just fine with the higher-inertia motor, although both laboured at times with up to 20bhp less than in 2014 – say 220bhp all in.

The Marelli MHT ECU of 2014, like everybody else's, had been replaced by the third round by the new cost-capped MLE system, with software thrown in for customer Kawasaki teams. The ECU main body had to be relocated, as it was bigger than the previous unit. Split ride-by-wire throttle bodies, 47mm diameter, controlled two sets of engine bores each.

Again, like nobody else except semi-supported Pedercini rider David Salom, KHI's team used Showa suspension front and back: new T551 forks with external cartridges. A Showa T551 BFR rear shock absorber lay almost flat behind the engine and in front of the rear wheel as part of Kawasaki's home-designed Horizontal Back Link rear suspension. A large alloy adjuster was one of a few detail changes, to meet the cost cap limit and still deliver the required quality.

Big 338mm Brembo T-type discs are were used almost all the time, with Brembo Evo calipers biting on the steel friction surfaces.

MV AGUSTA F4 RR

Almost an Evo bike in 2014, the new MV had been developed with an expectation of all-Evo and thus had some issues during the season with top-end output. Unlike the Supersport F3s, there were fewer problems of a technical nature that interrupted sessions or races. The variable inlet tracts for the radial cylinder head, with four valves per 79 x 50.9mm cylinder, made the F4-RR a very potent street bike.

With titanium inlet and exhaust valves in stock form, the MV was a bike of great potential, given the 2015 requirement to use only stock materials, or materials of the same size and weight as stock.

MV employed their 2014 electronics in the first two rounds, in line with the dispensation granted to all teams intending to use the slightly delayed new MLE Marelli ECUs.

The bike did not hit the 168kg limit at the beginning of the season; it was estimated to be perhaps 5kg heavier than optimum, and a hoped-for modified chassis had not quite arrived by season's end.

The tubular-steel top chassis section was mated to two alloy side plates that carried the swing-arm. A new swing-arm design, which altered the rear link layout, appeared relatively early in the year. It was much bigger and close to the tyre, but had more flex when leaned over in corners.

Brembo brakes and Marchesini wheels were used, again specially made for the MV and its single-sided rear swing-arm.

SUZUKI GSX-R1000K14

It was possibly the final fling for the Suzuki and its 74.5 x 57.3mm engine. Despite the stock or near-stock engine limits for the bottom end and rods, etc, Yoshimura and Suzuki found more horsepower in 2015 than in 2014, perhaps even 225bhp or more by season's end.

A new and deeper oil pan required a new exhaust layout, but it still exited on the right in conventional manner. In fact, the entire bike was very conventional, even old school. Yet it was still podium capable early on.

Before the two-round amnesty extensions for pre-cost-capped kit electronics, the bike used a Motec M170 ECU to power Lowes to a podium in Chang.

The team's take on a twin throttle system had one bank of throttle bodies controlled by the ECU and another directly controlled by a spring-loaded cable throttle. This was claimed to deliver better rider feel and feedback, yet still allow engine braking and all other strategies to be controlled by the ECU.

Suzuki used Ohlins suspension and Brembo brake callipers, but had Sunstar discs as a result of a technical support and sponsorship package. Forks were the best 42mm RSP25s.

The underslung rear swing-arm of 2014 was used again, as it had been voted a success; it imbued the Suzuki with a more modern look and feel.

Stripped down, however, the Suzuki showed its age, with its wide chassis spars and engine position. Ironically, it was the work needed to adapt to the new Marelli MLE-based electronics that killed the push of the Suzuki towards potential winning status again.

2015 Major Technical Regulations

Major limits were placed on all machines, requiring them to use many stock materials inside the engine and restricting the amount of adjustment and/or tolerances to the key chassis dimensions. Significant cost-capping initiatives spread from suspension and brake units – as in 2014 – to include electronics and ride-by-wire. In summary, the main rule changes were:

Minimum weight increased to 168kg, no tolerance.

Cost-capped race kit or approved-supplier ride-by-wire throttle system at 2,500 euros.

Cost-capped race kit or one approved-supplier ECU and all associated displays, extra sensors, wiring, software and updates at 8,000 euros per set.

Valves, valve guides, cylinders, pistons, rings and clips to remain as homologated.

Con-rods could be changed for alternatives of same length, weight and material. Con-rod bolts were free. Camshafts were free, but had to remain in homologated position.

Five per cent maximum reduction in crankshaft weight (previously 15 per cent).

One set of freely chosen gearbox ratios per rider, per season.

Steering-stem axis and position could be altered by moving steering head bearings +/- 6mm in respect of the original bearings.

Swing-arm pivot could be moved +/- 5mm in any direction from the homologated axis.

Restriction to one bike at any one time remained, but a spare motorcycle could be built and be ready for use if the original proved beyond repair.

PHILLIP ISLAND

ROUND 1 · AUSTRALIA

Above: Rea leads Davies, Haslam and Torres in race one.

Right: Troy Bayliss came out of retirement to replace the injured Giugliano.

Centre right: New boy. Jordi Torres on the Aprilia.

Opposite page, from top: Bayliss scored points in race one on the Ducati Panigale; Leon Haslam celebrated a win in race two; Randy de Puniet made his debut on the Suzuki; Race one was just the first of many wins for Rea in 2015.

Below right: Haslam leads Rea, Davies and van der Mark in race two.

Below far right: Michael van der Mark looked the part on his debut.
Photos: Gold & Goose

W ITH a whole new technical landscape for the 2015 ENI FIM Superbike World Championship, there were more question marks than usual to be rubbed out by the opening round.

On a history-making weekend for the Aussie circuit, celebrating 25 WSBK events in total, there was a real feel-good factor at work at what is always a favourite venue. Add the dramatic reappearance of three-times champion and long-time WSBK retiree Troy Bayliss as a replacement for the injured Davide Giugliano (Aruba.it Racing – Ducati World Superbike), plus a host of rider and team changes in the winter months, and anticipation was at high pitch.

In 2014, Kawasaki and Aprilia had fought for supremacy, and it was obvious that in 2015 the on-track battles would feature those two big hitters, plus a rejuvenated Ducati effort thanks to the tech changes bringing them closer to the best four-cylinders in terms of top speed.

The result of each PI race was a near photo finish, as has been usual at the majestic 4.445km circuit since the start of WSBK racing in 1988. As season starts go, it was go-go-go.

All the top riders bar Bayliss having enjoyed the usual two days of official testing, practice and qualifying were mostly about preparing for race day. With Jonathan Rea (Kawasaki Racing Team) scoring only his fifth career pole on Saturday, there was no surprise that he won his very first race for Kawasaki.

The first race was an Island classic, with audacious late passes and a last lap of full risk for all involved. Rea not only had to work hard for his win, but also had to summon every ounce of his racing experience to hold off another seasoned WSBK rider in a new team, Leon Haslam (Aprilia Racing Red Devils). Haslam finished only 0.039 second down, emerging from Rea's slipstream just too late.

In what was an early demonstration of British rider power, Chaz Davies (Aruba.it Racing – Ducati World Superbike) rode his big V-twin to within 0.496 second of the win itself.

Less than two seconds behind, Moto2 refugee Jordi Torres, Haslam's team-mate, made a great start to his WSBK career in fourth.

Another WSBK rookie, but this time a WSS promotee, took fifth place. Michael van der Mark (Pata Honda) came to Superbike as WSS champion and looked an immediate threat.

In a troubled sixth place, 2013 champion Tom Sykes (Kawasaki Racing Team) had found his new Ninja ZX-10R, neutered by the regulations, unsuited to his stop-and-squirt style; being run off track by van der Mark at one stage did not help either.

In the second race, also over the full scheduled 22 laps, van Der Mark was in the leading mix, riding hungry and fast, but he crashed out with a handful of laps to go.

Up front at the end was the same trio of Albion adventurers, but this time Haslam made his final-curve calculations to perfection and passed Rea over the line – by 0.010 second. Davies was even closer than in race one, 0.298 second behind.

Fourth-placed Sykes was 'only' 5.242 seconds behind the win this time, not over 13 as he had been in race one.

Another recent world champion, Sylvain Guintoli (Pata Honda), overcame his longstanding neck injury from a winter test crash in Spain to score fifth, one slot ahead of another Spanish rider for 2015, 125cc champion of old Nico Terol (Althea Racing Ducati).

Former GP riders proliferated in 2015's version of WSBK racing, with Randy de Puniet (Voltcom Crescent Suzuki) seventh in race two in Oz.

For Bayliss, his astoundingly popular return delivered only 13th and 16th places, with an unplanned tyre change midway through race two. He needed the testing he had missed.

BURIRAM

ROUND 2 · THAILAND

Top: Under the huge stand, the bikes blast away for race two.

Above: Newin Chidchob, in charge of proceedings at Buriram.

Above right: Chang Circuit – the destination of speed.

Above far right: South African wildcard Greg Gildenhuys just missed out on the points in both races.

Right: Race-two battle between Pata Honda team-mates and rivals van der Mark and Guintoli.

Photos: Gold & Goose

THE flat and featureless Chang International Circuit in Buriram, Thailand – all 4.554km of it – will win no awards for clever track layout. Most assuredly, however, it is already a winner in terms of facilities, infrastructure, local enthusiasm and feel-good factor, as was attested by the large and enthusiastic crowd on race day..

Two local wild-cards even joined the WSBK gang for what were two tough races. Tough for everybody except new championship leader Jonathan Rea that is.

With the Superpole win, two fastest laps and then two start-to-finish race wins, Rea was operating in a different zone of competitiveness.

Again, the other podium places were taken by British riders.

Leon Haslam doubled his second-place finishes for Aprilia, but still left trailing Rea in the points. He had been 6.329 seconds down after race one and 4.946 seconds back after race two.

Compared to a podium-less Australia, third in race one and then fifth in race two were strong results for Tom Sykes, although he was far from satisfied. He had run higher than his eventual placings, but had been forced to drop back, fighting successfully with rookie rider Torres to keep third in race one, but losing fourth to him in race two.

A new dawn for the talented Alex Lowes came in the meeting where his team were allowed to use their 2014 Motec electronics for the last time, before everyone had to have their chosen 2015 units in place for Aragon. His push to an eventual third in race two came after a hard nudge past Sykes, and after the first of two falls, but no submissions, from PI podium perennial Chaz Davies.

Davies was well out of sorts, the normally placidly spoken Welshman seething at his big V-twin's lack of corner exit punch, which left him pushing too hard on braking and into corners to stay in contention. He remounted to finish 11th in race one, and again in race two for 15th.

Lowes fell in the first event, remounted way down and then was pinged for passing a rider under a yellow flag, dropping from sixth to seventh.

The second and last 2015 innings by Aussie Troy Bayliss led to eighth in race one, before he was dropped back to ninth by the stewards, for the same misdemeanour as Lowes. In race two, he was 11th.

An uncivil war between the Fireblade duo of Guintoli and van der Mark was saved for the second race, after VDM's machine stopped with an electrical issue in race one. Guintoli was fifth in that 20-lap opener. In the second full-distance fight, VDM passed his team-mate around the outside, but left the track to do it, being relegated to seventh, allowing Guintoli to scoop up sixth.

In the privateer world, with no Evo class-within-a-class in 2015, Matteo Baiocco took his Althea Racing Ducati to a superb sixth, behind Guintoli, in race one. His eighth in race two was a few seconds closer to Rea than his technically better result in race one.

With Davies toiling and tripping himself up this weekend, privateer Ducati riders did better than they may have expected. Leandro Mercado (Barni Racing Ducati) had moved up from Superstock for 2015 and scored two tenths. Nico Terol was a less impressed 12th in each race, after a decent start with Althea in Australia.

Leon Camier had the frustration of two no-scores at Buriram on his official MV Agusta Reparto Corse F4, after two brighter starts in Australia.

Arm-pump stopped Suzuki's de Puniet from performing in race one, and he fell in race two.

Disaster dogged the Hero EBR team when technical issues caused both riders – Larry Pegram and Niccolo Canepa – to retire in race one and then withdraw from race two, just to be on the safe side.

Above: Matteo Baiocco made a big impression, with sixth in race one and eighth in race two.

Top: Tom Sykes heads Haslam during race two.

Above centre: David Salom leads de Puniet and Terol.

Left: Two wins for Rea.

Right: Alex Lowes took a podium place in race two.

Photos: Gold & Goose

SUPERBIKE WORLD CHAMPIONSHIP
ARAGON
ROUND 3 · SPAIN

Top: Davies and Rea locked in combat in race one.

Above: A rare Superpole for Haslam.

Above right: A pensive Paul Denning.

Right: More like a village fete than a bike racing event.

Photos: Gold & Goose

FOR the first time, the WSBK riders were to ride Motorland Aragon's full MotoGP layout and length. This meant that the harsh final hairpin and chicane of the previous layout were replaced by a more sweeping final left-hander, which made the track length 5.077km.

Thus the old lap records were preserved in aspic. The new track best was 1m 49.664s, set by Leon Haslam and Aprilia, which gave the English rider only the second Superpole of his long career. He had expected little beforehand, so taking his first pole since 2010 was an early bonus. He was joined on the front row by Davies and Sykes.

Sykes led the first race for 12 of the planned 18 laps, with Davies and Rea just behind. Both were in front with a handful of circuits remaining, however, and they battled it out for the win. Davies had a go into the final corner, but Rea won the drag to the flag and secured four race victories in five goes. He won by only 0.051 of a second, despite suffering from a fever.

Sykes faded to third, but was over ten seconds ahead of Haslam, who in turn was battling hard with team-mate Jordi Torres, just ahead of speedy Giugliano replacement Xavi Fores.

In the second race, with the track temperature having doubled from the cool first race (started at 10.30am), there was no final-corner action between Rea and Davies. To the surprise of many, Davies won by a relatively vast 3.190 seconds, beating Rea hands down in a start-to-finish rampage of pace and perseverance.

Warmer track temperatures had helped Davies to a degree, and under the new rules the Ducati was at no huge top-speed disadvantage – compared to previous seasons at least. Small set-up changes were made to his machine between races, but as the rider himself said, that was all he needed to get more grip, and to turn nearly there in the opener to emphatically there in race two.

He set the fastest lap of the second race, but could not get close to the new lap record of Sykes from the first, a 1m 50.890s. The Welshman broke an unwanted record, ending the longest gap – 58 races – between wins for a manufacturer as he gave the Ducati Panigale R its first ever victory at this level.

For one of the few manufacturers in WSBK with a direct factory team (albeit with sub-contracted logistics), there was as much relief as there was elation.

The final podium places were filled by Rea and Haslam, the latter taking even more benefits from a warmer track than Davies, if not in terms of points.

Torres was fourth, Fores fifth and Kawasaki Team Pedercini semi-official rider David Salom sixth at his home round.

Sykes did not feature this time, as he had high-sided while chasing Haslam at turn 15, the problem later being traced to an electronics glitch. That was little consolation for the heavily battered Sykes, who now was fourth in the overall rankings, and with a race meeting the very next weekend.

Another former champion crashed in race two: Sylvain Guintoli's run of 42 consecutive points scores in WSBK came to an end in the gravel of turn 14.

In addition to the factory duo, Ducati privateers were beginning to show well on the Panigale, with Nico Terol seventh in race one for former champions Althea Racing, and Leandro Mercado eighth, then seventh, for his rookie WSBK Barni Racing Team.

The small, but well-entertained Spanish crowd left to a backdrop of three manufacturers having won races in the opening three rounds, but with Rea howling away from the rest in the championship fight. Haslam performed damage limitation in Spain, but already was 26 points adrift after just six races.

Above: Davies was ecstatic with his victory in the second race.

Above left: Xavi Fores was a speedy stand-in for injured Davide Giugliano. He was sixth in race one; fifth in race two.

Top: Eighth and seventh places were a good day's work for Argentinian Leandro Mercado and BARNI Racing Team Ducati.

Right: Leon Haslam grabbed a podium for Aprilia in race two.

Photos: Gold & Goose

ASSEN is one of the most historic circuits in the entire sphere of motor-cycle racing, but it is very much a place of living history, having been heavily altered and modernised over the decades. Local fans at 'the Cathedral' even had a new moto-messiah on their side, preaching to the masses from the mount of the podium after two Madijk tricks from the man they call Mikey.

Pole, to no surprise, was taken by Sykes, who beat front-row fellows Rea and Haslam. Local boy Michael van der Mark was in the middle of row two and ready for another run with the front men, like in race two at Phillip Island.

Another early 10.30am start and a cool track temperature welcomed the 24 starters, and an early breakaway group included van der Mark.

Rea led and would head all 21 laps. Van der Mark was up to third with 15 laps to go, scrapping with Davies and then Haslam.

A bizarre incident at turn one sent Lowes off track on the escape road, trying to slow to recover the circuit. Then his team-mate, Randy de Puniet, crashed under braking, just behind. The sliding Frenchman hit Lowes's ma-chine, and both riders scored a DNF.

With Sykes going backwards to an eventual fifth, Davies and Rea were out in front, with Haslam and VDM some way behind as they approached the flag.

Rea closed out his race-one deal by just over a second from Davies, but the biggest reaction was behind, where VDM became the first ever Dutch rider to secure a podium placing in WSBK with third, just over four seconds from the win and only just ahead of Haslam. Sykes's drop-off from potential podium grace was stark, but he had a good cushion back to sixth-placed Jordi Torres.

Race two provided an identical top six, but it was altogether closer and played out on only marginally warmer asphalt than race one.

This time, Sykes got the bit between his teeth and led for 12 laps, sure he could find the solution to race one's mid-race fade, but he was unable to pull away enough to make his break stick.

Once again, VDM was in the leading mix, even clipping the back of Davies's rear wheel in the middle of the final chicane with nine laps to run, but he stayed on to recover his composure and position.

Rea had squeezed out a gap on his pursuers after passing Sykes, but Davies was chasing hard, if not quite quickly enough. He lost out by 0.439 second as Rea set a new lap record of 1m 35.889s on the penultimate lap. This was Rea's second double of the season and well deserved as he took his tally of Assen race wins to seven.

VDM had squeezed Haslam as he dived inside at the final chicane, putting the latter on the dirt and himself on the artificial grass. The results stood, however, and he earned a remarkable second podium on a Honda that was clearly benefiting little from the 2015 rule changes.

Haslam, in fourth, was only just less than three seconds from Rea, but Sykes was six seconds back, toiling to beat Torres by half a second.

Guintoli could not match his younger team-mate's heady hometown hero-ics, but a lonely seventh was proof that things were at least moving forward, for both him and Honda.

Behind the leading riders, the midfield contained Fores on a Ducati in eighth; Lowes ninth as his team struggled with their new Marelli EFI system (introduced by regulation at Motorland); and Leon Camier in the same tenth position he had taken in race one for his official MV Agusta squad.

With news that the EBR factory in the USA had gone into administration, the Hero EBR team swallowed the bad news, pluckily took to the track anyway and competed for what was the final time in 2015. It was a tough break for Larry Pegram's American team. They had been making real progress between too-frequent bouts of mechanical mishap.

Top: Michael van der Mark scored a double podium to please the fans at his home round.

Above: The indefatigable Imre Toth on his BMW.

Above left: The last stand. Larry Pe-gram and his Hero EBR team.

Left: Niccola Canepa grabbed a point for Hero EBR in race one.

Below left: Magic Michael enjoys his first podium appearance in WSBK.

Right: Tom Sykes shows attitude, but he had a somewhat disappoint-ing time at Assen.

Top far left: Fans get a fabulous view at the Cathedral of Speed.

Far left: Rea leads Davies, Sykes and Haslam in race one.
Photos: Gold & Goose

Left: Guintoli was back from injury and grabbed Superpole.

Below left: Ronald Ten Kate.

Far left: Sykes leads Rea in race one, but the latter would triumph.

Centre row, from left: Mercardo continued his strong run of form; Michel Fabrizio was called back into action with Althea Racing; Niccolo Canepa found himself a new place with Grillini, but would have to wait until Donington to race their Kawasaki; Matteo Baiocco leads van der Mark and co in race one.

Bottom far left: Guintoli and Badovini battle it out for fifth place in race one.

Bottom left: Giugliano chases the Kawasakis in race two.

Bottom right: Jordi Torres was a distant third, behind Rea and Sykes in race two.

Photos: Gold & Goose

A S Jonathan Rea prepared for his attempt to pour himself another double fizz at the top of the Imola podium, one regular WSBK factory rider was merely glad to be celebrating his return to action after recovering from serious vertebrae fractures suffered during the opening round in Australia.

Davide Giugliano cemented his place in the WSBK paddock in a mind-blowing manner by taking pole position on Saturday. At the circuit closest to Ducati's home base in Borgo Panigale, this was a virtual fairy-tale.

Kawasaki kids Sykes and Rea were second and third on the grid, but the first start ultimately was a false one. The two Ducatis and Kawasaki were chasing each other around until fourth-placed qualifier Davies went out with a tech issue. Torres was also out with gearbox issues, and when the red flags came out after David Salom crashed, neither he nor Davies made the restart.

Sykes and Rea hit the front, and the latter, who had struggled in the abandoned race, was well in the hunt for a sprint win after making set-up changes. He slipped past Sykes after only two laps.

The slowing Giugliano followed the leaders, losing ground in a race that lasted just 10 minutes and 43 seconds. His podium was still more than he or anybody else had expected after such a long period of recovery, most of it spent immobile.

Rea's margin of victory was 0.482 second; Sykes remained second, but was a threat to the end.

Haslam placed fourth, four seconds from third place, while a great recovery from 15th on the grid allowed Sylvain Guintoli to rip through to fifth. Ayrton Badovini (BMW Motorrad Italia SBK) was sixth – just behind Guintoli and just ahead of impressive 2014 Superstock 1000 champion Leandro Mercado.

In the second race, a full 19-lap effort, Rea won again. The Ulsterman made his empathy with Imola tell, finishing 4.399 seconds ahead of Sykes.

Kawasaki's dominance on race day was particularly clear, given that the nearest challenger to the 1-2 Ninja riders was Imola rookie Torres, fully 26 seconds from the win. He made no secret of his dislike for Imola and understood well that he had really inherited third after Davies had suffered another technical problem; the tiring Giugliano finished fourth.

Guintoli went out of the race with a fall, the second of the year, as did his team-mate van der Mark much later.

Haslam had been struggling and dropped to seventh, clashing with van der Mark at the Rivazzas before the Dutch rider ran off and fell. At the Tamburello next time around, Haslam also had his very own fast off.

With some top riders out of the running, Badovini was fifth, and former Ducati test rider Matteo Baiocco (Althea Racing Ducati) sixth. Spanish privateer Roman Ramos – one of a flood of Spanish riders topping up WSBK in 2015 – took his rookie Team Go Eleven to seventh at their home round. Only 13 riders finished race two.

The second race was Rea's 150th WSBK start, the culmination of his third double of the year and a consecutive double at this undulating circuit. He had won both Imola races for Pata Honda in 2014.

He was not so much running off with the championship lead as strolling away with it. Eight wins from ten races was greatness in the making.

With Davies's Ducati having let him down after his accumulating progress at the previous two rounds, and Haslam having been off the podium pace and then unlucky in race two, Rea's cause was helped to the max by his rivals' general misfortunes. Only Sykes challenged him at Imola – he was about to do more than that at the next round.

THE circuit used for the first ever WSBK race weekend in 1988, Donington Park has always been a great motorcycle racing venue. Tom Sykes enjoys its 4.023km undulations and flows, even more than ever now that he lives nearby, having 'emigrated' from Yorkshire a few years ago. He had also won the previous four Donington WSBK races, after all.

Just to add some extra pepper to the increasingly dominant Kawasaki mill, the rider who had won there immediately before Sykes was Jonathan Rea. On his Ninja, given the way his 2015 season had been going, JR was in a position to do it all again.

A good weekend for many of the British riders began with Leon Camier being fastest in FP1 on Friday. He finished Superpole seventh, one of six Brits inside the top places on the grid. Fastest of all was Sykes, at a new track-best pace of 1m 27.071s, from Rea and Italian interloper Giugliano.

A high-noon start to race one led to the British trio of Haslam, Sykes and Rea sharing the lead, which changed five times across the stripe over race distance. Alex Lowes (in fetching Union Jack leathers and helmet) was part of an all-British top five for a time, with Sykes, Rea, Haslam and Davies. Giugliano had been forced to pit to take on new rubber and finished 17th.

Up front, as the Kawasaki pairing ran away, Rea let Sykes through, waving him past after he became too close for comfort exiting Goddards with nine laps left.

Sykes had enough in his rear tyres this weekend and made his pace tell all the way, winning by 3.743 seconds, his first race victory of the year. Rea, in turn, was over 11 seconds ahead of Davies. Haslam completed the British battering of the others, 18 seconds from the win and suffering painfully with broken ribs sustained in his Imola fall.

Ayrton Badovini was a strong fifth for BMW, having beaten Lowes by half a second. Torres placed seventh and Guintoli eighth after team-mate van der Mark had fallen.

In the second race, started at 3pm, Sykes piled in early, setting a new lap record of 1m 27.640s on lap two. That was more than a quarter of a second less than the record set by Rea in race one just a few hours earlier. All this pace on a cool track surface of 21°C.

Haslam was Sykes's early challenger, Rea behind and almost off even as his race had barely begun. A near high-side at the fast right of Coppice forced him way out wide. He lost a heel plate as he smashed back down, but he stayed on, now down in seventh.

An early fight between Davies and Camier was ended when the MV runner fell on lap four, at the Foggy Esses. He rejoined, but had to pit, eventually to retire. In a busy race for incidents, van der Mark had entered the pit lane and gone right into his pit garage; he was black-flagged after he rejoined the race later on. Terol suffered a high high-side on his Ducati at Coppice, at third race distance.

With a clear track ahead and his championship worries behind him for a day, Sykes just moved onward and upward, while Rea had to ride at his best to come back from sixth place.

Using tighter, faster lines than most, Rea sliced past his opponents. Davies was also on the move forward, passing Giugliano and Lowes in quick order. The pair took some time to get to Haslam, but when they did they passed with relative ease.

In taking his double win, Sykes had recorded six consecutive Donington WSBK victories, and each race produced another Kawasaki 1-2, Sykes and Rea from Davies and Haslam each time. Giugliano was fifth, Lowes sixth, Torres seventh, Guintoli eighth, Badovini ninth and Baiocco tenth.

Above: Leon Camier took his MV Agusta to ninth in race one.

Top: Roman Ramos leads David Salom in their private Kawasaki battle in race two.

Top left: Sykes finally got the better of team-mate Rea to score a double win at Donington.

Far left: Alex Lowes took sixth in both races. Wearing suitably patriotic leathers, the Suzuki rider battles Giugliano and Davies in race two.

Left, from top: BMW Motorrad Italia boss Petro Guidi; the team's sporting director Berti Hauser; Brian Gillen, MV Agusta team manager.

Right: The podium positions were identical for both races, with Davies acting as support for the dominant Kawasaki pair.

Photos: Gold & Goose

PORTIMAO

ROUND 7 · PORTUGAL

Top: The field streams past the VIP Tower on the opening lap.

Above: Ayrton Badovini and Roman Ramos in race two.

Above right: Davies battles Haslam for third place in race two.

Right: Sykes and Rea vie for position on wets during race one.

Photos: Gold & Goose

THE Portimao race finally went ahead, despite some worries about financial backing. Everyone was happy about its retention on the calendar, as the brilliantly conceived venue is an architectural triumph, its intense circuit layout both a physical challenge and a test of concentration – in wet or dry conditions. And we had some of each on race day..

There was even a full-on official test on the day after the race action, which meant that any celebrations of another double win for Jonathan Rea had to be relatively muted.

On the other side of the Kawasaki Racing Team garage, however, any cork popping was very much on hold, as Sykes suffered problems in each of the races – which guaranteed he would be second in race one and eighth in the second 20-lapper.

Italian speed king Giugliano was on pole, Sykes and Davies on the second works Ducati alongside. Despite having to endure Superpole 1, Alex Lowes (Suzuki) went to fourth on the real grid. Rea had crashed in Superpole and thus was eighth on the grid.

Rea started both races well, but it was Sykes who led the first, as his rivals squabbled behind him. Rea soon closed up, but Sykes remained in the lead for the first 11 laps, until Rea passed him.

With six laps to go, rain started to fall, heavily enough for riders to start to come in for wet-weather tyres. Sykes stayed out too long, however, rueing his decision as finally he had to make a slow lap on slicks before heading back out. He met Rea, who had endured his own moment of worry, meaning that the two KRT riders were set for a duel for the last few laps.

It was not to be for Sykes, despite having taken the lead for another two laps, as his rear wheel sensor played up, letting Rea escape before it came on line again and his traction control started working well enough to start helping in the wet conditions. He was almost ten seconds down at the flag, but over four seconds up on Davies. Giugliano was well back in fourth, heading wet-weather guru Sylvain Guintoli.

Baiocco was sixth on his Ducati, just ahead of another damp-track specialist, Ayrton Badovini (BMW).

Despite the arrival of the wet weather, tyre changes and the tricky nature of Portimao, with its swathe of blind corner entries, 20 of the 22 riders finished.

Lowes ran wide after he and Rea had come too close in turn one of race two, on a dry track that would stay dry all race long.

Rea was having some issues, running wide more than once, but he got his rhythm back as he passed Giugliano. One-time leader Sykes was swallowed up by Giugliano and then by most riders in the leading half of the race. A leaking wheel rim had caused him to drop back, and he finished eighth.

It was a case of keeping on to the happy ending for Rea, who took yet another double win as he crossed the line 5.416 seconds up on a determined, but outpaced Giugliano. Haslam, desperate to make up for his race-one problems, played it hard enough, passing Davies to go third; the Welsh rider was fourth.

In a battle of the Pata Hondas, Michael van der Mark smashed his way to fifth, 0.143 second up on French team-mate Guintoli. First-time Portimao runner Torres secured seventh on his Aprilia, with a luckless Sykes three seconds adrift and with less than half the normal tyre pressure in the rear Pirelli.

Happiness personified, Rea had helped his Catalan team celebrate the victory Barcelona CF had enjoyed in the Champions' League Final the night before, in the best way possible, with a double win. Race two was his tenth individual race win of the year, and it made his the best ever start to any WSBK championship season.

Above: Honda pair Guintoli and van der Mark wheelie in formation during race two.

Left: Althea's Genesio Bevilaqua.

Below: Alex Lowes still on slicks as the rain begins to fall in race one.

Bottom: Davide Giugliano scorched to Superpole.

Below right: Rea sported a Barcelona replica shirt as a tribute to his Spanish crew.

Photos: Gold & Goose

MISANO
ROUND 8 · ITALY

Above: The 'Roman Emperor' was the centre of attention.

Right: The lensman catches Biaggi's attention during a photoshoot.

Centre right: Michele Pirro was a wild-card on the third Arube.it Racing Ducati.

Below right: Tom Sykes is chased by Giugliano and Rea in race two.

Photos: Gold & Goose

SOMETHING old (Max Biaggi), something new (the entire track surface), something borrowed (Michele Pirro) and something blue (the skies, for most of race weekend by the Adriatic coast). So goes a paraphrase for what a bride should wear on her wedding day.

There certainly seemed to be more fuss and attention paid to former double WSBK champion Max Biaggi at the Misano round than to any bride this side of royalty. The former king of the paddock, and four-time 250cc GP world champion, Biaggi was attempting to wind back the clock a few seasons to when he had been a potential race winner almost every weekend.

No doubt about it, after a test at Misano in readiness for the second Italian round of the series, Biaggi would be quick. But fastest overall on Friday?

Under the rules, as a wild-card, he could have any gearbox he liked, and he used that to full effect. He got to understand the new tarmac before anybody else, too, including the newly cambered sections. But even the fact that he was Aprilia's regular test rider, and therefore still used to riding at racing speeds – unlike Bayliss who had no tests or recent worthwhile WSBK riding experience to draw on before PI and Thailand – could not mitigate how well Max did in practice and most of qualifying. Even fifth on the grid after Superpole was an achievement for somebody who was about to turn 44 years old within a few days.

Sykes was on pole, Haslam second, Giugliano third and Rea fourth, alongside Biaggi.

Max's presence threatened to overshadow what was going on around him, but it was 1-2 business as usual for Kawasaki, in race one at least.

Guintoli, only 15th in qualifying, clashed with Biaggi early on lap one of race one, and Torres pushed himself out of contention with a crash on lap two. Rea moved up to chase Sykes and Davies in the leading two places, going through Davies with two laps remaining. Ducati's latest British star (although only 11th in qualifying), with more grip and more guile than Giugliano in the opener, took Ducati's 800th podium place, but he could do nothing about Rea on the final corner. Neither could he touch race winner Sykes, who was a whopping 3.613 seconds ahead, taking the best from his rear tyre.

Haslam was fifth, only just ahead of Biaggi, who looked like he might not have tried too hard to pass the full-time Aprilia rider.

The second 21-lap race, in warmer track conditions, saw Rea on the same rear tyre choice as his team-mate this time, making a top-three group with Sykes and Giugliano early in the race.

Giugliano took to the front for nine laps, while Sykes dropped down the order, although he had thought the hotter track would have helped him more, not less.

Rea's 25th career race win was as sweet as any previous victory. He was transcending the norms of the WSBK class, having scored either first or second in all 16 races in his first year of Kawasaki competition.

Giugliano was a neat and ordered second, while Haslam won the final-corner duel with Davies to take third, his second podium in as many weekends.

Biaggi held off Torres for his second sixth place of the day, and another ex-GP rider finished eighth – in both races – Michele Pirro. He was a late call-up to replace the once-more injured Luca Scassa on the planned third Aruba.it Racing Ducati for Misano.

Race two saw the top seven riders home finish within 7.075 seconds, an unusually close situation in any big-capacity racing class after 21 laps. Only Assen's race two had come close to that level so far in 2015, with seven seconds covering the top six.

At a sunny and feel-good Misano, the big prizes of the weekend went to Rea and Sykes, but the real public focus was very much on the return of Max.

Top: After giving best to Sykes in the first race, Rea emerged victorious in race two.

Above centre: Despite the beautiful weather, the crowd was sparse.

Above: Haslam (91) leads Davies in their battle for third in race two.

Left: Romano Albesiano of Aprilia.

Left: All smiles from Paul Denning and Freddie Sheene.

Right: A season-best second place for Davide Giugliano in race two.

Photos: Gold & Goose

Above: Camier leads de Puniet in their race-two battle.

Left and below left: "I wish they all could be California girls."

Far left: Chaz Davies leads the field on the first lap of race 1.

Below: Nicky Hayden was rumoured to be heading to WSBK in 2016.
Photos: Gold & Goose

Above: Davies celebrates his race-one victory. The Welshman would repeat his dominance in race two.

Left: Torres led the Aprilia challenge.

Far left: Davies heads the Kawasakis and the Aprilias down the Corkscrew in race two.

Right: Sykes had the upper hand over team-mate Rea.
Photos: Gold & Goose

HERE can be few tracks in the world that rival Laguna Seca for intensity and gradient changes, but there is much more to a Monterey WSBK weekend than the famous Corkscrew and its tricky sister corners at the short 3.610km race-track.

The most important thing is that it is located in the USA, and at the centre of many aspects of America's bike industry and culture, California. With all the new long-haul WSBK destinations, present and future, being introduced by Dorna, it would have been a reversal in status not to go back to America, and specifically Laguna.

These considerations simply pale, however, in the light of the deaths of two MotoAmerica Superbike championship riders – Spaniards Bernat Martinez and Daniel Rivas – that occurred in the same horrible multi-rider incident after the WSBK races had been completed. This particular weekend will rightly be remembered for the best and the worst realities of racing.

The two WSBK races went full distance at the first time of asking, unlike in 2014.

Ducati rider Chaz Davies not only beat the unstoppable Rea both times, but also beat Sykes, who in turn got the better of team-mate and champion elect Rea in each race.

Two third places were Rea's 'worst' results of the season so far. But in finishing just over, and then just under, two seconds behind Davies, his slip from top-step glory was hardly an abdication of ambition. It simply had not been his day to shine, but he still came away with useful points.

After two incredibly adept races, having also secured Superpole on Saturday, Davies really earned his second and third race wins on the Panigale. He led each race from the start to the 25th lap.

At Laguna, a circuit that really tests the concentration, it was never as easy as Davies made it look, even given that it is probably his favourite venue. This was especially true in race two, when light rain started to fall for a time, first in one sector and then in all of them.

His team-mate, Davide Giugliano, fell around this time and ended up in the medical centre, having hurt his back once more.

The Laguna big three of Davies, Sykes and Rea were virtually untouchable to the others, with fourth-placed finishers Giugliano (race one) and Jordi Torres (race two) 15.9 and 16.5 seconds respectively behind Chaz, and not much less adrift of his chasing green shadows.

Rea challenged Sykes for second, but could not make it stick and settled for his unaccustomed bronzes. Perhaps he was considering the bigger overall prize for the first time.

In the opening Laguna race, Voltcom Suzuki's Alex Lowes was sixth for Suzuki, his best result since Donington, while Sylvain Guintoli clearly won the battle of the Pata Hondas to take seventh.

Leon Haslam, who had fallen in race one and rejoined for 13th, was just over a second behind fellow Aprilia rider Torres for fifth in race two; Ayrton Badovini went sixth and Michael van der Mark seventh.

Guintoli was out of the second running, after he collected Lowes. As the Suzuki man pulled over to the pit lane exit to retire, Guintoli was lining him up for a possible pass on that side into the final turn. He said Lowes had moved over without any signal and down he went.

Niccolo Canepa, who had started the season on the now defunct Hero EBR machine, got to ride in America after all, but on a Ducati from his own nation, not an American version of a V-twin. He scored eighth in race two, after a DNF in the opener.

It was like old times for Ducati, not only winning, but also supplying lots of top-ten privateers.

Leandro Mercado's rookie Barni Racing Ducati team were enamoured with his race-one ninth, and his identical follow-up in race two.

SUPERBIKE WORLD CHAMPIONSHIP
SEPANG
ROUND 10 · MALAYSIA

Above and inset: Chaz Davies makes his last-corner lunge to snatch the race-two win from Rea.

Right: Tom Sykes picks up his bike to recover to 11th in race two.

Centre right: Gianluca Vizziello was given a ride on the Grillini Kawasaki.

Below and below centre: Sylvain Guintoli runs into Max Biaggi in the first-corner scrum, leaving the Italian down and out of race two.

Photos: Gold & Goose

Above: A handshake between Davies and Sykes after their close finish in race one.

Left: Torres was delighted with a podium in race two.

Below: Matteo Baiocco notched up solid points for Althea Racing again.

Below right: A podium for old master Max Biaggi in race one.

Photos: Gold & Goose

UNDER the new technical rules, everybody was supposed to be on a level playing field in terms of costs and competitiveness. As is the way in racing, however, some equals are more equal than others.

For most of 2015, the three most factory of factory teams had been gripping the whip hand tightest. Now it seemed to be a two-manufacturer fight, with Kawasaki squaring up to Ducati, while Aprilia trailed in third.

Surely at Sepang, the Aprilias would begin to perform like their 2014 counterparts, which had gathered up their piston-skirts and grip levels best when racing in hot conditions.

It was not to be for the RSV4 regulars again in Malaysia, however, in terms of challenging for wins at least.

The phenomenon that is Max Biaggi, now 44 years old and with a big Sepang pre-race test session under his belt, was back again. Sykes stretched his Kawasaki's legs to take yet another win in Superpole (28 and counting) from Jordi Torres and a bubbling Sylvain Guintoli. Biaggi was hiding in plain sight, in fourth.

Rea was seventh after almost falling on his fast lap, Davies only sixth, so the game looked on for some upsets.

Sykes certainly finished race one very upset.

We had seen Sykes blast away out in front, going too hard said Rea, setting times most others could only do on qualifying rubber in Superpole. Predictably, he dropped back to finish fifth, some 17 seconds from the win, after Davies and Rea had passed him with four laps to go. None other than Max Biaggi and then Sylvain Guintoli would also take Sykes on the final tour. Biaggi gained his 71st podium finish as a result, an upset to some, but an inevitability once Sykes had slowed so dramatically.

The fact that Rea won the opener, if only by 0.121 seconds from Davies, was no upset at all; just a thrilling finale after Chaz had led from lap 12 to 15.

A last-lap sort-out at the final corner resulted in JR snatching back victory from the counterattacking Davies, but only after the Kawasaki rider had made a mistake by running wide into the final curve.

Biaggi had been confident of finishing even closer in race two. So he said after no-scoring, having been knocked off by a combination of Guintoli and Sykes in the very first corner.

Guintoli had gone inside after Sykes and Biaggi had each left a gap by running slightly wide. Both tried to return to the inside for the next left. Biaggi found Guintoli there and stopped his inward move; Sykes was on his way in already, and the Kawasaki and Aprilia hit hard. Sykes stayed on, with brake lever damage, but Biaggi was out.

Max's last WSBK race may have ended with scuffs on his leathers, but his Roman legionary's breastplate was burnished brighter than ever.

Sykes dropped back, worked his way forward, fell at turn nine, restarted right at the back and battled forward for a second time to finish 14th.

Up front, Davies and Rea contested the 1-2 again, but this time race-long leader Davies undid Rea's last-lap approach work. The advancing Rea had passed him on the straight into the final corner, but Davies shifted to the inside and made a big lunge from behind. There was distinct contact between the red and green machines, but even in defeat Rea (0.091 second behind) forgave his rival. He even said he would have done the same.

Had Rea won the race, he would have been champion, six races and three rounds early. Davies's aggression, therefore, had saved the ignominy of the championship being decided before the long summer break had even started.

Torres was a strong third, but five seconds adrift, Guintoli an impressive fourth, having beaten van der Mark in the inter-Honda stakes. Haslam, with too little pressure in his rear tyre, was sixth.

JEREZ
ROUND 11 · SPAIN

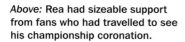

Above: Rea had sizeable support from fans who had travelled to see his championship coronation.

Above right: Canepa posted a surprise third fastest in Superpole.

Top: Rea and Sykes lead away at the start of race two. Neither Kawasaki rider would feature on the podium, however.

Right: Michael van der Mark took a race-one podium for Pata Honda.
Photos: Gold & Goose

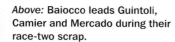

Above: Baiocco leads Guintoli, Camier and Mercado during their race-two scrap.

Left: Wearing a neck brace, the injured Giugliano was in attendance.

Below left: Michele Pirro was drafted in to ride the Italian's Ducati once more.

Below: The Aprilias of Torres and Haslam lead Sykes, van der Mark and Rea in race two.

Below right: Costume change number one for Jonathan Rea.

Photos: Gold & Goose

A T the spiritual home of modern-day MotoGP racing in Spain, Dorna's once-Italian ENI FIM Superbike World Championship series dusted off its castanets after six weekends of inaction and got down to the serious business of going through the motions to crown its latest world champion.

Jonathan Rea only needed six points, in any order of delivery, to leave Spain with the big trophy stuffed inside his green leathers.

A formality? Well, yes; just not in the way he or anybody else expected.

Oddly, Pirelli had not brought Jonathan's favoured stiff front tyre. It took a very persuasive argument to get Rea off an old, but trusted front option at the best of times, and tyres in general would be a major talking point on race day.

Sykes on pole was becoming almost *de rigueur*, his fifth of the year, and with a new track best lap of 1m 40.292s. Amazing what 20bhp less than 2014 could do for a lap time.

Rea was chilled out and even confident of two winning challenges on Sunday, in the second grid slot, whatever front tyre he had to use. Niccolo Canepa's privateer Ducati in third place was a surprise, while Michael van der Mark came through Superpole 1 and 2 to go fourth on the grid, a kind of positive shock therapy for his Ten Kate line-up with its rebooted backroom.

Clearly some weirdness was afoot. It would be apparent again on Sunday, and bring friends.

Flagged off at 10.30am, race one was a Sykes benefit, the 2013 champion showing that when he had the tyres and set-up, he was still as potent a racer as ever. He led all 20 laps and saw off a second-half challenge from Davies, who had expected Sykes to slow from halfway.

Ride of the day may have come from van der Mark, who finished third, having fended off an attacking Haslam and then finished nearly 2.5 seconds up on a clearly struggling Rea.

Having set a new lap record of 1m 41.136s on lap two, which would survive the day, it looked rosy for champion-elect Rea. But, calamitous front tyre issues meant that he could not hold a line and was forced to run very wide, unable to defend as other riders outmanoeuvred him. Only his world championship best allowed him to finish fourth, for his first off-podium ride of the year.

He had still achieved his lifelong ambition after just one of the two Jerez races, however, and went through his well-rehearsed and executed celebration slowdown lap at his team's 'home' round. He stopped and donned TT F2 champion Brian Reid's old helmet and received a new number plate with a big gold '1' on it. Then he stopped at another corner for TT F1 champion Joey Dunlop's old helmet. He finally stopped at the turn 11 grandstand, where he was feted by his travelling support from Northern Ireland as he put on his own gold winner's helmet.

Like his two friends and heroes, he had just become a world champion from Northern Ireland.

There was no escaping, however, that it had not come along in the way he had planned – off the podium through no fault of his own.

There would be a hollow and false fourth in race two as well, for seemingly the same reason, and this time Kawasaki's joy at winning its first ever manufacturers' championship was dulled by Sykes dropping to fifth, having overruled his crew chief's advice on choice of front tyre.

The first non-Kawasaki podium of the year allowed Davies to take a strong win, while after a no-holds-barred Aprilia tussle Torres was second, his best result yet in WSBK racing. Haslam was third, and behind the stranded Kawasaki duo of Rea and Sykes, Matteo Baiocco planted his privateer Althea flag in sixth place.

It was a riveting, exhausting, uplifting, deflating 'finale' to the season – and for the neutrals, all the drama and big title deciders had happened two rounds too early.

SUPERBIKE WORLD CHAMPIONSHIP
MAGNY-COURS
ROUND 12 · FRANCE

Above: Scassa and Torres were locked in combat in both races.

Above right: Niccolo Canepa.

Top: Jonathan Rea takes the applause from his pit crew after his race-one win.

Right: Sykes and Davies, braking hard, are shadowed by eventual winner Rea in race two.

Photos: Gold & Goose

A WARM start to the weekend preceded a wet and cold finish, as first Superpole and then race day were afflicted with the precipitation typical of a French October. With the weather turning just before Superpole, it was Leon Haslam who splashed his way to the free watch, his second pre-race win of the year and only the third of his long WSBK career. He had fallen shortly after setting his best time, but Jonathan Rea had slowed down in the final risky sector, so he remained on top.

Race one was wet, race two quite dry, meaning it was just one of those disturbed days. Especially after wild-card Markus Reiterberger's Van Zon Re-meha BMW leaked oil on to the surface around much of the track during morning warm-up, its rider having ignored the signals from the pit lane.

The delay was so significant that race one was late getting under way, while the Supersport and Stock 1000 riders would get no morning warm-up at all.

In the wet, Rea led the opener, then Tom Sykes went to the front. He had crashed in Superpole and been on the back of the third row of the grid, but he looked the race winner despite this handicap, until Rea got moving near the end.

It was evident that no KRT team orders were in place, so there was no chance of Sykes's bitter rival Rea giving him the extra five points for the win. Rea even passed him hard enough for Sykes to lose his line, and any chance of a riposte.

JR was ravenously hungry for more wins, desperate to make up for two off-podium Spanish misadventures and – volubly in his post-race interview – out to break Colin Edwards's all-time record points haul of 552 by season's end in Qatar.

With Sykes second, Sylvain Guintoli earned a precious Honda podium, his reputation as a wet-weather specialist being underlined in sodden red, white and blue lines. His bronze-medal position was a real boost for the French crowd, out in decent numbers again despite the rains and the return of the Bol d'Or to the iconic Le Castellet just one week before.

Fourth went to the ever improving Michael van der Mark, while fifth was a season best so far for Leon Camier and the legendary name of MV Agusta.

Davies, with a half-wet/half-dry chassis set-up, battled against this issue all race and finished sixth in a shortened 19-lap race.

The second French contest was held in basically dry conditions and went the full distance of 21 laps. The outcome was another win for Rea. Naturally. On his favoured SC2 front tyre, which gave him more support going into and around corners, he was on his own plane of existence again.

Davies tried to run down Rea's advantage for a long time, but stopped before the end, realising it was too risky. Instead, he opted for a safe second and making up some ground on Sykes. Third place for the 2013 champion would have been a good result at the start of the year, but he spun back to third overall and left Magny-Cours 16 points behind Davies.

In taking his second fourth place of the day, van der Mark demonstrated that his rookie season was laced with greater consistency, regardless of the conditions.

Fifth for Haslam was a horrible outcome to a race in which he had started from pole again. When added to 16th in the first race, when he had experienced the same issues to an even worse degree, the highlight of his day was leading race two for two laps.

Guintoli was sixth in race two, Niccolo Canepa seventh, his best race after finishing the wet Superpole sessions in third place.

Jordi Torres's day had been a relative disaster: he had qualified 12th and then matched that performance in race one. He was only able to improve slightly in race two, to eighth.

Above: A lonely ride into third place for Guintoli in race one.

Left: The first, and only podium for the outgoing champion in 2015.

Top and above centre: Fifth in race one was the best result of the year for Leon Camier, and MV's loyal band of supporters showed their appreciation.

Right: Sykes was the 'bridesmaid' once again, as team-mate Rea took his 13th win of the year in race one.

Photos: Gold & Goose

Above: Torres leads Rea in race one.

Top: Arabian nights, at their illuminated best.

Right: Haslam leads Davies and Sykes across the finish line in race two.

Above right: Haslam's joy is obvious after his win in the last race of the 2015 season.

Photos: Gold & Goose

Left: It was the final Honda ride for 2014 champion Guintoli.

Below left: Hungarian Gabor Rizmayer picked up points in both races for Team Toth's BMW squad.

Below centre left: Sykes took the Superpole win yet again, for 30 career pole positions in all.

Below: Davies leads Haslam in the second race.

Bottom: Aprilia on top again in Qatar: Jordi Torres and the team celebrate his maiden win.

Below right: Decent points for Randy de Puniet and Suzuki.

Photos: Gold & Goose

IN its second iteration as a night race, 2015's floodlit WSBK finale in Qatar provided more shocks, and ambitions achieved or dashed, than its lowly billing as a race with no value would have suggested.

Jonathan Rea and Kawasaki had already become top dogs, after all, in their respective championships. Instead, the Losail races were necessary for sifting out second place, with Tom Sykes trying to undermine the 16-point advantage that Chaz Davies had brought to the Gulf.

There was also the not-so-small matter of Rea looking to become the highest ever points scorer, and needing 'only' 25 to do it. As his previous worst weekend score had been 32 points, his chances were better than good.

Davies increased his final advantage by one point in relation to Sykes, despite the Kawasaki rider finishing on the podium twice in Losail. In coming home a struggling fourth and then a greatly improved second in the 17-lap races, Davies took his deserved second overall, driving a red wedge between the seemingly all-conquering Kawasakis. After two no scores (Imola) and two virtual no-scores (Buriram), it was a feat that had seemed about as likely as splitting the atom with a Meccano set.

Sykes and Davies had deserved to fight for the runner-up spot behind the imperious Rea, who had set himself up for the all-time points record in brilliantly combative form. He had taken 20 points in race one and was only 0.726s off the winner, despite his favoured SC2 front tyre not being in the allocation again at this round.

The 2015 race winners' club endured a relatively barren opening race, with Leon Haslam struggling again on an Aprilia that felt heavy and sluggish and took him to only sixth, behind Michael van der Mark's Honda.

A new, distinctly non-British name appeared on the race winners' list – Jordi Torres. Rea had said that he was the man to watch after examining his race pace all weekend, and the new champion was right. Rea was not quite able to repass the slow-starting Torres on the final lap, even after an audacious attempt around the outside on the final curve.

After a tough rookie year on an Aprilia that was not in the same league as 2014's missile, Torres was a welcome non-British winner. The first and last of 2015.

Sykes was third in race one, by over six seconds, after leading for some time, a machine glitch having held back his final push. Worse was to come for Kawasaki in race two, if not for Sykes this time.

With Rea leading and then in the mix for the podium places, he only needed five more points to go ahead of Colin Edwards's all-time best of 552. Even if he finished on the end of a six-rider early fight, he would get ten points. Even 11th would put him in the history books for yet another feat of arms in his remarkable season. But his bike quit on him after four laps and he had to roll back to the pits, four points short of even a share of the record points haul.

It was an ignominious end to a truly brilliant season for Rea; a championship performance that will surely live in the collective memory of WSBK long after the final day's dud has been archived into the deepest vaults.

There was a final victory firework of pure joy in the night skies over Losail, however, in the form of Haslam's black-and-graphite Aprilia. Some chassis changes between races had given him a bike he could flick like a switchblade knife and still keep ahead of his rivals down the straights.

Davies was second, Sykes a very close third and van der Mark fourth, while 2014's Losail miracle man, Sylvian Guintoli, left his number-one plate behind at its point of origin with a respectable fifth.

Compiled by Peter McLaren

| Round 1 | **PHILLIP ISLAND, Australia** · 22 February, 2015 · 2.762-mile/4.445km circuit · WEATHER: Race 1 · Dry · Track 42°C · Air 30°C; Race 2 · Dry · Track 38°C · Air 31°C |

Race 1: 22 laps, 60.764 miles/97.790km

Time of race: 33m 58.385s · **Average speed:** 107.315mph/172.707km/h

Pos.	Rider	Nat.	No.	Entrant	Machine	Tyres	Time & Gap	Laps
1	**Jonathan Rea**	GBR	65	Kawasaki Racing Team	Kawasaki ZX-10R	P		22
2	**Leon Haslam**	GBR	91	Aprilia Racing Team - Red Devils	Aprilia RSV4 RF	P	0.039s	22
3	**Chaz Davies**	GBR	7	Aruba.it Racing-Ducati SBK Team	Ducati Panigale R	P	0.496s	22
4	**Jordi Torres**	ESP	81	Aprilia Racing Team - Red Devils	Aprilia RSV4 RF	P	2.259s	22
5	**Michael VD Mark**	NED	60	PATA Honda World Superbike Team	Honda CBR1000RR SP	P	9.838s	22
6	**Tom Sykes**	GBR	66	Kawasaki Racing Team	Kawasaki ZX-10R	P	13.761s	22
7	**Sylvain Guintoli**	FRA	1	PATA Honda World Superbike Team	Honda CBR1000RR SP	P	14.021s	22
8	**Nicolas Terol**	ESP	18	Althea Racing	Ducati Panigale R	P	15.954s	22
9	**Alex Lowes**	GBR	22	VOLTCOM Crescent Suzuki	Suzuki GSX-R1000	P	21.106s	22
10	**Leon Camier**	GBR	2	MV Agusta Reparto Corse	MV Agusta 1000 F4	P	24.771s	22
11	**Matteo Baiocco**	ITA	15	Althea Racing	Ducati Panigale R	P	28.920s	22
12	**Leandro Mercado**	ARG	36	BARNI Racing Team	Ducati Panigale R	P	35.929s	22
13	**Troy Bayliss**	AUS	21	Aruba.it Racing-Ducati SBK Team	Ducati Panigale R	P	40.315s	22
14	**Jed Metcher**	AUS	77	Race Center - Demolition Plus	Kawasaki ZX-10R	P	45.090s	22
15	**Sylvain Barrier**	FRA	20	BMW Motorrad Italia SBK Team	BMW S1000 RR	P	46.444s	22
16	Roman Ramos	ESP	40	Team Go Eleven	Kawasaki ZX-10R	P	53.331s	22
17	Randy de Puniet	FRA	14	VOLTCOM Crescent Suzuki	Suzuki GSX-R1000	P	58.811s	22
18	Larry Pegram	USA	72	Team Hero EBR	EBR 1190 RX	P	1m 06.071s	22
19	Santiago Barragan	ESP	51	Grillini SBK Team	Kawasaki ZX-10R	P	1m 06.110s	22
20	Imre Toth	HUN	10	BMW Team Toth	BMW S1000 RR	P	1 Lap	21
	Niccolo Canepa	ITA	59	Team Hero EBR	EBR 1190 RX	P	DNF	15
	Christophe Ponsson	FRA	23	Grillini SBK Team	Kawasaki ZX-10R	P	DNF	9

Fastest race lap: Leon Haslam on lap 16, 1m 31.826s, 108.283mph/174.264km/h.

Race 2: 22 laps, 60.764 miles/97.790km

Time of race: 33m 58.711s · **Average speed:** 107.298mph/172.680km/h

Pos.	Rider	Time & Gap	Laps
1	**Leon Haslam**		22
2	**Jonathan Rea**	0.010s	22
3	**Chaz Davies**	0.298s	22
4	**Tom Sykes**	5.242s	22
5	**Sylvain Guintoli**	14.649s	22
6	**Nicolas Terol**	16.025s	22
7	**Randy de Puniet**	22.300s	22
8	**Leon Camier**	23.606s	22
9	**Matteo Baiocco**	23.818s	22
10	**Roman Ramos**	35.775s	22
11	**Leandro Mercado**	39.929s	22
12	**Sylvain Barrier**	46.267s	22
13	**Santiago Barragan**	57.893s	22
14	**Larry Pegram**	1m 02.676s	22
15	**Christophe Ponsson**	1m 05.262s	22
16	Troy Bayliss	1 Lap	21
17	Imre Toth	1 Lap	21
	Michael VD Mark	DNF	18
	Jordi Torres	DNF	17
	Jed Metcher	DNF	3
	Alex Lowes	DNF	1

1	Rea	1m 31.212s
2	Davies	1m 31.238s
3	Haslam	1m 31.507s
4	VD Mark	1m 31.613s
5	Lowes	1m 32.042s
6	Terol	1m 32.081s
7	Torres	1m 32.243s
8	Sykes	1m 32.265s
9	Guintoli	1m 32.446s
10	Baiocco	1m 32.841s
11	Salom	No Time
12	Mercado	No Time
13	De Puniet	1m 31.885s
14	Bayliss	1m 32.201s
15	Camier	1m 32.668s
16	Metcher	1m 32.727s
17	Canepa	1m 32.998s
18	Barrier	1m 33.057s
19	Walters	1m 33.477s
20	Ramos	1m 33.716s

Fastest race lap: Chaz Davies on lap 2, 1m 31.725s, 108.402mph/174.456km/h.

Lap record: Chaz Davies, GBR (Ducati), 1m 30.949s, 109.327mph/175.945km/h (2014).

Points

1, Haslam 45; 2, Rea 45; 3, Davies 32; 4, Sykes 23; 5, Guintoli 20; 6, Terol 18; 7, Camier 14; 8, Torres 13; 9, Baiocco 12; 10, VD Mark 11; 11, De Puniet 9; 12, Mercado 9; 13, Lowes 7; 14, Ramos 6; 15, Barrier 5; 16, Barragan 3; 17, Bayliss 3; 18, Pegram 2; 19, Metcher 2; 20, Ponsson 1.

Round 2 — BURIRAM, Thailand · 22 March, 2015 · 2.830-mile/4.554km circuit · WEATHER: Race 1 · Dry · Track 50°C · Air 33°C; Race 2 · Dry · Track 48°C · Air 32°C

Race 1: 20 laps, 56.594 miles/91.080km
Time of race: 31m 33.852s · **Average speed:** 107.580mph/173.133km/h

Pos.	Rider	Nat.	No.	Entrant	Machine	Tyres	Time & Gap	Laps
1	**Jonathan Rea**	GBR	65	Kawasaki Racing Team	Kawasaki ZX-10R	P		20
2	**Leon Haslam**	GBR	91	Aprilia Racing Team - Red Devils	Aprilia RSV4 RF	P	6.329s	20
3	**Tom Sykes**	GBR	66	Kawasaki Racing Team	Kawasaki ZX-10R	P	8.183s	20
4	**Jordi Torres**	ESP	81	Aprilia Racing Team - Red Devils	Aprilia RSV4 RF	P	8.513s	20
5	**Sylvain Guintoli**	FRA	1	PATA Honda World Superbike Team	Honda CBR1000RR SP	P	20.502s	20
6	**Matteo Baiocco**	ITA	15	Althea Racing	Ducati Panigale R	P	26.118s	20
7	**Alex Lowes**	GBR	22	VOLTCOM Crescent Suzuki	Suzuki GSX-R1000	P	26.149s	20
8	**David Salom**	ESP	44	Team Pedercini	Kawasaki ZX-10R	P	27.925s	20
9	**Troy Bayliss**	AUS	21	Aruba.it Racing-Ducati SBK Team	Ducati Panigale R	P	28.174s	20
10	**Leandro Mercado**	ARG	36	BARNI Racing Team	Ducati Panigale R	P	32.610s	20
11	**Chaz Davies**	GBR	7	Aruba.it Racing-Ducati SBK Team	Ducati Panigale R	P	37.330s	20
12	**Nicolas Terol**	ESP	18	Althea Racing	Ducati Panigale R	P	37.902s	20
13	**Randy de Puniet**	FRA	14	VOLTCOM Crescent Suzuki	Suzuki GSX-R1000	P	41.722s	20
14	**Sylvain Barrier**	FRA	20	BMW Motorrad Italia SBK Team	BMW S1000 RR	P	50.099s	20
15	**Roman Ramos**	ESP	40	Team Go Eleven	Kawasaki ZX-10R	P	59.457s	20
16	Greg Gildenhuys	RSA	43	Team Pedercini	Kawasaki ZX-10R	P	1m 20.519s	20
17	Santiago Barragan	ESP	51	Grillini SBK Team	Kawasaki ZX-10R	P	1m 20.931s	20
18	Imre Toth	HUN	10	BMW Team Toth	BMW S1000 RR	P	1 Lap	19
19	Ireneusz Sikora	POL	5	BMW Team Toth	BMW S1000 RR	P	1 Lap	19
	Larry Pegram	USA	72	Team Hero EBR	EBR 1190 RX	P	DNF	16
	Anucha Nakcharoensri	THA	9	YSS TS Racing	Honda CBR1000RR	P	DNF	13
	Michael VD Mark	NED	60	PATA Honda World Superbike Team	Honda CBR1000RR SP	P	DNF	6
	Christophe Ponsson	FRA	23	Grillini SBK Team	Kawasaki ZX-10R	P	DNF	4
	Niccolo Canepa	ITA	59	Team Hero EBR	EBR 1190 RX	P	DNF	3
	Leon Camier	GBR	2	MV Agusta Reparto Corse	MV Agusta 1000 F4	P	DNF	1
	Chanon Chumjai	THA	53	RAC Oil Racing Team	BMW S1000 RR	P	DNF	0

Fastest race lap: Jonathan Rea on lap 2, 1m 33.969s, 108.408mph/174.466km/h.

Race 2: 20 laps, 56.594 miles/91.080km
Time of race: 31m 31.173s · **Average speed:** 107.732mph/173.378km/h

Pos.	Rider	Time & Gap	Laps		Superpole	
1	**Jonathan Rea**		20	1	Rea	1m 33.382s
2	**Leon Haslam**	4.946s	20	2	Haslam	1m 33.393s
3	**Alex Lowes**	8.701s	20	3	Lowes	1m 33.738s
4	**Jordi Torres**	10.628s	20	4	Sykes	1m 33.841s
5	**Tom Sykes**	14.326s	20	5	Torres	1m 34.080s
6	**Sylvain Guintoli**	21.060s	20	6	Davies	1m 34.084s
7	**Michael VD Mark**	21.246s	20	7	Bayliss	1m 34.334s
8	**Matteo Baiocco**	23.868s	20	8	VD Mark	1m 34.514s
9	**David Salom**	25.744s	20	9	Guintoli	1m 34.562s
10	**Leandro Mercado**	29.692s	20	10	Mercado	1m 34.674s
11	**Troy Bayliss**	34.533s	20	11	Salom	1m 34.961s
12	**Nicolas Terol**	38.323s	20	12	Baiocco	1m 35.024s
13	**Sylvain Barrier**	45.834s	20			
14	**Roman Ramos**	45.955s	20	13	Barrier	1m 35.115s
15	**Chaz Davies**	1m 00.898s	20	14	Terol	1m 35.255s
16	Greg Gildenhuys	1m 23.943s	20	15	Camier	1m 35.267s
17	Anucha Nakcharoensri	1m 38.125s	20	16	De Puniet	1m 35.578s
18	Imre Toth	1 Lap	19	17	Ramos	1m 36.226s
19	Ireneusz Sikora	1 Lap	19	18	Canepa	1m 36.466s
20	Chanon Chumjai	1 Lap	19	19	Ponsson	1m 36.788s
	Santiago Barragan	DNF	13	20	Barragan	1m 37.536s
	Leon Camier	DNF	10			
	Randy de Puniet	DNF	5			
	Christophe Ponsson	DNF	0			

Fastest race lap: Jonathan Rea on lap 2, 1m 33.817s, 108.584mph/174.749km/h (record).
Previous lap record: New circuit.

Points

1, Rea 95; 2, Haslam 85; 3, Sykes 50; 4, Guintoli 41; 5, Torres 39; 6, Davies 38; 7, Lowes 32; 8. Baiocco 30; 9, Terol 26; 10, Mercado21; 11, VD Mark 20; 12, Salom 15; 13, Bayliss 15; 14, Camier 14; 15, De Puniet 12; 16, Barrier 10; 17, Ramos 9; 18, Barragan 3; 19, Pegram 2; 20, Metcher 2; 21, Ponsson 1.

Round 3 — ARAGON, Spain · 12 April, 2015 · 3.155-mile/5.077km circuit · WEATHER: Race 1 · Dry · Track 18°C · Air 12°C; Race 2 · Dry · Track 32°C · Air 18°C

Race 1: 18 laps, 56.785 miles/91.386km
Time of race: 33m 36.937s · **Average speed:** 101.354mph/163.113km/h

Pos.	Rider	Nat.	No.	Entrant	Machine	Tyres	Time & Gap	Laps
1	**Jonathan Rea**	GBR	65	Kawasaki Racing Team	Kawasaki ZX-10R	P		18
2	**Chaz Davies**	GBR	7	Aruba.it Racing-Ducati SBK Team	Ducati Panigale R	P	0.051s	18
3	**Tom Sykes**	GBR	66	Kawasaki Racing Team	Kawasaki ZX-10R	P	4.977s	18
4	**Leon Haslam**	GBR	91	Aprilia Racing Team - Red Devils	Aprilia RSV4 RF	P	15.088s	18
5	**Jordi Torres**	ESP	81	Aprilia Racing Team - Red Devils	Aprilia RSV4 RF	T	15.290s	18
6	**Xavi Fores**	ESP	112	Aruba.it Racing-Ducati SBK Team	Ducati Panigale R	P	16.655s	18
7	**Nicolas Terol**	ESP	18	Althea Racing	Ducati Panigale R	P	17.365s	18
8	**Leandro Mercado**	ARG	36	BARNI Racing Team	Ducati Panigale R	P	25.527s	18
9	**Sylvain Guintoli**	FRA	1	PATA Honda World Superbike Team	Honda CBR1000RR SP	P	31.464s	18
10	**Leon Camier**	GBR	2	MV Agusta Reparto Corse	MV Agusta 1000 F4	P	43.013s	18
11	**Santiago Barragan**	ESP	51	Grillini SBK Team	Kawasaki ZX-10R	P	43.627s	18
12	**Matteo Baiocco**	ITA	15	Althea Racing	Ducati Panigale R	P	44.893s	18
13	**Roman Ramos**	ESP	40	Team Go Eleven	Kawasaki ZX-10R	P	47.663s	18
14	**Christophe Ponsson**	FRA	23	Grillini SBK Team	Kawasaki ZX-10R	P	1m 11.843s	18
15	**Niccolo Canepa**	ITA	59	Team Hero EBR	EBR 1190 RX	P	1m 15.919s	18
16	Javier Alviz	ESP	90	Team Pedercini	Kawasaki ZX-10R	P	1m 20.816s	18
17	Larry Pegram	USA	72	Team Hero EBR	EBR 1190 RX	P	1m 22.279s	18
18	Imre Toth	HUN	10	BMW Team Toth	BMW S1000 RR	P	1 Lap	17
19	Gabor Rizmayer	HUN	75	BMW Team Toth	BMW S1000 RR	P	1 Lap	17
	Alex Lowes	GBR	22	VOLTCOM Crescent Suzuki	Suzuki GSX-R1000	P	NC	13
	Ayrton Badovini	ITA	86	BMW Motorrad Italia SBK Team	BMW S1000 RR	P	DNF	16
	Michael VD Mark	NED	60	PATA Honda World Superbike Team	Honda CBR1000RR SP	P	DNF	9
	Randy de Puniet	FRA	14	VOLTCOM Crescent Suzuki	Suzuki GSX-R1000	P	DNF	7
	David Salom	ESP	44	Team Pedercini	Kawasaki ZX-10R	P	DNF	6

Fastest race lap: Tom Sykes on lap 2, 1m 50.890s, 102.416mph/164.823km/h (record).

Race 2: 18 laps, 56.785 miles/91.386km
Time of race: 33m 34.669s · **Average speed:** 101.468mph/163.297km/h

Pos.	Rider	Time & Gap	Laps		Superpole	
1	**Chaz Davies**		18	1	Haslam	1m 49.664s
2	**Jonathan Rea**	3.190s	18	2	Davies	1m 49.697s
3	**Leon Haslam**	3.712s	18	3	Sykes	1m 49.863s
4	**Jordi Torres**	14.216s	18	4	Rea	1m 50.053s
5	**Xavi Fores**	20.524s	18	5	Fores	1m 50.449s
6	**David Salom**	25.878s	18	6	Badovini	1m 50.670s
7	**Leandro Mercado**	25.939s	18	7	Torres	1m 50.735s
8	**Michael VD Mark**	26.075s	18	8	Lowes	1m 50.924s
9	**Ayrton Badovini**	27.253s	18	9	Terol	1m 51.146s
10	**Nicolas Terol**	28.666s	18	10	Mercado	1m 51.243s
11	**Matteo Baiocco**	41.038s	18	11	VD Mark	1m 51.510s
12	**Roman Ramos**	41.983s	18	12	Salom	1m 52.016s
13	**Randy de Puniet**	42.961s	18			
14	**Alex Lowes**	43.057s	18	13	Baiocco	1m 51.404s
15	**Leon Camier**	43.375s	18	14	Guintoli	1m 51.481s
16	Christophe Ponsson	59.139s	18	15	Camier	1m 52.526s
17	Santiago Barragan	59.296s	18	16	Canepa	1m 52.970s
18	Niccolo Canepa	1m 16.004s	18	17	Ponsson	1m 53.065s
19	Larry Pegram	1m 33.714s	18	18	Ramos	1m 53.138s
20	Imre Toth	1 Lap	17	19	De Puniet	1m 53.477s
	Javier Alviz	DNF	7	20	Barragan	1m 53.830s
	Sylvain Guintoli	DNF	5			
	Tom Sykes	DNF	4			
	Gabor Rizmayer	DNS	0			

Fastest race lap: Chaz Davies on lap 4, 1m 51.156s, 102.171mph/164.428km/h.
Previous lap record: New circuit layout.

Points

1, Rea 140; 2, Haslam 114; 3, Davies 83; 4, Sykes 66; 5, Torres 63; 6, Guintoli 48; 7, Terol 41; 8, Baiocco 39; 9, Mercado 38; 10, Lowes 34; 11, VD Mark 28; 12, Salom 25; 13, Fores 21; 14, Camier 21; 15, Ramos 16; 16, De Puniet 15; 17, Bayliss 15; 18, Barrier 10; 19, Barragan 8; 20, Badovini 7; 21, Ponsson 3; 22, Pegram 2; 23, Metcher 2; 24, Canepa 1.

WORLD SUPERBIKE CHAMPIONSHIP · 2015

Race 1: 21 laps, 59.268 miles/95.382km

Time of race: 33m 48.898s · **Average speed:** 105.162mph/169.242km/h

Pos.	Rider	Nat.	No.	Entrant	Machine	Tyres	Time & Gap	Laps
1	**Jonathan Rea**	GBR	65	Kawasaki Racing Team	Kawasaki ZX-10R	P		21
2	**Chaz Davies**	GBR	7	Aruba.it Racing-Ducati SBK Team	Ducati Panigale R	P	1.098s	21
3	**Michael VD Mark**	NED	60	PATA Honda World Superbike Team	Honda CBR1000RR SP	P	4.140s	21
4	**Leon Haslam**	GBR	91	Aprilia Racing Team - Red Devils	Aprilia RSV4 RF	P	4.517s	21
5	**Tom Sykes**	GBR	66	Kawasaki Racing Team	Kawasaki ZX-10R	P	6.140s	21
6	**Jordi Torres**	ESP	81	Aprilia Racing Team - Red Devils	Aprilia RSV4 RF	P	11.007s	21
7	**Xavi Fores**	ESP	112	Aruba.it Racing-Ducati SBK Team	Ducati Panigale R	P	15.029s	21
8	**Sylvain Guintoli**	FRA	1	PATA Honda World Superbike Team	Honda CBR1000RR SP	P	17.718s	21
9	**Nicolas Terol**	ESP	18	Althea Racing	Ducati Panigale R	P	22.706s	21
10	**Leon Camier**	GBR	2	MV Agusta Reparto Corse	MV Agusta 1000 F4	P	22.867s	21
11	**Leandro Mercado**	ARG	36	BARNI Racing Team	Ducati Panigale R	P	29.884s	21
12	**Matteo Baiocco**	ITA	15	Althea Racing	Ducati Panigale R	P	36.816s	21
13	**Roman Ramos**	ESP	40	Team Go Eleven	Kawasaki ZX-10R	P	37.190s	21
14	**David Salom**	ESP	44	Team Pedercini	Kawasaki ZX-10R	P	46.675s	21
15	**Niccolo Canepa**	ITA	59	Team Hero EBR	EBR 1190 RX	P	1m 14.271s	21
16	Christophe Ponsson	FRA	23	Grillini SBK Team	Kawasaki ZX-10R	P	1m 14.296s	21
17	Santiago Barragan	ESP	51	Grillini SBK Team	Kawasaki ZX-10R	P	1m 15.979s	21
18	Gabor Rizmayer	HUN	75	BMW Team Toth	BMW S1000 RR	P	1 Lap	20
	Ayrton Badovini	ITA	86	BMW Motorrad Italia SBK Team	BMW S1000 RR	P	DNF	11
	Imre Toth	HUN	10	BMW Team Toth	BMW S1000 RR	P	DNF	9
	Alex Lowes	GBR	22	VOLTCOM Crescent Suzuki	Suzuki GSX-R1000	P	DNF	8
	Randy de Puniet	FRA	14	VOLTCOM Crescent Suzuki	Suzuki GSX-R1000	P	DNF	8
	Larry Pegram	USA	72	Team Hero EBR	EBR 1190 RX	P	DNF	5
	Javier Alviz	ESP	90	Team Pedercini	Kawasaki ZX-10R	P	DNF	0

Race 2: 21 laps, 59.268 miles/95.382km

Time of race: 33m 51.013s · **Average speed:** 105.053mph/169.066km/h

Pos.	Rider	Time & Gap	Laps		Superpole	
1	**Jonathan Rea**		21	1	Sykes	1m 34.789s
2	**Chaz Davies**	0.439s	21	2	Rea	1m 34.920s
3	**Michael VD Mark**	2.831s	21	3	Haslam	1m 35.336s
4	**Leon Haslam**	2.992s	21	4	Davies	1m 35.425s
5	**Tom Sykes**	6.508s	21	5	VD Mark	1m 35.619s
6	**Jordi Torres**	7.092s	21	6	Lowes	1m 35.722s
7	**Sylvain Guintoli**	11.190s	21	7	Fores	1m 35.786s
8	**Xavi Fores**	15.636s	21	8	Torres	1m 35.855s
9	**Alex Lowes**	16.402s	21	9	Guintoli	1m 36.118s
10	**Leon Camier**	18.505s	21	10	Mercado	1m 36.394s
11	**Matteo Baiocco**	21.459s	21	11	Camier	1m 36.402s
12	**Ayrton Badovini**	21.977s	21	12	Terol	1m 36.555s
13	**David Salom**	22.082s	21			
14	**Leandro Mercado**	22.928s	21	13	Baiocco	1m 36.392s
15	**Roman Ramos**	41.801s	21	14	Badovini	1m 36.711s
16	Christophe Ponsson	1m 06.835s	21	15	Ramos	1m 36.847s
17	Javier Alviz	1 Lap	20	16	Salom	1m 37.033s
18	Gabor Rizmayer	1 Lap	20	17	Canepa	1m 37.273s
	Niccolo Canepa	DNF	20	18	De Puniet	1m 37.654s
	Imre Toth	DNF	15	19	Ponsson	1m 38.326s
	Santiago Barragan	DNF	11	20	Barragan	1m 38.977s
	Larry Pegram	DNF	7			
	Randy de Puniet	DNF	5			
	Nicolas Terol	DNF	3			

Fastest race lap: Jonathan Rea on lap 20, 1m 35.889s, 105.957mph/170.522km/h (record).

Fastest race lap: Chaz Davies on lap 18, 1m 35.992s, 105.844mph/170.339km/h.
Previous lap record: Tom Sykes, GBR (Kawasaki), 1m 35.893s, 105.956mph/170.520km/h (2013).

Points

1, Rea 190; 2, Haslam 140, 3, Davies 123; 4, Sykes 88; 5, Torres 83; 6, Guintoli 65; 7, VD Mark 60; 8, Terol 48; 9, Baiocco 48; 10, Mercado 45; 11, Lowes 41; 12, Fores 38; 13, Camier 33; 14, Salom 30; 15, Ramos 20; 16, De Puniet 15; 17, Bayliss 15; 18, Badovini 11; 19, Barrier10; 20, Barragsn 8; 21, Ponsson 3; 22, Pegram 2; 23, Metcher 2; 24 Canepa 2.

Race 1: 6 laps, 18.403 miles/29.616km

Time of race: 10m 43.252s · **Average speed:** 102.991mph/165.748km/h

Pos.	Rider	Nat.	No.	Entrant	Machine	Tyres	Time & Gap	Laps
1	**Jonathan Rea**	GBR	65	Kawasaki Racing Team	Kawasaki ZX-10R	P		6
2	**Tom Sykes**	GBR	66	Kawasaki Racing Team	Kawasaki ZX-10R	P	0.482s	6
3	**Davide Giugliano**	ITA	34	Aruba.it Racing-Ducati SBK Team	Ducati Panigale R	P	3.945s	6
4	**Leon Haslam**	GBR	91	Aprilia Racing Team - Red Devils	Aprilia RSV4 RF	P	7.455s	6
5	**Sylvain Guintoli**	FRA	1	PATA Honda World Superbike Team	Honda CBR1000RR SP	P	11.925s	6
6	**Ayrton Badovini**	ITA	86	BMW Motorrad Italia SBK Team	BMW S1000 RR	P	12.074s	6
7	**Leandro Mercado**	ARG	36	BARNI Racing Team	Ducati Panigale R	P	12.789s	6
8	**Matteo Baiocco**	ITA	15	Althea Racing	Ducati Panigale R	P	13.712s	6
9	**Michael VD Mark**	NED	60	PATA Honda World Superbike Team	Honda CBR1000RR SP	P	13.863s	6
10	**Michel Fabrizio**	ITA	84	Althea Racing	Ducati Panigale R	P	14.637s	6
11	**Roman Ramos**	ESP	40	Team Go Eleven	Kawasaki ZX-10R	P	16.990s	6
12	**Alex Lowes**	GBR	22	VOLTCOM Crescent Suzuki	Suzuki GSX-R1000	P	21.123s	6
13	**Santiago Barragan**	ESP	51	Grillini SBK Team	Kawasaki ZX-10R	P	32.443s	6
14	**Christophe Ponsson**	FRA	23	Team Pedercini	Kawasaki ZX-10R	P	32.977s	6
15	**Imre Toth**	HUN	10	BMW Team Toth	BMW S1000 RR	P	39.711s	6
16	Gabor Rizmayer	HUN	75	BMW Team Toth	BMW S1000 RR	P	40.821s	6
	Leon Camier	GBR	2	MV Agusta Reparto Corse	MV Agusta 1000 F4	P	DNF	3
	David Salom	ESP	44	Team Pedercini	Kawasaki ZX-10R	P	DNS	0
	Jordi Torres	ESP	81	Aprilia Racing Team - Red Devils	Aprilia RSV4 RF	P	DNS	0
	Chaz Davies	GBR	7	Aruba.it Racing-Ducati SBK Team	Ducati Panigale R	P	DNS	0
	Randy de Puniet	FRA	14	VOLTCOM Crescent Suzuki	Suzuki GSX-R1000	P	DNS	0

Race 2: 19 laps, 58.275 miles/93.784km

Time of race: 34m 6.825s · **Average speed:** 102.495mph/164.949km/h

Pos.	Rider	Time & Gap	Laps		Superpole (Wet)	
1	**Jonathan Rea**		19	1	Giugliano	1m 46.382s
2	**Tom Sykes**	4.399s	19	2	Sykes	1m 46.466s
3	**Jordi Torres**	26.020s	19	3	Rea	1m 46.503s
4	**Davide Giugliano**	30.853s	19	4	Davies	1m 46.672s
5	**Ayrton Badovini**	35.379s	19	5	Haslam	1m 46.854s
6	**Matteo Baiocco**	38.818s	19	6	Torres	1m 47.394s
7	**Roman Ramos**	40.663s	19	7	Mercado	1m 47.628s
8	**Leandro Mercado**	42.067s	19	8	Badovini	1m 48.147s
9	**Michel Fabrizio**	55.722s	19	9	VD Mark	1m 48.225s
10	**Alex Lowes**	56.990s	19	10	Salom	1m 48.524s
11	**Santiago Barragan**	1m 29.613s	19	11	Lowes	1m 48.730s
12	**Imre Toth**	1 Lap	18	12	Camier	No Time
13	**Gabor Rizmayer**	1 Lap	18			
	Chaz Davies	DNF	14	13	Fabrizio	1m 48.148s
	Leon Haslam	DNF	8	14	Baiocco	1m 48.174s
	Michael VD Mark	DNF	8	15	Guintoli	1m 48.567s
	Leon Camier	DNF	5	16	Ramos	1m 49.685s
	Randy de Puniet	DNF	4	17	De Puniet	1m 50.378s
	Christophe Ponsson	DNF	3	18	Barragan	1m 51.398s
	Sylvain Guintoli	DNF	0	19	Ponsson	1m 51.786s
				20	Canepa	No Time

Fastest race lap: Tom Sykes on lap 5, 1m 46.707s, 103.475mph/166.527km/h (record).

Fastest race lap: Jonathan Rea on lap 12, 1m 47.198s, 103.001mph/165.764km/h.
Previous lap record: Tom Sykes, GBR (Kawasaki), 1m 47.274s, 102.928mph/165.647km/h (2013).

Points

1, Rea 240; 2. Haslam 153; 3, Sykes 128; 4, Davies 123; 5, Torres 99; 6, Guintoli76; 7, VD Mark67; 8, Baiocco66; 9, Mercado 62; 10, Lowes 51; 11, Terol 48; 12, Fores 38; 13, Ramos 34; 14, Camier 33; 15, Badovini 32; 16, Salom 30; 17, Giugliano 29; 18, Barragan 16; 19, De Puniet 15; 20, Bayliss 15; 21, Fabrizio 13; 22, Barrier 10; 23, Toth 5; 24, Ponsson 5; 25, Rizmayer 3; 26, Pegram 2; 27, Metcher 2; 28, Canepa 2.

Round 6 — **DONINGTON PARK, Great Britain** · 24 May, 2015 · 2.500-mile/4.023km circuit · WEATHER: Race 1 · Dry · Track 21°C · Air 15°C; Race 2 · Dry · Track 21°C · Air 14°C

Race 1: 23 laps, 57.495 miles/92.529km

Time of race: 33m 59.865s · Average speed: 101.468mph/163.297km/h

Pos.	Rider	Nat.	No.	Entrant	Machine	Tyres	Time & Gap	Laps
1	Tom Sykes	GBR	66	Kawasaki Racing Team	Kawasaki ZX-10R	P		23
2	Jonathan Rea	GBR	65	Kawasaki Racing Team	Kawasaki ZX-10R	P	3.743s	23
3	Chaz Davies	GBR	7	Aruba.it Racing-Ducati SBK Team	Ducati Panigale R	P	15.140s	23
4	Leon Haslam	GBR	91	Aprilia Racing Team - Red Devils	Aprilia RSV4 RF	P	18.304s	23
5	Ayrton Badovini	ITA	86	BMW Motorrad Italia SBK Team	BMW S1000 RR	P	20.362s	23
6	Alex Lowes	GBR	22	VOLTCOM Crescent Suzuki	Suzuki GSX-R1000	P	20.848s	23
7	Jordi Torres	ESP	81	Aprilia Racing Team - Red Devils	Aprilia RSV4 RF	P	21.807s	23
8	Sylvain Guintoli	FRA	1	PATA Honda World Superbike Team	Honda CBR1000RR SP	P	24.346s	23
9	Leon Camier	GBR	2	MV Agusta Reparto Corse	MV Agusta 1000 F4	P	30.570s	23
10	David Salom	ESP	44	Team Pedercini	Kawasaki ZX-10R	P	39.074s	23
11	Leandro Mercado	ARG	36	BARNI Racing Team	Ducati Panigale R	P	44.023s	23
12	Nicolas Terol	ESP	18	Althea Racing	Ducati Panigale R	P	46.925s	23
13	Roman Ramos	ESP	40	Team Go Eleven	Kawasaki ZX-10R	P	50.871s	23
14	Randy de Puniet	FRA	14	VOLTCOM Crescent Suzuki	Suzuki GSX-R1000	P	1m 06.993s	23
15	Niccolo Canepa	ITA	59	Grillini SBK Team	Kawasaki ZX-10R	P	1m 09.883s	23
16	Christophe Ponsson	FRA	23	Team Pedercini	Kawasaki ZX-10R	P	1m 26.098s	23
17	Davide Giugliano	ITA	34	Aruba.it Racing-Ducati SBK Team	Ducati Panigale R	P	1 Lap	22
18	Gabor Rizmayer	HUN	75	BMW Team Toth	BMW S1000 RR	P	1 Lap	22
19	Imre Toth	HUN	10	BMW Team Toth	BMW S1000 RR	P	1 Lap	22
	Santiago Barragan	ESP	51	Grillini SBK Team	Kawasaki ZX-10R	P	DNF	17
	Matteo Baiocco	ITA	15	Althea Racing	Ducati Panigale R	P	DNF	13
	Michael VD Mark	NED	60	PATA Honda World Superbike Team	Honda CBR1000RR SP	P	DNF	8

Race 2: 23 laps, 57.495 miles/92.529km

Time of race: 33m 52.649s · Average speed: 101.828mph/163.877km/h

Pos.	Rider	Time & Gap	Laps		Superpole	
1	Tom Sykes		23	1	Sykes	1m 27.071s
2	Jonathan Rea	9.772s	23	2	Rea	1m 27.308s
3	Chaz Davies	12.304s	23	3	Giugliano	1m 27.344s
4	Leon Haslam	15.601s	23	4	Haslam	1m 27.535s
5	Davide Giugliano	15.779s	23	5	Lowes	1m 27.554s
6	Alex Lowes	23.136s	23	6	Davies	1m 27.710s
7	Jordi Torres	26.674s	23	7	Camier	1m 28.011s
8	Sylvain Guintoli	27.206s	23	8	Baiocco	1m 28.188s
9	Ayrton Badovini	31.469s	23	9	Guintoli	1m 28.370s
10	Matteo Baiocco	34.659s	23	10	Salom	1m 28.620s
11	Roman Ramos	36.298s	23	11	Badovini	1m 28.701s
12	David Salom	36.682s	23	12	VD Mark	1m 28.715s
13	Leandro Mercado	1m 17.739s	23			
14	Randy de Puniet	1m 24.434s	23	13	Torres	1m 28.689s
15	Santiago Barragan	1m 24.601s	23	14	Terol	1m 28.827s
16	Gabor Rizmayer	1 Lap	22	15	Mercado	1m 28.991s
17	Imre Toth	1 Lap	22	16	Ramos	1m 29.436s
	Christophe Ponsson	DNF	7	17	Ponsson	1m 29.668s
	Nicolas Terol	DNF	6	18	De Puniet	1m 29.686s
	Niccolo Canepa	DNF	4	19	Canepa	1m 29.783s
	Michael VD Mark	DNF	4	20	Barragan	1m 30.839s
	Leon Camier	DNF	3			

Fastest race lap: Jonathan Rea on lap 9, 1m 27.914s, 102.363mph/164.738km/h.

Fastest race lap: Tom Sykes on lap 2, 1m 27.640s, 102.683mph/165.253km/h (record).
Previous lap record: Tom Sykes, GBR (Kawasaki), 1m 28.074s, 102.178mph/164.439km/h (2013).

Points

1, Rea 280; 2, Haslam 179; 3, Sykes178; 4, Davies 155; 5, Torres 117; 6, Guintoli 92; 7, Baiocco 72; 8, Lowes 71; 9, Mercado 70; 10, VD Mark 67; 11, Terol 52; 12, Badovini 50; 13, Ramos 42; 14, Giugliano 40; 15, Salom 40; 16, Camier 40; 17, Fores 38; 18, De Puniet 19; 19, Barragan 17; 20, Bayliss 15; 21, Fabrizio 13; 22, Barrier 10; 23, Toth 5; 24, Ponsson 5; 25, Rizmayer 3; 26, Canepa 3; 27, Pegram 2; 28, Metcher 2.

Round 7 — **PORTIMAO, Portugal** · 7 June, 2015 · 2.853-mile/4.592km circuit · WEATHER: Race 1 · Wet · Track 29°C · Air 25°C; Race 2 · Dry · Track 21°C · Air 14°C

Race 1: 20 laps, 57.067 miles/91.840km

Time of race: 37m 10.092s · Average speed: 92.122mph/148.256km/h

Pos.	Rider	Nat.	No.	Entrant	Machine	Tyres	Time & Gap	Laps
1	Jonathan Rea	GBR	65	Kawasaki Racing Team	Kawasaki ZX-10R	P		20
2	Tom Sykes	GBR	66	Kawasaki Racing Team	Kawasaki ZX-10R	P	9.384s	20
3	Chaz Davies	GBR	7	Aruba.it Racing-Ducati SBK Team	Ducati Panigale R	P	13.753s	20
4	Davide Giugliano	ITA	34	Aruba.it Racing-Ducati SBK Team	Ducati Panigale R	P	27.818s	20
5	Sylvain Guintoli	FRA	1	PATA Honda World Superbike Team	Honda CBR1000RR SP	P	28.141s	20
6	Matteo Baiocco	ITA	15	Althea Racing	Ducati Panigale R	P	39.665s	20
7	Ayrton Badovini	ITA	86	BMW Motorrad Italia SBK Team	BMW S1000 RR	P	40.829s	20
8	Leandro Mercado	ARG	36	BARNI Racing Team	Ducati Panigale R	P	43.401s	20
9	Michael VD Mark	NED	60	PATA Honda World Superbike Team	Honda CBR1000RR SP	P	59.025s	20
10	Alex Lowes	GBR	22	VOLTCOM Crescent Suzuki	Suzuki GSX-R1000	P	1m 01.388s	20
11	Jordi Torres	ESP	81	Aprilia Racing Team - Red Devils	Aprilia RSV4 RF	P	1m 02.769s	20
12	Leon Haslam	GBR	91	Aprilia Racing Team - Red Devils	Aprilia RSV4 RF	P	1m 04.152s	20
13	Randy de Puniet	FRA	14	VOLTCOM Crescent Suzuki	Suzuki GSX-R1000	P	1m 39.537s	20
14	David Salom	ESP	44	Team Pedercini	Kawasaki ZX-10R	P	1m 43.681s	20
15	Nicolas Terol	ESP	18	Althea Racing	Ducati Panigale R	P	1m 45.940s	20
16	Roman Ramos	ESP	40	Team Go Eleven	Kawasaki ZX-10R	P	1m 49.326s	20
17	Niccolo Canepa	ITA	59	Grillini SBK Team	Kawasaki ZX-10R	P	1 Lap	19
18	Christophe Ponsson	FRA	23	Team Pedercini	Kawasaki ZX-10R	P	1 Lap	19
19	Gabor Rizmayer	HUN	75	BMW Team Toth	BMW S1000 RR	P	1 Lap	19
20	Imre Toth	HUN	10	BMW Team Toth	BMW S1000 RR	P	5 Laps	15
	Santiago Barragan	ESP	51	Grillini SBK Team	Kawasaki ZX-10R	P	DNF	15
	Leon Camier	GBR	2	MV Agusta Reparto Corse	MV Agusta 1000 F4	P	DNF	2

Race 2: 20 laps, 57.067 miles/91.840km

Time of race: 34m 33.783s · Average speed: 99.065mph/159.430km/h

Pos.	Rider	Time & Gap	Laps		Superpole	
1	Jonathan Rea		20	1	Giugliano	1m 41.764s
2	Davide Giugliano	5.416s	20	2	Sykes	1m 41.880s
3	Leon Haslam	6.689s	20	3	Davies	1m 42.123s
4	Chaz Davies	10.445s	20	4	Lowes	1m 42.198s
5	Michael VD Mark	14.122s	20	5	Haslam	1m 42.217s
6	Sylvain Guintoli	14.265s	20	6	Baiocco	1m 42.468s
7	Jordi Torres	16.213s	20	7	Guintoli	1m 42.641s
8	Tom Sykes	19.384s	20	8	Rea	1m 42.902s
9	Leandro Mercado	19.998s	20	9	Torres	1m 42.975s
10	Matteo Baiocco	27.332s	20	10	Badovini	1m 43.067s
11	Roman Ramos	28.904s	20	11	Mercado	1m 43.327s
12	Ayrton Badovini	31.138s	20	12	Salom	1m 43.609s
13	Alex Lowes	34.252s	20			
14	Christophe Ponsson	56.181s	20	13	VD Mark	1m 43.272s
15	Nicolas Terol	1m 02.679s	20	14	Camier	1m 43.468s
16	Randy de Puniet	1m 03.200s	20	15	Ramos	1m 43.488s
17	Niccolo Canepa	1m 03.488s	20	16	De Puniet	1m 44.273s
18	Gabor Rizmayer	1 Lap	19	17	Terol	1m 44.992s
19	Imre Toth	1 Lap	19	18	Ponsson	1m 45.066s
	Santiago Barragan	DNF	8	19	Barragan	1m 45.640s
	David Salom	DNF	4	20	Canepa	1m 45.674s
	Leon Camier	DNF	1			

Fastest race lap: Jonathan Rea on lap 3, 1m 42.637s, 100.081mph/161.065km/h.

Fastest race lap: Jonathan Rea on lap 2, 1m 43.034s, 99.695mph/160.444km/h.
Lap record: Tom Sykes, GBR (Kawasaki), 1m 42.475s, 100.239mph/161.319km/h (2013).

Points

1, Rea 330; 2, Sykes 206; 3, Haslam 199; 4, Davies 184; 5, Torres 131; 6, Guintoli 113; 7, Baiocco 88; 8, VD Mark 85; 9, Mercado 85; 10, Lowes 80; 11, Giugliano 73; 12, Badovini 63; 13, Terol 54; 14, Ramos 47; 15, Salom 42; 16, Camier 40; 17, Fores 38; 18, De Puniet 22, 19, Barragan 17; 20, Bayliss 15; 21, Fabrizio 13, 22, Barrier 10; 23, Ponsson 7; 24, Toth 5; 25, Rizmayer 3; 26, Canepa 3; 27, Pegram 2; 28, Metcher 2.

WORLD SUPERBIKE CHAMPIONSHIP · 2015

Race 1: 21 laps, 55.144 miles/88.746km

Time of race: 33m 30.813s · **Average speed:** 98.726mph/158.884km/h

Pos.	Rider	Nat.	No.	Entrant	Machine	Tyres	Time & Gap	Laps
1	**Tom Sykes**	GBR	66	Kawasaki Racing Team	Kawasaki ZX-10R	P		21
2	**Jonathan Rea**	GBR	65	Kawasaki Racing Team	Kawasaki ZX-10R	P	3.613s	21
3	**Chaz Davies**	GBR	7	Aruba.it Racing-Ducati SBK Team	Ducati Panigale R	P	4.178s	21
4	**Davide Giugliano**	ITA	34	Aruba.it Racing-Ducati SBK Team	Ducati Panigale R	P	5.944s	21
5	**Leon Haslam**	GBR	91	Aprilia Racing Team - Red Devils	Aprilia RSV4 RF	P	12.155s	21
6	**Max Biaggi**	ITA	3	Aprilia Racing Team	Aprilia RSV4 RF	P	12.352s	21
7	**Ayrton Badovini**	ITA	86	BMW Motorrad Italia SBK Team	BMW S1000 RR	P	18.145s	21
8	**Michele Pirro**	ITA	55	Aruba.it Racing-Ducati SBK Team	Ducati Panigale R	P	18.328s	21
9	**Sylvain Guintoli**	FRA	1	PATA Honda World Superbike Team	Honda CBR1000RR SP	P	20.088s	21
10	**Michael VD Mark**	NED	60	PATA Honda World Superbike Team	Honda CBR1000RR SP	P	20.282s	21
11	**Leandro Mercado**	ARG	36	BARNI Racing Team	Ducati Panigale R	P	24.195s	21
12	**Alex Lowes**	GBR	22	VOLTCOM Crescent Suzuki	Suzuki GSX-R1000	P	26.625s	21
13	**Leon Camier**	GBR	2	MV Agusta Reparto Corse	MV Agusta F4 RR	P	26.719s	21
14	**Roman Ramos**	ESP	40	Team Go Eleven	Kawasaki ZX-10R	P	31.898s	21
15	**Matteo Baiocco**	ITA	15	Althea Racing	Ducati Panigale R	P	32.643s	21
16	Markus Reiterberger	GER	11	VanZon Remeha BMW	BMW S1000 RR	P	36.833s	21
17	David Salom	ESP	44	Team Pedercini	Kawasaki ZX-10R	P	42.514s	21
18	Christophe Ponsson	FRA	23	Team Pedercini	Kawasaki ZX-10R	P	1m 10.247s	21
19	Santiago Barragan	ESP	51	Grillini SBK Team	Kawasaki ZX-10R	P	1m 10.536s	21
20	Gianluca Vizziello	ITA	45	Grillini SBK Team	Kawasaki ZX-10R	P	1m 28.191s	21
21	Gabor Rizmayer	HUN	75	BMW Team Toth	BMW S1000 RR	P	1m 38.856s	21
22	Imre Toth	HUN	10	BMW Team Toth	BMW S1000 RR	P	1 Lap	20
	Niccolo Canepa	ITA	59	Althea Racing	Ducati Panigale R	P	DNF	14
	Randy de Puniet	FRA	14	VOLTCOM Crescent Suzuki	Suzuki GSX-R1000	P	DNF	10
	Jordi Torres	ESP	81	Aprilia Racing Team - Red Devils	Aprilia RSV4 RF	P	DNF	2

Fastest race lap: Davide Giugliano on lap 3, 1m 34.855s, 99.660mph/160.388km/h.

Race 2: 21 laps, 55.144 miles/88.746km

Time of race: 33m 31.716s · **Average speed:** 98.681mph/158.812km/h

Pos.	Rider	Time & Gap	Laps	Superpole	
1	**Jonathan Rea**		21	1 Sykes	1m 34.214s
2	**Davide Giugliano**	1.290s	21	2 Haslam	1m 34.426s
3	**Leon Haslam**	2.436s	21	3 Giugliano	1m 34.442s
4	**Chaz Davies**	2.514s	21	4 Rea	1m 34.459s
5	**Tom Sykes**	5.694s	21	5 Biaggi	1m 34.463s
6	**Max Biaggi**	5.911s	21	6 Torres	1m 34.551s
7	**Jordi Torres**	7.075s	21	7 Lowes	1m 34.811s
8	**Michele Pirro**	10.159s	21	8 Badovini	1m 34.881s
9	**Sylvain Guintoli**	17.476s	21	9 Guintoli	1m 35.061s
10	**Michael VD Mark**	17.589s	21	10 Pirro	1m 35.139s
11	**Ayrton Badovini**	21.744s	21	11 Davies	1m 35.473s
12	**Niccolo Canepa**	26.599s	21	12 Baiocco	1m 35.862s
13	**Markus Reiterberger**	30.402s	21		
14	**Roman Ramos**	36.000s	21	13 Mercado	1m 35.285s
15	**David Salom**	36.186s	21	14 Canepa	1m 35.464s
16	Leon Camier	37.572s	21	15 VD Mark	1m 35.642s
17	Randy de Puniet	55.983s	21	16 Reiterberger	1m 35.658s
18	Christophe Ponsson	1m 10.593s	21	17 Ramos	1m 36.205s
19	Gianluca Vizziello	1m 16.119s	21	18 Camier	1m 36.247s
20	Santiago Barragan	1m 16.177s	21	19 De Puniet	1m 36.262s
21	Gabor Rizmayer	1m 31.041s	21	20 Salom	No Time
22	Imre Toth	2 Laps	19		
	Matteo Baiocco	DNF	15		
	Alex Lowes	DNF	8		
	Leandro Mercado	DNF	3		

Fastest race lap: Jonathan Rea on lap 2, 1m 34.720s, 99.803mph/160.617km/h (record).

Previous lap record: Tom Sykes, GBR (Kawasaki), 1m 35.629s, 98.854mph/159.090km/h (2014).

Points

1, Rea 375; 2, Sykes 242; 3, Haslam 226; 4, Davies 213; 5, Torres 140; 6, Guintoli 127; 7, Giugliano 106; 8, VD Mark 97; 9, Mercado 90; 10, Baiocco 89; 11, Lowes 84; 12, Badovini 77; 13, Terol 54; 14, Ramos 51; 15, Salom 43; 16, Camier 43; 17, Fores 38; 18, De Puniet 22; 19, Biaggi 20; 20, Barragan 17; 21, Pirro 16; 22, Bayliss 15; 23, Fabrizio 13; 24, Barrier 10; 25, Canepa 7; 26, Ponsson 7; 27, Toth 5; 28, Reiterberger 3; 29, Rizmayer 3; 30, Pegram 2; 31, Metcher 2.

Race 1: 25 laps, 56.079 miles/90.250km

Time of race: 35m 15.693s · **Average speed:** 95.422mph/153.567km/h

Pos.	Rider	Nat.	No.	Entrant	Machine	Tyres	Time & Gap	Laps
1	**Chaz Davies**	GBR	7	Aruba.it Racing-Ducati SBK Team	Ducati Panigale R	P		25
2	**Tom Sykes**	GBR	66	Kawasaki Racing Team	Kawasaki ZX-10R	P	1.798s	25
3	**Jonathan Rea**	GBR	65	Kawasaki Racing Team	Kawasaki ZX-10R	P	2.107s	25
4	**Davide Giugliano**	ITA	34	Aruba.it Racing-Ducati SBK Team	Ducati Panigale R	P	15.954s	25
5	**Jordi Torres**	ESP	81	Aprilia Racing Team - Red Devils	Aprilia RSV4 RF	P	19.661s	25
6	**Alex Lowes**	GBR	22	VOLTCOM Crescent Suzuki	Suzuki GSX-R1000	P	24.431s	25
7	**Sylvain Guintoli**	FRA	1	PATA Honda World Superbike Team	Honda CBR1000RR SP	P	26.971s	25
8	**Michael VD Mark**	NED	60	PATA Honda World Superbike Team	Honda CBR1000RR SP	P	35.428s	25
9	**Leandro Mercado**	ARG	36	BARNI Racing Team	Ducati Panigale R	P	41.261s	25
10	**Leon Camier**	GBR	2	MV Agusta Reparto Corse	MV Agusta F4 RR	P	44.383s	25
11	**Randy de Puniet**	FRA	14	VOLTCOM Crescent Suzuki	Suzuki GSX-R1000	P	52.748s	25
12	**Roman Ramos**	ESP	40	Team Go Eleven	Kawasaki ZX-10R	P	54.906s	25
13	**Leon Haslam**	GBR	91	Aprilia Racing Team - Red Devils	Aprilia RSV4 RF	P	1m 18.150s	25
14	**Christophe Ponsson**	FRA	23	Team Pedercini	Kawasaki ZX-10R	P	1m 20.220s	25
15	**Gianluca Vizziello**	ITA	45	Grillini SBK Team	Kawasaki ZX-10R	P	1 Lap	24
16	Imre Toth	HUN	10	BMW Team Toth	BMW S1000 RR	P	1 Lap	24
	David Salom	ESP	44	Team Pedercini	Kawasaki ZX-10R	P	DNF	24
	Santiago Barragan	ESP	51	Grillini SBK Team	Kawasaki ZX-10R	P	DNF	19
	Gabor Rizmayer	HUN	75	BMW Team Toth	BMW S1000 RR	P	DNF	14
	Ayrton Badovini	ITA	86	BMW Motorrad Italia SBK Team	BMW S1000 RR	P	DNF	3
	Matteo Baiocco	ITA	15	Althea Racing	Ducati Panigale R	P	DNF	0
	Niccolo Canepa	ITA	59	Althea Racing	Ducati Panigale R	P	DNF	0

Fastest race lap: Chaz Davies on lap 5, 1m 23.739s, 96.435mph/155.197km/h.

Race 2: 25 laps, 56.079 miles/90.250km

Time of race: 35m 13.816s · **Average speed:** 95.507mph/153.703km/h

Pos.	Rider	Time & Gap	Laps	Superpole	
1	**Chaz Davies**		25	1 Davies	1m 22.101s
2	**Tom Sykes**	1.406s	25	2 Giugliano	1m 22.297s
3	**Jonathan Rea**	1.982s	25	3 Torres	1m 22.414s
4	**Davide Giugliano**	16.551s	25	4 Sykes	1m 22.526s
5	**Leon Haslam**	17.772s	25	5 Rea	1m 22.854s
6	**Ayrton Badovini**	31.735s	25	6 Haslam	1m 22.991s
7	**Michael VD Mark**	34.446s	25	7 Canepa	1m 23.256s
8	**Niccolo Canepa**	38.048s	25	8 Lowes	1m 23.285s
9	**Leandro Mercado**	41.755s	25	9 Guintoli	1m 23.406s
10	**Leon Camier**	49.105s	25	10 Camier	1m 23.990s
11	**Randy de Puniet**	56.249s	25	11 Salom	1m 23.998s
12	**Roman Ramos**	1m 01.630s	25	12 Badovini	1m 24.663s
13	**Matteo Baiocco**	1m 12.647s	25		
14	**Gianluca Vizziello**	1 Lap	24	13 Baiocco	1m 24.146s
15	**Christophe Ponsson**	1 Lap	24	14 Mercado	1m 24.166s
16	Gabor Rizmayer	1 Lap	24	15 VD Mark	1m 24.461s
17	Imre Toth	2 Laps	23	16 Ramos	1m 24.619s
18	Santiago Barragan	3 Laps	22	17 De Puniet	1m 24.771s
	Alex Lowes	DNF	6	18 Ponsson	1m 25.485s
	David Salom	DNF	3	19 Rizmayer	1m 26.489s
	Davide Giugliano	DNF	1	20 Barragan	1m 26.968s
	Sylvain Guintoli	DNF	1		

Fastest race lap: Tom Sykes on lap 10, 1m 23.842s, 96.316mph/155.006km/h.

Lap record: Davide Giugliano, ITA (Ducati), 1m 23.403s, 96.823mph/155.822km/h (2014).

Points

1, Rea 407; 2, Sykes 282; 3, Davies 263; 4, Haslam 240; 5, Torres 164; 6, Guintoli 136; 7, Giugliano 119; 8, VD Mark 114; 9, Mercado 104; 10, Lowes 94; 11, Baiocco 92; 12, Badovini 87; 13, Ramos 59; 14, Camier 55; 15, Terol 54; 16, Salom 43; 17, Fores 38; 18, De Puniet 32; 19, Biaggi 20; 20, Barragan 17; 21, Pirro 16; 22, Canepa 15; 23, Bayliss 15; 24, Fabrizio 13; 25, Barrier 10; 26, Ponsson 10; 27, Toth 5; 28, Reiterberger 3; 29, Rizmayer 3; 30, Vizziello 3; 31, Pegram 2; 32, Metcher 2.

Round 10   SEPANG, Malaysia · 2 August, 2015 · 3.447-mile/5.543km circuit · WEATHER: Race 1 · Dry · Track 43°C · Air 31°C; Race 2 · Dry · Track 39°C · Air 31°C

Race 1: 16 laps, 55.108 miles/88.688km

Time of race: 33m 33.964s · **Average speed:** 98.507mph/158.532km/h

Pos.	Rider	Nat.	No.	Entrant	Machine	Tyres	Time & Gap	Laps
1	**Jonathan Rea**	GBR	65	Kawasaki Racing Team	Kawasaki ZX-10R	P		16
2	**Chaz Davies**	GBR	7	Aruba.it Racing-Ducati SBK Team	Ducati Panigale R	P	0.121s	16
3	**Max Biaggi**	ITA	3	Aprilia Racing Team	Aprilia RSV4 RF	P	10.695s	16
4	**Sylvain Guintoli**	FRA	1	PATA Honda World Superbike Team	Honda CBR1000RR SP	P	15.433s	16
5	**Tom Sykes**	GBR	66	Kawasaki Racing Team	Kawasaki ZX-10R	P	17.983s	16
6	**Alex Lowes**	GBR	22	VOLTCOM Crescent Suzuki	Suzuki GSX-R1000	P	23.758s	16
7	**Leon Haslam**	GBR	91	Aprilia Racing Team - Red Devils	Aprilia RSV4 RF	P	24.854s	16
8	**Matteo Baiocco**	ITA	15	Althea Racing	Ducati Panigale R	P	28.306s	16
9	**Niccolo Canepa**	ITA	59	Althea Racing	Ducati Panigale R	P	31.098s	16
10	**Jordi Torres**	ESP	81	Aprilia Racing Team - Red Devils	Aprilia RSV4 RF	P	34.105s	16
11	**David Salom**	ESP	44	Team Pedercini	Kawasaki ZX-10R	P	37.107s	16
12	**Randy de Puniet**	FRA	14	VOLTCOM Crescent Suzuki	Suzuki GSX-R1000	P	37.378s	16
13	**Leon Camier**	GBR	2	MV Agusta Reparto Corse	MV Agusta F4 RR	P	39.656s	16
14	**Roman Ramos**	ESP	40	Team Go Eleven	Kawasaki ZX-10R	P	43.451s	16
15	**Leandro Mercado**	ARG	36	BARNI Racing Team	Ducati Panigale R	P	48.476s	16
16	Christophe Ponsson	FRA	23	Team Pedercini	Kawasaki ZX-10R	P	1m 01.166s	16
17	Gabor Rizmayer	HUN	75	BMW Team Toth	BMW S1000 RR	P	1m 24.006s	16
18	Alex Phillis	AUS	48	Grillini SBK Team	Kawasaki ZX-10R	P	1m 31.093s	16
19	Imre Toth	HUN	10	BMW Team Toth	BMW S1000 RR	P	2m 02.124s	16
	Gianluca Vizziello	ITA	45	Grillini SBK Team	Kawasaki ZX-10R	P	DNF	7
	Michael VD Mark	NED	60	PATA Honda World Superbike Team	Honda CBR1000RR SP	P	DNF	7

Race 2: 16 laps, 55.108 miles/88.688km

Time of race: 33m 36.466s · **Average speed:** 98.385mph/158.335km/h

Pos.	Rider	Time & Gap	Laps
1	**Chaz Davies**		16
2	**Jonathan Rea**	0.091s	16
3	**Jordi Torres**	5.008s	16
4	**Sylvain Guintoli**	13.130s	16
5	**Michael VD Mark**	15.801s	16
6	**Leon Haslam**	15.970s	16
7	**David Salom**	24.561s	16
8	**Alex Lowes**	26.526s	16
9	**Matteo Baiocco**	28.528s	16
10	**Roman Ramos**	31.598s	16
11	**Niccolo Canepa**	33.568s	16
12	**Leon Camier**	34.806s	16
13	**Randy de Puniet**	46.521s	16
14	**Tom Sykes**	48.964s	16
15	**Leandro Mercado**	49.865s	16
16	Christophe Ponsson	1m 04.171s	16
17	Gianluca Vizziello	1m 24.837s	16
18	Gabor Rizmayer	1m 25.068s	16
19	Alex Phillis	1m 34.051s	16
20	Imre Toth	2m 00.907s	16
	Max Biaggi	DNF	0

	Superpole	
1	Sykes	2m 03.240s
2	Torres	2m 03.510s
3	Guintoli	2m 03.836s
4	Biaggi	2m 03.948s
5	Lowes	2m 04.018s
6	Davies	2m 04.179s
7	Rea	2m 04.207s
8	Haslam	2m 04.214s
9	Canepa	2m 04.654s
10	Baiocco	2m 05.000s
11	De Puniet	2m 05.100s
12	Badovini	No Time
13	VD Mark	2m 05.004s
14	Camier	2m 05.051s
15	Ramos	2m 06.145s
16	Mercado	2m 06.261s
17	Salom	2m 06.707s
18	Vizziello	2m 07.525s
19	Ponsson	2m 08.289s
20	Rizmayer	2m 09.112s

Fastest race lap: Tom Sykes on lap 2, 2m 3.654s, 100.274mph/161.376km/h (record).

Fastest race lap: Chaz Davies on lap 3, 2m 4.707s, 99.427mph/160.013km/h.

Previous lap record: Marco Melandri, ITA (Aprilia), 2m 4.884s, 99.377mph/159.931km/h (2014).

Points

1, Rea 452; 2, Davies 308; 3, Sykes 295; 4, Haslam 259; 5, Torres 186; 6, Guintoli 162; 7, VD Mark 125; 8, Giugliano 119; 9, Lowes 112; 10, Baiocco 107; 11, Mercado 106; 12, Badovini 87; 13, Ramos 67; 14, Camier 62; 15, Salom 57; 16, Terol 54; 17, De Puniet 39; 18, Fores 38; 19, Biaggi 36; 20, Canepa 27; 21, Barragan 17; 22, Pirro 16; 23, Bayliss 15; 24, Fabrizio 13; 25, Barrier 10; 26, Ponsson 10; 27, Toth 5; 28, Reiterberger 3; 29, Rizmayer 3; 30, Vizziello 3; 31, Pegram 2; 32, Metcher 2.

Round 11   JEREZ, Spain · 20 September, 2015 · 2.748-mile/4.423km circuit · WEATHER: Race 1 · Dry · Track 29°C · Air 25°C; Race 2 · Dry · Track 43°C · Air 29°C

Race 1: 20 laps, 54.966 miles/88.460km

Time of race: 34m 14.685s · **Average speed:** 96.306mph/154.990km/h

Pos.	Rider	Nat.	No.	Entrant	Machine	Tyres	Time & Gap	Laps
1	**Tom Sykes**	GBR	66	Kawasaki Racing Team	Kawasaki ZX-10R	P		20
2	**Chaz Davies**	GBR	7	Aruba.it Racing-Ducati SBK Team	Ducati Panigale R	P	2.865s	20
3	**Michael VD Mark**	NED	60	PATA Honda World Superbike Team	Honda CBR1000RR SP	P	6.665s	20
4	**Jonathan Rea**	GBR	65	Kawasaki Racing Team	Kawasaki ZX-10R	P	9.059s	20
5	**Leon Haslam**	GBR	91	Aprilia Racing Team - Red Devils	Aprilia RSV4 RF	P	9.318s	20
6	**Michele Pirro**	ITA	55	Aruba.it Racing-Ducati SBK Team	Ducati Panigale R	P	10.466s	20
7	**Alex Lowes**	GBR	22	VOLTCOM Crescent Suzuki	Suzuki GSX-R1000	P	15.945s	20
8	**Matteo Baiocco**	ITA	15	Althea Racing	Ducati Panigale R	P	18.020s	20
9	**Leon Camier**	GBR	2	MV Agusta Reparto Corse	MV Agusta F4 RR	P	18.654s	20
10	**Sylvain Guintoli**	FRA	1	PATA Honda World Superbike Team	Honda CBR1000RR SP	P	19.510s	20
11	**David Salom**	ESP	44	Team Pedercini	Kawasaki ZX-10R	P	24.441s	20
12	**Jordi Torres**	ESP	81	Aprilia Racing Team - Red Devils	Aprilia RSV4 RF	P	29.247s	20
13	**Roman Ramos**	ESP	40	Team Go Eleven	Kawasaki ZX-10R	P	35.768s	20
14	**Leandro Mercado**	ARG	36	BARNI Racing Team	Ducati Panigale R	P	37.933s	20
15	**Ayrton Badovini**	ITA	86	BMW Motorrad Italia SBK Team	BMW S1000 RR	P	40.147s	20
16	Randy de Puniet	FRA	14	VOLTCOM Crescent Suzuki	Suzuki GSX-R1000	P	40.275s	20
17	Niccolo Canepa	ITA	59	Althea Racing	Ducati Panigale R	P	45.846s	20
18	Gabor Rizmayer	HUN	75	BMW Team Toth	BMW S1000 RR	P	1m 15.451s	20
19	Alex Phillis	AUS	48	Grillini SBK Team	Kawasaki ZX-10R	P	1 Lap	19
20	Imre Toth	HUN	10	BMW Team Toth	BMW S1000 RR	P	1 Lap	19
21	Christophe Ponsson	FRA	23	Team Pedercini	Kawasaki ZX-10R	P	3 Laps	17
22	Gianluca Vizziello	ITA	45	Grillini SBK Team	Kawasaki ZX-10R	P	3 Laps	17

Race 2: 20 laps, 54.966 miles/88.460km

Time of race: 34m 29.546s · **Average speed:** 95.615mph/153.877km/h

Pos.	Rider	Time & Gap	Laps
1	**Chaz Davies**		20
2	**Jordi Torres**	1.840s	20
3	**Leon Haslam**	2.335s	20
4	**Jonathan Rea**	7.619s	20
5	**Tom Sykes**	11.500s	20
6	**Matteo Baiocco**	12.705s	20
7	**Michele Pirro**	12.995s	20
8	**Leon Camier**	15.332s	20
9	**Sylvain Guintoli**	18.411s	20
10	**Leandro Mercado**	21.544s	20
11	**Niccolo Canepa**	23.448s	20
12	**David Salom**	27.790s	20
13	**Michael VD Mark**	31.948s	20
14	**Ayrton Badovini**	33.001s	20
15	**Christophe Ponsson**	55.353s	20
16	Gabor Rizmayer	1m 09.045s	20
17	Gianluca Vizziello	1m 24.797s	20
18	Alex Lowes	1m 37.110s	20
19	Alex Phillis	1m 42.754s	20
20	Imre Toth	1m 43.004s	20
	Roman Ramos	DNF	19
	Randy de Puniet	DNF	5

	Superpole	
1	Sykes	1m 40.292s
2	Rea	1m 40.500s
3	Canepa	1m 40.508s
4	VD Mark	1m 40.956s
5	Torres	1m 40.974s
6	Davies	1m 41.155s
7	Pirro	1m 41.185s
8	Baiocco	1m 41.415s
9	Lowes	1m 41.427s
10	Guintoli	1m 41.467s
11	Haslam	1m 41.512s
12	Salom	No Time
13	Camier	1m 41.745s
14	Mercado	1m 41.908s
15	De Puniet	1m 42.486s
16	Ramos	1m 42.584s
17	Badovini	1m 42.714s
18	Ponsson	1m 42.774s
19	Vizziello	1m 43.746s
20	Rizmayer	1m 43.826s

Fastest race lap: Jonathan Rea on lap 2, 1m 41.136s, 97.828mph/157.439km/h (record).

Fastest race lap: Tom Sykes on lap 2, 1m 42.238s, 96.774mph/155.742km/h.

Previous lap record: Tom Sykes, GBR (Kawasaki), 1m 41.691s, 97.294mph/156.580km/h (2013).

Points

1, Rea 478; 2, Davies 353; 3, Sykes 331; 4, Haslam 286; 5, Torres 210; 6, Guintoli 175; 7, VD Mark 144; 8, Baiocco 125; 9, Lowes 121; 10, Giugliano 119; 11, Mercado 114; 12, Badovini 90; 13, Camier 77; 14, Ramos 70; 15, Salom 66; 16, Terol 54; 17, De Puniet 39; 18, Fores 38; 19, Biaggi 36; 20, Pirro 35; 21, Canepa 32; 22, Barragan 17; 23, Bayliss 15; 24, Fabrizio 13; 25, Ponsson 11; 26, Barrier 10; 27, Toth 5; 28, Reiterberger 3; 29, Rizmayer 3; 30, Vizziello 3; 31, Pegram 2; 32, Metcher 2.

SBK TISSOT
OFFICIAL TIMEKEEPER

Round 12 · **MAGNY-COURS, France** · 4 October, 2015 · 2.741-mile/4.411km circuit · WEATHER: Race 1 · Wet · Track 15°C · Air 11°C; Race 2 · Dry · Track 19°C · Air 14°C

Race 1: 19 laps, 52.076 miles/83.809km
Time of race: 36m 29.856s · Average speed: 85.611mph/137.777km/h

Pos.	Rider	Nat.	No.	Entrant	Machine	Tyres	Time & Gap	Laps
1	**Jonathan Rea**	GBR	65	Kawasaki Racing Team	Kawasaki ZX-10R	P		19
2	**Tom Sykes**	GBR	66	Kawasaki Racing Team	Kawasaki ZX-10R	P	4.711s	19
3	**Sylvain Guintoli**	FRA	1	PATA Honda World Superbike Team	Honda CBR1000RR SP	P	14.683s	19
4	**Michael VD Mark**	NED	60	PATA Honda World Superbike Team	Honda CBR1000RR SP	P	22.772s	19
5	**Leon Camier**	GBR	2	MV Agusta Reparto Corse	MV Agusta F4 RR	P	30.136s	19
6	**Chaz Davies**	GBR	7	Aruba.it Racing-Ducati SBK Team	Ducati Panigale R	P	31.528s	19
7	**Matteo Baiocco**	ITA	15	Althea Racing	Ducati Panigale R	P	32.129s	19
8	**Alex Lowes**	GBR	22	VOLTCOM Crescent Suzuki	Suzuki GSX-R1000	P	39.034s	19
9	**Leandro Mercado**	ARG	36	BARNI Racing Team	Ducati Panigale R	P	1m 01.396s	19
10	**Niccolo Canepa**	ITA	59	Althea Racing	Ducati Panigale R	P	1m 07.845s	19
11	**Gianluca Vizziello**	ITA	45	Grillini SBK Team	Kawasaki ZX-10R	P	1m 09.622s	19
12	**Jordi Torres**	ESP	81	Aprilia Racing Team - Red Devils	Aprilia RSV4 RF	P	1m 16.782s	19
13	**Luca Scassa**	ITA	99	Aruba.it Racing-Ducati SBK Team	Ducati Panigale R	P	1m 19.531s	19
14	**Ayrton Badovini**	ITA	86	BMW Motorrad Italia SBK Team	BMW S1000 RR	P	1m 26.459s	19
15	**Roman Ramos**	ESP	40	Team Go Eleven	Kawasaki ZX-10R	P	1m 30.260s	19
16	Leon Haslam	GBR	91	Aprilia Racing Team - Red Devils	Aprilia RSV4 RF	P	1 Lap	18
17	Gabor Rizmayer	HUN	75	BMW Team Toth	BMW S1000 RR	P	1 Lap	18
18	Christophe Ponsson	FRA	23	Team Pedercini	Kawasaki ZX-10R	P	1 Lap	18
19	Alex Phillis	AUS	48	Grillini SBK Team	Kawasaki ZX-10R	P	1 Lap	18
20	Imre Toth	HUN	10	BMW Team Toth	BMW S1000 RR	P	1 Lap	18
21	Markus Reiterberger	GER	11	VanZon Remeha BMW	BMW S1000 RR	P	2 Laps	17
	Pawel Szkopek	POL	19	Szkopek POLand Position	Yamaha YZF R1	P	DNF	14
	Randy de Puniet	FRA	14	VOLTCOM Crescent Suzuki	Suzuki GSX-R1000	P	DNF	10
	David Salom	ESP	44	Team Pedercini	Kawasaki ZX-10R	P	DNF	5

Fastest race lap: Jonathan Rea on lap 16, 1m 53.247s, 87.129mph/140.221km/h.

Race 2: 21 laps, 57.558 miles/92.631km
Time of race: 34m 40.147s · Average speed: 99.613mph/160.312km/h

Pos.	Rider	Time & Gap	Laps		Superpole	
1	**Jonathan Rea**		21	1	Haslam	1m 56.404s
2	**Chaz Davies**	2.848s	21	2	Rea	1m 56.408s
3	**Tom Sykes**	6.551s	21	3	Canepa	1m 56.912s
4	**Michael VD Mark**	10.202s	21	4	Davies	1m 57.049s
5	**Leon Haslam**	12.921s	21	5	Guintoli	1m 57.839s
6	**Sylvain Guintoli**	19.885s	21	6	Scassa	1m 57.991s
7	**Niccolo Canepa**	24.248s	21	7	Camier	1m 59.768s
8	**Jordi Torres**	27.248s	21	8	Badovini	2m 00.676s
9	**Luca Scassa**	29.220s	21	9	Sykes	2m 01.144s
10	**Alex Lowes**	32.799s	21	10	Reiterberger	2m 01.800s
11	**Matteo Baiocco**	37.183s	21	11	Lowes	2m 02.227s
12	**Leandro Mercado**	37.347s	21	12	Torres	2m 02.379s
13	**Markus Reiterberger**	43.676s	21			
14	**David Salom**	45.943s	21	13	Baiocco	1m 59.117s
15	**Leon Camier**	47.982s	21	14	Mercado	1m 59.446s
16	Roman Ramos	59.663s	21	15	VD Mark	2m 00.528s
17	Gianluca Vizziello	1m 15.160s	21	16	Szkopek	2m 02.809s
18	Randy de Puniet	1m 15.533s	21	17	Vizziello	2m 03.982s
19	Christophe Ponsson	1m 35.502s	21	18	Ramos	2m 04.796s
20	Gabor Rizmayer	1 Lap	20	19	De Puniet	2m 06.621s
21	Imre Toth	1 Lap	20	20	Salom	No Time
22	Alex Phillis	2 Laps	19			
	Ayrton Badovini	DNF	10			
	Pawel Szkopek	DNF	9			

Fastest race lap: Jonathan Rea on lap 15, 1m 38.500s, 100.174mph/161.214km/h.
Lap record: Tom Sykes, GBR (Kawasaki), 1m 37.932s, 100.755mph/162.149km/h (2013).

Points
1, Rea, 528; 2, Davies 383; 3, Sykes 367; 4, Haslam 297; 5, Torres 222; 6, Guintoli 201; 7, VD Mark 170; 8, Baiocco 139; 9, Lowes 135; 10, Mercado 125; 11, Giugliano 119; 12, Badovini 92; 13, Camier 89; 14, Ramos 71; 15, Salom 68; 16, Terol 54; 17, Canepa 47; 18, De Puniet 39; 19, Fores 38; 20, Biaggi 36; 21, Pirro 35; 22, Barragan 17; 23, Bayliss 15; 24, Fabrizio 13; 25, Ponsson 11; 26, Scassa 10; 27, Barrier 10; 28, Vizziello 8; 29, Reiterberger 6; 30, Toth 5; 31, Rizmayer 3; 32, Pegram 2; 33, Metcher 2.

Round 13 · **LOSAIL, Qatar** · 18 October, 2015 · 3.343-mile/5.380km circuit · WEATHER: Race 1 · Dry · Track 37°C · Air 32°C; Race 2 · Dry · Track 34°C · Air 31°C

Race 1: 17 laps, 56.831 miles/91.460km
Time of race: 33m 40.883s · Average speed: 101.238mph/162.927km/h

Pos.	Rider	Nat.	No.	Entrant	Machine	Tyres	Time & Gap	Laps
1	**Jordi Torres**	ESP	81	Aprilia Racing Team - Red Devils	Aprilia RSV4 RF	P		17
2	**Jonathan Rea**	GBR	65	Kawasaki Racing Team	Kawasaki ZX-10R	P	0.726s	17
3	**Tom Sykes**	GBR	66	Kawasaki Racing Team	Kawasaki ZX-10R	P	6.579s	17
4	**Chaz Davies**	GBR	7	Aruba.it Racing-Ducati SBK Team	Ducati Panigale R	P	7.889s	17
5	**Michael VD Mark**	NED	60	PATA Honda World Superbike Team	Honda CBR1000RR SP	P	13.512s	17
6	**Leon Haslam**	GBR	91	Aprilia Racing Team - Red Devils	Aprilia RSV4 RF	P	17.755s	17
7	**Xavi Fores**	ESP	112	Aruba.it Racing-Ducati SBK Team	Ducati Panigale R	P	23.590s	17
8	**David Salom**	ESP	44	Team Pedercini	Kawasaki ZX-10R	P	26.417s	17
9	**Leandro Mercado**	ARG	36	BARNI Racing Team	Ducati Panigale R	P	26.489s	17
10	**Sylvain Guintoli**	FRA	1	PATA Honda World Superbike Team	Honda CBR1000RR SP	P	27.979s	17
11	**Ayrton Badovini**	ITA	86	BMW Motorrad Italia SBK Team	BMW S1000 RR	P	28.120s	17
12	**Randy de Puniet**	FRA	14	VOLTCOM Crescent Suzuki	Suzuki GSX-R1000	P	34.064s	17
13	**Gabor Rizmayer**	HUN	75	BMW Team Toth	BMW S1000 RR	P	1m 09.123s	17
14	**Christophe Ponsson**	FRA	23	Team Pedercini	Kawasaki ZX-10R	P	1m 10.996s	17
15	**Gianluca Vizziello**	ITA	45	Grillini SBK Team	Kawasaki ZX-10R	P	1m 13.892s	17
16	Alex Phillis	AUS	48	Grillini SBK Team	Kawasaki ZX-10R	P	1m 30.797s	17
17	Imre Toth	HUN	10	BMW Team Toth	BMW S1000 RR	P	1 Lap	16
	Niccolo Canepa	ITA	59	Althea Racing	Ducati Panigale R	P	DNF	10
	Roman Ramos	ESP	40	Team Go Eleven	Kawasaki ZX-10R	P	DNF	7
	Alex Lowes	GBR	22	VOLTCOM Crescent Suzuki	Suzuki GSX-R1000	P	DNF	6
	Leon Camier	GBR	2	MV Agusta Reparto Corse	MV Agusta F4 RR	P	DNF	0

Fastest race lap: Tom Sykes on lap 2, 1m 57.317s, 102.583mph/165.091km/h (record).

Race 2: 17 laps, 56.831 miles/91.460km
Time of race: 33m 45.745s · Average speed: 100.995mph/162.536km/h

Pos.	Rider	Time & Gap	Laps		Superpole	
1	**Leon Haslam**		17	1	Sykes	1m 56.821s
2	**Chaz Davies**	0.110s	17	2	Rea	1m 56.997s
3	**Tom Sykes**	0.388s	17	3	Fores	1m 57.384s
4	**Michael VD Mark**	7.653s	17	4	Davies	1m 57.406s
5	**Sylvain Guintoli**	14.487s	17	5	Haslam	1m 57.449s
6	**Leandro Mercado**	19.363s	17	6	Torres	1m 57.601s
7	**Randy de Puniet**	22.468s	17	7	Lowes	1m 57.638s
8	**Niccolo Canepa**	22.530s	17	8	De Puniet	1m 57.644s
9	**David Salom**	27.596s	17	9	VD Mark	1m 58.034s
10	**Ayrton Badovini**	29.294s	17	10	Mercado	1m 58.565s
11	**Christophe Ponsson**	1m 02.181s	17	11	Baiocco	1m 58.741s
12	**Gianluca Vizziello**	1m 05.246s	17	12	Salom	1m 59.289s
13	**Gabor Rizmayer**	1m 05.256s	17			
14	**Imre Toth**	2m 04.813s	17	13	Guintoli	1m 58.768s
15	**Alex Phillis**	2 Laps	15	14	Canepa	1m 58.941s
	Roman Ramos	DNF	16	15	Badovini	1m 59.229s
	Jordi Torres	DNF	15	16	Camier	1m 59.256s
	Jonathan Rea	DNF	4	17	Ponsson	1m 59.339s
	Leon Camier	DNF	4	18	Ramos	1m 59.928s
	Alex Lowes	DNF	0	19	Vizziello	2m 01.565s
				20	Rizmayer	2m 02.827s

Fastest race lap: Leon Haslam on lap 3, 1m 58.068s, 101.930mph/164.041km/h.
Previous lap record: Sylvain Guintoli, FRA (Aprilia), 1m 57.906s, 102.070mph/164.266km/h (2014).

Points
1, Rea 548; 2, Davies 416; 3, Sykes 399; 4 Haslam 332; 5 Torres 247; 6, Guintoli 218; 7, VD Mark 194; 8, Mercado 142; 9, Baiocco 139; 10, Lowes 135; 11, Giugliano 119; 12, Badovini 103; 13, Camier 89; 14, Salom 83; 15, Ramos 71; 16, Canepa 55; 17, Terol 54; 18, De Puniet 52; 19, Fores 47; 20, Biaggi 36; 21, Pirro 35; 22, Ponsson 18; 23, Barragan 17; 24, Bayliss 15; 25, Fabrizio 13; 26, Vizziello 13; 27, Scassa 10; 28, Barrier 10; 29, Rizmayer 9; 30, Toth 7; 31, Reiterberger 6; 32, Pegram 2; 33, Metcher 2; 34, Phillis 1.

2015 · FINAL POINTS TABLE

Position	Rider	Nationality	Machine	Phillip Island/1	Phillip Island/2	Buriram/1	Buriram/2	Aragon/1	Aragon/2	Assen/1	Assen/2	Imola/1	Imola/2	Donington/1	Donington/2	Portimao/1	Portimao/2	Misano/1	Misano/2	Laguna Seca/1	Laguna Seca/2	Sepang/1	Sepang/2	Jerez/1	Jerez/2	Magny-Cours/1	Magny-Cours/2	Losail/1	Losai/2l	Total Points
1	Jonathan Rea	GBR	Kawasaki	25	20	25	25	25	20	25	25	25	25	20	20	25	25	20	25	16	16	25	20	13	13	25	25	20	–	**548**
2	Chaz Davies	GBR	Ducati	16	16	5	1	20	25	20	20	–	–	16	16	16	13	16	13	25	25	20	25	20	25	10	20	13	20	**416**
3	Tom Sykes	GBR	Kawasaki	10	13	16	11	16	–	11	11	20	20	25	25	20	8	25	11	20	20	11	2	25	11	20	16	16	16	**399**
4	Leon Haslam	GBR	Aprilia	20	25	20	20	13	16	13	13	13	–	13	13	4	16	11	16	3	11	9	10	11	16	–	11	10	25	**332**
5	Jordi Torres	ESP	Aprilia	13	–	13	13	11	13	10	10	–	16	9	9	5	9	–	9	11	13	6	16	4	20	4	8	25	–	**247**
6	Sylvain Guintoli	FRA	Honda	9	11	11	10	7	–	8	9	11	–	8	8	11	10	7	7	9	–	13	13	6	7	16	10	6	11	**218**
7	Michael VD Mark	NED	Honda	11	–	–	9	–	8	16	16	7	–	–	–	7	11	6	6	8	9	–	11	16	3	13	13	11	13	**194**
8	Leandro Mercado	ARG	Ducati	4	5	6	6	8	9	5	2	9	8	5	3	8	7	5	–	7	7	1	1	2	6	7	4	7	10	**142**
9	Matteo Baiocco	ITA	Ducati	5	7	10	8	4	5	4	5	8	10	–	6	10	6	1	–	–	3	8	7	8	10	9	5	–	–	**139**
10	Alex Lowes	GBR	Suzuki	7	–	9	16	–	2	–	7	4	6	10	10	6	3	4	–	10	–	10	8	9	–	8	6	–	–	**135**
11	Davide Giugliano	ITA	Ducati	–	–	–	–	–	–	–	–	16	13	–	11	13	20	13	20	13	–	–	–	–	–	–	–	–	–	**119**
12	Ayrton Badovini	ITA	BMW	–	–	–	–	–	7	–	4	10	11	11	7	9	4	9	5	–	10	–	–	1	2	2	–	5	6	**103**
13	Leon Camier	GBR	MV Agusta	6	8	–	–	6	1	6	6	–	–	–	7	–	3	–	–	6	6	3	4	7	8	11	1	–	–	**89**
14	David Salom	ESP	Kawasaki	–	–	8	7	–	10	2	3	–	–	6	4	2	–	–	1	–	–	5	9	5	4	–	2	8	7	**83**
15	Roman Ramos	ESP	Kawasaki	–	6	1	2	3	4	3	1	5	9	3	5	–	5	2	2	4	4	2	6	3	–	1	–	–	–	**71**
16	Niccolo Canepa	ITA	EBR/Kaw/Duc	–	–	–	–	1	–	1	–	–	–	1	–	–	–	–	4	–	8	7	5	–	5	6	9	–	8	**55**
17	Nicolas Terol	ESP	Ducati	8	10	4	4	9	6	7	–	–	–	4	–	1	1	–	–	–	–	–	–	–	–	–	–	–	–	**54**
18	Randy de Puniet	FRA	Suzuki	–	9	3	–	–	3	–	–	2	2	3	–	–	–	–	–	5	5	4	3	–	–	–	–	4	9	**52**
19	Xavi Fores	ESP	Ducati	–	–	–	–	10	11	9	8	–	–	–	–	–	–	–	–	–	–	–	–	–	–	–	–	9	–	**47**
20	Max Biaggi	ITA	Aprilia	–	–	–	–	–	–	–	–	–	–	–	–	10	10	–	–	–	–	16	–	–	–	–	–	–	–	**36**
21	Michele Pirro	ITA	Ducati	–	–	–	–	–	–	–	–	–	–	–	–	8	8	–	–	–	–	–	–	10	9	–	–	–	–	**35**
22	Christophe Ponsson	FRA	Kawasaki	–	1	–	–	2	–	–	–	2	–	–	–	2	–	–	–	2	1	–	–	–	1	–	–	2	5	**18**
23	Santiago Barragan	ESP	Kawasaki	–	3	–	–	5	–	–	–	3	5	–	1	–	–	–	–	–	–	–	–	–	–	–	–	–	–	**17**
24	Troy Bayliss	AUS	Ducati	3	–	7	5	–	–	–	–	–	–	–	–	–	–	–	–	–	–	–	–	–	–	–	–	–	–	**15**
25	Michel Fabrizio	ITA	Ducati	–	–	–	–	–	–	–	–	6	7	–	–	–	–	–	–	–	–	–	–	–	–	–	–	–	–	**13**
26	Gianluca Vizziello	ITA	Kawasaki	–	–	–	–	–	–	–	–	–	–	–	–	–	–	–	–	1	2	–	–	–	–	5	–	1	4	**13**
27	Luca Scassa	ITA	Ducati	–	–	–	–	–	–	–	–	–	–	–	–	–	–	–	–	–	–	–	–	3	7	–	–	–	–	**10**
28	Sylvain Barrier	FRA	BMW	1	4	2	3	–	–	–	–	–	–	–	–	–	–	–	–	–	–	–	–	–	–	–	–	–	–	**10**
29	Gabor Rizmayer	HUN	BMW	–	–	–	–	–	–	–	–	–	3	–	–	–	–	–	–	–	–	–	–	–	–	–	–	3	3	**9**
30	Imre Toth	HUN	BMW	–	–	–	–	–	–	–	–	1	4	–	–	–	–	–	–	–	–	–	–	–	–	–	–	–	2	**7**
31	Markus Reiterberger	GER	BMW	–	–	–	–	–	–	–	–	–	–	–	–	–	–	3	–	–	–	–	–	–	–	3	–	–	–	**6**
32	Larry Pegram	USA	EBR	–	2	–	–	–	–	–	–	–	–	–	–	–	–	–	–	–	–	–	–	–	–	–	–	–	–	**2**
33	Jed Metcher	AUS	Kawasaki	2	–	–	–	–	–	–	–	–	–	–	–	–	–	–	–	–	–	–	–	–	–	–	–	–	–	**2**
34	Alex Phillis	AUS	Kawasaki	–	–	–	–	–	–	–	–	–	–	–	–	–	–	–	–	–	–	–	–	–	–	–	–	–	1	**1**

SCORE FOUR

By GORDON RITCHIE

Above: The main men: Sofuoglu leads Cluzel at Imola.

Above right: Cluzel and Sofuoglu clashed again at Assen.

Right: Sofuoglu took his fourth Supersport title to cement his place as the most successful rider in the history of the class.

Far right: Jules Cluzel's season was curtailed by a double leg fracture.

Bottom far right: American rider PJ Jacobsen was the Supersport runner-up.

Photos: Gold & Goose

IN probably its last season as a free-electronics class, the FIM Supersport World Championship transmitted rock-and-roll radio on a number of different manufacturer frequencies. The sheer numbers on the grids were far from record breaking, but the quality towards the top remained strong and varied.

After a tough 2014 with machine problems, a move to the Kawasaki Puccetti Racing squad gave three-times champion Kenan Sofuoglu the chance to aim for a fourth title. The Turkish star did not miss, winning it a round early, but he admitted that his closest and most persistent rival, Jules Cluzel (MV Agusta Reparto Corse), could have been champion, had things worked out differently towards the end.

The third eventual genuine title challenger was America's Patrick 'PJ' Jacobsen. He started well, if not spectacularly, on a Kawasaki Intermoto Ponyexpres Ninja ZX-6R, until the collapse of that Czech-based team. Then he went even further east and joined the Core" Motorsport Thailand Honda squad. His season really took off after that, but he had too much to do to catch Sofuoglu.

In winning his fourth WSS Championship, Sofuoglu raised his statistical dominance of the class to new and rarefied altitudes. With 104 starts under his belt, he took his tally to 32 wins, 69 podiums, 23 pole positions, 82 front-row starts, 25 fastest laps and 1,669 career points. All of these totals are WSS records; he is the unquestioned GOAT of the class.

Despite his feats on track, Sofuoglu's latest winning season was made unimaginably difficult and painful because of

the sudden illness and eventual passing of his first-born son, Hamza. He dedicated his championship win to him in a moving speech at Magny-Cours.

On track, Sofuoglu found the upwardly mobile Puccetti Racing Team and his official status as a Kawasaki rider to be two very strong pillars of support. His great rival, Cluzel, to whom he was sometimes verbally combative and sometimes glowingly respectful, won the first race in Australia, out in a league of his own after some brilliant action in the early laps.

It became a bit too combative at times, notably when Kyle Smith (Pata Honda) and Sofuoglu had a moment on the ultra-fast straight that caused the Kawasaki rider to run off at full pace. He remained upright through the sand, however, and was able to rejoin.

With the MVs showing improved pace, even on their fast 2014 spec, Cluzel was over three seconds ahead of teammate Zanetti at the flag, with Gino Rea (CIA Landlords Insurance Honda) back on the podium after his recent Moto2 adventures. Smith was right behind in fourth. Sofuoglu rode back to sixth, behind the Core" Motorsport Thailand Honda of Ratthapark Wilairot.

It was a home round next for Wilairot, at the new and well-appointed Buriram circuit. He won it, to the surprise of many, including himself, his all-new Thai-operated (but British and Dutch staffed) team and Ten Kate Racing Products, who supplied and fettled the machinery between races. It was proving an effective way to go racing at a higher level in WSS.

After the early sifting of pace between the leaders, Cluzel

had it all sewn up again, until his bike failed, leaving the fired-up Wilairot as leader. He simply rode for his life as the laps counted down, with a massive local crowd enjoying their first WSBK/WSS experience way more than many had imagined. His win was the first by a Thai rider, at the first ever Thai round.

Sofuoglu mugged fellow Kawasaki rider Jacobsen for second, right on the final corner. The top three were covered by 1.860 seconds.

Back in Europe, at the Motorland Aragon circuit (on the hairpin-free MotoGP layout for the first time), Sofuoglu and Cluzel went for it, but the latter suffered another tech failure from the MV.

Sofuoglu won his first victory of 2015 by 3.224 seconds from Jacobsen, with Smith third this time and Rea well down in fourth.

A trip north to Assen for round four resulted in the almost regular Sofuoglu-Cluzel leading battle going all the way, and over the edge on the final lap. Both riders desperately wanted to win in their first real head-to-head, which led to some bumping and barging through the race and then another famous incident at the infamous final chicane.

Cluzel went inside on the brakes, made a clean pass, but ran a little wide in the middle section, and Sofuoglu gassed it inside. They touched as their trajectories crossed. Cluzel was on the grass, Sofuoglu away and clear; and Cluzel was only just a second ahead of the following rider, Smith. The leading pair spat out gesticulations and verbals after the flag, and the season went from hot to overheated.

The undulations and sweeps of Imola always make for great, if risky, racing. After their usual close Kawasaki vs MV fight, Sofuoglu won by 0.883 second from Cluzel, leaving third-placed rider Zanetti nearly ten seconds back.

Originally, Sofuoglu was not going to race in Italy, as his son Hamza had been taken seriously ill a few days before. But, knowing all that could be done for the boy was being done, he came to win. After he did so, he promptly left to be with his family. Suddenly, the racing itself, though thrilling, was not at the forefront of the paddock's thoughts.

Come Donington, two weekends later, and there was no Wilairot in the Core" Motorsports Thailand Team: he and his team boss had fallen out terminally. The seat was given to local rider Andy Reid for the weekend; he finished tenth.

Another British competitor, a pure wild-card on his own Pacedayz European Trackdayz Yamaha, Kyle Ryde would be glad he came along. So was the crowd, as he finished third, behind four-in-a-row Sofuoglu and Cluzel.

In overcast conditions, Kyle Smith had crashed out, Ryde flew to third, but Sofuoglu was unstoppable once more, just less than a second ahead of Cluzel.

The Frenchman really needed to start winning to get back into contention with Sofuoglu, and he did just that at the following round in Portugal. On pole, Cluzel had to deal with new permanent Core" Motorsport Thailand Honda signing Jacobsen, who had swapped his Ninja ZX-6R for a CBR.

Cluzel broke free eventually, while Sofuoglu passed the new Honda rider, but there was nothing he could do about the pace of his rival. The MV rider's first win since the opener in Australia was a sweet victory, and he would build even more pressure on Sofuoglu at the next round in Misano.

Above: Rookie Kyle Smith beat the stars in the season finale at Qatar.

Right: First race in Thailand had a Thai winner – a surprise for Wilairot. Here he leads Jacobsen, Smith and Sofuoglu.

Centre right: Moto2 refugee Gino Rea.

Top right: Cluzel's team-mate Zanetti finished third overall.

Far right: Superstock 1000 champion Lorenzo Savadori.

Bottom right: Young Turk. Superstock 600 champion Razgatlioglu.

Photos: Gold & Goose

Seeing his main rival get so far ahead in the lead at the Italian track, and with Jacobsen and Zanetti in front stealing more points from him, Sofuoglu upped his struggling pace, but he paid the price by falling. He restarted, but could take only 11th.

Cluzel won, his second in a row, 1.525 seconds clear of Jacobsen and eight seconds from fellow MV rider Zanetti.

Gino Rea, in fourth, had a good finish after some bad luck, but he was 23 seconds from the fastest rider on the day.

Sofuoglu's cushion of points was now becoming more of a hard seat, although 20 points was still a handy gap before the series headed for yet another flyaway – Malaysia – but only after a long break in the action.

A subsequent second win for the new Core" team, and a first ever for Jacobsen, proved that it was not only going to be about Cluzel and Sofuoglu from now on. After a fight with the French MV rider, Jacobsen obviously had overcome his late fading issues and he craftily nipped inside Cluzel on the exit of the very last corner, winning by 0.091 second. In another thriller behind, Zanetti aced Sofuoglu over the line, cutting his once healthy championship lead to 13 points.

With three rounds left, Sofuoglu had to start beating Cluzel again, as finishing behind him in second each time would not be enough. The interfering fates returned from their second long summer slumber to ruin Cluzel's season, however, as he suffered a nasty double lower leg fracture in practice.

Now with a clear run, but genuine regret that his great rival was out, Sofuoglu remained clear of Jacobsen in the Jerez race, just over a second ahead, which put him back into a commanding position, some 33 points ahead of new second-place man Jacobsen. Third in the race was Zanetti, keeping MV hopes alive for the manufacturers' title.

The penultimate race, at Magny-Cours, was cut to only 11 laps after a massive oil spill halted the first attempt. The truncated contest was still a fight for a time, but Sofuoglu thought better of it when Jacobsen made his final pass to lead. The latter went on to take his second win since joining the Core" team.

In finishing second, however, Sofuoglu made himself the champion yet again.

Third was Lucas Mahias (MG Competition Yamaha), continuing his recovery from the mid-season failure of the Kawasaki Intermoto Ponyexpres team. In front of his home crowd, a podium was a pleasure.

Zannetti's fourth, having won a fight with Smith, made it four different makes in the top four places.

In the final race of the year, at Losail, Pata Honda rookie Smith, a Spanish-resident Yorkshireman, started behind the leaders, but finished ahead of even Sofuoglu, if only by 0.971 second. As Smith slid and spun to his victory, Sofuoglu had to fight Zanetti for second, blocking his attempted slipstreaming pass to the line with an overly risky swerve to take the 20 points.

It had been a year of huge contrasts for Sofuoglu, but on his fast, stable and reliable bike (compared to his troubled 2014 machine), in a team that made a giant leap from se-

rial Superstock champions to Supersport greats in one year, it was a title he deserved, for guts and professionalism under pressure as much as for his evergreen pace.

Superstock 1000 FIM Cup

went all the way to the finish to determine the overall winner.

Lorenzo Savadori (Nuova M2 Racing Aprilia) made up for losing at the last race by winning the title in France. A host of new models, an extension of the age of permitted participants and more manufacturer interest than in some previous years made for a thrilling and generally unpredictable podium spectacle each round, even if Savadori won half the races.

Runner-up, by 22 points, was three-times race winner Roberto Tamburini (Team MotoxRacing BMW), who was 21 points ahead of top Ducati rider Raffaele de Rosa (Althea Racing) in third.

The final win of the year, at Magny-Cours, came from home hero Jeremy Guarnoni (Team Trasimeno). It was the first victory in this class for the new Yamaha YZF-R1M.

Superstock 600 FIM European Championship

The tendency in recent years for the champion to be a runaway winner continued as Turkish rider Toprak Razgatlioglu (Kawasaki Puccetti Racing) simply dominated the class. Five wins in the first five races put him in position to win the title outright at Misano, and in finishing third he did just that – two rounds early.

Even after missing Jerez with a cracked collarbone, suffered in a training accident, his third place in the final round at Magny-Cours gave him a 59-point advantage over Michael Ruben Rinaldi (San Carlo Team Italia Kawasaki). Federico Caricasulo (Pata Honda Junior Team) finished third overall, and Augusto Fernandez (Pata Honda Junior) fourth. The chasing three behind Razgatlioglu took one race win each.

FULL ON, FULL BORE!

By MICHAEL GUY

Above: Ian Hutchison set the Superbike practice pace on the Kawasaki, but his two wins came in Supersport.

Right: Michael Dunlop's love affair with the Milwaukee Yamaha was short-lived.

Photos: David Collister/photocycles.com

Far right: Hutchy's return to Island success after a long injury fight-back yielded three more wins.

Bottom far right: The top step once again eluded fans' favourite Guy Martin.

Photos: Bernd Fischer-faceCatcher.com

AFTER an off-season of team and rider changes, the Isle of Man TT took on an all-new look in 2015. Having dominated the 2014 event with four wins, Michael Dunlop had appeared set to continue his formidable partnership with the BMW-supported Buildbase team. But instead of signing a lucrative new deal to continue his TT winning ways, the 11-times victor was unceremoniously dumped by the German manufacturer at the end of the year. The news shocked the road-racing world. How could BMW, the manufacturer who had celebrated their first official ever TT win for 75 years, let the supreme talents of Dunlop go?

The reason stemmed from Dunlop's reluctance to play a starring role in BMW's PR campaign, along with the decision to switch their official support from Dunlop's Buildbase BMW team, who had also taken Ryuichi Kiyonari to runner-up spot in BSB, to the Northern Irish Tyco squad.

For a short while, Dunlop's racing future remained uncertain. There was talk about him running his own team or continuing with Buildbase BMW without official support. It was even rumoured that he would not race at all. But the prospect of a man of Dunlop's pedigree sitting idle was too much for Yamaha, and he joined Shaun Muir's Milwaukee Yamaha squad to campaign the all-new R1. On paper, it looked like a match made in heaven – the man of the moment aboard a bike that had the potential to rewrite the Superbike rulebook. In reality, it became a partnership that was strained from the first Spanish test and never recovered.

A disastrous NW200, in which the R1 was shrouded in smoke due to an ongoing technical issue that caused oil to be sucked into the air box, meant that Dunlop left his homeland with no wins and firmly on the back foot on the eve of the TT.

With the start of practice week under way, Dunlop was off the pace and hugely frustrated with both bike and team. Adamant that he would be unable to win aboard the R1, and simply not prepared to ride around making up the numbers, he took the unprecedented decision to quit the Milwaukee Yamaha team midway through practice week. He put Plan B into operation, and his 2014 winning Buildbase team, who weren't even supposed to be coming to the Island, were deployed from Mallory Park in a bid to rescue his TT. After receiving the call, the Buildbase crew worked on the Superbike until 1am at the workshops before driving to Heysham to catch the ferry.

With fellow race favourites John McGuinness and Bruce Anstey remaining with their respective Honda Racing and Padgetts teams, the other big shake-up in the paddock was the Tyco-backed TAS Racing team's switch to BMW power.

Tyco had been synonymous with Suzuki, but having been unable to fight at the front of the TT on the ageing GSXR-1000 and give Guy Martin his first win, they made the switch to BMW.

For fans' favourite Martin, the switch to the German contender after years with Suzuki was seen as a giant step towards the TV star securing his much anticipated and overdue

first Island win. With the GSXR regarded as a spent force and the S1000RR proven in the hands of Michael Dunlop in 2014, Guy was expected to up his game. William, the elder Dunlop brother, joined him in the team. Both men were full of praise for the new bike, but after only managing average results at the NW200, they acknowledged that they needed more laps to get the S1000RR dialed into the uniquely demanding 37.75-mile TT circuit.

Practice week was seriously hampered by heavy rain and gale-force winds, which changed the planned schedule beyond all recognition. The opening evening practice session was cancelled, and while the second evening session did finally get under way, it was classed as untimed due to the Mountain section being wet. On the Wednesday night, the first timed practice session took place, and the lack of laps earlier in the week played into the hands of riders who already had intimate knowledge of their bikes – such as Honda men Anstey and McGuinness.

It was 46-year-old Kiwi Anstey who topped the time sheets, posting an impressive 128.441mph lap aboard his Valvoline-backed Padgetts Honda CBR1000RR. McGuinness also made a positive start, finishing second with a 128.596 best, showing that he was back in strength, following the disappointment of 2014, when he had been forced to ride injured after a heavy Enduro bike crash.

Former 2010 five-in-a-week TT hero Ian Hutchinson was another who started the week strongly, benefiting from time spent competing in the British Superbike Championship on the PBM Kawasaki ZX-10R. He finished third fastest, ahead of Martin, with an encouraging 127.453 on the BMW.

The second Superbike practice session got under way on Thursday, and it was a resurgent Hutchinson who made his race-week intentions clear by becoming the first man to post a 130mph lap. It was Hutchy's first since 2010, and it put him ahead of early pace-setters Anstey and McGuinness.

Dunlop's controversial midweek switch from Yamaha to BMW was vindicated when he went over 4mph faster first time out on the S1000RR than he'd managed on the R1. He was fourth fastest – an achievement made even more impressive by the fact that he wasn't even riding his Superbike, his best lap coming on his Superstock-spec BMW.

At the end of practice week, Hutchinson set the fastest Superbike lap, taking a psychological edge into the opening Superbike race. His 130.266mph best pipped McGuinness,

the only other man to run 130mph; Anstey was third. Tyco BMW pairing William Dunlop and Guy Martin were fourth and fifth fastest, with Michael Dunlop sixth overall aboard his Buildbase BMW.

Incredibly, Superstock qualifying honours went to Michael Dunlop, despite his team switch. The 26-year-old Ballymoney man had demonstrated in 2014 that he was capable of pushing a Superstock bike firmly into Superbike territory. His 129.659mph lap was quicker than his Superbike time and more than enough to keep his rivals at bay. Hutchinson was second on the PBM Kawasaki, albeit 1.351mph slower. Australian Dave Johnson powered his Smith Racing BMW to third, ahead of Quattro Plant Kawasaki rider James Hillier. Bruce Anstey rounded out the top five, with John McGuinness eighth riding the EMC Honda – a bike and team that he had put together himself after leaving Padgetts Honda following a clash of sponsors.

In Supersport, Bruce Anstey made his intentions clear on the Valvoline Padgetts Honda CBR600RR by posting a 125.218mph benchmark. He was run a close second by Hutchinson, who had made a last-minute change of teams and machinery on the eve of the TT. Hutchy had been due to ride the Tsingtao-backed MV Agusta triple, but then persuaded Prodigy front man Keith Flint to back his Team Traction Control Yamaha R6, used in the British Supersport championship. Hutchy only managed a total of three laps on the R6 during practice week, making his second-fastest time an ominous warning.

McGuinness showed his pace to go third fastest on the Jackson Racing CBR600RR, ahead of Mar-Train Yamaha pairing Dean Harrison and Gary Johnson. William Dunlop qualified sixth on another Yamaha, with younger brother Michael seventh aboard his own MD Racing Honda. Guy Martin concluded practice week ninth at 123.082mph on the Smiths Racing Triumph. Martin had moved to the 2014 Supersport winning team after his regular Tyco team switched from Suzuki to BMW. Since BMW did not build a Supersport bike, Tyco were unable to offer him a ride in the class.

TT returnee Ryan Farquhar set the pace in the Lightweight class with an impressive 117.432mph lap on his own SGS/KMR Kawasaki. He was pushed all the way by Gary Johnson (WK Bikes CF Moto), Ivan Lintin (RC Express Kawasaki) and James Hillier (Quattro Plant Kawasaki), who all lapped within 1mph of the leader.

Above: Bruce Anstey got out of bed on the right side to take a long-awaited win in the Superbike race.

Top right: Anstey's winning Honda flanked by the Kawasakis of Hillier (left) and runner-up Hutchinson.
Photos: Gavan Caldwell

Above right: Guy Martin's best was third on the Supersport Triumph.
Photo: Bernd Fischer-faceCatcher.com

Right: Hutchison was dominant in both Supersport races on his Yamaha.
Photo: David Collister/photocycles.com

In the electric TT Zero classification, McGuinness set the benchmark with a 113mph lap, while his Mugen team-mate, Bruce Anstey, failed to complete a lap after breaking down.

Qualifying for the sidecar race led to an intense final session, where 17-time TT winner Dave Molyneux set the pace, albeit a fraction slower than John Holden's time set during Thursday's practice session.

SUPERBIKE

"The win I've always wanted," was how Bruce Anstey described his Superbike TT victory in *parc fermé* at the end of an intense six-lap battle.

Anstey had an incredible TT record, having secured at least one podium at the event for the previous 13 years, but a big-bike win had eluded him until now. He remains one of the fiercest competitors on track, yet one of the most laid back off it. If Anstey gets out of the bed on the right side, he is simply unstoppable. He has also gained a reputation for becoming stronger and stronger during the course of a race, but often he leaves himself too much to do after making a slow start.

Knowing full well that he would have to attack from the moment the flag dropped, initially Anstey trailed fast-starter Ian Hutchinson, but remained firmly in contention, just 1.2s behind at the end of the opening lap. As the race progressed, he let his impeccably prepared Valvoline Padgetts Honda glide around the mountain circuit to gradually close down and pass Hutchy on lap five.

With everything going to plan, it looked like nothing would stand in his way – until Michael Dunlop, 20 seconds behind on corrected time, overtook him on the road on the final lap. The move rattled Anstey and caused him to make a number of mistakes, before finally regrouping and repassing the BMW man.

The race was cut short by a red flag when Michael Dunlop subsequently collided with back-marker Scott Wilson, who had crashed at The Nook. Dunlop, who was on schedule to secure third place, escaped any broken bones, but was left battered and bruised by the heavy crash.

With Hutchinson showing he was back to his best by finishing second, it was Quattro Plant Kawasaki man James Hillier who prospered from Dunlop's crash to secure the final place on the podium.

For Anstey, the win clearly meant a lot, but there was no enlightenment as to how it had happened: "I haven't done anything different, but I have been really relaxed this year. There has been no more training or time on the bike. I have been having a little bit more sleep, and maybe I just got out of bed on the right side this morning!"

John McGuinness was never in contention for victory, but he did secure a solid fourth, while Guy Martin's Tyco BMW debut lasted just three miles, his S1000RR having ground to a halt with an electrical problem.

SUPERSPORT – Race One

Hutchinson went one better to claim an emotional victory in the opening Supersport race. Aboard the Team Traction Control Yamaha R6, after only three laps in practice, he dominated the race from start to finish, winning by 7.723 seconds.

The 35-year-old was unable to hold back the tears after his hugely significant victory. Five years earlier, the Bingley man had become the first to win five TTs in a week, but within weeks had been involved in a sickening British Supersport crash at Brands Hatch, which nearly cost him his leg. Now, after 30 operations and a number of failed comebacks, he had arrived at the TT under the radar, with all the hype and expectation sitting on the shoulders of his rivals, McGuinness, Dunlop and Martin. But when the flag dropped, for the first time in five years he was ready to race. His opening two laps of 126mph laid down a marker that none of his rivals could match.

Anstey didn't make it easy for his rival. Fresh from his Superbike win, the Padgetts Honda man mounted a serious final-lap charge, but Hutchy simply upped his game each time to take the victory.

Asked about the hell he had been through to get back to

being a TT winner, Hutchy said, "I never stopped believing. If I had, I would never have got here would I? There's never been a back-up plan; I always knew it was going to take time, I just had to be patient."

With Anstey securing second, 2014 Supersport race winner Gary Johnson took third, having switched from the Smith Racing Triumph squad to the Mar-Train Yamaha team.

SUPERSPORT – Race Two

If Hutchinson's rivals had been stunned by his pace in the opening Supersport race, they were left reeling when the quietly-spoken Yorkshireman continued his utter domination of the class. This time, his winning advantage was almost doubled – 14.82s against 7.72s. And this time, team owner Keith Flint was there to celebrate.

In a hard-fought opening lap, he had to overhaul early leader James Hillier, before coming under pressure from Anstey. But on the second lap, Hutchy upped the ante with a 127.093mph lap, fastest of the race, to open a lead of 3.8 seconds. On lap three, this continued to grow, before an assertive attack from Anstey closed the gap from ten to eight seconds. But with accurate pit boards and information being conveyed to Hutchy around the lap, he was able to respond, up the pace and increase his lead again.

"I'm enjoying riding my bike so much at the moment, it didn't even feel like a race, more like a four-lap evening practice," he said. "I'm loving it. I'm back!"

Anstey wrapped up his second Supersport runner-up spot of the week with another accomplished performance and was the first to acknowledge Hutchy's unmatchable pace. "I went as hard as I could for the four laps. It was a perfect race, I was flat out all the way. That was as fast as I could

go on the day and Hutchy … well Hutchy just smoked us."

Guy Martin managed to extract some redemption from what had been an all-round difficult and disappointing TT by securing third aboard the Smiths Racing Triumph. He had benefited from staying in the tow of Hutchy when he was passed on the road to stay ahead of James Hillier in the closing stages. Like Anstey, he was quick to heap praise on Hutchy, but also lamented what could have been: "I think this bike is better than that, better than third place. The team is mega and it goes like stink. I should have pulled my finger out my backside and cracked on, but that was as hard as I wanted to go today."

SIDECAR – Races One & Two

Brothers Ben and Tom Birchall made the 2015 TT their own by winning both races on their Manx Gas LCR outfit. They won the opening race by a comfortable 24.113s to set a new Sidecar race record and notch up their second TT victory. Second place went to John Holden and Dan Sayle, with Conrad Harrison, father of solo front-runner Dean Harrison, and passenger Mike Aylott in third.

The expected challenge from sidecar legend Dave Molyneux ended on the opening lap. The veteran racer led early on, but was forced to retire at Brandish.

The second Sidecar TT was a classic, and while the Birchalls were able to wrap up victory number two, it was a fiercely contested battle at lap-record speed.

A 115.549mph first lap allowed the Birchalls to open up an early advantage over Molyneux, with Holden in third. On the second lap, all three teams lapped in excess of 116mph, before going even faster on the final circuit. With the Birchalls' advantage hovering at around seven seconds over Molyneux, the brothers produced a stunning 116.783mph final circuit, a new lap record – only to see it immediately broken by Molyneux with a 116.785mph best.

"There was nothing left on that last lap. I knew Dave was on one and he was closing the gap. But what a way to win another TT and what a man to beat," said Ben Birchall.

SUPERSTOCK

Having set the fastest time in practice, Michael Dunlop was the man with a target on his back as the flag dropped to signal the start of the four-lap Superstock TT. Despite riding injured, a result of his heavy Superbike race crash earlier in the week, the 26-year-old BMW rider set the early pace to lead the opening lap. His 130.932mph lap from a standing start was enough to take control, but only just, with both Hutchinson and Guy Martin also scorching to 130mph opening laps.

Lap two was more of the same, blisteringly fast times and nothing between Dunlop and Hutchy, but as they came in at the end of the second lap, separated by 1.9s, things were about to change. Due to Superstock bikes not being allowed to run quick-release wheel systems, tyres are not generally changed, but Hutchy's PBM Kawasaki team had other ideas. Having devised a completely legal system to keep wheel spacers and brake callipers in situ, PBM mechanic Sam Neate soaked up the intense pressure and calmly changed the rear wheel, finishing well before the ZX-10R had been refueled.

The motivation was not only to give Hutchy new rubber, but also to reduce fuel consumption, as the team knew that they would be very tight on fuel on the final lap. The new tyre, with its extra grip, reduced wheel spin, which in turn gave the advantage of increased mpg. This gave Hutchy a distinct advantage, and over the final two laps he eased away from Dunlop to win by a commanding 17.139 seconds.

Dunlop's second-place finish ended up being the highlight of his 2015 TT, since the Ulsterman was unable to secure any victories to add to his existing tally of 11 TT wins.

The battle for third was far more intense. Martin having been forced out of contention when his Tyco BMW was re-

luctant to start after the pit stop, James Hillier and Lee Johnston became embroiled in a battle royal for the final podium place. In the end, it was Johnston who claimed the coveted spot by just 0.270s, but it took a 130.851mph lap to do it on his East Coast Construction BMW.

In only his second visit to the TT, fastest ever newcomer Peter Hickman rounded out the top five on his Briggs BMW.

TT ZERO

The one-lap Zero TT was always going to be a battle of the Mugen men, McGuinness and Anstey. McGuinness had won in 2014 with a 117mph lap, and the talk preceding the race was all about the possibility of him topping 120mph. He came close, setting a 119.279mph lap to beat Anstey by just 4.042 seconds.

Lee Johnston rounded out the podium, having ridden Victory's stunning new machine. The American manufacturer had announced their entry into the race just weeks before the TT and made their intentions clear by setting an impressive 111.620mph lap at their first attempt.

Guy Martin finished fourth aboard the second Victory, a last-minute replacement for William Dunlop, who had crashed out of a one-lap practice session on Monday night riding his Superstock-spec Tyco BMW.

McGuinness was forced to fend off the now regular criticism of the race, many racers and fans questioning the credibility of the class and arguing that it should not be classed as a TT win. McGuinness dealt with such comments with his usual candour, saying, "If you don't think it should be classed as a TT win, grab a seat on the back and I'll take you for a lap."

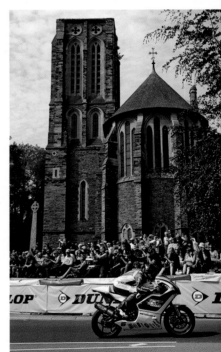

LIGHTWEIGHT

Lincolnshire rider Ivan Lintin secured his first TT victory by winning the Lightweight TT aboard his RC Express Racing Kawasaki. He had gone head to head with former Lightweight TT winner James Hillier, and both men smashed the lap record.

Going into the last lap, it was all to play for. Lintin's final circuit at 120.845mph became the new benchmark, only to be beaten by Hillier's stunning 120.848mph best. But his momentous effort was not enough to overhaul Lintin, who won by 3.875 seconds.

"I'm really happy with that! The speeds we're going aren't bad for a shopping bike you can go out and buy for £5k! I was getting good pit boards around the lap and they were up to plus five seconds at one point, but then James started reeling me back in. I had 30 miles still to go, I was determined to make the dream happen, so I dug in and got the job done," said Lintin.

Michael Rutter proved his undisputed TT credentials once again to secure third place on the Team ILR Patton.

SENIOR

Having won three TTs, the momentum going into the 2015 Senior was firmly riding with PBM Kawasaki man Hutchinson. Valvoline Padgetts Honda rider Anstey was also tipped for the top, following his Superbike win and double Supersport runner-up spot. The man who had been forgotten, however, was the greatest living TT racer on the planet – John McGuinness.

Having failed to make his mark during race week, the 22-times winner arrived on the start grid with the number-one plate, but he was still the forgotten man. The bookies had written him off, making him an 18:1 outsider, but behind the laid-back façade, McGuinness's fire was raging.

The race got under way in near-perfect conditions, but subsequently was red-flagged on the opening lap, following a crash at the 11th milestone involving front-runner Jamie Hamilton. The 24-year-old suffered serious injuries, from which he continued to make a strong recovery as MOTOCOURSE went to press.

A reinvigorated McGuinness made his intentions clear from the off, and after trailing a fast-starting James Hillier, the Honda man moved into the lead, posting a stunning 131.850mph lap – the fastest ever from a standing start. Despite the incredible time, McGuinness remained under intense pressure from Hutchinson, who trailed the Morecambe rider by just 1.2s at the end of the lap.

On lap two, McGuinness posted a new outright TT record of 131.701mph, which included slowing down for his single pit stop.

"I knew from the way the crowd were shouting and cheering that it must have been a pretty good lap," said McGuinness after the race. TV cameras caught him riding as smoothly as ever, but with a certain urgency about his work, backing his Honda into corners and leaving black lines on the exit, short-circuit style.

The result of his new lap record was a 10.2s lead, and after pinching more valuable time through his slick pit stop, he picked up where he had left off by laying down two more near-perfect laps.

After a week when he'd been written off, McGuinness showed that he remained a TT great, walking away with the big prize and a new outright lap record.

"It was a four-lap dash, shit or bust, all in. And in 1 hour 9 minutes it was done. There was no time to dither, from the word go, it was full on, full bore.

"People have short memories. I didn't forget how to ride a bike overnight. I was ready this year, I was fit and I was mentally strong. My week wasn't perfect but I'm not going to roll over am I?" he said defiantly.

James Hillier proved once again that he is capable of running at the very front at the TT, finishing a brilliant second, ahead of three-in-a-week man Hutchy. Despite securing the final podium spot, Hutchinson found it hard to hide his dejection at being beaten. A split exhaust header had compromised his race in the closing laps, but it was more the determination and sheer bloody mindedness of McGuinness that had left the Kawasaki man scratching his head.

Guy Martin may not have been able to win or get on the podium, but his fourth-place finish was highly creditable given the pedigree racing at the TT. He also joined a very exclusive club by becoming one of only five men to have posted a 132mph lap of the TT. The other four were John McGuinness, Michael Dunlop, James Hillier and Bruce Anstey.

Above: The return of the master: John McGuinness and Honda took victory in the Senior.
Photo: Gavan Caldwell

Top left: Gary Johnston (BMW) took a hard-earned third in Superstock.
Photo: Dave Collister/photocycles.com

Above left: The sidecar family. Top three finishers in race two, John Holden and Dan Sayle, double-winning Burchall brothers and Benjamin Binns with Dave Molyneux.
Photo: Mark Walters

Left: Lightweight winner Ivan Lintin (Kawasaki).
Photo: Dave Collister/photocycles.com

Bottom left: McGuinness added to his TT tally with a win in the one-lap TT Zero.
Photo: Gavan Caldwell

BRITISH SUPERBIKE REVIEW

CHAMPION AT LAST

By OLLIE BARSTOW

IF the 2015 MCE British Superbike Championship were to be compared to a football match, this was the title showdown many had been waiting for. In a season of two halves, while defending champion Byrne may have kicked off his campaign in race-winning style, it was Brookes's almost perfect possession of the podium's top step in the second half of the year that led to him being crowned champion at full time.

With no repeat of the fumbles, missteps and fouls that had stymied previous title bids, it may have taken until round six for Brookes to put his first win on the leaderboard, but goal after goal thereafter proved more than enough to take him to the top of the table.

Indeed, though Brookes's route to the 2015 BSB title may have taken time to gather momentum, from the moment he took the chequered flag at Brands Hatch in July, an unstoppable surge of 13 victories in 16 races was as relentless as it was definitive.

A run of form so crushing that it effectively negated the impact of the three-round, seven-race Title Showdown format, designed to keep the championship fight alive to the end, Brookes's success marked the end of a six-year wait for a BSB crown that so often had been just agonisingly out of reach.

Indeed, though the Australian couldn't have been considered anything less than a title contender going into 2015, his failure to close out previous campaigns had left the odd question mark, even before his candidacy was considered amid a myriad of worthy rivals in a talent-laden field just as capable of mounting a title tilt.

Then again, with the much anticipated all-new Yamaha R1 at his disposal, and a second season under the stewardship of the Milwaukee-backed Shaun Muir Racing team, many – including the man himself – considered the 2015 season to be his best chance yet.

Fresh from wrapping up a record-breaking fourth British Superbike title in 2014, Byrne began the season with his sights set firmly on furthering his status as the most successful BSB rider of all time with a fifth success, the 61-times race winner having teamed up again with Paul Bird Kawasaki.

With the evergreen ZX-10R still proving the bike of choice for a significant number of the teams, Kawasaki once again had strength in numbers, its quantity tempered by the quality of its impressive roll call of riders. Not least of these was Stuart Easton on the second PBM bike and multiple race winner James Ellison on the JG Speedfit-backed GBmoto entry, while the likes of Supersport standout Luke Mossey and 2014 race winner Howie Mainwaring (Quattro Plant), Richard Cooper (Anvil Hire TAG), Jack Kennedy (WD-40), Chris Walker and Danny Buchan (Be Wiser) bolstered the manufacturer's talented supporting cast.

Spurred on by the breakthrough success of its 2014 campaign, in which a rejuvenated Ryuichi Kiyonari had landed the manufacturer its first win en route to a surprise title challenge, BMW increased its involvement for 2015 by throwing its support behind the Tyco-backed TAS Racing outfit, which had switched from long-time collaborators Suzuki over the winter and lured Michael Laverty from MotoGP to join Tommy Bridewell.

Kiyonari, meanwhile, opted not to dilute a winning formula by staying with the Buildbase team to race alongside Superstock graduate Lee Jackson, while Peter Hickman stuck with the race winning RAF Reserves team, which also swapped machinery from Honda to BMW. Supersport champions Billy McConnell and Smiths Racing stepped up with their own S1000RR entry.

Following a sabbatical in 2014, Honda Racing returned to the BSB ranks for 2015, the manufacturer – champions in 2013 with Alex Lowes – entrusting its fortunes to new signing Dan Linfoot and its Superstock standout Jason O'Halloran, while fast female Jenny Tinmouth completed its bold three-rider line-up.

Elsewhere, Brookes had experienced fellow Australian Broc Parkes to measure himself against on the Milwaukee Yamaha, while the Bennetts-backed Halsall Racing team assumed Suzuki's BSB effort to run Christian Iddon alongside

two-times race winner Josh Waters. Finally, Moto Rapido ensured that Ducati were still represented in BSB, initially with Jakub Smrz, before enticing fan favourite John Hopkins later in the year.

With 26 races over 12 rounds once again outlining the twists and turns of the path towards title glory, in a break from tradition, Donington Park heralded the start of the 2015 season, the Leicestershire venue playing host to a massive grid bristling with hopes and expectations.

As testament to the strength of a championship arguably in the rudest of health, more than 30 riders across seven manufacturers and 11 nationalities would take their place on the grid over the course of the season. The inaugural plunge through Craner Curves was a sight to behold as BSB 2015 officially burst into action.

For all of the pre-season predictions and posturing, though, familiar faces drew the first blood, with many of the front-runners from 2014 straight on the pace. However, it was Ellison who had the honour of kicking off the 2015 season with a fine victory, the Kendal rider getting the better of Byrne and Brookes to notch up a first ever win for the JG Speedfit GBmoto outfit, not to mention his own first BSB success in two years.

Ellison might have been able to challenge for a double in race two had technical issues not intervened, but his absence elevated the omnipresent Byrne to the top spot for a 62nd career win that further swelled his record-breaking BSB victory tally.

Not that he wasn't made to work for victory. He came up against a formidable foe in Linfoot, the surprise 2014 Title Showdown contender making an eye-catching impression on Honda's return to BSB competition to notch up only his second career podium with a plucky performance. Easton, meanwhile, complemented PBM's efforts with a measured ride to third.

After the disappointment of being unable to challenge for a double triumph at Donington Park, Ellison had another opportunity at Brands Hatch, emerging as the man to beat once more around the Indy layout of the Kent venue.

Two composed rides in both races proved as convincing a double as Ellison could have envisaged, the JG Speedfit rider leading both races from the start, constantly extending his advantage and then keeping his nerve when each time his margin was eroded by safety car interventions.

Landmark weekends don't come so often for riders as experienced as Ellison, but after four races, he appeared to be the man with momentum on his side, while the presence of Byrne and Brookes on the podium in each race allowed the trio to establish an edge over the competition at this early stage in the season.

It was on to the challenging undulations of the exhilarating Oulton Park circuit for round three, and two eventful races yielded two unexpected winners in Tommy Bridewell and Stuart Easton.

Bridewell was reacquainting himself with the BMW machinery he had last ridden in 2012, though both he and Laverty had endured an indifferent start to the season as Tyco Racing got to grips with the tricky S1000RR after so many years fettling Suzukis. The first race at Oulton Park offered the first glimmers of potential for both man and machine.

Going up against Brookes for the victory in an engaging head-to-head between two former team-mates and foes, Bridewell's steely defence of the lead justly rewarded him with only his second career win, ahead of the Yamaha rider and an unusually distant Byrne in third.

Bridewell's high would soon be paired with a frustrating low, however, as he crashed out of the second race early on while leading, a set of results somewhat symptomatic of a

Above: James Ellison was strong early on, but his season was interrupted by injury. He finished a close third overall.

Left: Defending champion Shane Byrne (Paul Bird Kawasaki) was Brookes's main rival.

Photos: Clive Challinor Motorsport Photography

Above: Michael Laverty returned from MotoGP to campaign the Tyco BMW.

Top right: Former champion Ryuichi Kiyonari didn't see out the season on the Buildbase BMW.

Above right: Stuart Easton scored an emotional win at Oulton Park, before his season was marred by yet another injury.

Right: Flame-out for Peter Hickman's RAF Reserves BMW.

Photos: Clive Challinor Motorsport Photography

season of peaks and troughs, without the measured consistency that had characterised his previous campaigns.

That said, Bridewell's season at least proved more measured than that of BMW counterpart Kiyonari, who had begun the season as a cautious favourite following his remarkable re-emergence as a title contender in 2014. However, though the Japanese rider began 2015 fairly well, with a handful of top-five finishes – albeit tempered by sizeable crashes at Donington Park and Brands Hatch – the second race at Oulton Park kick-started a descent from which he wouldn't recover when he took out Byrne while disputing the lead on the final lap.

Thereafter, Kiyonari would bother the top five just once more, before leaving both Buildbase and BSB before the year was out, his career once again seemingly in the balance just 12 months after his glorious return to form.

Despite the bitter disappointment for Kiyonari and Byrne, few would have begrudged the fortuitous spoils going the way of Easton. The Scot resisted a determined Ellison and Brookes in the final corners to seal an emotional first win since 2010, and his first BSB triumph since the horrific road racing accident of 2011 that had nearly ended his career.

With three rounds down, Byrne's Oulton Park DNF had allowed Ellison to nose ahead at the top of the standings, seven points clear of his fellow Kawasaki rider, while Brookes's consistent podiums kept him in the hunt just 15 points off the top spot, but seemingly with more to come.

Spurred on by the disappointment of his dramatic Oulton Park exit, Byrne duly gave a champion's response next time

out at Snetterton, the Kent rider producing an imperious performance to win both races around the Norfolk circuit from pole. He went on to repeat the double north of the border at Knockhill, the four-times champion tallying yet more race-winning credits to propel him towards the end-of-season Title Showdown, not to mention firm his credentials as favourite for a landmark fifth BSB title.

Indeed, while Ellison had gone into round four clutching the championship lead, three DNFs from the ensuing four races at Snetterton and Knockhill caused his challenge to dwindle significantly, the JG Speedfit rider plummeting from eight points ahead to 83 points in arrears.

With Byrne striding ahead in typically convincing fashion, Brookes continued to build momentum on the still developing Yamaha. The Australian favoured a relatively steady approach to learning his way around the new R1, knowing full well that the end-of-year Title Showdown would be the pivotal moment to put the year's knowledge into action.

Indeed, with nine podiums from the opening ten races giving a glimpse of the bike's potential – unlike disappointing team-mate Parkes, who was struggling to crack the top ten – Brookes's method of allowing the bike to develop towards him would reap dividends in the most spectacular way during round six at Brands Hatch.

Returning to the familiar surroundings of the Kent circuit, this time on the grand prix layout, Brookes finally found the sweet spot of his Yamaha and swept to a resounding first win of the season, before following it up with a similarly ominous victory in race two. Furthermore, his sharp upturn in per-

formance coincided with a disparate shift in fortunes for the PBM Kawasaki team, with both Easton and Byrne suffering mammoth crashes in the same race, albeit with differing consequences.

Remarkably, despite the severity of his tumble, Byrne was able to bounce back in race two, rewarding the hard work of his stretched PBM crew in fixing his bike by following Brookes home in second. Easton, on the other hand, effectively had his season curtailed by the crash. It was a cruel setback for a rider who appeared to be finding his best form again.

If Brookes's comprehensive double success at Brands Hatch came as relatively little surprise to those who had watched both man and machine systematically develop into a formidable package since the start of the season, few could have realised in that moment the torrent of domination it would unleash in the ensuing rounds.

With just three rounds remaining before the Title Showdown got under way, Brookes quickly underlined his new-found momentum at the high-speed Thruxton circuit – scene of his first ever BSB win in 2010 – with two more resounding victories, which moved him ahead of Byrne in the overall standings for the first time.

Indeed, if Byrne was beginning to feel the pressure of his revitalised rival, then round eight at Cadwell Park would prove particularly telling, as Brookes escaped to another pair of dominant wins from pole position to confirm his elevation from erstwhile title pretender to title favourite at the expense of the out-of-sorts Kawasaki rider.

By contrast, Byrne was struggling to rediscover his form on the ZX-10R, an unusually lacklustre run of results yielding just a single podium at Thruxton and Cadwell Park as he surrendered his formerly healthy advantage. This prompted an entire rebuild of his Kawasaki ahead of Oulton Park – the final round before the Title Showdown – in the hope of justifying the downturn. Although Byrne was not in danger of missing out on the three-round Shootout, pride and momentum were very much at stake ahead of the all-important final push for the title.

For the most part, Byrne would claw back some crucial ground, winning two of the three races around the Cheshire circuit, although rare mechanical problems consigned him to a costly DNF in the other. Meanwhile, Brookes's weekend was shaped by an engine failure in qualifying that put him

last on the grid, though the Australian still sent out a signal to his rivals with a marvellous fight back to fourth place, before getting back to his increasingly accustomed spot at the top of the podium in race two.

With Byrne finally defeating Brookes in a straight fight in race three, however, the scene was set for what appeared to be a dramatic head-to-head between two long-time foes.

Elsewhere, the fight to join them in the Title Showdown descended into a war of attrition between the remaining riders as injuries and inconsistencies threw the top-six battle wide open across the midfield.

Though unable to maintain his rapid early-season form, Ellison remained on course for a spot inside the top six, until a crash on oil at Thruxton left him with a broken wrist and forced him out for four races. Fortunately for him at least, three of his closest rivals also had their progress hampered by injuries, with Easton unable to recover fully from his Brands Hatch smash, while Honda Racing's O'Halloran – who had manoeuvred himself into position with a brace of podiums at Snetterton – also saw his season end abruptly, just as it was gaining momentum, when he suffered a broken femur in a crash at Thruxton.

Meanwhile, O'Halloran's team-mate, Linfoot, spent much of his season on the comeback trail after a crash during round two at Brands Hatch had consigned him to the sidelines for four races. On his return, however, the Yorkshireman was back to form, making a determined late push for the top six with podiums at Thruxton and Oulton Park to squeeze the absent Easton out of the Title Showdown reckoning at the last moment.

Completing the top six contenders – more through perseverance than headline-grabbing performances, Tommy Bridewell's form peaked enough to secure his place for Tyco BMW, while team-mate Michael Laverty also earned a spot, despite not being one of a remarkable 13 riders to step on the podium in the run-up to the cut-off point.

With the points equalised and podium credits tallied, Byrne and Brookes's seven wins apiece put them almost level ahead of the Showdown, the Yamaha rider having the

edge on 553 points, just two ahead of his main rival. Behind them, Ellison kicked off his renewed title bid on 522 points, with Tommy Bridewell and Dan Linfoot on 507 each, and Michael Laverty starting from 500, but all eyes were on only Brookes and Byrne.

Now a firm fixture on the BSB calendar, the annual jaunt to the iconic Assen circuit in the Netherlands would kick off the Title Showdown once more.

A venue synonymous with close competition, the 'Cathedral' lived up to its reputation for intense racing, but despite close competition, some plucky midfielders finding late-season form and even the elements threatening to throw a curve ball, Brookes remained finely poised as Byrne fumbled.

Prevailing in two closely contested races to secure a critical maximum haul of 50 points, Brookes twice led home a rejuvenated Ellison – now back to full strength after his wrist injury – while Laverty finally secured a return to the podium with a third in race one, and the ever improving Mossey led briefly on the way to the rostrum in race two for Quattro Plant Kawasaki.

Byrne, on the other hand, found himself mired in the pack for much of the day, en route to fourth- and fifth-place results, which dropped him 28 points in arrears with just five races remaining. That meant he would go to the pivotal penultimate round at Silverstone knowing that only wins would keep him in the title hunt, not just in terms of points, but also in terms of interrupting Brookes's seemingly relentless momentum.

However, an unflustered Brookes continued to pile on the pressure by winning once again in race one, keeping his cool as a more ragged Byrne and Ellison both failed to trip up their rival with some boisterous racing.

With race two proving a 'now or never' moment for Byrne, his early pace appeared to have the measure of Brookes, whose poor start left him down in eighth for a time. However, in a race arguably representative of the entire title battle, Brookes's sheer confidence on the Yamaha allowed him to ascend effortlessly to the front of the field, while an embattled Byrne faded to fifth.

Above: Luke Mossey clinched the BSB Riders' Cup as the top non-Showdown rider. The Quattro Plant Kawasaki scored two podiums in a strong year.

Top: In their cups: after 13 race wins, Milwaukee Yamaha's Shaun Muir and Josh Brookes celebrate a dominant season with their giant trophies.

Photo: Clive Challinor Motorsport Photography

It was a fitting result for Brookes, but a damning one for Byrne. A fourth straight win put the Yamaha rider tantalisingly close to the crown with one round and three races remaining at Brands Hatch. Indeed, with a sizeable 47-point cushion, Brookes went into the finale needing to out-score Byrne by just three points in the weekend's first race alone to take the championship.

And so it proved. Byrne did his utmost to unsettle Brookes around his home circuit, only for the Yamaha rider to pick his moment to grab a lead he would multiply to the chequered flag, crossing the line as the race winner and – finally – the British Superbike champion.

Brookes emphasised his new-found dominance over the competition with a 13th win of the season in race two. Although a self-inflicted tumble in race three stopped him from making it a stunning clean sweep of the Title Showdown, it did not diminish the spectacular completion of long awaited title win, having come so close every year since his debut in 2009.

It was a second BSB title win for Shaun Muir Racing in collaboration with Yamaha, four years after Tommy Hill's suc-

cess. Brookes ended the season with 13 wins, 23 podiums and 12 pole positions from 26 races, but these statistics only partly explain a title campaign that snowballed into an unstoppable avalanche of second-half dominance.

Though unable to halt the charge of his longstanding rival, nevertheless Byrne could turn his attention to 2016 and a new challenge, PBM bringing its successful tenure with Kawasaki to a close to become Ducati's official factory representative. No doubt the erstwhile champion will be more determined than ever to reclaim his throne.

Though overshadowed by the rampant Brookes and never quite able to build on his spectacular start to the season, Ellison's three podiums in the Showdown allowed him to seal third position in the standings for the JG Speedfit team, his best overall BSB finish since 2009.

Having clinched the final race win of the season, Laverty snatched fourth in the standings to conclude a solid, if not spectacular return to the BSB ranks. Meanwhile, Linfoot and Bridewell couldn't mount a renewed challenge once the Title Showdown got under way, but at least they still finished 2015 having cracked the all-important top six for a second successive year.

Indeed, in a season in which a remarkable 15 riders took to the podium, the midfield battle proved more evenly matched than ever. Outside the top six, young Mossey clinched the BSB Riders' Cup as the top non-Showdown rider, the Quattro Plant Kawasaki rider's form soaring as he got to grips with Superbike machinery, culminating in two podium finishes. He finished ahead of Richard Cooper, who picked up two podiums on the Anvil Hire TAG Kawasaki, before a mid-season switch to Buildbase BMW – replacing the out-of-sorts Ryuichi Kiyonari – yielded more positive results en route to eighth overall.

Three well-deserved podiums also came the way of Peter Hickman on the RAF Reserves BMW, while Christian Iddon rounded out the top ten on the Bennetts Suzuki, the former World Supersport front-runner missing the rostrum, but showing positive late-season form on the ageing Gixxer.

Elsewhere, the injured Easton, Buchan – whose eye-catching pace was negated by too many costly crashes – the sidelined O'Halloran, the consistent Jackson and surprise Cadwell podium winner McConnell completed the top 15, just ahead of Hopkins, whose triumphant late-season return on the Moto Rapido Ducati was highlighted by four top-five finishes and a popular first podium since 2011.

Motorpoint British Supersport Championship

Five years after making his British Supersport Championship debut, Luke Stapleford finally had his hard graft come together as he swept to a dominant maiden title win for Profile Racing.

Having made the step up to the intermediate category in 2011, Stapleford may have gone on to become a relative veteran of the Supersport class in the ensuing years, but in a series accustomed to close competition and end-of-season title deciders, his route to the 2015 title on the evergreen Triumph 675R was as timely as it was impressive. He strolled to the 2015 crown with unnerving consistency and limited reliability issues, clinching the championship with a round to spare by collecting 14 race wins, six further podiums and 15 pole positions.

In a field of talented, yet evenly-matched riders, though there was no obvious title favourite from the initial line-up, it didn't take long for Stapleford to mark himself as the rider to beat, winning the Donington Park curtain-raiser to establish a championship lead he would largely retain all the way to the final race.

Stapleford's closest competition came from Jake Dixon on the 2014 title-winning Smiths Triumph, graduating British Superstock 600 champion Kyle Ryde on the PacedayZ Trackdays Yamaha and Gearlink Kawasaki's Glenn Irwin. While each showcased race-winning pace, however, none could muster the Profile Triumph rider's sheer consistency. Indeed, despite the early rivalries, the characteristic of Stapleford's championship was his unwavering regularity of being towards the top of every session and every race. Moreover, he failed to finish on the rostrum on just four occasions.

For Stapleford, everything clicked into place with a run of five consecutive wins in the middle of the season – at Brands Hatch, Thruxton and Cadwell Park. That and his constant presence on the podium in later races allowed him to wrap up the title with three races to spare at the penultimate Silverstone round.

Though his form would plateau just as Stapleford was forging clear at the head of the standings, closest rival and two-times race winner Ryde did enough to take the runner-up spot in his first season of Supersport racing. The youngster also picked up an eye-catching podium in a one-off World Supersport wild-card outing, too.

Dixon's 14 rostrums, including four wins, were punctuated by too many crashes and mechanical woes, and his title challenge stuttered in third, while Irwin's pace on the Gearlink Kawasaki fluctuated too wildly to keep him involved in the title reckoning en route to fourth.

James Rispoli made gradual improvements over the course of the season with Keith Flint's Team Traction Con-

trol. Though a maiden win eluded the American rider, he did take four second-place finishes. His late-season gains allowed him to secure fifth overall, ahead of Gearlink Kawasaki stalwart Ben Wilson and Profile Triumph's Sam Hornsey.

Luke Hedger, 2013 Superstock 600 champion, pinched eighth in the championship in the final race of the year, at the expense of the injured Andy Reid, who had broken his wrist at Oulton Park after crashing out in a last-corner battle for victory a day after claiming an emotional maiden win at the Cheshire venue.

Joe Collier claimed tenth in the standings and won the EVO crown with 14 class wins and seven further podiums, comfortably ahead of Marshall Neill and Matthew Paulo.

Pirelli National Superstock 1000

Josh Elliott came out on top of a fierce three-way battle for the Pirelli National Superstock 1000 crown, having steered his Morello Racing Kawasaki machinery to the podium in all but one race in 2015. Despite a fraught fight with Tyco BMW's Alastair Seeley and Trik-Moto BMW's Hudson Kennaugh for the majority of the campaign, his remarkable consistency left his rivals powerless to stop the Irishman from charging away.

With 2014 Superstock 1000 champion Danny Buchan having stepped up to BSB, the No. 1 plate was up for grabs as the three title favourites all graced the podium in the season-opener at Donington Park.

The championship battle was defined by some tight and aggressive clashes on track, but Elliott kept his nose clean to persistently find his way to the podium, finishing no lower than second in all but one race – at Brands Hatch, where he crashed while disputing the lead.

However, while five wins and six runner-up finishes, punctuated by that single crash, appeared to make Elliot the clear championship favourite, the omnipresence of both Seeley and Kennaugh kept the title fight alive into the closing stages of the season. Nonetheless, despite the best efforts of his rivals, Elliot ultimately prevailed with a round to spare, clinching his first ever national title against some accomplished competition.

Having missed out on a second career SSTK 1000 title, Seeley held on to second place, ahead of another former Superstock 1000 champion, Kennaugh. Both were comfortably clear of the chasing pack of Luke Quigley (Formwise Washrooms/Bathams BMW) and Adam Jenkinson (Northern Escalator Installations Yamaha).

Elsewhere, James East made positive improvements to take fifth with Downshift Motorsport Kawasaki, ahead of Jesse Trayler (MSS Colchester Kawasaki) and veteran Scots-

Above: In Supersport, Luke Stapleford and his Triumph 675R were the ones to beat.

Above right: Amassing a total of 14 wins, Stapleford overwhelmed the opposition in the Motorpoint British Supersport Championship.

Top far right: Robbie Brown took the honours in the Ducati TriOptions Cup.

Above far right: Joe Collier (11) rode his Triumph to the Supersport Evo Cup title.

Right: Josh Elliott, on the Morello Kawasaki, beat off a stern challenge from Alastair Seeley to emerge victorious in the Pirelli National Superstock 1000 class.

Right, clockwise from top left: Dutch youngster Scott Deroue won the Motostar title on his KTM; Mason Law (20) took the Superstock 600 crown on his Kawasaki; Cameron Fraser lifted the 2015 KTM Junior Cup title at Silverstone; Motostar 125cc honours went to the dominant Josh Owens.

Bottom right: Ricky Stevens and Ryan Charlwood were convincing winners in the Sidecar class, with 12 wins from 18 races

Photos: Clive Challinor Motorsport Photography

man Michael Robertson (MRR Kawasaki). Josh Wainwright (Connect Kawasaki) and Dominic Usher (DU Racing BMW) completed the top ten.

Pirelli National Superstock 600

Continuing the theme for the support classes in 2015, the Pirelli National Superstock 600 Championship was also decided long before the final flag had flown, as Mason Law clinched his title at the penultimate round in a season that had yielded ten podiums from 12 races.

The NMT No Limits Kawasaki rider stamped his authority on a title challenge by claiming four wins in the first four races, only to give title chaser Ben Currie some added motivation by crashing at Snetterton, which chopped his points lead to 13.

An instant return to the podium re-established some of Law's healthy advantage at Knockhill, before two more wins and three podiums in the final five races allowed him to wrap things up before the conclusion at Brands Hatch.

Despite finishing 59 points off the champion, PacedayZ Trackdays Yamaha's Currie kept hold of the runner-up spot, ahead of Tarran Mackenzie (Stauff Connect Academy Kawasaki), son of three-times BSB champion Niall, who notched up two wins in the final three races.

HEL Performance Motostar British Championship

Dutch rider Scott Deroue wrapped up the HEL Motostar British 2015 Championship in some style with 12 victories, clinching the title at the penultimate Silverstone round.

With Bradley Ray notching up a win and a second place at the Donington Park season-opener, before defecting to the Superstock 600 class, Deroue was left to fight in a league of his own, taking the title by 119 points and only missing out on the podium twice in 22 races.

Elsewhere, Josh Owens was an equally convincing title winner in the 125GP class. He also won on 12 occasions, beating Mark Clayton and Andrew Sawford.

Ducati TriOptions Cup

Robbie Brown became the one-make Ducati TriOptions Cup winner after prevailing in a tight scrap at the final round with Leon Morris. Despite dominating much of the year with eight wins, Brown only held a slender three-point cushion over 2014 runner-up Morris ahead of the final two races, but a victory and a second place at Brands Hatch gave him the title.

Santander Consumer Finance KTM British Junior Cup

A new addition to the BSB support line-up, the Santander Consumer Finance KTM British Junior Cup created another rung on the ladder for youngsters. Its inaugural title winner was Cameron Fraser, who took four wins to end the year with a comfortable margin over runner-up Kevin Keyes and Chris Taylor.

Hyundai Heavy Industries British Sidecar Championship

The Hyundai Heavy Industries British Sidecar Championship maintained its support billing in 2015. The experienced duo of Ricky Stevens and Ryan Charlwood claimed the title for Assured Office Solutions/Be Wiser Kawasaki with 12 wins from 18 races.

MAKING HISTORY

By JOHN McKENZIE

THE 2015 season looked as though it was going to be the most closely fought for some time, with the return of four-times Finnish world champion Pekka Paivarinta, who had sat out 2014 without a deal. The former ice racer had enlisted partner Kirsi Kainulainen as passenger and was in a position to provide some stiff competition for current and five-times champion Tim Reeves, and 2009 champions Ben and Tom Birchall.

Three world champions on the grid. What could possibly go wrong? With the benefit of hindsight, arguably the season was all but decided in a controversial opener at Donington.

Round 1: Donington Park, Great Britain

The championship got under way at a very breezy Donington Park with an action-packed curtain-raiser.

Pole qualifiers Ben and Tom Birchall, who had posted a 1m 09.668s on the Mitchells of Mansfield LCR Suzuki, were quick starters, with wild-cards Ricky Stevens and Ryan Charlwood in their wheel tracks going into Redgate, closely followed by the pairings of Reeves/Gregory Cluze, and Paivarinta/Kainulainen.

The jostling for position was soon curtailed when the red flags came out on the second lap, following an incident that put John Holden and Andy Winkle in hospital, after a tangle with Uwe Gurke and Manfred Weschelberger.

At the restart – to be run over 19 laps – the same names bunched into the first corner – Birchall, Stevens, Reeves and Paivarinta.

Birchall and Reeves managed to get away from the pack and engaged in a hard-fought battle, parrying with each other and swapping the lead. Everything came to a head on the penultimate lap, when the Birchall brothers had the lead, Going into Redgate, Reeves tried an unsuccessful passing manoeuvre and the pair clashed. This resulted in the rear tyre on Birchall's LCR Suzuki deflating and coming off the rim, leaving him with no choice but to retire from the race.

Birchall's retirement handed second place to wild-card Stevens, who followed Reeves home. It was the best sidecar debut since Alain Michel's 1976 second place at Le Mans, and further joy awaited them.

After a lengthy inquiry, the FIM stewards ruled that Reeves's behaviour throughout the race had been unacceptable and that he had been responsible for the crash with Birchall. He was disqualified.

That decision elevated Stevens to a win on his championship debut.

Third over the line, but now second, was Paivarinta. Passenger, Kirsi Kainulainen, became the first female in a rostrum place since the legendary Dana Rowe at Clermont Ferrand way back in 1974. The final place went to another wild-card team, Ben Holland and Lee Watson on their Cat Finning LCR Kawasaki.

Ben Birchall was furious: "We as a team are disgusted with the behaviour of a fellow racer, which has caused damage to our outfit and an injury to Tom's hand. When he hit me at Redgate, I was very lucky to be able to save the outfit from turning on to its roof, which would have been a disaster. This has put our next race in jeopardy, as we have to assess the damage and try to get the outfit up and running in such a short timescale."

Two days later, the Birchalls issued a statement explaining their decision to withdraw from the series:

"Whilst we are more than prepared to continue confronting the inherent dangers of our sport for the thrill of racing wheel to wheel with true honest competitors in pursuit of success, we can no longer participate in an event which in our view does not deal seriously enough with renegade participants that continually flout the rules of racing, and in doing so make a mockery of true and fair competition. We have therefore reluctantly taken the decision to withdraw from the FIM 2015 World Championship."

Round 2: Le Mans, France

With Donington winner Stevens absent to concentrate on domestic racing, the 18-lap race got under way under a warm sun, and it was Paivarinta and Kainu-lainen on their 44-Racing LCR BMW who out-dragged the field, at least until Reeves and Cluze snuck up the inside going into the fast uphill chicane, with Bennie Streuer tucked in third place.

Reeves soon got the break and raced away to an unchallenged win, posting a fastest lap of 1m 42.460s in the process. The pair were delighted.

Some way back, Paivarinta and the always improving Streuer fought for the runner-up spot, but the Finn's experience held out to take second from the Dutchman, and an 11-point championship lead.

Round 3: Rijeka, Croatia

After a two-month break, the show resumed at the always hot and rubber-savaging 4.168km Grobnik circuit for the first two-race weekend of the year.

Despite driver Tim Reeves struggling with a back injury, the Team E-Aide Motorsport LCR Kawasaki outfit took the win in Saturday's ten-lap Sprint Race. With pole (in 1m 34.433s) and a fastest lap, again they left Paivarinta and Streuer to fight for the remaining rostrum places. Paivarinta claimed second.

For Sunday's 18-lap Gold Race, Reeves repeated the process with fearsome efficiency.

With Reeves off at the front, it was John Holden and Ashley Hawes who assumed second, with Paivarinta, Gurck and Streuer squabbling for the advantage.

Streuer passed Paivarinta, but the Finn powered back, allowing Gurck to get back in the mix.

At the flag, Paivarinta held on, and his consistency from four second places gave him the championship lead on 80 points, five clear of pace-setter Reeves.

Round 4: Pannoniaring, Hungary

Once again, Reeves took pole at this new track for sidecar racing, with Paivarinta and Streuer making up the front row.

In Saturday's ten-lap Sprint Race, Reeves was pushed very hard by Paivarinta. Suspecting potential tyre problems, he rode clinically – just enough to re-

Above: Fateful encounter: Tim Reeves and Gregory Cluze lead the Birchalls at Donington Park. It was the brothers' first and last race.

Above right: Pekka Paivarinta and Kirsi Kainulainen took third overall.

Left: No beard, but otherwise it was 'like father, like son'. Gold medals for Geert Koerts and Bennie Streuer.

Far left: Streuer/Koerts lead the pack.

Photos: Mark Walters

Round 7: Oschersleben, Germany

The championship would be decided in one climactic weekend at Oschersleben. With so much at stake, the atmosphere in the paddock became tense as the start for the opening 12-lap sprint race drew near.

Reeves was on his sixth consecutive pole position, with a time of 1m 31.340s, and at the green light he used it to full advantage to escape from the attentions of Streuer and Paivarinta, building a buffer.

As the laps counted down, Streuer began to reel in Reeves, who was suffering gearbox problems, but he managed to hold on. Streuer took second and set the fastest lap of the race: 1m 31.530s.

Paivarinta's third left him happy and looking forward to the final.

The positions gave Streuer 160 points, Paivarinta 152 and the on-form Reeves 150.

On Sunday morning, the weather was perfect for the battle about to unfold.

Andy Peach and Charlie Richardson, starting from third, grabbed the lead, but Reeves was soon on to them, chased by Paivarinta, who ran off the track before recovering and getting back into sixth.

Peach held the lead, with Reeves close at hand, while Streuer watched in third. Paivarinta was held back by Gurck for five laps before he could attempt to challenge the leading trio.

Reeves seized his chance, passed Peach and started to accelerate away. Then Streuer caught Peach, but was unable to do anything about Reeves's lead.

Streuer knew what was at stake and sensibly played it safe. Knowing the title was within grasp and that Paivarinta was too far back to affect the outcome, he kept Peach at bay.

Reeves took a clear and convincing win, but the best he could hope for was second in the championship, and he was gracious in conceding his 2014 crown: "We're disappointed, but so pleased for Bennie and Geert. They are our rivals on track, but we are all great friends on and off track, too."

For Streuer and Koerts, second was theirs, as was the World Championship, earned with 180 points

Third place for Peach and Richardson was marred when Richardson slipped from the chair just after taking the flag. He rolled spectacularly down the track, luckily collecting just a few bruises.

Paivarinta and Kainulainen were fourth, knowing that their error on the first lap had cost them dear, and a possible second place overall. Peach also earned a rare honour in taking rostrum places both as a passenger (with Ian Guy) and a driver.

Kirsi Kainulainen's championship third with Paivarinta also made her the first woman to take a world championship road racing medal.

But it was a hugely popular and well-deserved victory for the son of the 1984–86 world champion. Season-long consistency – they were the only team to score in every one of the ten races, never finishing below fourth – was the key.

Reeves did win every race he finished, and if he had not been disqualified from victory at the opening round at Donington, the title could perhaps have been his. But what if the Birchalls had stayed?

---

tain both grip and the race lead. He led Paivarinta under the flag by 0.142 second, the Finn having recorded the fastest lap in his efforts to match him. With five of the ten-race series now completed, the two teams were level on 100 points each.

Uwe Gurck took third place after a monumental battle with Streuer.

For Sunday's 15-lap Gold Race, a wet race was declared and everyone started on wet tyres.

Reeves imperiously took the lead from the start and was never threatened, romping home with a comfortable 13.141-second margin from Paivarinta. Bennie Streuer and Geert Koerts took third.

Five wins in a row gave Reeves a five-point lead over Paivarinta, and he was beginning to look unstoppable. The Briton's home track was coming next.

Round 5: Brands Hatch, Great Britain

In perfect weather, a combined grid of world championship and British F1 championship contenders made up the field. That gave Ricky Stevens and Ryan Charlwood – also claiming a home-track advantage – a second chance to shine in their first involvement with the series since Donington.

The race turned out to be a game changer for all.

It went wrong for Reeves on the first lap with a broken gear shifter. A frenzied pit stop got them back on the track, but two laps down.

In the meantime, Andy Peach and Charlie Richardson (LCR Kawasaki) had gained a healthy lead over Stevens and Charlwood, with Holden and Hawes lying third. Peach's hopes of glory were dashed on lap six, when rear brake problems forced them out.

At two-thirds distance – lap 12 – the proceedings unravelled. Reeves had fought back to 12th, albeit a lap in arrears, but then Holden and Hawes crashed out, flipping their outfit. With yellow flags out, Reeves was unable to move forward to pass the pairing of Garry Bryan and Jamie Winn. Then Bryan locked the back wheel and spun in front of Reeves just as he was trying to pass. The latter had nowhere to go except

into the gravel and out of the race.

A lap later, the race was red-flagged when Paivarinta turned his outfit over. Kirsi Kainulainen suffered a broken rib and spent the night in hospital.

With 13 laps run, the race was deemed completed. That put Bennie Streuer and passenger Geert Koerts on the top step of the podium for the first time, and one of sidecar racing's most famous names back in the spotlight.

Second went to Mike Roscher and Anna Burkard, their best result to date, with third to Slovenian Milan Spendal and French passenger Freddy Lelubez.

Both Reeves and Paivarinta having crashed out, the points table suddenly closed up. Reeves remained on 125, Paivarinta was on 120, but Streuer was up to 115 and maybe just beginning to wonder.

Round 6: Assen, Netherlands

After winning in England, Bennie Streuer faced the biggest race of his career to date, and expectations ran high for the local boy among a huge partisan crowd. Qualifying second fastest gave him the centre spot on the grid, with Reeves on pole again.

Jacob Rutz's LCR Yamaha developed an electrical problem on the grid, and its removal to the pit lane caused the race to be reduced to 16 laps.

At the start, Reeves shot away, followed by Streuer, Paivarinta and Seb Delannoy.

With six laps to go, Reeves was looking comfortable, but then he suffered a major engine blow-up, which caused a fire when the fuel line was damaged.

His sudden retirement gifted the lead to Streuer, but on lap 11 the red flags came out after an incident involving Colin Nicholson and Ilse de Haas, and the result was declared, giving Streuer his second win on the track where his father had had so many great battles. The victory also put him on top of the points table at 140, with two races to go.

Second went to Seb Delannoy, with Paivarinta third after a brave show from Kirsi Kainulainen, still not 100 per cent fit after Brands.

YOUTH OVER EXPERIENCE

By LARRY LAWRENCE

Cameron Beaubier shaded defending champion and Yamaha team-mate Josh Hayes for the first MotoAmerica crown.

Above: Roger Hayden was main rival to the Yamahas. Here his Suzuki is sandwiched between title winner Beaubier and defender Hayes.

Top and above centre right: In Memoriam – a tragic first year for MotoAmerica saw Daniel Rivas *(above)* and Bernat Martinez *(below)* die in a first-lap disaster at Laguna Seca.

Photos: Gold & Goose

Above right: Popular Superstock star Dane Westby died in a pre-season road accident.

Bottom right: Josh Hayes leads the way in the season opener at COTA. His title defence failed by just four points.

Photos: MotoAmerica/Brian J. Nelson

FOR several years, Cameron Beaubier has been pegged as America's next great hope for MotoGP. He showed tremendous promise in 2013, dominating the Daytona Sportbike support class, but his 2014 Superbike rookie season had highs and lows. He finished third and showed great promise with three wins.

In 2015, it all came together for Beaubier in the summer. He was consistently strong all season and, thanks to a few miscues by his veteran Yamaha team-mate and defender, Josh Hayes, he fulfilled his promise and won the MotoAmerica/AMA Superbike Championship by a narrow four-point margin over Hayes (372–368).

In spite of swiping the title, Beaubier didn't clearly establish himself as America's top road racer. A cursory look at the numbers confirms this fact. While he outscored Hayes for the title, he ended the season with eight victories to Hayes's ten. It was not a resounding title win, but Beaubier did what he had to do for his first MotoAmerica/AMA Superbike Championship and added his name to a prestigious list of AMA Superbike title holders, which includes such road racing luminaries as Eddie Lawson, Fred Merkel, Wayne Rainey, Doug Chandler, Doug Polen, Troy Corser, Nicky Hayden, Mat Mladin and Ben Spies.

He was the 20th rider to win the AMA Superbike championship, which began in 1976. At 22 years old (plus nine months), he was the fourth youngest, after Fred Merkel, Ben Spies and Nicky Hayden, youngest ever at 21. It's notable that all three went on to win world championships.

Monster Energy/Graves Motorsports Yamaha's record was perfect: they won every round. Hayes pushed his numbers ever higher, finishing the season with 58 career Superbike wins, second on the all-time list to Mladin.

Yamaha has now won seven AMA Superbike Championships, behind Suzuki with 13, Kawasaki with nine and Honda with eight. Their current streak of six-consecutive titles is the second longest manufacturer's winning streak, behind only Suzuki's amazing 2003 to 2009 run of seven straight wins.

Yoshimura Suzuki being shut out was the other story of the season – the first time the team had finished with no wins since 2002, and it's not like Suzuki wasn't competitive. Roger Hayden, who finished third in the series, was on the podium 15 times in 18 races and took so many second-place finishes by under a second it makes your head spin. The youngest of the three racing brothers could hardly believe his rotten luck as he contemplated his winless season.

The year was also marked with tragedy. One of America's brightest up-and-coming road racers, Dane Westby, was killed in a street accident before the start of the season. Westby was the fastest Superstock 1000 rider in pre-season testing, and his absence was sorely felt. Then a horrific multi-bike incident on the first lap at Laguna Seca on 19th July took the lives of Spaniards Bernat Martinez (35) and 27-year-old Daniel Rivas. It was one of the darkest days in the history of the series.

Yamaha also swept the board in the support classes, winning the Superstock 1000 title with Jake Gagne, the Supersport title with JD Beach and the Superstock 600 class with Joe Roberts. Gage McAllister took home the KTM RC390 Cup crown.

Circuit of the Americas – 11–12 April

The inaugural MotoAmerica/AMA FIM North America Road Racing Championship event kicked off alongside MotoGP at Circuit of the Americas in mid-April. Yamaha flexed its muscles early, with Hayes and Beaubier splitting wins on their factory R1s and leaving the weekend tied atop the standings. Hayes won the series opener in the rain by 5.2 seconds over pole-sitter Beaubier. The latter came back to even the score in the dry, edging his team-mate by four-tenths in race two.

The only serious challengers, Yoshimura Suzuki with Hayden and series rookie Jake Lewis, were off the pace. Hayden led briefly in both races and eventually managed a pair of podium finishes, but he was 18 and seven seconds back respectively.

It was clear that Yoshimura had some work to do.

Jake Gagne showed just what a well-sorted Superstock machine could do. The RoadRace Factory/Red Bull Yamaha rider dominated, easily outpacing his Superstock 1000 competition by over half a minute in both races, and twice finishing fourth overall (the classes ran concurrently). Gagne's performance in Texas showed early on that the remainder of the Superstock 1000 field was racing for scraps.

Part-time flat-tracker JD Beach took the win in the Supersport opener by 5.5 seconds over Garrett Gerloff. It marked his first national road-race victory in five years, but it wouldn't be his last.

Road Atlanta – 19 April

Road Atlanta was the first stand-alone MotoAmerica race, and the riders had to deal with rain nearly all weekend. In a wet race one, Hayden seemed determined this time to do battle with the Yamahas, but after swapping the lead back and forth with Hayes, he crashed in the early going. In the tricky conditions, Beaubier gradually inched away from Hayes, and was 4.6 seconds ahead when the race was red-flagged for a second time and called complete.

One bright spot for Suzuki was rookie Lewis taking his first Superbike podium in race one; he was third behind the Yamaha pair.

Race two proved pivotal in the championship battle, as Hayes crashed out early. "I just felt a little bump in the front and the next thing I knew, I was sliding on my head," he said.

That left Hayden alone, but he also crashed out while leading by over three seconds. The two DNFs dropped Hayden to seventh in the standings and put an immediate damper on any championship aspirations.

Lewis led briefly, before being passed by Beaubier, who pulled way to a 3.7-second victory, completing a weekend

sweep and building a commanding early 30-point lead in the standings over Hayes.

In Superstock 1000, newly signed Josh Day took an emotional race-one victory aboard the Yamalube/Westby Yamaha. He was joined on the podium by team owner Tryg Westby, who'd lost his son just weeks earlier. Gagne, who crashed in race one, took victory in race two and notably finished third overall in the combined Superbike/Superstock 1000 race.

Josh Herrin, the castaway from Moto2 a year earlier, began repairing his battered racing career with a Supersport race-one victory in a close battle with pole-starter Gerloff, who came back to win race two with ease by 8.6 seconds over Herrin in wet-to-drying conditions, taking over the series lead from Beach.

Road Atlanta was also the venue for the first round of MotoAmerica Superstock 600, and Joe Roberts took commanding victories in both races aboard his Wheels in Motion/ Motosport.com/Meen Yamaha R6. It would establish a pattern that would hold for most of the year, causing some to criticise the highly experienced Roberts for racing in a class designed for newer, less-established riders.

Virginia International Raceway – 17 May

The premier series returned to the picturesque VIR for the first time in five years, and it proved to be one of the better attended races of the season. Josh Hayes regained major ground on Beaubier, dominating the weekend by winning both rounds.

After a big crash on Friday and an overnight rebuild by his crew, Hayes got away early and pulled out to an eventual 3.282-second victory over his team-mate. Hayden finished a distant third. It was a milestone 50th AMA Superbike win for Hayes. He had built an 8.5-second lead before a red flag

just before half-distance. Ultimately, the red flag didn't hinder him, as he pulled away quickly after the restart.

In race two, he pulled away methodically again, for a massive 13.368-seconds on Hayden. Beaubier finished third after trying to challenge Hayden, but coming up short. The sweep for Hayes chopped Beaubier's series lead nearly in half, from 30 points coming in to just 16.

Long-time AMA campaigner Taylor Knapp finally broke through to score his first pro road-race victory in the Superstock class in race one. Gagne, who had retired from race one with a slipping clutch, came back to take an easy 34.8-second victory over Josh Day in race two, lifting his series lead to six points over Knapp.

Josh Herrin and JD Beach split wins in Supersport action. In the first race, Herrin edged Beach by just a tenth of a second. The latter's comeback to victory in race two earned him a one-point lead in the standings over Jake Gagne as the series left Virginia.

After his dominating performance at Road Atlanta, pundits were talking series sweep for Joe Roberts in Superstock 600, but after winning race one, he made an error and crashed out in the second, handing victory to Mexican road racing champ Richie Escalante. That gave Escalante the series lead by three points over Roberts.

Road America – 31 May

The four-mile Road America in Elkhart Lake, Wisconsin, is perhaps the most picturesque circuit in the series, and the faithful Upper Midwest fans always show up in droves.

The Yamaha pair were battling for the lead on lap five of race one when Hayes crashed. That left Beaubier to fend off the Suzukis of Hayden and Lewis. In the end, he edged Hayden by 0.136 second, Lewis having dropped back late in the race. Hayes minimised the damage somewhat, remounting

for sixth. He was helped by the fact that there were only nine Superbikes still in the race at the end.

Hayes came back to dominate race two, beating Beaubier by 4.586 seconds. The Suzukis of Lewis and Hayden finished third and fourth, Hayden troubled by electronics issues.

Hayes's crash helped Beaubier push his series lead back to 26 points, more than a race win's worth of a cushion.

Gagne also began to open up a gap in Superstock, with two massive wins to leave Elkhart Lake with a 30-point lead over Knapp.

In wet conditions, Herrin dominated the first Supersport race to take a temporary series lead. JD Beach made what seemed an impossible save in the wet race one, recovering to finish fourth. That save proved important when he came back to slipstream both Herrin and Gerloff along the straight on the final lap to steal the victory in race two. It was a spectacular race, with the top three separated by just 12-hundredths. Beach and Herrin were now tied on points.

Millennium Technologies/KWR Yamaha rider Travis Wyman took a surprise victory in the wet in a close battle with Joe Roberts in the first Superstock 600 race. Roberts came back to take a hard-fought win over Richie Escalante in race two, reclaiming the series lead.

The KTM RC390 Cup debuted at Road America. Gage McAllister, 19, opened the season with a victory after rivals Anthony Mazziotto and Hayden Schultz crashed out while battling McAllister for the lead. McAllister made it a clean sweep by winning race two after fighting an epic late-race battle with 15-year-old Canadian Braeden Ortt and 16-year-old Jody Barry.

Barber Motorsports Park – 14 June

Blazing heat greeted the riders for event at the well-manicured Barber Motorsports Park in Alabama. Superbike race

MotoAmerica – Year One
ON THE RIGHT TRACK
by Larry Lawrence

IT'S not hyperbole to say that professional motorcycle road racing in America was near death. Sure the series under the old Daytona Motorsports Group may have limped on in some form or fashion, but few if any riders were making money and just a couple of manufacturers were hanging on – and at least one of those was making noises that it was going to leave.

That was the backdrop of the sport facing a new entity called MotoAmerica, which took over the management of America's professional motorcycle road racing series at the beginning of 2015. The US motorcycle industry was holding its collective breath.

KRAVE Group is a Costa Mesa, California-based organisation that includes former multi-champion Wayne Rainey; Chuck Aksland, a former racer and 20-year manager of Team Roberts, who previously had served as vice president of motorsport operations at Circuit of The Americas; Terry Karges, a former motorsports marketing executive and team owner, who had spent 17 years at Roush Performance before being named executive director of the Petersen Museum; and Richard Varner, a motorcycle manufacturer, energy sector entrepreneur, philanthropist and businessman.

The Rainey connection was all important. Wayne Rainey is arguably one of the most beloved personalities in all of motorcycle racing. He was a two-times AMA Superbike champion and then three-times 500cc Grand Prix world champion before being paralysed in a GP crash in 1993. Later he became the team manager for Marlboro Yamaha and was inducted into the Motorcycle Hall of Fame in 1999.

If there is one person who could unite the various entities in motorcycling, it is Rainey. He had a tall task, but most felt that he and his partners came through mostly with flying colours in the organisation's first season.

There were hiccups early on with timing, scoring and

TV, but those were quickly ironed out. Instead of staying in the background, Rainey was a constant and highly-visible presence at the races. He and the rest of the MotoAmerica staff forged solid relationships with the teams and the riders, and did their best to reinvigorate the fans' interest.

MotoAmerica at least seemed to stop the downward slide of road racing in America. Whether or not they can bring the sport back to health remains to be seen. While the economy in America has improved from the depths of the recession, motorcycle sales have been slow to recover. Efforts to get more manufacturers involved in MotoAmerica, most importantly Honda, haven't yet borne fruit.

And then there are the challenges of keeping a full calendar. With Indianapolis off the MotoGP schedule, MotoAmerica is scrambling to find a replacement. Getting a decent national television contract continues to be a goal; if accomplished, that could help bring back more manufacturers and teams.

The universal question is this: are there younger fans out there to replace the aging Baby Boomers, who carried the sport to its heights in America from the mid-1990s to the mid-2000s? That will be the challenge MotoAmerica faces in the coming years as they try to revive what once was the most important domestic road racing championship in the world.

Above: Happy Herrin: back from a Moto2 struggle, Josh Herrin heads for the Supersport podium at Barber.

Top: JD Beach took the Supersport Series by the scruff of the neck.

Above left: Midfield maul: Josh Day, Chris Fillmore and Sheridan Morais battle it out at the Miller Motorsports Park in Utah.

Inset, top right: No figurehead: Wayne Rainey was an inspirational leader for the new MotoAmerica series.

Left: Joe Roberts dominated Superstock 600s; moved to Supersports for a last-race win in New Jersey.

Photos: MotoAmerica/Brian J. Nelson

one was shaping up to be a great fight between Hayes and Hayden in the closing laps, but a red flag on lap 16 (due to fluid on the track) ruined a possible last-lap battle. Thus Hayes scored his fifth victory of the season by less than half a second. Superstock 1000 rider Jake Gagne finished third overall on the RoadRace Factory Yamaha.

The biggest story of the day was that series leader Cameron Beaubier crashed out of the lead on lap eight on the curbing between turns eight and nine, his bike spinning on the ground while Hayes was forced to go heavy on the binders to avoid the machine. That allowed Hayden to sneak underneath to take the lead. Eventually Hayes found his way back to the lead to score the victory, instantly closing up the championship chase. Hayes moved to within a single point of Beaubier in the standings.

Beaubier came back in race two to hold off Hayes by 0.128 second; Hayden was third. He had run with the Yamahas, but fell off the pace in the closing laps.

"That was an awesome race," Beaubier said. "Roger and Josh and I were pushing each other the whole way, and it was so hot out there. I was happy to get the win and to make it up to my team that race after crashing in the first."

His lead was now down to six points.

Gagne's double victory earned a 44-point lead in the Superstock 1000 Championship – over Knapp by 16.9 seconds and then by 14.2 seconds over South African rider Sheridan Morais, who'd recently joined the Aprilia HSBK Racing team.

JD Beach won the first, then found just enough speed on the final lap of the second Supersport race to hold off a determined pair of Herrin and Bobby Fong. It was his fifth win of the season, putting him ten points ahead of Herrin.

Joe Roberts faced stiffer competition from Escalante in race one, but still managed to rack up another pair of victories in the Bazzaz Superstock 600 at Barber. In race one, Roberts edged Escalante; then in race two, after an early

battle with Bryce Prince, Roberts cleared out and won by 6.505 seconds, his sixth win. It extended his series lead to 20 points over Escalante.

Mazziotto beat Hayden Schultz to the line in the red-flag-shortened KTM RC 390 Cup race one by just 0.081 of a second. Race two was hard fought, with a final-lap showdown between McAllister, Mazziotto and Schultz, the more experienced McAllister topping his younger rivals. His third win extended his series lead.

Miller Motorsports Park – 28 June

Hayes swept both races at Utah's expansive desert circuit and regained the points lead. It was a straight-up battle in the first race, with Hayes making his move on the last lap, leaving his young team-mate unable to respond. He was even stronger in race two, crossing the finish line 4.2-seconds ahead of Beaubier. Hayden was third in both races, but out of touch.

The result was that Hayes regained the points lead for the first time since the opening race.

Josh Day scored a sweep in the Superstock 1000 class after series leader Gagne fought electrical problems in both races, the second time resulting in a crash. Fortunately for Gagne, he had benefited from a massive lead coming into Utah, and in spite of two DNFs, he escaped still leading by 17 points over Knapp.

If you were to point to one race weekend where JD Beach definitively broke out of the pack and began looking very much like a champion in waiting, it would have been the Supersport races in Utah. He dominated both, winning by 5.567 seconds in race one over Gerloff, and then by a whopping 9.979 seconds over Fong in the second race. That standout performance pushed his series lead over Herrin from ten to 44 points.

Above: Jake Gagne was the convincing Superstock winner.

Top: Gage McAllister took the KTM RC390 Cup title.

Top left: Yamahas in control – JD Beach leads Josh Herrin in the Supersport race at the Virginia International Raceway.

Above left: McAllister heads the pack at Road America in the closely fought KTM RC390 Cup.

Above far left: Cameron Beaubier was crowned 2015 Superbike champion in New Jersey.

Left: Roger Hayden's Yoshimura Suzuki heads the retro-liveried Yamahas of Hayes and Beaubier at New Jersey.

Photos: MotoAmerica/Brian J. Nelson

Ditto for Joe Roberts in Superstock 600, where his sweep, albeit much closer than Beach's massive margins of victory, increased his series lead to 37 points over Richie Escalante.

McAllister and Ortt traded wins in the KTM RC390 Cup, with McAllister pulling away in the series.

Laguna Seca – 18–19 July

The racing at the combined World Superbike/MotoAmerica weekend at Laguna Seca was overshadowed by the tragic deaths of Spanish Superbike riders Dani Rivas and Bernat Martinez, after a horrific five-rider, chain-reaction pile-up at the start of the second Superbike race. Rivas's BMW lost power soon after he launched. He threw his hand in the air, but while some riders, tucked in and speeding forward, were able to avoid him, others following had no time to react and that started the pile-up.

In Superbike, Hayes and Beaubier split wins, and the two left Laguna tied on points as Suzuki and Hayden began to make inroads, finishing a close second to Beaubier and just ahead of Hayes in race two.

British former World Superbike competitor Mark Heckles took victory in Superstock 1000 race one in tricky wet-to-dry conditions. On the advice of WSBK rider Jonathan Rea, Heckles ran slicks, which turned out to be the right choice. Series leader Gagne chose rain tires and struggled as the track dried.

Gagne came back and won the second race by nearly ten seconds from Sheridan Morais. His lead over Knapp (third in both races) was now 20 points.

Beach scored another runaway victory in Supersport and was looking more and more like a champion in waiting.

There would be no more waiting for Joe Roberts, who clinched the Superstock 600 class championship with the combination of a victory and a crash by his nearest rival, Escalante.

McAllister was on the verge of taking the KTM RC390 Cup title, but he was forced to wait to loft the No. 1 plate after his machine popped a chain. Ortt took a second straight win after a race-long battle with Mazziotto.

Indianapolis Motor Speedway – 8–9 August

It was AMA Superbike tests that initially paved the way for motorcycle racing at the Indianapolis Motor Speedway, but it took years for the series to finally race at the Brickyard in a combined MotoGP/MotoAmerica affair. It turned out to be worth the wait.

Race one featured a fantastic scrap from start to finish, between Beaubier and Hayden. The two swapped the lead several times and had some amazing turn one shut-off battles during the 18-lap race. In the end, a small slip by Hayden was all the Yamaha rider needed to take over the lead on the final lap and hold off a last-second draft attempt to win by 0.040 second. It was Beaubier's seventh win of the season and helped it push his lead to nine points over third-placed Hayes with three rounds remaining. Hayes was six seconds back from the leaders and had his hands full with Suzuki rookie Lewis.

Superbike race two was called after 15 of a scheduled 18 laps when light rain became heavier. In another thriller, Beaubier's margin of victory over Hayden was 0.015 second, while Hayes was a close third.

Beaubier would carry an 18-point lead into the series finale. Hayes was no longer in control of his own destiny.

Gagne won Superstock 1000 race one, overcoming issues with tyres spinning on the rim. Josh Day was second among the Superstock riders, and Knapp third, in spite of a loose clip-on handlebar. Gagne won race two as well, his 11th victory in 16 races. That pushed his lead over Knapp to a nearly insurmountable 43 points.

Gerloff came out on top of the six-lap MotoAmerica Supersport sprint race for his second win of the season. He had won the battle, but team-mate Beach had won the war, securing his first MotoAmerica Supersport championship a weekend early, after Herrin had crashed on the restart of a red-flagged race.

New Jersey Motorsports Park – 13 September

The factory Yamahas sported special 60th-anniversary yellow-and-black livery in the series finale. That anniversary would end on a high note after Beaubier broke through to win his first Superbike title.

Senior team-mate Hayes did all he could by winning both races. In the rain-shortened race one, Beaubier was second and Hayden a close third.

Both Hayes and Hayden had major motivation to win the final: Hayes to keep his slim title hopes alive; Hayden to finally earn the victory that had eluded him all season. Meanwhile, would-be champ Cameron Beaubier had every reason in the world to just hang back and not get involved in the fray. He had a 13-point lead coming in and needed only to finish third or better.

In the end, Hayes took a narrow victory for a clean sweep of the weekend, while Beaubier cruised home to earn the series title.

"I would have rather crashed than not get this win," Hayes said afterwards. "I'm proud of my season and the ten wins. I had a few mistakes over the year that were hard to overcome, but I think this is about Cameron and the great year he's had. One thing is for sure, I want to come back and try to get him next year."

Beaubier's need only to finish for the lead was a mixed blessing. "I was up there with those guys in the beginning," he explained. "At first, I was thinking I would just keep Josh and Roger in sight, but then I made a mistake and slipped one time, and that was it for me. I decided just to back it off and get it to the finish. It feels great to win this championship. The team gave me such a great bike all year, and I couldn't have asked for anything more."

Gagne closed out his title with a pair of Superstock 1000 wins in New Jersey. All season he had shown that a well-prepped Yamaha Superstock-spec machine could run with, and often beat, the Superbikes; his stock as a rider certainly rose in his first season competing on 1000s.

Joe Roberts only proved what many pundits had been saying throughout the season: that he belonged in the Supersport Championship rather than the underling Superstock 600 class. Having already clinched the Superstock 600 title, he raced Supersport in the Jersey finale weekend and dominated in the rain in race one. It was his first victory in the Supersport class in just his third appearance in the series in 2015.

While the final margin was just over six seconds, actually he had backed it off in the later laps, having built a 15-second lead mid-race.

Herrin ended his season on a high note, winning the final Supersport race of 2015 after a four-way dogfight on the last lap from team-mate Roberts, Gerloff and champion Beach. That victory jumped him to second in the final standings, ahead of Gerloff.

Champion Roberts's switch to Supersport left the Superstock 600 class wide open. HB Racing's Michael Gilbert took advantage and earned his first victory of the year, and the first of his pro career, in race one. Bryce Prince closed out the season with a win in race two.

McAllister took the win and the title in race one of the KTM RC390 Cup. He had been in a battle for the duration, however, though that tussle ended up being between two riders by the end of the race. At that point, it was McAllister versus New Jersey's own, Mazziotto, with the former drafting past the latter over the line to take the victory by just 0.079 of a second. Even so, New Jersey fans went home happy after Mazziotto secured the top spot on the podium in the final race of the season.

MAJOR RESULTS

OTHER CHAMPIONSHIP RACING SERIES WORLDWIDE

Compiled by PETER McLAREN

MOTOAMERICA/AMA Championship Road Race Series (Superbike/ Superstock 1000)

** Indicates Superstock 1000 machine.*

CIRCUIT OF THE AMERICAS, Austin, Texas, 11–12 April, 12 Laps, 41.1 miles/ 66.182km
Race 1
1 Josh Hayes (Yamaha); **2** Cameron Beaubier (Yamaha); **3** Roger Hayden (Suzuki); **4** Jake Gagne (Yamaha)*; **5** Dustin Dominguez (Aprilia)*; **6** Tyler O'Hara (Yamaha)*; **7** Bernat Martinez (Yamaha); **8** Mark Heckles (Yamaha)*; **9** Devon McDonough (Aprilia)*; **10** Taylor Knapp (Yamaha)*.

Race 2
1 Cameron Beaubier (Yamaha); **2** Josh Hayes (Yamaha); **3** Roger Hayden (Suzuki); **4** Jake Gagne (Yamaha)*; **5** Jake Lewis (Suzuki); **6** Chris Fillmore (KTM); **7** Dustin Dominguez (Aprilia)*; **8** Taylor Knapp (Yamaha)*; **9** Geoff May (Yamaha)*; **10** Elena Myers (Suzuki).

ROAD ATLANTA, Braselton, Georgia, 19 April, 22 Laps, 55.88 miles/89.930km
Race 1 (12 laps, red flag)
1 Cameron Beaubier (Yamaha); **2** Josh Hayes (Yamaha); **3** Jake Lewis (Suzuki); **4** Joshua Day (Yamaha)*; **5** Tyler O'Hara (Yamaha)*; **6** Taylor Knapp (Yamaha)*; **7** Mark Heckles (Yamaha)*; **8** Devon McDonough (Aprilia)*; **9** Bernat Martinez (Yamaha); **10** Chris Ulrich (Suzuki).

Race 2 (16 laps, rain)
1 Cameron Beaubier (Yamaha); **2** Jake Lewis (Suzuki); **3** Jake Gagne (Yamaha)*; **4** Tyler O'Hara (Yamaha)*; **5** Taylor Knapp (Yamaha)*; **6** Mark Heckles (Yamaha)*; **7** Bernat Martinez (Yamaha); **8** Chris Ulrich (Suzuki); **9** Dustin Dominguez (Aprilia)*; **10** Shane Narbonne (Yamaha)*.

VIRGINIA INTERNATIONAL RACEWAY, Danville, Virginia, 17 May, 25 Laps, 56.25 miles/ 90.525km
Race 1 (19 laps)
1 Josh Hayes (Yamaha); **2** Cameron Beaubier (Yamaha); **3** Roger Hayden (Suzuki); **4** Danny Eslick (Honda); **5** Taylor Knapp (Yamaha)*; **6** Jake Lewis (Suzuki); **7** Chris Ulrich (Suzuki); **8** Mark Heckles (Yamaha)*; **9** Dustin Dominguez (Aprilia)*; **10** Frankie Babuska (Suzuki)*.

Race 2
1 Josh Hayes (Yamaha); **2** Roger Hayden (Suzuki); **3** Cameron Beaubier (Yamaha); **4** Jake Lewis (Suzuki); **5** Jake Gagne (Yamaha)*; **6** Danny Eslick (Honda); **7** Josh Day (Yamaha)*; **8** Mark Heckles (Yamaha)*; **9** Tyler O'Hara (Yamaha)*; **10** Chris Ulrich (Suzuki).

ROAD AMERICA, Elkhart Lake, Wisconsin, 31 May, 56 miles/90.123km
Race 1
1 Cameron Beaubier (Yamaha); **2** Roger Hayden (Suzuki); **3** Jake Lewis (Suzuki); **4** Jake Gagne (Yamaha)*; **5** Danny Eslick (Honda); **6** Chris Fillmore (KTM); **7** Josh Hayes (Yamaha); **8** Sheridan Morais (Aprilia)*; **9** Shane Narbonne (Yamaha)*; **10** Mark Heckles (Yamaha)*.

Race 2
1 Josh Hayes (Yamaha); **2** Cameron Beaubier (Yamaha); **3** Jake Lewis (Suzuki); **4** Roger Hayden (Suzuki); **5** Jake Gagne (Yamaha)*; **6** Danny Eslick (Honda); **7** Chris Fillmore (KTM); **8** Taylor Knapp (Yamaha)*; **9** Sheridan Morais (Aprilia)*; **10** Tyler O'Hara (Yamaha)*.

BARBER MOTORSPORTS PARK, Birmingham, Alabama, 14 June, 47.6 miles/76.604km
Race 1 (15 laps due to red flag)
1 Josh Hayes (Yamaha); **2** Roger Hayden (Suzuki); **3** Jake Gagne (Yamaha)*; **4** Jake Lewis (Suzuki); **5** Danny Eslick (Honda); **6** Taylor Knapp (Yamaha)*; **7** Chris Fillmore (KTM); **8** Tyler O'Hara (Yamaha)*; **9** Mark Heckles (Yamaha)*; **10** Chris Ulrich (Suzuki).

Race 2
1 Cameron Beaubier (Yamaha); **2** Josh Hayes (Yamaha); **3** Roger Hayden (Suzuki); **4** Jake Gagne (Yamaha)*; **5** Jake Lewis (Suzuki); **6** Sheridan Morais (Aprilia)*; **7** Danny Eslick (Honda); **8** Taylor Knapp (Yamaha)*; **9** Chris Fillmore (KTM); 10. Joshua Day (Yamaha)*.

MILLER MOTORSPORTS PARK, Tooele, Utah, 28 June, 54.9 miles/88.352km
Race 1
1 Josh Hayes (Yamaha); **2** Cameron Beaubier (Yamaha); **3** Roger Hayden (Suzuki); **4** Jake Lewis (Suzuki); **5** Josh Day (Yamaha)*; **6** Chris Fillmore (KTM); **7** Danny Eslick (Honda); **8** Taylor Knapp (Yamaha)*; **9** Sheridan Morais (Aprilia)*; **10** Bernat Martinez (Yamaha).

Race 2
1 Josh Hayes (Yamaha); **2** Cameron Beaubier (Yamaha); **3** Roger Hayden (Suzuki); **4** Jake Lewis (Suzuki); **5** Josh Day (Yamaha)*; **6** Chris Fillmore (KTM); **7** Sheridan Morais (Aprilia)*; **8** Taylor Knapp (Yamaha)*; **9** Danny Eslick (Honda); **10** Mark Heckles (Yamaha)*.

LAGUNA SECA, Monterey, California, 19 July, 51.5 miles/82.881km
Race 1
1 Josh Hayes (Yamaha); **2** Cameron Beaubier (Yamaha); **3** Roger Hayden (Suzuki); **4** Jake Lewis (Suzuki); **5** Mark Heckles (Yamaha)*; **6** Steve Rapp (BMW)*; **7** Chris Ulrich (Suzuki); **8** Taylor Knapp (Yamaha)*; **9** Shane Narbonne (Yamaha)*; **10** Cory Call (BMW)*.

Race 2 (18 laps)
1 Cameron Beaubier (Yamaha); **2** Roger Hayden (Suzuki); **3** Josh Hayes (Yamaha); **4** Jake Gagne (Yamaha)*; **5** Sheridan Morais (Aprilia)*; **6** Taylor Knapp (Yamaha)*; **7** Josh Day (Yamaha)*; **8** Jake Lewis (Suzuki); **9** Tyler O'Hara (Yamaha)*; **10** Chris Ulrich (Suzuki).

INDIANAPOLIS MOTOR SPEEDWAY, Indianapolis, Indiana, 8–9 August, 47.2 miles/ 75.925km
Race 1
1 Cameron Beaubier (Yamaha); **2** Roger Hayden (Suzuki); **3** Josh Hayes (Yamaha); **4** Jake Lewis (Suzuki); **5** Jake Gagne (Yamaha)*; **6** Josh Day (Yamaha)*; **7** Taylor Knapp (Yamaha)*; **8** Sheridan Morais (Aprilia)*; **9** Steve Rapp (BMW)*; **10** Shane Narbonne (Yamaha)*.

Race 2 (15 laps)
1 Cameron Beaubier (Yamaha); **2** Roger Hayden (Suzuki); **3** Josh Hayes (Yamaha); **4** Jake Lewis (Suzuki); **5** Jake Gagne (Yamaha)*; **6** Josh Day (Yamaha)*; **7** Sheridan Morais (Aprilia)*; **8** Tyler O'Hara (Yamaha)*; **9** Taylor Knapp (Yamaha)*; **10** Chris Ulrich (Suzuki).

NEW JERSEY MOTORSPORTS PARK, Millville, New Jersey, 13 September, 56.25 miles/ 90.525km
Race 1 (5 laps, rain and red flag)
1 Josh Hayes (Yamaha); **2** Cameron Beaubier (Yamaha); **3** Roger Hayden (Suzuki); **4** Jake Gagne (Yamaha)*; **5** Kyle Wyman (Yamaha)*; **6** Josh Day (Yamaha)*; **7** Taylor Knapp (Yamaha)*; **8** Danny Eslick (Aprilia)*; **9** Shane Narbonne (Yamaha)*; **10** Geoff May (Honda).

Race 2
1 Josh Hayes (Yamaha); **2** Roger Hayden (Suzuki); **3** Jake Gagne (Yamaha)*; **4** Taylor Knapp (Yamaha)*; **5** Josh Day (Yamaha)*; **6** Cameron Beaubier (Yamaha); **7** Kyle Wyman (Yamaha)*; **8** Danny Eslick (Aprilia)*; **9** Chris Ulrich (Suzuki); **10** Chris Fillmore (KTM).

Final Championship Points:
Superbike

1	Cameron Beaubier	372
2	Josh Hayes	368
3	Roger Hayden	281
4	Jake Lewis	223
5	Elena Myers	152
6	Chris Ulrich	148

7 Bernat Martinez, 127; **8** Chris Fillmore, 102; **9** Danny Eslick, 92; **10** Mathew Orange, 40.

Superstock 1000

1	Jake Gagne	344
2	Taylor Knapp	284
3	Mark Heckles	225
4	Josh Day	203
5	Tyler O'Hara	169

Supersport

1	JD Beach	310
2	Josh Herin	255
3	Garrett Gerloff	250
4	David Anthony	158
5	Tomas Puerta	137

Superstock 600

1	Joe Roberts	245
2	Richie Escalante	185
3	Travis Wyman	182
4	Wyatt Farris	143
5	Bryce Prince	139

KTM RC390 Cup

1	Gage McAllister	172
2	Anthony Mazziotto	137
3	Braeden Ortt	124
4	Hayden Schultz	88
5	Justin McWilliams	86

Endurance World Championship

24 HEURES MOTO, Le Mans Bugatti Circuit, France, 18–19 April 2015.
FIM Endurance World Championship, Rnd 1. 833 laps of the 2.600-mile/4.185km circuit, 2166.2 miles/3486.1km
1 Suzuki Endurance Racing Team: Vincent Philippe, Anthony Delhalle, Etienne Masson (Suzuki), 24h 1m 35.527s.
2 SRC Kawasaki: Grégory Leblanc, Matthieu Lagrive, Fabien Foret (Kawasaki), 826 laps; **3** Team Bolliger Switzerland: Horst Saiger, Roman Stamm, Daniel Sutter (Kawasaki), 821 laps; **4** Junior Team LMS Suzuki: Baptiste Guittet, Gregg Black, Romain Maitre (Suzuki), 821 laps; **5** GMT94 Yamaha: David Checa, Kenny Foray, Mathieu Gines (Yamaha), 819 laps; **6** Team Traqueur Louit Moto 33: Julien Pilot, Emeric Jonchiere, Morgan Berchet (Kawasaki), 816 laps; **7** BMW Motorrad France Team Penz13: Markus Reiterberger, Gareth Jones, Pedro Vallcaneras (BMW), 816 laps; **8** Tati Team Beaujolais Racing: Julien Enjolras, Cédric Tangre, Michaël Savary (Kawasaki), 813 laps; **9** AM Moto Racing Competition: Anthony Loiseau, Alexandre Ayer, Robin Camus (Suzuki), 811 laps; **10** Team April Moto Motors Events: Grégory Fastré, Julien Diguet, Axel Maurin (Suzuki), 808 laps; **11** BMRT 3D Endurance: Kevin Denis, Jimmy Maccio, Anthony Violland (Kawasaki), 807 laps; **12** MACO Racing Team: Gianluca Vizziello, Marko Jerman, Anthony Dos Santos (Yamaha), 806 laps; **13** Starteam PAM-Racing: Kevin Longearet, Jonathan Hardt, Claude Lucas (Suzuki), 804 laps; **14** National Motos: Greg Junod, Valentin Debise, Louis Bulle (Honda), 798 laps; **15** Qatar Endurance Racing Team: Alex Cudlin, Mashel Al Naimi, Arturo Tizon (Kawasaki), 797 laps.
Fastest lap: Monster Energy Yamaha YART: Max Neukirchner, Ivan Silva, Sheridan Morais, 1m 38.381s, 95.13mph/153.1km/h (lap 354).
Championship points: 1 Suzuki Endurance Racing Team, 60; **2** SRC Kawasaki, 42; **3** Team Bolliger Switzerland, 41; **4** GMT94 Yamaha, 36; **5** Junior Team LMS Suzuki, 33; **6** Team Traqueur Louit Moto 33, 28.

SUZUKA 8 HOURS, Suzuka, Japan, 26 July 2015.
FIM Endurance World Championship, Rnd 2. 204 laps of the 3.617-mile/5.821km circuit, 737.9 miles/1187.5km
1 Yamaha Factory Racing Team: Katsuyuki Nakasuga, Pol Espargaro, Bradley Smith (Yamaha), 8h 0m 29.708s.
2 FCC TSR Honda: Josh Hook, Kyle Smith, Dominique Aegerter (Honda), +1m 17.411s; **3** Team Kagayama: Yukio Kagayama, Noriyuki Haga, Ryuichi Kiyonari (Suzuki), 203 laps; **4** Suzuki Endurance Racing Team: Vincent Philippe, Anthony Delhalle, Etienne Masson (Suzuki), 202 laps; **5** Yoshimura Suzuki Shell Advance: Takuya Tsuda, Alex Lowes, Josh Waters (Suzuki), 201 laps; **6** GMT94 Yamaha: David Checa, Kenny Foray, Mathieu Gines (Yamaha), 201 laps; **7** Honda Endurance Racing: Julien Da Costa, Sebastien Gimbert, Freddy Foray (Honda), 201 laps; **8** Honda Suzuka Racing Team: Daijiro Hiura, Kamei, Yudai Takashi Yasuda (Honda), 200 laps; **9** Team Green: Akira Yanagawa, Haji Ahmad Yudhistira, Kazuki Watanabe (Kawasaki), 199 laps; **10** MotoMap Supply: Yoshihiro Konno, Nobuatsu Aoki, Hideyuki Ogata (Suzuki), 199 laps; **11** EVA RT Trickstar: Osamu Deguchi, Hitoyasu Izutsu, Erwan Nigon (Kawasaki), 199 laps; **12** Team Bolliger Switzerland: Nicolas Salchaud, Roman Stamm, Daniel Sutter (Kawasaki), 199 laps; **13** Teluru Kohara RT: Kazuma Watanabe, Tetsuta Nagashima, Kousuke Akiyoshi (Honda), 198 laps; **14** Toho Racing with Moriwaki: Tatsuya Yamaguchi, Toni Elias, Ratthapark Wilairot (Honda), 198 laps; **15** Confia Flex Motorad39: Daisaku Sakai, Shinya Takeishi, Takatoshi Ohnishi (BMW), 197 laps.
Fastest lap: Yamaha Factory Racing Team: Katsuyuki Nakasuga, Pol Espargaro, Bradley Smith, 2m 8.496s, 101.33mph/163.08km/h (lap 6).
Championship points: 1 Suzuki Endurance Racing Team, 81; **2** GMT94 Yamaha, 52; **3** Team Bolliger Switzerland, 50; **4** SRC Kawasaki, 42; **5** Yamaha Factory Racing Team, 35; **6** Junior Team LMS Suzuki, 33.

OSCHERSLEBEN 8 HOURS, Oschersleben, Germany, 22 August 2015.
FIM Endurance World Championship, Rnd 3. 312 laps of the 2.297-mile/3.696km circuit, 716.5 miles/1153.2km
1 GMT94 Yamaha: David Checa, Kenny Foray, Mathieu Gines (Yamaha), 8h 1m 9.771s.
2 Suzuki Endurance Racing Team: Vincent Philippe, Anthony Delhalle, Etienne Masson (Suzuki), +18.773s; **3** Monster Energy Yamaha - YART: Broc Parkes, Ivan Silva, Sheridan Morais (Yamaha), 309 laps; **4** Junior Team LMS Suzuki: Baptiste Guittet, Gregg Black, Romain Maitre (Suzuki), 308 laps; **5** Honda Racing: Julien Da Costa, Sébastien Gimbert, Freddy Foray (Honda), 306 laps; **6** BMW Motorrad France Team Penz13: Markus Reiterberger, Bastien Mackels, Pedro Vallcaneras (BMW), 306 laps; **7** Starteam PAM-Racing: Kevin Longearet, Jonathan Hardt, Claude Lucas (Suzuki), 305 laps; **8** MACO Racing Team: Gianluca Vizziello, Marko Jerman, Anthony Dos Santos (Yamaha), 305 laps; **9** National Motos: Sébastien Suchet, Greg Junod, Louis Bulle (Honda), 304 laps; **10** Team Traqueur Louit Moto 33: Julien Pilot, Emeric Jonchiere, Morgan Berchet (Kawasaki), 304 laps; **11** R2CL: Gwen Giabbani, Jimmy Storrar, Nina Prinz (Suzuki), 303 laps; **12** AM Moto Racing Competition: Anthony Loiseau, Alexandre Ayer, Robin Camus (Suzuki), 300 laps; **13** Flembbo Leader Team: Janez Prosenik,, Maxime Cudeville, Emiliano Bellucci (Kawasaki), 300 laps; **14** Aprilia Grebenstein: Ralf Uhlig, Holger-Jens Schwarz, Jan Bühn (Aprilia), 300 laps; **15** RS Speedbikes Racing: Lars Albrecht, Rico Löwe, Tobias Kollan (BMW), 299 laps.
Fastest lap: BMW Motorrad France Team Penz13: Markus Reiterberger, Bastien Mackels, Pedro Vallcaneras, 1m 26.816s, 95.26mph/ 153.3km/h (lap 6).
Championship points: 1 Suzuki Endurance Racing Team, 110; **2** GMT94 Yamaha, 87; **3** Team Bolliger Switzerland, 55; **4** Junior Team LMS Suzuki, 54; **5** SRC Kawasaki, 42; **6** Team Traqueur Louit Moto 33, 39.

BOL D'OR (24 hours), Paul Ricard - Le Castellet, France, 19–20 September 2015.
FIM Endurance World Championship, Rnd 4. 684 laps of the 3.598-mile/5.791km circuit, 2461.3 miles/3961.0km
1 SRC Kawasaki: Gregory Leblanc, Matthieu Lagrive, Fabien Foret (Kawasaki), 24h 1m 22.895s.
2 GMT94 Yamaha: David Checa, Kenny Foray, Mathieu Gines (Yamaha), 682 laps; **3** Suzuki Endurance Racing Team: Vincent Philippe, Antony Delhalle, Etienne Masson (Suzuki), 677 laps; **4** Tati Team Beaujolais Racing: Julien Enjolras, Cédric Tangre, Michel Savary (Kawasaki), 673 laps; **5** Team Traqueur Louit Moto 33: Julien Pilot, Emeric Jonchiere, Morgan Berchet (Kawasaki), 672 laps; **6** BMW Motorrad France Team Penz13: Markus Reiterberger, Bastien Mackels, Lucas Pesek (BMW), 669 laps; **7** Völpker NRT 48 & Penz13 By Schubert: Marco Nekvasil, Stefan Kerschbaumer, Dominik Vincon (BMW), 668 laps; **8** Team 3ART Yam'Avenue: Alex Plancassagne, Gabriel Pons, Olivier Depoorter (Yamaha), 664 laps; **9** Atomic 68: Stéphane Egea, Kenny Riedmann, Maxime Gucciardi (Suzuki), 662 laps; **10** Team Aprilmoto Motors Events: Grégory Fastre, David Perret, Julien Diguet (Suzuki), 660 laps; **11** Flembbo Leader Team: Janez Prosenik, Emiliano Bellucci, Maxime Cudeville (Kawasaki), 660 laps; **12** AM Moto Racing Competition: Anthony Loiseau, Alexandre Ayer, Robin Camus (Suzuki), 655 laps; **13** Ecurie Chrono Sport 1: Stéphane Pagani, Baptiste Perdriat, Guillaume Saive (Kawasaki), 654 laps; **14** MACO Racing Team: Anthony Dos Santos, Marko Jerman, Pedro Vallcaneras (Yamaha), 647 laps; **15** Tecmas Racing Team: Dominique Platet, Clive Rambure, Camille Hedelin (BMW), 640 laps.
Fastest lap: SRC Kawasaki: Gregory Leblanc, Matthieu Lagrive, Fabien Foret, 1m 58.979s, 108.86mph/175.2km/h (lap 26).

Final Endurance World Championship points:

1	Suzuki Endurance Racing Team	154
2	GMT94 Yamaha	132
3	SRC Kawasaki	100

4 BMW Motorrad France Team Penz13 71
5 Team Traqueur Louit Moto 33 68
6 Team Bolliger Switzerland 55
7 Junior Team LMS Suzuki, 54; **8** Tati Team Beaujolais Racing, 53; **9** Honda Endurance Racing, 50; **10** Monster Energy Yamaha YART, 41; **11** Yamaha Factory Racing Team, 35; **12** National Motos, 33; **13** MACO Racing Team, 33; **14** AM Moto Racing Competition, 31; **15** FCC TSR Honda, 29.

Isle of Man Tourist Trophy Races

ISLE OF MAN TOURIST TROPHY COURSE, 7–12 June 2015, 37.73-mile/60.72km circuit. RST Superbike TT (6 laps, 226.38 miles/ 364.32km)
1 Bruce Anstey (Honda), 1h 45m 29.902s, 128.749mph/207.201km/h.
2 Ian Hutchinson (Kawasaki), 1h 45m 40.879s; **3** James Hillier (Kawasaki), 1h 46m 29.410s; **4** John McGuinness (Honda), 1h 46m 42.757s; **5** William Dunlop (BMW), 1h 47m 41.221s; **6** Michael Rutter (BMW), 1h 48m 4.608s; **7** Dan Kneen (Honda), 1h 30m 20.463s; **8** Peter Hickman (BMW), 1h 30m 50.199s; **9** Lee Johnston (BMW), 1h 31m 1.982s; **10** David Johnson (BMW), 1h 31m 6.559s; **11** Jamie Hamilton (Suzuki), 1h 31m 41.955s; **12** Steve Mercer (Honda), 1h 32m 28.759s; **13** Daniel Hegarty (Kawasaki), 1h 32m 30.956s; **14** Russ Mountford (Kawasaki), 1h 33m 21.989s; **15** Daniel Cooper (Honda), 1h 33m 25.168s.
Fastest lap: Bruce Anstey (Honda), 17m 10.587s, 131.797mph/212.107km/h (lap 6).
Superbike TT lap record: Bruce Anstey (Honda), 17m 6.682s, 132.298mph/212.913km/h (2014).

Sure Sidecar TT Race 1 (3 laps, 113.19 miles/ 182.16km)
1 Ben Birchall/Tom Birchall (LCR), 58m 39.776s, 115.770mph/186.314km/h.
2 John Holden/Dan Sayle (LCR), 59m 3.889s; **3** Conrad Harrison/Mike Aylott (Shelbourne Honda), 59m 35.636s; **4** Ian Bell/Carl Bell (LCR), 1h 0m 36.205s; **5** Alan Founds/Tom Peters (LCR Suzuki), 1h 0m 56.899s; **6** Gary Bryan/Jamie Winn (Baker), 1h 0m 56.906s; **7** Gary Knight/ Jason Crowe (DMR Kawasaki), 1h 1m 42.389s; **8** Matt Dix/Shaun Parker (Baker Yamaha), 1h 2m 10.797s; **9** Robert Handcock/Aki Aalto (Baker), 1h 2m 11.953s; **10** Wayne Lockey/Mark Sayers (Ireson Honda), 1h 2m 19.958s; **11** Tony Baker/ Fiona Baker-Milligan (Suzuki), 1h 2m 29.144s; **12** Steve Ramsden/Matty Ramsden (LCR), 1h 2m 37.249s; **13** Michael Grabmuller/Manfred Wechselberger (Yamaha), 1h 2m 49.463s; **14** John Saunders/Robert Lunt (Shelbourne), 1h 2m 51.183s; **15** Gordon Shand/Frank Claeys (Honda), 1h 3m 23.955s.
Fastest lap: Ben Birchall/Tom Birchall (LCR), 19m 30.321s, 116.030mph/186.732km/h (lap 2).
Sidecar lap record: Nick Crowe/Daniel Sayle (LCR Honda), 19m 24.240s, 116.667mph/ 187.757km/h (2007).

Monster Energy Supersport TT Race 1 (4 laps, 150.92 miles/242.88km)
1 Ian Hutchinson (Yamaha), 1h 12m 10.872s, 125.451mph/201.894km/h.
2 Bruce Anstey (Honda), 1h 12m 18.595s; **3** Gary Johnson (Yamaha), 1h 12m 35.811s; **4** Lee Johnston (Triumph), 1h 12m 48.591s; **5** Guy Martin (Triumph), 1h 12m 58.110s; **6** James Hillier (Kawasaki), 1h 13m 24.531s; **7** John McGuinness (Honda), 1h 13m 29.156s; **8** Conor Cummins (Honda), 1h 13m 51.604s; **9** Dan Kneen (Honda), 1h 14m 12.448s; **10** Michael Rutter (Kawasaki), 1h 14m 22.389s; **11** David Johnson (Triumph), 1h 14m 30.461s; **12** Ivan Lintin (Kawasaki), 1h 14m 39.667s; **13** Cameron Donald (Honda), 1h 14m 51.998s; **14** Daniel Cooper (Honda), 1h 15m 0.880s; **15** Jamie Hamilton (Honda), 1h 15m 3.753s.
Fastest lap: Ian Hutchinson (Yamaha), 17m 44.728s, 127.571mph/205.306km/h (lap 4).
Supersport lap record: Michael Dunlop (Honda), 17m 35.659s, 128.666mph/207.069km/h (2013).

RL360 Superstock TT (4 laps, 150.92 miles/ 242.88km)
1 Ian Hutchinson (Kawasaki), 1h 10m 5.298s, 129.197mph/207.922km/h.
2 Michael Dunlop (BMW), 1h 10m 22.437s; **3** Lee Johnston (BMW), 1h 10m 30.677s; **4** James Hillier (Kawasaki), 1h 10m 30.947s; **5** Peter Hickman (BMW), 1h 10m 50.444s; **6** David Johnson (BMW), 1h 11m 0.805s; **7** Guy Martin (BMW), 1h 11m 10.217s; **8** John McGuinness (Honda), 1h 11m 35.129s; **9** Bruce Anstey (Honda), 1h 11m 47.731s; **10** Conor Cummins (Honda), 1h 11m 50.172s; **11** Michael Rutter (BMW), 1h 11m 53.302s; **12** Dan Kneen (Honda), 1h 12m 9.576s; **13** Dean Harrison (Yamaha), 1h 12m 16.958s; **14** Ivan Lintin (Kawasaki), 1h 12m 34.395s; **15** Daniel Cooper (Honda), 1h 12m 52.536s.
Fastest lap: Michael Dunlop (BMW), 17m 17.392s, 130.932mph/210.715km/h (lap 1).
Superstock lap record: Michael Dunlop (Honda), 17m 15.114s, 131.220mph/211.178km/h (2013).

SES TT Zero (1 lap, 37.73 miles/60.72km)
1 John McGuinness (Mugen), 18m 58.743s, 119.279mph/191.961km/h (record).
2 Bruce Anstey (Mugen), 19m 2.785s; **3** Lee Johnston (Victory), 20m 16.881s; **4** Guy Martin (Victory), 20m 37.987s; **5** Robert Wilson (Sarolea), 21m 15.256s; **6** Michael Sweeney (University of Nottingham), 30m 56.695s.
Previous TT Zero lap record: John McGuinness (Mugen), 19m 17.300s, 117.366mph/ 188.882km/h (2014).

Monster Energy Supersport TT Race 2 (4 laps, 150.92 miles/242.88km)
1 Ian Hutchinson (Yamaha), 1h 11m 58.750s, 125.803mph/202.460km/h.
2 Bruce Anstey (Honda), 1h 12m 13.570s; **3** Guy Martin (Triumph), 1h 12m 30.775s; **4** James Hillier (Kawasaki), 1h 12m 39.835s; **5** Gary Johnson (Yamaha), 1h 12m 53.400s; **6** Lee Johnston (Triumph), 1h 13m 7.207s; **7** Conor Cummins (Honda), 1h 13m 27.145s; **8** John McGuinness (Honda), 1h 13m 27.187s; **9** Dan Kneen (Honda), 1h 13m 29.162s; **10** David Johnson (Triumph), 1h 13m 31.628s; **11** Peter Hickman (MV Agusta), 1h 13m 37.747s; **12** Ivan Lintin (Kawasaki), 1h 14m 24.409s; **13** Cameron Donald (Honda), 1h 14m 24.619s; **14** Jamie Hamilton (Honda), 1h 14m 28.190s; **15** Daniel Cooper (Honda), 1h 14m 32.340s.
Fastest lap: Ian Hutchinson (Yamaha), 17m 43.224s, 127.751mph/205.595km/h (lap 2).
Supersport lap record: Michael Dunlop (Honda), 17m 35.659s, 128.667mph/207.069km/h (2013).

Sure Sidecar TT Race 2 (3 laps, 113.19 miles/ 182.16km)
1 Ben Birchall/Tom Birchall (LCR), 58m 24.971s, 116.259mph/187.101km/h.
2 Dave Molyneux/Benjamin Binns (Suzuki), 58m 32.555s; **3** John Holden/Dan Sayle (LCR), 58m 44.836s; **4** Conrad Harrison/ Mike Aylott (Shelbourne), 1h 0m 00.881s; **5** Ian Bell/Carl Bell (LCR), 1h 0m 58.065s; **6** Matt Dix/Shaun Parker (Baker Yamaha), 1h 1m 51.854s; **7** Wayne Lockey/ Mark Sayers (Ireson Honda), 1h 2m 37.392s; **8** Steve Ramsden/Matty Ramsden (LCR), 1h 2m 52.696s; **9** Robert Handcock/Aki Aalto (Baker), 1h 3m 3.752s; **10** Tony Baker/ Fiona Baker-Milligan (Suzuki), 1h 3m 14.313s; **11** Colin Buckley/ Robbie Shorter (Suzuki), 1h 3m 23.084s; **12** Gordon Shand/Frank Claeys (Honda), 1h 3m 43.391s; **13** Mike Roscher/ Manuel Hirschi (Other), 1h 4m 18.734s; **14** Mike Cookson/Alun Thomas (Honda), 1h 4m 27.389s; **15** Pete Alton/Keith Brotherton (Yamaha), 1h 4m 30.003s.
Fastest lap: Dave Molyneux/Benjamin Binns (Suzuki), 19m 23.056s, 116.785mph/ 187.947km/h (lap 3) (record).
Previous Sidecar lap record: Nick Crowe/ Daniel Sayle (LCR Honda), 19m 24.240s, 116.667mph/187.757km/h (2007).

Bennetts Lightweight TT (3 laps, 113.19 miles/ 182.16km)
1 Ivan Lintin (Kawasaki), 57m 6.070s, 118.936mph/191.409km/h.
2 James Hillier (Kawasaki), 57m 9.945s; **3** Michael Rutter (Paton), 57m 43.318s; **4** James Cowton (Kawasaki), 58m 5.032s; **5** Jamie Hamilton (Kawasaki), 58m 15.457s; **6** Daniel Cooper (Kawasaki), 58m 19.594s; **7** Michael Russell (Kawasaki), 59m 5.750s; **8** Mark Miller (Kawasaki), 59m 53.262s; **9** Connor Behan (Kawasaki), 59m 56.166s; **10** Daniel Webb (Kawasaki), 59m 58.353s; **11** Derek McGee (Kawasaki), 1h 0m 9.093s; **12** James Ford (Kawasaki), 1h 0m 23.136s; **13** Tuukka Korhonen (Kawasaki), 1h 0m 26.549s; **14** Bjorn Gunnarsson (Kawasaki), 1h 0m 31.952s; **15** David Johnson (Kawasaki), 1h 0m 39.100s.
Fastest lap: James Hillier (Kawasaki), 18m 43.955s, 120.848mph/194.486km/h (lap 3) (record).
Previous Lightweight TT record: James Hillier (Kawasaki), 19m 0.168s, 119.130mph/ 191.721km/h (2013).

PokerStars Senior TT (4 laps, 150.92 miles/ 242.88km)
1 John McGuinness (Honda), 1h 9m 23.903s, 130.481mph/209.989km/h.
2 James Hillier (Kawasaki), 1h 9m 38.117s; **3** Ian Hutchinson (Kawasaki), 1h 9m 44.730s; **4** Guy Martin (BMW), 1h 9m 52.148s; **5** Michael Dunlop (BMW), 1h 10m 3.010s; **6** Conor Cummins (Honda), 1h 10m 7.202s; **7** Peter Hickman (BMW), 1h 10m 9.836s; **8** Bruce Anstey (Honda), 1h 10m 13.264s; **9** David Johnson (BMW), 1h 10m 20.869s; **10** Michael Rutter (BMW), 1h 10m 23.255s; **11** Dean Harrison (Yamaha), 1h 11m 13.345s; **12** Gary Johnson (Kawasaki), 1h 11m 13.487s; **13** Dan Kneen (Honda), 1h 11m 18.705s; **14** Martin Jessopp (BMW), 1h 12m 3.432s; **15** Alan Bonner (Kawasaki), 1h 12m 27.235s.
Fastest lap & new outright TT record: John McGuinness (Honda), 17m 3.567s, 132.701mph/213.562km/h (lap 2).
Previous Senior TT lap record: Michael Dunlop (BMW), 17m 11.591s, 131.668mph/ 211.899km/h (2014).

British Championships

DONINGTON PARK, 6 April 2015, 2.487-mile/ 4.002km circuit. MCE British Superbike Championship With Pirelli, Round 1 (2 x 20 laps, 49.740 miles/80.049km)
Race 1
1 James Ellison (Kawasaki), 31m 5.460s, 95.92mph/154.37km/h.
2 Shane Byrne (Kawasaki); **3** Josh Brookes (Yamaha); **4** Dan Linfoot (Honda); **5** Peter Hickman (BMW); **6** Tommy Bridewell (BMW); **7** Christian Iddon (Suzuki); **8** Chris Walker (Kawasaki); **9** Michael Laverty (BMW); **10** Richard Cooper (Kawasaki); **11** Stuart Easton (Kawasaki); **12** Robbin Harms (BMW); **13** Lee Jackson (BMW); **14** Ryuichi Kiyonari (BMW); **15** Luke Mossey (Kawasaki).
Fastest lap: Byrne, 1m 29.512s, 100.03mph/ 160.99km/h.

Race 2
1 Shane Byrne (Kawasaki), 30m 15.457s, 98.57mph/158.63km/h.
2 Dan Linfoot (Honda); **3** Stuart Easton (Kawasaki); **4** Peter Hickman (BMW); **5** Christian Iddon (Suzuki); **6** Josh Brookes (Yamaha); **7** Michael Laverty (BMW); **8** Tommy Bridewell (BMW); **9** Billy McConnell (BMW); **10** Chris Walker (Kawasaki); **11** Jason O'Halloran (Honda); **12** James Ellison (Kawasaki); **13** Lee Jackson (BMW); **14** Howie Mainwaring Smart (Kawasaki); **15** Josh Waters (Suzuki).
Fastest lap: Byrne, 1m 29.967s, 99.53mph/ 160.17km/h.
Championship points: 1 Byrne, 45; **2** Linfoot, 33; **3** Ellison, 29; **4** Brookes, 26; **5** Hickman, 24; **6** Easton, 21.

Motorpoint British Supersport Championship & Supersport Evo, Round 1
Race 1 (6 laps 14.922 miles/24.015km)
1 Luke Stapleford (Triumph), 9m 17.713s, 96.08mph/154.63km/h.
2 Jake Dixon (Triumph); **3** Glenn Irwin (Kawasaki); **4** Kyle Ryde (Yamaha); **5** Andy Reid (Yamaha); **6** Ben Wilson (Kawasaki); **7** Joe Collier (Triumph); **8** Dean Hipwell (Triumph); **9** Marshall Neill (Yamaha); **10** Jamie Perrin (Yamaha); **11** Sam Hornsey (Triumph); **12** Levi Day (Kawasaki); **13** Sam Coventry (Kawasaki); **14** Bjorn Estment (Triumph); **15** Luke Jones (MV Agusta).
Fastest lap: Dixon, 1m 31.676s, 97.67mph/ 157.19km/h.

Race 2 (18 laps 44.766 miles/72.044km)
1 Jake Dixon (Triumph), 27m 44.386s, 96.75mph/155.7km/h.
2 Luke Stapleford (Triumph); **3** Kyle Ryde (Yamaha); **4** Glenn Irwin (Kawasaki); **5** Andy Reid (Yamaha); **6** Ben Wilson (Kawasaki); **7** James Rispoli (Yamaha); **8** Harry Hartley (Yamaha); **9** Joe Collier (Triumph); **10** Danny Webb (Yamaha); **11** Marshall Neill (Yamaha); **12** Levi Day (Kawasaki); **13** Bjorn Estment (Triumph); **14** Josh Day (Triumph); **15** Freddy Pett (Triumph).
Fastest lap: Dixon, 1m 31.680s, 97.67mph/ 157.18km/h.
Championship points: 1 Stapleford, 45; **2** Dixon, 45; **3** Irwin, 29; **4** Ryde, 29; **5** Reid, 22; **6** Wilson, 20.

HEL British Motostar Championship, Rnd 1. Race 1 (10 laps 24.870 miles/40.024km)
1 Brad Ray (KTM), 16m 40.844s, 89.33mph/ 143.76km/h.
2 Taz Taylor (KTM); **3** Edward Rendell (Honda); **4** Georgina Polden (KTM); **5** Joe Thomas (Honda); **6** Joseph Thompson (Repli-Cast Moto3); **7** Vasco Van Der Valk (Honda); **8** Elliot Lodge (Honda); **9** Brian Slooten (Honda); **10** Joel Marklund (Honda); **11** Andrew Sawford (Aprilia); **12** Tomas De Vries (Honda); **13** Ryan Longshaw (Honda); **14** Mark Clayton (Honda); **15** Wesley Jonker (Luyten Honda).
Fastest lap: Taylor, 1m 38.847s, 90.58mph/ 145.78km/h.

Race 2 (14 laps 34.818 miles/56.034km)
1 Scott Deroue (KTM), 23m 9.030s, 90.15mph/ 145.08km/h.
2 Brad Ray (KTM); **3** Taz Taylor (KTM); **4** Edward Rendell (Honda); **5** Dani Saez (Repli-Cast Moto3); **6** Jorel Boerboom (Kalex KTM); **7** Joe Thomas (Honda), **8** Charlie Nesbitt (Repli-Cast Moto3); **9** Brian Slooten (Honda); **10** Elliot Lodge (Honda); **11** Joseph Thompson (Repli-Cast Moto3); **12** Vasco Van Der Valk (Honda); **13** Jake Archer (Honda); **14** Josh Owens (Honda); **15** Edmund Best (Honda).
Fastest lap: Taylor, 1m 38.218s, 91.16mph/ 146.72km/h.
Moto3 points: 1 Ray, 45; **2** Taylor, 36; **3** Rendell, 29; **4** Deroue, 25; **5** Thomas, 20; **6** Thompson, 15.

BRANDS HATCH INDY, 19 April 2015, 1.208-mile/1.944km circuit. MCE British Superbike Championship With Pirelli, Rnd 2.
Race 1 (33 laps 39.864 miles/64.155km)
1 James Ellison (Kawasaki), 26m 16.502s, 91.02mph/146.48km/h.
2 Shane Byrne (Kawasaki); **3** Josh Brookes (Yamaha); **4** Ryuichi Kiyonari (BMW); **5** Jason O'Halloran (Honda); **6** Stuart Easton (Kawasaki); **7** Howie Mainwaring Smart (Kawasaki); **8** Broc Parkes (Yamaha); **9** Billy McConnell (BMW); **10** Chris Walker (Kawasaki); **11** Richard Cooper (Kawasaki); **12** Luke Mossey (Kawasaki); **13** Michael Laverty (BMW); **14** Danny Buchan (Kawasaki); **15** Josh Waters (Suzuki).
Fastest lap: Ellison, 45.313s, 95.96mph/ 154.44km/h.

Race 2 (25 laps 30.200 miles/48.602km)
1 James Ellison (Kawasaki), 19m 24.226s, 93.37mph/150.26km/h.
2 Shane Byrne (Kawasaki); **3** Josh Brookes (Yamaha); **4** Ryuichi Kiyonari (BMW);5 Stuart Easton (Kawasaki); **6** Tommy Bridewell (BMW); **7** Howie Mainwaring Smart (Kawasaki); **8** Danny Buchan (Kawasaki); **9** Billy McConnell (BMW); **10** Jason O'Halloran (Honda); **11** Broc Parkes (Yamaha); **12** Christian Iddon (Suzuki); **13** Chris Walker (Kawasaki); **14** Peter Hickman (BMW); **15** Richard Cooper (Kawasaki).
Fastest lap: Ellison, 45.212s, 96.18mph/ 154.79km/h.
Championship points: 1 Byrne, 85; **2** Ellison, 79; **3** Brookes, 58; **4** Easton, 42; **5** Linfoot, 33; **6** Bridewell, 28.

Motorpoint British Supersport Championship & Supersport Evo, Rnd 2.
Race 1 (18 laps 21.744 miles/34.994km)
1 Kyle Ryde (Yamaha), 14m 5.306s, 92.59mph/ 149.01km/h.
2 Glenn Irwin (Kawasaki); **3** Luke Stapleford (Triumph); **4** Jake Dixon (Triumph); **5** Sam Hornsey (Triumph); **6** Ben Wilson (Kawasaki); **7** Danny Webb (Yamaha); **8** Dean Hipwell (Triumph); **9** Bjorn Estment (Triumph); **10** Joe Collier (Triumph); **11** Jamie Perrin (Yamaha); **12** Marshall Neill (Yamaha); **13** Sam Coventry (Kawasaki); **14** Luke Jones (MV Agusta); **15** Levi Day (Kawasaki).
Fastest lap: Ryde, 46.368s, 93.78mph/ 150.93km/h.

Race 2 (20 laps 24.160 miles/38.882km)
1 Luke Stapleford (Triumph), 15m 36.606s, 92.85mph/149.43km/h.
2 Kyle Ryde (Yamaha); **3** Jake Dixon (Triumph); **4** Glenn Irwin (Kawasaki); **5** James Rispoli (Yamaha); **6** Ben Wilson (Kawasaki); **7** Danny Webb (Yamaha); **8** Bjorn Estment (Triumph); **9** Harry Hartley (Yamaha); **10** Joe Collier (Triumph); **11** Luke Jones (MV Agusta); **12** Sam Coventry (Kawasaki); **13** Jamie Perrin (Yamaha); **14** Niall Campbell (Yamaha); **15** Josh Day (Triumph).
Fastest lap: Ryde, 46.176s, 94.17mph/ 151.55km/h.
Championship points: 1 Stapleford, 86; **2** Dixon, 74; **3** Ryde, 74; **4** Irwin, 62; **5** Wilson, 40; **6** Collier, 28.

HEL British Motostar Championship, Rnd 2. Race 1 (15 laps, 18.120 miles/29.161km)
1 Taz Taylor (KTM), 12m 41.954s, 85.60mph/ 137.76km/h.
2 Scott Deroue (KTM); **3** Edward Rendell (Honda); **4** Charlie Nesbitt (Repli-Cast Moto3); **5** Christoph Beinlich (Honda); **6** Jorel Boerboom (Kalex KTM); **7** Alex Persson (Kalex KTM); **8** Dani Saez (Repli-Cast Moto3); **9** Jake Archer (Honda); **10** Joel Marklund (Honda); **11** Elliot Lodge (Honda); **12** Brian Slooten (Honda); **13** Joseph Thompson (Repli-Cast Moto3); **14** Joe Thomas (Honda); **15** Vasco Van Der Valk (Honda).
Fastest lap: Taylor, 50.070s, 86.85mph/ 139.77km/h.

Race 2 (18 laps, 21.744 miles/34.994km)
1 Scott Deroue (KTM), 14m 57.688s, 87.19mph/140.32km/h.
2 Taz Taylor (KTM); **3** Edward Rendell (Honda); **4** Jorel Boerboom (Kalex KTM); **5** Alex Persson (Kalex KTM); **6** Christoph Beinlich (Honda); **7** Dani Saez (Repli-Cast Moto3); **8** Georgina Polden (KTM); **9** Brian Slooten (Honda); **10** Jake Archer (Honda); **11** Elliot Lodge (Honda); **12** Joe Thomas (Honda); **13** Josh Owens (Honda); **14** Asher Durham (KTM); **15** Vasco Van Der Valk (Honda).
Fastest lap: Deroue, 49.3s, 88.20mph/ 141.95km/h.
Moto3 points: 1 Taylor, 81; **2** Deroue, 70; **3** Rendell, 61; **4** Ray, 45; **5** Boerboom, 33; **6** Saez, 28.

OULTON PARK, 4 May 2015, 2.692-mile/ 4.332km circuit.
MCE British Superbike Championship With Pirelli, Rnd 3 (2 x 18 laps, 48.456 miles/ 77.982km)
Race 1
1 Tommy Bridewell (BMW), 28m 43.914s, 101.19mph/162.85km/h.
2 Josh Brookes (Yamaha); **3** Shane Byrne (Kawasaki); **4** Stuart Easton (Kawasaki); **5** Ryuichi Kiyonari (BMW); **6** James Ellison (Kawasaki); **7** Jason O'Halloran (Honda); **8** Michael Laverty (BMW); **9** Howie Mainwaring Smart (Kawasaki); **10** Richard Cooper (Kawasaki); **11** Chris Walker (Kawasaki); **12** Josh Waters (Suzuki); **13** James

Westmoreland (Kawasaki); **14** Billy McConnell (BMW); **15** Lee Jackson (BMW).
Fastest lap: Brookes, 1m 35.107s, 101.89mph/163.99km/h.

Race 2
1 Stuart Easton (Kawasaki), 28m 46.890s, 101.01mph/162.56km/h.
2 James Ellison (Kawasaki); **3** Josh Brookes (Yamaha); **4** Michael Laverty (BMW); **5** Jason O'Halloran (Honda); **6** Howie Mainwaring Smart (Kawasaki); **7** Richard Cooper (Kawasaki); **8** Billy McConnell (BMW); **9** Chris Walker (Kawasaki); **10** Lee Jackson (BMW); **11** James Westmoreland (Kawasaki); **12** Josh Waters (Suzuki); **13** Luke Mossey (Kawasaki); **14** Martin Jessopp (BMW); **15** Christian Iddon (Suzuki).
Fastest lap: Byrne, 1m 35.007s, 102.00mph/164.16km/h.
Championship points: 1 Ellison, 109; **2** Byrne, 101; **3** Brookes, 94; **4** Easton, 80; **5** Bridewell, 53; **6** O'Halloran, 42.

Motorpoint British Supersport Championship & Supersport Evo, Rnd 3.
Race 1 (8 laps 21.536 miles/34.659km)
1 Luke Stapleford (Triumph), 13m 13.016s, 97.76mph/157.33km/h.
2 Glenn Irwin (Kawasaki); **3** Kyle Ryde (Yamaha); **4** Andy Reid (Yamaha); **5** Joe Collier (Triumph); **6** Luke Hedger (Kawasaki); **7** Dean Hipwell (Triumph); **8** Danny Webb (Yamaha); **9** Harry Hartley (Yamaha); **10** Jamie Perrin (Yamaha); **11** Sam Coventry (Kawasaki); **12** Josh Day (Triumph); **13** Levi Day (Kawasaki); **14** Marshall Neill (Yamaha); **15** Matthew Paulo (Yamaha).
Fastest lap: Stapleford, 1m 38.109s, 98.78mph/158.97km/h.

Race 2 (15 laps 40.380 miles/64.985km)
1 Jake Dixon (Triumph), 25m 33.437s, 94.79mph/152.55km/h.
2 Kyle Ryde (Yamaha); **3** Andy Reid (Yamaha); **4** Glenn Irwin (Kawasaki); **5** Joe Collier (Triumph); **6** Ben Wilson (Kawasaki); **7** Sam Hornsey (Triumph); **8** Dean Hipwell (Triumph); **9** Danny Webb (Yamaha); **10** Josh Day (Triumph); **11** Marshall Neill (Yamaha); **12** Levi Day (Kawasaki); **13** Bjorn Estment (Triumph); **14** Matthew Paulo (Yamaha); **15** Phil Wakefield (Yamaha).
Fastest lap: Reid, 1m 38.100s, 98.79mph/158.98km/h.
Championship points: 1 Stapleford, 111; **2** Ryde, 110; **3** Dixon, 99; **4** Irwin, 95; **5** Reid, 51; **6** Wilson, 50.

HEL British Motostar Championship, Rnd 3.
Race 1 (14 laps 37.688 miles/60.653km)
1 Taz Taylor (KTM), 24m 54.009s, 90.81mph/146.14km/h.
2 Edward Rendell (Honda); **3** Alex Persson (Kalex KTM); **4** Scott Deroue (KTM); **5** Jake Archer (Honda); **6** Jorel Boerboom (Kalex KTM); **7** Georgina Polden (KTM); **8** Dani Saez (Repli-Cast Moto3); **9** Charlie Nesbitt (Repli-Cast Moto3); **10** Elliot Lodge (Honda); **11** Joel Marklund (Honda); **12** Christoph Beinlich (Honda); **13** Brian Slooten (Honda); **14** Joe Thomas (Honda); **15** Vasco Van Der Valk (Honda).
Fastest lap: Taylor, 1m 45.345s, 91.99mph/148.05km/h.
Moto3 points: 1 Taylor, 106; **2** Deroue, 83; **3** Rendell, 81; **4** Ray, 45; **5** Boerboom, 43; **6** Saez, 36.

SNETTERTON, 21 June 2015, 2.969-mile/4.778km circuit.
MCE British Superbike Championship With Pirelli, Rnd 4 (2 x 16 laps, 47.504 miles/76.450km)
Race 1
1 Shane Byrne (Kawasaki), 29m 6.649s, 97.90mph/157.55km/h.
2 Josh Brookes (Yamaha); **3** Jason O'Halloran (Honda); **4** Tommy Bridewell (BMW); **5** Dan Linfoot (Honda); **6** Chris Walker (Kawasaki); **7** Stuart Easton (Kawasaki); **8** Howie Mainwaring Smart (Kawasaki); **9** Luke Mossey (Kawasaki); **10** Richard Cooper (Kawasaki); **11** Broc Parkes (Yamaha); **12** Peter Hickman (BMW); **13** Danny Buchan (Kawasaki); **14** Josh Waters (Suzuki); **15** Jack Kennedy (Kawasaki).
Fastest lap: Byrne, 1m 48.041s, 98.92mph/159.20km/h.

Race 2
1 Shane Byrne (Kawasaki), 29m 31.765s, 96.51mph/155.32km/h.
2 Josh Brookes (Yamaha); **3** Jason O'Halloran (Honda); **4** Michael Laverty (BMW); **5** Tommy Bridewell (BMW); **6** Stuart Easton (Kawasaki); **7** James Ellison (Kawasaki); **8** Filip Backlund (Kawasaki); **9** Christian Iddon (Suzuki); **10** Dan Linfoot (Honda); **11** Broc Parkes (Yamaha); **12** Richard Cooper (Kawasaki); **13** Luke Mossey (Kawasaki); **14** Billy McConnell (BMW); **15** Peter Hickman (BMW).
Fastest lap: Byrne, 1m 47.912s, 99.04mph/159.39km/h.
Championship points: 1 Byrne, 151; **2** Brookes, 134; **3** Ellison, 118; **4** Easton, 99; **5** Bridewell, 77; **6** O'Halloran, 74.

Motorpoint British Supersport Championship & Supersport Evo, Rnd 4.
Race 1 (10 laps 29.690 miles/47.781km)
1 Luke Stapleford (Triumph), 18m 43.008s, 95.17mph/153.16km/h.
2 Kyle Ryde (Yamaha); **3** Andy Reid (Yamaha); **4** James Rispoli (Yamaha); **5** Glenn Irwin (Kawasaki); **6** Luke Hedger (Kawasaki); **7** Danny Webb (Yamaha); **8** Marshall Neill (Yamaha); **9** Joe Collier (Triumph); **10** Dean Hipwell (Triumph); **11** Levi Day (Kawasaki); **12** Matthew Paulo (Yamaha); **13** Freddy Pett (Triumph); **14** Jamie Perrin (Yamaha); **15** Phil Wakefield (Yamaha).
Fastest lap: Stapleford, 1m 50.689s, 96.55mph/155.39km/h.

Race 2 (15 laps 44.535 miles/71.672km)
1 Glenn Irwin (Kawasaki), 28m 9.350s, 94.90mph/152.73km/h.
2 James Rispoli (Yamaha); **3** Luke Hedger (Kawasaki); **4** Danny Webb (Yamaha); **5** Jake Dixon (Triumph); **6** Joe Collier (Triumph); **7** Levi Day (Kawasaki); **8** Jamie Perrin (Yamaha); **9** Luke Jones (My Agusta); **10** Matthew Paulo (Yamaha); **11** Josh Daley (Kawasaki), **12** Sam Coventry (Kawasaki); **13** Freddy Pett (Triumph); **14** Niall Campbell (Yamaha); **15** Phil Wakefield (Yamaha).
Fastest lap: Stapleford, 1m 50.806s, 96.45mph/155.23km/h.
Championship points: 1 Stapleford, 136; **2** Irwin, 131; **3** Ryde, 130; **4** Dixon, 110; **5** Reid, 67; **6** Collier, 67.

HEL British Motostar Championship, Rnd 4.
Race 1 (8 laps 23.752 miles/38.225km)
1 Scott Deroue (KTM), 16m 17.458s, 87.47mph/140.77km/h.
2 Dani Saez (Repli-Cast Moto3); **3** Edward Rendell (Ten Kate Honda); **4** Alex Persson (Kalex KTM); **5** Christoph Beinlich (Honda); **6** Charlie Nesbitt (Repli-Cast Moto3); **7** Elliot Lodge (Honda); **8** Georgina Polden (KTM); **9** Joseph Thompson (Repli-Cast Moto3); **10** Mike Brouwers (Honda); **11** Brian Slooten (Honda); **12** Vasco Van Der Valk (Honda); **13** Tomas De Vries (Honda); **14** Joe Thomas (Honda); **15** Josh Owens (Honda).
Fastest lap: Taylor, 2m 0.910s, 88.39mph/142.26km/h.

Race 2 (12 laps 35.628 miles/57.338km)
1 Taz Taylor (KTM), 24m 23.603s, 87.63mph/141.03km/h.
2 Scott Deroue (KTM); **3** Edward Rendell (Ten Kate Honda); **4** Jorel Boerboom (Kalex KTM); **5** Charlie Nesbitt (Repli-Cast Moto3); **6** Christoph Beinlich (Honda); **7** Alex Persson (Kalex KTM); **8** Dani Saez (Repli-Cast Moto3); **9** Vasco Van Der Valk (Honda); **10** Brian Slooten (Honda); **11** Joseph Thompson (Repli-Cast Moto3); **12** Edmund Best (Honda); **13** Mike Brouwers (Honda); **14** Joe Thomas (Honda); **15** Tomas De Vries (Honda).
Fastest lap: Deroue, 2m 0.214s, 88.90mph/143.08km/h.
Moto3 points: 1 Taylor, 131; **2** Deroue, 128; **3** Rendell, 113; **4** Saez, 64; **5** Persson, 58; **6** Boerboom, 56.

KNOCKHILL, 5 July 2015, 1.267-mile/2.039km circuit.
MCE British Superbike Championship With Pirelli, Rnd 5.
Race 1 (30 laps 38.010 miles/61.171km)
1 Shane Byrne (Kawasaki), 25m 4.244s, 90.96mph/146.39km/h.
2 Stuart Easton (Kawasaki); **3** Josh Brookes (Yamaha); **4** Michael Laverty (BMW); **5** Jason O'Halloran (Honda); **6** Danny Buchan (Kawasaki); **7** Tommy Bridewell (BMW); **8** Luke Mossey (Kawasaki); **9** James Westmoreland (Kawasaki); **10** Peter Hickman (BMW); **11** Lee Jackson (BMW); **12** Billy McConnell (BMW); **13** Michael Rutter (Kawasaki); **14** Broc Parkes (Yamaha); **15** Jed Metcher (Kawasaki).
Fastest lap: Ellison, 48.415s, 94.20mph/151.61km/h.

Race 2 (11 laps 13.937 miles/22.429km)
1 Shane Byrne (Kawasaki), 8m 56.056s, 93.59mph/150.62km/h.
2 Stuart Easton (Kawasaki); **3** Josh Brookes (Yamaha); **4** Ryuichi Kiyonari (BMW); **5** Jason O'Halloran (Honda); **6** Michael Laverty (BMW); **7** Danny Buchan (Kawasaki); **8** James Westmoreland (Kawasaki); **9** Peter Hickman (BMW); **10** Christian Iddon (Suzuki); **11** Lee Jackson (BMW); **12** Dan Linfoot (Honda); **13** Richard Cooper (Kawasaki); **14** Broc Parkes (Yamaha); **15** Josh Waters (Suzuki).
Fastest lap: Byrne, 48.252s, 94.52mph/152.12km/h.
Championship points: 1 Byrne, 201; **2** Brookes, 166; **3** Easton, 139; **4** Ellison, 118; **5** O'Halloran, 96; **6** Bridewell, 86.

Motorpoint British Supersport Championship & Supersport Evo, Rnd 5.
Race 1 (18 laps 22.806 miles/36.703km)
1 Glenn Irwin (Kawasaki), 15m 3.162s, 90.90mph/146.29km/h.
2 Luke Stapleford (Triumph); **3** Kyle Ryde (Yamaha); **4** Sam Hornsey (Triumph); **5** James Rispoli (Yamaha); **6** Luke Hedger (Kawasaki); **7** Danny Webb (Yamaha); **8** Matthew Paulo (Yamaha); **9** Joe Collier (Triumph); **10** Levi Day (Kawasaki); **11** Marshall Neill (Yamaha), **12** Bjorn Estment (Triumph); **13** Dean Hipwell (Triumph); **14** Sam Coventry (Kawasaki); **15** Paul Curran (Triumph).
Fastest lap: Dixon, 49.632s, 91.89mph/147.89km/h.

Race 2 (26 laps 32.942 miles/53.015km)
1 Kyle Ryde (Yamaha), 22m 26.732s, 88.05mph/141.7km/h.
2 Jake Dixon (Triumph); **3** Glenn Irwin (Kawasaki); **4** Luke Stapleford (Triumph); **5** Sam Hornsey (Triumph); **6** James Rispoli (Yamaha); **7** Joe Collier (Triumph); **8** Luke Hedger (Kawasaki); **9** Marshall Neill (Yamaha); **10** Matthew Paulo (Yamaha); **11** Levi Day (Kawasaki), **12** Danny Webb (Yamaha); **13** Dean Hipwell (Triumph); **14** Niall Campbell (Yamaha); **15** David Allingham (MV Agusta).
Fastest lap: Dixon, 49.525s, 92.09mph/148.21km/h.
Championship points: 1 Irwin, 172; **2** Ryde, 171; **3** Stapleford, 169; **4** Dixon, 130; **5** Collier, 83; **6** Webb, 74.

HEL British Motostar Championship, Rnd 5.
Race 1 (16 laps 20.272 miles/32.625km)
1 Taz Taylor (KTM), 14m 22.955s, 84.56mph/136.09km/h.
2 Scott Deroue (KTM); **3** Dani Saez (Repli-Cast Moto3); **4** Edward Rendell (Ten Kate Honda); **5** Charlie Nesbitt (Repli-Cast Moto3); **6** Elliot Lodge (Honda); **7** Alex Persson (Kalex KTM); **8** Vasco Van Der Valk (Honda); **9** Richard Kerr (Honda); **10** Joe Thomas (Honda); **11** Joel Marklund (Honda); **12** Mike Brouwers (Honda); **13** Tomas De Vries (Honda); **14** Georgina Polden (KTM); **15** Edmund Best (Honda).
Fastest lap: Saez, 53.297s, 85.57mph/137.72km/h.

Race 2 (22 laps 27.874 miles/44.859km)
1 Taz Taylor (KTM), 20m 50.626s, 80.23mph/129.12km/h.
2 Scott Deroue (KTM); **3** Edward Rendell (Ten Kate Honda); **4** Jorel Boerboom (Kalex KTM); **5** Alex Persson (Kalex KTM); **6** Dani Saez (Repli-Cast Moto3); **7** Vasco Van Der Valk (Honda); **8** Charlie Nesbitt (Repli-Cast Moto3); **9** Elliot Lodge (Honda); **10** Georgina Polden (KTM); **11** Richard Kerr (Honda); **12** Joel Marklund (Honda); **13** Edmund Best (Honda); **14** Cameron Horsman (EE125); **15** Tomas De Vries (Honda).
Fastest lap: Deroue, 55.717s, 81.86mph/131.74km/Hayden
Moto3 points: 1 Taylor, 181; **2** Deroue, 168; **3** Rendell, 142; **4** Saez, 90; **5** Persson, 78; **6** Boerboom, 69.

BRANDS HATCH GP, 19 July 2015, 2.433-mile/3.916km circuit.
MCE British Superbike Championship With Pirelli, Rnd 6 (2 x 20 laps, 48.660 miles/78.311km)
Race 1
1 Josh Brookes (Yamaha), 30m 20.450s, 96.23mph/154.87km/h.
2 Richard Cooper (Kawasaki); **3** James Ellison (Kawasaki); **4** Tommy Bridewell (BMW); **5** Michael Laverty (BMW); **6** John Hopkins (Ducati); **7** Luke Mossey (Kawasaki); **8** Dan Linfoot (Honda); **9** James Westmoreland (Kawasaki); **10** Billy McConnell (BMW); **11** Broc Parkes (Yamaha); **12** Lee Jackson (BMW); **13** Christian Iddon (Suzuki); **14** Jack Kennedy (Kawasaki); **15** Filip Backlund (Kawasaki).
Fastest lap: Brookes, 1m 26.095s, 101.74mph/163.74km/h.

Race 2
1 Josh Brookes (Yamaha), 28m 53.720s, 101.05mph/162.62km/h.
2 Shane Byrne (Kawasaki); **3** Richard Cooper (Kawasaki); **4** James Ellison (Kawasaki); **5** Michael Laverty (BMW); **6** Billy McConnell (BMW); **7** Luke Mossey (Kawasaki); **8** Christian Iddon (Suzuki); **9** Jason O'Halloran (Honda); **10** Broc Parkes (Yamaha); **11** Lee Jackson (BMW); **12** Jack Kennedy (Kawasaki); **13** Peter Hickman (BMW); **14** James Westmoreland (Kawasaki); **15** Martin Jessopp (BMW).
Fastest lap: Brookes, 1m 26.072s, 101.77mph/163.78km/h.
Championship points: 1 Byrne, 221; **2** Brookes, 216; **3** Ellison, 147; **4** Easton, 139; **5** O'Halloran, 103; **6** Bridewell, 99.

Motorpoint British Supersport Championship & Supersport Evo, Rnd 6.
Race 1 (12 laps 29.196 miles/46.986km)
1 Luke Stapleford (Triumph), 17m 42.397s, 98.94mph/159.23km/h.
2 Kyle Ryde (Yamaha); **3** Andy Reid (Yamaha); **4** James Rispoli (Yamaha); **5** Sam Hornsey (Triumph); **6** Luke Hedger (Kawasaki); **7** Ben Wilson (Kawasaki); **8** Dean Hipwell (Triumph); **9** Joe Collier (Triumph); **10** Bjorn Estment (Triumph); **11** Jamie Perrin (Yamaha), **12** Freddy Pett (Triumph); **13** Sam Coventry (Kawasaki); **14** Niall Campbell (Yamaha); **15** Levi Day (Kawasaki).
Fastest lap: Stapleford, 1m 27.737s, 99.84mph/160.68km/h.

Race 2 (18 laps 43.794 miles/70.48km)
1 Luke Stapleford (Triumph), 26m 37.728s, 98.68mph/158.81km/h.
2 Kyle Ryde (Yamaha); **3** Andy Reid (Yamaha); **4** James Rispoli (Yamaha); **5** Sam Hornsey (Triumph); **6** Jake Dixon (Triumph); **7** Luke Hedger (Kawasaki); **8** Glenn Irwin (Kawasaki); **9** Ben Wilson (Kawasaki); **10** Joe Collier (Triumph); **11** Dean Hipwell (Triumph), **12** Sam Coventry (Kawasaki); **13** Marshall Neill (Yamaha); **14** Freddy Pett (Triumph); **15** Matthew Paulo (Yamaha).
Fastest lap: Stapleford, 1m 27.993s, 99.55mph/160.21km/h.
Championship points: 1 Stapleford, 219; **2** Ryde, 211; **3** Irwin, 180; **4** Dixon, 140; **5** Rispoli, 100; **6** Reid, 99.

HEL British Motostar Championship, Rnd 6.
Race 1 (12 laps 29.196 miles/46.986km)
1 Taz Taylor (KTM), 15m 52.525s, 91.96mph/148.00km/h.
2 Scott Deroue (KTM); **3** Charlie Nesbitt (Repli-Cast Moto3); **4** Dani Saez (Repli-Cast Moto3); **5** Jorel Boerboom (Kalex KTM); **6** Alex Persson (Kalex KTM); **7** Jake Archer (Honda); **8** Edward Rendell (Ten Kate Honda); **9** Vasco Van Der Valk (Honda); **10** Elliot Lodge (Honda); **11** Mike Brouwers (Honda); **12** Georgina Polden (KTM); **13** Brian Slooten (Honda); **14** Joe Thomas (Honda); **15** Edmund Best (Honda).
Fastest lap: Taylor, 1m 33.940s, 93.24mph/150.07km/h.

Race 2 (10 laps 24.330 miles/39.155km)
1 Scott Deroue (KTM), 18m 56.751s, 92.47mph/148.82km/h.
2 Taz Taylor (KTM); **3** Edward Rendell (Ten Kate Honda); **4** Dani Saez (Repli-Cast Moto3); **5** Jorel Boerboom (Kalex KTM); **6** Mike Brouwers (Honda); **7** Elliot Lodge (Honda); **8** Georgina Polden (KTM); **9** Vasco Van Der Valk (Honda); **10** Joe Thomas (Honda); **11** Brian Slooten (Honda); **12** Cameron Horsman (EE125); **13** Josh Owens (Honda); **14** Tomas De Vries (Honda); **15** TJ Toms (Repli-Cast Moto3).
Fastest lap: Taylor, 1m 33.113s, 94.07mph/151.40km/h.
Moto3 points: 1 Taylor, 226; **2** Deroue, 213; **3** Rendell, 166; **4** Saez, 116; **5** Boerboom, 91; **6** Persson, 88.

THRUXTON, 2 August 2015, 2.356-mile/3.792km circuit.
MCE British Superbike Championship With Pirelli, Rnd 7.
Race 1 (15 laps 35.340 miles/56.874km)
1 Josh Brookes (Yamaha), 19m 3.878s, 111.22mph/178.99km/h.
2 Dan Linfoot (Honda); **3** James Westmoreland (Kawasaki); **4** Shane Byrne (Kawasaki); **5** Howie Mainwaring Smart (Kawasaki); **6** Luke Mossey (Kawasaki); **7** Jack Kennedy (Kawasaki); **8** Billy McConnell (BMW); **9** Michael Laverty (BMW); **10** Martin Jessopp (BMW); **11** Filip Backlund (Kawasaki); **12** Adam Jenkinson (Yamaha); **13** Ian Hutchinson (Kawasaki); **14** Josh Waters (Suzuki); **15** Chris Walker (Kawasaki).
Fastest lap: Linfoot, 1m 15.106s, 112.92mph/181.74km/h.

Race 2 (20 laps 47.120 miles/75.832km)
1 Josh Brookes (Yamaha), 25m 59.029s, 108.80mph/175.10km/h.
2 Shane Byrne (Kawasaki); **3** Luke Mossey (Kawasaki); **4** Tommy Bridewell (BMW); **5** Dan Linfoot (Honda); **6** Michael Laverty (BMW); **7** Howie Mainwaring Smart (Kawasaki); **8** Martin Jessopp (BMW); **9** Lee Jackson (BMW); **10** Josh Waters (Suzuki); **11** Ian Hutchinson (Kawasaki); **12** Chris Walker (Kawasaki); **13** Adam Jenkinson (Yamaha); **14** Filip Backlund (Kawasaki); **15** Billy McConnell (BMW).
Fastest lap: Brookes, 1m 14.884s, 113.26mph/182.27km/h.
Championship points: 1 Brookes, 266; **2** Byrne, 254; **3** Ellison, 147; **4** Easton, 139; **5** Laverty, 115; **6** Bridewell, 112.

Motorpoint British Supersport Championship & Supersport Evo, Rnd 7.
Race 1 (12 laps 28.272 miles/45.499km)
1 Luke Stapleford (Triumph), 15m 27.422s, 109.74mph/176.61km/h.
2 Kyle Ryde (Yamaha); **3** James Rispoli (Yamaha); **4** Sam Hornsey (Triumph); **5** Andy Reid (Yamaha); **6** Glenn Irwin (Kawasaki); **7** Luke Hedger (Kawasaki); **8** Ben Wilson (Kawasaki); **9** Danny Webb (Yamaha); **10** Jake Dixon (Triumph); **11** Marshall Neill (Yamaha), **12** Bjorn Estment (Triumph); **13** Jamie Perrin (Yamaha); **14** Joe Collier (Triumph); **15** Keith Farmer (MV Agusta).
Fastest lap: Rispoli, 1m 16.247s, 111.23mph/179.02km/h.

Race 2 (18 laps 42.408 miles/68.249km)
1 Luke Stapleford (Triumph), 23m 34.598s, 107.92mph/173.68km/h.
2 Andy Reid (Yamaha); **3** Jake Dixon (Triumph); **4** Glenn Irwin (Kawasaki); **5** Luke Hedger (Kawasaki); **6** Kyle Ryde (Yamaha); **7** Ben Wilson (Kawasaki); **8** Sam Hornsey (Triumph); **9** Danny Webb (Yamaha); **10** Dean Hipwell (Triumph); **11** Joe Collier (Triumph), **12** Jamie Perrin (Yamaha); **13** Bjorn Estment (Triumph); **14** Marshall Neill (Yamaha); **15** Matthew Paulo (Yamaha).
Fastest lap: Stapleford, 1m 16.432s, 110.96mph/178.58km/h.

Championship points: 1 Stapleford, 269; **2** Ryde, 241; **3** Irwin, 203; **4** Dixon, 162; **5** Reid, 130; **6** Rispoli, 116.

HEL British Motostar Championship, Rnd 7.
Race 1 (10 laps 23.560 miles/37.916km)
1 Taz Taylor (KTM), 13m 45.660s, 102.72mph/165.31km/h.
2 Scott Deroue (KTM); **3** Dani Saez (Repli-Cast Moto3); **4** Charlie Nesbitt (Repli-Cast Moto3); **5** Jake Archer (Honda); **6** Georgina Polden (KTM); **7** Alex Persson (Kalex KTM); **8** Mike Brouwers (Honda); **9** Edmund Best (Honda); **10** Jorel Boerboom (Kalex KTM); **11** Vasco Van Der Valk (Honda); **12** Elliot Lodge (Honda); **13** Joe Thomas (Honda); **14** Josh Owens (Honda); **15** Brian Slooten (Honda).
Fastest lap: Deroue, 1m 21.176s, 104.48mph/168.15km/h.

Race 2 (12 laps 28.272 miles/45.499km)
1 Scott Deroue (KTM), 16m 20.496s, 103.80mph/167.05km/h.
2 Charlie Nesbitt (Repli-Cast Moto3); **3** Dani Saez (Repli-Cast Moto3); **4** Taz Taylor (KTM); **5** Edward Rendell (Ten Kate Honda); **6** Jake Archer (Honda); **7** Alex Persson (Kalex KTM); **8** Jorel Boerboom (Kalex KTM); **9** Mike Brouwers (Honda); **10** Georgina Polden (KTM); **11** Edmund Best (Honda); **12** Vasco Van Der Valk (Honda); **13** Elliot Lodge (Honda); **14** Joe Thomas (Honda); **15** Richard Kerr (Honda).
Fastest lap: Nesbitt, 1m 20.252s, 105.68mph/170.08km/h.
Moto3 points: 1 Taylor, 264; **2** Deroue, 258; **3** Rendell, 177; **4** Saez, 148; **5** Nesbitt, 117; **6** Persson, 106.

CADWELL PARK, 23 August 2015, 2.180-mile/3.508km circuit.
MCE British Superbike Championship With Pirelli, Rnd 8 (2 x 18 laps, 39.240 miles/63.151km)
Race 1
1 Josh Brookes (Yamaha), 26m 58.694s, 87.27mph/140.45km/h.
2 Peter Hickman (BMW); **3** Billy McConnell (BMW); **4** Tommy Bridewell (BMW); **5** Michael Laverty (BMW); **6** Shane Byrne (Kawasaki); **7** Luke Mossey (Kawasaki); **8** Richard Cooper (BMW); **9** Christian Iddon (Suzuki); **10** Dan Linfoot (Honda); **11** Jack Kennedy (Kawasaki); **12** Lee Jackson (BMW); **13** James Westmoreland (Kawasaki); **14** Ryuichi Kiyonari (BMW); **15** Howie Mainwaring Smart (Kawasaki).
Fastest lap: Brookes, 1m 27.150s, 90.05mph/144.92km/h.

Race 2
1 Josh Brookes (Yamaha), 26m 19.043s, 89.46mph/143.97km/h.
2 Peter Hickman (BMW); **3** Tommy Bridewell (BMW); **4** Shane Byrne (Kawasaki); **5** Luke Mossey (Kawasaki); **6** Billy McConnell (BMW); **7** Richard Cooper (BMW); **8** Danny Buchan (Kawasaki); **9** James Westmoreland (Kawasaki); **10** Dan Linfoot (Honda); **11** Lee Jackson (BMW); **12** Martin Jessopp (BMW); **13** Christian Iddon (Suzuki); **14** Jack Kennedy (Kawasaki); **15** Chris Walker (Kawasaki).
Fastest lap: Brookes, 1m 26.911s, 90.30mph/145.32km/h.
Championship points: 1 Brookes, 316; **2** Byrne, 277; **3** Ellison, 147; **4** Bridewell, 141; **5** Easton, 139; **6** Laverty,126.

Motorpoint British Supersport Championship & Supersport Evo, Rnd 8.
Race 1 (10 laps 21.800 miles/35.084km)
1 Luke Stapleford (Triumph), 14m 58.862s, 87.31mph/140.51km/h.
2 Kyle Ryde (Yamaha); **3** Jake Dixon (Triumph); **4** James Rispoli (Yamaha); **5** Glenn Irwin (Kawasaki); **6** Andy Reid (Yamaha); **7** Ben Wilson (Kawasaki); **8** Luke Hedger (Kawasaki); **9** Matthew Paulo (Yamaha); **10** Bjorn Estment (Triumph); **11** Harry Hartley (Yamaha); **12** Joe Collier (Triumph); **13** Marshall Neill (Yamaha); **14** Sam Coventry (Kawasaki); **15** Freddy Pett (Triumph).
Fastest lap: Dixon, 1m 28.886s, 88.29mph/142.09km/h.

Race 2 (16 laps 34.880 miles/56.134km)
1 Jake Dixon (Triumph), 23m 54.029s, 87.56mph/140.91km/h.
2 Luke Stapleford (Triumph); **3** Kyle Ryde (Yamaha); **4** James Rispoli (Yamaha); **5** Ben Wilson (Kawasaki); **6** Luke Hedger (Kawasaki); **7** Glenn Irwin (Kawasaki); **8** Sam Hornsey (Triumph); **9** Matthew Paulo (Yamaha); **10** Harry Hartley (Yamaha); **11** Marshall Neill (Yamaha), **12** Danny Webb (Yamaha); **13** Keith Farmer (MV Agusta); **14** Dean Hipwell (Triumph); **15** Josh Daley (Kawasaki).
Fastest lap: Stapleford, 1m 28.746s, 88.43mph/142.31km/h.
Championship points: 1 Stapleford, 314; **2** Ryde, 277; **3** Irwin, 223; **4** Dixon, 203; **5** Rispoli, 142; **6** Reid, 140.

HEL British Motostar Championship, Rnd 8 (2 x 10 laps 21.800 miles/35.084km)
Race 1
1 Taz Taylor (KTM), 15m 47.175s, 82.85mph/133.33km/h.
2 Scott Deroue (KTM); **3** Charlie Nesbitt (Repli-Cast Moto3); **4** Jake Archer (Honda); **5** Jorel Boerboom (Kalex KTM); **6** Vasco Van Der Valk (Honda); **7** Edmund Best (Honda); **8** Mike Brouwers (Honda); **9** Elliot Lodge (Honda); **10** Brian Slooten (Honda); **11** Georgina Polden (KTM); **12** Cameron Horsman (EE125); **13** Tomas De Vries (Honda); **14** Josh Owens (Honda); **15** Richard Kerr (Honda).
Fastest lap: Nesbitt, 1m 33.217s, 84.19mph/135.49km/h.

Race 2
1 Scott Deroue (KTM), 17m 36.550s, 74.28mph/119.54km/h.
2 Jorel Boerboom (Kalex KTM); **3** Richard Kerr (Honda); **4** Jake Archer (Honda); **5** Vasco Van Der Valk (Honda); **6** Mike Brouwers (Honda); **7** Elliot Lodge (Honda); **8** Georgina Polden (KTM); **9** Tomas De Vries (Honda); **10** Edmund Best (Honda); **11** Brian Slooten (Honda); **12** TJ Toms (Repli-Cast Moto3); **13** Josh Owens (Honda); **14** Andrew Sawford (Aprilia); **15** Joe Thomas (Honda).
Fastest lap: Deroue, 1m 41.616s, 77.23mph/124.29km/h.
Championship points: 1 Deroue, 303; **2** Taylor, 289; **3** Rendell, 177; **4** Saez, 148; **5** Boerboom, 136; **6** Nesbitt, 133.

OULTON PARK, 6 September 2015, 2.692-mile/4.332km circuit.
MCE British Superbike Championship With Pirelli, Rnd 9 (3 x 18 laps, 48.456 miles/77.982km)
Race 1
1 Shane Byrne (Kawasaki), 28m 48.122s, 100.94mph/162.45km/h.
2 James Ellison (Kawasaki); **3** Danny Buchan (Kawasaki); **4** Josh Brookes (Yamaha); **5** Dan Linfoot (Honda); **6** Luke Mossey (Kawasaki); **7** Richard Cooper (BMW); **8** Lee Jackson (BMW); **9** Michael Laverty (BMW); **10** Peter Hickman (BMW); **11** Chris Walker (Kawasaki); **12** Martin Jessopp (BMW); **13** Filip Backlund (Kawasaki); **14** Josh Waters (Suzuki); **15** Ryuichi Kiyonari (BMW).
Fastest lap: Byrne, 1m 35.158s, 101.84mph/163.90km/h.

Race 2
1 Josh Brookes (Yamaha), 28m 40.621s, 101.38mph/163.16km/h.
2 Danny Buchan (Kawasaki); **3** Dan Linfoot (Honda); **4** Luke Mossey (Kawasaki); **5** James Ellison (Kawasaki); **6** Peter Hickman (BMW); **7** Michael Laverty (BMW); **8** Richard Cooper (BMW); **9** Christian Iddon (Suzuki); **10** James Westmoreland (Kawasaki); **11** Lee Jackson (BMW); **12** Ryuichi Kiyonari (BMW); **13** Chris Walker (Kawasaki); **14** Martin Jessopp (BMW); **15** Josh Waters (Suzuki).
Fastest lap: Brookes, 1m 34.607s, 102.43mph/164.85km/h.

Race 3
1 Shane Byrne (Kawasaki), 29m 36.071s, 98.21mph/158.05km/h.
2 Josh Brookes (Yamaha); **3** Tommy Bridewell (BMW); **4** Danny Buchan (Kawasaki); **5** James Ellison (Kawasaki); **6** Dan Linfoot (Honda); **7** Richard Cooper (BMW); **8** Christian Iddon (Suzuki); **9** Ryuichi Kiyonari (BMW); **10** Howie Mainwaring Smart (Kawasaki); **11** Luke Mossey (Kawasaki); **12** Michael Laverty (BMW); **13** Lee Jackson (BMW); **14** James Westmoreland (Kawasaki); **15** Billy McConnell (BMW).
Fastest lap: Brookes, 1m 34.483s, 102.57mph/165.07km/h.

The top six BSB riders in points after Oulton Park qualified for 'The Showdown', to decide the championship over the last three rounds. These title fighters had their points equalised at 500 and then podium credits added from their main season results (5 points for each 1st place, 3 points for 2nd, 1 point for 3rd).

Championship points for start of Showdown: 1 Brookes, 553; **2** Byrne, 551; **3** Ellison, 522; **4** Bridewell, 507; **5** Linfoot, 507; **6** Laverty, 500.

Motorpoint British Supersport Championship & Supersport Evo, Rnd 9.
Race 1 (12 laps 32.304 miles/51.988km)
1 Andy Reid (Yamaha), 19m 44.933s, 98.14mph/157.94km/h.
2 Jake Dixon (Triumph); **3** Luke Stapleford (Triumph); **4** Sam Hornsey (Triumph); **5** James Rispoli (Yamaha); **6** Ben Wilson (Kawasaki); **7** Harry Hartley (Yamaha); **8** Luke Hedger (Kawasaki); **9** Danny Webb (Yamaha); **10** Joe Collier (Triumph); **11** Marshall Neill (Yamaha), **12** Matthew Paulo (Yamaha); **13** Bjorn Estment (Triumph); **14** Sam Coventry (Kawasaki); **15** Keith Farmer (MV Agusta).
Fastest lap: Reid, 1m 37.666s, 99.22mph/159.69km/h.

Race 2 (15 laps 40.380 miles/64.985km)
1 Jake Dixon (Triumph), 25m 37.676s, 94.53mph/152.13km/h.
2 James Rispoli (Yamaha); **3** Luke Stapleford (Triumph); **4** Glenn Irwin (Kawasaki); **5** Ben Wilson (Kawasaki); **6** Luke Hedger (Kawasaki); **7** Dean Hipwell (Triumph); **8** Keith Farmer (MV Agusta); **9** Joe Collier (Triumph); **10** Matthew Paulo (Yamaha); **11** Marshall Neill (Yamaha), **12** Sam Coventry (Kawasaki); **13** Bjorn Estment (Triumph); **14** Niall Campbell (Yamaha); **15** Tommy Philp (Yamaha).
Fastest lap: Stapleford, 1m 37.360s, 99.54mph/160.19km/h.
Championship points: 1 Stapleford, 346; **2** Ryde, 277; **3** Dixon, 248; **4** Irwin, 236; **5** Rispoli, 173; **6** Reid, 165.

HEL British Motostar Championship, Rnd 9 (12 laps 32.304 miles/51.988km)
1 Scott Deroue (KTM), 21m 9.954s, 91.57mph/147.37km/h.
2 Jake Archer (Honda); **3** Charlie Nesbitt (Repli-Cast Moto3); **4** Dani Saez (Repli-Cast Moto3); **5** Jorel Boerboom (Kalex KTM); **6** Edward Rendell (Ten Kate Honda); **7** Vasco Van Der Valk (Honda); **8** Mike Brouwers (Honda); **9** Georgina Polden (KTM); **10** Brian Slooten (Honda); **11** Elliot Lodge (Honda); **12** Cameron Horsman (EE125); **13** TJ Toms (Repli-Cast Moto3); **14** Wesley Jonker (Luyten Honda); **15** Liam Delves (Honda).
Fastest lap: Taylor, 1m 44.044s, 93.14mph/149.90km/h.
Moto3 points: 1 Deroue, 328; **2** Taylor, 289; **3** Rendell, 187; **4** Saez, 161; **5** Nesbitt, 149; **6** Boerboom, 147.

ASSEN, 20 September 2015, 2.822-mile/4.452km circuit.
MCE British Superbike Championship With Pirelli, Rnd 10.
Race 1 (18 laps 50.796 miles/81.748km)
1 Josh Brookes (Yamaha), 29m 24.231s, 103.66mph/166.82km/h.
2 James Ellison (Kawasaki); **3** Michael Laverty (BMW); **4** Shane Byrne (Kawasaki); **5** John Hopkins (Ducati); **6** Richard Cooper (BMW); **7** Christian Iddon (Suzuki); **8** Tommy Bridewell (BMW); **9** Peter Hickman (BMW); **10** Danny Buchan (Kawasaki); **11** Billy McConnell (BMW); **12** Lee Jackson (BMW); **13** Jack Kennedy (Kawasaki); **14** Dan Linfoot (Honda); **15** Josh Waters (Suzuki).
Fastest lap: Brookes, 1m 36.904s, 104.84mph/168.73km/h.

Race 2 (15 laps 42.330 miles/68.124km)
1 Josh Brookes (Yamaha), 25m 48.595s, 98.41mph/158.38km/h.
2 James Ellison (Kawasaki); **3** Luke Mossey (Kawasaki); **4** Richard Cooper (BMW); **5** Shane Byrne (Kawasaki); **6** Christian Iddon (Suzuki); **7** Jack Kennedy (Kawasaki); **8** Chris Walker (Kawasaki); **9** Michael Laverty (BMW); **10** Jakub Smrz (Yamaha); **11** John Hopkins (Ducati); **12** Danny Buchan (Kawasaki); **13** Peter Hickman (BMW); **14** Josh Waters (Suzuki); **15** Martin Jessopp (BMW).
Fastest lap: Brookes, 1m 37.719s, 103.97mph/167.32km/h.
Championship points: 1 Brookes, 603; **2** Byrne, 575; **3** Ellison, 562; **4** Laverty, 523; **5** Bridewell, 515; **6** Linfoot, 509.

Motorpoint British Supersport Championship & Supersport Evo, Rnd 10.
Race 1 (12 laps 33.864 miles/54.499km)
1 Luke Stapleford (Triumph), 20m 3.229s, 101.32mph/163.06km/h.
2 James Rispoli (Yamaha); **3** Jake Dixon (Triumph); **4** Sam Hornsey (Triumph); **5** Glenn Irwin (Kawasaki); **6** Kyle Ryde (Yamaha); **7** Ben Wilson (Kawasaki); **8** Danny Webb (Yamaha); **9** Joe Francis (Yamaha); **10** Ben Stafford (Kawasaki); **11** Marshall Neill (Yamaha), **12** Dean Hipwell (Triumph); **13** David Allingham (MV Agusta); **14** Freddy Pett (Triumph); **15** Cliff Kloots (Yamaha).
Fastest lap: Stapleford, 1m 39.159s, 102.46mph/164.89km/h.

Race 2 (13 laps 36.686 miles/59.04km)
1 Luke Stapleford (Triumph), 23m 21.260s, 94.25mph/151.68km/h.
2 Jake Dixon (Triumph); **3** Glenn Irwin (Kawasaki); **4** Sam Hornsey (Triumph); **5** Kyle Ryde (Yamaha); **6** Ben Wilson (Kawasaki); **7** Danny Webb (Yamaha); **8** Joe Francis (Yamaha); **9** Luke Hedger (Kawasaki); **10** Marshall Neill (Yamaha); **11** Dean Hipwell (Triumph), **12** Harry Hartley (Yamaha); **13** Matthew Paulo (Yamaha); **14** Joe Collier (Triumph); **15** Matt Truelove (Yamaha).
Fastest lap: Stapleford, 1m 39.966s, 101.63mph/163.56km/h.
Championship points: 1 Stapleford, 396; **2** Ryde, 298; **3** Dixon, 284; **4** Irwin, 263; **5** Rispoli, 193; **6** Reid, 165.

HEL British Motostar Championship, Rnd 10.
Race 1 (10 laps 28.220 miles/45.416km)
1 Taz Taylor (KTM), 18m 1.393s, 93.95mph/151.2km/h.
2 Scott Deroue (KTM); **3** Dani Saez (Repli-Cast Moto3); **4** Ernst Dubbink (Honda); **5** Jake Archer (Honda); **6** Jorel Boerboom (Kalex KTM); **7** Mike Brouwers (Honda); **8** Vasco Van Der Valk (Honda); **9** Edward Rendell (Ten Kate Honda); **10** Charlie Nesbitt (Repli-Cast Moto3); **11** Brian Slooten (Honda); **12** Dennis Koopman (Honda); **13** Christoph Beinlich (Honda); **14** Elliot Lodge (Honda); **15** Georgina Polden (KTM).
Fastest lap: Taylor, 1m 46.526s, 95.37mph/153.49km/h.

Race 2 (6 laps 16.932 miles/27.249km)
1 Scott Deroue (KTM), 11m 22.856s, 89.27mph/143.67km/h.
2 Edward Rendell (Ten Kate Honda); **3** Jorel Boerboom (Kalex KTM); **4** Jake Archer (Honda); **5** Dani Saez (Repli-Cast Moto3); **6** Vasco Van Der Valk (Honda); **7** Mike Brouwers (Honda); **8** Georgina Polden (KTM); **9** Ernst Dubbink (Honda); **10** Cameron Horsman (EE125); **11** Elliot Lodge (Honda); **12** Brian Slooten (Honda); **13** Josh Owens (Honda); **14** Walid Soppe (Honda); **15** Joe Thomas (Honda).
Fastest lap: Deroue, 1m 52.061s, 90.66mph/145.91km/h.
Moto3 points: 1 Deroue, 373; **2** Taylor, 314; **3** Rendell, 214; **4** Saez, 188; **5** Boerboom, 173; **6** Nesbitt, 155.

SILVERSTONE, 4 October 2015, 3.667-mile/5.902km circuit.
MCE British Superbike Championship With Pirelli, Rnd 11 (2 x 14 laps, 51.338 miles/82.621km)
Race 1
1 Josh Brookes (Yamaha), 29m 33.139s, 104.24mph/167.76km/h.
2 Shane Byrne (Kawasaki); **3** Peter Hickman (BMW); **4** John Hopkins (Ducati); **5** James Ellison (Kawasaki); **6** Michael Laverty (BMW); **7** Dan Linfoot (Honda); **8** Christian Iddon (Suzuki); **9** Tommy Bridewell (BMW); **10** Jakub Smrz (Yamaha); **11** Lee Jackson (BMW); **12** Richard Cooper (BMW); **13** Billy McConnell (BMW); **14** Howie Mainwaring Smart (Kawasaki); **15** Josh Waters (Suzuki).
Fastest lap: Byrne, 2m 5.458s, 105.23mph/169.35km/h.

Race 2
1 Josh Brookes (Yamaha), 25m 35.464s, 104.10mph/167.53km/h.
2 Michael Laverty (BMW); **3** Dan Linfoot (Honda); **4** Christian Iddon (Suzuki); **5** Shane Byrne (Kawasaki); **6** Richard Cooper (BMW); **7** Tommy Bridewell (BMW); **8** Peter Hickman (BMW); **9** Lee Jackson (BMW); **10** Luke Mossey (Kawasaki); **11** Howie Mainwaring Smart (Kawasaki); **12** Luke Stapleford (Kawasaki); **13** Jakub Smrz (Yamaha); **14** Danny Buchan (Kawasaki); **15** Julien Da Costa (Honda).
Fastest lap: Ellison, 2m 5.267s, 105.39mph/169.61km/h.
Championship points: 1 Brookes, 653; **2** Byrne, 606; **3** Ellison, 573; **4** Laverty, 553; **5** Linfoot, 534; **6** Bridewell, 531.

Motorpoint British Supersport Championship & Supersport Evo, Rnd 11.
Race 1 (10 laps 36.670 miles/59.015km)
1 Luke Stapleford (Triumph), 21m 33.693s, 102.05mph/164.23km/h.
2 James Rispoli (Yamaha); **3** Glenn Irwin (Kawasaki); **4** Jake Dixon (Triumph); **5** Kyle Ryde (Yamaha); **6** Sam Hornsey (Triumph); **7** Ben Wilson (Kawasaki); **8** Joe Francis (Yamaha); **9** Luke Hedger (Kawasaki); **10** Joe Collier (Triumph); **11** Marshall Neill (Yamaha), **12** Jamie Perrin (Yamaha); **13** Matthew Paulo (Yamaha); **14** Dean Hipwell (Triumph); **15** Freddy Pett (Triumph).
Fastest lap: Stapleford, 2m 8.571s, 102.68mph/165.25km/h.

Race 2 (12 laps 44.004 miles/70.818km)
1 Glenn Irwin (Kawasaki), 26m 14.896s, 100.59mph/161.88km/h.
2 James Rispoli (Yamaha); **3** Sam Hornsey (Triumph); **4** Ben Wilson (Kawasaki); **5** Kyle Ryde (Yamaha); **6** Luke Hedger (Kawasaki); **7** Danny Webb (Yamaha); **8** Joe Francis (Yamaha); **9** Jamie Perrin (Yamaha); **10** Marshall Neill (Yamaha); **11** Joe Collier (Triumph), **12** Freddy Pett (Triumph); **13** Sam Coventry (Kawasaki); **14** Matthew Paulo (Yamaha); **15** Dean Hipwell (Triumph).
Fastest lap: Rispoli, 2m 9.010s, 102.33mph/164.69km/h.
Championship points: 1 Stapleford, 421; **2** Ryde, 320; **3** Irwin, 304; **4** Dixon, 297; **5** Rispoli, 233; **6** Reid, 165.

HEL British Motostar Championship, Rnd 11.
Race 1 (8 laps 29.336 miles/47.212km)
1 Scott Deroue (KTM), 18m 40.784s, 94.23mph/151.65km/h.
2 Taz Taylor (KTM); **3** Edward Rendell (Ten Kate Honda); **4** Jake Archer (Honda); **5** Jorel Boerboom (Kalex KTM); **6** Vasco Van Der Valk (Honda); **7** Elliot Lodge (Honda); **8** Mike Brouwers (Honda); **9** Brian Slooten (Honda); **10** Georgina Polden (KTM); **11** Edmund Best (Honda); **12** Josh Owens (Honda); **13** Tomas De Vries (Honda); **14** Wesley Jonker (Luyten Honda); **15** Richard Kerr (Honda).
Fastest lap: Archer, 2m 19.341s, 94.74mph/152.48km/h.

Race 2 (10 laps 36.670 miles/59.020km)
1 Scott Deroue (KTM), 23m 7.481s, 95.15mph/153.13km/h.
2 Taz Taylor (KTM); **3** Edward Rendell (Ten Kate Honda); **4** Jorel Boerboom (Kalex KTM); **5** Vasco Van Der Valk (Honda); **6** Jake Archer (Honda); **7** Elliot Lodge (Honda); **8** Brian Slooten (Honda); **9** Mike Brouwers (Honda); **10** Georgina Polden (KTM); **11** Richard Kerr (Honda); **12** Tomas De

Vries (Honda); **13** Josh Owens (Honda); **14** Joe Thomas (Honda); **15** Edmund Best (Honda).
Fastest lap: Deroue, 2m 17.574s, 95.96mph/154.44km/h.
Moto3 points: 1 Deroue, 423; **2** Taylor, 354; **3** Rendell, 246; **4** Boerboom, 197; **5** Saez, 188; **6** Nesbitt, 155.

BRANDS HATCH GP, 18 October 2015, 2.433-mile/3.9126km circuit.
MCE British Superbike Championship With Pirelli, Rnd 12.
Race 1 (20 laps 48.660 miles/78.311km)
1 Josh Brookes (Yamaha), 28m 52.991s, 101.09mph/162.69km/h.
2 Shane Byrne (Kawasaki); **3** John Hopkins (Ducati); **4** Christian Iddon (Suzuki); **5** Lee Jackson (BMW); **6** James Ellison (Kawasaki); **7** Luke Mossey (Kawasaki); **8** Danny Buchan (Kawasaki); **9** Michael Laverty (BMW); **10** Jakub Smrz (Yamaha); **11** Tommy Bridewell (BMW); **12** Peter Hickman (BMW); **13** Dan Linfoot (Honda); **14** Howie Mainwaring Smart (Kawasaki); **15** Billy McConnell (BMW).
Fastest lap: Brookes, 1m 25.500s, 102.45mph/164.88km/h.

Race 2 (19 laps 46.227 miles/74.395km)
1 Josh Brookes (Yamaha), 27m 26.648s, 101.07mph/162.66km/h.
2 Shane Byrne (Kawasaki); **3** Michael Laverty (BMW); **4** John Hopkins (Ducati); **5** James Ellison (Kawasaki); **6** Lee Jackson (BMW); **7** Luke Mossey (Kawasaki); **8** Christian Iddon (Suzuki); **9** Danny Buchan (Kawasaki); **10** Dan Linfoot (Honda); **11** Tommy Bridewell (BMW); **12** Peter Hickman (BMW); **13** Howie Mainwaring Smart (Kawasaki); **14** Jakub Smrz (Yamaha); **15** Martin Jessopp (BMW).
Fastest lap: Brookes, 1m 25.959s, 101.90mph/164.00km/h.

Race 3 (20 laps 48.660 miles/78.311km)
1 Michael Laverty (BMW), 28m 58.931s, 100.74mph/162.13km/h.
2 James Ellison (Kawasaki); **3** Shane Byrne (Kawasaki); **4** Dan Linfoot (Honda); **5** Christian Iddon (Suzuki); **6** Luke Mossey (Kawasaki); **7** Danny Buchan (Kawasaki); **8** John Hopkins (Ducati); **9** Jakub Smrz (Yamaha); **10** Howie Mainwaring Smart (Kawasaki); **11** Peter Hickman (BMW); **12** Tommy Bridewell (BMW); **13** Martin Jessopp (BMW); **14** Luke Stapleford (Kawasaki); **15** Robbin Harms (Kawasaki).
Fastest lap: Mainwaring Smart, 1m 26.207s, 101.61mph/163.53km/h.

Motorpoint British Supersport Championship & Supersport Evo, Rnd 12.
Race 1 (7 laps 17.031 miles/27.409km)
1 Luke Stapleford (Triumph), 10m 24.068s, 98.25mph/158.12km/h.
2 Jake Dixon (Triumph); **3** Sam Hornsey (Triumph); **4** James Rispoli (Yamaha); **5** Kyle Ryde (Yamaha); **6** Joe Francis (Yamaha); **7** Ben Wilson (Kawasaki); **8** Joe Collier (Triumph); **9** Luke Hedger (Kawasaki); **10** Jamie Perrin (Yamaha); **11** Bjorn Estment (Triumph); **12** Marshall Neill (Yamaha); **13** Danny Webb (Yamaha); **14** Matthew Paulo (Yamaha); **15** Sam Coventry (Kawasaki).
Fastest lap: Stapleford, 1m 27.927s, 99.62mph/160.33km/h.

Race 2 (18 laps 43.794 miles/70.480km)
1 Luke Stapleford (Triumph), 26m 34.884s, 98.86mph/159.1km/h.
2 Jake Dixon (Triumph); **3** Glenn Irwin (Kawasaki); **4** Kyle Ryde (Yamaha); **5** Ben Wilson (Kawasaki); **6** James Rispoli (Yamaha); **7** Joe Francis (Yamaha); **8** Luke Hedger (Yamaha); **9** Danny Webb (Yamaha); **10** Joe Collier (Triumph); **11** Jamie Perrin (Yamaha); **12** Bjorn Estment (Triumph); **13** Sam Coventry (Yamaha); **14** Sam Thompson (Triumph); **15** Freddy Pett (Triumph).
Fastest lap: Stapleford, 1m 27.675s, 99.91mph/160.79km/h.

HEL British Motostar Championship, Rnd 12.
Race 1 (10 laps 24.330 miles/39.155km)
1 Taz Taylor (Honda), 16m 2.625s, 90.99mph/146.43km/h.
2 Scott Deroue (KTM); **3** Dani Saez (Repli-Cast Moto3); **4** Edward Rendell (Ten Kate Honda); **5** Mike Brouwers (Honda); **6** Jake Archer (Honda); **7** Vasco Van Der Valk (Honda); **8** Jorel Boerboom (Kalex KTM); **9** Elliot Lodge (Honda); **10** Chris Taylor (KTM); **11** Charlie Nesbitt (Repli-Cast Moto3); **12** Bradley Ray (EE125); **13** Brian Slooten (Honda); **14** Ryan Longshaw (Kalex KTM); **15** Christoph Beinlich (Honda).
Fastest lap: Deroue, 1m 34.719s, 92.48mph/148.83km/h.

Race 2 (12 laps 29.196 miles/46.986km)
1 Scott Deroue (KTM), 19m 5.532s, 91.76mph/147.67km/h.
2 Taz Taylor (Honda); **3** Dani Saez (Repli-Cast Moto3); **4** Jorel Boerboom (Kalex KTM); **5** Charlie Nesbitt (Repli-Cast Moto3); **6** Vasco Van Der Valk (Honda); **7** Elliot Lodge (Honda); **8** Bradley Ray (EE125); **9** Brian Slooten (Honda); **10** Chris Taylor (KTM); **11** Ryan Longshaw (Kalex KTM); **12** Georgina Polden (KTM); **13** Tomas De Vries (Honda); **14** Josh Owens (Honda); **15** Joe Thomas (Honda).

Fastest lap: Taylor, 1m 33.605s, 93.58mph/150.60km/h.

Final British Superbike Championship points:
1	Josh Brookes,	703
2	Shane Byrne,	662
3	James Ellison,	614
4	Michael Laverty,	601
5	Dan Linfoot,	556
6	Tommy Bridewell,	545

7 Luke Mossey, 168; **8** Richard Cooper, 156; **9** Peter Hickman, 150; **10** Christian Iddon, 146; **11** Stuart Easton, 139; **12** Danny Buchan, 125; **13** Jason O'Halloran, 103; **14** Lee Jackson, 101; **15** Billy McConnell, 98.

Final British Supersport Championship points:
1	Luke Stapleford,	471
2	Kyle Ryde,	344
3	Jake Dixon,	337
4	Glenn Irwin,	320
5	James Rispoli,	256
6	Ben Wilson,	185

7 Sam Hornsey, 181; **8** Luke Hedger, 168; **9** Andy Reid, 165; **10** Joe Collier, 147; **11** Danny Webb, 135; **12** Marshall Neill, 97; **13** Dean Hipwell, 87; **14** Matthew Paulo, 64; **15** Jamie Perrin, 64.

Final British Motostar Moto3 Championship points:
1	Scott Deroue,	473
2	Taz Taylor,	354
3	Edward Rendell,	262
4	Dani Saez,	228
5	Jorel Boerboom,	222
6	Charlie Nesbitt,	174

7 Jake Archer, 162; **8** Vasco Van Der Walk, 158; **9** Elliot Lodge, 143; **10** Georgina Polden, 121; **11** Mike Brouwers, 119; **12** Alex Persson, 106; **13** Brian Slooten, 105; **14** Joe Thomas, 67; **15** Christoph Beinlich, 52.

Final British Motostar 125GP Championship points:
1	Josh Owens,	435
2	Mark Clayton,	270
3	Andrew Sawford,	255
4	Liam Delves,	249
5	Wesley Jonker,	246
6	Cameron Horsman,	228

7 Tasia Rodink, 183; **8** Stephen Campbell, 179; **9** Jamie Edwards, 176; **10** Jamie Ashby, 141; **11** Ryan Longshaw, 131; **12** Louis Valleley, 63; **13** Taz Taylor, 50; **14** David Wales, 46; **15** Bradley Ray, 40.

Supersport World Championship

PHILLIP ISLAND, Australia, 22 February 2015, 2.762-mile/4.445km circuit.
Supersport World Championship, Rnd 1 (18 laps, 49.716 miles/80.010km)
1 Jules Cluzel, FRA (MV Agusta), 28m 19.638s, 105.303mph/169.469km/h.
2 Lorenzo Zanetti, ITA (MV Agusta); **3** Gino Rea, GBR (Honda); **4** Kyle Smith, GBR (Honda); **5** Ratthapark Wilairot, THA (Honda); **6** Kenan Sofuoglu, TUR (Kawasaki); **7** Alex Baldolini, ITA (MV Agusta); **8** Roberto Rolfo, ITA (Honda); **9** Dominic Schmitter, SUI (Kawasaki); **10** Patrick Jacobsen, USA (Kawasaki); **11** Christian Gamarino, ITA (Kawasaki); **12** Marco Faccani, ITA (Kawasaki); **13** Aiden Wagner, AUS (Yamaha); **14** Glenn Scott, AUS (Honda); **15** Fabio Menghi, ITA (Yamaha).
Fastest lap: Kenan Sofuoglu, TUR (Kawasaki), 1m 33.409s, 106.448mph/171.311km/h.
Championship points: 1 Cluzel, 25; **2** Zanetti, 20; **3** Rea, 16; **4** Smith, 13; **5** Wilairot, 11; **6** Sofuoglu, 10.

BURIRAM, Thailand, 22 March 2015, 2.830-mile/4.554km circuit.
Supersport World Championship, Rnd 2 (17 laps, 48.105 miles/77.418km)
1 Ratthapark Wilairot, THA (Honda), 27m 57.523s, 103.235mph/166.141km/h.
2 Kenan Sofuoglu, TUR (Kawasaki); **3** Patrick Jacobsen, USA (Kawasaki); **4** Lucas Mahias, FRA (Kawasaki); **5** Ratthapong Wilairot, THA (Honda); **6** Roberto Rolfo, ITA (Honda); **7** Marco Faccani, ITA (Kawasaki); **8** Martin Cardenas, COL (Honda); **9** Alex Baldolini, ITA (MV Agusta); **10** Gino Rea, GBR (Honda); **11** Decha Kraisart, THA (Yamaha); **12** Kevin Wahr, GER (Honda); **13** Christian Gamarino, ITA (Kawasaki); **14** Glenn Scott, AUS (Honda); **15** Dominic Schmitter, SUI (Kawasaki).
Fastest lap: Jules Cluzel, FRA (MV Agusta), 1m 37.887s, 104.069mph/167.483km/h (record).
Championship points: 1 Wilairot, 36; **2** Sofuoglu, 30; **3** Cluzel, 25; **4** Jacobsen, 22; **5** Rea, 22; **6** Zanetti, 20.

ARAGON, Spain, 12 April 2015, 3.155-mile/5.077km circuit.
Supersport World Championship, Rnd 3 (16 laps, 50.475 miles/81.232km)
1 Kenan Sofuoglu, TUR (Kawasaki), 30m 47.195s, 98.371mph/158.313km/h.
2 Patrick Jacobsen, USA (Kawasaki); **3** Kyle Smith, GBR (Honda); **4** Gino Rea, GBR (Honda); **5** Lorenzo Zanetti, ITA (MV Agusta); **6** Alex Baldolini, ITA (MV Agusta); **7** Fabio Menghi, ITA (Yamaha); **8** Dominic Schmitter, SUI (Kawasaki); **9** Christian Gamarino, ITA (Kawasaki); **10** Roberto Rolfo, ITA (Honda); **11** Riccardo Russo, ITA (Honda); **12** Kevin Wahr, GER (Honda); **13** Vladimir Ivanov, RUS (Yamaha); **14** Marcos Ramirez, ESP (Yamaha); **15** Luigi Morciano, ITA (Honda).
Fastest lap: Patrick Jacobsen, USA (Kawasaki), 1m 54.605s, 99.096mph/159.480km/h (record).
Championship points: 1 Sofuoglu, 55; **2** Jacobsen, 42; **3** Wilairot, 36; **4** Rea, 35; **5** Zanetti, 31; **6** Smith, 29.

ASSEN, Holland, 19 April 2015, 2.822-mile/4.542km circuit.
Supersport World Championship, Rnd 4 (18 laps, 50.801 miles/81.756km)
1 Kenan Sofuoglu, TUR (Kawasaki), 29m 44.434s, 102.488mph/164.938km/h.
2 Jules Cluzel, FRA (MV Agusta); **3** Kyle Smith, GBR (Honda); **4** Patrick Jacobsen, USA (Kawasaki); **5** Roberto Rolfo, ITA (Honda); 6 Lorenzo Zanetti, ITA (MV Agusta); **7** Lucas Mahias, FRA (Kawasaki); **8** Marco Faccani, ITA (Kawasaki); **9** Alex Baldolini, ITA (MV Agusta); **10** Riccardo Russo, ITA (Honda); **11** Martin Cardenas, COL (Honda); **12** Fabio Menghi, ITA (Yamaha); **13** Dominic Schmitter, SUI (Kawasaki); **14** Gino Rea, GBR (Honda); **15** Luigi Morciano, ITA (Honda).
Fastest lap: Jules Cluzel, FRA (MV Agusta), 1m 38.184s, 103.481mph/166.536km/h (record).
Championship points: 1 Sofuoglu, 80; **2** Jacobsen, 55; **3** Cluzel, 45; **4** Smith, 45; **5** Zanetti, 41; **6** Rea, 37.

IMOLA, Italy, 10 May 2015, 3.067-mile/4.936km circuit.
Supersport World Championship, Rnd 5 (17 laps, 52.140 miles/83.912km)
1 Kenan Sofuoglu, TUR (Kawasaki), 31m 38.539s, 98.869mph/159.114km/h.
2 Jules Cluzel, FRA (MV Agusta); **3** Lorenzo Zanetti, ITA (MV Agusta); **4** Patrick Jacobsen, USA (Kawasaki); **5** Marco Faccani, ITA (Kawasaki); **6** Ratthapark Wilairot, THA (Honda); **7** Gino Rea, GBR (Honda); **8** Riccardo Russo, ITA (Honda); **9** Martin Cardenas, COL (Honda); **10** Roberto Rolfo, ITA (Honda); **11** Christian Gamarino, ITA (Kawasaki); **12** Fabio Menghi, ITA (Yamaha); **13** Dominic Schmitter, SUI (Kawasaki); **14** Aiden Wagner, AUS (Honda); **15** Kyle Smith, GBR (Honda).
Fastest lap: Jules Cluzel, FRA (MV Agusta), 1m 51.101s, 99.383mph/159.941km/h (record).
Championship points: 1 Sofuoglu, 105; **2** Jacobsen, 68; **3** Cluzel, 65; **4** Zanetti, 57; **5** Wilairot, 46; **6** Smith, 46.

DONINGTON PARK, Great Britain, 24 May 2015, 2.500-mile/4.023km circuit.
Supersport World Championship, Rnd 6 (20 laps, 49.996 miles/80.460km)
1 Kenan Sofuoglu, TUR (Kawasaki), 30m 20.711s, 98.853mph/159.089km/h.
2 Jules Cluzel, FRA (MV Agusta); **3** Kyle Ryde, GBR (Yamaha); **4** Lorenzo Zanetti, ITA (MV Agusta); **5** Patrick Jacobsen, USA (Kawasaki); **6** Luke Stapleford (Triumph); **7** Sam Hornsey, GBR (Triumph); **8** Gino Rea, GBR (Honda); **9** Niki Tuuli, FIN (Yamaha); **10** Andy Reid, GBR (Honda); **11** Roberto Rolfo, ITA (Honda); **12** Riccardo Russo, ITA (Honda); **13** Martin Cardenas, COL (Honda); **14** Christian Gamarino, ITA (Kawasaki); **15** Kieran Clarke, GBR (Honda).
Fastest lap: Jules Cluzel, FRA (MV Agusta), 1m 30.425s, 99.521mph/160.164km/h.
Championship points: 1 Sofuoglu, 130; **2** Cluzel, 85; **3** Jacobsen, 79; **4** Zanetti, 70; **5** Rea, 54; **6** Wilairot, 46.

PORTIMAO, Portugal, 7 June 2015, 2.853-mile/4.592km circuit.
Supersport World Championship, Rnd 7 (18 laps, 51.360 miles/82.656km)
1 Jules Cluzel, FRA (MV Agusta), 31m 54.954s, 96.554mph/155.388km/h.
2 Kenan Sofuoglu, TUR (Kawasaki); **3** Patrick Jacobsen, USA (Honda); **4** Gino Rea, GBR (Honda); **5** Lorenzo Zanetti, ITA (MV Agusta); **6** Kyle Smith, GBR (Honda); **7** Christian Gamarino, ITA (Kawasaki); **8** Roberto Rolfo, ITA (Honda); **9** Martin Cardenas, COL (Honda); **10** Fabio Menghi, ITA (Yamaha); **11** Marcos Ramirez, ESP (Honda); **12** Marco Faccani, ITA (Kawasaki); **13** Glenn Scott, AUS (Honda); **14** Dominic Schmitter, SUI (Kawasaki); **15** Miguel Praia, POR (Honda).
Fastest lap: Kenan Sofuoglu, TUR (Kawasaki), 1m 45.411s, 97.447mph/156.826km/h.
Championship points: 1 Sofuoglu, 150; **2** Cluzel, 110; **3** Jacobsen, 95; **4** Zanetti, 81; **5** Rea, 67; **6** Smith, 56.

MISANO, Italy, 21 June 2015, 2.626mile/4.226km circuit.
Supersport World Championship, Rnd 8 (19 laps, 49.892 miles/80.294km)
1 Jules Cluzel, FRA (MV Agusta), 31m 19.621s, 95.558mph/153.785km/h.
2 Patrick Jacobsen, USA (Honda); **3** Lorenzo Zanetti, ITA (MV Agusta); **4** Gino Rea, GBR (Honda); **5** Alex Baldolini, ITA (MV Agusta); **6**

Smith, GBR (Honda); **4** Gino Rea, GBR (Honda); **5** Lorenzo Zanetti, ITA (MV Agusta); **6** Alex Baldolini, ITA (MV Agusta); **7** Fabio Menghi, ITA (Yamaha); **8** Dominic Schmitter, SUI (Kawasaki); **9** Christian Gamarino, ITA (Kawasaki); **10** Roberto Rolfo, ITA (Honda); **11** Riccardo Russo, ITA (Honda); **12** Kevin Wahr, GER (Honda); **13** Vladimir Ivanov, RUS (Yamaha); **14** Marcos Ramirez, ESP (Yamaha); **15** Luigi Morciano, ITA (Honda).
Fastest lap: Patrick Jacobsen, USA (Kawasaki), 1m 54.605s, 99.096mph/159.480km/h (record).
Championship points: 1 Sofuoglu, 55; **2** Jacobsen, 42; **3** Wilairot, 36; **4** Rea, 35; **5** Zanetti, 31; **6** Smith, 29.

ASSEN, Holland, 19 April 2015, 2.822-mile/4.542km circuit.
Supersport World Championship, Rnd 4 (18 laps, 50.801 miles/81.756km)
1 Kenan Sofuoglu, TUR (Kawasaki), 29m 44.434s, 102.488mph/164.938km/h.
2 Jules Cluzel, FRA (MV Agusta); **3** Kyle Smith, GBR (Honda); **4** Patrick Jacobsen, USA (Kawasaki); **5** Roberto Rolfo, ITA (Honda); 6 Lorenzo Zanetti, ITA (MV Agusta); **7** Lucas Mahias, FRA (Kawasaki); **8** Marco Faccani, ITA (Kawasaki); **9** Alex Baldolini, ITA (MV Agusta); **10** Riccardo Russo, ITA (Honda); **11** Martin Cardenas, COL (Honda); **12** Fabio Menghi, ITA (Yamaha); **13** Dominic Schmitter, SUI (Kawasaki); **14** Gino Rea, GBR (Honda); **15** Luigi Morciano, ITA (Honda).
Fastest lap: Jules Cluzel, FRA (MV Agusta), 1m 38.184s, 103.481mph/166.536km/h (record).
Championship points: 1 Sofuoglu, 80; **2** Jacobsen, 55; **3** Cluzel, 45; **4** Smith, 45; **5** Zanetti, 41; **6** Rea, 37.

IMOLA, Italy, 10 May 2015, 3.067-mile/4.936km circuit.
Supersport World Championship, Rnd 5 (17 laps, 52.140 miles/83.912km)
1 Kenan Sofuoglu, TUR (Kawasaki), 31m 38.539s, 98.869mph/159.114km/h.
2 Jules Cluzel, FRA (MV Agusta); **3** Lorenzo Zanetti, ITA (MV Agusta); **4** Patrick Jacobsen, USA (Kawasaki); **5** Marco Faccani, ITA (Kawasaki); **6** Ratthapark Wilairot, THA (Honda); **7** Gino Rea, GBR (Honda); **8** Riccardo Russo, ITA (Honda); **9** Martin Cardenas, COL (Honda); **10** Roberto Rolfo, ITA (Honda); **11** Christian Gamarino, ITA (Kawasaki); **12** Fabio Menghi, ITA (Yamaha); **13** Dominic Schmitter, SUI (Kawasaki); **14** Aiden Wagner, AUS (Honda); **15** Kyle Smith, GBR (Honda).
Fastest lap: Jules Cluzel, FRA (MV Agusta), 1m 51.101s, 99.383mph/159.941km/h (record).
Championship points: 1 Sofuoglu, 105; **2** Jacobsen, 68; **3** Cluzel, 65; **4** Zanetti, 57; **5** Wilairot, 46; **6** Smith, 46.

DONINGTON PARK, Great Britain, 24 May 2015, 2.500-mile/4.023km circuit.
Supersport World Championship, Rnd 6 (20 laps, 49.996 miles/80.460km)
1 Kenan Sofuoglu, TUR (Kawasaki), 30m 20.711s, 98.853mph/159.089km/h.
2 Jules Cluzel, FRA (MV Agusta); **3** Kyle Ryde, GBR (Yamaha); **4** Lorenzo Zanetti, ITA (MV Agusta); **5** Patrick Jacobsen, USA (Kawasaki); **6** Luke Stapleford (Triumph); **7** Sam Hornsey, GBR (Triumph); **8** Gino Rea, GBR (Honda); **9** Niki Tuuli, FIN (Yamaha); **10** Andy Reid, GBR (Honda); **11** Roberto Rolfo, ITA (Honda); **12** Riccardo Russo, ITA (Honda); **13** Martin Cardenas, COL (Honda); **14** Christian Gamarino, ITA (Kawasaki); **15** Kieran Clarke, GBR (Honda).
Fastest lap: Jules Cluzel, FRA (MV Agusta), 1m 30.425s, 99.521mph/160.164km/h.
Championship points: 1 Sofuoglu, 130; **2** Cluzel, 85; **3** Jacobsen, 79; **4** Zanetti, 70; **5** Rea, 54; **6** Wilairot, 46.

PORTIMAO, Portugal, 7 June 2015, 2.853-mile/4.592km circuit.
Supersport World Championship, Rnd 7 (18 laps, 51.360 miles/82.656km)
1 Jules Cluzel, FRA (MV Agusta), 31m 54.954s, 96.554mph/155.388km/h.
2 Kenan Sofuoglu, TUR (Kawasaki); **3** Patrick Jacobsen, USA (Honda); **4** Gino Rea, GBR (Honda); **5** Lorenzo Zanetti, ITA (MV Agusta); **6** Kyle Smith, GBR (Honda); **7** Christian Gamarino, ITA (Kawasaki); **8** Roberto Rolfo, ITA (Honda); **9** Martin Cardenas, COL (Honda); **10** Fabio Menghi, ITA (Yamaha); **11** Marcos Ramirez, ESP (Honda); **12** Marco Faccani, ITA (Kawasaki); **13** Glenn Scott, AUS (Honda); **14** Dominic Schmitter, SUI (Kawasaki); **15** Miguel Praia, POR (Honda).
Fastest lap: Kenan Sofuoglu, TUR (Kawasaki), 1m 45.411s, 97.447mph/156.826km/h.
Championship points: 1 Sofuoglu, 150; **2** Cluzel, 110; **3** Jacobsen, 95; **4** Zanetti, 81; **5** Rea, 67; **6** Smith, 56.

MISANO, Italy, 21 June 2015, 2.626mile/4.226km circuit.
Supersport World Championship, Rnd 8 (19 laps, 49.892 miles/80.294km)
1 Jules Cluzel, FRA (MV Agusta), 31m 19.621s, 95.558mph/153.785km/h.
2 Patrick Jacobsen, USA (Honda); **3** Lorenzo Zanetti, ITA (MV Agusta); **4** Gino Rea, GBR (Honda); **5** Alex Baldolini, ITA (MV Agusta); **6**

Fabio Menghi, ITA (Yamaha); **7** Christian Gamarino, ITA (Kawasaki); **8** Riccardo Russo, ITA (Honda); **9** Marco Faccani, ITA (Kawasaki); **10** Martin Cardenas, COL (Honda); **11** Kenan Sofuoglu, TUR (Honda); **12** Roberto Rolfo, ITA (Honda); **13** Dominic Schmitter, SUI (Kawasaki); **14** Kevin Wahr, GER (Honda); **15** Glenn Scott, AUS (Honda).
Fastest lap: Jules Cluzel, FRA (MV Agusta), 1m 38.239s, 96.227mph/154.863km/h (record).
Championship points: 1 Sofuoglu, 155; **2** Cluzel, 135; **3** Jacobsen, 115; **4** Zanetti, 97; **5** Rea, 88; **6** Rolfo, 58.

SEPANG, Malaysia, 2 August 2015, 3.447-mile/5.543km circuit.
Supersport World Championship, Rnd 9 (14 laps, 48.220 miles/77.602km)
1 Patrick Jacobsen, USA (Honda), 30m 21.294s, 95.312mph/153.389km/h.
2 Jules Cluzel, FRA (MV Agusta); **3** Lorenzo Zanetti, ITA (MV Agusta); **4** Kenan Sofuoglu, TUR (Kawasaki); **5** Kyle Smith, GBR (Honda); **6** Roberto Rolfo, ITA (Honda); **7** Martin Cardenas, COL (Honda); **8** Gino Rea, GBR (Honda); **9** Christian Gamarino, ITA (Kawasaki); **10** Alex Baldolini, ITA (MV Agusta); **11** Dominic Schmitter, SUI (Kawasaki); **12** Fabio Menghi, ITA (Yamaha); **13** Kevin Wahr, GER (Honda); **14** Aiden Wagner, AUS (Honda); **15** Marcos Ramirez, ESP (Honda).
Fastest lap: Kenan Sofuoglu, TUR (Kawasaki), 2m 9.338s, 95.868mph/154.284km/h.
Championship points: 1 Sofuoglu, 168; **2** Cluzel, 155; **3** Jacobsen, 140; **4** Zanetti, 113; **5** Rea, 88; **6** Rolfo, 68.

JEREZ, Spain, 20 September 2015, 2.748-mile/4.423km circuit.
Supersport World Championship, Rnd 10 (19 laps, 52.218 miles/84.037km)
1 Kenan Sofuoglu, TUR (Kawasaki), 33m 17.651s, 94.103mph/151.444km/h.
2 Patrick Jacobsen, USA (Honda); **3** Lorenzo Zanetti, ITA (MV Agusta); **4** Kyle Smith, GBR (Honda); **5** Nico Terol, ESP (MV Agusta); **6** Marco Faccani, ITA (Kawasaki); **7** Alex Baldolini, ITA (MV Agusta); **8** Christian Gamarino, ITA (Kawasaki); **9** Kevin Wahr, GER (Honda); **10** Roberto Rolfo, ITA (Honda); **11** Dominic Schmitter, SUI (Kawasaki); **12** Marcos Ramirez, ESP (Honda); **13** Aiden Wagner, AUS (Honda); **14** Martin Cardenas, COL (Honda); **15** Janos Chrobak, HUN (Honda).
Fastest lap: Patrick Jacobsen, USA (Honda), 1m 44.177s, 94.973mph/152.844km/h.
Championship points: 1 Sofuoglu, 193; **2** Jacobsen, 160; **3** Cluzel, 155; **4** Zanetti, 129; **5** Rea, 88; **6** Smith, 80.

MAGNY-COURS, France, 4 October 2015, 2.741-mile/4.411km circuit.
Supersport World Championship, Rnd 11 (11 laps, 30.150 miles/48.521km)
1 Patrick Jacobsen, USA (Honda), 19m 14.983s, 93.974mph/151.237km/h.
2 Kenan Sofuoglu, TUR (Kawasaki); **3** Lucas Mahias, FRA (Yamaha); **4** Lorenzo Zanetti, ITA (MV Agusta); **5** Kyle Smith, GBR (Honda); **6** Kevin Wahr, GER (Honda); **7** Gino Rea, GBR (Honda); **8** Martin Cardenas, COL (Honda); **9** Christian Gamarino, ITA (Kawasaki); **10** Marco Faccani, ITA (Kawasaki); **11** Roberto Rolfo, ITA (Honda); **12** Dominic Schmitter, SUI (Kawasaki); **13** Aiden Wagner, AUS (Honda); **14** Nico Terol, ESP (MV Agusta); **15** Xavier Pinsach, ESP (Honda).
Fastest lap: Patrick Jacobsen, USA (Honda), 1m 43.569s, 95.271mph/153.324km/h.
Championship points: 1 Sofuoglu, 213; **2** Jacobsen, 185; **3** Cluzel, 155; **4** Zanetti, 142; **5** Rea, 97; **6** Smith, 91.

LOSAIL, Qatar, 18 October 2015, 3.343-mile/5.380km circuit.
Supersport World Championship, Rnd 12 (15 laps, 50.145 miles/80.700km)
1 Kyle Smith, GBR (Honda), 30m 44.036s, 97.895mph/157.546km/h.
2 Kenan Sofuoglu, TUR (Kawasaki); **3** Lorenzo Zanetti, ITA (MV Agusta); **4** Lucas Mahias, FRA (Yamaha); **5** Patrick Jacobsen, USA (Honda); **6** Nico Terol, ESP (MV Agusta); **7** Roberto Rolfo, ITA (Honda); **8** Alex Baldolini, ITA (MV Agusta); **9** Marco Faccani, ITA (Kawasaki); **10** Fabio Menghi, ITA (Yamaha); **11** Dominic Schmitter, SUI (Kawasaki); **12** Sergio Gadea, ESP (Honda); **13** Nacho Calero, ESP (Honda); **14** Abdulaziz Binladin, KSA (Kawasaki); **15** Kevin Manfredi, ITA (Honda).
Fastest lap: Kyle Smith, GBR (Honda), 2m 2.122s, 98.547mph/158.596km/h.

Final World Supersport Championship points:
1	Kenan Sofuoglu, TUR,	233
2	Patrick Jacobsen, USA,	196
3	Lorenzo Zanetti, ITA,	158
4	Jules Cluzel, FRA,	155
5	Kyle Smith, GBR,	116
6	Gino Rea, GBR,	97

7 Roberto Rolfo, ITA, 88; **8** Alex Baldolini, ITA, 67; **9** Marco Faccani, ITA, 66; **10** Christian Gamarino, ITA, 62; **11** Martin Cardenas, COL, 55; **12** Lucas Mahias, FRA, 51; **13** Ratthapark Wilairot, THA, 46; **14** Dominic Schmitter, SWI, 46; **15** Fabio Menghi, ITA, 44.